THE TRUE STORY OF THE VENDETTA OF THE

47

Ronin from Akó

THOMAS HARPER

Leete's
Island
Books

Library of Congress Number: 2019932656

ISBN: 978-0-918172-77-8 (paper)

Copyright © 2019 G. G. Rowley

Cover Design: Karen Davidson

Design: Karen Davidson and Ingrid Bromberg Kennedy

Leete's Island Books, Box 1 Sedgwick, Maine 04676

First Edition

For Gaye,
with whom it all began.

武士が義理を不存候而ハ大形盗賊同前ニ而御座候へとも、
左様申候へハいなものニ罷成、其上ニわる口ものの名を取候而ハ、
其身の害に罷成候間口をとち罷成事ニ候.

A warrior with no sense of honor is hardly better than a bandit—
although if you say that nowadays, you'll only be thought a crackpot.
Besides, it does you no good to be known as a knocker. I just keep
my mouth shut.

       Hazama Kihei to Ōishi Gozaemon,
       LETTER DATED 1688, NINTH MONTH, 10TH DAY

CONTENTS

THE VENDETTA OF THE 47 RONIN FROM AKŌ

Nur das Gründliche wahrhaft unterhaltend sei.
Only the exhaustive can be truly interesting.
Thomas Mann, *Der Zauberberg*

This book is as true to fact as I have been able to make it. It is closely based upon contemporary documents. All the events it relates actually took place. All the people involved in them really existed. Even the dialogue is drawn from documentary sources, either verbatim or reconstructed from reported speech. I have invented nothing.

This is not to suggest, though, that I have succeeded in telling the whole truth. For even those who participated in the vendetta could report only what little of the whole they themselves had seen, and their perceptions of those events sometimes differ markedly from those of their comrades. And even contemporary attempts to tell the whole story—the "true records," as they called them—must be read not so much as history but as something more like newspapers: reports not of what actually happened but of what people heard, thought, or were saying had happened.

With all this in mind, I have labored to construct a narrative as complete, precise, and factually correct as the sources permit, and to resist the urge to portray people as I would wish them to have been rather than as they were. To this end, I have indulged in one small fiction, which I must declare here: I tell the story not in my own voice but that of a narrator who grew up among samurai, and who knew well the documents upon which this story must be based. Ōhashi Yoshizō was a real person, who will introduce himself in the prologue to the story. Although the author of several books, including two on the assassination of Ii Kamon-no-Kami Naosuke (1815–1860), Yoshizō never wrote a word about the Akō vendetta. But by attempting to inhabit his persona, I aim to avoid saying anything that he would not have said if he had told his own tale. I hope that his presence will keep me honest. As the old saying goes, "Some fictions can lead us to the truth." I hope this is one of them.

ACKNOWLEDGMENTS

This book has been a long time coming, and I owe many debts to many people, some of them friends as well as benefactors, some of them scholars and samurai who must be revered across a distance of centuries for the treasures of industry and erudition they have left us. These are debts that I can never repay. My bibliography, I hope, will acknowledge the magnitude of what I owe those who are survived by only their works; those still with us I wish to thank individually.

Two constant (in all senses of the word) and extraordinarily congenial companions on this journey have been Henry Smith, professor of history at Columbia University, and W. J. Boot, professor of Japanese and long-time colleague at the University of Leiden. In the early days of the project, when my own efforts were more in the nature of a neophyte's groping than anything that could be called research, Henry was a generous and knowledgeable interlocutor and guide. And when I reached the stage at which I could begin writing, Wim, voluntarily, spent vast amounts of his time reading, and commenting upon, every chapter as it was completed. Without Wim and Henry to talk with about our mutual friends the ronin, I would have been far more poorly prepared to write about them. Their wisdom and generosity have made this a better book.

I am grateful, too, to Professor Kasaya Kazuhiko of the International Research Center for Japanese Studies, who not only knew the answer to every question I ever asked him (and there were many), but seemed always to have a beautifully organized lecture on the subject at the tip of his tongue.

To Professor Yokoyama Toshio of Kyoto University, whose knowledge of the city of Kyoto, past and present, seems inexhaustible, and whose ready sharing of that knowledge has been invaluable to this project.

To Professor Nakano Mitsutoshi for arranging entrée to the Kyushu University Library, and especially for making available its copy of *Ehon Chūshingura*, one of the very few complete sets of the work still extant.

To Dr. Brian Powell of the University of Oxford for sharing his vast knowledge of the "Chūshingura" dramatic tradition and, in particular, for introducing me to both Mayama Seika's perceptive reading of the incident and his invaluable gazetteer, *Chūshingura chishi*.

To Dr. James McMullen of the University of Oxford for helping me to place the ruminations of my characters in the larger contexts of Edo-period thought and, especially, Confucianism in its Japanese permutations.

To Professor Glenn Stockwell of Waseda University for explaining and demonstrating the proper procedure (*kata*) for *kaishaku* as prescribed in the traditions of the Musō Jikiden Ryū of *Iaidō*, of which Professor Stockwell is the current *Iemoto*.

To Jeroen Veldhuisen (now Yamashita Noboru) for demonstrating the technique (*kata*) of disarming a man wielding a sword that Kajikawa Yosōbei probably would have used.

To Okumura Shizuo, a native of Akō, for countless nuggets of local lore and guidance of a depth that only someone born to the region could give.

And to Koizumi Yōichi, the premier dealer in Gishiana at the gate to the temple Sengakuji, who has been an extremely generous guide to sites, little-known source materials, and valuable lore of many sorts.

I am particularly grateful to two scholars whom I have never met, but whose work ranks among the very best in this field to appear in recent years. Satō Makoto and Tanaka Mitsurō are the moderators of internet websites devoted principally to the Akō Incident, both of which are rich sources of accurate information, intelligent comment, and unbiased analysis.

Peter Neill, founder of Leete's Island Books, without hesitation undertook to publish a massive manuscript that large corporate publishers had either declined as "too long for today's market" or offered to help me cut in half. And Irene Pavitt, despite having retired only recently from her responsibilities as an editor at Columbia University Press, not only agreed cheerfully to edit this Monster (as we've come to call it), but maintained to the very end of that long process the acuity of vision and incisive judgment for which she is known. I doubt that many authors feel as deeply grateful to their publisher and editor as I do.

And finally, I should be terribly remiss did I not at least attempt to thank Dr. Yano Hideaki and his superb team of young surgeons at the National Center for Global Health and Medicine in Tokyo. Their meticulous execution of an extremely complex procedure, fraught with unforeseen complications, has given me the extra time I needed to complete this book. "But I need ten more years," I said, only faintly hopeful. They gave me that gift of life, my gratitude for which can hardly be expressed in mere words. But I must try; so in the words of the men I know best: *Katajikenaku zonji-tatematsuri-sōrō!*

It is the dedicatee of this book, my wife, Gaye Rowley, who first struck the spark of interest that grew into such an obsession that it forced me to attempt to tell this vast story. In the thirty years since striking that spark, she has lived almost daily with this obsession and has contributed to its shaping in ways far too various and significant to enumerate. This book would not exist without her.

NOTE TO THE READER

Any attempt to re-create the world of Edo-period samurai for readers of a modern European language will be fraught with myriad "translation problems," most of them far more complex than mere linguistic difficulties. Many writers have tried many different solutions, and I have learnt a great deal from them. Where I depart from past practice, I mean no criticism of that practice. It is simply that all usage is subject to the demands of context. What works well in a book on one subject may not work as well in another context. In the notes that follow, I describe some of these problems and the ways I have attempted to cope with them.

Names and Titles

+ The names by which people address one another, in any culture, weave a web of considerable complexity. But in Edo-period samurai society, that web was particularly intricate and thus requires some explanation. In this narrative, I follow contemporary practice to the greatest extent possible, and depart from it only where it might create confusion for readers unfamiliar with Japanese usage.

+ At the simplest level, this means that surnames precede given names. In Europe, this should cause no confusion, as the same format is still followed there in many contexts, and even North American readers will be familiar with rosters and directories arranged alphabetically by surname.

+ Every man of samurai rank had four names: a surname, indicating the family or house to which he belonged (*myōji*); a familiar name, which his family, friends, and colleagues used (*tsūshō* or, in some cases, *kanmei*); a clan or lineage name (*uji*); and a formal name (*imina* and various alternative designations). The full name of Ōishi Kuranosuke, for example, was Ōishi Kuranosuke Fujiwara Yoshitaka.

✦ The "proper" pronunciations of the surnames of some of the characters in this narrative are unknown. The reason for this is that many Japanese names, although written identically, can be pronounced in a number of ways, all quite correct. Only by asking the person in question can one know which pronunciation is preferred in his or her family. But if the person in question lived three hundred or more years ago, and there is no written record of how he pronounced his name, one can only speculate. For example, the young ronin known in this narrative as Yatō Emoshichi 矢頭右衛門七 is elsewhere called Yakōbe, Yagashira, or Yazu Emoshichi. All are "correct" pronunciations, but no record survives of how Emoshichi and others in his family pronounced their surname. In such cases, I have tried to ascertain what that person's near contemporaries called him. In *Kanadehon Chūshingura* (1748), for example, the Emoshichi character is called Satō Yomoshichi; and in another play based upon the Akō incident (*Yotsuya kaidan*, 1825), the name is written with different characters, 矢藤, that can only be pronounced "Yatō." Guided by this evidence that Edo-period playwrights considered Yatō the correct pronunciation of Emoshichi's surname, I have followed their lead.

✦ Given names, too, can be problematic, especially those derived from titles in the old Palace Guard units (Hyōe). Originally, names bearing this suffix were pronounced "-hyōe" or "-byōe," depending upon the syllables that preceded it. By the beginning of the eighteenth century, however, a creeping tendency to informality gave rise to the use of the simpler Sino-Japanese pronunciation of the same characters, "-hei" and "-bei," making it impossible at times to tell which pronunciation is intended. For example, we know from letters addressed to women, and thus written in phonetic script, that Horibe Yahyōe and his son Horibe Yasubyōe signed their correspondence thus, on the basis of which purists insist that these are the *only* correct pronunciations of their given names. Yet we know from other sources that their contemporaries also called them Yahei and Yasubei—rather like an Anglophone who is known as Tom to all his friends, but signs formal letters as and writes under the name Thomas (unless he is a British academic of informalitarian pretensions). Certain forms may have been preferred in certain contexts, but neither form was exclusively correct or exclusively incorrect. Fortunately, not all given names are subject to such ambiguity; Kuranosuke and Jūnai, for example, can be pronounced only one way. But where ambiguity does exist, the writer of an alphabetic language must make a choice. In this book, I use the more formal pronunciation where written evidence indicates that this was intended; elsewhere, I have been guided by the evidence of Edo-period practice, including that in the writings of the Edo/Meiji-period historian Shigeno Yasutsugu and, of course, my narrator, Ōhashi Yoshizō. For an interesting (though nonprescriptive) discussion of this problem, see also Tanaka Mitsurō, "'Yasubei'? soretomo 'Yasubyōe'?," *Rongaibi* 6.

+ As a final authority, this book follows the pronunciations of both surnames and given names listed in the Akō Historical Museum's catalogue *Kenshō: Akō jiken* 2:124–26, and reprinted in *Egakareta Akō gishi*, 95–97. All these readings are corroborated by those in the online catalogue of the National Diet Library of Japan.

+ A lesser complication—not really a problem—with given names is that the long vowels in some names came to be pronounced as though they were short vowels. In this book, I have retained the macron indicating that these vowels were originally pronounced as long vowels. Some Japanese writers, however, gloss Saburōbei as Saburobei, Gorōbei as Gorobei, and Jirōzaemon as Jirozaemon. They are not mistaken; they are simply following custom rather than tradition.

+ Nicknames formed by the abbreviation of *tsūshō*—for example, Chūza for Chūzaemon, Sōu for Sōemon, and Kura for

Kuranosuke—are retained when the ronin themselves use them.

- ✦ I have retained all indications of respect and rank, such as Dono and Sama. Sama is, of course, the more respectful, and Dono is roughly analogous to the Italian/Spanish "Don." As in any language, however, the less respectful forms may indicate a greater degree of intimacy, just as, conversely, one can insult through an excess of respect.

- ✦ In women's names, I maintain the distinction between the honorific prefix "O-" and the name itself. A woman whom others address as O-Tan, were she to mention her own name at all, would introduce herself simply as Tan, and never as Otan—an error that actors are too often made to commit in Japanese historical dramas.

- ✦ Since the Shogunate and the Corps of Vassals of the several daimyo domains were originally fighting units that were later transformed into military governments, wherever possible the functions and titles of government officials have been translated with military rather than courtly equivalents. For example, Yanagisawa Yoshiyasu is identified as Tokugawa Tsunayoshi's Chief Adjutant rather than Grand Chamberlain, the more usual courtly title.

Calendar and Dates

- ✦ No attempt has been made to convert the dates of the lunar calendar to those of the solar-based Gregorian calendar. To do so grossly misrepresents the contemporary perception of an event's place within the year. Instead, the numbered designations of the months are construed as proper nouns and capitalized; days are rendered as numerals for ease in distinguishing them from months; and years are designated by their era titles, followed (in one small concession to Eurocentrism) by the corresponding year in the Western calendar—for example, Genroku 14 (1701), Third Month, 14th Day. The slight discrepancy between the boundaries of the lunar and solar years is ignored.

Time

- It is usually impossible to determine with even moderate precision the time at which an event took place. Most people, most of the time, had only a rough idea what time of day it was. Mechanical timekeeping devices were very expensive, and thus scarce, and the systems these devices served were complex and confusing.

- Two systems of telling time were in use simultaneously. Both were based on what Endymion Wilkinson, in *Chinese History*, aptly calls the "double-hour" division of the day into twelve parts, but in different ways.

  In the older system, the divisions of the day were named after the twelve animals of the zodiac: Rat, Ox, Tiger, and so on. And each double-hour was considered to span the point in time for which it was named. The Hour of the Rat, for example, began at what we call 11:00 P.M., spanned midnight, and ended at 1:00 A.M. This system served well enough until the introduction of time drums and bells, which required the use of numbers.

  The newer numerical system, however, was not simply an updated set of names for the hours of the zodiacal system. It made little sense for a bell to toll the midpoint of a double-hour, and so the hours of the numerical system were construed as beginning at the sounding of the bell or drum. The Ninth Hour, therefore, did not span midnight; it began at midnight and extended until 2:00 A.M. And the numbers used in this system did not begin at one and progress from there; they began at nine and regressed to four, and then at noon began again at nine.

  In addition, there was a system of variable hours that could be superimposed on either the zodiacal or the numerical system— provided one had access to variable timekeeping devices. In this system, sunrise and sunset were considered constants, and thus the double-hours of the day varied in length, depending upon the season. In summer, daylight hours were long and nighttime hours short; in winter, the reverse.

- Matters were further complicated by confusion arising from the mixed use and misuse of the two systems. It is not unusual to encounter a Genroku-era writer who tells time by both the zodiacal and numerical systems in the same document. Neither is it unusual for a writer to use the zodiacal system as though it were numerical or the numerical system as though it were zodiacal. And the reader almost never knows whether a writer is reckoning time correctly or incorrectly, or in hours of variable or uniform length. Given all the unanswerable questions that these ambiguities raise, all references to time in this book are treated as though they are based on the "correct" use of the zodiacal or the numerical system, with no attempt to adjust for the possibility of variation in the length of hours.

- One further source of confusion for Western readers is that the new day was regarded as beginning not at midnight but at sunrise. Modern historians sometimes describe the attack of the ronin as taking place early on the morning of the 15th Day; but to the ronin themselves, it was still the night of the 14th Day.

Age

- The ages of people in this narrative are given as stated in contemporary sources, and thus are calculated according to the "year-counting" (*kazoedoshi*) system. This number indicates the number of calendar years in which they have lived, rather than the number of twelve-month periods of life that they have completed. And so, unless a person was born at the very beginning of a New Year, he may have lived in forty-five calendar years, but have completed only forty-four twelve-month periods. In the year-counting system, he is said to be forty-five, but by Western count only forty-four.

Weather

- Most references to the weather are taken from the text being used. When a description of the weather seems essential to the narrative, but is not mentioned in the source text, it is taken from contemporary sources: for Edo, the *Goji'in nikki*, and for Kyoto, the *Edo-Meiji Kyōto no tenki hyō: Nijō-ke nainai gobansho hinami no ki*. The latter is complete for virtually the entire span of the narrative, but there are gaps in the former. Thus occasionally (though very rarely), I have followed the advice of the editor of *Hinami no ki* and ventured a guess on the assumption that Kyoto's weather usually moves in an easterly direction and arrives in Edo a day or two later.

Money, Land Value, and Income

+ As a general rule, money in the east of Japan was made of gold, and in the west of silver. A further difference was that gold coins were of standard weights, whereas each quantity of silver had to be weighed separately to determine its value. These differences made the business of money changing (*ryōgae*) indispensable to the conduct of financial transactions between eastern and western Japan.

+ The value of land was calculated in terms of its yield measured in *koku* of rice, 1 *koku* being a bit more than five bushels. A medium-size domain such as Akō was valued at 53,000 *koku*, whereas the Asano main house in Hiroshima, which held the entire province of Aki and much of Bingo, was valued at 430,000 *koku*.

+ The stipendiary allotments of samurai, too, were measured in *koku*, this being a vestige of the days when samurai were granted individual fiefdoms and lived on the land they held. After Toyotomi Hideyoshi forced all samurai to leave the land and reside in castle towns, this system of calculating income remained in place, although there was considerable variation in the degree to which samurai income was tied to particular plots of land. In some domains, samurai still held specific villages, even though they no longer lived there; in other domains, enfeoffment was only nominal, and *koku* was simply a convenient measure of income.

+ In the lower ranks of samurai, there were some who were not even nominally enfeoffed and were paid in *kuramai* (storehouse rice), which was measured not in *koku* of unhulled rice, but in *hyō* (bales of polished rice).

Translated Texts

* In attempting to construct a coherent narrative that incorporates a great many translations of texts written in the seventeenth and eighteenth centuries, I have occasionally, as Edward Gibbon (1737–1794) put it, "used some slight freedom" in adapting the texts to fit their context better. In most cases, this involved little more than compensating for the fact that these writers—particularly writers of letters—lacked the opportunities to edit themselves that computers now give us. Sentences could not be moved about, infelicitous phrases reworded, redundancies eliminated, repetitious vocabulary varied. Occasionally, I have provided editorial assistance of this sort on their behalf, but as sparingly as possible. In those rare instances when a text seemed to require extensive editing, I have preferred to paraphrase rather than translate.

EDO

These locations are only approximate. This map, although drawn in 1727, is based upon an imprecise original dated 1702.

1. Edo Castle
2. Teppōzu, Akō Asano Upper Mansion
3. Honjo, Kira Mansion
4. Sakurada, Uesugi Upper Mansion
5. Kuranosuke's inn
6. Sengoku Hōki-no-Kami, Official Mansion
7. Sengakuji
8. Tamura Ukyō-no-Daibu, Lower Mansion
9. Hosokawa Etchū-no-Kami, Middle Mansion
10. Hisamatsu Oki-no-Kami, Middle Mansion
11. Mōri Kai-no-Kami, Middle Mansion
12. Mizuno Kenmotsu, Middle Mansion

47

TOKYO, 1915

If I take these out to the hinterlands,
they'll never again see the light of day.

Nabeta Shōzan

This is the story of a story—a story that most people think they already know. All they really know, of course, is the prancing and posturing of a troupe of Kabuki actors, not one of whom has ever held a real sword, much less contemplated using one.

It was my good fortune to learn the story from a different source—not from the theater, but from the work of an old samurai who had spent most of his life investigating what really happened. It was ill fortune, I suppose, that I was only a child when he was nearing the end of life; I couldn't have understood much of what he had to say about honor, fealty, or the Principle of Equal Punishment. But an image of the old man remains with me, which somehow leaves me feeling that I share his closeness to the world and the people he studied. I don't mean the feeling you get from reading a novel, that you yourself are there, watching it all happen. It is more like reading a schoolbook description of some great battle—the war with Russia, say, or the Meiji Revolution—and then later learning that your uncle or your grandfather had fought in it. Suddenly, that corner of history becomes intensely personal. That battle becomes a part of your own life, almost as though you yourself could remember it.

This is the way I feel about the vendetta of the forty-seven ronin from the domain of Akō. And that, I suppose, is why, sixty years later, I've become so obsessed with reconstructing the old man's tale. I want to tell it as he would have told it, using the same documents that he spent his life collecting. But that is the end of the story. To tell it properly, we must go back to the beginning.

◆ ◆ ◆

My father was Ōhashi Totsuan, and my grandfather was Shimizu Sekijō. Those names won't mean much to anyone alive today; but in their time, both men were moderately well known as teachers of military science. If the Shogunate had not been overthrown in 1867, I too, would have learnt their profession and followed in their footsteps.

But it is neither my ancestors nor myself that I want to tell you about. We live in a different world now; I make my living as a writer and editor and can't even imagine myself as a samurai, carrying two swords in my sash wherever I go. I speak of these things only because the old man I mentioned a moment ago had been a disciple of both my father and my grandfather. Along with his profession, Father had inherited a small but loyal following, many of whom were fiercely devoted to the lost cause of "expelling the foreign barbarians and revering the Emperor." Those were days, you must understand, when some still thought that we had a choice. Nabeta Shōzan, the old samurai who collected the documents spread out here on my desk, was one of my father's followers—but hardly one of the revolutionary sort. His interest in military matters was strictly antiquarian.

By rights, I shouldn't even describe him as a "follower"; Father never did. Shōzan was at least thirty years older than my father, and probably had known him as a baby. When my grandfather died and my father took over the school, Shōzan remained in the fold, as loyal to the young heir as to his first teacher. But to Father, Shōzan was no mere disciple. He considered him a senior colleague, and they always addressed each other as "Sensei."

◆ ◆ ◆

It must have been in 1853 or 1854, for no one was talking of anything but the "Black Ships" from America and the ferociously bearded Commodore who had warned the Shogun that he would blow us to bits if we did not open the country to trade. It must have been fairly early in the morning, too, for the housemaids were still bustling about, beating air into the bedding and noisily stacking dishes in the kitchen. Father's friends did not normally call at this hour; but in those times, nothing was normal. And so there in the vestibule stood Shōzan Sensei, tall and erect, every crease in his clothing pressed to perfection, and with him a manservant who carried two large bundles. He had come to ask a favor, Shōzan said. Father, of course, replied that he would do anything he could for the old man and invited him into the sitting room, where they could talk more comfortably.

The favor that Shōzan asked was simple enough, although strange-seeming. Might he leave two bundles of books in Father's care—the two great bundles that his servant bore? Father knew immediately what books they were. Shōzan was a great admirer of the forty-seven samurai from Akō, who in 1702 had staged a spectacular vendetta to avenge an insult to their late liege lord. In his way, you see, the old man was as much an idealist as anyone in Father's circle. Over the past forty or fifty years, he had spent his every spare moment tracking down every document he could find that had any connection whatever with his paragons of loyalty. He had unearthed letters that the dead men's descendants had forgotten they possessed; he had found diaries of people who had known the ronin, and eyewitness accounts of their attack and their deaths; he had somehow gained access to the official records of some of those charged with handling the case. Every scrap of evidence he could lay his hands on, he copied out in his own hand. You can imagine the amount of time this took. Time to follow up empty rumors as well as solid leads; time to travel to distant towns and villages; time to arrange meetings with the owners of the evidence; time to persuade the wary to let him study their possessions; and, above all, time to copy—and copy carefully, so as not to miss or mistake a single word.

Fortunately, Shōzan's employment allowed him the time he needed to pursue his obsession. He was a personal attendant to Andō Tsushima-no-Kami, one of the highest-ranking vassals of the Shogun. This placed Shōzan in the middle rank of samurai, with a comfortable income of 250 koku per year. More importantly, however, it permitted him to live permanently in Edo. Andō's fief was the remote northeastern domain of

Taira, surrounded by mountains, facing a rugged seacoast, removed from any of the main highways. But as a high-ranking official in the Shogun's inner circle, Andō was exempt from the round of alternate attendance required of most lords. For Shōzan, this meant that he need not spend every other year of his career in a rural castle town. And even in Edo, his presence was not required on a daily basis, for his place of duty was Andō's Middle Mansion in Koishikawa, not the Upper Mansion, adjacent to the castle, where the lord of a domain must spend most of his time.

It was precisely this that made Shōzan's visit seem so strange. Why would someone so ideally situated suddenly decide to rid himself of these forty hand-bound volumes, filled with the documents it had taken him a lifetime to collect?

"But why?" Father asked.

Shōzan's answer was short and direct: "I've been transferred—permanently—back to the castle in Taira." What before had seemed only strange, now seemed vaguely ominous. For a samurai in direct attendance upon his lord, such an assignment amounted to banishment. Shōzan was seventy-three years old. He would never see the city of Edo again.

Father could only repeat his question, "Why?" although with considerably more feeling this time.

"One doesn't ask, does one?" Shōzan replied. "As Nyoraishi says, 'A samurai who complains will one day betray his lord.' There is a grain of truth in that maxim, and I would not have such a thing thought of me. In any case, it no longer matters where I go. What matter are these." His eyes indicated the forty volumes of manuscript; "If I take these back to Taira, they will only rot there." There was no need to add that a man in his mid-seventies could expect to die soon and that with equal certainty he could expect his rural relatives to forget that his forty volumes ever existed.

"But shouldn't you publish them?" Father asked. "No one alive knows anywhere near as much about this as you do. There's no other collection like it."

Shōzan had had the same thought long ago. He had approached several publishers. Every one had turned him down. Times had changed. People were no longer reading books about the heroes of yesteryear. It could ruin a publisher to bring out a forty-volume collection of undigested documents. A hundred years earlier, it might have broken records. But now—certain financial disaster. Shōzan had done all that he could. My father was his last hope.

"This can't go on forever," Shōzan said. "Once this problem of the foreigners is resolved, things will return to normal. You are young. I'm sure you'll see a day when such things will be appreciated again. And when the time seems right, if you could just put them in the hands of a good publisher . . ." In the end, Father had to agree that this was probably the best plan.

A few weeks later, Shōzan set out for the castle town of Taira, his "home" beyond the mountains in the north. We never saw him again. A few years later, word came that he had died—content, I like to think, that his life's work would one day be given its due.

◆ ◆ ◆

But history plays mischievous tricks. In attempting to protect his documents, Shōzan had unwittingly placed them in great danger—although neither he nor Father could have known it at the time.

As I've said, Shōzan's liege lord, Andō Tsushima-no-Kami, was a member of the innermost circle of power in the Shogunate, a protégé of the Chief Elder, Ii Kamon-no-Kami. At the time of Shōzan's "transfer," Andō was thirty-three and already a Commissioner of Temples and Shrines, one of the small elite who reported directly to the Shogun. The following year, he was promoted to the Shogun's Junior Council, and two years later to the pinnacle of power, membership in the Council of Elders.

By all reports, Andō was a man of high principles—open to reason and incorruptible. But his principles were not shared by my father and his circle. Andō, like his patron, was far too hospitable to the foreign barbarians for their taste. What most infuriated them, however, was a rumor that cast doubt upon Andō's motives in promoting the marriage of Princess Kazu to the young Shogun. The ostensible purpose of this marriage was to strengthen the nation in a time of crisis by uniting the house of the Emperor with the house of the Shogun. But many, my father included, suspected that the real motive was to make a hostage of the Princess, and then do away with the Emperor altogether.

I doubt there was the slightest bit of truth in that rumor. But in a world that was changing as rapidly as ours in those days, even the wildest nonsense could somehow seem plausible. Father and his friends decided that drastic action was called for.

Any history book will tell you that on the 15th Day of the First Month of 1862, just as Andō, the new Elder, was about to enter the Sakashita Gate of Edo Castle, he was ambushed by a band of fanatic "barbarian-expellers." What is not so well known is that the attack was planned by my father. For the first and only time in his life, he had put his expertise in military matters to practical use—and failed miserably. Andō was wounded, but his bodyguards were alert and skilled. The would-be assassins were slaughtered on the spot. My father escaped death only because he was already in prison, having been arrested on suspicion of conspiracy two days earlier. It would have been better if he had died with his fellow conspirators. For over the next six months, he was interrogated and tortured continually. But he never confessed, and he never divulged the name of anyone not already dead. When it was clear that he would die before he would talk, they sent him home to us, a broken man with but a few more hours to live. I remember asking my mother when Father would come home. I remember the shock of seeing his shattered body. I remember watching him die.

◆ ◆ ◆

By now, you may be wondering what all of this has to do with those forty volumes of documents relating to the vendetta that old Nabeta Shōzan left behind. Well, for one thing, these intrigues make me suspect that Shōzan's "transfer" was not a punishment but an act of percipient kindness. At the time, neither Shōzan nor my father would have dreamt that seven years hence Father would attempt to assassinate Shōzan's liege lord. But someone may well have sensed the potential for conflict in the company that Shōzan was keeping. Shōzan's loyalty was beyond question. He had served the Andō house faithfully for more than fifty years. At the slightest hint of conflict, he would have broken with Father's school immediately. But what if a compromising situation should develop before the old antiquary was even aware of it? I suspect that someone—an Elder of the Andō house or a Liaison Officer—thought it best to move him out of harm's way before any danger did develop, move him back to the castle in Taira. He was told nothing because nothing could be told without seeming to blame an esteemed retainer. The order was issued, and whatever pain it caused, it at least saved the old man from an embarrassing conflict between duty and friendship.

I tell you my father's fate, too, simply to demonstrate the dangers that Shōzan's documents, against all odds, survived. What Father did with the documents after Shōzan left Edo, I have no idea. Probably he put them in the fireproof storehouse at the back of the garden. And probably they lay there untouched for the next few years. Perhaps other things—scrolls, tea bowls, unused furnishings—piled up around them, eventually concealing the two blue-wrapped bundles from casual notice.

One does wonder, though, by what fortunate accident they survived destruction when Father was arrested. And not because of what the Inspectorate or the City Magistrate's men might have done with them, but because of my own mother's vigilance. The moment Father was taken away, she burnt every scrap of paper she could find. She even snatched a letter from his desk while the house was swarming with Inspectors, wadded it to make it look as though she had just blown her nose on it, and in full view of everyone took it into the garden and burnt it. If Shōzan's forty volumes had been standing in plain sight, I'm sure that they, too, would have gone up in flames, lest in some unaccountable way they should incriminate Father. But they were not burnt, which probably means that by 1862, when Father died, they had been forgotten. And if by then they were merely forgotten, the Meiji Revolution five years later must have obliterated every trace of their memory. Yet still they lay there, somewhere. I had known of them from stories my mother told me as a child; yet to my memory, she never mentioned them again before her death in 1881. By the turn of the century, I was the only living member of the family who might have recalled Shōzan and his collection. Yet I didn't. It was only the chance remark of a friend that brought it all back to me.

✦ ✦ ✦

My friend had attended a lecture given by the historian Professor Shigeno Yasutsugu. "Dr. Demolition" was Shigeno's nickname, for he had imbibed to the full, via his colleague Ludwig Rieß, the exalted view of primary documents as well as the ruthless professionalism of Leopold van Ranke, and would reject any source that could not be proved beyond all doubt to show *wie es eigentlich gewesen* (what actually happened). This must have imposed severe limits on the sources available for Shigeno's own work, but it created infinite opportunities to demolish some of the most cherished episodes in our nation's history, which he did with great delight. He even had the courage to demolish the myth of the warrior-monk Benkei. The professor's zeal may at times have been excessive, but it made him a very entertaining lecturer.

At any rate, Shigeno's subject on the night that my friend went to hear him was the vendetta of the forty-seven ronin from Akō in 1702. As usual, he spent more than his allotted hour demolishing every foundation stone of the beloved tale, but what stuck in my friend's mind was a casual comment made near the end of the lecture. Shigeno seems to have remarked that an excellent collection of documents was rumored to survive in the family of the late Ōhashi Totsuan. "But no one has ever seen them," he added, "and we don't know if they still exist—if ever they did exist."

"If ever they *did* exist": that was pure Shigeno—and not a very kind comment. It must have been my father himself who told him of Shōzan's collection when they were colleagues at the old Confucian Academy. But it was in that instant, when my friend repeated Shigeno's remark, that I knew—after fifty years of not knowing—that most certainly they *had* existed, because fifty-some years before, I had seen them. I had seen them carried into the house, two great bundles neatly wrapped in dark-blue cotton. I had watched the old man untie the bundles and leaf through volume after volume as he explained a bit about what they contained. The mind is a capricious instrument. I had witnessed the old man's farewell to the fruits of a life's work, and I had eradicated the event, totally, from my memory. Now it all came back.

✦ ✦ ✦

But did the documents *still* exist? Obviously they did, or I wouldn't be telling you this. But there was a span of about half an hour, while searching our storehouse, when I came close to giving up. Then I lifted yet another box, set it aside, and there they were. It was at that moment, I think, that I first began to feel something of the fascination that these documents held for the old man who had collected them. The bundles turned out to be nowhere near as large as my child's mind had imagined them, which is probably the reason I'd failed to notice them at first. Fifty years earlier, they must have stood almost as tall as I did. Now, resting at the rear of a bottom shelf, obscured but not hidden by a cluster of paulownia-wood storage boxes, it was their shape and not their size that told me they contained two stacks of books equal in height. I lifted them to the floor. The blue fabric was covered with dust but not faded; when I undid the knots, folded down the corners of the cloth, and opened the cover of the topmost volume, the paper was like new. Oblivion had been a benevolent protector. No one else had even looked at these pages since Shōzan handed over the bundles to Father.

Unfortunately, I was never able to show the collection to Professor Shigeno. He was in his eighties when he gave the lecture my friend attended, and he died not long thereafter. Nor had I, at first, any more success in finding a publisher than old Shōzan himself had had. Eventually, though, through my connections as a journalist, I did manage to publish some of the more interesting pieces serially in a newspaper; after which the response to these documents persuaded the National Publications Society to bring out a handsome, three-volume edition of Shōzan's collection, more than half a century after the old man had parted with his life's work. As a courtesy, I was asked to write a short afterword. This I gladly did, if only to express my delight that the old man's work was now safe from destruction. But safety from destruction is one thing; proper appreciation is another. I have survived a devastating earthquake that forced us to move out of the city and across the river; I have lived through a revolution, albeit a short one; and I have watched the world of my childhood and youth all but totally disappear.

Who in this new world we now live in reads old documents of this sort? The more I read them myself, though, the more I came to feel that it was my duty to save not merely the texts themselves but also the tale that the old man spent his life trying to reconstruct from them—which is to say, the true story of the Akō vendetta.

As I write, I wish I could say, *This is what I remember; this is what the old man told my father.* For I did see the old samurai, standing straight and tall in the vestibule with his great bundles of documents—this much my mother told me. I may even have noticed the great calluses on his elbows for which he was famous—the sign of a truly inveterate reader. But I have no clear memory of these things; I was too young. All I can say is that in the months that followed my "discovery," I read every one of the volumes he left with us, some of them several times over. I can't claim to know them as thoroughly as the man who spent his life collecting and copying them. But I certainly can feel the power of the spell they cast over him, and I hope they may say to me in my old age some of the same things they said to Nabeta Shōzan.

◆ ◆ ◆

The story begins on New Year's Day of the year Genroku 14 (1701).

ŌHASHI YOSHIZŌ

PART I

Year of the Serpent

Genroku 14 (1701)

CHAPTER

1

━━◗▭▬━━━━━━━

*This New Year appears
not to augur well.*

Edo, New Year's Season, Genroku 14 (1701)
As always, there were those who said that catastrophe was certain to strike this year, but for once the doomsayers seem to have had some evidence for their dire predictions. On the eve of the New Year, the citizens of Edo, as was their custom, had remained awake throughout the night. Then, in the hour before dawn, dressed in their holiday best, they thronged to the heights and to the seashore, to Takanawa and Shiba, to Atago and Kanda, and especially to the strand in Fukagawa, hoping to greet the first rays of the rising sun and to pray that the Great Peace, which the whole land now enjoyed, would continue. Instead, they found the sky heavily overcast, and no sooner had the clouds begun to lighten than they were suddenly turned black by a near-total eclipse of the sun—80 percent to be precise—plunging the city back into almost total darkness. Astronomers at the Official Observatory were well aware that this eclipse would occur; for them, it was a predictable astronomical event. Yet predictable or no, to the multitude, it remained an omen, and the Shogun's Junior Council of Elders had already ordered rites to counteract its effects at several of the larger temples. Science notwithstanding, they knew from experience that the appearance of concern was important.

But the magic didn't work. No sooner had light returned to the city than news began to spread of a ghastly discovery in the house of a respected military family, the Ōkōchi by name, who lived near the new Eitai Bridge. In the vestibule to their home, whither they had gone to open their doors to the first visitors of the New Year, they found the severed head of a woman lying in a pool of blood. Who the woman was and how her head had got there were never subsequently explained. The Ōkōchi did their best to put a propitious interpretation on the event. For a military house, they said, nothing could bring greater good fortune than to take a head on the 1st Day of the New Year. They even built a little shrine to honor their happy find. But they knew as well as anyone that finding the head of a strange woman in their vestibule was not the same as decapitating an enemy on the battlefield.

No, the fourteenth year of Genroku did not get off to a good start. But what future misfortunes might these omens portend? That was still anyone's guess. The New Year's season being as hectic as it is, most people just forgot them.

But not everyone. An old man living in retirement on the fringes of the city received the following New Year's greeting from his younger kinsman, the Chief Elder of the domain of Akō in the western province of Harima:

> As this New Year appears not to augur well, I trust you will take particular care to keep in good health. Please rest assured that all of us here, as we grow another year older, remain well. We send you our most cordial good wishes for the New Year's season.
>
> FIRST MONTH, 1ST DAY   Ōishi Kuranosuke [monogram]
> To: Ōishi Mujin Sama and family

✦ ✦ ✦

The hectic pace of the New Year's season—sometimes I think that that alone could be the cause of catastrophe. Even a beggar becomes a busy man with the coming of the New Year, at least as long as people continue to throng the temples and shrines. Before long, however, the crowds dwindle, along with their spirit of generosity, and his life returns to normal. A respectable townsman, however, can count on spending the better part of a month discharging his duties and fulfilling his obligations. For a samurai, it can take longer, depending upon his rank—added to which, he has far more demanding standards of decorum. But imagine what it must be like for the Shogun and those involved in the discharge of his obligations. I despair of giving you anything like a precise account of the fifth Shogun's movements on that morning of the 1st Day of 1701. The documentation is so cryptic, so fragmentary, and so much changes from year to year. But since everything that transpired thereafter traces back to this day, I feel I must at least try.

At dawn on New Year's Day, the Shogun begins a grueling stint of three full days in which he must receive and reciprocate the greetings of all his clansmen, his vassals, his allied lords, and his liegemen—not to mention the numberless groups of eminent merchants and craftsmen who are not of samurai rank, but whose services he depends upon.

♦ ♦ ♦

Long before first light, the upper mansions of the great and powerful are alive with preparations for their lords' progress to the castle. In the lamp-lit inner rooms, the lord himself is being dressed in his most formal court attire. In the long barrack blocks that enclose the property, his vanguard, his Corps of Pages, and his Horse Guards are arming and outfitting themselves. In the storage rooms, lackeys and menials are assembling the equipment of their assigned tasks—the halberds and the lances that identify the house, the umbrellas, the seating mats for the long wait at the dismounting ground, the crested trunks. In the stables, horses are being curried, caparisoned, and saddled. And in the kitchens, tea and rations for the whole procession are being prepared and packed.

Finally, as the night sky turns gray and then crimson, the lord's palanquin, borne by four men in livery and followed by four more in reserve, is carried to the formal entry hall of the mansion, while in the white-graveled court before it, the procession forms up. When the signal to march is given, His Lordship emerges from his quarters and boards his conveyance; the trunk bearers, in perfect unison, grasp the poles of their burdens, flip them smartly into the air, and settle them upon their shoulders; the gates swing open; the guide of the column takes his place at its head, strides out of the gate, and turns smartly in the direction of the castle.

It is a stirring sight to watch these columns converge upon the main gate of the Shogun's castle, just as the sun is about to rise above the city for the first time in the New Year. They have been ordered to arrive at dawn, and precisely at dawn they arrive—their movements synchronized by the beat of the time drum in its tower on the ramparts of the castle. There are not as many great lords today as on a day of general audience, but those whose appointed day it is are the grandest of grand. One moment, the square is empty, an immaculately swept open ground presided over by the exquisitely fashioned sprays of pine and bamboo that flank the gates of the mansions facing it. The next moment, the streets begin to fill with the precise and purposeful steps of the long trains of the premier military houses of the land. To a man, they are clad in their New Year's best and groomed to perfection; yet even in their finery, they look as ready for action as for ceremony. Their formal trousers are bloused up above their knees, revealing the muscled calves of men who can—and regularly do—march the length of the land. Their lances look as tall as the masts of ships; the hilts of their swords protrude menacingly; their stance is wide, and their pace firm; their fingers are curled in a loose fist, their elbows tensed, their arms swinging smartly in time with their pace; their gaze is straight and steady, and their faces stern, as though to say, "Touch me, and I'll kill you; come near me, and I'll knock you flat."

Here, in its full glory, is the might that a Shogun can command. The spotter, who runs to the guardhouse and cries out the name of lord and domain as each column approaches, is trained to identify every noble house in the land by the shape of the plumes and scabbards atop its lances. His cries, in turn, send other foot soldiers running to direct the course of the converging columns. Amid all this running about and shouting of commands, these great bodies of warriors move in almost total silence to their appointed places on the dismounting ground. They form up into units, arrange their equipment in neat rows, spread their mats, and take their seats. For all but a few, this is the terminus of their march. Here, for the next four hours or more, they will wait while their lord fulfills his duties in the castle. Inevitably, the mood shifts as the concentration of the march gives way to the resignation of waiting. As ever among warriors too long at their ease, quarrels and fights break out between the lower ranks of the several houses. But these are remarkably few. The better sort of samurai more likely takes a book from the folds of his kimono—perhaps a volume of old poems or, more often, a critique of new offerings at the theaters or even a guide to the ladies of the pleasure quarters. The lackeys sit down on the trunks they have borne here and gossip and smoke. And before long, peddlers of saké and snacks and sweets come weaving through the crowd, doing their best to eke out a living by easing the boredom of their captive market. At the fringes of the ground, small clusters of sightseers appear. Some can be seen turning the pages of the latest Military Register, trying to identify the several lords from the crests on their trunks or the plumes atop their lances. Others—perhaps beggars or country folk—just stand with their mouths agape at the splendor of it all.

Yet while most settle down to a long wait, a few must prepare for the next stage of their lord's progress. Six of his closest attendants gather around his palanquin—two on either side and two before it—while at the rear, there follow two trunk bearers, the sandal bearer, and the umbrella bearer. When all is in order, His Lordship's palanquin is again hoisted to the shoulders of its bearers, and they cross the moat to the main gate. It is a deceptively modest gate, designed not to withstand attack, but to draw an enemy into the heavily fortified trap of stone walls that lie behind its doors. Once within this bastion, the small suite quickly vanishes from the sight of the force left behind on the dismounting ground. It turns to the right; passes through a massive inner gate; emerges into the Third Perimeter, the outermost of the moated enclosures; turns sharply to the left; and traverses another broad yard to the Alighting Bridge. Here, again, the procession must halt, in front of the long guardhouse of the Company of One Hundred, and it may go no farther. An attendant crouches and slides open the door to the palanquin. Then the sandal bearer, from a position to the rear of the conveyance where he will not violate His Lordship's line of vision, takes aim and with the easy skill of long practice tosses his lord's sandals—first the right, then the left—so that they land in perfect alignment and in the precise position where His Lordship will step as he emerges. For

figure 1
The dismounting ground at the main gate of Edo Castle.
(*Tokugawa seiseiroku*, 1889)

even a lord whose domain covers an entire province and more must cross this bridge on foot.

From here on, His Lordship is attended by only his Commander of the Bodyguard, his Liaison Officer, his sandal bearer, and one of the trunk bearers—and if it is raining, his umbrella bearer as well. They cross the Alighting Bridge, at the far end of which they pass through the Third Gate into another fortified enceinte. Here they exit to the left, into the yard of the Second Perimeter; pass yet another guardhouse; and then veer to the right toward the Middle Gate, the only one of the six inner gates that does not open into a stone-walled trap. At this gate, the trunk bearer must halt and wait.

Once through the Middle Gate, the lord and his attendants ascend the long winding causeway rising to the Central Perimeter. Finally, they enter the last of the fortified enclosures, and when they emerge from the Great Shoin Gate on the far side of it, they are within sight of the entryway to the palace. Here the lord must leave behind even the last remnants of his entourage. A samurai of good lineage, sent ahead for the purpose, takes his long sword, and when His Lordship steps up into the entry hall, the sandal bearer retrieves his sandals. But only one member of his entourage, usually his Liaison Officer, is allowed actually to enter the palace. And even this man may not accompany his lord; he must wait in the Fern-Palm Room until the ceremonies are over, at which time it is his duty to receive and carry away the gifts that his lord has been given by the Shogun. In the meantime, the Commander of the Bodyguard, the Keeper of the Sword, and the lackeys withdraw. His Lordship enters the palace, armed with only his short sword and attended by only a Palace Usher with shaven head, one of that great host of hundreds known familiarly, at least to their superiors, as the Tea Monks.

And so, one after another, the great lords arrive, traveling in pomp and splendor as far as the castle gates, and then gradually shedding the protection of their entourage as they penetrate deeper into the maze of walls and moats and finally are ushered, alone and disarmed, to their appointed places in the palace, there to await their turn to greet the Shogun.

◆ ◆ ◆

In the meantime, the Shogun himself has been quite as busy as any of the lords now arriving. Well before the sun rises over the ramparts, his preparations are nearly complete. His body bathed, his teeth cleaned, his hair dressed, and his regalia laid out in readiness, it remains only for his personal attendants to help him dress.

His first destination is the Women's Palace, where he exchanges greetings with his wife. This visit requires only a middling level of formal costume—a standard blue kimono with crosshatched midriff, a heavily starched linen vest with sharply pointed shoulders, and linen trousers with extra-long legs that extend a yard or so beyond his feet. Thus clad, he strides through the locked door—through which he and he alone may pass—and down the long "bell corridor," past rows of women of all ranks, all with heads bowed to the floor, and takes his seat in the upper level of the audience chambers, where he is joined, on the same level, by his wife.

"My felicitations on the advent of this New Year," he says. "And may you enjoy many more such years to come."

"I offer you my heartiest greetings of the New Year," she replies. "And may it ever be thus."

Whereupon, they both rise, leave the room, and proceed farther down the corridor to the Altar Room, where they pay their respects to the mortuary tablets of their departed ancestors. In their absence, there is a flurry of activity in the audience chambers, for when the couple return, the rooms will be filled with an array of sweets and the meats of fowls and fishes—the Toso Repast, a menu meant to ward off illness in the coming year and to lengthen their span of life in years to come. The first dish, however, is a thin, unappetizing soup, flavored with only unseasoned slices of a great white radish, the purpose of which is to remind them of those long lean years that the House of Tokugawa endured before rising to its present eminence.

"Particularly tasty this year," the Shogun enthuses, and, turning to his wife, "My Lady, do have another bowl!" His Highness himself, however, has no time to linger over the more truly delectable offerings to follow, for he must return to his own apartments and change into formal court costume for the more public ceremonials at which his presence is required.

◆ ◆ ◆

About an hour later, his attendants make the final adjustments to his robe of imperial purple and knot the cord of his tall black-lacquered court cap. Followed by two Page Boys, one bearing his sword, His Highness leaves his quarters in the middle reaches of the palace and strides to the most formal of his audience chambers, the Whitewood Rooms. There, a member of his Council of Elders awaits him. The Elder slides open the door, and the Shogun enters and takes his seat, facing south at the front of the uppermost of the two chambers. The Elder follows him in, slides the door shut, and takes his place in the Lower Chamber, to the Shogun's right. The long day can now begin.

The heads of the three cadet branches of the Tokugawa house— Owari, Kii, and Mito—are the first to be received. These are the Shogun's closest relatives, to whom he turns for counsel in times of crisis—and for an heir as well, should his own line be barren of male issue. And waiting with them in the corridor is Matsudaira Kaga-no-Kami, head of the House of Maeda, the most formidable of the Shogun's allies. Needless to say, the preeminence of these four gentlemen entitles them to enter the presence individually, in the order of their respective ranks. When all is in readiness, an Inspector General bows to them and in a low voice gives the signal: "This way, please."

The lord of Owari enters, bearing before him at eye level a white-wood platform tray over which is draped a neatly inscribed list of his New Year's gifts to the Shogun, weighed down by a short ceremonial sword—or, more precisely, I should say a replica of a sword, for by this time these gift swords were no longer made of steel, but of wood. When he reaches the division between mats to which his rank entitles him to advance, he kneels, places the tray as far before himself as he can reach, and bows low. As he does so, the Elder announces him: "The Owari Grand Counselor." The lord of Owari then rises and moves to a seat in the Lower Chamber at the Shogun's left.

In like manner, the remaining three lords enter and, although their rank does not entitle them to advance quite so far into the room, they too present their offerings and make obeisance. When all have been

figure 2
Tosa Mitsuoki's portrait of Tokugawa Tsunayoshi in formal court costume.
(Tokugawa Art Museum, Nagoya)

announced, and all have taken their seats on the Shogun's left, the Elder speaks again: "The Owari Grand Counselor, the Kii Middle Counselor, the Mito Middle Counselor, and Matsudaira Kaga-no-Kami make bold to offer their greetings upon the advent of this New Year."

The Shogun turns to them, inclines his head slightly, and replies, "Felicitations." At this signal, four Masters of Military Protocol enter and remove the trays bearing the lists of gifts and ceremonial swords. They are followed immediately by three Masters of Court Protocol carrying whitewood platform trays, upon each of which rests a shallow unglazed cup—one for saké, one for the hare broth so auspicious to the Tokugawa house, and one into which any excess droplets from the other two may be deposited. These are placed before the Shogun, whereupon two more Masters of Court Protocol enter with the vessels of saké and broth from which they will pour. The Shogun, of course, is served first. He takes his sip of saké in three drafts and hands the cup back to the Master of Court Protocol. It is filled again and placed upon a tray that a Captain of the Corps of Pages carries to the Owari Major Counselor. The Lord of Owari, too, drains the cup in three drafts and replaces it on the tray, upon which it is carried back to where it began its felicitous circuit. Any remaining droplets are tapped into the third cup, and the pouring of another such exchange may begin.

And so it goes until His Highness has imbibed both saké and broth with all four of his most exalted callers of the day. This done, the implements are removed to the anteroom, and the Shogun's gifts to the gentlemen, suits of seasonal robes displayed on long whitewood trays, are carried in and set before them by members of the Shogun's Corps of Pages. The gentlemen bow and rise to retreat, followed by the Pages who bear their gifts to the Fern-Palm Room, where they hand them to the Liaison Officers of the four lords.

✦ ✦ ✦

Now the Shogun must betake himself to the more spacious rooms of the Great Hall, where he will receive another illustrious group, also his relatives, but related more distantly or by marriage. First come the Ikeda of Tottori, the Matsudaira of Fukui, and the Matsudaira of Tsuyama.

"This way please . . ." They enter and are announced individually, although not by an Elder but by a Master of Military Protocol; they present their gifts, albeit from a greater distance than did their more exalted kinsmen. "Felicitations . . ." Congratulatory cups are exchanged; suits of seasonal clothing bestowed. And being less closely related to His Highness, these lords are allowed—indeed, required—to take their cups home with them as mementos of their audience. They wrap them in fine paper brought for the purpose, place them gently within the folds of their robes, and retreat. A member of the Shogun's Corps of Pages follows, bearing the Shogun's gifts of seasonal clothing, which he will hand to a Palace Usher at the end of the corridor, who will, in turn, give them to the lords' Liaison Officers in the Fern-Palm Room.

The next group is a mixture of kinsmen still more distantly related, as well as liegemen of long standing, all of Junior Fourth Rank: the Matsudaira of Takasu, of Saijō, of Moriyama, and of Fuchū and the Ii of Hikone. "This way please . . ." Then come the Matsudaira of Aizu, of Takamatsu, of Matsuyama, of Kuwana, of Maebashi, and of Akashi, followed by the Tōdō of Tsu and the Maeda of Daishōji. "Felicitations . . ." Cups wrapped, these lords, too, take their leave.

◆ ◆ ◆

While all of this has been going on, a much larger assembly of lords has been waiting behind closed doors in a long space, known simply as Rooms Two and Three, adjacent to the Great Hall. Those in the front rows are daimyo of Junior Fifth Rank, and behind them kneel the Shogun's higher-ranking bannermen, each with his list of gifts, weighed down by a sword, spread across a tray before him. These men the Shogun will receive collectively. He leaves his seat and walks down to the lower level of the chamber, where he stands facing the doors. "This way, please," an Inspector General says to the assembly; whereupon, two members of the Council of Elders slide open the doors behind which the Shogun stands. As one, the entire assembly bows, brows to the floor; whereupon, one of the Elders who opened the doors declares, "One and all proffer you their greetings on the advent of this New Year." "Felicitations," the Shogun replies, still standing. "We are all most grateful to Your Highness for your salutation," the Elder replies; whereupon, both Elders slide the doors shut again.

One would be tempted to describe the scene as a sort of dramatic performance, were it not that the curtain remains open for but a few seconds and the audience sees almost nothing of the action on stage. And for those in the middle to rear rows, this brief glimpse of His Highness is the only sight of him they will catch throughout the entire year. Those in the front rows, however, some of them lords of sizable domains, will now be allowed to present their greetings (and gifts) in person. Not individually, of course, but in groups of three or five.

Under the direction of the same Inspector General who guided them to their assigned seats and alerted them when the doors were about to open, they begin to exit Room Two, three by three, into the polished corridor, from which they enter the presence of the Shogun, who by now has returned to his seat on the upper level of the Great Hall. Saké is served by the Commanders of the Life Guards and the Corps of Pages; cups are wrapped and slipped within robes. The trio then moves to the west side of the room, and in unison bow. As they rise, three Officers of Shogunal Benefaction approach and place a suit of seasonal robes on the left shoulder of each lord, all three of whom, again in unison, place their left hands upon their benefaction as they withdraw. Then come the next three daimyo and the next and the next.

Finally come the bannermen, who rank below the daimyo, but high enough nonetheless to enter the presence of the Shogun—"Wearers of the Hunting Cloak," as they are called. These men enter in groups of five, are served their saké by members of the Corps of Pages, and receive no gifts whatever. They simply wrap their cups and depart.

◆ ◆ ◆

And so it goes throughout the entire day, throughout the 2nd Day, and throughout the 3rd. The heirs of the Three Cadet Houses, the heirs of the more distant Tokugawa relatives, the lords of domains comprising an entire province or more—the Hosokawa, the Asano, the Shimazu, the Daté, and at least ten more—must be greeted in the Whitewood Rooms. They are followed by representatives of those lords who for reasons of illness or absence or youth are unable to greet the Shogun in person. If the Keeper of the Shogun's castle in Osaka happens to be in Edo, he, too, offers his felicitations on this day. Then the Elders of the greatest noble houses are felicitated in the long Pine Gallery. Heirs apparent, newly succeeded to their domains, are welcomed in the Hall of T'ang Emperors. And in an anteroom to the Blackwood Rooms, the Elders of the several commoners' wards of Edo; the Upper and Lower wards of Kyoto; and the cities of Osaka, Sakai, Nara, and Fushimi; as well as representatives of the guilds of the Yodo River boatmen, the silversmiths, the moneychangers, and the makers of vermillion ink. The list goes on and on, and comprises just about every category of official, craftsman, artist, and merchant one can think of.

And in the evenings and intervals of these highly formal exchanges, there come the celebrations of myriad "Firsts"—chief among them, the First Chanting of the Nō, performed by several of the greatest lords in the land, but also the First Sweeping of the Palace, the First Mounting of the Horse, and so on and so forth. I'll not even attempt a summary of this multitude of festivities.

+ + +

After the first three days, the pace slackens somewhat. The governance of the realm cannot be neglected for days on end, and the officials involved have their own obligations to be discharged. Even so, the end of the New Year's season is still a long way off. Not until the 1st Day of the Second Month does the Prince-Abbot of the Shogunal Temples at Ueno and Nikko come to offer his greetings for the New Year. And behind-the-scenes preparations are under way for an observance far more extended and complicated than any other of the season—the transmission of the Shogun's greetings to the one person in the land who, nominally at least, ranks above him: the Emperor in Kyoto. The complexity of this exchange is due not only to the logistics of long-distance travel, but also to the fact that it must be conducted according to the protocols of the Imperial Court, which differ greatly from those of the Shogun's court.

So great are the differences, in fact, that a small corps of specialists in court ceremonial is required to handle the Shogunate's business with the Imperial Court. These are the gentlemen of the so-called Exalted Houses. As you can tell from their names—Kira, Ōtomo, Oda, Takeda, Shinagawa, Hatakeyama—most of them are descended from the once-great clans that were defeated in the wars that raged before Tokugawa Ieyasu brought peace to the land. In this sense, perhaps, they are indeed "exalted"—but in no other. For these are the clans that lost all their wealth, all their lands, and all the power of their armed might. Yet Ieyasu, in yet another instance of his seemingly boundless practical wisdom, saw a use for these shattered remnants of the once "exalted." Their knowledge of the language and the customs and the ceremonies of the Emperor and his court—gained from years of aping the court—could be put to good use in keeping the Emperor and his courtiers from meddling in affairs of state.

The Emperor's palace was refurbished, and his courtiers were given small estates that would provide them with a comfortable, although far from opulent, income. And then they were commanded to devote their time exclusively to the noble pursuits of scholarship and poetry. There was to be no direct contact between any military house and the houses of the nobility. All business was to be conducted through a strictly defined channel of communication that always must pass through the office of the Shogunal Deputy for Kyoto. On the side of the court, two gentlemen of good family were to be appointed as Military Liaison Officers, at a stipend of 250 bales of polished rice per year, to be paid by the Shogunate. On the side of the Shogunate, a few gentlemen of the "Exalted Houses" would be appointed Masters of Court Protocol. In this way, all relations between Shogun and Emperor could be conducted according to the highest standards of decorum—and under the strictest supervision. When the court had business with the Shogun, it would first go to the Shogunal Deputy. If it was then deemed advisable that the Military Liaison Officers travel to Edo, they would be accommodated there in a lodge built especially for the purpose, a daimyo would be appointed to see to their every need, and they would be treated according to the customs and usages of their own court. And conversely, when the Shogun had business with the court, he would send his exalted

Master of Court Protocol to Kyoto, where, under the supervision of the Shogunal Deputy, he could deal with the court in the manner to which it was accustomed. Accordingly, these exalted gentlemen were given court rank even higher than that of most daimyo. They were not themselves daimyo, however, as their forebears had been; their stipendiary fiefs yielded less than half the income of even the lowest-ranking daimyo. Neither were they permitted to learn any of the martial arts. Nor did they have any voice in the exercise of authority. But in rank, and in the company they kept, they were exalted indeed, these Masters of Court Protocol. As you can imagine, the New Year's season, with its multitude of ceremonies, was their season of greatest glory; and the greatest honor of the season was to carry the Shogun's felicitations to the Emperor.

In the fourteenth year of Genroku (1701), this long process was set in train on the 7th Day of the First Month. The Masters of Court Protocol had, of course, been serving in secondary roles from the very beginning of the hectic round of New Year's observances. But on this day, duties were assigned that only they, with their unique knowledge of Imperial Court custom, would be competent to perform. A delegation would be dispatched as the Shogun's representatives to the Great Shrine at Ise, as would another delegation to the tomb of the founding Shogun in Nikkō. The most important task, however, was that of the Shogun's emissary to the Emperor. It was this official who must travel to Kyoto and present the Shogun's felicitations for the New Year to the Emperor and the Retired Emperor; upon his return to Edo, it would be he who must oversee the round of ceremonies and entertainments that would ensue when the Emperor's envoys came to Edo to return His Majesty's greetings to the Shogun. This task would span a period of more than two months. It was assigned to Kira Kōzuke-no-Suke Yoshinaka.

At the time of the fifth Shogun, some five gentlemen of the Exalted Houses held appointments as Masters of Court Protocol, and several more were assigned to the Reserve Force to await future openings. Of this number, Kira Kōzuke-no-Suke was the acknowledged doyen. At the age of sixty-one, not only was he the eldest member of his corps, but his experience in office totaled more than forty years. Nor had he wasted any of that time. He had grown extremely learned in every aspect of court lore, and his knowledge of the minutiae of courtly ceremony was unsurpassed. Whatever duty might be assigned him, Kira could be counted on to perform it with practiced grace and perfect decorum.

Kira was, moreover, extremely well connected. Two centuries or so in the past, in the dynasty preceding the Tokugawa, the Kira were the premier kinsmen of the Ashikaga Shogun and the first to be called upon to provide a successor when the Ashikaga Shogun was without issue. When we follow the Kira genealogy down to the early years of the present dynasty, we find that Kira's great-grandfather was a son of the great-aunt of Tokugawa Ieyasu. Nor did his glory lie entirely in the past. Kira's wife was the sister of Uesugi Tsunakatsu, and Kira's son had been adopted into the Uesugi house as the heir to Tsunakatsu. This young man had, in turn, married a daughter of the Kii branch of the Tokugawa house, a lady whose brother was married to the only daughter of the ruling Shogun, Tokugawa Tsunayoshi. Kira's own daughters, moreover, had married into three of the greatest houses of their day: the Shimazu, the Sakai, and the Tsugaru. The lines of relationship are complicated, but their results can be summed up easily enough: Kira was descended of a house that once could have produced a Shogun; he himself was a blood relative of the founding Shogun; and through ties of marriage, he was related to the ruling Shogun. He was also the father of one of the most powerful lords in the land, the father-in-law of another, and a more distant kinsman of two more.

It was rumored as well that the Shogun had compelling reasons to appoint this particular man to carry his greetings to Kyoto in this particular year—reasons that had nothing to do with celebrating the New Year.

The fifth Shogun, you may know, was a devotee of the doctrines of Confucius, and not merely in the sense that he listened dutifully to the lectures of the scholars he patronized. Those who remember him for only the severity and capriciousness of his legislation lose sight of the fact that this Shogun was as extreme in his virtues as he was in his flaws. He was himself a learned scholar, who could—and did—lecture on the Confucian canon. In consequence, his practice of the doctrine of devotion to one's parents went far beyond the careful observance of forms. His devotion to his mother, Keishōin, was as extravagant as it was sincere. And having lavished upon her every form of devotion that he himself could command, he now desired that she be promoted to First Rank in the imperial hierarchy—an honor that could be granted only by command of the Emperor. But, alas, the Shogun's mother was not a lady of distinguished birth. In the normal course of things, it probably would never have occurred to the Emperor or his advisers to raise her to such high rank. It was, of course, within the Shogun's power simply to demand the favor. Yet to do so would only rob the honor of its value. It must seem—to the court as much as to the world—to be granted in the free exercise of goodwill. It must be arranged delicately and diplomatically by someone who enjoyed the confidence of the Imperial Court. This, they say, was Kira's unstated mission in Kyoto. In his round of visits to the ranking nobles of the court, he would drop veiled allusions to the Shogun's highly virtuous desire, as well as to the gratitude that would be shown those contributing to its realization. Appropriately timed and carefully chosen, these few words should, within a year or so, yield the desired effect. To execute such a mission, there was no one more competent than Kira.

Shortly after dawn on the 11th Day of the First Month, four days after his appointment as the Shogun's emissary to the Emperor, Kira and his suite of twenty-seven attendants set out from his home near the enceinte at the Kajibashi Bridge. They stopped briefly at the castle to pick up the Shogun's New Year's gifts to the Emperor, and then made a direct route for the Eastern Sea Road. Depending on the weather and the depth of the rivers that must be forded, they could expect to enter the imperial city of Kyoto within twelve to fifteen days.

✦ ✦ ✦

Well after Kira's departure, further preparations for the Shogun's exchange of greetings with the Emperor were set in motion. It was the practice of the Shogunate to grant the honor of entertaining the Imperial Envoys to two of their daimyo allies. This was by no means a coveted honor. It was a long and stressful task, both for the daimyo themselves and for their vassals who were resident in Edo. It also involved, in the words of one lord so honored, "massive expenditure." The burdens were enormous.

In the fourteenth year of Genroku, the Council of Elders decided that this year the entertainment of the Emperor's envoys would be entrusted to Asano Takumi-no-Kami Naganori, lord of the domain of Akō, a cadet branch of the great House of Asano in Hiroshima. The envoy of the Retired Emperor Reigen would be entertained by Daté Sakyō-no-Suke Muneharu, the young lord of the domain of Yoshida in the province of Iyo, a cadet branch of the house descended from that fearsome warrior of an earlier century, the "One-eyed Dragon," Daté no Masamune.

CHAPTER

2

*We understand that in recent years, these
entertainments have been tending to extravagance.
We trust that this year, you will proceed,
shall we say, somewhat more lightly.*

Monstrous events can arise from the most mundane beginnings. All it took this time was an unwitting mismatch of two men to turn a tedious routine, performed countless times past without mishap, into a bloody tumult. Were it not for their horrendous consequences, the procedures described here would hardly be worth reading about. But if we are to comprehend what happened in the Third Month, we must first look back at events in the Second Month. I shall be as brief as possible.

Edo, Second Month, 3rd Day
On the morning of this day, a messenger arrived at the Upper Mansion of Asano Takumi-no-Kami bearing a directive from the Council of Elders and signed by all five Elders. The missive itself does not survive, but the gist of it is recorded in the Asano house records: "Tomorrow the 4th, at mid–Fifth Hour (9:00 a.m.), you are to present yourself at the castle in connection with matters of official business." No hint of the nature of that business was given.

Edo, Second Month, 4th Day
At 9:00 a.m., both Asano Takumi-no-Kami and Daté Sakyō-no-Suke appeared at the castle as directed and took their assigned seats in the Willow Room of the palace, whence they were shown into the presence of the full Council of Elders in the Hall of T'ang Emperors. Akimoto

Tajima-no-Kami, the Duty Elder for the Second Month, then informed Asano that he had been appointed official host to the two envoys from the Emperor, and Daté that he was to host the envoy from the Retired Emperor. Both men, with heads bowed to the floor, expressed their gratitude for the honor accorded them, following which Tajima-no-Kami offered them some advice: "The entertainment of court nobles has always been conducted in accord with court precedents of long standing. I would advise you, therefore, to consult with the Masters of Court Protocol—in particular, Kira Kōzuke-no-Suke—to ensure that all goes as prescribed." To which he added, "We understand that in recent years, these entertainments have been tending to extravagance. We trust that this year, you will proceed, shall we say, somewhat more lightly." Nothing more is recorded of this conference.

◆ ◆ ◆

The man they had been advised particularly to consult, Kira Kōzuke-no-Suke, was, of course, not available. In recent years, he had been in the habit of leaving Edo on the 13th Day of the First Month and returning on the 24th of the Second Month. This year, he had departed two days earlier, but even as the end of the Second Month approached, there still was no news of his return. There was, nonetheless, much to be getting on with in his absence.

First of all, there were the courtesy calls. Each of the five Elders must be visited individually and thanked for the bestowal of this distinguished appointment. These visits had to be made by Takumi-no-Kami himself, even though none of the Elders would be present in person, and so appropriate letters were written to leave with a Steward at each Elder's official mansion. And then each of the three ranking Masters of Court Protocol must be called upon, this time with letters protesting total ignorance of such esoteric lore as court ceremony and begging the benefit of their erudition and experience in the performance of this duty.

But, of course, no daimyo would ever entrust his fate entirely to the goodwill of a Master of Court Protocol. He would first gather as much inside information as he could from relatives and friends who had performed the same task in recent years, as well as from those of his vassals who might have contacts of their own. This was not the first time Takumi-no-Kami had served as host to the Imperial Envoys. On the previous occasion (1683), though, he had been but a youth of seventeen. His best source of intelligence would not be memory but the fresher experience of others.

The first to come to his aid were his in-laws. Five years earlier, in 1696, his wife's nephew, Asano Tosa-no-Kami Nagazumi, lord of the Asano cadet house in Miyoshi, had served as host to the Imperial Envoys, and his Liaison Officers had kept careful records. This year, Tosa-no-Kami was absent from Edo owing to illness. But his father, Shikibu-no-Shō Nagateru, Lady Asano's elder brother, was living in retirement at the Akasaka Middle Mansion of the Miyoshi house. As soon as he heard of Takumi-no-Kami's appointment, he sent him these valuable volumes. They were, I am sure, of considerable practical value; but for those of us who know what was to happen a month or so later, the most interesting, and significant, advice he was given came in the form of earnest, if unavailing, warnings from friends—in particular, Katō Tōtōmi-no-Kami Yasutane: "Last year, on the fiftieth anniversary of the death of the third Shogun, Iemitsu, I escorted Kira to the Tokugawa tombs in Nikkō. He is an overbearing man who delights in hurting others. There were many times when I wished I could kill him. Upon reflection, though, I realized that it would be an act of disloyalty to disrupt an official rite of such importance, just for the sake of a personal grievance. So I restrained myself. His treatment of you is bound to be just as rude. But he's not worth wasting your time on. I do hope, for the sake of your domain, that you'll be able to bear up under it. When it is all over, you'll be glad you did."

Takumi-no-Kami replied, "I'm very grateful for your advice and would be loath to reject it. But there are some things that must never be borne. I can't really promise that I shall do as you did."

There are reports of other such warnings, less well attested than this one. There is no need to repeat them, however, for they all suggest the same potential for tempestuous conflict: a haughty and disdainful official, one of those men for whom pride must serve as a substitute for power, finds himself briefly in a position to dictate to a castellan and lord of a domain of 53,000 koku—but in this case, a lord who happened to have a stubborn streak of his own. They warn, too, of Kira's avarice, another vice for which he was notorious. As an Elder of the great Satake house wrote in his diary that year:

> Kira Dono is a flagrantly arrogant man and underhanded as well. There are any number of people he has duped into giving him things. Just this last year, when he visited Izumi Dono for the first time and was banqueted there, he made off with a triptych of paintings by Sesshū [1420–1506]. So when he visits our mansion, we keep a close eye on his entourage and are under strict orders to display nothing of any value.

Takumi-no-Kami himself was well aware of Kira's reputation for greed—that "the more meager the gifts, the more meager his willingness to help." Yet when his Liaison Officers and Adjutants urged him to do as other daimyo were doing—shower Kira with gifts—Takumi-no-Kami refused. "Once I have completed my duties as official host," he said, "I shall send him appropriate gifts. But I think it quite inappropriate to send a plethora of gifts in advance." Only such gifts as customary formalities required were sent before Kira's return from Kyoto, but nothing in excess thereof. If only he could have heeded the warning of the anonymous satirist who wrote:

> yoku no kawa atsuki koto koso dōri nare
> kiritemo kirenu kōzuke no tsura
> Greed is nothing if not thick-skinned;
> such is just its nature. Cut you may,
> but you'll never cut through the brazen face of Kōzuke.

Edo, Second Month, 15th Day

To congratulate Takumi-no-Kami on his appointment as official host to the Imperial Envoys, the Asano main house in Hiroshima sent a gift of five hundred candles and unspecified auspicious delicacies.

But from this point forward, until the arrival of the Imperial Envoys in Edo, neither the Asano house records nor any other surviving account of this incident mentions anything done during these twenty-some days of frantic activity and fraught negotiation. We know that Kira returned somewhat later than he had been expected, on the 29th Day. But of why he had remained away so long, we know nothing. We can be sure that Takumi-no-Kami had been waiting impatiently for Kira's return and that his meeting with him would have been a tense one, what with Takumi's frustration and Kira's fatigue. But of that, too, there is no written record.

What we do know, though, from the records of another daimyo house, is that these days were filled with intense activity, involving just about every member of the Akō Corps of Vassals then resident in Edo. A journal compiled more than a hundred years later by an Elder of the House of Tamura Sakyō-no-Daibu cannot be presumed to replicate those activities in every particular, but the order and nature of such ceremonies changed very little. These records thus afford us a rare glimpse of how any daimyo assigned this duty busied himself during these days.

◆ ◆ ◆

Tamura had had a good deal more time in which to accomplish his preparations than did Takumi-no-Kami. Two full months elapsed between the time Sakyō-no-Daibu was informed of his appointment and the arrival of the envoys from Kyoto.

Once the initial courtesies had been observed, however, the Tamura vassals turned immediately to more practical matters. First there was the matter of food. This was no small matter. Each of the three envoys was to be accompanied by an entourage of eighty-three attendants (more than a few of them, I suspect, simply enjoying a free trip to Edo that the Tamura were forced to finance); there would be at least 250 mouths to feed. A daimyo could not ask his own kitchen and provisioning staff to take on the task; he had to contract with private caterers for the procurement, preparation, and serving of the meals.

Then there was the matter of the venue. The Imperial Envoys and at least some of their staff would be housed in the Military Liaison Lodge, immediately adjacent to the Military Tribunal, at a sharp bend in the moat known as the Dragon's Mouth. The daimyo serving as host to the nobles would also lodge here for the duration of the visit, together with a number of his vassals. It was necessary, therefore, that courtesy calls be paid to the permanent custodians of both the lodge and the tribunal. At the lodge, in particular, there would be many details to discuss, but fire prevention is the only one mentioned specifically.

Another matter that required considerable advance preparation was the day, midway through the visit, that would be devoted entirely to the entertainment of the nobles. A full program of five Nō plays, interlaced with comic Kyōgen interludes, was to be staged for their delectation. And then they would be served a lavish banquet, the menu for which survives. Fortunately for the Tamura, it was not a part of their duty to plan the menu, decide the program of the Nō, and make arrangements with the performers; those tasks were performed by the caterers and by the Shogun's own staff. But it was essential to the Tamura to know the details of these arrangements, so they might guide their charges without mishap through that long day.

As the arrival of the envoys drew nearer, preparations grew ever more concretely practical. First the buildings of the Military Liaison Lodge were inspected "in detail," no doubt to determine who would be housed where and how their movements would be directed (the floor plan indicating these assignments survives). The Tamura also undertook responsibility for the long tenement blocks in which the lesser members of the delegation would be quartered. Moreover, the task of cleaning the entire complex fell to the temporary occupants and not the permanent staff of the lodge, after which one of the Masters of Court Protocol inspected their work.

Once the Tamura had taken possession of the Military Liaison Lodge, their next responsibility was to furnish it. For the lodge was but an empty shell; it provided nothing. All the utensils required for cooking, all the dishes and trays needed for serving, all the equipment indispensable to ceremonial tea, every mattress and cushion and quilt, and even the scrolls and screens that would adorn the rooms in which the nobles were quartered had to be supplied from the stores of the official host.

The Tamura also made use of this interim before the arrival of their guests to practice some of the functions they were to perform at the lodge. The most important of these seems to have been the service of meals. The caterers were called in, together with the service staff they had recruited, and put through a dress rehearsal of an entire repast. The same day, the caterers submitted their proposed menus for approval, on the basis of which a list was drawn up of all the foodstuffs that must be procured. Five days later, the service staff was recalled, and the most presentable were singled out to serve the most exalted of the nobles. Orders had already been placed for new livery jackets bearing the Tamura crest, to be worn by these servitors and other lesser functionaries.

By this time, word had come by express-relay courier that the Imperial Envoys and their entourage had left Kyoto and would arrive in Edo ten days hence, on the 26th. It was by no means certain, however, that they would arrive on precisely that date. Four major rivers as well as several lesser streams had to be forded along the way, at any one of which they might be delayed by high water. Provision was made, therefore, to track their progress day by day from Numazu and Mishima over the last five days until their arrival in Edo. To this end, several "notification billets" of uniform size, 6.5 inches high and 3.5 inches wide, were cut from heavy paper, and on each was inscribed a stage in the progress of the envoys. Thus, for example, when the procession arrived in Mishima, a relay runner set out for Edo bearing a number of billets inscribed, "Lord Sanjō has just arrived in Mishima"; and when the procession set out again the next morning, another runner was dispatched bearing billets stating that "Lord Sanjō has just departed Mishima." As soon as these billets arrived at the Military Liaison Lodge, an officer on duty distributed them to the various parties who required this information. And so the process continued until the arrival of the envoys at Shinagawa, just outside the city. It was just as well, too, that such a system was employed, for the procession was indeed delayed by high water at the Ōi River and did not arrive in Edo until the 28th, two days later than planned.

This was also the time when the Tamura vassals most directly involved in entertaining the envoys moved from the Tamura Upper Mansion to the Military Liaison Lodge, taking with them all the equipment necessary to the execution of their many tasks. And, finally, on the day preceding the arrival of the envoys, a detail designated the Rear Guard moved into the inn in Shinagawa where the envoys would lodge on the last night of their journey; there they would welcome the travelers on behalf of their lord and then escort them on their progress through the city. On the same day, Tamura Sakyō-no-Daibu himself moved to quarters in the Military Liaison Lodge. Everything and everyone was now in place and prepared for the pageant to begin.

◆ ◆ ◆

When we return to the point at which we left off in the Asano records, we learn little more than that in the interim, "a certain discord had arisen between Takumi-no-Kami and Kōzuke-no-Suke" and that "time and again, Kōzuke-no-Suke treated him badly, often so much so as to anger Takumi-no-Kami Sama." They would have met frequently during the hurried round of preparations at the Military Liaison Lodge, which this year was more frenetic than usual, owing to Kira's tardy return from Kyoto. And we have it on good authority that Kira did speak abusively to Takumi-no-Kami in the course of their work there. Meanwhile, however, much else was going on.

Edo, Third Month, 10th Day

Before dawn, Tominomori Suke'emon and Takada Gunbei, both members of the Asano Horse Guards, departed the Military Liaison Lodge and set out for Shinagawa, on the outskirts of the city. These men were to serve as Rear Guards for the procession of the Imperial Envoys, which was scheduled to arrive in Shinagawa that day.

In the latter part of the morning, an advance unit of the envoys' procession arrived in Shinagawa. They were escorted to the Asano Upper Mansion, where at midday they were greeted by Takumi-no-Kami himself, and then were served a meal.

In the meantime, all who in any way were to be involved in entertaining the envoys left their quarters in the Asano mansion and moved to the Military Liaison Lodge. Takumi-no-Kami, too, now moved to the lodge. All secondary gates to the mansion were then barred, leaving only the main gate open to traffic.

Late in the afternoon, the envoys arrived in Shinagawa and were shown to the Honjin, the official inn reserved for those of exalted rank traveling on official business. The remainder of the day, they relaxed, while their attendants saw to the final preparations for their progress into Edo.

Edo, Third Month, 11th Day

Another very early start. According to the Asano house records, the procession was formed up and moving well before sunrise. About two hours after dawn, they arrived at the Military Liaison Lodge. Dark, heavy clouds hung low over the city throughout the day, but no rain fell.

Fortunately, this was to be a day of rest for the envoys, for Takumi-no-Kami was not feeling his best. Ever since his assignment to this duty, he had been busy night and day, and the strain had brought on a recurrence of the chronic chest pangs from which he suffered. His personal physician, Terai Genkei, prepared a brew of medicaments, and His Lordship was able to rest and recover his strength somewhat in preparation for the next day.

In the afternoon, a member of the Council of Elders and one of the Masters of Court Protocol, as emissaries of the Shogun, called at the lodge to welcome the Imperial Envoys and discuss with them their activities for the next few days.

Edo, Third Month, 12th Day

Rain today. At the Hour of the Serpent (ca. 9:00 a.m.), the Imperial Envoys were escorted by Takumi-no-Kami to the Shogun's palace within the Central Perimeter of the castle. There they were met by one of the Masters of Court Protocol and were taken to meet the full Council of Elders. Thereafter, they were shown to their retiring room at the head of the Pine Gallery, where they awaited their "face-to-face audience" with the Shogun in the nearby Whitewood Rooms. This meeting was the first of a pair of formal exchanges that constituted the principal reason for the envoys' journey to Edo. This day, they returned the greetings of the Emperor and other members of the Imperial Court to the Shogun, and presented the gifts that accompanied their good wishes. Two days hence, the Shogun would reciprocate.

Unfortunately, no detailed description of this rite survives, but the outlines of it are clear enough. After the envoys took their places in the Lower Chamber of the Whitewood Rooms, the Shogun entered and took his seat in the Upper Chamber, while in the adjacent room several high-ranking lords looked on. The senior envoy, Yanagiwara Sukekado, then presented the gifts of the Emperor—the traditional "sword and list" displayed on a platform tray—while the junior envoy, Takano Yasuharu, declaimed the formal greeting that accompanied the gifts. The gifts were accepted with due deference and placed on display in the alcove of the Upper Chamber. Thereafter, the gifts of the Retired Emperor ("sword and list") and the Empress Mother (a sum of gold) were presented by Seikanji Dainagon, the Retired Emperor's Liaison Officer, whereupon the junior Imperial Envoy declaimed their greetings. These, too, were displayed in the alcove. Then the gift of the Imperial Consort and Honorary Empress (gold) was likewise presented, received, and displayed. Finally, the three envoys, one by one, expressed their personal greetings to the Shogun, and retreated to the left-hand wall of the Lower Chamber. The Shogun responded and retired. The envoys then were seen off by one of the Elders, their day's duty done.

*Now you'll remember,
won't you?*

For the past year, Kajikawa Yosōbei Yoriteru had held a post on the staff of the Warden of Edo Castle. For a man of advanced age and middling station—which Yosōbei was—it was an excellent post. His home stood on one of the larger allotments in the Wardens' Quarter. He held a small fief in Adachi, a few leagues north of the city, that brought him a comfortable income of 720 koku per year. His duties were light, involving mainly day-to-day management of the business of the ladies of the Women's Palace. In short, Yosōbei was enjoying the fullness of his reward for thirty-three years of service in the Shogun's Life Guards. His was not a post, however, that a young man ambitious of advancement would envy. Nor was it a post that Yosōbei himself would have coveted a hundred or more years earlier, when so many castles were under siege.

Unenviable honor, in one form or another, has always been the lot of the Warden of a castle. Even in times of war, when his function was of supreme importance, the Warden was not a man to be envied. When the castellan rode forth to battle, he of course took most of his warriors with him. The Warden had to remain behind with only a skeleton force and defend the fortress against surprise attack. In the best of circumstances, the presence of this force deterred the enemy from attacking. The Warden and his men survived, but they also missed a chance to perform the feats of arms that brought advancement and increased income. If the enemy did attack, the Warden and his men were at a disadvantage from the start. Their first mission was to get word out, to their own side or to an ally, and then hold the gates and ramparts until relief arrived. If their messages were intercepted or the castle was breached before they were relieved, then every last man was doomed to a horrible death. Some were blown off the walls by musket and cannon fire. Others were slaughtered and beheaded when the gates were battered down. Those who still remained would set fire to the great keep, and while the flames were rising, they would murder all the hostages. Most of them were young women—daughters of potential enemies, to be sure, but so long in their midst that they had come to think of them as sisters and cousins. In better times, many eventually would have married into the clan; now all of them had to die. Then, finally, with that distasteful task accomplished, the last remaining defenders sat down together, slit open their own bellies, and waited for the flames, or the explosion of a powder magazine, to put an end to their agony.

Peace, of course, totally transformed the office and duties of the Warden. The sheer size of Edo Castle demanded not one Warden but a Grand Warden, six Commanders of the Watch, and a staff five times the size of that in any earlier castle. Yet no army had ever set forth to battle from Edo Castle. By the time Kajikawa Yosōbei was appointed to his post, the Great Peace had lasted nearly a hundred years. By then, it had begun to seem that defending the castle would be the last thing the Warden and his men would be called upon to do. Indeed, defense had become so minimal a priority that the post of Grand Warden had been abolished two years previously, leaving only the six Commanders of the Watch. Their duties still included maintenance of the armory in a state of readiness for attack. But more and more of their time was taken up with the care of the occupants of the Women's Palace. These women were no longer hostages, of course; the real hostages were the wives and children of the daimyo, who, although confined to the city of Edo, lived in their own homes. Even so, any woman in the service of the Shogun who had been given permission to leave the castle had to carry with her documents declaring her destination as well as the reason for and the duration of her absence. These documents were issued by the Warden, a time-consuming task in a castle that housed perhaps 1,000 women.

Thus it was that in the Third Month of the fourteenth year of Genroku, Kajikawa Yosōbei, Duty Watch Officer for the Warden of

Edo Castle, was assigned to carry greetings and gifts from the wife of the Shogun to the envoys of the Emperor and the Retired Emperor. And by accident of this ceremonial assignment, he was the only person who actually saw what happened that morning in the castle. Fortunately, he wrote it all down.

Edo, Third Month, 12th Day

Shortly before the envoys were to be received by the Shogun in the Whitewood Rooms, Yosōbei reported to the Wardens' duty room. He was expecting to join his colleague Kinzaemon there, but found Tōjūrō instead. Tōjūrō told him that Kinzaemon didn't like wearing a court cap, as one must in the presence of such dignitaries, so he had asked Tōjūrō to take the watch in his stead. As the Hour of the Serpent (9:00 a.m.) approached, Tōjūrō finished adjusting his cap and costume and left to take his place in the ceremonial formation. Yosōbei remained in the duty room, alone. He turned to his desk, took up a brush, and began composing a circular memorandum announcing the next day's business:

> FOR GENERAL CIRCULATION:
>
> *All members of staff are to be in attendance on the morrow for a program of Nō plays to be presented for the entertainment of the imperial envoys, scheduled to begin at . . .*

Edo, Third Month, 13th Day

Midway through the Fifth Hour (9:00 a.m.), the Nō began with Ōkura Chōdayū's performance of the auspicious dance Shiki Sanba. The envoys were seated in the Second Room of the Great Hall, directly opposite the stage. In the same room, immediately to their left, but separated from them by a standing screen, were their official hosts, who were probably more concerned with seeing that all proceeded smoothly, properly, and on time than with watching the Nō. Behind them all sat Kira, his two senior colleagues Ōtomo and Hatakeyama, and three lesser members of their "exalted" fraternity.

It was a full program of four dramas to which the nobles were treated: Takasago, Tamura, Tōboku, and Kasuga Ryūjin, interspersed with the comic interludes Fuku-no-Kami and Kombu Uri. And, finally, in the early afternoon, Chōdayū intoned the congratulatory chant that brought the program to an end, whereupon everyone proceeded to his appointed place for the banquet that was to follow. Yosōbei and his colleagues dined in the Center Room. Immediately thereafter, he sought out Kira Kōzuke-no-Suke to confirm the arrangements for his mission the next morning.

"I shall be representing Her Highness on the morrow," he said to Kira. "Would you be so kind as to inform the nobles?"

"I've already told them," Kira replied. "But as soon as His Highness has tendered his response to the Emperor, the nobles will proceed to the Council of Elders; after that, my colleagues and I will see them off. You'd better not wait too long before you leave for the lodge. It would make a bad impression if you were to arrive late."

"I plan to go as soon as Sagami-no-Kami leaves to escort them to the lodge," Yosōbei assured him. "Everything will be done according to proper procedure."

That settled, it remained only to arrange to pick up the list of Her Highness's gifts to the envoys. Kira told Yosōbei that he would have to arrange that with the duty member of the Junior Council, Katō Etchu-no-Kami; Katō, in turn, told him that the document would be issued by the Secretariat and that Yosōbei should pick it up there. At the same time, Inaba Tango-no-Kami, one of the five Elders, reminded him that he should inform Her Highness's Ladies-in-Waiting that he would be undertaking the mission.

"Yes, sir, and I'll note down the names of the Military Liaison Officers and the emissary of the Retired Emperor for the ladies," Yosōbei said. "In the morning, I'll go to the Lady-in-Waiting on duty, show her my orders, and tell her that I am the one who'll be going."

It was past the Seventh Hour (4:30 p.m.) when Yosōbei returned to the Wardens' duty room. His colleague Naitō Kinzō was composing the circular memorandum announcing the next day's business:

For general circulation:

On the morrow, the Shogun's reply to the Emperor's New Year's greetings . . .

Yosōbei could see that all preparations were well in hand; he left the office and went home.

Edo, Third Month, 14th Day

Kajikawa Yosōbei left his home at the usual hour, so as to arrive at the castle by the Fifth Hour (8:00 a.m). This morning, however, he went by a route that took him more directly to the reception rooms of the Women's Palace. This was the day of his mission, and he had to ascertain the correct wording of the message he would carry for Her Highness to the Imperial Envoys and pick up the wrapping paper for her gifts. He announced himself, and a Lady-in-Waiting named Hirō Dono came out to receive him. She recited a rough version of the greeting, which Yosōbei copied down, transposing it as he wrote into the stock phrases of formal correspondence. On the way out, he encountered his former colleague Tsuchiya Kansuke, Captain of the Life Guards.

"I understand from Kazue Dono that you're to deliver Her Highness's greetings today. You know, don't you, that there's a letter of felicitation to go as well?" Kansuke's query was well meant. This was Yosōbei's first assignment to the New Year's mission. It would have been unkind to allow him to overlook an unfamiliar detail.

"Quite so," Yosōbei said, pleased to be able to show that all was under control. "I have it with me." He did not stop to discuss the matter further, but continued on his way to the menservants' work room to the right of the gate. Here Yosōbei handed over the wrapping paper with instructions for the preparation of the gift. From there, he went directly to his own room, stowed his long sword in the rack, and proceeded to the Wardens' duty room.

"Yosōbei Dono." The Commander of the Watch, Matsudaira Kazue-no-Kami, called to him. "Kira Dono has just sent word that your mission today is to begin earlier than planned."

"I'll get the details," Yosōbei said, and left the room again, thinking that he might find Kira in the Center Room. But the only person there was Okado Denpachirō, Duty Watch Officer of the Inspectorate. Yosōbei asked him if he knew the whereabouts of the Masters of Court Protocol, but he did not know.

"Have the nobles arrived in the Courtiers' Reception Room?" Yosōbei asked.

"I think they've already moved on to their retiring room," Denpachirō said. This meant that they would be in the Upper Chamber, facing the Pine Gallery, waiting for the ceremony to begin.

"In that case, Kira should be nearby—in the Pine Gallery, perhaps?"

"Perhaps; I couldn't say for certain, though."

"Well, then, I'll go to the Pine Gallery and see if he's there," Yosōbei said as he left the room. He strode toward the southern end of palace; through the Kerria Room, the Chrysanthemum Room, and the Autumn Leaves Room; and down the Willow Gallery on the opposite side of the open court from the Pine Gallery. He had walked almost the entire length of the public rooms of the palace by the time he reached the corridor at the rear of the Great Hall. As he continued down the hallway to the point where it joins the Pine Gallery, he noticed that he was followed by two of the Tea Monks who served as ushers in the palace. One of them turned in at the door to the Great Hall; the other continued straight on to the Pine Gallery and was just behind Yosōbei at the point where the gallery makes a sharp turn to the right. There Yosōbei stopped for a moment. At the near end of the gallery, before the sliding doors that were delicately painted with a scene of seaside pines, sat the two official hosts: Asano Takumi-no-Kami and Daté Sakyō-no-Suke. At the far end of the gallery, 5 or 6 yards (4.5 or 5.4 meters) from the door to the Whitewood Rooms, stood Kira and his colleagues. Yosōbei turned to the Tea Monk coming up behind him.

"Would you call Lord Kira for me, please?" The usher hurried to the end of the hall, but then turned and came back alone.

"Lord Kira has been summoned by the Council of Elders," the man reported. "He'll be busy for a short while."

"In that case, would you call Lord Takumi for me, please?"

Takumi-no-Kami rose and crossed to the open side of the gallery. Yosōbei spoke to him with the deference due a daimyo: "I shall be serving as Her Highness's representative to the Military Liaison mission today. I beg your kind cooperation in this matter."

"Of course." Takumi nodded assent as he spoke, and then returned to his seat. Yosōbei looked again toward the far end of the Pine Gallery, and this time saw Kira emerging from the Whitewood Rooms. Again, he sent the usher to fetch him. Yosōbei could see the old man incline his head toward the monk, listen for a moment, and then turn and start walking in his direction. Yosōbei reciprocated and set out to meet him. Between the sixth and seventh pillars of the gallery, they met.

"I understand that I'm to leave earlier than was planned," Yosōbei said. But before Kira could reply, a shout from behind him cut short their conversation.

"Now you'll remember, won't you—all those times you've offended me?" This cry was followed by what seemed an unnaturally loud rush of wind, which Yosōbei did not immediately recognize as the swish of a slim shaft of steel. The blade struck Kira on the back of his right shoulder.

"Wha . . . What . . . ?" Startled and stricken with fear, Kira wheeled about. The blade flashed again, this time aimed directly at his skull. Kira made no attempt to evade it. He clapped his hands to his face, as though to staunch the flow of blood, and then turned to flee. But before he could take a step, his body wilted and crumpled to the floor. Twice more, the assailant slashed out, but his prey had fallen out of reach of his short sword.

Yosōbei now found himself face to face with an apparent madman. To his amazement, it was Asano Takumi-no-Kami, who had spoken to him so calmly only moments before. Yosōbei never paused to consider what he ought to do. The instincts of years of training took control, and he reacted instantly and effortlessly. His legs flexed at the knee, and his arms rose to cover his midsection. From the clumsy swordplay, he could see that the man he faced was no master of any of the martial arts. At fifty-five, Yosōbei was no longer a young man, but he was still reckoned one of the most powerful and formidable of the Shogun's bannermen. His own hands would be weapon enough. Two quick steps forward,

figure 3
An unknown artist's portrait of Asano Takumi-no-Kami Naganori.
(Kagakuji, Akō)

then a hop to clear the body. As he landed, Yosōbei pivoted left, out of the way of the blade. His right hand came down hard upon the knuckles of the hand holding the sword. In the same movement, he thrust his arm forward until his fingers hit the hilt. His grip tightened; his elbow locked. Then his left hand, palm open and fingers spread, shot up from below. The heel of his hand slammed Takumi's shoulder blade, and his thumb hooked under his armpit. Then gripping the shoulder muscle, Yosōbei drove the body forward. The sword fell; Takumi lurched out of balance, his whole arm paralyzed with pain. At this point, Yosōbei could have wrenched the arm out of its socket. Instead, he allowed the elbow to bend and drew the forearm behind Takumi's back, maintaining just enough pressure to prevent movement.

Asano Takumi-no-Kami now lay pinioned, his face to the floor. Behind him lay Kira, unconscious, his head in the center of a spreading pool of blood. For a moment, there was silence and calm, before the full force of the event could be grasped by those who had seen it. Then began the babbling and shouting, as a crowd of Kira's colleagues, Palace Ushers, and other participants in the day's rites rushed to see what all the commotion was about. Some of them seemed to think that Yosōbei had started the fight and began tugging at his arms.

"I am not the one," he snapped. "The quarrel is between these two gentlemen." He could not see that Kira was already being dragged away.

◆ ◆ ◆

After his brief conversation with Yosōbei in the Center Room, Okado Denpachirō had returned to his post in the Inspectors' duty room at the head of the central corridor. He and Ōkubo Gonzaemon were the Duty Watch Officers of the day. But in view of the importance of the occasion, all twenty-four Inspectors had been ordered to stand by in case of need. Contrary to what any of them had expected, they were indeed needed.

Running footsteps halted abruptly outside the Inspectors' room, the door slid open, and a breathless messenger knelt before them. Before he could complete his report, another entered and then another. There had been a quarrel in the Pine Gallery. Swords had been drawn. The Master of Court Protocol had been wounded, but no one knew who had attacked him. The next instant, Denpachirō and his colleagues were on their feet and running toward the Pine Gallery.

They passed below the Whitewood Rooms, where the ceremony was to take place, and turned into the Cherry Blossom Room, which opened onto the Pine Gallery. There staggering across the veranda came Kira Kōzuke-no-Suke, bloodied, still bleeding, and bellowing like a madman.

"A doctor, a doctor! Get a doctor, someone!" He might have saved his breath; the Duty Inspector General, Sengoku Hōki-no-Kami, had long since sent for the palace physicians.

Kira's colleagues Shinagawa Buzen-no-Kami and Hatakeyama Shimōsa-no-Kami had been the first to come to his aid. They had raised the dazed old man to his feet and half carried, half dragged him in the direction of the doctors' duty room. Now, halfway there, he was again fully conscious. "A doctor, a doctor!" His voice quavered, but lacked nothing in volume. Denpachirō and his men hardly paused as they passed him on their way to the scene of the affray.

◆ ◆ ◆

You can imagine the confusion of the crowd that the Inspectors now had to push their way through. Virtually everyone within earshot of the attack had come running to see what was afoot—including even the great lords, who had just taken their places in the Hall of T'ang Emperors. One of them, however, remained seated. This was Matsudaira Izumi-no-Kami Norimura, lord of Toba Castle in Ise, who at the time was only sixteen. Instead of running with the crowd, the youth was berating his fellow daimyo, most of whom were at least twice his age.

"Get back!" he shouted. "Back to your assigned positions! What is the duty of a vassal if not to stand firm and defend his liege lord in time of danger? Now get back, and await the report of the Inspectors!" It was at just that moment that Kira staggered past the entrance to their room, still bleeding and supported on the shoulders of his colleagues. Izumi-no-Kami smiled sardonically at the sight and turned to the lord seated next to him, Wakizaka Awaji-no-Kami.

"One doesn't often see blood on a warrior's robes these days," he said. "Rather a handsome sight, isn't it?" I don't know who reported this scene, but his comment on the young man's character was certainly to the point: "As they say: 'A tiger, by the time it is three days old, already has the urge to devour an ox.' Here was a promising young man."

◆ ◆ ◆

The path of Kira's progress from the far end of the Pine Gallery was marked by great splotches of blood, in some places so broad that it was hard to find a way through without stepping in them. Denpachirō could now identify the miscreant by the large crest of crossed hawk's feathers on his court costume, the wearer of which still lay under the grip of Yosōbei. Takumi-no-Kami's face was flushed with anger, but unlike his victim he spoke with dignity.

"I'm not at all deranged," he was saying. "You've done right to thwart me, but you may now release me."

Yosōbei neither replied nor relaxed his grip.

"I am a castellan and lord of a domain of 50,000 koku. That I acted in disregard of these august precincts, I deeply regret. But I am attired as an official of the Shogunate, and to be detained in such an undignified position is an insult to that attire. I have no grievance whatever against those in authority. I am not going to attack anyone. It's unfortunate that I failed to kill him, but there's nothing I can do about that now." To Denpachirō, it seemed that Takumi-no-Kami spoke sensibly and articulately, but Yosōbei kept him pinned to the floor, his arm twisted behind his back. Denpachirō approached Yosōbei and told him that he and his fellow Inspectors would now take custody of the prisoner.

Takumi-no-Kami rose, flexed his right arm, and adjusted his court cap and crested robes. As he did so, Yosōbei extracted the empty scabbard from his sash, retrieved the fallen sword, and sheathed it. Then Denpachirō and three of his colleagues, followed by a growing crowd, led the daimyo away in the direction of the Fern-Palm Room. Yosōbei fell in behind them, carrying the sword. Four other Inspectors went to take custody of Kira, while the rest of their number strode off to report the disturbance to the Shogun.

◆ ◆ ◆

Takumi-no-Kami, still in a state of agitation, talked ceaselessly as they led him away: "I've been furious with Kira for days now. It was dreadful of me to do this in the palace, and on such an august occasion. But I simply had to kill him. That was that." The procession left the Pine Gallery, trekked past the Great Hall, and traversed the antechamber of the Willow Room, and still Takumi was repeating the same phrases at ever louder volume: "I simply had to kill him. That was that." It was as though he were trying to justify himself to Kira's colleagues, some of whom had joined the motley crowd. No one was responding; but finally, as they passed through the wooden door to the Fern-Palm Room, one of Kira's colleagues spoke to him in a conciliatory voice: "It's all over now; there's no need to speak so loud, is there?"

That was all it took. Takumi-no-Kami fell silent. The four Inspectors led him to a seat in the southwest corner of the Fern-Palm Room. A partition of folding screens was erected around him. The crowd dispersed. Yosōbei handed the sword to a Palace Usher who happened to be there doing a bit of last-minute sweeping. The Inspectors took it in turns to guard their prisoner until they should receive further orders.

◆ ◆ ◆

The arrival of the palace physicians likewise helped to silence Kira's unseemly demonstration, but their medical ministrations were nowhere near as successful. Tsugaru Isan, a general practitioner, administered internal medicines; Sakamoto Yōkei, a surgeon, attended to his wounds. But nothing they could do seemed to staunch the flow of blood. Kira's strength was ebbing rapidly. The Duty Inspector General, after quick consultation with the Elders, told Kira's senior colleague, Hatakeyama Shimōsa-no-Kami, to send immediately for a specialist, Kurisaki Dōyū. A letter was drafted, and two Sub-Inspectors carried it speedily to Dōyū's home in Nagasawa-chō, near Hatchōbori. Dōyū, unfortunately, was out on a house call, but an apprentice who knew his whereabouts set out immediately to carry the summons to his mentor.

CHAPTER

4

The Kurisaki line had been annihilated.
Almost.

Kurisaki Dōyū was trained in a branch of medicine no longer as widely practiced as it had been in the past. He was a specialist in European methods for the treatment of sword wounds, an art in which his family had excelled for more than a hundred years, from the time of Dōyū's grandfather Kurisaki Dōki.

The family had not always been medical men. As best we can tell, the Kurisaki were a small clan of rural warrior gentry in the western reaches of Kyushu. Their village, Kurisaki, from which they took their name, controlled one of the approaches to the fortress in Uto, which, in turn, formed a link in the network of outposts that ringed the great castle in Kumamoto. Like most country clans in the sixteenth century, the Kurisaki were caught up in an endless series of battles, first between their own regional overlords, and then against the great armies of Oda Nobunaga and Toyotomi Hideyoshi as these men fought to extend their hegemony over the entire land. For a time, however, it looked as though the embattled gentry might eventually be able to settle down peaceably on their smallholdings. The castellan at Uto, Hōki Sahyōe Akitaka, had saved his own skin by surrendering his fortress to Hideyoshi without a battle. Hideyoshi, in return, had issued written orders to the new lord of the province of Higo that the fifty-two houses of local gentry were to be confirmed in their holdings and that no new survey or reallocation of lands was to take place for at least three years. Yet no sooner had Sassa Mutsu-no-Kami Narimasa taken possession of the castle in Kumamoto than survey teams were sent out and new land allocations promulgated.

The local gentry were, with good reason, outraged. Within less than a month, rebellions were flaring up throughout the province; Higo was again a province at war.

Hideyoshi was so incensed at Sassa's ineptitude, insolence, and disobedience that he recalled him to Osaka, intercepted him en route, and commanded him to take his own life. But the damage that Sassa had done in Kyushu was irreparable. The next new lord, Katō Kazueno-Kami Kiyomasa, could not let the rebels go unpunished; he had no choice but to hunt them down and exterminate them. Their severed heads, they say, were on display at every crossroads. But one last group, holed up in the old fort at Komorida and determined to fight to the death, was going to require more concerted action. These men, as fate would have it, were the Uto gentry and their liegemen, led by Izuno Shōgen and including, of course, the Kurisaki. Against this force, Kiyomasa himself led the attack. "I'll crush them with my own hands," he said. "That should open the eyes of everyone in this province."

It must have been a chilling sight as the men of Uto looked down from Mount Kinoha and saw five hundred musketeers and two hundred mounted samurai advancing up the slope from the river, their commander crowned with a fantastic 3-foot-tall helmet of burnished silver-gray steel, its crown rakishly bent like that of a warrior's court cap and emblazoned with the bright-red ball of a rising sun. Kiyomasa first set fire to the Uto stronghold, then pelted its occupants with lead, and finally cut down any who attempted to counterattack or escape. Even so, it was no easy victory. Kiyomasa himself was wounded twice by musket fire, and 140 of his men came close enough to death to merit commendation for their bravery. But by sundown, all 130 defenders of Komorida were dead. The Kurisaki line had been annihilated.

Almost. For at some point during this awful massacre, the nursemaid of Kurisaki Utanosuke, the seven-year-old heir to the house, managed to spirit the boy out of their village and make a clean escape. How she managed it we shall never know, but she was obviously a brave and resourceful woman. Fleeing first to Nagasaki, the two fugitives managed to evade capture there for two years. But then, someone who knew their secret betrayed them to the enemy—or as one account poetically puts it,

"Rain began to leak through the leaves of the tree under which they had sheltered." And so, before they could be apprehended, they took passage aboard a ship about to sail for Luzon, laden with cargo destined for the next Manila Galleon. With good winds, sailing roughly southwest by south (± 215°), they would have cleared the Cape of Engaño in fifteen or sixteen days, and two days later entered Manila Bay.

Why she felt that she had to flee so far, we have no idea. It may simply be that she had to leave by the first ship available, whatever its destination. Or, as some suggest, the family may have had Christian connections and she and Utanosuke could no longer feel safe anywhere in Kyushu now that Hideyoshi had disenfeoffed the Jesuits of Nagasaki. Whatever her reasons, Utanosuke's nursemaid provided well for the boy's future during their years of exile. They would have found a welcome refuge in "Campo Japón," the large Japanese community that had grown up in Dilao, just outside the eastern portal to the new city of Manila, near the Franciscan monastery and mission house, La Candelaria.

Over the next few years, Utanosuke must have acquired considerable competence in both written and spoken Spanish, and probably Latin as well, for in his fourteenth year he was accepted as an apprentice to a Manila surgeon who specialized in the treatment of sword wounds, an art in which the Spanish were unsurpassed. His apprenticeship extended over the next eight years, following which he remained in Manila for several years more. Then, in 1617, two years after the fall of Osaka Castle, Kurisaki Dōki Masamoto, as he now styled himself, decided that it should now be safe—or expedient or wise—to return to Nagasaki. The Spanish had never been entirely welcoming of the Japanese in Manila. They were happy to enlist Japanese skill at arms in the cause of their own conquests, but wary of the presence of such independent-minded warriors in their midst. Yet whatever Kurisaki's reasons for leaving when he did, he found that the skills he had acquired in his twenty-some years abroad were much in demand at home.

The port of Nagasaki had not yet been closed to foreign ships. Hardly a night passed when carousing did not give way to brawling, and then, all too often, to swordfights. Nagasaki was Japan's Wild West in those days, but a city of opportunity for a practitioner of sword-wound surgery. The Shogunal Magistrate in Nagasaki awarded Dōki a grant of government land and a house in Yorozuya-machi, commissioned him to treat the samurai on the staff of the magistracy, and licensed him to treat foreign residents and visitors to the city. Dōki's fame spread, his practice flourished, and soon he was training apprentices of his own, four of whom were his own sons. He was, moreover, revered as the only exponent of European medical practice who could actually read the treatises of that tradition—indeed, the only surgeon in all Japan who had learnt his art abroad. On the basis of this, Dōki was granted an official patent permitting him to establish the "Kurisaki School, Authorized Guardians of Familial Traditions for the Treatment of Wounds Incurred in Battle."

In the years thereafter, his progeny and disciples appear to have maintained scrupulously their founder's high standards. His eldest son entered the service of the Echizen Tokugawa; his second son, that of the Matsura of Hirado. His fourth son, the first Kurisaki Dōyū, by command of the Shogunal Magistrate, remained to carry on the practice in Nagasaki. And in 1691, a century after his grandfather's flight to Luzon, Kurisaki Dōyū Masayuki was summoned from Nagasaki to Edo and appointed to the Shogun's staff of attendant physicians at a stipend of 200 bales per year, later increased to 350. It was in this capacity that Dōyū was summoned to the castle to treat the wounds of Kira Kōzuke-no-Suke.

◆ ◆ ◆

It was not forbidden for personal physicians of the Shogun to treat private patients, as long as it did not interfere with their official duties. Unfortunately for Iseya Hanshichi, a saké dealer who lived near the Myōjin Shrine in Kanda, the official duties of his eminent physician were about to interfere with the treatment of his illness. When the letter from the castle reached him, Dōyū was at Hanshichi's home, treating a painfully suppurating boil. As soon as he saw the inscription and the seal, Dōyū knew that this was a summons that would brook no delay. He broke the seal, opened the letter, and read it immediately:

Lord Kira Kōzuke-no-Suke having been unexpectedly wounded in the palace, you are requested, by order of the Duty Inspector

*General, Sengoku Hōki-no-Kami, to proceed to the castle immedi-
ately and with all haste.*

THIRD MONTH, 14TH DAY   *Hatakeyama Shimōsa-no-Kami*
To: Kurisaki Dōyū Sama

Dōyū was being summoned to practice the art in which he was specialized and on a case of sufficient importance to involve the highest ranks
of officialdom. He left Hanshichi and his oozing boil in the care of an
apprentice, gathered his instruments, and headed directly for the castle.

CHAPTER
5

*But . . . you're not to refrain from
speaking your mind.*

The Shogun was in his bath when the Inspectors sent to report the attack to him thundered down the corridor into his private quarters in the center of the palace. The Shogun did not normally bathe at this hour, nor was his bath this morning merely a matter of personal cleanliness. It was a mark of the extreme solemnity and respect with which he prepared himself for this final stage in his exchange of felicitations with the Emperor, that he should speak his greeting in a state of great bodily purity. His ablutions were timed to end only moments before the Imperial Envoys entered his presence. Having abstained from meat and fish and women since the previous evening, he would rise from the waters in as immaculate a state as the human body can attain, don fresh robes, proceed directly to the Whitewood Rooms, and, in this pristine condition, receive the Imperial Envoys and acknowledge the greetings from Kyoto that they had conveyed to him two days earlier.

If the Inspectors, as they ran through the labyrinth of corridors, thought that they would be permitted to interrupt these almost sacral ablutions merely to report an attempted murder, they were badly mistaken. They were met at the door to the bathing chambers by one of the most powerful men in the palace, the Shogun's Chief Adjutant, Yanagisawa Dewa-no-Kami Yasuaki. Yanagisawa did not even evince surprise when told of the incident. "Such matters must not interrupt His Highness's purification," he told them. He then sent two of the men back to the scene of the disturbance, carrying interim orders, and told the others to return to their duty room. Their report must wait until the

Shogun was fully bathed and dressed.

It is said that the coolness, dispatch, and discretion with which Yanagisawa handled this utterly unexpected emergency were typical of the qualities that had won him such rapid advancement. For Yanagisawa Dewa-no-Kami was not one of those officials who owed his position to the battlefield exploits of an ancestor a hundred or more years in the past. He had succeeded to his father's modest post in the Corps of Pages while the fifth Shogun was still lord of the mountain domain of Kōfu; his rise to high office was entirely the result of the consummate skill with which he executed the tasks assigned him.

Today, too, Yanagisawa's handling of a difficult situation had been perfect. He arrogated to himself none of the decisions that were the Shogun's own prerogative, yet neither did he neglect to issue any of the orders that lay within his own responsibility.

In the meantime, His Highness had risen from the cedar-scented waters of his wooden tub and taken his seat on the slatted platform where one of his corps of personal attendants, clad in a close-fitting undergarment of pure white cotton, stood ready to scrub his body. Eight cotton sachets filled with fragrant rice bran had been laid out in readiness—one sachet for each arm and hand, one for each leg and foot, one for the chest and one for the back, one for the lower torso, one for the neck and face—so that no part of His Highness's body should go uncleansed by the rich emulsion of starches, oils, and proteins that the bran secretes. The samurai whose duty it was to scrub His Highness performed his task with vigor and care; then, with equal care, he rinsed the milky solution from the Shogun's body with bucket after bucket of warm water—the final step in the long process of purification. Now the Shogun rose again and stepped from the wooden slats of the bathing room onto the tatami mats of the drying room. Here, on a shelf, lay a stack of ten freshly laundered drying robes of white cotton. His pages, who awaited him here, keeping guard over his swords, now helped him into and out of this succession of dry robes, until every drop of moisture on his skin had been absorbed. Then His Highness proceeded to the dressing room, where his court robes lay on lacquered trays awaiting the final stage of his preparation. And when at last His Highness was

figure 4
Kanō Tsunenobu's portrait of Yanagisawa Dewa-no-Kami Yasuaki.
(Ichirenji, Kōfu)

fully dressed, another attendant carefully combed out his hair, drew it back tightly, tied it securely at the base, smoothed out the topknot with a fresh application of fragrant oils, and placed it neatly upon the freshly shaved crown of His Highness's pate. Finally, his court cap was lowered onto his head and the cord carefully knotted. Only then, when His Highness was fully prepared to leave his private quarters and proceed to the public areas of the palace, did Yanagisawa speak.

"Your Highness," he said calmly, "I must report that Asano Takumi-no-Kami has just attacked Kira Kōzuke-no-Suke in the Pine Gallery and wounded him with his sword. His wounds are not fatal, and so I've ordered that Takumi-no-Kami be detained, that Kira be given medical attention, and that the gallery be cleansed of blood pollution. But may I ask whom Your Highness wishes to appoint to take over the duties of official host? And does Your Highness wish that the ceremony take place in the Whitewood Rooms as planned?"

His Highness was furious, as well he might be when so much care had been taken to perform these rites to perfection. But he did not lose his good sense as a commander. Before leaving the bathing rooms to proceed to his private quarters, he gave three orders:

1. The Imperial Envoys were to be advised of the nature of the delay and asked if they would object to continuing the ceremonies as planned. If there were no objections, the venue was to be changed to the Blackwood Rooms in order to avoid the Pine Gallery.

2. The Inspectors were to investigate the reasons for the attack.

3. Asano Takumi-no-Kami was to be replaced as official host by Toda Noto-no-Kami.

The task of executing the Shogun's first command fell to two of the younger Masters of Court Protocol, Hatakeyama Minbu and Toda Nakatsukasa. They went immediately to the Upper Chamber, where the three envoys still waited.

"As you know, blood has been spilled," Minbu said. "His Highness wonders, therefore, owing to the pollution, whether you feel that the Imperial Response should be postponed."

"Not at all," Sukekado replied. "There's been no death pollution, so we see no reason that it should not proceed as planned. Kindly tell His Highness that we are agreeable to whatever he may think best."

In that case, they were told, the venue would be changed to the Blackwood Rooms, which they could reach without traversing the Pine Gallery. Needless to say, their hosts were much relieved to learn that there need be no further disruption. And when news of this reached the Emperor in Kyoto, he is said to have been mightily pleased that Sukekado had had the presence of mind to make this fine distinction; for once, it put the Shogunate in the debt of the court.

◆ ◆ ◆

Despite all the confusion, the change of venue seems to have been managed with extreme efficiency and speed. The Official Daily Records tell us that the Imperial Response had already begun midway through the Hour of the Serpent (ca. 10:00 a.m.).

Today, it was incumbent upon the Shogun to enter the chamber first, which he did, preceded by one of the Elders to "clear the way" and followed by two Masters of Court Protocol bearing his swords. Once he had taken his seat in the upper level, the three envoys, one at a time, entered the lower level. As each was announced, he took his seat at the left of the chamber. The two senior envoys were then summoned before the Shogun, to whom they reiterated the Emperor's felicitations, in response to which the Shogun, in somewhat effusive terms, expressed his gratitude. The Emperor's envoys having retired, it was then the turn of the Retired Emperor's envoy to enter, be announced, be seated, and repeat the same exchange with the Shogun. The two Imperial Envoys were then recalled to the presence, whereupon the Shogun proclaimed his gratitude to the Empress Mother, the Retired Empress, and the Imperial Consort. That done, the Shogun declared the festivities at an end and granted the nobles his permission to return to Kyoto.

Thereafter, the Elders and nobles retreated to the anteroom, where the Elders enumerated the gifts of the Shogunate to the various imperials and the several members of their court. Finally, seated again in the lower level, the Elders slid open the doors to the adjacent chamber, revealing the Shogun standing before the ranks of his vassal daimyo in a final parting flourish. The Shogun then retreated to the inner rooms of the palace. He had many other matters he must attend to that day.

◆ ◆ ◆

It was only a matter of moments before rumors of a swordfight began to spread outward from the palace, rather like the sparkling tip of a fuse snaking its way toward a powder keg. Suddenly, Palace Ushers were seen rushing about even more frantically than was usual on ceremonial occasions. A guardsman asked one of them what was afoot. A moment later, that guardsman was dispatched to the gates, bearing orders that all doors be shut and bolted and that no one be allowed to pass. A retainer of one of the lords in attendance in the palace overheard the conversation. He told his comrades, and they passed the word to the retainers of other lords. Men were sent to carry the "news" to their comrades waiting at the intermediate gates, who, in turn, rushed out to the entourage waiting patiently on the broad expanse of the dismounting ground. Here lay the powder keg, and it exploded.

No one knew for certain who had attacked whom. But everyone knew that the penalty for drawing a sword within the castle walls was death, and everyone knew the ancient Principle of Equal Punishment: in any quarrel, regardless of who was at fault, both parties were deemed guilty. Thus everyone knew that if either party to this quarrel should be his lord, he would soon be without a lord. Without a lord, without employment, without income, without a home. He would become a ronin, the worst possible fate for a samurai in peacetime. Small wonder that when the spark of rumor touched that quiet crowd, tumult arose. Who had attacked whom? The future of every samurai on that broad expanse hung upon the answer to that question. They rushed to the gates to find out, but the guards knew no more than did those waiting without. A few of the more desperate and brash pushed their way past the guards and pursued their quest to the doors of the palace itself. The guards doubted that they could withstand the press much longer without resorting to force. This was no ordinary mob; it was a throng of armed and trained warriors in a state of extreme agitation. If the names of the assailant and his victim were not soon forthcoming, the tumult could turn to slaughter. Word went out to the Inspectorate that the situation outside the gates was growing dangerous.

✦ ✦ ✦

The moment the ceremonies were completed and the envoys had departed the Blackwood Rooms, the Shogun strode back to his personal quarters and summoned the full Council of Elders, the full Junior Council of Elders, and the six Inspectors General to a meeting in the Clock Room. His Highness invited no discussion at this meeting. There was to be an immediate investigation. The Elders were to question any eyewitnesses, the Inspectorate was to interrogate Takumi-no-Kami and Kōzuke-no-Suke, and the information so gathered was to be relayed directly to the Shogun. These commands delivered, he turned and left the room. Those who remained immediately set about executing his orders. Tsuchiya Sagami-no-Kami, Duty Officer of the month for the Council of Elders, sent an usher to find Kajikawa Yosōbei. The Junior Council, under whose jurisdiction the Inspectorate fell, appointed two interrogation teams to be headed by the Duty Watch Officers of the day, Okado Denpachirō and Ōkubo Gonzaemon; their assistants were to be Kondō Heihachirō and Kuru Jūzaemon. Amano Denshirō and Soné Gorōbei were assigned to maintain direct surveillance at the site of interrogation.

✦ ✦ ✦

These orders had only just reached Denpachirō when two Deputy Inspectors, Mizuno Mokuzaemon and Machida Ihei, burst into the Inspectors' duty room.

"They're unable to restrain the crowds at the gates!" they cried. Some samurai had even managed to force their way in as far as the main entrance to the palace, and the central entrance at the rear; others were likely to follow. "What shall we do?"

Denpachirō saw immediately what the problem was. These were men desperate to know whether their lord had been involved in this quarrel.

"Go straight to the carpentry shop," Denpachirō said. "Tell the carpenters that they're to make notice boards—of the standard pine, but large ones—and inscribe both sides, as follows, in a large hand:

ASANO TAKUMI-NO-KAMI HAS ATTACKED KIRA KŌZUKE-NO-SUKE

BOTH PARTIES ARE NOW BEING INTERROGATED

ONE AND ALL ARE TO REFRAIN FROM CREATING ANY

DISTURBANCE

These are to be erected at every dismounting ground—immediately!"

Reports soon came back that the tumult had died down, although, of course, the retainers of Takumi-no-Kami and Kōzuke-no-Suke were in an even greater state of agitation than before. Denpachirō duly reported the incident and his handling of it to the Council of Elders and the Junior Council. The Elders saw immediately that their next task must be to quiet the Asano retainers and prevent the spread of violence beyond the castle walls. Kira's retainers would pose little threat. They were fewer in number, and they were city samurai. But Asano's men would number a hundred or more, and many of them were rough-hewn provincials who knew only one solution to every problem—their swords. Those stationed in the Military Liaison Lodge must be removed immediately, and those in the Asano mansion at Teppōzu must be warned strictly against fomenting any disturbance. The Elders summoned the Duty Inspector General, Sengoku Hōki-no-Kami, and charged him with this assignment.

◆ ◆ ◆

Kajikawa Yosōbei was now uncertain what the status of his assigned mission might be after this chaotic interlude. He wasn't even sure whom he should ask to find out. At this point, he thought, the best thing would be to return to the Whitewood Rooms. He turned right at the next corridor and was walking past the Willow Room when a thought occurred to him: he was certain to be interrogated in the investigation of this incident. It would be embarrassing if he were not to know the name of the usher to whom he had given Takumi-no-Kami's sword. He had seen the man often enough, but had never known his name. He had better find out now. Yosōbei retraced his steps and fortunately was able to find the usher not far from where they had parted.

"Indeed," the monk concurred, "you've seen every detail of the whole incident. You're certain to be asked." His name was Kyūwa, he said, Seki Kyūwa.

Again, Yosōbei set out for the Whitewood Rooms, and again he failed to reach his destination. This time, he was stopped by another usher sent by Katō Etchū-no-Kami of the Junior Council. Yosōbei was wanted immediately in the Clock Room, the deliberation chamber of the Council of Elders. When Yosōbei entered the anteroom, he realized that the investigation was already in progress. Four of the five Elders were there, all four of the Junior Elders, and all six Inspectors General.

Yosōbei was invited to describe his experience of the event in full detail, from beginning to end. The board listened attentively and did not interrupt him. After he had finished, Sagami-no-Kami was the first to speak: "How severely was Kōzuke-no-Suke wounded?"

"He was wounded in two or three places, but not severely, I think."

Bungo-no-Kami continued the questioning: "When he was attacked, did Kōzuke-no-Suke draw his sword or place his hand on the hilt?"

"As far as I could see, he did not put his hand on his sword." There were no further questions. No one had wanted to know the name of the Tea Monk to whom he had given the sword.

Before he left the room, however, Yosōbei asked the question that he had determined to ask in the first place: Should he now carry on with his mission on behalf of Her Highness? He should indeed, Etchū-no-Kami told him.

♦ ♦ ♦

The interrogation of both parties to the quarrel was to take place in the Cypress Room, the anteroom to the doctors' chambers, whither Takumi-no-Kami had been taken under the guard of six Sub-Inspectors.

When Denpachirō arrived, accompanied by Kondō Heihachirō, he began with the statutory declaration: "In connection with today's incident, we two have been assigned to take your testimony. You must understand, therefore, that, in accordance with the law, we shall dispense with all deferential forms of address." The Inspectors would now speak in the stead of the Shogun; not even a daimyo could expect to be addressed as a superior.

"You attacked and wounded Kōzuke-no-Suke in total disregard of your presence in the palace. What were your reasons for doing so?"

At first Takumi-no-Kami said nothing, as though he had not even heard the question. Then, after a long silence, he replied, "I bear no ill will whatever toward those in authority, but I did have a personal grievance. It was on this account that I lost control of myself. I wanted to kill him, and so I attacked him. Whatever punishment may be meted out to me, I have nothing further to say in my defense. My only regret is that I failed to kill Kōzuke-no-Suke." That said, he asked a question of his own: "Speaking of whom, how does he fare?"

"His wounds are not deep," Denpachirō replied, "but he is old, and he has lost a great deal of blood, especially from the wound on his head. It's still uncertain whether he'll recover."

A look that could only be described as one of great joy spread over Takumi-no-Kami's face: "I'm sorry that I've no further testimony to offer you. I ask nothing more than to be punished as the law prescribes."

The two Inspectors rose, signaling the end of the interview, and escorted the daimyo back to the Fern-Palm Room.

◆ ◆ ◆

Not long after this first party had left the room, two more Inspectors, Kuru Jūzaemon and Ōkubo Gonzaemon, arrived with orders to interrogate Kira. Jūzaemon began: "A short time ago, Asano Takumi-no-Kami, apparently bearing a personal grudge, attacked and wounded you. We have been ordered to investigate the circumstances of this incident. In accordance with the law, therefore, we shall dispense with all deferential forms of address. Tell us then: What was Takumi-no-Kami's grievance that made him attack you in total disregard of his presence in the palace? Surely you must remember. Tell us precisely what happened."

"I've no recollection of any cause for resentment between us," Kira replied. "It seemed to me that Takumi-no-Kami was utterly deranged. After all, I'm just an old man. What could there be to resent? No, I haven't the least recollection of any resentment. There is nothing more I can say."

Kira's reply was in total contradiction to that of his assailant, neither had it the least ring of sincerity or truth. But the Inspectors pressed him no further. They had asked a specific and pointed question; he gave them an evasive reply. They rose and left to report this to their superiors.

♦ ♦ ♦

Whatever differences these two men had—and they must have been considerable—both were determined not to reveal them, although for very different reasons. Takumi-no-Kami probably felt that to defend his disruption of a solemn ceremony on the basis of a private grievance would detract from his honor. While for Kira, to reveal the cause of Takumi's grievance—or even his own awareness of a grievance—would implicate him as the instigator of the quarrel. Thus we shall never know precisely what Kira did or said to anger Takumi, or why.

♦ ♦ ♦

Before departing to deliver the gifts and greetings of the Shogun's wife, Yosōbei went directly to his room and changed his clothes. There were slight flecks of blood on his costume, and it would not do to undertake so important an assignment in tainted garb. After he had changed, as a further precaution, he reported again to the Duty Elder, Sagami-no-Kami. Yosōbei was determined that the Elders not overlook the fact that he had come under blood pollution, only to regret their oversight after the damage had been done. He needn't worry about a little blood, he was told; but given the interruption, he had better wait a bit longer before leaving the castle.

♦ ♦ ♦

When the four Inspectors had completed their interrogations, they reported to the Duty Inspector General, Sengoku Hōki-no-Kami, and his colleague Andō Chikugo-no-Kami, whence they were shunted progressively up the chain of command. The Inspectors General decided that the four men should report their findings directly to the Junior Council of Elders. And when the Junior Council heard the testimony they had elicited, they agreed that the Inspectors should report in person to the Council of Elders. And when the Elder Ogasawara Sado-no-Kami heard what they had to say, he ordered the Inspectors to inform the Chief Adjutant in their own words. The Adjutant, who would himself carry the report to the Shogun, told the four men to stand by in the Inspectors' duty room and await further orders there.

+ + +

Not long after all the reports were in, the Shogun himself decided the fate of the two parties to the quarrel in the Pine Gallery. Perhaps he had decided even before the reports were delivered, for he consulted with no one in making his decision, neither his Chief Adjutant nor his Council of Elders. The private thoughts of a ruling Shogun seldom find their way into the records of his day, with the result that we have no idea what arguments or, more likely, what passions swayed the mind of Tokugawa Tsunayoshi on this day. And what was secret then remains secret still. Lacking any documents, therefore, we can rely on only the narrative imagination of one Sugimoto Yoshichika, a samurai in the service of the Kaga domain, whose efforts to ascertain the truth, if not totally successful, at least seem entirely genuine. This, as Sugimoto tells it, is how the matter was handled:

The Shogun summoned the entire Council of Elders and with no preliminary explanation told them that, effective immediately, Asano Takumi-no-Kami was to be remanded to the custody of one of his fellow daimyo, and, once safely in custody, he was to commit seppuku. One imagines that the Elders, for a moment at least, were at a loss for words. But presently, Inaba Tango-no-Kami ventured to speak: "That Takumi-no-Kami should behave so unmindfully, of both the augustness of the occasion and his presence in the palace, seems to me totally deranged. Might I suggest, therefore, that we defer pronouncing sentence upon him for the time being?"

And then, emboldened perhaps by his junior colleague, Akimoto Tajima-no-Kami said, "I quite agree with Tango-no-Kami."

The Shogun's face darkened with displeasure, and he showed no inclination to discuss the matter further. He rose abruptly and turned for the door; yet as he did, he looked back and said, "But Tajima-no-Kami, you're not to refrain from speaking your mind." At least his departure was not to be taken as censure.

Once back in his private quarters, the Shogun summoned Tsuchiya Sagami-no-Kami, Duty Officer of the month for the Elders, and told him simply, "Takumi-no-Kami is sentenced to commit seppuku." Sagami-no-Kami was to attend to the details. Orders were passed to the Junior Council. The Inspectorate was activated. Two decrees were dictated and transcribed in the Secretariat—one addressed to Takumi-no-Kami and the other to Kira Kōzuke-no-Suke.

*No one, even unto those of the lowest rank,
is to create the slightest disturbance.*

The commotion outside the entry hall of the palace, although not as unruly as that at the outer gates, was no less intense. Every man gathered there was on the closest of terms with his liege lord, either by virtue of the office he held or through personal intimacy. These were not the sort of men who were subject to mindless frenzies of devotion, but their concern for their lords was likely to be only the more steadfast for being conscious and reasoned. The Inspectorate was quick to recognize that these men, at the very door to the palace, must be informed immediately of events within. Two Inspectors hurried to the entry hall and called for the retainers of Takumi-no-Kami: Takebe Kiroku, Isogai Jūrōzaemon, and Nakamura Sei'emon. There had been a quarrel, they were told, and Takumi-no-Kami had for the time being been remanded to the custody of Tamura Ukyō-no-Daibu. They were to take his swords and return to the Asano Upper Mansion in Teppōzu. No record of their response remains. We know only that they re-formed his entourage around his empty palanquin and set out, their tall plumed lances lowered. They were probably the first to bear the news of what soon came to be called the Catastrophe.

◆ ◆ ◆

Toda Uneme-no-Kami Ujisada, lord and castellan of the 100,000-koku domain of Ōgaki, was one of the Shogun's vassal daimyo who had been commanded to attend His Highness at the morning's Imperial Response. As it happened, he was also a first cousin of Asano Takumi-no-Kami.

And so, when the commotion broke out in the Pine Gallery, Uneme-no-Kami was already seated in the Hall of T'ang Emperors, just a short distance from the scene of the attack. All sorts of dire thoughts must have crossed his mind when he learnt that his own kinsman had caused this uproar, but his immediate reaction was to excuse himself from the room and speak to one of the Inspectors, Itsumi Gozaemon: "I am a cousin of Asano Takumi. I wonder if I should refrain from participating in this ceremony."

"Yes. That may be best," Gozaemon agreed. And so Uneme-no-Kami betook himself to the Cypress Room, some distance down the corridor, where he awaited further orders. He may even have expected to be implicated in his cousin's crime. But far from it. Instead, the Duty Inspector General, Sengoku Hōki-no-Kami, came to enlist his aid. The Council of Elders, he said, desired Uneme-no-Kami to go immediately to the Military Liaison Lodge and urge that there be no unruly reaction by the Asano vassals on duty there. A detail from the Inspectorate, led by Suzuki Gengoemon, had already been sent. But the authority of a close relative of high rank was essential to ensure the submission of this large body of men, who may even have witnessed their lord's humiliation. For it was here, they say, that the friction between Kira and Takumi began to rub raw. We have no eyewitness descriptions of any of their contretemps. But Horibe Yahei, the now-retired Edo Liaison Officer of the Akō domain, tells us quite plainly:

> At the Military Liaison Lodge, Kira Kōzuke-no-Suke Dono rebuked him on several occasions, yet in deference to the gravity of his duties, Takumi-no-Kami endured these indignities patiently. In the palace, however, in full view of several of his peers, Kira slandered him so severely as to sully his honor as a warrior. Had he allowed the man to escape after that, it would have shamed him forever thereafter. And so he decided in advance that he must strike. Slander, after all, is tantamount to murder.

Yahei may well have witnessed the incidents he mentions, for it is likely that his presence would have been required at the lodge. And his report is confirmed by Kira's physician, Kurisaki Dōyū, who knew both men and had been involved in the incident almost from the start:

> They had never got on well, but especially so at the Military Liaison Lodge. Kira was the most senior Master of Court Protocol; Takumi was young and inexperienced in dealing with court nobles. He was totally dependent upon Kira, who for some reason treated him with insufferable arrogance. . . . Takumi had always been short tempered, and when Kira turned up in front of the Plover Room, he must have lost control of himself.

And even the official history of the Tokugawa house, though compiled years later, says:

> It has long been said that because Kira Kōzuke-no-Suke had held this office through several successive reigns, and had years of experience in dealing with the Imperial Court, there was no one whose knowledge of court and military ceremonial was the equal of his. And thus even the greatest of houses bent to his will and submitted to instruction from him. As a result, he grew greedy for bribes, and his house grew rich from them. But Naganori refused to truckle to him or enrich him. Yoshinaka secretly resented this and on several occasions withheld instruction from him, so that Naganori often mistook the timing or failed to perform properly. This angered him—and thus he did what he did.

Whatever the fears of the Elders, they proved groundless. When Uneme-no-Kami arrived at the Military Liaison Lodge, he and the Inspectors summoned the two Asano Elders then resident in Edo, Yasui Hikoemon and Fujii Matazaemon, as well as Takumi's adjutants, Okumura Chūemon and Kasuya Kanzaemon. He told them: "We have been sent here to maintain order and discipline. No one, even unto those of the lowest rank, is to create the slightest disturbance. A new official host is to be appointed imminently, and as soon as his people arrive at the lodge, you are to hand over your duties to them and withdraw in the most peaceable manner possible."

As best we can tell, these orders were followed faithfully—no doubt because no one yet suspected that their lord's enemy was still alive. No details of their withdrawal survive, but from later reports we know that it was Hara Sōemon, a Company Commander of Foot Soldiers, who took charge of the move. Somehow, Sōemon managed to assemble a flotilla of small boats, load them, and send them wending their way through the network of canals to the Asano Upper Mansion, each boat bedecked with a banner bearing the crossed feathers of the Asano crest. It was a huge job. Everything the Asano people had transported to the Military Liaison Lodge in the days leading up to the arrival of the envoys—folding screens and vases and scrolls, bedding, kitchen utensils and serving trays and even soup bowls—had to be removed and was removed within an hour past midday. It was a minor triumph of logistics in a day of irreparable disaster. But an empty triumph, for by the time the boats reached their destination, more than half their cargo had been pilfered. With so much else on their minds, no one even considered attempting to recover the stolen property.

◆ ◆ ◆

As the ripples of admonition spread out from the castle—from palace to dismounting ground to Military Liaison Lodge—they soon reached Takumi-no-Kami's own upper mansion in Teppōzu (Musket Strand) a quarter that stood amidst the network of canals that crisscrossed the reclaimed lands at the river's edge.

Two Inspectors, Amano Denshirō and Shindō Heihachirō, leading a sizable contingent of Deputy Inspectors and Sub-Inspectors, arrived at Teppōzu in the latter half of the Hour of the Ram (ca. 2:00--3:00 p.m.). Their message was the same as that sent to everyone else: Takumi-no-Kami had committed an outrage in the palace for which he had been remanded to the custody of Tamura Ukyō-no-Daibu; no one was to foment any disturbance of any sort. By then, this was old news to the residents of the mansion, but it was their first official notification. The Elders of the house thus decided that now they must send word to the home domain in Akō, 155 leagues (388 miles, 620 kilometers) to the west. The fastest way to accomplish this was by "express conveyance," an extraordinary mode of transport that I shall explain in a later chapter.

◆ ◆ ◆

Not least of those to be notified of events in the palace was Asano Aki-no-Kami Tsunanaga, head of the Asano main house in Hiroshima and lord of a domain of 440,000 koku, the lands of which comprised the entire province of Aki. Wealth was not the only reason that Aki-no-Kami must be accorded special treatment. He was also the great-great-great-grandson of Asano Nagamasa, progenitor of the Asano line and a special ally of the founding Shogun, Tokugawa Ieyasu.

Nagamasa had begun his career as an archer in the service of Nobunaga and was married to a sister of the wife of Hideyoshi, who had begun his career, even more humbly, as sandal bearer to Nobunaga. But as Hideyoshi schemed and fought his way to the top after the assassination of Nobunaga, his brother-in-law Nagamasa rose with him. It was thus a stroke of great good fortune for Tokugawa Ieyasu that Nagamasa decided to side with him before the decisive battle of Sekigahara, rather than with his relatives, the heirs of Hideyoshi. Now, a century later, it remained a matter of importance that Tokugawa Tsunayoshi, the great-grandson of Ieyasu, not appear to treat the great-great-great-grandson of Nagamasa in an offhand manner in the delicate matter of his kinsman's misbehavior.

The Elders must have given careful thought to their choice of an emissary to carry the news. They sent not an Inspector General or even an Inspector. On such a mission, the arrival of an official of that rank might seem a veiled threat. With a vassal daimyo, such as Toda Uneme-no-Kami, there was no need to veil the threat. But with an old and trusted ally, it was better to assume his complete understanding of the situation and send a man of no official standing within the Shogunal house. They chose a Tea Monk, Yoshino Eiden, one of the Palace Ushers who customarily saw to the needs of Aki-no-Kami when on duty and who was a frequent visitor to the Asano mansion when off duty. Eiden's arrival at the Asano mansion, just opposite the great Sakurada Gate, aroused no alarm. But alas, he was unable to discharge his duty. Aki-no-Kami was not at home; he was attending a celebration of the completion of his son's new mansion in Aoyama, where he himself would play a leading role in a program of Nō plays to be performed on the new stage. The duty watch at the Sakurada mansion took careful note of Eiden's report, and then dispatched two men to carry the news to Aki-no-Kami: the Inspector Katō Saheita Masafumi and the Company Commander of Archers, Niwa Genbei Shigetsune. Unfortunately, they arrived too late. The play had begun, and Aki-no-Kami was already on stage, masked and robed, chanting the role of the Rokujō Consort, the regal but wronged mistress of the hero of *The Tale of Genji*. Saheita and Genbei could only watch and wait until the first act had run its course.

LADY ROKUJŌ (Asano Aki-no-Kami):
Chill is the autumn wind that blows,
Chill is the autumn wind that blows,
Through the grove of this Shrine in the Fields,
Piercing one to the bone; while vanished, too,
Are autumn's tints which once so pierced the heart.
Why, I cannot but wonder, why do I come here,
Back to this transient world, so shrouded in memories?
Bitter it is to return,
Bitter it is to return.

A WANDERING MONK (actor unknown): *In the shade of this grove, as I calm my thoughts and ponder times past, suddenly there appears this most alluring woman. Pray tell, madam, who might you be?*

ROKUJŌ: *Who am I, you ask? I would ask the same of you. For this is that very Shrine in the Fields where long ago, the Imperial Vestal would lodge for a time on her way to Ise. That custom has long since lapsed; yet every year, on this 7th Day of the Longest [Ninth] Month, for old time's sake and unbeknownst to anyone, I come to purify this shrine and worship here—only to be disturbed now by the untoward arrival of one who comes whence I know not. Quickly, I say, quickly! Away with you!*

WANDERING MONK: *Nay, nay! I shall cause you no concern. I am but a monk, one who has abandoned this world wherein we know not*

whither we are bound. Yet what might those memories of times past be,
that bring you back to this ruin every year on this same day?

ROKUJŌ: *Today it was, this 7th Day of the Longest Month,*
When the Shining Genji journeyed here;
When, bearing a sprig of the Sacred Tree,
He slipped it within these sacred confines.
And today it was, that the Consort replied,
kamigaki wa shirushi no sugi mo naki mono o
    ikani magaete oreru sakaki zo
"Within these sacred confines stand no tall cedars to guide you hither;
    How then dare you presume to pluck from this sacrosanct tree?"

WANDERING MONK: *Truly a beautiful verse; and the hue of that sprig,*
which you now hold, remains unchanged from of yore.

At this point in the play, Aki-no-Kami and the Chorus lapsed into a
long and lyrical recapitulation of Genji's affair with the Rokujō Lady
and the tragic consequences of his inconstancy, which so wounded her
pride. For Katō Saheita and Niwa Genbei, the moments must have
passed like hours until finally began the finale of the act:

CHORUS: *Hearing your story, it is clear you are no common villager.*
Pray tell your name.

ROKUJŌ: *To tell my name, for one so worthless as I, would bring but*
shame. Yet if my shame must be known, then so be it. Still I would ask,
if you please, that you pray for me as one nameless, one no longer of
this world.

CHORUS: *"No longer of this world," you say? How strange! Then—*
from this world . . .

ROKUJŌ: *I have long since departed, leaving only a name.*

CHORUS: *The Consort herself . . .*

ROKUJŌ: *. . . am I!*

CHORUS: *As night falls and the autumn wind begins to blow,*

And the moon's pale gleam, sifting through the grove,
Lights her way beneath the trees,
She steps between the dark pillars of the gate,
Into the shadows, and vanishes from sight;
She steps between the dark pillars of the gate,
Into the shadows, and vanishes from sight.

At long last, Aki-no-Kami turned and retreated, shuffling slowly to the chant of the Chorus, down the bridgeway to the Mirror Room. Even before the curtain rose and then fell behind him, Saheita and Genbei were rushing behind the scenes to the rear entrance. Moments later, it was announced that the remainder of the performance had been canceled.

◆ ◆ ◆

I have often wondered just when in the course of that long day the Elders (and the Junior Elders and the Inspectors General as well) came to realize that their greatest difficulty was no longer seeing the ceremonial visit of the Imperial Envoys through to a dignified end, but having to oversee the confiscation of a daimyo's castle and domains against the will of a corps of angry and well-armed vassals.

The sentence of death to a daimyo meant automatic disenfeoffment, and disenfeoffment meant the loss of livelihood for every member of the abolished house. Not only could the lord's heir not inherit, but every samurai, foot soldier, lackey, and menial in his service would be turned out of his home and his enfeoffment or stipend terminated. This had happened many times before. The law was harsh, but it was respected and accepted. Disenfeoffment alone was not the problem. The problem this time was that another law had been flouted, the Principle of Equal Punishment.

For the past three centuries and more, it had been customary practice that both parties to any quarrel were to be punished equally. Who was "right" and who was "wrong" had nothing to do with the case. In choosing to quarrel, both men abandoned reason and rational discussion, and thus were a threat to peace. Both were in the wrong, and both must be punished, usually by death. But Kira was not to be punished. Instead, he would be extolled by the Shogun himself for having refrained from drawing his sword—which everyone must have understood was more an act of cowardice than of restraint. Equal Punishment was no longer enshrined in the written codes of Tokugawa law; but the concept still carried the force of customary law. This case of disenfeoffment would require particular delicacy.

The disenfeoffment of one of the Shogun's own vassals could be handled entirely by the Shogun's own officials. But the disenfeoffment of an ally—indeed, the progeny of one of the founding Shogun's most trusted allies—must be managed more diplomatically. The Shogun's officials might plan and administer the process, but all commands and coercion—should coercion be called for—must come from kinsmen and colleagues. This time, coercion might indeed be called for. For the Elders knew well that the moment the Akō samurai learned of Kira's reprieve, they would be furious that he had not suffered the same punishment as their lord.

The plan, therefore, was not simply to rely upon Shogunal decrees, but to hold Takumi-no-Kami's closest relatives responsible for the execution of those decrees. The very magnitude of what these lords had to lose, should they fail in this responsibility, was the best possible guarantee of its fulfillment.

◆ ◆ ◆

Once Toda Uneme-no-Kami had discharged his duties at the Military Liaison Lodge, he returned to his own upper mansion, only a short distance away on the same street. From there, he sent two of his senior officers, Nakagawa Jingobei and Kano Jibuemon, back to the lodge to act as his representatives while he himself awaited further word from the Council of Elders. He did not have to wait long. At the Hour of the Monkey (3:00–4:00 p.m.), he was summoned to the official residence of the Duty Elder, Tsuchiya Sagami-no-Kami. There, Uneme-no-Kami was joined by another close relative, Asano Mino-no-Kami, a bannerman of the Shogun. These two gentlemen were then dispatched to the Asano Upper Mansion bearing a Shogunal decree that was to be proclaimed to all Asano vassals then resident in Edo.

About an hour later, they were joined by two more lords, Asano

Daigaku, the younger brother and heir of Takumi-no-Kami, and Mizuno Kenmotsu, a daimyo delegated by the Council of Elders to oversee the entire process, and if necessary to exercise armed persuasion upon any recalcitrant vassals of the Asano house (for which purpose, a large force that Mizuno had led hither waited outside). By this time, most of the Asano vassals had returned from the lodge, and all present were summoned to the main reception rooms of the mansion. There, Toda Uneme-no-Kami advised them verbally of the Elders' warning, after which Mino-no-Kami read aloud the decree they had brought with them:

> *Asano Takumi-no-Kami, reportedly bearing a personal grudge against Kira Kōzuke-no-Suke, has committed an outrage within the palace. Under the circumstances, this was deemed inexcusable. By reason thereof, his domains are to be confiscated, and he is commanded this evening to commit seppuku. You are advised that if his vassals create any disturbance of any sort, his kinsmen shall be held responsible. I trust we may count upon your compliance on this occasion.*

So far, however, none of the Akō vassals was aware that Kira was still alive and likely to recover from his wounds. Most of them assumed that he was dead, and the rest did not even bother to wonder. They had more immediate worries on their minds. And so they raised not the slightest protest. Uneme-no-Kami, Mino-no-Kami, and Mizuno Kenmotsu could see that no further persuasion or coercion would be needed.

Uneme-no-Kami decided that he would spend the night at Teppōzu, but dismissed the force that he had brought with him. The other gentlemen withdrew, along with all the men they had brought with them. The inhabitants of the Asano mansion were at last left to the management of their own affairs. Their first act on their own behalf was to send a second pair of messengers to Akō by express conveyance, this time to convey the sad news of their lord's sentence of death and their own disenfeoffment.

CHAPTER
7

Such was a journey
by express conveyance.

News of the domain's impending doom had to travel a distance of 155 leagues before anyone in Akō could do anything about it. In modern measure, that is about 388 miles (620 kilometers), and by modern means of transport, it takes no more than an overnight train trip to cover the distance. In the Genroku era, however, it was normally a journey—on foot, of course—of seventeen days from Edo to Akō. This was far too slow for news of such moment. The message could be speeded considerably if sent by relay courier. But neither would that do. It was essential not only that written word reach the domain, but that it be carried by men who could explain all the details of this series of events and answer some of the questions that were bound to arise. The only way of fulfilling both requirements was to send two men, of sturdy constitution, by an expensive and complicated mode of transport known as *hayakago* (express conveyance).

The conveyance itself can be simply described. It was the same light-weight litter that anyone could hire in the streets of any city. It consisted of a timber bar, perhaps 5 or 6 feet long, from which was suspended a basket-like seat woven of strips of bamboo and padded with an ordinary cushion. The whole thing was light enough to be carried on the shoulder of one man; with a passenger in the seat, it could be borne easily by two men.

What made this simple conveyance "express" is a more complex matter. The first complexity was the number of bearers required. Instead of two men, one had to hire anywhere from four to seven, for the increased speed of the express version was gained by an increase in manpower. There were several ways in which this manpower could be brought to bear. The most common method was to attach a crosspiece to each end of the bar from which the seat hung. This made it possible for four men to share the load and thus move at a livelier trot than two alone could manage. A further increase could be gained by attaching a rope to the front end of the bar that would be towed by a fifth man running ahead of the bearers; if a sixth was hired, he could push at the rear of the bar. And a seventh, if available and affordable, could periodically relieve each of the others, allowing them, one by one, to run for a time unburdened.

A further complication, of course, was the distance to be traveled. All transport of any sort was hired for the distance of one post station to the next. At each station along the way, new litters had to be prepared and new men engaged to bear them. If time was of no concern, the chance for passengers to rest and refresh themselves at each stop would probably be a welcome interlude. But in this case, time was of the essence. It was thus necessary, at each station along the way, to hire an unencumbered courier who would run on ahead of the travelers to warn the manager of the next station to prepare new litters and assemble the men needed to bear them. In this way, the Akō samurai, at each stop, could simply roll out of one litter and into another, and continue on their way. This agonizing process had to be repeated at sixty-some post stations between Edo and Akō.

Then there was the problem of payment. Without institutional backing, an individual traveler would have to negotiate and pay for such services at each station along the way, and carry with him the cash to do so. Fortunately, however, some foresighted vassal of the Akō house, in preceding years, had arranged that generous annual gratuities be sent to certain merchants in the transport business in Edo—just in case. Now this generosity paid off. The author of this wise policy had only to mention to his beneficiaries what was needed, and almost immediately he was provided not only with the first of the express conveyances for the journey, but also with letters of credit that would ensure payment to every post station between Edo and Akō.

Finally, we must not ignore the agonies of such a journey. It was not simply that the travelers were allowed no rest at the way stations. The journey was accomplished in record time, only four and a half days. Thus these men could not have slept for four and a half days. And not only could they not have slept, but they would have been jounced about with every step of their bearers, forced to bite down on a bit of twisted rag to prevent damage to their teeth, and hold tight to a rope attached to the bar above them to keep from being tossed onto the road. By the time they reached Akō, they would have been so exhausted and so debilitated that there are hardly words to describe the desperate state of their condition. Such was a journey by express conveyance.

♦ ♦ ♦

The first two bearers of bad tidings, Hayami Tōzaemon, a member of the Horse Guards, and Kayano Sanpei, a samurai of no enfeoffment, left directly from the Military Liaison Lodge, without even changing out of their formal robes, late in the Hour of the Ram (ca. 2:30 p.m.). News of the full horror of the Catastrophe, however, was entrusted to men of higher rank, Hara Sōemon, a Company Commander of Foot Soldiers, and Ōishi Sezaemon, a member of the Horse Guards. Sōemon was loath to leave until they could learn whether Kira had died or was still alive. But Yasui Hikoemon and Fujii Matazaemon, the two Asano Elders in Edo, were insisting that they be gone immediately.

"Time's a-wasting," they said. "You've got to get going—now!"

"We'll make up for lost time on the road," Sōemon replied. "We can't leave until we know for certain."

"In that case, we'll send an express courier as soon as we hear any news."

"Very well, then," Sōemon said, and they set off sometime "before midnight."

The two Elders never sent any word of any sort.

figure 5
Nagayasu Gasan's painting of a peasant couple watching messengers
rushing to Akō. (Akō Municipal Museum of History)

CHAPTER
8

With all due respect, . . . we beg to register our objection
to this sentence of same-day seppuku.

The four Inspectors who had interrogated Asano Takumi-no-Kami and
Kira Kōzuke-no-Suke had been on standby in their duty room since
the Council of Elders had instructed them to return there and await
further orders. Now their orders had come, this time carried by the
Commander of the Tea Monks, Nagakura Chin'ami. Chin'ami told them
that Takumi-no-Kami, for having attacked Kōzuke-no-Suke within the
precincts of the palace, had been remanded to the custody of Tamura
Ukyō-no-Daibu and would be sentenced to commit seppuku. Kira, for
his exemplary behavior in not drawing his sword, had been exonerated
and was free to return home at any time in the company of his doctors
and colleagues. The four Inspectors thus would be required to supervise
the execution of these judgments.

The Inspectors acknowledged receipt of their orders with due
respect, but their acquiescence to these orders was not immediately
forthcoming. They themselves had gathered the evidence upon which,
presumably, the Shogun's judgment was based. But the judgment they
were being asked to execute seemed to them utterly at odds with the evidence. After some discussion among themselves, they asked Chin'ami to
convey the following message: they would straightaway carry out their
duties in connection with Takumi-no-Kami's confinement. Concerning
other aspects of the judgment, however, they asked permission to postpone their response. And in order to explain their reasons for this delay,
they requested an audience with the Junior Council of Elders, under
whose jurisdiction the Inspectorate worked.

✦ ✦ ✦

By early afternoon, when Kurisaki Dōyū reached the Ōtemon Gate, every entrance to the castle had been shut and bolted and closed to all traffic from either direction. Dōyū had only to mention his mission and show his official summons, however, and he was admitted without delay. At the inner gate, he was met by a squad of Deputy Inspectors, who took him directly to the doctors' duty room, where Kira now lay, just across the long hallway from the Cypress Room. The duty physician and surgeon sat on either side of the bleeding patient. Suddenly, just as Dōyū stepped into the room, Kira's breath began to quicken faintly. Was he about to expire? Were these his last gasps? Dōyū reached immediately for a sachet of medicine that he had prepared in advance and immersed it. He then turned to examine the wounds. At first he applied a lime-based styptic, but the blood only welled up beneath it and burst forth from between the lips of the wounds. There was no time to send for better equipment. Dōyū tore a long strip from the sleeve of Kira's white under-robe, folded it lengthwise, spread a poultice over the gashes, and bound them tightly. Almost immediately, the bleeding stopped. Dōyū then gave Kira the potion he had prepared, which seemed to revive him a bit. When Dōyū was certain that the flow of blood had been staunched, he loosened the band on Kira's forehead and pressed the edges of the wound together more tightly with his fingers; then he restored the pressure and, with the help of Kira's men, propped up the patient in a more comfortable position. For the moment, nothing more could be done. Dōyū left the room and went to wash his hands and clean up a bit.

On the way back to his patient, passing through the Hearth Room, Dōyū chanced to encounter Sengoku Hōki-no-Kami, the Inspector General who had authorized his summons. He took the opportunity to report his progress with the case: "I've stopped the bleeding and revived him, but I've yet to treat the wounds comprehensively. Eventually, they'll have to be cleansed and stitched."

"The Council of Elders will wish to hear of this," Hōki-no-Kami said, adding that in the meantime Dōyū should stand by for further orders. This suited Dōyū perfectly; it gave him the time he needed for the next step of his treatment, the execution of which he could not speak of quite so openly.

♦ ♦ ♦

The Junior Council agreed to hear the dissent of the four Inspectors immediately, and delegated two of their number, Katō Etchū-no-Kami and Inagaki Tsushima-no-Kami, to confer with the Inspectors. Okado Denpachirō, as the Duty Watch Officer of the day, spoke on behalf of the group.

"As I reported in some detail following our interrogations," Denpachirō explained, "Takumi-no-Kami bore no enmity whatever toward his superiors, but he was deeply resentful of Kōzuke-no-Suke. He lost control of himself, and, despite his presence in the palace, he attacked Kira. He expressed deep remorse for this grave offence, and said that whatever punishment might be meted out to him, he could offer no excuse for his actions. His answers to all our questions were prompt and straightforward.

"Now, we must remember that Takumi-no-Kami is lord of a domain of 50,000 koku and is a castellan as well. What is more, his house is a branch of one of the greatest in the land. If he is sentenced to commit seppuku this very same day, it is certain to seem cavalier justice for a man of his stature. Although we ourselves are but minor officials, we have been charged with the duties of official Inspectors; it would thus be an act of disloyalty were we not to point out this oversight on the part of His Highness. With all due respect, therefore, we beg to register our objection to this sentence of same-day seppuku.

"Next, as regards Kōzuke-no-Suke: his conduct may well have been exemplary, but if he aroused such resentment in Takumi-no-Kami that he should cast away the domain of 50,000 koku of which he is lord and bring ruin to the house of which he is head; if, whether deranged or not, Takumi-no-Kami should so totally lose control of himself that he would draw his sword and attack with no thought for his presence in the palace, it is hard to imagine that Kōzuke-no-Suke could be totally blameless.

"We perhaps overestimate the importance of the information gathered in our investigation of the motives of these men. Even so, the lord of the Asano main house, being an ally of the Shogun rather than his vassal, may still feel that we have handled this incident in too offhand a manner.

"We suggest therefore, that before Takumi-no-Kami is sentenced to commit seppuku, there should be further investigation by both the Inspectors General and ourselves. After a seemly number of days have passed, he may then be sentenced to whatever punishment seems appropriate. Until such time, Kōzuke-no-Suke, too, should be placed under Domiciliary Confinement. If upon subsequent investigation it should appear that his conduct was indeed exemplary, that he was not the object of personal resentment, that Takumi-no-Kami's attack was entirely an act of insanity, then Kōzuke-no-Suke may be accorded due praise. But to praise him on the very day of the incident does seem excessive. Such are the recommendations we presume to proffer."

Throughout this long and complex exposition, the Junior Elders listened attentively and patiently. Their reply was: "Your arguments make a great deal of sense. It is apparent, too, that you have performed your duties as Inspectors with great diligence. We shall present your recommendations to the Council of Elders."

♦ ♦ ♦

All was much as Dōyū had left it when he returned to the room. His patient was resting quietly; the Sub-Inspectors still kept their watch. The time was right. Dōyū turned to the Inspectors and spoke softly: "You know, I left the house very early this morning, and I've had nothing to eat since then."

"Why, of course!" The Inspectors seemed almost apologetic that this had not occurred to them: "Why don't you go straight to the kitchens and have the cook prepare something for you there." This was precisely what Dōyū was hoping they would suggest.

"Thank you," Dōyū said, "I'll do that, if I may." In fact, Dōyū himself had no desire to eat. He wanted food for his patient. Kira probably had risen before dawn that morning; at least eight hours had passed since his last meal. If he was to recover from the severe loss of blood he had suffered, he would need nourishment, and he would need it soon.

Normally, this would present no problem. But today, if only symbolically, the Shogun was host to the Emperor. To be sure, he would never travel to meet the Emperor in person, but he took these symbolic meetings very seriously. Every participant in the ceremony was beholden to avoid any sort of impurity. If Dōyū were to let it be known that he wished food for someone under blood pollution, he was sure to be denied. Never mind that the food was needed for a patient in danger of dying of sword wounds; in the view of many, the fact that he had been wounded in an unseemly quarrel would only make the pollution seem more odious. Dōyū thought it best, therefore, that Kira's need for nourishment not be mentioned.

When the surgeon stepped out of the room, he accosted the first Palace Usher who passed his way and asked him to fetch two or three sheets of paper. There was no need to discuss the use to which these would be put. He merely thanked the monk and proceeded on his way to the interior of the palace.

The kitchens were under guard today. But since Dōyū, with at least partial honesty, could present his request as a command from the Inspectorate, he was served immediately. When Dōyū produced his three sheets of paper and began wrapping leftovers in them, though, the kitchen Inspectors began eyeing him suspiciously.

"What are you intending to do with these, may we ask?" said one of the Inspectors.

"I left the house very early this morning, and this is the first I've eaten since then. But my samurai and my servant are still on duty in the doctors' room, and they've had nothing at all to eat. I thought I'd at least wrap up some of my leftovers to hold them until we can send for replacements." Dōyū seems to have been as skilled an actor as he was a surgeon. The Inspectors not only believed his tale but, most inconveniently, offered to help: "In that case, we'll have a meal prepared from the remains of yesterday's banquet and have it sent to your men." Their kindness was becoming more dangerous than their suspicion.

"Oh no," Dōyū protested, "there's no need for you to go to so much trouble." And before the Inspectors could renew their offers of assistance, he picked up two pairs of chopsticks, tucked them in the folds of his robe along with the packet of food, and left the room.

But if Dōyū thought that the complications of treating his patient were now overcome, he was mistaken. Upon leaving the kitchens, his route again took him through the Hearth Room, where once more he encountered the Inspector General Sengoku Hōki-no-Kami.

More than three hours had passed since the Council of Elders had authorized Hōki-no-Kami to send for Dōyū. Although the Elders were still a long way from penetrating all the mysteries of this case, certain fundamental facts had emerged. What had seemed the unpremeditated attack of a madman on an innocent official was turning out to be no such thing. Takumi-no-Kami had been angry, but by no means deranged. Kira had provoked him. And although neither party seemed willing to reveal the cause of their quarrel, a quarrel there had been. Whatever else might come of this revelation, it had immediate effects upon the arrangements for Kira's medical care. This was what Hōki-no-Kami had come to discuss with Dōyū.

"As you know," the Inspector General began, "it was on orders from the Council of Elders that I sent for you to treat Kira. I've now been ordered to tell you that you need treat him no longer." The Elders, it seems, had at first considered Kira to be an innocent victim attacked in the line of duty. Accordingly, they had assumed full responsibility for his treatment. It was clear now, however—to the Elders, at least— that Kira himself had provoked the attack; the treatment of his wounds, therefore, was his own responsibility, which must be borne at his own expense. Private quarrels must be privately financed.

"I've just informed Kira and his colleagues of this decision, and they're asking permission to retain your services on a private basis. The Elders are prepared to grant that request. It was you, after all, who revived him and stopped his bleeding. You are free to continue treating him as a private patient, if you so desire."

To Dōyū's credit, he did not take the opportunity of an easy escape. He conferred with Kira's colleagues to confirm the patient's wishes. He dismissed the other two physicians as gracefully as possible, apologizing to the duty surgeon for keeping him so long from his other duties and begging permission of the internist to consult with him further should the need arise. Finally, he reported back to the Inspector General that if the Elders approved, he would remain on the case. The Elders, of course, approved, and Dōyū, at long last, was free to continue treating his patient.

The wound on Kira's forehead was less than 4 inches long, but the blade had cut into the bone. He was lucky that it was not deeper and longer. Fortunately, though, the blow had been deflected by the metal band in his court cap. Dōyū sent for boiling water, and after he had cleansed the wound, he drew the edges together with six sutures of fine silk. He then bathed the wound in a weak solution of tea and applied a thin sprinkling of a powdered medication. The wound on his back was more than 6 inches long, but not deep. Only three stitches were needed to hold it together. Dōyū treated it as he had the other wound, and bandaged them both with strips of white cotton torn from Kira's under-robe.

The doctors' room, so immaculate when Kira had been brought there, was now smeared with blood and strewn with discarded garments and the litter of surgery. Dōyū was appalled to see that Kira's men were doing nothing.

"Whatever are you doing with yourselves?" the doctor demanded. "Palace officials soon will be coming. You can't expect them to sit in a room that's befouled with blood. Now, pick up his clothing and put it in the luggage trunk. Let's get busy and make this room presentable."

Kira himself was resting quietly. Now at last there was time for the final stage of Dōyū's treatment. He sent for hot water, a tea bowl, and some salt. When they arrived, he took the food that he had gone to such trouble to spirit out of the kitchens, mixed it with the salt and water, and made a thin gruel. Kira downed two bowls of it and before long was looking almost as strong as ever. Dōyū had been right. What had seemed Kira's last gasps had been caused as much by lack of nourishment as by loss of blood. He was also right in predicting that Kira would soon have official visitors.

Kira's men were just finishing their task when Sengoku Hōki-no-Kami appeared at the door.

"I won't come in," the Inspector General said, peering inquiringly at the patient, but apparently apprehensive lest he come in contact with blood pollution.

Dōyū rose to meet him: "You're welcome to come in if you wish. I've been expecting interrogation officers and have seen to it that there be no trace of pollution when they arrive."

Hōki-no-Kami stepped into the room and seemed pleased to find it so unexpectedly clean: "I'd heard that blood had been gushing in here, but there's not a trace of it to be seen now. You'd hardly know that the man had been wounded. You've done a fine job. I shall make a detailed report of this to the Council of Elders." But it was not curiosity about the victim's well-being that had brought the Inspector General to the doctors' room. Neither was there to be any further interrogation. Hōki-no-Kami had come at the behest of the Council of Elders to convey a Shogunal decree to Kira Kōzuke-no-Suke. And as he was speaking to Dōyū, another figure entered the room. It was none other than the Shogun's Chief Adjutant, Yanagisawa Dewa-no-Kami. The Inspector General then took out the decree and read it:

Kira Kōzuke-no-Suke

Asano Takumi, heedless of his presence in the palace and the august nature of the occasion, attacked you without provocation. This was considered an offense of the gravest sort, and thus it has been commanded that Takumi be duly punished. You, Kōzuke-no-Suke, are absolved of all blame and are commanded to devote yourself to the care of your wounds.

YEAR OF THE SERPENT, THIRD MONTH, 14TH DAY

To this, the Chief Adjutant added in his own words that His Highness also hoped that once Kira had recovered, he would not hesitate to return to his duties as doyen of the Masters of Court Protocol. The Elders had changed their minds about Kira's guilt, but the Shogun had not changed his.

◆ ◆ ◆

Not long after the Inspector General and the Chief Adjutant had departed the doctors' room, another officer of the Inspectorate appeared at the door. His name was Nakajima Hikoemon, he said, and he had been sent to assist in transporting the patient to his home. Kira's colleague Shinagawa Buzen-no-Kami would, of course, accompany him, but there were practical matters to be attended to that might lie beyond the experience of such an exalted gentleman.

"We're to leave from the Hirakawa Gate," Hikoemon said. In Edo Castle, the Hirakawa Gate is designated the Gate of the Unclean, the only gate through which women, the wounded, the dead, and even bad tidings might pass. It made for a roundabout route, approximately doubling the distance to be covered, but Kira was under blood pollution. He must leave from the Hirakawa Gate.

"As you know, the Elders wish you to accompany your patient," Hikoemon said to Dōyū, "but they ask that you proceed on foot and not board your palanquin until we reach the gate." Apparently, even unpolluted members of the procession were expected to exercise restraint when traveling in the company of the tainted.

The route by which they would travel was also a matter of concern. Dōyū naturally suggested that it would be best for his patient to return by the most direct route, bearing right as they exited through the Hirakawa Gate, following the moat around to the main gate, crossing the bridge at the Dragon's Mouth, and then turning into the avenue that would take them past the Military Liaison Lodge and thence straight to Kira's home just within the Gofukubashi Gate.

"I would advise against that," Hikoemon said. "It will take us a bit out of our way, but we had best avoid the neighborhood of the Military Liaison Lodge." Dōyū understood immediately. The lodge had been swarming with Takumi-no-Kami's men, some of whom might still be there. There was no telling what sort of trouble might ensue if they were to see Kira, alive and free and on his way home. The Council of Elders had provided a large contingent of armed men to guard the procession. In addition to Hikoemon and his fellow Inspectors, a company of lancers was to surround Kira, Buzen-no-Kami, and Dōyū; both front and rear of the train would be guarded by Deputy Inspectors and Sub-Inspectors. Still, there was no need to provoke a battle; they would take the long route.

As they made their way from the palace to the Hirakawa Gate, Dōyū kept close behind Kira's palanquin, checking at frequent intervals to see whether the movement was causing any change in his patient's condition. Even after passing through the gate, he maintained this position, lest an emergency catch him unprepared. As Hikoemon suggested, they followed a zigzag route though the quarter on the far side of the moat from the Military Liaison Lodge. Only when they reached the square at the Tokiwabashi Gate did they feel that they might relax their guard a bit. Here Dōyū boarded his palanquin, although he did leave the window open, and Hikoemon mounted his horse to lead them across the square and over the Zenigame Bridge to the rear entrance of Kira's mansion.

✦ ✦ ✦

What the Elders thought of the Inspectors' recommendations to the Junior Elders was never recorded, perhaps never even expressed—for all discussion was preempted by the Shogun's Chief Adjutant, Yanagisawa Dewa-no-Kami. He heard the report through and answered it in two curt sentences: "The matter is already decided. Tell the Inspectors that their orders stand as issued."

The two Junior Elders were deeply chagrined when they returned to the duty room where the Inspectors waited. They reiterated their own opinion, that the Inspectors' recommendations were eminently sensible, but Yanagisawa Dewa-no-Kami had already authorized the sentence. The matter was decided; they had gone as high in the chain of command as they dared. Denpachirō, however, was only the more adamant.

"If Dewa-no-Kami has decided this on his own initiative," said Denpachirō, "then I must beg you to resubmit our recommendations. This sentence is excessively one-sided. It's a disgrace even to think what the allied daimyo will make of it. We beg you to submit our recommendations once more. Please tell Dewa-no-Kami that if this has been reported to His Highness and he has approved the sentence, then we accept the fact that nothing further can be done. But if Dewa-no-Kami has authorized this on his own, then I must insist upon submitting our report to higher authority."

If Denpachirō had previously performed his duty as an Inspector with diligence, he was now performing it with daring. The only higher authority to whom he could appeal was the Shogun himself. But Denpachirō was not indulging in idle threats. Every fully fledged Inspector had the right—indeed, the duty—to report any malfeasance by any person, no matter how high his station or rank, directly to the Shogun. It was a prerogative that was seldom exercised in time of peace, but a right and duty of the greatest importance. The lord of a domain was in many ways a blind man, cut off from contact with the people he ruled by his elevated position and prevented from knowing the true thoughts of his officials, whether for better or worse, by their desire to flatter him. His Inspectors had to be his eyes and ears. Yet no matter how carefully they might watch and listen, if they were to report their findings through the normal chain of command, then only the most innocuous bits of intelligence would ever reach the ruler. And so, in the middling ranks of officialdom, the Inspectors alone were granted direct access to their lord and immunity from punishment for criticizing their superiors. Obviously, one's Inspectors must be chosen with the greatest of care. They must be intelligent, fearless, fair, and incorruptible. Evidently, the Junior Elders considered Denpachirō to be such a person, for Tsushima-no-Kami and Etchū-no-Kami went again to present his arguments to the Shogun's Chief Adjutant. This time, Yanagisawa fairly exploded with anger: "Whether this recommendation has been transmitted to His Highness or not, I fail to comprehend how anyone can challenge the authority of an officer charged with the execution of His Highness's orders. Denpachirō is to be relieved of his duties at once and restricted to the duty room until further notice."

♦ ♦ ♦

When Kira arrived home, he was greeted by a crowd of relatives and close friends, a veritable army sent by his son Uesugi Danjō, as well as three more doctors, two of whom were colleagues of Dōyū. They helped Kira into his sitting room, taking special care that he be positioned properly and giving him another dose of a medicine of Dōyū's own concoction. At this point, the Inspector in charge, Nakajima Hikoemon, came in to check on the patient and tell Dōyū that he would now be leaving to report to the Duty Elder and the Duty Junior Elder. Dōyū, too, allowed as how he ought to be leaving to attend to another patient, besides which, he, too, must report to the Elders and Junior Elders. And so it was arranged that Kira be given a light evening meal of gruel. Later that night, Dōyū said, he would return and check Kira's wounds before he retired. With that he left, went about his business, made his reports, and returned home.

CHAPTER
9

Sooner even than these blossoms,
beckoned by the breeze, I, too, must fall.

Tamura Ukyō-no-Daibu Takeaki, lord of Ichinoseki, a domain of 30,000 koku that lay in the deep north 155 leagues from Edo, was but one of the many vassal daimyo who had been commanded to attend the Shogun at that morning's Imperial Response. His sole duty had been to join the ranks of his fellow daimyo, seated behind the Shogun, when they were displayed to the envoys in the closing flourish to their audience. Now there was nothing to deter him from leaving the castle. He did hold the office of Master of Military Protocol, but it was not his turn to serve as Duty Officer that day. Normally, he would now have done precisely as his colleagues were doing—change out of ceremonial attire, alert his men waiting at the inner and outer gates, and go home.

But it had not been a normal day. The corridors still swarmed with ushers and officials running to and fro on assignments connected with the attack in the Pine Gallery. As a vassal daimyo and an officeholder, it might be best, he thought, if he were to delay his departure, just in case he should be needed to assist in some way. His colleagues might think it presumptuous, and even self-serving, that he should linger when his presence had not been invited. But surely it was as much the part of a responsible official to anticipate duty as to discharge it. Let others say what they might; he would remain in the duty room just a little longer. Just in case.

As these thoughts passed through Tamura's mind, a Palace Usher entered the room with a query from the Duty Officer of the Junior Council of Elders, Inoue Yamato-no-Kami: "Who among the Masters of Military Protocol is still in attendance?"

"Other than the Duty Officer, only myself," Tamura replied. Moments later, the usher returned with yet another query: "Are you in any way related to Asano Takumi-no-Kami?" Tamura told him that he was not.

"In that case," the monk said, "I am to ask that you report to the Duty Officer of the Council of Elders." Tamura left immediately for the Clock Room. One wonders if Tamura was ever to regret his decision to remain behind, for had he left the duty room with his colleagues, he probably would have escaped one of the most unpleasant duties he would ever be required to perform.

It was well past midday when Tsuchiya Sagami-no-Kami welcomed him to the anteroom of the Elders' deliberation chamber. His orders were brief and—purposely, I suspect—vague.

"For the time being, Asano Takumi-no-Kami is to be placed in your custody," Tsuchiya told him. "You'll kindly arrange to take him away immediately."

Tamura had two questions concerning proper procedure: "Is it necessary that I accompany him en route? Or that I greet him upon arrival at my residence?"

"Neither will be necessary," the Elder said.

"Then I shall prepare immediately." As soon as he had taken leave of the Elder, Tamura strode back to the ceremonial precincts of the palace, summoned his Adjutant and sent him ahead to begin preparations, and then gathered his entourage and returned in haste to his upper mansion to muster his full force for the mission. By the midpoint of the Eighth Hour (3:00 p.m.), they were ready to march.

✦ ✦ ✦

In times of peace, it was sudden emergencies of just this sort that tested the mettle of a daimyo. In times of peace, the lord of a domain was expected not only to cultivate the arts of governance, but at the same time to maintain himself and his men at a high level of readiness in the arts of war. But lacking the requisite battles, these skills were never put to the ultimate test. Aged forty-six, Tamura Ukyō had been born some fifty-six years after the founding Shogun, Ieyasu, had put an end to what had seemed an endless succession of wars and almost forty years after the last brief bursts of rebellion in the early years of the Great Peace. He may well have known some of those very old men who had had brief experience of battle, but he himself had never led his men to war. He had never lived in a time of war; he had never inhaled the atmosphere of impending war. Now he was to be tested, if not in actual battle, at least in the ability to make ready for battle. How rapidly could he muster his force? How smartly would his men respond to their orders? Would they turn to their assigned tasks with discipline and assurance or in bumbling confusion? In what state of readiness would their equipment be? Would logistical needs be properly calculated and provided for? How smoothly would the whole operation be carried out? In short, if this had been a call to battle, would Tamura's response have inspired confidence of victory or premonition of defeat? These are questions that would have been asked no matter who was assigned the task. But they would excite particular interest in the case of a daimyo descended in the line of the great "One-eyed Dragon," Daté no Masamune, one of the few warriors whom the founding Shogun prudently decided not to challenge lest he jeopardize the peace.

◆ ◆ ◆

By all reports, the force mustered by Tamura and his senior officers was every bit as impressive and disciplined as one might expect of this illustrious house. The procession was led by the Edo Liaison Officer of the domain, clad in starched formal linens, mounted on his horse, flanked by two young samurai, and followed by the bearers of his lance and his sandals as well as by a guard of three foot soldiers.

Next came a Company Commander, similarly mounted and attended, leading thirty foot soldiers, all of whom, except their Sub-Commanders, were equipped with long, stout, hardwood staves and coils of rope.

In the center of the column came the palanquin, with its six bearers, in which the prisoner would be transported. Its inner walls were boarded tight and lined with a fine rope mesh through which only a snake could escape. On the outside, the door bore a heavy hasp that would be secured with an iron padlock when the time came and, finally, a second net of stout rope, now borne by a lackey, that would be thrown over the whole conveyance. This portable prison proceeded under the guard of fifteen unmounted samurai and their commander. To their rear marched the bearers of a luggage box and a sword case, which would be used to transport the prisoner's ceremonial attire and weapons. Each bearer was under the command of an unmounted samurai, and they were followed by a guard of three foot soldiers.

Then came a Captain at the head of another company of thirty foot soldiers, their two Sub-Commanders bringing up the rear, followed by a rank of three unmounted samurai.

And finally, there came an Inspector and a member of Lord Tamura's Horse Guards, both mounted, of course, and attended by a young samurai each and the bearers of their lances and sandals. And at the rear of the column marched two physicians, an internist and a surgeon, each with two servants to bear his medical kit and his sandals, and each under the protection of a Deputy Inspector.

All told, it was a force of 118 men that issued from the gates of the Tamura mansion near the foot of Mount Atago in the mid-afternoon of that day. They marched due north, swiftly and silently, headed for the Sakurada Gate. Clearly, the Tamura house was taking its responsibility seriously and was determined to show that it could perform it as though its survival depended upon it. It was to go down in history as a "magnificent" model of peacetime preparedness.

◆ ◆ ◆

When the Tamura force reached the castle, it was met at the Sakurada Dismounting Ground by a Deputy Inspector. Hikawa Gengo dismounted and announced himself and his mission: "This force has been dispatched hither under orders to take a certain gentleman into custody. We ask, therefore, that you instruct us where we are to proceed."

At this point, the force was divided. Those who had surrounded the palanquin were led within the Sakurada Gate, but the foot soldiers were left behind to await them on the dismounting ground—except for four or five of their number who were selected to guard the prisoner and were asked to leave their staves behind before entering the castle. The

Deputy Inspector then led this group through the gate as far as the Alighting Bridge, where they halted to await further orders. They then proceeded farther, through the Great Shoin Gate, past the main entry hall to the palace, and on to the central entrance, which was used by palace officials and functionaries. There they were told to stow the rope net inside the palanquin and carry the conveyance through the doors as though it were no different from an ordinary palanquin—which they did. Thereupon, the Inspector Soné Gorōbei, who was standing at one side of the entrance, sent word within that the prisoner might now be brought to board the conveyance. Once within the palace, the Tamura people were met by three Inspectors General—Andō Chikugo-no-Kami, Sengoku Hōki-no-Kami, and Shōda Shimōsa-no-Kami—who told them that they were to take the palanquin still farther into the palace, down the long corridor flanked by the private rooms of the highest officials, up into the inner hallway, and as far as the standing screen at the entrance to the Tea Monks' duty room. The bearers again shouldered their burden, carried it to the appointed place, set it down, and removed the rope net that had been stowed within it. The doors through which they had entered were then shut and barred, and Takumi-no-Kami was led from the room, surrounded by Deputy Inspectors. The four senior members of the Tamura force signified their acceptance of the prisoner, guided him politely to the palanquin, slid shut the door, and fastened the padlock through the hasp. They had been told that they need not cover the entire conveyance with the heavy rope net, but decided, probably for their own peace of mind, that they would do so anyhow. That accomplished, the bearers were summoned, and Takumi-no-Kami embarked upon his journey to the Tamura mansion. As they were leaving, a Deputy Inspector handed over Takumi's short sword, court cap, paper fold, and fan, which were duly placed in the luggage trunk brought for the purpose. Takumi himself was still wearing his ceremonial robes emblazed with the outsized crests of the Asano house.

◆ ◆ ◆

In the meantime, the foot soldiers, lackeys, and horses that had remained behind at the dismounting ground were led along the moat and around to the Hirakawa Gate, from which those within the castle would soon emerge. With their formation again intact, they proceeded back across the dismounting ground, out the Hibiya Gate, and through the maze of daimyo mansions between there and the Saiwaibashi Gate, whence it was a straight passage down "Daimyo Lane" to the Tamura mansion. One of their number rode ahead of the procession to explain their mission at the guard posts of the mansions they would pass along the way, so they would not be delayed. They entered the rear gate of the Tamura mansion sometime before the end of the Hour of the Monkey (ca. 5:00 p.m.).

At the Tamura mansion, too, the palanquin was carried directly into the house, through a series of five rooms, up to the very entrance of the chamber that had been prepared for Takumi-no-Kami's detention. Every sliding panel in this room had been nailed shut and then securely boarded over. Only a small section of the openwork above the transom was left uncovered to light the room, however minimally. Within, the room was furnished with the basic necessities of a confined life: bedding, a pillow, nightwear, a basin for washing, a comb and cord for dressing his hair, and a bucket to be used as a makeshift toilet. Every entrance to this wing of the house was guarded by foot soldiers, and every approach to the room was blocked.

Once within his makeshift cell, Takumi changed out of his ceremonial robes and into the more usual garb that the Tamura people had provided for him. He was then served a normal meal of one soup and five side dishes, but he could not stomach it and ate only two bowls of bland gruel.

Apparently, however, Takumi-no-Kami was not left incommunicado. Outside the door to his chamber was stationed an intermediary, Ikuta Magofusa by name, through whom he could communicate freely with his custodians. Magofusa, and everyone else in the household, had been instructed that if Takumi-no-Kami should inquire about Kōzuke-no-Suke, they were to reply: "We've been extremely busy here and so have no definite news, but we've heard that his wounds are serious and he is not likely to recover." But when Takumi struck up a conversation with Magofusa—a man with whom normally he would not have deigned to converse—he never raised that subject.

"I think I must have been born completely useless," he said. "And I have this chronic ailment; it sometimes leaves me feeling all choked up. Today in the palace, I lost control of myself and did something quite unforgivable. Now, here I am, enjoying the hospitality of you and your good comrades. But at least I did what I wanted to do to my enemy; that much I can claim. And by the way, might I trouble you to bring me some saké?"

"I'm afraid the law prohibits us from granting that request," Magofusa replied.

"How about tobacco, then?"

"That, too, I'm afraid."

And so, as a last resort, Takumi asked for tea, and that request was granted. By now, the color had returned to his face and his breath was even and slow.

"Do you happen to know how they've punished my brother Daigaku?" he asked. Magofusa, of course, knew nothing of such matters.

"I expect he's being held in custody, too."

Then he turned to Magofusa and said, "I should like to send a letter to my vassals."

"I'm afraid, sir, we're not in a position to permit that without consulting the Inspector General."

"Might I ask you, then, to convey a verbal message?"

Magofusa hesitated, but then in lowered voice asked, "To whom, sir?"

"To two of my men. Their names are Kataoka Gengoemon and Isogai Jūrōzaemon."

"And the message?"

"Only this: that 'I should have told you about this problem beforehand; but what happened today was sudden and unavoidable, so I could not. I expect that you'll find it all rather mysterious.'" This much of his message was indeed recorded and transmitted, through an unnamed vassal of Asano Daigaku, the Tamura people say. But was there more? Some think that there must have been—some explanation of the "mysterious" deed. But if there was more, it may have been considered too sensitive and thus was suppressed. We shall never know.

◆ ◆ ◆

Now that Takumi-no-Kami had been safely ensconced in his custody, Tamura Ukyō-no-Daibu's thoughts turned to concerns of his own. He addressed a letter of inquiry to the Duty Elder, Tsuchiya Sagami-no-Kami:

> Item. *While the detainee is in my custody, will there be any objection to my presence in the palace in order to attend to my duties there?*
>
> Item. *Shall I continue to take my turn on fire watch in the Second Perimeter of the castle?*
>
> Item. *Is it permissible to provide the detainee with the usual implements that are provided to those in detention?*

Sagami-no-Kami's reply said simply: "You will soon be visited by the Inspector General Shōda Shimōsa-no-Kami, who will answer all your questions personally."

Strange to say, Tamura Ukyō-no-Daibu had not been told that he was host to a man who would be dead before the day was done. But why not? For although it was normal that a prisoner should be told his fate only when the formal sentence was read to him, his custodian usually was informed in advance, so that appropriate preparations could be made. Why did the Council of Elders deny Tamura Ukyō this courtesy? The only reason I can imagine is that the Elders may still have held a thread of hope that the Shogun's mind might yet be changed. If so, it was a false hope, held far too long.

◆ ◆ ◆

The sun had sunk low in the sky and the corridors of the palace were almost silent when a directive from the Junior Council of Elders was delivered to Okado Denpachirō, who was still confined to the duty room of the Inspectorate. Denpachirō was ordered to report immediately to Akimoto Tajima-no-Kami, a member of the Council of Elders, who told him: "A short while ago, you submitted a report recommending reconsideration of the case of Asano Takumi-no-Kami's attack on Kira Kōzuke-no-Suke. We thought your opinion eminently sensible and your concern for those in authority exemplary. It was perhaps ill advised to urge the Shogun's Chief Adjutant to change his mind, but your opinion was legitimately advanced in the line of duty. You certainly do not merit being placed under restriction. We wish you to return to your duties immediately."

Returning to duty, of course, meant joining the party being sent to the mansion of Tamura Ukyō-no-Daibu to oversee the sentence of death against which he had just protested. But if such was now to be his duty, then Denpachirō would perform it no less diligently than he had in opposing the sentence. He returned immediately to his comrades and asked what arrangements had been made for Takumi-no-Kami's suicide during the period of his restriction, and where it was to take place. The detail would be led, they told him, by the Inspector General Shōda Shimōsa-no-Kami.

So he was going to meet the famous glutton—the man who could eat eighty slices of charcoal-broiled eel and six bowls of rice at one sitting; whose father had demonstrated his capacity before the Shogun Iemitsu himself, by eating a hundred persimmons and ten pounds of sugar; whose grandfather had won a noodle-eating contest by devouring the equivalent of fifty bowls, which he topped off with a brimming bowl of gruel after his opponent collapsed. A noble lineage, the Shōda house! Denpachirō left to report to Shimōsa-no-Kami.

"I've been on restriction until just now," he explained, "and have been out of touch. I understand that you are to lead the party, and I've been appointed second-in-command. Everything is under control, I expect. But should we perhaps check to see that Lord Tamura's preparations are progressing properly?"

"I've looked into that already," Shimōsa-no-Kami replied. "I doubt there'll be any problem."

It remained only to change into proper attire for the occasion and muster their entourage. Each Inspector was to be attended by an unmounted samurai and four Constables from the City Magistrate's office. Shortly before the Hour of the Cock (ca. 5:00 p.m.), they were ready to leave the castle.

The Inspector General led the procession, followed by Denpachirō, who, in turn, was followed by his fellow Inspector Ōkubo Gonzaemon. At the Sakurada Gate, they were met by a party of Tamura's men who had come to guide them to the Tamura mansion. From there, they moved on to the Saiwaibashi Gate, through which they passed over the outer moat into the avenue that led to their destination. At the gate to the mansion, they were met by three Elders and three Adjutants of the Tamura house. These men escorted the three Inspectors to the entry hall, where Lord Tamura himself welcomed them into his reception rooms.

After the preliminary civilities had been exchanged, Shimōsa-no-Kami's first task was to disillusion Lord Tamura of the assumption that his guest was to remain in his custody "for the time being," as he had been told, and then to tell him that he must prepare to oversee the rite of seppuku. This came as a great surprise to Tamura and his vassals and threw the entire household into "a sudden tumult."

When Shimōsa-no-Kami returned to his colleagues and announced that preparations had begun, Denpachirō and Gonzaemon assumed, logically enough, that their next duty would be to inspect the site of the rite. Their suspicions were aroused, therefore, when Shimōsa-no-Kami told them that this would not be necessary, as he had already perused a plan of the site.

Denpachirō was the first to question this expedient: "While I was restricted to the duty room, I had no chance to examine this plan. As you may recall, I inquired about what preparations had been made, to which you replied that everything was under control, and we would discuss the matter later. And so we left everything in your hands. But you are not the only officer assigned to this mission. As second-in-command, I'd be terribly remiss if something should go wrong and I hadn't even looked at the floor plan. You may feel that you've fulfilled your duty by inspecting a drawing; I must insist upon inspecting the site."

"When the commander of a mission has given his approval," Shimōsa-no-Kami replied, none too pleased with this reference to his laxity, "it is not the place of his second-in-command to contradict him. But you are an Inspector; I can hardly order you not to inspect. Inspect whatever you please! When the job is done, we shall both be free to submit our separate reports. That will be your opportunity to report whatever little flaws you may find. As I said, do as you please!"

Shimōsa-no-Kami's sarcasm betrays his awareness that he was in no position to command his colleagues other than as head of their present mission. Purely in terms of rank, an Inspector General did stand higher in the overall hierarchy than an Inspector. But they were not in the same chain of command. An Inspector General reported to the Council of Elders, whereas Inspectors reported to the Junior Council. And despite his lower rank, an Inspector still had the right of direct appeal to the Shogun. It was a right that he must exercise with discretion, but an undisputed right. Thus when Shimōsa-no-Kami insisted upon his right to command, Denpachirō made it clear that his obedience would be only provisional.

Denpachirō and Gonzaemon soon discovered why their portly superior had not cared to have his preparations scrutinized. The site that had been prepared was grimly, almost indecently, austere. A layer of rough reed matting had been spread out in the garden, upon which lay three white-edged tatami mats covered with a bolt of red felt and shielded on three sides by white curtains. It was a gross breach of military decorum to force a daimyo to commit seppuku out of doors, as though he were a common samurai. Whatever his crime, a gentleman of this rank must at least be granted the dignity of killing himself indoors. This was too egregious a lapse to be relegated to an official report, Denpachirō decided; they must take up the matter directly with the lord of the mansion, Tamura Ukyō-no-Daibu.

Tamura was visibly displeased when Denpachirō asked him whether he had actually discussed the matter with Shimōsa-no-Kami or had just done as the Inspector General told him to do. "After all," Denpachirō added, "a garden, no matter how finely outfitted, is still a garden; and a reception room, no matter how poorly prepared, nonetheless remains a reception room." Tamura was mollified, however, when Denpachirō pointed out that Takumi-no-Kami had not been stripped of his rank and titles before he was sentenced. He had not been forced to resume his old name, Mataichirō, but was still a daimyo of the Fifth Rank and a castellan, and he deserved to be treated as a daimyo.

As it happened, the Tamura, too, had assumed that Takumi must commit seppuku indoors. But there was a problem, an architectural problem. All the rooms in the Tamura mansion that were suitable for such a ceremony were on the same level. Nowhere was there a dais that would allow the Shogun's emissaries to witness the rite from a vantage 6 inches higher than the victim. It was quickly decided, therefore, that they would construct a temporary dais in the main reception room. But at just this point, Shōda Shimōsa-no-Kami had intervened. There was no need to do anything of the sort, he told them. Before leaving the castle, he had inspected the plan of their mansion and discussed this problem with the Duty Elder, Tsuchiya Sagami-no-Kami, who had assured him—so he claimed—that there would be no objection to conducting the rite on the gravelly expanse in the garden.

Denpachirō could see that the debate was now at an end. They must proceed as Shimōsa-no-Kami had commanded.

＋ ＋ ＋

Takumi-no-Kami was informed that his presence was required on orders from the Shogun, for which he should dress more formally, with starched linen vest and broad trousers over the kimono he was now wearing. Ideally, he should change into a kimono bearing his own family crest, but under the circumstances, that was impossible. The required garments were, of course, provided by the Tamura house.

It was a little past the Sixth Hour (6:00 p.m.) when the Inspectors took their seats at the head of the main reception room and requested that Takumi-no-Kami be summoned. He was led to the threshold of the room by three Deputy Inspectors, right, left, and rear, and seated there. Shōda Shimōsa-no-Kami then unfolded the Shogunal decree and read it aloud:

Asano Takumi

Reportedly bearing a personal grudge, you have perpetrated an unprovoked attack with your sword upon Kira Kōzuke-no-Suke. For this most extraordinary outrage, committed in disregard of your

presence within the palace and the august nature of the occasion, you
are hereby commanded to commit seppuku.

Takumi-no-Kami replied, "For my unseemly behavior today, I would
be deserving of any punishment that might be meted out to me. I
am extremely grateful, therefore, that I shall be permitted to commit
seppuku."

Thereupon, the panels opening onto the garden were slid open,
revealing the site that had been prepared. The three Deputy Inspectors
escorted their charge down the steps and into the garden and seated him
upon the red felt, facing the room where he had just been sentenced.
The three Inspectors, Lord Tamura, and his son then moved to seats
facing the garden.

The Tamura house records, despite the great detail of their descriptions of preparations for the event, seem strangely reticent to describe
the event itself. One text tells us that a low-ranking samurai named
Aizawa Sōemon carried the blade to Takumi-no-Kami on a platform
tray and that the Second did his work and then held up the severed
head for inspection—and nothing in between. Another says that the
Second did his work well, and thereafter everyone who had come from
the castle left. The Asano, however, are far more forthcoming, which at
first I found puzzling—for how could the Asano know anything about
it? But then I read in the Asano house records an interlinear note that
revealed that the wife of Tominomori Suke'emon, one of Takumi-no-
Kami's Horse Guards, was the daughter of Suga Jizaemon, a Company
Commander of Foot Soldiers in the Tamura house. Jizaemon was one of
the four senior officers assigned to take Takumi-no-Kami into custody
and oversee the arrangements for his suicide. He was a direct participant in everything that took place, from beginning to end. And after it
was over, he told his daughter and her husband everything that he had
seen and heard. This is how his story is recorded by Ochiai Yozaemon,
the chamberlain of Takumi's wife:

Takumi seated himself in the center of the three mats in the garden
facing the reception room. He was dressed in a white under-robe, a

deep-blue kimono crosshatched at the waist, and a formal starched linen vest and trousers. Once he was seated, a blade was brought to him on a platform tray, wrapped in stiff white paper that was secured with thin, tightly twisted paper twine. About 2 inches of the blade protruded. He drew the tray toward himself, slipped the vest off his shoulders, withdrew his arms from the sleeves of his robes, and folded the fabric down far enough to expose his abdomen. He then leaned forward, reached out, and took the sword in his right hand. His left hand probed his abdomen lightly to locate the lowest rib and guided the tip of the sword to a point just below it. Then in a single movement, Takumi drove home the blade and, with both hands on the hilt, began to draw it across to the right. When the blade reached the end of its horizontal traverse, Takumi paused and spoke weakly.

"Assistance, please."

At that instant, Isoda Budayū brought the blade of his long sword crashing down upon him.

And then? Again, the Tamura house records are silent. But the Asano vassals who went to fetch the remains of their lord say that they found a great gash on his head just behind his left ear. And that rumors were leaking out to the streets that Budayū's first blow had missed its mark, that Takumi had neither cried out nor moved, that Budayu had quickly collected himself and with a second blow severed the head. Who can say where the truth lies?

✦ ✦ ✦

Here, again, I must digress, for anyone who knows anything at all of this story will by now be wondering why I have failed to mention Takumi-no-Kami's famous death poem, the composition of which Okado Denpachirō himself describes so movingly:

After Takumi-no-Kami had taken his seat, he said, "I have a favor to ask of the Inspectors. I expect that my sword has been entrusted to your care. I should like the Second to use that sword in discharging his duty. And after it is over, I should like to present the sword as a gift to the Second." Shōda Shimōsa-no-Kami turned to me and asked, "What does my second-in-command the Inspector think?" I said. "I think his request should be granted," whereupon a man was sent to fetch the weapon. In the meantime, Takumi-no-Kami asked for writing implements and paper, and while he was waiting for the sword to be brought, he took up the brush and wrote:

kaze sasou hana yori mo nao ware wa mata
haru no nagori o ikani to ka semu
Sooner even than these blossoms, beckoned
by the breeze, I too must fall;
but those last vestiges of spring—
what to do about them?

The sword was handed to the Second, Isoda Budayū, who waited in readiness. A Deputy Inspector took the poem and presented it to Tamura Ukyō-no-Daibu. The Second performed his task in accord with long-established tradition, and the rite was brought to an end.

It is such a poignant poem, and so appropriate to the occasion, that one hates to cast doubt upon its authenticity; yet nowhere in the records of either the Tamura house or the Asano house is there any mention of it. I would like to think it authentic, but can offer no evidence that would prove it so; lacking such corroboration, I can see why a professional historian like Professor Shigeno Yasutsugu rejects it outright as apocryphal.

◆ ◆ ◆

Immediately after the rite "was brought to an end," the Inspectors and their entourage departed and returned to the castle. In the garden, a spread was thrown over the body, and a white folding screen placed before the open side of the site. Several lanterns mounted on tall poles were positioned around the curtains to illumine the garden, and a guard of foot soldiers and samurai was posted. Notification was sent to the Council of Elders, the Junior Council, and the Shogun's Chief Adjutant, and finally a letter was composed to be carried to Asano Daigaku:

> *Today Shōda Shimōsa-no-Kami, Ōkubo Gonzaemon, and Okado*
> *Denpachirō presented themselves at my residence and commanded*
> *Asano Takumi to commit seppuku. The aforementioned three*
> *gentlemen likewise assure us that we are free to hand over his body*
> *to his next of kin. As the matter has already been reported to the*
> *Council of Elders, we request that you proceed hither at your earliest*
> *convenience to collect his remains. Herewith the foregoing.*

THIRD MONTH, 14TH DAY   *Tamura Ukyō-no-Daibu*
To: Asano Daigaku Sama

It was after the Fourth Hour (10:00 p.m.) that night that a delegation from the Asano house arrived. It was led by two men who appeared to be his close personal attendants and who were accompanied by four or five others, the Tamura records say; the sight of them placing the body of their lord in his palanquin was pitiful to witness.

The Asano records are more detailed: dusk had already turned to darkness when the party arrived at the gates of the Tamura mansion. They were first shown to the veranda of the reception room, where they were greeted with due courtesy. Thereafter, they were invited to descend to the garden, and as they proceeded thither, the white folding screen was removed from the entrance to the enclosure, revealing several samurai who had maintained total silence throughout the exchange of greetings and continued to do so. This force stood guard over the body of Takumi-no-Kami, who lay where he had died, his severed head resting beside his left shoulder. Without a word, his men lifted him into his burial urn. The Tamura then handed over to them their lord's personal effects—his court robes, his swords, the short sword with which he had attacked Kira, as well as his fan and paper fold. These, "in accord with long-established tradition," they lay atop his body. Finally, they placed the urn in his palanquin, fell into formation, and marched slowly toward the rear gate that led out from the riding ground. From there, they proceeded directly to the temple Sengakuji. The burial rite was simple and short, with only three monks at the graveside to chant the sutras. At the end of it, his four close personal attendants—Kataoka Gengoemon, Isogai Jūrōzaemon, Tanaka Sadashirō, and Nakamura Sei'emon—drew their short swords, cut off their topknots, and cast them into the grave atop the burial urn, symbolically joining their lord (and former lover) in death.

CHAPTER
10

Insolent scum! I could cut down every one of you for this!
Nor will I hesitate to do so if I must!

The Tamura vassals who welcomed the Asano delegation were right to guess that this group was led by Takumi-no-Kami's "close personal attendants"—although they were perhaps unaware of how close these men had been to their lord. Four of them, Kataoka Gengoemon, Isogai Jūrōzaemon, Tanaka Sadashirō, and Nakamura Sei'emon, were former Page Boys (which is not the same as being a member of the Corps of Pages). Page Boys were handsome youths who, before they came of age, served as the boy lovers of their lord. When they came of age, they shaved their forelocks, married, and lived much like any other samurai. Yet although they no longer shared their lord's bed, they remained on close personal terms with him and often were more handsomely rewarded than their fellow samurai. No opprobrium attached to such a relationship. For the most part, these were boys of samurai birth to whom no other opportunities were open—second or third sons, sons of mistresses, orphans. Yet as one wag put it, this was a career that put "a life of ease within the grasp of their bums"; one could hardly blame a boy of no prospects for grasping such a chance. Kataoka Gengoemon, for instance, the senior member of this group, was the son of his father's mistress. Now, aged thirty-five, he was married, had two daughters, and had risen to be Takumi-no-Kami's Confidential Secretary and Commander of Page Boys, for which his reward was 350 koku per year, more than triple what his father had earned.

Such, then, were the men at the core of the group that had come to the Tamura mansion. Natural enough, we might think. Yet Horibe

Yasubei took a rather dubious view of it all: "Neither Yasui Hikoemon nor Fujii Matazaemon, both of them Elders of the Asano house, went with the group to receive the body, nor did they attend the funeral at the temple Sengakuji. This I find utterly incomprehensible." Yasubei was not the only one to express misgivings of this sort. Did the Elders actually care so little for their lord that they would not even see him to his grave? Or had the former Page Boys asserted their rights of "possession" and forcibly excluded the Elders? As we shall see from the subsequent behavior of all these people, either was possible. But we shall never know for certain why the Elders chose to absent themselves.

◆ ◆ ◆

Throughout the night that followed that long day, Horibe Yasubei had remained awake and on duty. He had been charged with the security of all the entrances to the Asano Upper Mansion. The main gate and two subordinate gates opened onto the avenue that followed the broad canal—the Prince-Abbot's Canal, as the townsfolk called it—surrounding the block of reclaimed land upon which the great temple Honganji still stands. A fourth gate, appropriately called the Watergate, opened almost directly onto the tributary canal that ran south to the estuary of the River Sumida. On any other night, a detail of eight or ten foot soldiers and lackeys, standing alternate watches, would have provided sufficient security. That night, however, the whole city knew of Takumi-no-Kami's seppuku. They knew, too, that his death meant the certain abolition of the Akō branch of the Asano house and the confiscation of all its properties. In a matter of days, the mansion would be emptied, turned over to a custodian, and ultimately assigned to a new occupant. It may also have been known that most of the foot soldiers of the Asano house had been assigned to duties at the lower mansions in Akasaka and Honjo. Tonight, in short, the Asano Upper Mansion was dangerously vulnerable to thieves. For if some of the good citizens of Edo could find it in their hearts to sympathize with the men who were about to be turned out of their home, there were only too many others who thought more of how they might help empty the house.

At the Hour of the Boar (9:00 p.m.), the main gate was shut tight and bolted, anyone requesting passage through the wicket was required to identify himself, and no one who was not a member of the household was to be admitted. With this gap in their defenses closed, it should have been an easy matter to monitor traffic at the three smaller gates. And it would have been if, as the occupants thought, the odd sneak thief was all they had to contend with. What actually happened was nothing that anyone could have predicted.

In the middle of the night, a small flotilla of boats slipped up to the quayside steps outside the Watergate and landed a band of forty or fifty townsmen, who simply marched into the mansion and proceeded to make off with everything light enough to carry. Which they were able to do because at just this moment, the guard posted at the Watergate decided that he would leave his post and stroll over to the rear gate for a chat with one of his comrades.

The first warning of the invasion to reach Yasubei was the raucous shouts and bellowing of a band of fifty looters. He was furious at the dereliction of his sentry and furious at his own failure to detect it, but there was no time now for anything but action. Yasubei ran in the direction of the shouts, and the devastation that he discovered only whetted his anger. "It was a disgusting sight," he wrote to his late father's friend in Shibata. "Here our lord had given his utmost to uphold his honor as a warrior and yet had met a most lamentable end. If now we must surrender his mansion, I was determined that we should at least do so in orderly fashion." There was only one way to put a stop to this.

Yasubei drew his sword and raged at the mob: "Insolent scum! I could cut down every one of you for this! Nor will I hesitate to do so if I must!" The intruders could hardly have known that the man they faced had, seven years earlier, become something of a hero for challenging a band of armed ruffians and killing most of them. They must have sensed, though, that he was fully prepared to make good on his threat. Besides which, they were not samurai themselves; typical townsmen that they were, they ran straight for their boats and rowed off as fast as they could go. Yasubei immediately posted a new guard and ordered the Watergate shut and locked.

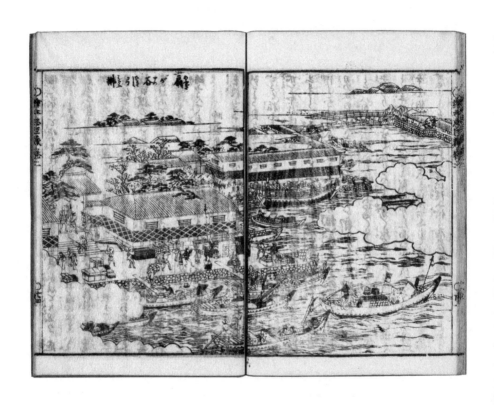

figure 6
The Watergate of the Asano Upper Mansion in Teppōzu.
(*Ehon Chūshingura*, Waseda University Library, Tokyo)

But this was by no means the end of the problem. In this vast property covering more than 7 acres, the only enfeoffed warriors in attendance were the Edo Elders and Adjutants, Yasubei, and two or three more samurai. All the other men were either absent on some mission or another, or quartered in the two lower mansions. The band of looters he had just routed may well have known this. A better organized raid might not be so easily withstood. Yasubei thus reported the incident to Toda Uneme-no-Kami, who was spending the night there. Toda immediately sent for a company of sixty foot soldiers to secure the Watergate throughout the rest of the night; the following morning, he called in another hundred foot soldiers under the command of five samurai. Yet another hundred foot soldiers and fifteen samurai were sent from the mansion of the Hiroshima main house of the Asano clan. All four gates could now be secured around the clock by this force.

◆ ◆ ◆

Throughout the day and into the night, deep within the Asano mansion in a separate establishment of her own, Lady Asano would have been receiving regular reports on the progress of the Catastrophe. But women of her rank led exceedingly protected lives, so it is hardly surprising that we know almost nothing of her response to these reports. What we do know, however, is that after the departure of the emissaries from the Shogunate, Asano Daigaku went immediately to the inner rooms of his brother's wife. What passed between them seems to have been overheard by people sent earlier from the Hiroshima main house. One of them, Otani Benzen, was a friend of Muro Kyūsō, a scholar from Kaga, and later he told Kyūsō all about it.

On the morning of the 14th, according to Kyūsō's account, Lady Asano could see that her husband was upset and sensed that something was seriously wrong. She walked with him to the door of her apartments.

"Please," she said as he was about to leave, "come straight back and see me as soon as you've done your duties at the palace." She could hardly have imagined that those would be the last words she would ever speak to him. She seemed prepared for the worst, though, when Daigaku entered her rooms and told her what had happened.

"Who was it?" she demanded. "Is he dead?"

"I don't really know," Daigaku said. "The Council of Elders commanded me to come here and warn everyone that they must create no disturbance. I came immediately."

"You don't really know? How can you say such a thing? Your own brother is about to die, and you can't be bothered to find out whether his enemy is still alive? 'You come from the Council of Elders,' you say, 'to warn us not to make a fuss.' How can you even mouth such drivel at a time like this?"

She said not another word. As the Hiroshima people tell it, she just turned her back on him and left the room.

✦ ✦ ✦

We wish that we knew more about this affectionate but fiercely principled woman, Lady Asano. But apart from what Kyūsō reports, facts are hard to come by. Popular accounts claim that she was betrothed at the age of two and married at ten. Both claims are false. But if you work your way through the *Records of a Dutiful Progeny*, a sparse but more nuanced and plausible outline of her life begins to emerge.

Aguri was born deep in the mountains of Bingo, in the domain of Miyoshi, in the ninth year of Kanbun. Her father was Asano Inaba-no-Kami Nagaharu, lord of this domain. Of Aguri's mother, we know for certain only that her name was O-Ishi, that her other surviving daughter married a court noble in Kyoto, and that she herself was, as the chronicler puts it, "a lady of the house." The phrase leaves considerable margin for interpretation. But the status accorded her daughters, as well as her connection with the temple Zuikōin, give credence to the genealogy that traces her ancestry, through a line of second sons, to the Yamazaki house, vassals of Nobunaga, Hideyoshi, and the ill-fated Fukushima Masanori. When Masanori was disenfeoffed from Hiroshima, O-Ishi's father may well have lost his position and remained behind in the Hiroshima area—which could account for her connection with the new lords of Hiroshima, the Asano. To be sure, she was not Inaba-no-Kami's principal wife. That lady was required to live permanently in Edo, as a "surety"—which is to say, a hostage—to the

Shogun. But O-Ishi does seem to have been mistress of the domainal establishment in Miyoshi, where Inaba-no-Kami spent every other year. Over the years, she bore him a son and four daughters. Only two of the girls survived long enough to be married: Aguri, born in 1669 when her mother was thirty-eight, and Yoshi, born two years later in 1671. Four years later, Inaba-no-Kami died unexpectedly in Edo, aged sixty-two. On the 15th Day of the New Year, he awoke in the night, soaked in sweat, with a sharp pain in his ear. On the 17th, he lapsed into a coma, and on the 19th he expired. By a strange coincidence, this was the very day of Aguri's *himo-otoshi* in Miyoshi, a fête celebrated by girls of warrior birth in their seventh year, when they cease to secure their robes with cord and for the first time don the broad obi.

After her father's death, Aguri was taken into the Hiroshima house and not long thereafter was moved to Edo in preparation for her marriage to Naganori. Three years later, her younger sister (now Tsuru) was moved to Kyoto, where she was to be married to the court noble Kawabata Suenori. With all her children gone, O-Ishi, too, now a nun, left Miyoshi to live with her cousin, the monk Yōho, in Kyoto, where he was Superior of the family temple, Zuikōin. And there she died, in 1696, aged sixty-five. She hadn't seen her daughter Aguri since the girl left for Edo twenty years earlier.

◆ ◆ ◆

There is a story, too, that Itō Bai'u tells, about the man responsible for Aguri's upbringing, which may offer a clue to her character.

The man's name was Yonemura Gon'emon, and he began his career as the sandal bearer to Ōno Shuri-no-Suke Harunaga, commander of the defending force in the siege of Osaka Castle. In his early days, as the lowest of the low, Gon'emon would not have been allowed even to enter the field of vision of his lord; he would have learnt to toss his commander's sandals into position from beyond the range of his peripheral vision. Yet in one way and another, Shuri-no-Suke came to realize that Gon'emon, despite his humble origins, was a youth of considerable intelligence and courage. Prior to the battle of Osaka Castle, Shuri-no-Suke rewarded his lowly favorite, raising him to the rank of samurai. And when the castle fell, and Shuri-no-Suke was about to take his own life, it was Gon'emon to whom he entrusted his young daughter, commanding him to spirit her away and rear her in hiding. For a time, Gon'emon seems to have evaded the dragnet of the victors, but eventually he was caught and imprisoned in Edo. He would have been high on the list of wanted fugitives, for they suspected that he knew where the vast stores of gold and silver of the Toyotomi war chest had been hidden. Under interrogation, Gon'emon flatly denied any such knowledge.

"Come now, we know that you were a favorite of Shuri-no-Suke. Yet you say that you know nothing?" The interrogator turned to his men. "If he insists that he knows nothing, then put him to the ordeal and we'll question him again."

Until then, Gon'emon had kept his brow pressed to the earth, but when he heard this, he raised his head and spoke: "I must say, I am astonished to hear a senior officer of this great house talk such non-sense. I am a man of humble birth. Shuri-no-Suke singled me out for promotion, and I now rank among his samurai. When Shuri-no-Suke was in Osaka, he was in overall command of the castle and its defense. From morning to night, his mind was filled with nothing but matters of life and death. Gold and silver meant nothing to him. And those of us under his command—well, we thought of nothing but killing you people and cutting off your heads. We hadn't a moment to think of any-thing else.

"So if I may, let me point out something that should be obvious to you: when there's a battle raging in a castle, what does it matter if you do have hundreds of millions in gold and silver? What good does that do you if you lose your head? Yet if you win, then everything is yours, even unto the swords of the enemy commanders. Without ever seeking wealth, you end up with so much that you don't know what to do with it. So why would we even think about gold and silver? Winning was all that mattered to us.

"If there was anything more I could tell you, I would not hesitate to tell you, right here and now. But there is nothing more. So what am I sup-posed to say, even if you rip open my mouth and tear out my tongue? 'Put him to the ordeal,' you say, 'and then question him again.' What nonsense!"

He spoke so fearlessly that the Tokugawa officials could see that he was a man of incredible bravery. Instead of torturing him, they released him, and then took him into their own service, as preceptor to the young Tokugawa scion Hyōe Hitachi. Gon'emon, they say, always dressed plainly and ate simple food, but he kept his weapons in sparkling condition. And despite his new duties, he remained true to his promise to rear the daughter of his late lord, Ōno Shuri-no-Suke.

Years later, when his young charge was grown and had a family of her own, Gon'emon was transferred to the service of Asano Inaba-no-Kami Nagaharu. Inaba-no-Kami, too, entrusted him with the upbringing of his daughters. One of these girls was Aguri. It is no great stretch, I think, to hear echoes of old Gon'emon's voice in Lady Asano's rebuke of her brother-in-law Daigaku. Were the old warrior still alive, he would have been proud of her.

◆ ◆ ◆

After Daigaku had left her presence, Lady Asano remained in complete control of herself and the situation. At first, she busied herself assembling the trifles that she would need over the next few days, sending her women to fetch one thing and then another. Then came word from the Tamura house of her husband's suicide. She turned to the waiting woman at her side: "Fetch me my sword." The woman did as she was told and brought the weapon to her mistress.

"Now cut off my hair and be quick about it." At this command, her waiting woman baulked.

"Wouldn't it be best to wait until we arrive at the Miyoshi mansion? Surely that's not too long a delay?"

Lady Asano said nothing. She took the sword and, with her own hand, slashed to shoulder length her long black tresses, which had taken so many years to grow. She was a widow now; henceforth, she would live as a nun, dedicated to the performance of devotions on behalf of her late husband.

◆ ◆ ◆

One of the first things that Asano Aki-no-Kami had done after returning from his disrupted performance at his son's new mansion was to submit two official inquiries to the Council of Elders:

1. Should he refrain from attending the bimonthly general audience at the palace on the morrow?
2. Might he arrange for Lady Asano to move from Teppōzu to the mansion of the family of her birth, the Miyoshi cadet house?

The Elders responded positively to both questions: Aki-no-Kami was still welcome to appear in the presence of the Shogun, and Lady Asano might move wherever she wished. This, of course, was why Aki-no-Kami's men were within earshot when Her Ladyship berated her brother-in-law. They were assisting with preparations for her removal to Akasaka. By the beginning of the Hour of the Tiger (ca. 3:00 a.m.), all was at last in readiness.

From the moment she first heard of the incident until late that night, when she boarded her palanquin to leave Teppōzu for the last time, Lady Asano had betrayed no sign of inner turmoil. She remained as calm as though this were just another ordinary day, her people said. But now it was time to leave. Her elder brother, Asano Shikibu-no-Shō, had sent a detail to fetch her back to the Miyoshi mansion in Akasaka—a very small detail of only fifteen men, as he, too, was apprehensive lest he provoke the authorities. And only after this small procession was in motion, marching through the night on the way to Akasaka, did those closest to her conveyance hear the sound of muffled sobs. No one spoke, but before long the eyes of every man in her entourage were wet with tears. At the rear of the procession, Nakazawa Yaichibei (of whom we shall never hear again) wept audibly all the way, and then returned alone to Teppōzu; this was the last time in his life that he would guard his mistress on her outings.

When Lady Asano reached the home of her brother, they say, she shut herself in her rooms and for long refused to emerge.

CHAPTER
11

He's—not dead,
you say?

In the dark of night, every village or hamlet looks the same. The long procession of pines that lines the highway halts; the shadow of a farmer's shed appears. Then a low wall, almost within arm's reach. A jumping line of ragged thatch. You're too low to see the roofs above it. Now and again, a sign jumps out of a lane. Too dark to read it. No, that one said "tea." The first dog sounds the alarm. Then all the dogs. Everywhere the dogs. You shift off the numb side of your bottom; time for the other side to go numb.

At the last change of relay, Hayami Tōzaemon and Kayano Sanpei had carried their dread news as far as Odawara, some 20 leagues (50 miles, 80 kilometers) from Edo, the tenth of fifty-three post stations on the Eastern Sea Road. Now, as the sky began to gray, they could make out the dim contours of Futagoyama, the twin peaks toward which the road was tending. Soon they would begin the long, slow climb through Hakone Pass to the checkpoint that guarded the western gateway to the Kantō Plain.

Edo, Third Month, 15th Day
Thieves were not the only ones who sought entry to the Asano mansion. When news of the Akō disaster reached the upper mansion of Ikeda Iyo-no-Kami, lord of Okayama, it was received not as an item of idle gossip but as a matter that could have repercussions in the Ikeda home domains. Okayama lay immediately to the west of Akō and shared with it a long stretch of the border between the provinces

of Harima and Bizen. It was a much larger domain than Akō, rated at more than 310,000 koku, six times the yield of its small neighbor. Still, it would not do to be unprepared if trouble should threaten to spill over the border. There was constant traffic and trade between the two domains, and unrest among peasants had a way of ignoring territorial borders. There was no immediate threat, but the situation demanded close observation. Kagano Densuke, a Deputy Inspector in the House of Ikeda, was summoned. He was to penetrate the Asano mansion in Teppōzu, the Elders told him, and gather every scrap of information he could for transmission to Okayama. Further steps would be taken in other quarters, depending upon how the situation developed.

Early in the morning, Densuke strolled along the south bank of the canal that emptied into the estuary at Akashibashi. About halfway up the canal, his route brought him to a point where his line of vision opened into a narrow lane at the rear of the Asano mansion, on the far bank of the channel. Densuke paused, took a rough count of the foot soldiers clustered about the gate, and continued his stroll. A few steps farther, and he had a clear view through the Watergate. He could take in the situation there without interrupting his easy pace. Where the tributary that he followed joined the broader stream of the Prince-Abbot's Canal, there were two bridges. The one to the right led directly to the thoroughfare that passed the main gate of the Asano mansion. Densuke crossed the other bridge to the far side of the broad canal; from there, he could survey the main gate without attracting the attention of the knot of armed men who guarded it. What he saw convinced him that it would be impossible to enter any of the four gates without being apprehended as an interloper. All told, there were more than a hundred foot soldiers in evidence, and probably more within the walls. This deterred him only slightly. Intelligence was his profession, and he had his sources. Nor was it only chance that one of these sources happened to have ready access—in what capacity, we know not—to the Asano mansion. By the end of the day, Densuke had prepared a full report, copies of which were submitted to Iyo-no-Kami and dispatched to Okayama by relay courier.

◆ ◆ ◆

At the Kira household, all remained well with the wounded patient. But for Dōyū, the man was becoming as much a diplomatic as a medical problem. A messenger had come to him in the morning bearing word from Kira's son, Uesugi Danjō, that his father's wounds seemed to be healing well. This was only to be expected, for as Dōyū himself says, Kira, though in his sixties, had always been strong and healthy. The scar on his forehead would be inconspicuous, and both wounds probably would heal completely in fourteen or fifteen days. But for Uesugi Danjō, this seemed to pose a problem. The incident was already the talk of the town, and before long the news would spread throughout the land. If it became known that Kira's wounds were light and that he was recovering rapidly, public opinion could turn against him. Therefore, the Uesugi messenger requested, would Dōyū be so kind as to describe Kira's wounds as "grave" and "serious"? And would he also be so kind as to visit the patient every day for the next thirty or forty days? Dōyū did not refuse the request for this unnecessary attention; in fact, he visited Kira daily for the next sixty days. But he tells us that the family's real concern was not the welfare of his patient, but to avoid arousing the anger of Takumi's vassals, which might prompt them to finish the job that their liege lord had begun. The Uesugi, too, were aware that the Principle of Equal Punishment had been flouted.

◆ ◆ ◆

Nowadays, we are likely to think of the Shogunate as a massive bureaucracy, as inert as those we ourselves are accustomed to. Perhaps in some ways, it did over the years grow inert. We must remember, however, that before it became a government, the Shogunate was a military force; when matters of great moment were at stake, it could still act with astonishing, even ruthless, military efficiency. Which it did on the morning and early afternoon of the 15th, less than a full day after the Shogun had decreed that Takumi-no-Kami must commit seppuku.

Toda Uneme-no-Kami had spent almost the entire night at the Asano mansion, returning home only after Lady Asano had departed for Akasaka, sometime in the latter half of the Hour of the Tiger (ca. 4:00–5:00 a.m.). Even then, he was allowed no sleep. Immediately after his return, he sent a messenger to the Duty Elder, Tsuchiya Sagami-no-Kami, informing him of his whereabouts and inquiring what further involvement in the affair would be required of him. Not long thereafter, in the Hour of the Dragon (ca. 8:00 a.m.), he returned to Teppōzu, where his first duty was to write to the ten Asano relatives who would be required to wear mourning for Takumi-no-Kami—three uncles, six cousins, and a father-in-law—and inform them that they were now under sentence of Restraint. For the time being, they were to refrain from appearing in the presence of the Shogun and from performing duties of a public nature. A more drastic form of punishment was to be meted out to Takumi's closest male relative, Asano Daigaku.

◆ ◆ ◆

The 15th Day of every month was a day of general audience at the castle. But as soon as their ceremonial duties in this ritual were fulfilled, both the Council of Elders and the Council of Junior Elders convened in their separate chambers in the public sector of the palace. And well before the throng had dispersed, two of the daimyo present, Wakizaka Awaji-no-Kami and Kinoshita Higo-no-Kami, were advised that their presence would be required by the Elders in the Clock Room. There, Akimoto Tajima-no-Kami informed them of their appointment as official enforcers of the confiscation of the lands and castle of the Akō domain. The choice of these gentlemen was determined geographically. Tatsuno, the domain of the Wakizaka house, lay less than a day's march to the east of Akō; Ashimori, the domain of the Kinoshita house, less than two days to the west. On the appointed day of the surrender, they were told, their forces were to advance upon Akō in a pincer movement, fully armed and prepared for action—just in case there should be any resistance from the Akō vassals. Thereafter, Tsuchiya Sagami-no-Kami presented both daimyo with written instructions that specified the size of the force that would be required of them. The Wakizaka were to send some 3,500 men and the Kinoshita, 1,500. And after the surrender was complete, the Wakizaka were to garrison the domain until a new lord was appointed.

At the same time, four of the Shogun's bannermen were summoned to the Kerria Room, where the Junior Council was in session. Araki Jūzaemon, a Herald, and Kusakabe Sanjūrō, a member of the Corps of Pages, were appointed Supervisory Inspectors of the surrender process; Okada Shōdayū and Ishihara Shinzaemon were appointed Resident Deputies, who would remain in Akō thereafter, handling the day-to-day business of the domain in place of the departing vassals. Ishihara, however, declined to accept his appointment because he was distantly related to Takumi-no-Kami's mother; he was excused and replaced by another member of the Corps of Pages, Sakakibara Uneme.

There would be several subsequent discussions among these men as they worked out the details of this operation, but plans for the attainder of Akō were now in motion.

◆ ◆ ◆

At about the Hour of the Ram, sometime after 1:00 p.m., two men, one the prisoner of the other, arrived at the court of the Military Tribunal, a short distance from the main gate to Edo Castle and immediately adjacent to the Military Liaison Lodge. Toda Izu-no-Kami was a Unit Commander in the Shogun's Corps of Pages. He was also an uncle of the late Takumi-no-Kami—although only through ties of adoption and marriage, which exempted him from the restraints placed upon blood relatives. In his custody was Asano Daigaku Nagahiro, the younger brother and adoptive heir of Takumi-no-Kami. Their business at the tribunal was quickly accomplished. The Inspector General Mizoguchi Settsu-no-Kami, in the presence of his colleagues the Inspectors Kuru Jūzaemon and Hanabusa Kan'emon, and by order of the Council of Elders, sentenced Asano Daigaku to Domiciliary Confinement, duration unstated. This meant that until the Shogunate should decide otherwise, Daigaku would be detained under house arrest, the gates to his residence closed to all traffic, and any comings and goings of his retainers restricted to the rearmost gate after dark. Normally, the statutes of guilt by relation would not have punished a younger brother so severely; but after a near fatal attack of smallpox, Takumi-no-Kami,

who after twelve years of marriage was still childless, had thought it prudent to adopt Daigaku as his heir. Now, instead of a domain of 53,000
koku, Daigaku would inherit only a much larger share of his brother's
guilt than should have been his lot. He was returned immediately to his
residence in Kobiki-chō, 4-Chōme, where all the gates were shut and
barred and all the windows facing outward were boarded.

♦ ♦ ♦

The Asano Upper Mansion in Teppōzu was a study in contrasts.
The vassals whose duty it was to clear the mansion of its furnishings,
weapons, and adornments, however agitated their private thoughts
may have been, bent diligently and deliberately to the tasks of packing,
labeling, and loading their cargo in boats at the Watergate. While for
the wives and children of those stationed permanently in Edo, it was as
though their whole world had been turned upside down. In the midst
of such turmoil, some seemed able only to sob distractedly. Others, no
less distressed but more in control of themselves, bade painful farewells
to their close friends or sought the aid of relatives in finding rooms to
rent. There were those who chose to remain in Edo, and others who
went elsewhere to live with kinfolk. The more fortunate were safe at
least "for the time being," or "until you can arrange other housing." But
there were some who simply set out for the countryside, probably not
knowing themselves where they would end up. And then there were
those samurai and foot soldiers who had departed for Akō. Back in the
domain, they at least could postpone the problem of their own and their
families' survival until after the surrender of the castle. At this point,
even the briefest respite was welcome.

♦ ♦ ♦

Who brought the news and when is not recorded. We know only that
it was someone from the outside whom Horibe Yasubei had reason to
trust and that Yasubei was still on duty at the Asano Upper Mansion
when his informant spoke to him. What the man said came as a staggering shock: Kira Kōzuke-no-Suke had not died. In fact, his wounds
were so slight that it was likely he would recover quite quickly—and he

had been absolved of all guilt by the Shogun himself.

Yasubei had had little time to ponder such matters this past night, and it took him a moment to digest the fact that this was not just another wild rumor he was hearing. That Kira was dead was the one thing none of them had thought to doubt. For even if he had survived the attack in the castle, he would have been sentenced to death under the Principle of Equal Punishment. Surely this was one "law" even the Shogun himself would be loath to set aside.

"He's—not dead, you say?" Yasubei had to make sure. For if true, this changed everything. If justice had not been done, then someone would have to see that justice was done. If Kira was still alive, Kira would have to be killed. That, as Yasubei now saw it, was his duty. Magodayū and Gunbei, his comrades in the Edo Horse Guards, could be counted on to join him. As soon as the mansion was transferred to its new custodians, the three of them would round up a force and plan their attack.

CHAPTER

12

~~~

That is a lie.
It was I who disarmed him.

Some of you, I expect, will recognize this poem by Tachibana no Tamenaka, written almost 850 years ago on his journey north as the newly appointed Governor of Mutsu. It's not one of the greatest poems in our language, but I couldn't help recalling it when I was calculating the progress of Hayami Tōzaemon and Kayano Sanpei on their journey to Akō by express conveyance:

> *tabine suru sayo no nakayama sayo naka ni*
> *shika mo naku nari tsuma ya koishiki*
> The traveler, awakened from fitful sleep at Sayo no Nakayama:
> does the stag too cry in the night, yearning for his mate?

If my calculations are correct, Tōzaemon and Sanpei would just have passed through Kanaya, the twenty-fourth post station, as day was dawning. The next station, Nissaka, was only 2 leagues farther on, but a long stretch of that distance was a steep climb over the pass at Sayo no Nakayama. Not quite as steep as Hiroshige depicts it in his Eastern Sea Road prints, but probably more tiring for those ten or twelve bearers than a level run of 3 or 4 leagues would be. And their passengers, Tōzaemon and Sanpei, must by now have been yearning for sleep of any sort, however fitful or however often broken by the moan of a lovelorn stag.

Edo, Third Month, 16th Day
Again, in the morning, Kajikawa Yosōbei was summoned to the chambers

~ 134 ~

of the Council of Elders, where he was again interrogated, this time before an additional group of Masters of Court Protocol, whose presence the Elders did not explain.

"Who arrived on the scene first, and who thereafter?"

"I can't say that I know," Yosōbei replied. "All the Tea Monks came running, of course."

"We understand that Takumi-no-Kami Dono said nothing of the nature of his grievance. But did Kōzuke-no-Suke Dono reach for the hilt of his sword?"

"I did not see him do so. If he had drawn his sword, I certainly would have seen; but he did not. After that first flurry, I looked about for him, but he was nowhere in sight."

"Who took him away?"

"I have no idea," Yosōbei replied.

All the Elders' questions thus far were the same as those asked before, as likewise were Yosōbei's answers.

"That's exactly what he said last time," said Shinagawa Buzen-no-Kami, as though his consistency were somehow blameworthy. Then another of the Masters of Court Protocol, Kyōgoku Tsushima-no-Kami, spoke up, in tones that were unmistakably accusatory: "And he says that it was he who wrested the sword from Takumi-no-Kami. That is a lie. It was I who disarmed him; since I did not wish to entrust the sword to a Tea Monk, I handed it over to Yosōbei."

Unfortunately, Yosōbei tells us nothing of the Elders' reaction to this charge or how the meeting ended; he says only that he was determined not to let Tsushima Dono's slanderous falsehood go unchallenged. After the Masters of Court Protocol had dispersed, Yosōbei went to the Secretariat, where he sought the assistance of a high-ranking witness, the Inspector General Andō Chikugo-no-Kami. Andō, of course, corroborated Yosōbei's testimony, and then, together with his colleague Sengoku Hōki-no-Kami, went to assure the Council of Elders that Tsushima-no-Kami was the liar, not Yosōbei. Why the man even attempted such a mad fabrication remains a mystery, but the next day he was forced to apologize abjectly, "palms to the floor."

Yosōbei was totally exonerated. Yet, as we shall see, the experience aroused nagging second thoughts about the rectitude of what he had done. Under interrogation, he was duty bound to speak the truth; yet in doing so, he had saved the very man who had driven Takumi to draw his sword in the palace.

♦ ♦ ♦

By now, virtually the entire population of the Asano Upper Mansion in Teppōzu had departed for new lodgings, or at least the scant shelter of the homeless. Only nine Akō vassals remained, all men of senior rank, whose presence would be required on the morrow at the official resumption of the property by the Shogunate. There were the two Edo Elders, of course, Yasui Hikoemon and Fujii Matazaemon; as well as two Adjutants, an Inspector, two Edo Liaison Officers, and two Samurai Commanders. Everyone else was a vassal of either Toda Uneme-no-Kami or Asano Aki-no-Kami. It was now the task of these men to secure the property against would-be raiders and to remove the treasures that these raiders coveted. Aki-no-Kami had hired thirty boats, and throughout the day they plied between the Watergate and the Hiroshima storehouses upriver in Tsukiji. By evening, the move was complete. Only two days after the death of Takumi-no-Kami, the Teppōzu mansion was ready to receive a new master.

♦ ♦ ♦

Where did they go, all these people so suddenly made homeless? Most vanished without a trace. But a few of those who play a part in the continuing story did leave a record of their whereabouts. Yasui and Fujii, the two Elders, moved only a short distance away, to Iida-machi, near the river's edge. Horibe Yahei, the retired Edo Liaison Officer, and his son Yasubei moved en famille to Yonezawa-chō, a neighborhood on the site of the Shogunate's old arrow arsenal, on the city side of the Ryōgoku Bridge.

One of the more interesting arrangements, though, was that made by Tominomori Suke'emon, a man aged thirty-two who had been permanently stationed in Edo, and thus lived with his wife and mother in one of the barrack blocks of the Asano mansion. It is said that Suke'emon possessed private means beyond his enfeoffment of 200 koku, which

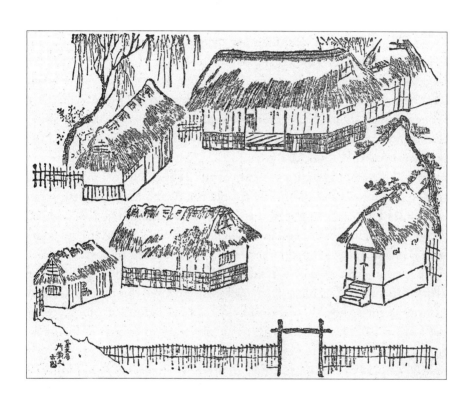

figure 7
Karube Gohei's farmstead in Hirama. (*Akō gishi zuihitsu*, 1855)

made it possible for him to keep a horse—a luxury that many "mounted" samurai could no longer afford. And having a horse, he had to feed it. This he managed through an arrangement with Karube Gohei, a farmer from the village of Hirama, on the far side of the Rokugō River, a short way upstream from Kawasaki.

We know very little about Farmer Gohei. Some writers describe him as "well-to-do," an Elder of the village or even the Headman, yet as far as I know, there is no documentary evidence for any of these claims. Still, the fact that he bore a surname, Karube, suggests that his ancestors had not always been peasants and that he may have owned a somewhat larger tract of land than did the average agriculturalist. But whatever Gohei's status, he and Suke'emon had mutually compatible needs. Gohei had to fertilize his fields; Suke'emon had to feed his horse. And so it was arranged that Gohei be granted the right to remove (by boat) the night soil generated by the residents of the Teppōzu mansion, in return for which Gohei would not only supply the Asano kitchens with fresh vegetables but also bring in fodder for Suke'emon's horse. (Something rather hard to imagine these days, when our bodily wastes have no commercial value and we must ourselves pay to have them removed.)

It appears, too, that this relationship between samurai and farmer grew into something more than just conveniently commercial. When disaster struck the Asano household, Gohei responded quickly to a request for laborers to help with the heavy work of emptying the mansion. And most touching of all, when Tominomori Suke'emon and his family were forced to vacate their quarters in Teppōzu, Gohei offered them a home on his farm in Hirama. They accepted, and their first (and only) son, Chōtarō, was born there the following year. We shall encounter all these people again as this story progresses.

CHAPTER

13

A daimyo in his domain . . . is like a potted tree,
whose roots are regularly trimmed and
can be moved about at will.

At this point, we lose sight—for the space of a day at least—of our bearers of bad tidings to Akō. As day was dawning, they would have arrived at Miya, the forty-first post station on the Eastern Sea Road, 88.5 leagues (221.25 miles, 354 kilometers) from Edo and 36.5 from Kyoto. Miya, they say, was the liveliest of the fifty-three stations, for here was a parting of the ways, with traffic coming and going in three directions instead of two. Which turn Tōzaemon and Sanpei took we do not know. If they chose to continue along the Eastern Sea Road, they would have taken ship for the Seven League Crossing of the Sea of Ise, from Miya to Kuwana, thus bypassing the multiple river fordings of the land route. This option also would have allowed them at least three hours of rest on shipboard, a much-needed respite at this point in their journey. But it also would have made it impossible to send word of their arrival to the next station, thus delaying considerably their departure from Kuwana. And so they may instead have decided to turn onto the Mino Highroad, which would have taken them through Nagoya and Ōgaki to the Middle Mountain Road, which they would have followed through the pass at Sekigahara and down the shore of Lake Biwa to rejoin the Eastern Sea Road at Kusatsu. Which route did they take? We have no idea where Tōzaemon and Sanpei were on this day.

Edo, Third Month, 17th Day
The official resumption of the Asano Upper Mansion was to take place

~ *139* ~

at the Hour of the Hare (ca. 6:00 a.m.). I say "resumption" because it was in the nature of the feudal system that even the grandest of the great lords were not the owners of their domains, but the custodians of lands granted them by the Shogun, who could take them back at any time and require them to move elsewhere—or even, if there were suitable reasons, disenfeoff them entirely. A daimyo in his domain, as one wise scholar put it, is like a potted tree, whose roots are regularly trimmed and can be moved about at will. The same was true, of course, of the upper, middle, and lower mansions that these lords were required to maintain in Edo. And so today, this particular jardiniere, the Asano Upper Mansion in Teppōzu, was about to be returned to its true owner, the Shogun.

It normally would have been the duty of Toda Uneme-no-Kami to represent the Asano house at the formal transfer of the property. He was still in residence at Teppōzu, in direct command of his vassals who guarded the gates and patrolled within the walls, but the conditions of his Restraint stipulated that he perform no official functions. So his kinsman by marriage Toda Izu-no-Kami, who was not under interdiction, rose soon after 3:00 a.m. to make one last round of inspection, to ensure the integrity and presentability of the property before the arrival of the Shogunal officials. Izu-no-Kami was pleased to find that in the main buildings, not a single tatami mat was missing and the final cleaning had been impeccable. He was shocked, however, to discover that many apartments in the barrack blocks were in a dreadful state, not merely of neglect, but deliberately vandalized. If this was the work of the men who had occupied these quarters, they were highly culpable, as they had countless times been enjoined to create no disturbance of any sort. But, then, there had been any number of merchants and day laborers in and out of the property, and there had been the raid of the marauding townsmen on the night of the 14th. At this point, it would be all but impossible to fix the blame for this damage with any certainty. In the end, Izu-no-Kami decided that, since the main buildings were in such excellent condition, he would refrain from probing further into the matter of the barrack blocks. But the transfer was delayed, until the Hour of the Dragon (ca. 8:00 a.m.). The condition of the barrack blocks required explanation, which Izu-no-Kami seems to have managed smoothly and successfully. The property was then turned over to the Shogun's Superintendent of Works, Okuda Hachirōemon, in the presence of a vassal of the mansion's interim custodian, Tozawa Kazusa-no-Suke of Shinjō.

◆ ◆ ◆

Like all daimyo from the west, Ikeda Iyo-no-Kami, lord of the domain of Okayama, was in attendance in Edo this year. He thus had read the report composed three days earlier by Kagano Densuke and had discussed the Akō disenfeoffment with his Elders and advisers a number of times since then. A decision had now been reached that a few armed units should be moved from the castle in Okayama to strategic points near the Akō border—just in case.

From the time of the founding Shogun, relations between the Ikeda and the Tokugawa had always been cordial. Still, it was never wise to leave any room for doubt about one's intentions in the movement of military forces. Iyo-no-Kami thought it best, therefore, to communicate his intentions to the Shogunate, emphasizing the peaceable aims of the mission and minimizing its magnitude. And so he instructed his Edo Liaison Officer, Yoshizaki Jinbei, to pay a "courtesy call" at the mansion of the Shogun's Chief Adjutant, Yanagisawa Dewa-no-Kami, ostensibly to deliver a gift and offer greetings of the season. But in the course of the visit, Jinbei might "casually" raise a question or two concerning this matter. Jinbei had long been acquainted with Yanagisawa's Chief Elder, Hiraoka Uemon, and, once they had exchanged the requisite pleasantries, he was able to broach the subject without letting on that it was the sole reason that he had come to call.

"Iyo-no-Kami doubts very much that this incident in Akō will in any way impinge upon the prestige of the Shogunate," Jinbei began. "Still, there is always the possibility that the peasants might use it as a pretext to incite protest of some sort. So it might be well, we think, to prepare ourselves for that eventuality. Our border with Akō is more than 10 leagues from the castle. And so we've been thinking of instructing Okayama to dispatch a few samurai to some of the villages near the border—nothing provocative, and all within our own domain, of course. I mention this because His Lordship specifically wanted you to know of it."

This was clearly the right move. Uemon went immediately to Yanagisawa Dewa-no-Kami, who gave him a direct reply: "I understand fully what His Lordship wishes to do, and agree totally with him. I've been meaning to take this up with the Council of Elders and recommend that they urge all neighboring daimyo to be just as attentive to their borders. Iyo-no-Kami is quite right."

As soon as detailed plans for the deployment could be drawn up, Iyo-no-Kami's orders would be sent by courier to Okayama. Yanagisawa, too, as we shall see, would take very thorough precautions to isolate the domain of Akō lest there be any outbursts from its borders.

◆ ◆ ◆

In the evening of the same day, Asano Aki-no-Kami sent an emissary to the widow of Takumi-no-Kami to inquire after her well-being and to present her with "gifts of great value," the nature of which is not specified. His emissary was also to bear a letter to her. This missive does not survive, but the gist of it is summarized in the Asano house records.

As we have seen, on the night of her husband's death, Lady Asano cut short her hair and assumed the habit of a nun. She also took the ecclesiastical name Jushōin. Whether this name was suggested to her by a religious of her acquaintance, or it was her own invention, we do not know. Aki-no-Kami was concerned, however, because the middle syllable of this name, "-shō-," was the same as the middle syllable of the Shogun's mother's ecclesiastical name, Keishōin. There was just a chance that this might seem presumptuous and thus give offense. Aki-no-Kami therefore urged Lady Asano to choose a new name that did not include that syllable. She, of course, complied. After the fifth of the seven obsequies for Takumi-no-Kami, she took the name Yōzei'in, which is how we shall know her henceforth.

CHAPTER
14

We ask . . . that you treat this
as a matter of urgency.

En Route to Akō, Third Month, 18th Day
Today, we must join Hayami Tōzaemon and Kayano Sanpei much earlier than usual and remain with them a much longer distance than usual;
for this was the last full day of their journey to Akō, and it was eventful
both in ways predictable and ways they could never have imagined.

Whichever route they decided to take out of Miya, they would have
passed through Kusatsu well before midnight, and from there on, they
could only have been traveling on the Eastern Sea Road. Thereafter,
we encounter Tōzaemon and Sanpei in Ōtsu, whence they sent ahead a
letter to Ōtsukaya Koemon in Fushimi. The document survives:

> *Having urgent business on behalf of Asano Takumi-no-Kami, we*
> *are en route to our home domain by express conveyance, and shall*
> *shortly arrive at your establishment. We would request, therefore,*
> *that you make immediate arrangements for two more such convey-*
> *ances to be in readiness upon our arrival. The account will be settled*
> *with all possible speed; we ask, therefore, that you treat this as a*
> *matter of urgency.*
>
> THIRD MONTH, NIGHT OF THE 17TH DAY   *Hayami Tōzaemon*
>   *Kayano Sanpei*
> To: Ōtsukaya Koemon Sama

As the date of the letter indicates, it was written well before dawn.
And almost directly on the heels of the courier who carried it, the

~ *143* ~

senders themselves would have set out over the pass through Mount Ausaka, scene of so many poetic partings and reunions in antiquity. For most travelers on the Eastern Sea Road, Ōtsu was the last post station before their final destination; it was only 3 leagues from there to the Sanjō Bridge in Kyoto. But Tōzaemon and Sanpei were still 30 leagues (75 miles, 120 kilometers) from Akō. Once over the pass, they had to turn off the highway and onto the Fushimi Road, which cut diagonally across the Yamashina Valley, a journey of about 4 leagues that would take about three hours.

I suspect that the reason this letter survives—the only one of the sixty-some that they must have sent—is that Ōtsukaya Koemon had a particularly close business relationship with the Asano of Akō. He was the proprietor of the Honjin in Fushimi, the premier inn reserved for those of exalted rank who were traveling on official business. Takumi-no-Kami himself often would have stayed there on his yearly journeys to and from Edo. But Ōtsukaya was more than merely an innkeeper to the Asano; he also supplied the domain's Kyoto Liaison Officer with fine saké and other commodities to be given as gifts when the occasion demanded. And, as we shall see, Ōtsukaya often proved himself a trustworthy transmitter of confidential communications that could not be entrusted to commercial postal services. For all these reasons, Ōtsukaya was paid a yearly retainer by the Asano house in addition to the fees for whatever services he might provide. Payment would now stop, of course, but Ōtsukaya remained a loyal friend.

It was still dark when Tōzaemon and Sanpei arrived in Fushimi. Their conveyances for the next leg of the journey were waiting; but first, there was another letter to be written, this one to Onodera Jūnai, the Akō Liaison Officer in Kyoto, for there wasn't time to make a stop in Kyoto and deliver the news in person. This missive does not survive, but its content could only have been a brief report of the Catastrophe. Jūnai's terse reply to Ōtsukaya reads:

> I have perused your gracious letter and am in receipt of the letter
> from Hara Sōemon and Ōishi Sezaemon. As you say, it was only to
> be expected that Takumi Dono should be punished as he was. This

*morning, I also received the letter from Hayami and Kayano. I shall
be in touch with you in due course. Respectfully,*

THIRD MONTH, 18TH DAY   *Onodera Jūnai [monogram]*

From Fushimi, Tōzaemon and Sanpei headed straight down the long
dike to the confluence of the Yodo and Katsura Rivers, boarded the ferry
at the Chinamen's Steps in Nōso, and crossed to Yamazaki, whence they
continued their journey on the Westlands Highroad.

From here on, the route veered away from the river, gently undulating
as it traced the edge of the foothills, tending in as westerly a direction
as the lay of the land allowed. The next post station was Akutagawa, 2
leagues distant. Then another 2 leagues to Kōriyama. Here, Tōzaemon
and Sanpei arranged with their bearers to make a brief stop in the
hamlet of Shiba, halfway to their next change in Segawa. As these men
hoisted the bars of the litters to their shoulders, the sky was lightening,
the shadows turning to shapes. The thin veil of mist that still hung low
over the brown stubble of the rice fields began to lift. The shades of
gray began to color faintly. Kayano Sanpei watched all of this intently.

For Sanpei, this was home. He knew every bend in the road, every
bridge, every tree. There, almost close enough to touch, was the bank of
the old irrigation pond that stretched along the north side of the road.
There, in the distance, beyond the fields, the indistinct outlines of a
few of the valley's villages; from this distance, they all looked the same,
but he knew their names: Ishimaru, Hakunoshima, Bōgashima. There,
the little stone carvings of the Three Monkeys, "See No Evil, Hear No
Evil, Speak No Evil"; Sanpei could still remember walking there with
his nursemaid. And there, closer in, the little cluster of hovels (it had
no name of its own) where the outcastes of the valley lived, thin wisps
of smoke rising above the thatch. All of this was familiar yet strange, in
the way such things can appear to an altered state of mind; and Kayano
Sanpei was exhausted. Only moments now before they reached the
hamlet of Shiba, Sanpei's birthplace, which lay roughly in the center of
the Kayano Valley.

◆ ◆ ◆

It was no accident that Kayano Sanpei bore the same name as this valley. Five centuries earlier, his ancestors, led by Minamoto Kamon-no-Suke Yoshimochi, had come here to assume control of lands assigned to them by Minamoto no Yoritomo as their reward for gallant service in the wars against the House of Taira. At first, Kamon-no-Suke was appointed Resident Intendant of the Kayano Estate, which he was to manage for its owners, the great Konoe house of the imperial court nobility. But as the power of these absentee aristocrats waned, their local managers came to control more and more of the estate in their own right, until they had become de facto landlords of the Kayano Valley. By the third generation of their tenure, the peasants had taken to calling their over-seer "Kayano Dono." The territorial epithet stuck and became the family name, but beyond this, we know very little of the first four hundred years of the House of Kayano in the Kayano Valley. In times of danger, they would strap on their armor and ride out to battle; in the lull, they would return to till the land. The reach of their control seems to have waxed and waned with the fortunes of war and the constant shifting of alliances. Some documents claim that they controlled 120 villages; some say 40-plus; some, fewer. But throughout the vicissitudes of those centuries, that cluster of 11 villages in the valley that gave them their name remained under their constant control.

With the triumph of Oda Nobunaga, however, the fortunes of the Kayano seemed again on the rise—although at the cost of their autonomy. Like most "local lords" in those early days of "unification," they were brought under the banner of a powerful regional overlord. The Kayano became vassals of Araki Murashige, who was a vassal of Nobunaga. They thus became rear vassals of Nobunaga and for a time enjoyed a small share in his successes. When Murashige was awarded the entire province of Settsu as his fief, the Kayano portion of this prize of battle increased their holdings to thirty-seven villages. It was not to last.

I suppose that we shall never know whether Murashige truly intended to betray Nobunaga or was the victim of groundless slander. To the Kayano, it made no difference. Nobunaga laid siege to Arioka Castle, Murashige's fortress at Itami, only to have Murashige escape ten months later, abandoning both his family and his vassals. Shortly thereafter, the castle fell. Their craven overlord was safe; the Kayano lost everything. Only in the next generation was it safe for the heir to the house to come out of hiding and resume the name Kayano. It was in this generation, too, that a strange stroke of fate, set in motion during the siege of Murashige's fortress, worked to unite the Kayano in a fortunate alliance with one of their former enemies.

Among the force sent by Nobunaga to besiege Arioka Castle was Ōshima Mohei Mitsumasa, a warrior from Mino. Like the Kayano, the Ōshima had become rear vassals of Nobunaga when their local over-lord, Saitō Shingorō, joined Nobunaga's Corps of Vassals. For their allegiance, they had been confirmed in their Mino holdings; for their part in Nobunaga's Echigo campaigns, they had been granted an addi-tional fief in that province. Now, with the fall of Murashige's fortress and his loss of the province of Settsu, the Kayano Valley, too, passed into the hands of the Ōshima.

When and how the Ōshima first made contact with the fugitive Kayano survivors is not recorded. I doubt that it would have been within the next five years, while Nobunaga was still alive. But after his assassi-nation, during the rule of Toyotomi Hideyoshi, the Kayano could safely have emerged from hiding. Their association with the Ōshima probably began soon thereafter. Certainly, the Ōshima had good reason to seek their help. With lands in three widely separated provinces, they would have needed capable and trustworthy managers to look after their inter-ests—especially now that Ōshima Mohei had been commanded to join Hideyoshi's invasion force bound for Korea. And who better to look after the Kayano Valley than the Kayano themselves—provided that they were willing. The details are lost, but it seems clear that the Ōshima went out of their way to make it attractive to the dispossessed local lord to oversee the lands they had managed so well for centuries, but no longer could call their own. Kayano Tsunetada was awarded a stipend of 80 *koku* per year; and some documents go so far as to say that he was treated as a "guest" of the Ōshima house rather than as a mere retainer.

Whatever the details of their relationship, it proved a cordial and long-lasting one. After Hideyoshi's death, Ōshima Mohei had wisely sided with Tokugawa Ieyasu at the battle of Sekigahara, and in his later years served Ieyasu in both winter and summer campaigns of the siege of Osaka Castle. In return, he was confirmed in all his previous enfeoffments, some of which were increased to make a total of more than 5,000 koku. The old warrior from Mino hadn't many years left to enjoy the fruits of his campaigning, but he had ensured that his heirs would stand among the highest-ranking bannermen of the new Shogunate. And he had built the foundation of a long-lasting relationship with the Kayano. By the generation of Ōsumi-no-Kami's great-grandson Kayano Tsuneshige, the family was again settled in its old homestead in Shiba in the Kayano Valley. And there the Kayano remained through the long years of peace that ensued—indeed, to the present day—no longer lords of the land, but still the little valley's first family.

♦ ♦ ♦

The litter lurched as the bearers braced themselves against the sudden dip in the road, then swayed left, and finally back again to the right, as they followed the bend at the bottom of the slope. This last turn brought into view the graceful curve of a great tiled roof, the temple Jōenji. Then Sanpei could hear the dull thump of five pairs of feet loping over two spans of earthen bridge. This would be the stream that marked the eastern boundary of Shiba. Then the slap of sandals on a stone bridge; slowing their pace as the road ascended to the right. Leaning out, Sanpei could see it now, on the left, the white plaster of the outbuildings that walled the Kayano homestead. He could make only the briefest of stops here. He must enter his old home, silence the clamor of surprise at his unexpected apparition, leave with his old parents the tragic news that he carried, and be off again. No time for civilities, no time for questions, no time for long explanations. But what was this just ahead? A cluster of people—doing what?

As Sanpei rose stiffly from the litter to enter the gate, he encountered not the surprised smiles of old servants and retainers, but a funeral cortege forming for the short journey to the temple graveyard. Expecting to shock, it was he himself who was shocked. Sanpei's mother was dead. He had arrived just as they were leaving to bury her.

Seldom is anyone forced to make so painfully stark a choice between duty to parents and duty to liege lord. Whether Sanpei had ever pondered what he might do in such a situation, whether he had ever mulled the question that, in its abstracted form, had exercised the thoughts of so many philosophers, who can say. Considered or not, his choice was instant. He must first do his duty as a samurai and hope that that would at least count as partial fulfillment of his filial duty. With hurried promises to his father that he would return as soon as he could, he resumed his cramped seat in the litter and signaled the bearers to proceed. The two flimsy conveyances and their occupants soon grew indistinct on the distant road, and then disappeared beyond the next bend. Before midday, they would reach the terminus of the Westlands Highroad at Nishinomiya and turn onto the Southern Mountain Road. In less than a day, they would be in Akō.

CHAPTER
15

Bitter the nettle, bitter the nettle,
Yet it ripens to a head of rich red.

Third Month, 19th Day

If the thick blanket of cloud under which they traveled in daylight should linger through the night, it could be difficult to spot the junction with the side road to Akō. But no matter. The team of bearers who took over at Shōjō knew where it was. It was early morning, and Tōzaemon and Sanpei were now less than 3 leagues from their destination.

The sky was passing from black to gray, and the dark line of hills began to show against it. By the side of the road, at the edge of the hamlet of Kuga, barely visible against the trunk of a great pine, stood a signpost marking a parting of the ways. The lead runner bent to make sure that it was the one they are looking for. "STRAIGHT AHEAD—SHIMONOSEKI AND KYUSHU; LEFT—AKŌ," it read. The bearers readjusted their load and swerved left, quickly regaining their pace. From here, the road passed through the villages of Naba and Sakata, and then wound upward through Takatori Pass, some of its last stretches, they say, carved out of precipitous cliffs. But when you finally reached the top, you saw spread out below a long narrow plain leading out to the sea. A river entered from the right, flowing the length of the valley, and 2 leagues in the distance, on its right bank, stood the castle town of Akō.

◆ ◆ ◆

Legend has it that Akō takes its name from a song sung 1,200 years ago by one Hata no Kawakatsu. This unfortunate man had once been a retainer of that paragon of wisdom Prince Shōtoku. After the death of his patron, Kawakatsu was hounded out of the capital by the Soga and driven down the coast, down the entire length of the province of Harima, until he reached the narrow plain at the mouth of what is now called the Chigusa River, just east of the border with the province of Bizen. There, 40 and more leagues from a home he would never see again, tilling the rough earth that had never before seen the blade of a tool, Kawakatsu nonetheless seems to have remained an optimist, singing,

> Bitter the nettle, bitter the nettle,
> Yet it ripens to a head of rich red.

Whether or not his sanguine hopes were fulfilled, we are not told, but the similitude of his song must have seemed somehow appropriate; forever thereafter—says the legend—the plain was called by the name Akaho, and later Akō, after the "rich red" head of ripening nettle in Kawakatsu's song. I suspect, though, that it was more the isolation of the place than the blessings of its soil that warmed the hopes of this fugitive of a millennium past.

◆ ◆ ◆

Akō stands at the end of a by-road that leads to the sea and stops there. Indeed, it stands at the end of three such roads, all of which lead though steep mountain passes—Takatori Pass, Inochi Pass, and Hosaka Pass—which is to say, it is situated on the way to nowhere. Nor is it a town with much history of its own. Standing as it does between two towering strongholds, it might one year be the western corner of the Himeji domain and another year the eastern corner of Okayama. Then, after the battle of Sekigahara, when both Himeji and Okayama passed into the hands of Ieyasu's great ally, Ikeda Terumasa, Akō was swallowed up into the midlands of the second largest fief in the land.

With the death of Terumasa, however, the Ikeda house slipped into a slow decline, helped along, it must be said, by the authorities in Edo. The last of Hideyoshi's descendants and allies had just been driven from their stronghold in Osaka Castle. Now that peace had come, this vast domain of the Ikeda began to seem more a threat to the Shogunate than a bulwark against rebellion. The Ikeda could not be dispossessed, of course, but it was arranged that Terumasa's domain—now comprising the whole of four provinces—be subdivided among his sons. In 1615, Terumasa's fifth son, Masatsuna, was enfeoffed with lands rated at 250,000 koku in and around the district of Akō. He established the seat of his rule in the village at the mouth of the Great River, a town began to grow, and for the first time Akō appears in the *Military Register* as a domain in its own right.

Masatsuna remained the lord of Akō until his death, but unfortunately he died without an heir, and the fief was amalgamated with that of his younger brother Teruoki, bringing the total to a rating of 540,000 koku. Teruoki brought yet another form of misfortune to the Ikeda house—madness. On the 15th Day of the Third Month of 1645, for reasons that remain a mystery, Ikeda Sakyō-no-Daibu Teruoki went on a rampage of slaughter, killing his wife, his daughter, and a number of their Ladies-in-Waiting. The episode was calamitous in territorial as well as human terms. No one could object to the disenfeoffment of a crazed murderer, nor did the Shogun's Council of Elders pass up the opportunity to do so. Teruoki was imprisoned in the castle of his kinsman at Okayama, and the central portion of his fief was reassigned to a cadet branch of the House of Asano, lords of the castle in Hiroshima. Akō, a fief unto itself for only thirty-one years, would now become the wedge that would pry apart the eastern and western halves of the old Ikeda domains.

＋ ＋ ＋

In 1645, the home domain of the Asano cadet house lay to the north of Edo, ruled from the castle in Kasama in the province of Hitachi. The origins of this enfeoffment go back to the year 1606, when Asano Nagamasa, head of the main house and staunch ally of Ieyasu, was granted a retirement fief in Hitachi rated at 50,000 koku. Five years later, upon Nagamasa's death in 1611, this domain passed to his third son, Nagashige, thus establishing a cadet branch of the House of Asano. Later still, as a reward for Nagashige's exploits in the battles for Osaka Castle, he was moved to the adjacent domain of Kasama, which made him not only a daimyo but also a castellan. In 1632, upon Nagashige's death, the domain passed to his son Asano Takumi-no-Kami Naganao. In 1645, as it happened, Naganao and a detachment of his vassals were on garrison duty in Osaka Castle when, with no prior warning, a messenger arrived bearing an extremely terse directive from the Council of Elders in Edo:

> *You are hereby directed to exchange domains, moving to Akō in the province of Harima. The details will be explained to you by Makita Kazuma. Respectfully,*
>
> SIXTH MONTH, 13TH DAY
>
> *Abe Tsushima-no-Kami*
> *Abe Bungo-no-Kami*
> *Matsudaira Izu-no-Kami*
> *[monograms]*
>
> To: Asano Takumi-no-Kami Dono

And with this directive there survives a record of the instructions that Makita delivered verbally:

> MEMORANDUM
>
> *Item. You are hereby directed to exchange domains. Akō being well situated, you are dispatched at an enfeoffment comparable to that of Kasama. The domain has as well the advantage of its proximity to that of your kinsman Matsudaira [Asano] Aki-no-Kami. For these several reasons, you are dispatched thither.*
>
> *Item. You are to proceed to Akō and take command there directly upon being relieved of your present garrison duties. You are to dispatch a messenger to Kasama with orders that your vassals there move immediately.*
>
> *Item. To date, Akō has had only a manor house. There is, however, a site of ample size that is well suited to the construction of a castle. Should you wish to build there, His Highness shall grant you permission to do so.*
>
> YEAR OF THE COCK [SHŌHŌ 2 (1645)], SIXTH MONTH, 13TH DAY

Thus it was that the first Asano to bear the title of Takumi-no-Kami became the first of his line to hold the fief of Akō. When Naganao was relieved of garrison duty and when he and his contingent left Osaka are not recorded. But by the 21st Day of the Seventh Month, little more than a month later, he had already taken possession of the domain of Akō. He never saw Kasama again.

◆ ◆ ◆

All the woodblock-print artists depict Akō as a quiet, tranquil place. No doubt, there was just as much bustle in the streets and on the wharves as in any other small harbor town, but those who have painted it— Hiroshige for one—seem not to have been as impressed by the life of the place as by the broad expanse of the salt flats; the tall columns of smoke rising listlessly from the thatched huts where the salt was processed; and the ships standing out to sea, their sails unfurled and the domain's banner fluttering at the stern, laden with salt for the markets in Osaka and Edo. Akō, as everyone knows, produces the best salt in the land—pure white, delicate in flavor, without a touch of bitterness. His Highness the Shogun cleaned his teeth every morning with this "flower of salt," and his attendants would allow no other within his chambers. For the lords of Akō, the salt industry was also a welcome source of additional income, which, so they say, eventually added another 20,000 koku to the value of the fief. Had it not been for the ill temper of one its lords, the domain would now be remembered for little more than its excellent salt.

◆ ◆ ◆

Day had still not fully dawned as Tōzaemon and Sanpei began their descent from the pass; by now, in the half-light of morning, they could make out the long white walls and the turrets of the castle, and the indistinct contours of the town nestled around it, still wrapped in haze, its back to the hills and its face to the sea.

The downward slope was less serpentine, and when it reached the valley, the road hugged the edge of the hills, leaving as much room as possible for productive fields. Tōzaemon and Sanpei passed between

figure 8
Utagawa Hiroshige III, *Saltern in Akō.* (1877)

the villages of Sagoshi and Takano and finally turned toward the river, just below the point where it forks. Here, there was a dam that doubled as a bridge, built of finely fitted stones that gave its surface a geometrical pattern resembling a turtle's shell—which is precisely what everyone called it. Having crossed the turtle's shell, the road then ran down the center of a long narrow islet. They passed through the village of Nonaka, through a fortified guard post, and finally turned right at the street that led across the bridge to the enceinte of the Eastern Portal. They exited the enceinte to the right, took a left turn and then another, made a quick stop at the public well to quench their thirst, and then detoured through the residential quarter to the Saltsheds Gate at the rear of the castle. For as bearers of bad tidings, they must not enter at the main gate.

Finally, after four and a half days of grueling, sleepless travel, they had arrived. Their first destination was the gate of the residence of the domain's Chief Elder, Ōishi Kuranosuke Yoshitaka, who at that point in the Hour of the Tiger (ca. 4:00 A.M.) must still have been sound asleep.

CHAPTER 16

Ōishi Kuranosuke

Ōishi Kuranosuke. We all know the name. But what sort of man was he, and where did he come from? The most ancient roots and the most recent roots of the House of Ōishi are reasonably well documented, but almost nothing survives from the intervening centuries. The genealogy that I have here bears a touching note in the margin: "Kinsmen! If you possess any documents, however fragmentary, pray seek them out and make them known." No one seems to have responded.

What the genealogy does tell us is this: the Ōishi are descended from Fujiwara no Hidesato, who lived sometime in the middle years of the tenth century. Nowadays, we think of Hidesato as something of a hero, one of the first great "Eastland Warriors," for it was he and Taira no Sadamori who in 940 put down the rebellion of Masakado. Indeed, it was Hidesato himself who cut off the rebel's head. In reward for this, the Emperor raised him to the rank of Shogun and made him lord of two great eastern provinces: Shimotsuke and Musashi.

What is conveniently forgotten, though, is that Hidesato was no easterner. He was born in the Tawara Pass where it opens into the Ōishi Valley, just over the hills south and east of Kyoto, less than a day's walk from the Imperial Palace. Hidesato was off in the Eastlands not by birth or by choice, but because he had been banished from the capital region for some transgression of which no record survives.

◆ ◆ ◆

The Ōishi Estate, as it was known in Hidesato's day, was not a large holding, but it was extremely well situated. It lay about 2 leagues down-stream from the point where Lake Biwa empties into the Seta River, and it commanded the main road through the mountains to Uji. Even now, you'll hear children of the valley singing, "Give me five coppers, I'll let you pass," a reminder that in earlier times the road through Ōishi was not only a convenience but a source of revenue.

But a well-watered and conveniently located estate is of little value if it cannot be defended against the greed of its neighbors. The Ōishi Estate, history shows, was virtually impregnable. It was all but surrounded by steep hills, some heavily wooded and some terraced with stone walls into tiny rice paddies. Once it has run the course of the valley, the river that irrigated the fields and provided smooth transport to markets along the lakeside becomes a roaring, impassable torrent. The hills are not high, but they rise straight up from the water. And the road that led to the cities on the far side of the mountains—little more than a path in some places—could quickly be transformed into a death trap.

Small wonder, then, that Hidesato was loath just to abandon Ōishi, even though he could no longer inhabit the land himself. The whole of his enfeoffment—from Tawara, south of the capital, to Kurimoto, over the mountains in Ōmi—was declared forfeit. Yet when he departed to go east, he somehow managed leave this one narrow valley in the hands of one of his sons. Like most such local lords, this young man and his progeny took the name of the place as the name of their family and called themselves the Ōishi; in later years, that name came to be counted as one of the "twelve branches of the House of Hidesato." From time to time, at the behest of their Fujiwara kinsmen in the Imperial Court, the Ōishi supplied details of armed men for guard duty at the palace and in the mansions of the nobility, as country cousins had always done. Even after the Genpei Wars, when rule of the land had passed from the hands of their noble kinsmen to the new Minamoto Shogunate in Kamakura, life went on much as it always had in the fields and hamlets of Ōishi. The impenetrable little valley was never overrun and never came under the jurisdiction of one of the new Military Governors.

In the latter years of the sixteenth century, however, Ōishi was to find itself standing in the line of advance of the mightiest armed force ever assembled in Japan. By this time, the land was again in turmoil.

Oda Nobunaga had begun his westward thrust from Komaki in the province of Owari. From there, he crossed the River Nagara into the province of Mino, razing fortress after fortress as he went, his army growing steadily as those who had the wisdom not to challenge him rushed to join him. When finally he conquered the stronghold at Mount Inaba and changed its name from Inokuchi to Gifu, only the province of Ōmi stood between him and the capital.

On the 7th Day of the Ninth Month of the eleventh year of Eiroku (1568), Nobunaga began his march on Kyoto. He set out from Gifu at the head of the great force he had assembled in the course of his conquest of Ise, Owari, Mikawa, and Mino. By the 13th, the castle at Kannonjiyama had fallen. And once the carnage had begun, no corner of the province, whatever its loyalties, was spared. When and how the Ōishi Estate fell is nowhere recorded. We know only that the "fortress," as they bravely call it in the genealogy, was razed and that Ōishi Kin'emon and all his men were "slain by Nobunaga." The little valley, proof for centuries against the depredations of rapacious neighbors, could not have held out long against an onslaught of such magnitude. Nobunaga himself may never even have known of this brief battle near the end of his campaign, but for the people of the valley, its effects were momentous. For the first time in nearly a millennium, the Ōishi Estate had fallen into the hands of a lord who did not bear the name Ōishi. But at least there survived two brothers, descended in a collateral line of the Ōishi. To them fell the task of regenerating the house.

♦ ♦ ♦

The elder brother, Ōishi Heizaemon Yoshisada, was taken into the service of the new lord of the valley, Yamaguchi Genba-no-Kami. After the assassination of Nobunaga, Genba-no-Kami allied himself with Toyotomi Hideyoshi, who sent him to Korea. In the course of those campaigns, Heizaemon seems to have won the reputation of a ferocious warrior. At any rate, he had a shocking assortment of scars that he was quick to display to anyone who might question his valor. He was also an embittered warrior. Genba-no-Kami had never rewarded him properly for any of his feats of arms. When the Korean campaign ended in failure, and the entire force withdrew to Japan, Heizaemon seized that opportunity to sever his ties with the house of Yamaguchi Genba-no-Kami. Pleading illness, age, and the pain of old wounds, he retired to the village of Ōishi with nothing to show for thirty-some years of warfare but his scars and three little girls he had brought back from Korea: Kii, Tsuru, and one whose name is no longer known, but was thought to have been the child of aristocrats because her ears were pierced. Twenty years later, Heizaemon's line came to an end when his only son was killed in the siege of Osaka Castle, fighting against the Sanada at Tennōji.

In the meantime, Heizaemon's younger brother, Ōishi Kyūemon Yoshinobu, had found what seemed to be a more promising career. He became a Herald in the entourage of Toyotomi Hidetsugu, the nephew and adoptive heir of Hideyoshi, in whose service he received the handsome stipend of 700 koku per year. But alas, Hidetsugu is the man who was to become known as the "Murderous Chancellor."

"If only ..." Those are the words that always come to mind when I think of Kyūemon. If only Hideyoshi had not finally succeeded in producing a son of his own. If only Hidetsugu had been less vicious and headstrong, he might still have ended up as his uncle's principal ally, rather than the object of his wrath. In either case, Ōishi Kyūemon, as one of Hidetsugu's senior retainers, might have become a man of consequence—the man to restore the fortunes of the House of Ōishi. As things fell out, Kyūemon had to count himself fortunate just to be alive, fortunate not to be among those purged when Hideyoshi commanded the suicide of his adoptive heir and displayed his severed head on the riverbed at Sanjō.

Kyūemon, too, retired to the village of Ōishi and devoted his last years to arranging the future of his sons, for whom he seems to have wished a less tumultuous life than his own. His firstborn was not the child of his wife, and so was given in adoption to a retainer of the Daté house in the distant northeast. Both sons of his wife, however, were to be made monks. Yoshikatsu was sent as a novice to Miyamoto-bō, one of thirty-some small temples clustered about the Imperial Temple Gokokuji, just below the Iwashimizu Hachiman Shrine, to the south of the capital. Nobutomo went to the Shōgoin in the Eastern Hills of Kyoto, then presided over by the aristocratic Abbot Dōchō, younger brother of Konoe Sakihisa.

* * *

You will wonder, I expect, how a former warrior living in enforced retirement was able to place his offspring in these aristocratic cloisters. The secret lay in his wife's connections. And a secret they attempted to keep it, although it could not have been long before everyone knew the truth.

Kyūemon's wife, Shimo, was ostensibly the daughter of his Fujiwara kinsman, Shindō Chikugo-no-Kami Nagaharu. But, in fact, Shimo was a "misplaced seed," an illegitimate child of the highest-ranking nobleman in the land, Konoe Sakihisa, courtier of the First Rank and Prime Minister to the Emperor.

Despite his lofty rank and resounding titles, Lord Sakihisa spent the greater part of his life as a fugitive, sometimes fleeing the ravages of war, sometimes just fleeing for his life. He roamed as far north as Echizen and as far west as Satsuma, and he took refuge with whatever military house might be willing to shelter him—the Uesugi, the Shimazu, the Toyotomi, and even the founder of the most recent Shogunal line, Tokugawa Ieyasu. Through all these years of wandering, he was accompanied by his faithful steward Shindō Chikugo-no-Kami—who was not at all the sort of samurai who were derided as "Kyoto warriors," more concerned to dress well than to fight well. The Shindō had served the Konoe for hundreds of years and had fought many a battle in their cause. His forebears defended the Yamashina Valley with a valor that has never been forgotten, and Chikugo-no-Kami himself has gone down in history for his single-handed defeat of a band of pirates near the harbor of Bōnotsu in Satsuma. Were it not for Chikugo-no-Kami's bravery and skill at arms, Lord Sakihisa might never have survived his fugitive years. Nor did his lordship fail to show his gratitude. Exalted in rank though he was, he lacked the resources to enrich his steward financially. But it was still within his power to grant him an honorary Governorship of the province of Chikugo and to raise him to Fourth Rank in the Imperial Court. In addition to this, he gave him his daughter Shimo, born in the year of Nobunaga's conquest of Ōmi, to raise as his own child—an arrangement that not only honored Shindō but also tidied up the life of His Lordship a bit. When Shimo was grown, Shindō Chikugo-no-Kami gave her in marriage to his kinsman and near neighbor Ōishi Kyūemon. Shimo bore Kyūemon two sons, Yoshikatsu and Nobutomo.

Without exception, the genealogists enjoin their kinsmen to total secrecy on this matter of Shimo's birth. It was nonetheless common knowledge that aristocratic blood of the highest rank flowed in the veins of these two boys. And given the opportunities that this made possible, it is hardly surprising that a father who knew the bitter rewards of warfare as well as Kyūemon did would prefer that his sons live the quiet life of noble clerics rather than follow in his own footsteps. It is just as well that Kyūemon did not live to see what actually became of them. For despite their father's benevolent intentions, and despite the obvious dangers, both boys decided that they would rather be warriors than monks. And Yoshikatsu made his escape in particularly dramatic fashion.

The year after Kyūemon's death—the year of the great battle at Sekigahara—his son Yoshikatsu turned fourteen, the age at which he was to take his final vows, shave his head, and begin his career as a fully fledged monk. In the depths of the night prior to this solemn rite, Yoshikatsu slipped out of the temple and fled. Although no one at the time would have imagined it, this act of rebellion was the first step in the restoration of the fortunes of the House of Ōishi.

Where Yoshikatsu's flight led that first night no one knows. Eventually, though, he decided to go east and seek his fortune in Edo, where the founding Tokugawa Shogun was building his massive new castle. There, in 1604, Ōishi Yoshikatsu was taken into the service of Asano Uneme-no-Kami Nagashige, the third son of Asano Nagamasa.

In the years following the battle of Sekigahara, Edo was a very different place from the city in which I was born. It was a brawling frontier town, populated by hardened warriors and merchants of the sort who seek to profit from war. The youth seems to have thrived there. In the Asano service, Yoshikatsu served first in the Corps of Pages and over the next decade gradually rose from a respectable stipend of 300 koku to 500 koku. But it was the siege of Osaka Castle in 1615 that was to propel him to the pinnacle of the Asano vassals. He fought so fiercely and so well in the struggle for the Tennōji Gate—returning with the heads of two Sanada warriors—that Nagashige raised him to the rank of Elder of the house, and then continued to promote him until he was receiving 1,500 koku and ranked as Chief Elder. After the advent of the Great Peace, such a career would be impossible: the second son of a minor military house, his family defeated and disenfeoffed, himself on the verge of being consigned to a cloister, absconds in the night and ends up the Chief Elder of a branch of one of the greatest houses in the land. Such was the life of the first Kuranosuke.

◆ ◆ ◆

But what of the last Kuranosuke, whom we shall get to know as the central figure of this story? What sort of a man was he? What did he look like? What did people think of him? Strange to say, we can answer these questions with a good deal more certainty than one would expect of a figure from so distant an age.

To begin with, he was not the sort of man whom one might imagine as the descendant of hardened battlefield warriors. He was a small man, even by the standards of his day: barely 5 feet tall, or 5 feet, 2 inches according to a more flattering description. And he was plump, though not fat. This we know because there survives a statuette of him carved by a craftsman who knew him well and strove to produce as lifelike an image of him as possible. We know, too, from written reports, that he was a quiet man who spoke seldom and softly and who never dressed ostentatiously. Which perhaps was why the street-corner storytellers of my childhood always described him as "useless as a lantern at midday." That epithet, however, we know to be false. For despite all that was physically unimpressive about him, he made a deep impression upon a great many people. He always had a friendly greeting and a kind word for his servants, a former retainer said, "even when their foreheads were pressed to the floor"; and he treated even the lowest-ranking samurai with all the respect due a warrior. Even the Adjutant of the main house in Hiroshima, Inoue Dan'emon, a man much higher in rank than Kuranosuke, once said that he inspired such respect that he was never able to address him merely by his name—which he had every right to do—but always called him "Kuranosuke Dono." Yet the qualities that those who knew and worked with him most often mentioned are the sheer competence with which he handled any task that he undertook, and his quiet but firm leadership of those he commanded. As Onodera Jūnai wrote to his cousin Onodera Jūbei: "Such has been Kuranosuke's performance that the entire Corps of Vassals is deeply impressed. They seem to place themselves entirely at his disposal. Even the young men show not the slightest resistance, but come every day, all day, to the castle, where they do whatever he tells them without the least complaint and do their work with great dispatch."

And finally, lest this seem a description of nothing more than a pleasant, efficient, and hard-working man, it must also be noted that Kuranosuke was more than a little fond of wine, women, and even song—ample evidence of which, along with his more decorous virtues, we shall see as this tale progresses.

I take the liberty to inform you,
via this hasty missive.

Akō, Third Month, 19th Day

It is a measure, I am sure, of the sheer force of the blow struck that dawn by the arrival of Tōzaemon and Sanpei that we lack any description of the event. Such a sudden and unimagined apparition could only portend catastrophe. Everyone sensed it immediately, and the shock was so overwhelming that not one of them ever thought to record what was said, what was thought, what was felt. All that those on the scene tell us is that Tōzaemon and Sanpei arrived toward the end of the Hour of the Tiger (ca. 4:30–5:00 A.M.) and that they reported immediately to Kuranosuke, told him what had happened, and handed him a letter from Asano Daigaku. The entire Corps of Vassals was then summoned to the castle, where Kuranosuke repeated the news from Edo and read aloud the letter:

> *I take the liberty to inform you, via this hasty missive, that today, the 14th, upon the arrival of the Imperial Envoys for their audience at the castle, Takumi Sama struck Kira Kōzuke-no-Suke Dono a blow with his sword. The Inspectors expressly inform us that Takumi Sama is unharmed. The foregoing is a matter of the utmost gravity. Mizuno Kenmotsu Dono and the Inspectors Kondō Heihachi Dono and Amano Denshirō Dono have come to the upper mansion bearing orders from the Council of Elders that all vassals exercise particular vigilance against fire and that they foment no disturbance. By the same token, strict orders must be issued to both*

the Corps of Vassals and the residents of the castle town that no disturbance there be instigated. The Samurai Commanders, too, are to be informed of my commands, as are all Company Commanders of Foot Soldiers and the several administrative officers. As there are only the two of you, there is no need whatever for you to come to Edo. Respectfully,

THIRD MONTH, 14TH DAY   *Asano Daigaku [monogram]*
To: Ōishi Kuranosuke Dono
Ōno Kurōbei Dono

P.S. Hayami Tōzaemon and Kayano Sanpei will explain matters in detail when they present this dispatch. It is of paramount importance that orders be given for the proper exchange of the domain's currency. Herewith, the foregoing.

Like many domains in the Genroku era, Akō had issued paper currency in order to facilitate the flow of peacetime commerce—in this case, transactions in the salt trade. The system had been introduced twenty-five years earlier by the second man to whom Daigaku's letter was addressed, Ōno Kurōbei. Over the years, Kurōbei had proved himself an astute financial manager (*too* astute, in the opinion of some), and for that talent, he had been made an Acting Elder of the house at a stipend of 600 koku. Under Kurōbei's management, Akō's currency remained sound and stable and had never been counterfeited, and thus circulated not only within the domain but in neighboring domains as well. Now, Asano Daigaku commanded, it must all be redeemed. Such a command could only mean that the domain itself was in danger, and not just the danger of financial collapse. Taken in tandem with the news of their lord's transgression and his subsequent confinement, this command could well mean that the domain was in imminent danger of attainder. The grip of panic that this thought aroused in the two hundred or more samurai gathered at the castle is not hard to imagine.

♦ ♦ ♦

Edo, Third Month, 19th Day

At about the same hour of the same day, Kajikawa Yosōbei received a summons to the castle. It was his off-duty day, and he was not told the reason that his presence was required. He left immediately from his home in the Wardens' Quarter, and not long after the striking of the Fourth Hour (10:00 A.M.), he entered the duty room and reported his arrival. Shortly thereafter, he was called by the Duty Junior Elder, Inoue Yamato-no-Kami, who told him that he should prepare himself for an audience with the Council of Elders—and that he was not dressed with sufficient formality for such an occasion. Fortunately, Yosōbei had the foresight to keep a suit of formal starched linens in his room at the palace, and so was able to change his clothing immediately. Having done so, he betook himself to the corridor leading from the Clock Room to the Paulownia Room to await his summons. He was called not long after midday. What Yosōbei thought the Elders might have in mind for him he does not say, but he seems to have been pleasantly surprised when he was told: "For your meritorious conduct in subduing Takumi-no-Kami on the occasion of his miscreant behavior, you are to be awarded an increase in your enfeoffment."

Yosōbei, of course, expressed his gratitude for this reward and thereafter thanked individually the staff officers of each of the Elders, as well as the Shogun's Chief Adjutant, Yanagisawa Dewa-no-Kami. It was not until later in the day, however, that the Duty Superintendent of Finance, Togawa Bizen-no-Kami, told him the actual amount of his increase.

"You are to be awarded an additional 500 koku," Togawa told him, "and you may choose whichever lands of this value that you wish in the vicinity of your present enfeoffment."

"As it happens," Yosōbei replied, "my present lands have no access to the river, which makes transport to markets something of a problem. If you could be so kind as to grant me lands with riverbank frontage, I should be most grateful."

One would think that this generous increase in Yosōbei's income, from 700 to 1,200 koku per year, would have been a source of great satisfaction to him. But Yosōbei's own thoughts on the matter seem to have been mixed:

As I think back upon these events, I realize now how mortified Takumi Dono must have felt when he failed to kill Kira Dono. It all happened so suddenly and so unexpectedly that I did what I did instinctively, without a moment's thought for what was happening or what the consequences might be. But these must remain my private thoughts, which I can mention to no one but my closest friends; I certainly would never discuss them with any of my superiors. Still— within this old man's mind of mine, I've had a great many second thoughts about what I did.

He may even have agreed with the unkind satirist who wrote:

yoi koto ni minu furi wa senu yosōbei
takumi kitta de kazō ichibai
Just because he couldn't let a good deed pass unnoticed:
Takumi cuts his belly for naught; Yosōbei doubles his income.

As a vassal of the Shogun, Yosōbei could hardly have done otherwise. Had he neglected to stop Takumi, he would have been derelict in his duty to maintain security in the castle; yet having done so, he must now live with the guilt of having prevented a fellow warrior from killing an enemy. These were thoughts that would trouble Yosōbei for years to come.

And if we can credit Okado Denpachirō, the 19th was not only a day of rewards but a day of reckoning of another sort. Following his description of the Junior Elders' inquiry into the conduct of Takumi-no-Kami's seppuku, Denpachirō states that "on the 19th, Shōda Shimōsa-no-Kami was dismissed from office and relegated to the Reserve Force, whereas Kajikawa Yosōbei, in reward for restraining Takumi-no-Kami, was awarded an increase of 500 koku. No other alterations in duty assignments were made." The trouble is that although Shōda's dismissal can be verified, the *Veritable Records* of the Shogunate dates it much later in the year, on the 21st Day of the Eighth Month. Still, it is not impossible that Denpachirō's report is correct in a certain sense, that Shōda was verbally relieved of his duties on the 19th, but only formally dismissed much later, together with a number of other officials who suffered the same punishment for "lax performance of their duties." The question of timing must remain open, but there can be no question that Shōda was punished for his cavalier handling of Takumi-no-Kami's suicide.

Akō, Third Month, 19th Day, Mid-morning

Bad news always travels fast, but news as bad as this—news of the Catastrophe—seems to have traveled at something like the speed of lightning. Curiously, though, it was not those hardest hit who reacted the most violently. The samurai and their wives and children, who could see that they would soon lose their hereditary income and be evicted from their homes, seem to have been too stunned to act—yet. It was the merchants, the shopkeepers, the moneylenders, the pawnbrokers, all those who had capital or savings, some part of which they held in the form of paper currency, who panicked first. They did not have to hear Asano Daigaku's letter to know that they had to cash in their banknotes immediately if they were to recoup any part of their value; for if the domain should run short of funds, their wealth would be worth no more than the strips of paper it was printed on. The result was almost instantaneous pandemonium at the Akō Currency Exchange. So many people descended so suddenly upon this office, demanding that their paper be exchanged for silver, that the guard had to be reinforced with five or six extra samurai, clad in chain mail and bearing unsheathed lances, just to keep the crowds from breaking down the door. With a bit of forethought, this mob might have realized that no exchange of any sort could be made without an audit of the domain's finances, but forethought doubtless seemed a luxury just then. Many of the disappointed decided that they would camp there until the morrow.

In the meantime, it was clear to Kuranosuke and Kurōbei that a great deal of accounting must be done in a great hurry. Supervision of this task fell to Okajima Yasoemon, the Officer in Charge of the Currency Exchange. The figures he came up with were these:

Face value of currency now in circulation:	12,000 gold pieces
Cash available for redemption of currency:	7,000 gold pieces
Shortfall:	5,000 gold pieces

And, of course, there were complications. The shortfall in part represented loans made to operators of the salt fields; astute businessmen that they were, these men were more likely to offer excuses, rather than payment at this juncture. Then, too, there would be further expenses when the Corps of Vassals dispersed, for it would be heartless to turn three hundred and some men loose in the world without giving them at least a small severance allowance to tide them over until they could find new homes and new livelihoods.

Kuranosuke's interim solution was to use all the cash on hand to redeem the paper currency at 60 percent of face value, and then to ask the main house in Hiroshima to "lend" them the money needed for further expenses. Tonomura Genzaemon would sail for Hiroshima on the evening tide carrying that request, the first appeal for financial assistance that the Akō cadet house had ever made.

Akō, Third Month, 19th Day, Hour of the Dog

If anyone still harbored hopes that the worst might yet be averted, those hopes were dashed that night toward the end of the Hour of the Dog (ca. 8:30–9:00 P.M.), upon the arrival of two more express conveyances from Edo, carrying Hara Sōemon and Ōishi Sezaemon. These two men bore the news that at sundown on the 14th, Takumi-no-Kami had committed seppuku at the mansion of Tamura Ukyō-no-Daibu, to whose custody he had been remanded earlier that day. They also carried copies of two letters, one from the Duty Elder, Tsuchiya Sagami-no-Kami, and addressed to Toda Uneme-no-Kami and Asano Mino-no-Kami announcing Takumi's sentence and enjoining his vassals, in both Akō and Edo, to "behave properly and foment no disturbance"; and the other from Lord Tamura addressed to Asano Daigaku inviting him to fetch the body of his brother "at your earliest convenience." There could now be no doubt about the fate of the domain of Akō. Both castle and lands were forfeit, which meant that 308 men of samurai rank as well as a large contingent of foot soldiers and lesser ranks would now become ronin, masterless warriors, bereft of home and income, left to fend for themselves in an age of peace when warriors were in scant demand.

Again, the entire Corps of Vassals was called to the castle, a convocation of which we know only that the foregoing two letters were read aloud to them. Few can have slept that night in Akō.

When two men quarrel, regardless of who is right or who is wrong, both parties shall be put to death.

There could hardly have been worse news for a samurai living in the second century of the Great Peace. I doubt that many samurai in Akō thought their present lives ideal. With no wars to fight, there was little room for advancement in a Corps of Vassals. And everywhere about them, they could see fellow warriors who were either wasting their days on frivolities or turning themselves into scheming bureaucrats, all the while mouthing brave platitudes about the Way of the Warrior. Which made the more principled samurai suspect that their very reason for being was coming into question. And yet . . . The lives they led were at least secure. Every vassal, in addition to his enfeoffment or stipendiary allowance, was allotted a house commensurate with his rank and a plot of land large enough to grow many of the vegetables that his family would need, and perhaps even cultivate a decorative garden. Few were more than moderately prosperous, but as members of the ruling class— nominally, at least—it was a reasonably dignified life for most warriors.

And now, *this*. Disenfeoffed. Everything they had was the gift of the lord they served, their reward for feats of arms performed by their forebears in battles long past. Now their lord was dead, his heir under house arrest, and his lands—the produce of which had fed, clothed, and housed them—declared forfeit. The Akō branch of the House of Asano was no more.

At first, no one seems to have thought beyond the immediate practical necessities of surviving this Catastrophe (as everyone was now calling it), into which they had so suddenly been cast. Where to go? What to take? What to sell? How to make a living? How to start an entirely new life? These were the questions that no one could escape, neither the Chief Elder of the domain nor the lowliest foot soldier.

But gradually, a more insidious question began to worm its way into the minds of some. I suspect that it was Kuranosuke who first began to wonder, for he was the first person to whom Hara Sōemon spoke when he arrived on the night of the 19th. He and Ōishi Sezaemon had meant to leave, Sōemon told him, as soon as word of their lord's death had come, but had delayed their departure in the hope of learning whether he had succeeded in killing his enemy. But to no avail. No news was forthcoming from any source. Finally, they could delay no longer; before they left, they had exacted a promise from the Edo Elders to send word by courier as soon as the facts could be ascertained. In Edo, they would certainly know by now; but in Akō, the crucial question remained unanswered: Was Kira dead, or was he still alive?

◆ ◆ ◆

At the outset, before they could recover from the initial shock, no one in Akō had questioned whether Takumi had killed Kira, nor was any objection raised against the justice of his punishment. For even if Takumi-no-Kami had failed, surely the Shogunate would have commanded Kira's death. But during those first two or three days, doubt began to creep in. Whether Kuranosuke raised the question in that late-night meeting with Sōemon is not recorded. We do know, though, that some of the Akō samurai were married to women from neighboring domains—Okayama, Himeji, even Takamatsu—and the news these women were hearing from their kinfolk back home was that Kira was *not* dead, that in fact his wounds were slight and he was recovering apace. Mere rumor, of course, but rumor from uncensored sources, originating in Edo, and thus sufficiently credible to be sound cause for doubt. And once doubt had been introduced, those to whom this question mattered found their lives and thoughts vastly more complicated and confused than before. Their problems were no longer merely practical, but now involved matters of high principle as well.

✦ ✦ ✦

These problems of principle were of several sorts, all intertwined, all turning upon points of samurai honor and morality.

In the first place, a truly loyal vassal could never surrender his lord's castle and lands unless commanded to do so by the lord himself. But what if his lord was dead and no heir had succeeded to his place? Was it not the samurai's duty to defend his dead lord's castle with his own life? For in the eyes of the Akō samurai, Takumi-no-Kami was no mere vassal of the Shogun; he was lord of a cadet branch of the great House of Asano, allies of Ieyasu at the battle of Sekigahara, but never his subjects. "Our lord's lord is not *our* lord," they would say. Successive Shoguns had tried their best to redefine this relationship, to transform their self-governing allies into obedient vassals, but as yet without much success. The Akō samurai were not prepared to accept such sophistry.

Somewhat more complex were the questions concerning loyalty itself. That loyalty was indispensable, every samurai agreed. But what should be the object of one's loyalty? The individual person of one's lord? The house over which one's lord ruled? The more abstract legacy of that house that passes from lord to lord? These are questions that were never articulated with perfect clarity, with the result that two people who thought they were discussing the same thing might fail to understand each other, because they had attached the same name to two different varieties of loyalty. We shall see many cases of this.

The most vexatious problem of principle, however, was the age-old Principle of Equal Punishment, which decreed that when two men quarrel, regardless of who is right or who is wrong, both parties shall be put to death. This had never been codified as a provision of the Laws of the Land. But for centuries, it had been so central to the codes of the great warrior clans, and was so universally regarded as just and beneficial, that, codified or no, in the minds of most samurai it ought never to be set aside. In this, they were ruled not by a code but by the unwritten customs of their class, by a powerful article of faith that persisted from beginning to end of this tale.

Such were the problems of principle that were beginning to gnaw at the minds and consciences of some Akō samurai, from the highest in rank to the lowest. Not everyone troubled themselves over problems of this sort. But for a few, these were ideas that mattered.

◆ ◆ ◆

In the meantime, the town was rapidly filling with outsiders whose thoughts were anything but principled. As we have seen, the holders of paper money were almost riotous in their demands for redemption and had to be held at bay by armed men to prevent them from storming the Currency Exchange.

Not far behind them came the bargain hunters: the dealers in second-hand clothing, furniture, antiques, weapons, armor, equestrian gear, and the like. For them, the expulsion of an entire Corps of Vassals was not a tragedy, but a business opportunity not to be missed. Almost every one of the more than three hundred samurai families would be forced to sell a great many of their possessions, and some, almost everything they could not carry. There would be scant room for haggling; it was a buyer's market. And the buyers were flocking to Akō not only from Okayama and Himeji, but from as far away as Kyoto and Osaka.

◆ ◆ ◆

Another more interesting group of interlopers strove to remain as inconspicuous as possible. These were the *shinobi* (undercover agents). In wartime—and, occasionally, even in peacetime—their mission might have been assassination, sabotage, abduction, or something equally nefarious. But this time, they had come simply as intelligencers, disguised as farmers, peddlers, or itinerants of the sort one might encounter anywhere on the highway. Most of them left no trace of their presence; they were hardly noticeable in a town suddenly filled with strangers. But miraculously—and, no doubt, unintentionally—the reports of one group of agents, from Okayama, survive intact.

The eastern border of the domain of Okayama lay barely 3 leagues from the town of Akō; the Elders of the House of Ikeda had not needed orders from Edo to decide that caution and close observation were called for. Word had reached them overnight of the Catastrophe in Akō, and their Elders had met immediately to discuss what their response should be. Above all, information was needed. Unrest has a way of ignoring political boundaries and can spread with alarming speed. Their first act, therefore, was to summon their Chief of Undercover Operations—who by a curious coincidence happened to be named Asano, Asano Sebei—and instruct him to send his men into the neighboring domain to gather firsthand intelligence.

Later that afternoon, two men dressed as itinerant peddlers, Seno Yaichibei and Imanaka Kirokurō, left the castle and made their way east over a little-traveled path. When darkness fell, they crossed the border into Akō. Well before midnight, they had covered the 13 leagues (32.5 miles, 52 kilometers) that separated the two castles, slipped into the town, and blended with the crowds. Their entry was easy and their cover perfect. Farmers and traders from the hinterlands of Akō and every neighboring province were flocking to the town to exchange their paper money for silver. No one was being checked for identity. No one took any notice of the strangers.

They themselves were more observant and had soon identified agents in disguise from both Himeji and Tatsuno, neighboring domains to the east of Akō. And one Okayama agent reported meeting "two of the Iga men"—which is to say, agents dispatched by the Shogunate—with whom he apparently conversed but did not exchange names. That did not matter. They were not working at cross-purposes and posed no threat to each other. All of them would pretend that none of them were there.

◆ ◆ ◆

More overtly, Ikeda Iyo-no-Kami, lord of Okayama, had moved quickly to seal his domain's eastern border against any intrusion from Akō. He also moved with greater military might than his Liaison Officer's "casual" report to Yanagisawa Dewa-no-Kami had implied. Tsuda Sagenta led a force of "thirty or forty samurai and about a hundred foot soldiers" to the post town of Katagami, 6 leagues from Okayama, and then sent a lesser detachment 3 leagues farther east to Mitsuishi, where the western road to Akō began. To the south, the domain Elder Iki Seibei led a force of six hundred men to the port town of Mushiake, 7 leagues from Akō on the seacoast. In between these strongpoints, "officials" were sent to all villages close to the border, presumably with suitable numbers of armed men in attendance.

Some members of the council had favored setting up guard posts on every road and path that crossed the border. After some discussion, however, this plan was set aside as too hostile-seeming. It would not do to be caught unprepared, but neither should one appear to threaten one's neighbors without provocation.

Within the domain, directives were sent to the Headmen of every village and hamlet in the eastern districts; they, in turn, erected signboards banning trade, or contact of any sort, with villagers and merchants from Akō until further notice. Samurai, of course, were strictly forbidden to communicate with anyone in Akō or even to visit the town of Akō.

◆ ◆ ◆

The Shogun's Chief Adjutant, Yanagisawa Dewa-no-Kami, must have convinced the Council of Elders that they should command other domains to do likewise. Before long, reports were arriving that Akō's neighbors in Tatsuno and Himeji had deployed men along their borders with Akō; still farther afield, the domains of Akashi, Imaichi, Okada, Niwase, Tsuyama, and even Tottori were on high alert. On the far side of the Inland Sea, Matsudaira Sanuki-no-Kami had sent a large fleet of "war boats" to sea, with Ōkubo Shuzen in command. And the lords of Tokushima, Matsuyama, and Marugame had followed suit, so that the banners of most domains in Shikoku could now be seen on armed vessels patrolling the waters off Akō.

Akō was now quite literally surrounded by contingents of armed men, most of them numbering in the hundreds, and all, according to one report, hoping for the worst. For if the samurai in Akō should resist surrendering their castle, their neighbors—some of whom felt that they had too long been denied the chance to fight a real war—were "prepared to attack and annihilate them."

CHAPTER
19

*It is of paramount importance that orders be given for
the proper exchange of the domain's currency.*

Akō, Third Month, 20th Day
The *next* day: the first day of a wholly new, and decidedly disagreeable,
way of living. We know what sorts of things went on that day, but very
few details of them survive. Everyone was still too stunned, and probably
perplexed, to make any record of what they did or what they thought.

♦ ♦ ♦

First of all, the Currency Exchange reopened. With so many disgruntled
holders of paper money camped outside it, any further delay could have
resulted in riot. There was just enough silver and gold in the domainal
coffers to cover 60 percent of the currency in circulation, and so it was
decided that all of it would be used to redeem the paper at 60 percent
of its face value. That was a very generous rate of redemption, certain
to be opposed by the more fiscally astute officials of the domain. For it
would leave nothing in reserve with which to pay a severance allowance
to the departing samurai, not to mention any other expenses that might
arise. But someone—almost certainly Kuranosuke—made the bold
choice and decided to take the risk of finding other funds to finance
other needs. All the domain's paper currency would be redeemed at 60
percent, and that of those who had come from other domains would be
redeemed first. How this was managed, even Okajima Yasoemon, the
Officer in Charge of the Currency Exchange, omits to tell us. We know,
though, that the process was far from orderly; the samurai in chain mail,
their lances lowered, were still required to hold the crowds at bay. And

the redeemed notes were burnt at the end of each day within the castle walls. We know nothing more.

Then there were the meetings in the castle. Here, I can at least say for certain that they were nothing like the meetings described by the street-corner storytellers of my childhood. As they told it, these were raucous affairs, with upward of two hundred samurai in a huge hall (such as probably never existed in Akō Castle), all shouting out their own opinions at the same time. I never tired of the story, but I now know that it was nothing but a story. It is true that, on the previous day, the 19th, everyone was twice summoned to the castle to be told of the news from Edo. But those were the only two times that the entire corps gathered there. Close attention to the sources makes it clear that only the highest ranking members of the Corps of Vassals took part in the deliberations and the decision-making process—the Elders, Samurai Commanders, Company Commanders, Adjutants, and occasionally other officials with special expertise.

And all the while this was going on, the town was filled with the din of the greedy, who now forced their way even into the narrow alleys of the off-street tenements, as they "combed" every corner of the town in search of cheap goods they could carry home and sell at twice or thrice the price they had paid.

Edo, Third Month, 20th Day

A gentleman came to call today at the residence of Kira Kōzuke-no-Suke, his colleague Ōtomo Ōmi-no-Kami. It is not impossible that Ōmi-no-Kami visited of his own free will, but his greeting sounds rather more like something he was sent to say, possibly even at the behest of the Shogun.

"How are your wounds healing?" Ōmi-no-Kami asked. "For once they have healed completely, you must not hesitate to return to your duties. Just take good care of yourself, and you'll soon recover, despite your age."

Kira himself, we are told, felt that he was indeed recovering apace. But if he thought that he would be permitted to resume his position as doyen of the Masters of Court Protocol, he was badly mistaken. The

Shogun would welcome him back. But his own kinsmen, the House of Uesugi, of which his son was the lord, would have none of it. It was not simply that public opinion had been unkind. His assailant had been a daimyo of 50,000 koku, head of a cadet branch of the great House of Asano. A man of this lineage had been punished unjustly, whereas Kira had been treated "far too kindly." And the Uesugi knew it. They knew, too, that if Kira should again appear in the limelight, the consequences for him could be fatal and for the House of Uesugi, dangerous. The family and their Elders quickly conferred and decided that Kira should as soon as possible resign his official position. This was the message that the Uesugi asked Ōtomo Ōmi-no-Kami to carry back to the Shogun. It was even rumored that Kira's wife, a daughter of the previous lord of the Uesugi house, had urged her husband to commit suicide—for the safety of their children, she said. As we shall see, she had a point.

◆ ◆ ◆

The 20th was also the seventh day since the seppuku of Takumi-no-Kami on the 14th, which meant that it was the first of the Seven Seventh-Days, the seven successive memorial rites that would be held at the temple Sengakuji, where he was buried. Many people still observe this custom with little thought of what it signifies. Originally, however, it had a practical purpose. Buddhist doctrine holds that the shade of the deceased lingers in limbo for forty-nine days while its fate in the next incarnation is being decided in the court of the King of the Netherworld, Enma-Ō. And since that court reviews the life of the person in question every seventh day following his death, finally rendering a decision in its seventh session, it is greatly to the advantage of the deceased to perform meritorious rites on his behalf on each of the seven days that the court is considering his case. If you take this notion at all seriously (or at least pretend to), it also constitutes a strong reason for attending every one of the seven obsequies.

As we might expect, Takumi-no-Kami's four former boy lovers—Kataoka Gengoemon, Tanaka Sadashirō, Isogai Jūrōzaemon, and Nakamura Sei'emon—were at Sengakuji today. These were the men who had gone to the mansion of Tamura Ukyō-no-Daibu to fetch the

figure 9
Paper currency for 10 *momme* of silver, dated 1695.
(Akō Municipal Museum of History)

body of their lord, and then had cut off their topknots and thrown them into his grave. But today? Instead of returning to their lodgings in the city, they turned right when they left the temple and set out on the Eastern Sea Road, bound for Akō. They would not be present at the remaining six obsequies for their lord. This did not pass unnoticed. Already, the former lovers had begun to set themselves apart from the rest of the Corps of Vassals.

*We shall now have to think of some place
whither to betake ourselves, but I am utterly at a loss
to imagine where we might go.*

If the chaos and confusion of the next three or four weeks are to be seen
with any clarity, we must keep constantly in mind that everyone in Edo
now *knew* that this case had been judged unjustly; that everyone in Akō
at least suspected that Kira was still alive; and that some people in both
places were determined to do something about it.

Once the Council of Elders had realized that Kira had not been
the innocent victim of a madman, that there had been a quarrel that
he himself had instigated, they immediately saw the potential for dissent against the Shogun's ill-considered ruling. The Elders thus began
to pressure the Asano main house and Takumi's closest kin to enforce
obedience in Akō, and these lords knew that their own domains could
be the price of their failure to do so. Tensions in Edo were building, and
the force of them would soon be felt in Akō.

Akō, Third Month, 21st Day

Records that survive in Akō note only that a courier from Edo arrived
today bearing news that on the 15th, Asano Daigaku had been sentenced
to Domiciliary Confinement. The undercover agents from Okayama
were more forthcoming. They reported that the gate to Daigaku's residence was to be "nailed shut," that the Akō samurai felt they must now
make up their minds what they would do once Daigaku's ultimate fate
was decided, and that fourteen of them "seem very strongly determined."

✦ ✦ ✦

"Very strongly determined"—but determined to do *what?* It is extremely difficult to piece together a coherent account of what went on in Akō in those early days of uncertainty. But by combining contemporaneous and retrospective accounts, a reasonably lucid framework begins to emerge within which to place isolated bits of information as we come across them. The overall picture looks something like this:

At first, there was no division of opinion. Their lord had committed a crime, for which he was duly punished—with unseemly haste, to be sure, but not unjustly. Everyone could agree upon this, and everyone had to do his part to make the consequences as bearable as possible. But then, as we have seen, doubt crept in. Rumors were reaching Akō that their lord's victim might *not* be dead; if that was true, then their lord's punishment was, in fact, quite unjust. Here lies the source of a schism that divided the members of the Akō Corps of Vassals until the very end.

On the one hand, there were those, most prominent among them Ōno Kurōbei, who maintained that loyalty to the House of Asano demanded that they comply with the commands of the Shogunate, be they just or unjust; to resist would only damage the future prospects of their lord's heir, Asano Daigaku. On the other hand, a group led by Ōishi Kuranosuke insisted that no samurai could endure the dishonor that he would incur by condoning an injustice to his lord. There was no room for compromise here. Everyone had to decide on which side of the fence he stood (or just pack up and leave, as many did), and that decision would determine which of two drastically divergent courses of action he would follow.

For the obedient, this was easy. You do as you are told and hope that your reward will be reinstatement of the domain, perhaps even with a place for you in the new order. But for those who felt they must resist? These people, understandably, were more secretive. With hindsight, however, we know that sometime in the course of these first days, those who sided with Kuranosuke formally pledged themselves to his cause. There is no record of Kuranosuke soliciting pledges, and no record if these promises were submitted individually or everyone signed a single document. Neither is there any record of what they pledged themselves to do. We know now, though, that at the outset, if Kira still lived, they were determined to defend Akō Castle against siege and that later, they decided instead to commit mass seppuku. In short, they were determined to die with honor, either in battle or by their own hands. To a modern sensibility, this perhaps seems a needless waste of life. But in the world these men inhabited, both plans made perfectly good sense.

◆ ◆ ◆

To understand why defending the castle against siege made good sense, we need only look back to the circumstances that brought the Asano main house to Hiroshima in the first place. In 1619, when the previous lord of Hiroshima Castle, Fukushima Masanori, fell afoul of the second Shogun, Tokugawa Hidetada, he was commanded to surrender his castle and his lands, rated at 500,000 koku, and move to a much smaller fief of only 45,000 koku. Just as in Akō, although on a much grander scale, the Shogunate surrounded Fukushima's domain with the armies of six of his neighbors. In response, Masanori's Chief Elder, Fukushima Tanba, mustered 4,000 men in Hiroshima Castle and commanded them to prepare for siege warfare. And when the emissaries of the Shogun sailed down the coast to Hiroshima to demand the surrender of castle and domain, they were intercepted at Ondo no Seto by the commander of this force, Ōhashi Moemon, accompanied by a hundred musketeers. Here the emissaries were told—politely, of course—that Masanori's fief could not be surrendered by his vassals without orders from Masanori himself. Orders from the Shogun alone would not suffice. In this particular year, however, Masanori was resident in Edo on alternate attendance. To obtain written orders in his own hand, a courier would have to be sent all the way to Edo and back, which would take several days and keep literally thousands of armed men on high alert all the while. In the interest of efficiency, could not the Fukushima vassals dispense with that formality, just this once? "No," Moemon told them, "we cannot." Their lord's lord was not *their* lord. At that point, some in the Shogunal entourage urged immediate attack.

Call in the forces that now lined the borders, lay siege to the castle, and take it by storm. Fortunately, wiser heads prevailed, and a courier was sent to Masanori in Edo. Days later, when he returned with written orders in their lord's own hand, Masanori's castle and lands were surrendered peaceably—and, most importantly, with honor. Fukushima Tanba, Ōhashi Moemon, and their men had laid their lives on the line, held their ground, and forced the Shogunate to meet the conditions they demanded. Their conduct elicited praise and admiration throughout the land and became the model for subsequent samurai unfortunate enough to suffer the same fate. Whether Kuranosuke ever likened his own situation to that of Fukushima Tanba, I have no idea. But he would surely have known of the incident, for after the surrender, Masanori's castle and most of his domain passed to Asano Naga'akira, whose descendants held it down to the time of the Meiji Revolution.

The situation in Akō, obviously, was not entirely analogous to that in Hiroshima eighty years earlier. There could be no written orders from the lord of Akō; he was dead. Nor from his heir, who had never succeeded and was under house arrest. Still there was good reason for resisting the Shogunate's demand for surrender. If Kira was still alive, only the threat of violence could persuade the Shogunate to bring him to justice under the Principle of Equal Punishment. And if, as was likely, their request should be spurned and the castle besieged, then at least they would die with honor, their point made.

◆ ◆ ◆

In the meantime, Kuranosuke, who like everyone else would soon be evicted from his home, had other more mundane matters to attend to. He began by writing to his adopted son Ōnishibō Kaku'un, present master of the same small temple at Iwashimizu from which his great-grandfather Ōishi Yoshikatsu had fled a hundred years earlier:

> By the time this reaches you, I expect that you will have heard what has befallen us here. You may well imagine the state in which this sudden shock has left us all. We shall now have to think of some place whither to betake ourselves, but I am utterly at a loss to imagine

where we might go. Concerning which: there will be fourteen or fifteen men of various ranks wishing to settle somewhere between Yamazaki and Yamashina. I am unfamiliar with the capital region. I'm not even sure but what it may be an unsuitable place for a ronin to reside, but I shall defer to your opinion in this matter, as I am also considering the Fushimi and Ōtsu areas. If it is all the same to you, though, I should prefer to live in your vicinity. Would you be so kind as to give us your thoughts on this matter? Yours respectfully,

THIRD MONTH, 21ST DAY   *Ō[ishi] Kuranosuke [monogram]*

To: Ōnishibō
Seishibō
Senjōbō
This note in haste.

~ *187* ~

*Not a single person they approached
would agree to join them.*

Rumor ran rife in Edo those first few days. Some were saying that Kira had been killed in the palace, while others said that he had not died until he returned home. Still others—though they, too, were only repeating rumors—spoke the truth: that Kira had not only survived, but been pardoned.

Yet there were also those who knew precisely what had happened and were doing their best to hide what they knew as long as they could, because in other hands this knowledge could do them harm. Toda Uneme-no-Kami knew perfectly well that Kira was alive. Had he wished to, he could have enlightened Hara Sōemon on that score before he set out for Akō to report Takumi-no-Kami's death, but he refrained from doing so. We have only to follow the movements of Horibe Yasubei to see why Uneme-no-Kami chose to remain silent.

◆ ◆ ◆

Horibe Yasubei, too, now knew the truth. Someone, whom he does not name, but whom he felt he could trust, had told him that Kira was not dead, that his wounds were light, and that he was certain to recover. This, Yasubei himself says, could not be overlooked. And so, once the Asano Upper Mansion in Teppōzu had been surrendered and his presence was no longer required there, he and two of his comrades in the Horse Guards, Okuda Magodayū and Takada Gunbei, decided that they would round up a group of like-minded men, break into the Kira mansion, and kill their lord's enemy. "If we can gather a group of twenty who are as determined as we are," Yasubei said, "we can mount an attack and settle the matter once and for all." But not a single person they approached would agree to join them.

Perhaps then, they thought, if they could persuade the Edo Elders to lead, others would be more likely to join. Yet the Elders would not even discuss the matter with them; whenever they came to call, the Elders were always "out" or "busy." For a time, they considered attempting the attack on their own. The idea was quickly abandoned. The Uesugi were maintaining day and night guard on the mansion of their kinsman Kira. For three men, however skilled with the sword, to attempt to penetrate those defenses would mean certain death. And there was no honor in dying a dog's death with never a hope of accomplishing their mission. There was only one course open to them now. They must make the journey to Akō. Surely they would find men of like mind there.

✦ ✦ ✦

But somehow, life seems never to go quite according to plan—even the simplest plan. For early on the morning of the 4th Day of the Fourth Month, a messenger appeared at the doorway of the Horibe tenement bearing a note from Kawamura Chūemon. If Yasubei were to be at home today, Chūemon wrote, he wondered if he might call upon him. As it happened, it was not a good day to be receiving callers. Yasubei, Gunbei, and Magodayu had already made plans to set out for Akō early on the morrow; there were last-minute preparations to make, colleagues to consult, and very little time in which to do so. But Chūemon was a cousin, the son of an elder sister of Yasubei's mother; to turn him away would be rude. And so Yasubei sent back a message, saying that if Chūemon could come that morning, he would wait at home for him. His cousin must have left as soon as his messenger returned; he arrived in Yonezawa-chō before midday, and he and Yasubei had "a leisurely conversation."

When Chūemon finally came to the point of his visit, he told Yasubei that on the evening of the 14th Day of the Third Month—the very evening of the Catastrophe, when virtually every warrior household in Edo must have buzzed with talk of Takumi and Kira—Mizoguchi

Shinano-no-Kami and his son Hōki-no-Kami were discussing Yasubei.

"This means that Yasubei is again a ronin," Shinano-no-Kami said, "and by now, he'll have dependents. I think that we had better recall him, lest all his people be left starving. Once the transfer of Akō Castle is completed, we must discuss this matter further."

Coming from the old daimyo, who years earlier had been the liege lord of Yasubei's father, this was tantamount to a command. And for Yasubei, it meant rescue from financial disaster. Chūemon was quick to explain that his visit was not to be construed as a formal offer; he had come simply to inform Yasubei confidentially what was afoot: "I am not the official emissary of Their Lordships; Akabori Tōemon will come and discuss the details with your father, Yahei."

Yahei, of course, was present in the room, and it now seemed that he should be the first to speak. His response was what one might expect of a former Liaison Officer: diplomatic, gracious—and noncommittal: "What with Yasubei's forebears so deeply indebted to their former lord, and with so many of his relatives still in the service of that great house, I am most honored that His Lordship should bestow such compassion upon us."

Yasubei, far less a diplomat (as he himself was aware), but no more keen to commit himself, said simply: "It is most gratifying that Their Lordships should so immediately think of us."

The conversation then turned for a time—or, perhaps, I should say that it was *turned*—to other topics of current gossip. But when the subject of Takumi's fate again came up, Yasubei decided it was time to put an end to this beating about the bush: "Even were I the recipient of our late lord's largesse for but a single day, I should still consider myself deeply in his debt. But beyond this, my entire family has for years been the beneficiaries of his kindness and care. As far as I am concerned, the distinction between hereditary vassals and newcomers is at this point irrelevant. My one and only desire is to dispel our late lord's wrath just as quickly as possible."

Chūemon spoke not another word. Without so much as a ritual fare-thee-well, he stood and left.

+ + +

Yasubei is now regarded as such a hero that many readers will find it difficult to understand why he should have been shunned by his own comrades in the mansion at Teppōzu. The reason, I suspect, lies in the young man's family history. Yasubei was not from Akō, and he was new to the Akō Corps of Vassals—a former ronin and an adopted son who had been taken into service only four years earlier. To those who were not stationed permanently in Edo, but who had come from Akō in the entourage of Takumi-no-Kami, Yasubei was a total stranger. Some may never even have spoken to him. It is hardly surprising that they should be wary of a stranger trying to recruit them to an attempt at assassination. Who was this man, then? And where did he come from? We need to know.

+ + +

Horibe Yasubei was not born a Horibe; he was born on the fringes of a far more illustrious lineage. But he had never before served as a samurai. If this seems a perverse way to describe a man later known as a quintessential samurai, I would protest that both facts are fundamental to an appreciation of what he later became and did.

Through his mother's line, Yasubei was a great-grandson of Mizoguchi Hōki-no-Kami Hidekatsu, founder of a line of powerful lords who ruled the distant northern domain of Shibata for nearly three hundred years. But shortly after Yasubei's birth, his mother died; and before her son had come of age, his father, Nakayama Yajiemon, had in some unknown way brought disgrace upon himself, been dismissed from the service of the Mizoguchi house, and in the same year (1683) died. It was not a good start in life. In his fourteenth year, Nakayama Yasubei was left an orphaned ronin, with no family of his own and no prospect of preferment.

Fortunately, there was a strong network of Mizoguchi kinfolk who were willing to take the boy in and care for him. At first, he went to live with his aged grandfather Mizoguchi Shirōbei, under whose guidance, they say, he first developed his passion for the art of swordsmanship.

But Shirōbei was to live only two more years, after which Yasubei had to move on, this time to the home of Nagai Saburōzaemon, Rural Overseer of a cluster of hamlets surrounding the village of Togashira. And through the Nagai, Yasubei was to meet Satō Jōemon, the man who would remain his closest friend throughout his short life.

Both Yasubei and Jōemon must have been about sixteen at the time. The wife of Yasubei's guardian in Togashira was the daughter of another Rural Overseer from the village of Kosudo, and thus her younger brother, Jōemon, was a frequent visitor to the Nagai household. The two boys took an immediate liking to each other and soon discovered that they had a great deal in common. As Yasubei himself says, "We were just like brothers." Both were the sons of ronin and had never served as samurai, but both were descended from warrior houses of which they were justifiably proud and hoped one day to find service that would restore the good names of their families. At the moment, though, their only prospects seemed to lie in that shadowy margin between the lowest ranks of samurai and the highest ranks of peasants.

The families they lived with were, at the village level, people of consequence; yet although they still bore surnames and wore two swords in their sashes, their duties had more to do with agriculture than with military matters. They were the well-to-do supervisors of village Headmen, intermediaries between the peasantry and the domain officialdom. But they lived among the villagers, far away from the castle town. It was not unusual for families of this sort to slip down the ladder and become what we now consider well-to-do peasants, no longer samurai at all. Yasubei and Jōemon aspired to something better, something more like the honor their ancestors had enjoyed—for which they had to leave their villages in Shibata and seek employment in the Shogun's capital, Edo.

Jōemon was the first to go. When he left is not recorded, but he quickly found employment there (albeit in a rather tenuous position) with Suwa Hyōbu, the Shogunal Magistrate for the city of Nagasaki. In the first year of Genroku (1688), Yasubei followed. Six years later, he was one of the most famous men in the city of Edo.

✦ ✦ ✦

In Koishikawa, at the top of a hill, hard by the western border of the villa of the lord of Mito, there stands a shrine dedicated to the ninth-century scholar and statesman Sugawara no Michizane—as well as to his ox. Veneration of Michizane himself had been common for nearly a millennium, ever since it was realized that his angry ghost had been the cause of a spate of destructive thunderstorms in Kyoto. But his ox was a relative newcomer to shrine worship. It was on this hill, legend has it, that Minamoto no Yoritomo, when he halted to rest on his march north, dozed and dreamt that Michizane appeared to him, riding an ox. Yoritomo was destined, the sage assured him, to conquer his enemies the Taira and become the first Shogun of the Kamakura period—a prophecy that not only came true, but also inspired the foundation of this new shrine to Michizane, mounted on his ox.

By happy coincidence, it was here, too, that Yasubei took his first steps toward making a name for himself in Edo. For at the foot of the hill where Yoritomo dreamt of Michizane and his ox (and the ox is still there, in the form of a stone that everyone agrees vaguely resembles a snoozing ox), in a narrow strip of land between two steep stone stairways to the shrine, the renowned swordsman Horiuchi Gendazaemon had built his training hall. Satō Jōemon, already one of his disciples, introduced Yasubei to his teacher; the rest, as we say, is history.

Gendazaemon was known for his no-nonsense approach to sword fighting. No fancy tricks, no mystical mudras or mantras, no secret initiations. His guiding principle was simple: in a massed battle, the longer your weapon, the greater your advantage. Your blade must be at least 3 feet in length, and preferably longer; then it's just a matter of learning how best to wield such a weighty piece of steel. Gendazaemon's own preferred weapon was the "great sword," which had not only a long blade but an even longer haft. This was a weapon that could stop even a galloping horse. A century or so earlier, Oda Nobunaga had kept a bodyguard of a hundred men armed with great swords. In Yasubei's day, there would hardly have been that many in the entire city of Edo who knew how to handle one. Of these, Horiuchi Gendazaemon was the acknowledged master.

It soon became apparent that this method of sword fighting was

Yasubei's true métier. He rose steadily in the ranking of Gendazaemon's disciples and eventually became one of the four leaders that his master rated highly enough to send out to students who required private instruction. This work is probably what enabled Yasubei to rent a small tenement of his own, in Ushigome Take-chō, and ultimately led, in an unexpected way, to his wider renown as a swordsman.

One student with whom Yasubei developed a particularly close relationship was a samurai in the service of Matsudaira Sakyō-no-Daibu Yorizumi, lord of the domain of Saijō (30,000 *koku*) in the province of Iyo. This student, Sugano Rokurōzaemon, was a man in his sixties, old enough to be Yasubei's grandfather. But the two men somehow developed a strong bond of intimacy. The older man offered to stand as the orphan's guardian and guarantor in his quest for employment, and then formalized his promise by exchanging vows with Yasubei as fictive uncle and nephew. This was a vow that was to change Yasubei's life in ways that he could never have imagined.

◆ ◆ ◆

In the year 1694, on the evening of the 7th Day of the Second Month, Rokurōzaemon attended a New Year's fête given by the commander of the unit in which he served. As the evening wore on and everyone grew steadily more inebriated, a quarrel broke out between Rokurōzaemon and one of his colleagues. Murakami Shōzaemon had spoken abusively, and Rokurōzaemon responded in kind. The other guests immediately intervened and persuaded the two to drink a toast to each other and smooth over their differences. Thereafter, everyone bade farewell to their host, and the matter seemed settled. But four days later, on the 11th, Shōzaemon sent a challenge to Rokurōzaemon, stating that he would await him late in the Hour of the Serpent (ca. 11:30 A.M.) at the Takadanobaba Mounted Archery Range for a duel to the death. Rokurōzaemon, despite his age, felt that he had no choice but to accept the challenge.

The fight—or, rather, the mêlée—that followed has become one of the more famous episodes in the history of Edo. And like all tales considered "famous," it has been told in so many different versions

figure 10
Horibe Yasubei and his great sword.
(Historiographical Institute, The University of Tokyo)

that one might think it impossible to say that any one of them is true. Fortunately, though, there also survive versions gleaned directly from the testimony of Yasubei and his friend Satō Jōemon. But first let me tell you the rather dramatic version preferred by most storytellers, and then modify it a bit in the light of more reliable evidence.

As I first heard it told, Rokurōzaemon, as he was leaving home to meet his adversary at the archery range, told his wife where he was going and why, and then said, "If I do not return, you must ask Yasubei's help in putting my affairs in order." But his wife, quite rightly, did not wait to learn her husband's fate; she sent a servant immediately to Yasubei, who, in turn, grabbed his swords and set out, running toward Takadanobaba—through Nijukki-machi, down the hill to Yanagi-chō, then back up through Hara-machi, and down again to Babashita, where he spied the saké shop Kokuraya. By this time, he had been running for at least twenty minutes and badly needed a drink. "A cup!" he shouted, and he was handed a brimming wooden measure of saké (Kokuraya still proudly displays the cup, actually a box). He downed it in a gulp or two and ran on to the Takadanobaba Mounted Archery Range, where the fight was already under way.

Alas, the more reliable sources are not so dramatic. Both state that Rokurōzaemon himself went to Yasubei's place in Take-chō.

"There is no one else I can talk to about this," he said to Yasubei, "so I've come to you. I'm going to go right now. Whether the other party will be there or not, I have no idea. If he is, I expect there'll be about six or seven of them, including his three brothers. I'll be taking my personal retainer Tsunoda Sajibei and my sandal bearer, but I don't expect that they'll be of much use once we get there. So if by chance I happen to be killed, I'd like to ask that you look after my wife and kill my enemies."

Yasubei was loath to make such grandiose promises, which he was certain he couldn't fulfill. "What I would rather do," Yasubei said, "is go with you. It doesn't matter how many of them there are. My arms and legs are stronger than yours. Just leave it to me; I'll cut down every one of them. I won't let them even come near your good self."

"Well, if that's how you feel, then come along," the old man said, and they set out together for Takadanobaba—with no mention of stopping for a drink at Kokuraya.

When they arrived at the Takadanobaba Mounted Archery Range, Yasubei tells us, they stopped and looked about, wondering whether their opponents were there; then Shōzaemon appeared at the far end of the south side. Yasubei turned to discuss the matter with Rokurōzaemon.

"I don't think that he's alone," Yasubei said, "but I can't see the others." Then one or two men emerged from the shade of the trees at the east end, probably Shōzaemon's brothers, Saburōemon and Nakatsugawa Yūken. And then four or five others who appeared to be their personal retainers.

"It looks like he's placed some of his men at the east end of the middle track, between the embankments," Yasubei said. So they called up Rokurōzaemon's retainer, and they all advanced toward the west, along the embankment. Yasubei said to Rokurōzaemon, "He seems to have divided his force; he wants to catch us in the middle. So let's have your man and your sandal bearer drop back and guard our rear; then you and I will move out together."

When Shōzaemon and Yasubei had closed to a distance of about 60 feet, Yasubei called out to him, "Well, isn't this a strange place that I should make your acquaintance?" "Strange, indeed," Shōzaemon replied. Yasubei then drew back toward Rokurōzaemon, intending to join him in attacking Shōzaemon. But then the brother Saburōemon emerged from the east, circled around, and came at Yasubei, wielding a very long sword. Yasubei met him with his sword in the overhead position and brought it down on the left side of his brow. Saburōemon faltered; fell back; and then, releasing his left hand from the haft, swung the sword with his right hand, aiming for Yasubei's arm. Yasubei stopped the blow with his sword guard; then pushing forward, he landed a direct frontal blow so powerful that it split the man's face in two. In the meantime, Rokurōzaemon's man Sajibei had stopped Nakatsugawa from attacking from the rear, and then cut him down.

Yasubei then pulled back to engage Shōzaemon. He was shocked to see that Rokurōzaemon was badly wounded on the forehead. But just as Yasubei was moving in on Shōzaemon, Rokurōzaemon attacked from the side and cut off Shōzaemon's right arm; then Sajibei cut off his left. Shōzaemon staggered back screaming, "No! No!"

"No! No! you say?" Yasubei shouted and drove his sword down on Shōzaemon's head. He dropped facing west.

"We've done it! We've done it!" Rokurōzaemon cried; then he, too, collapsed.

Yasubei and Sajibei lifted Rokurōzaemon, supported him on their shoulders, and prepared to leave. But even then, Shōzaemon seems still to have been alive. "Kill me! Kill me!" he was screaming. Yasubei turned to Sajibei: "There's no point in putting a man out of his misery when he's already been cut to pieces. But it's warrior's etiquette, so I'll do it."

None of the others who had come with the brothers was anywhere in sight now. Yasubei had slain one of them; the rest had fled. So Yasubei and Sajibei carried Rokurōzaemon home, purposely passing his dead enemy's gate in broad daylight. Sugano Rokurōzaemon died of his wounds later that day. There could be no doubt in anyone's mind that he had died an honorable death.

♦ ♦ ♦

For Nakayama Yasubei, however, this was far from the end of the affair. He, of course, continued his work giving private instruction to disciples of Horiuchi Gendazaemon. In the meantime, rumor rapidly spread news of the bloody battle at Takadanobaba and the exploits of the young hero of that fray—with the result that two or three months later (we do not know the precise date), Yasubei received a caller who had come to offer him not only adoption and marriage, but a respectable position as a samurai in the service of a daimyo. This story, too, has been told in countless versions, many of them highly fanciful and embellished. But one of them, told in 1702 by Yasubei's fellow vassal Kaiga Yazaemon—probably in Yasubei's presence—is surely the most reliable report of what took place.

♦ ♦ ♦

A few years earlier, Yazaemon began, when Yasubei had assisted his "uncle" and killed the man's enemy at Takadanobaba, Horibe Yahei, Liaison Officer of the Asano house in Edo, heard that he was living as a ronin in the vicinity of Kobinata, whereupon he called at Yasubei's

figure 11
The Takadanobaba Mounted Archery Range.
(*Edo meisho zue*, 1834–1836)

home, announced himself, and entered.

"Might the gentleman named Yasubei be your good self?" he asked.

"Indeed," he replied. "I am he."

"We have heard of your recent exploits when you assisted your uncle in his duel at Takadanobaba. In consequence—although I've no idea what your own feelings might be—a certain gentleman wishes to adopt you as his son-in-law. I am here because I've been asked to convey this message to you. The other party plans to retire within the next two or three years. His enfeoffment is 200 koku, which he hopes immediately to pass on to you, so that he can enjoy a comfortable retirement. And even though he himself will retire, there will be no reduction of his enfeoffment. His lord is a very generous gentleman and is certain to agree to this."

Yasubei replied, "I'm very grateful to you for conveying this kind offer to me. But if I were to join another family, that would mean relinquishing my original surname, which I should be most reluctant to do. So I must beg you to excuse me for not accepting."

"Of course! How very worthy that you should feel this way. But consider this: if you have children, then you could have your second son inherit your original name. So do, by all means, accept this proposal. When the other party hears that you are reluctant to relinquish your original name, I'm sure that he will think you only the more honorable and desire you all the more. What is more—unseemly though it is for an old man like me to speak of such things—the daughter is very good looking and highly intelligent, not at all a bad match, even for so fine a man as your good self. So please do consider all these factors in making your decision, which I hope you will do within the next few days."

Yasubei said, "Thank you very much for explaining all of this to me. Such being the case, I shall discuss the matter with my relatives and some of my closest friends and then reply to you."

When he said this, Yahei responded, "But if you yourself find this acceptable, there should be no need to discuss the matter with your honored family. For once you broach the subject, you'll then have to accept whatever they say, whether they approve or disapprove." He then went on to offer various other arguments to Yasubei, who in the end said, "In that case, let us proceed."

"Then I'll send for you tomorrow," the old man said. "And needless to say, as a ronin, there is no need for you to make any special preparations."

The next morning, he sent a man and a horse for Yasubei. And when they met, Yahei said, "I must confess that the 'other party' of whom I spoke is none other than myself. Ever since I heard of you, I've longed day and night to have you as my son-in-law."

We know now that negotiations between the two men took much longer and were far more complex than those Kaiga Yazaemon describes. Yet I can well imagine old Yahei saying something quite like this; for at this late point in his life, he was in serious need of a son and heir. He was over seventy, and two years earlier, his own son, Yaichibei, had been murdered by an enraged wastrel whose amorous advances the boy had spurned. Yahei avenged himself upon the murderer, but at his great age, his most immediate concern then became finding a suitable young man to succeed him. His application to adopt the younger brother of his second wife, for reasons unknown, had been rejected. But there could be no doubting the credentials of a warrior who had proved himself as dramatically and publicly as Yasubei had.

Yahei immediately lodged his petition with the appropriate officials, and as soon as it was approved, Yasubei married Yahei's daughter.

◆ ◆ ◆

Thus it was that Nakayama Yasubei Masatsune became the man we all know best as Horibe Yasubei Taketsune.

CHAPTER
22

If you have a different opinion,
I see no point in your remaining here.

Whatever the chaos and uncertainty of those first two or three days in Akō, it was nothing compared with what would follow. For when Tonomura Genzaemon set sail for Hiroshima on the night of the 19th, he set in motion a series of intrusions by Takumi's kinsmen whose first concern was that the Catastrophe in Akō do no damage to themselves.

Tonomura was dispatched to Hiroshima not merely to inform, but also to persuade the Asano main house to assist its cadet branch financially. He carried a request for a loan of 300 *kan* in silver, 200 of which would cover the shortfall at the Currency Exchange, the other 100 to be distributed as severance allowances to the departing vassals. Both parties would have known that this was a "loan" that could never be repaid. But as Genzaemon was careful to point out, this was the first time the Akō house had ever asked for assistance of any sort, and such a grant surely would redound to the credit of the Hiroshima house for helping its cadet branch to do the right thing. But unfortunately, His Lordship, Asano Aki-no-Kami Tsunanaga, was absent in Edo on alternate attendance. Genzaemon was received instead by Oki Gondayū Tadasuke, who was serving as Acting Elder in His Lordship's absence. After reading the letter from Kuranosuke and Kurōbei, Gondayū told Genzaemon that it was not within his power to authorize so large a loan without permission from Edo. In short, Genzaemon was politely turned away with a plausible excuse.

The next morning, the 23rd, Genzaemon proceeded 15 leagues (37.5 miles, 60 kilometers) inland to Miyoshi, the seat of the other Asano cadet house and the birthplace of Lady Asano. There, as it happened, Asano Tosa-no-Kami Nagazumi, lord of the domain, was in residence, having been excused from attendance in Edo this year on account of illness. He received Genzaemon as soon as he arrived. What Genzaemon told him—or asked of him—is not recorded, but His Lordship's answer was simply: "It is of the utmost importance that no disturbance of any sort be fomented within the domain." And immediately thereafter, he assigned Tokunaga Mataemon, a Company Commander of Musketeers, to carry that message directly to Akō.

No doubt, both Gondayū and Tosa-no-Kami commiserated courteously with Genzaemon, but their main concern was clear—that their own domains in no way be endangered by untoward behavior in Akō. This was the message that would repeatedly be hammered into the Akō samurai over the next month or so, with little apparent sympathy for the predicament they faced. Katashima Shin'enshi, the author of *Sekijō gishinden*, exaggerated only slightly when he said that the roads to Akō would soon be streaming with couriers from their fretful Asano kinsmen—"lined up like teeth on a comb."

◆ ◆ ◆

And all the while, the predicament itself was growing ever more complex. As the meetings of the senior officers in the castle continued, they produced no consensus but only a clearer definition of the lines of difference between them. On the one side, led by the Elder Ōno Kurōbei, were four Samurai Commanders—Okabayashi Mokunosuke, Tonomura Genzaemon, Itō Gozaemon, and Tamamushi Shichirōemon—as well as two Adjutants: Tanaka Seibei and Uemura Yogozaemon. While on the other side, led by Ōishi Kuranosuke, were one Samurai Commander, Okuno Shōgen, and four Company Commanders of Foot Soldiers: Kawamura Denbei, Shindō Genshirō, Hara Sōemon, and Oyama Gengoemon. One wishes for a record of the arguments that they hurled at one another, but none survives. There can be no doubt, though, that both sides were troubled not only by the arguments of their opponents, but by the failure—or refusal—of the two Edo Elders to send news of Kira's survival or demise. Any number of couriers had arrived from Edo in the meantime—from Asano Aki-no-Kami,

Asano Mino-no-Kami, and Toda Uneme-no-Kami—but not a word about Kira from Yasui Hikoemon and Fujii Hikoshirō.

✦ ✦ ✦

On the evening of the 23rd, Tokunaga Mataemon arrived in Akō from Miyoshi. He was the first of several emissaries from the various Asano kinsmen, and he lodged in the town rather than proceeding to the castle. The next morning, Kuranosuke and Kurōbei went immediately to welcome him.

"You're an emissary from Tosa-no-Kami Sama," Kuranosuke said. "You must come to the castle."

"You're terribly busy, I know," Mataemon replied. "I can just as well state my business here." Whereupon he said, "I'm to tell you that we were speechless to learn of Takumi-no-Kami Dono's misfortune and that we can well imagine how all of you must feel. Even so, you must permit no disturbance of any sort."

"We are very grateful for your kind words and hold your admonition in high esteem. You may rest assured that we shall pass this on to our Corps of Vassals and that we shall proffer you our formal acceptance on the morrow."

Kuranosuke and Kurōbei then returned to the castle. But later, long after nightfall, Kuranosuke did something very unusual. At midnight, he left his home entirely alone, without even his manservant to attend him, and walked quietly into town to Mataemon's lodging. Mataemon received him in his bedchamber.

Kuranosuke began, "I am very grateful to Tosa-no-Kami Sama for his thoughtfulness in sending you to us, as well as for your own kind understanding of our feelings. But we have yet to hear any word whether Kōzuke-no-Suke Dono is alive or dead. I can't imagine what our Elders in Edo might be thinking. They've sent us no word whatever. Yet surely Tosa-no-Kami Sama has heard whether he is alive or dead. Might I ask you to ask him—if only for the sake of his feelings for Takumi-no-Kami Dono—and to inform us secretly?"

"I certainly shall ask him," Mataemon replied.

"I beg that of you, most earnestly," Kuranosuke said, and immediately returned to his home. The following morning, Mataemon returned to Miyoshi.

◆ ◆ ◆

On the same day, the 25th, an emissary from Akō set out on the same route to Miyoshi that Mataemon had traveled in the opposite direction. He was Itō Goemon, a Samurai Commander and the younger brother of Ōno Kurōbei. What was his mission? No record of that survives in Akō, but we do know what he said when he arrived in Miyoshi and was received by Tosa-no-Kami, because someone in Miyoshi told someone in Hiroshima, through whom it found its way into the records of the Asano main house.

All seemed normal within the Corps of Vassals, Goemon said; the force that would take possession of the castle would arrive sometime in the middle of the next month, but in Akō they still had not heard whether Kōzuke-no-Suke Dono was alive or dead: "The vassals don't talk much about this, but some seem very concerned by it. Kurōbei says that now is not the time to be getting ideas about this. If we do, and we end up opposing the authorities, it will not be good for Daigaku Dono. Kuranosuke thinks that there is some merit in what Kurōbei says; yet under the circumstances, it does seem a shame to surrender the castle, which was built by the late Takumi-no-Kami Naganao. Still, it would not do to wage war against the Shogunate, he says, so there is nothing for it but to commit seppuku in the castle. Now, with Daigaku Dono under house arrest and Lord Toda Uneme-no-Kami Ujisada on restriction, not to mention the time it takes to communicate with Edo, if Your Lordship were to issue a written injunction, it could be used to calm the vassals and to make the Elders listen to reason. Either way, it should prevent the outbreak of any disturbance."

Tosa-no-Kami needed no convincing. He wrote:

> *Is all well with you concerning Takumi-no-Kami's misfortune? I trust that you will convey to your men of all ranks that they must neither oppose the authorities nor foment any disturbance. Herewith the foregoing. Respectfully,*

~ 205 ~

THIRD MONTH, 28TH DAY   *Asano Tosa-no-Kami [monogram]*
To: Ōishi Kuranosuke Dono
Ōno Kurōbei Dono

Whether Kuranosuke had been consulted concerning the dispatch of Goemon is not recorded. But clearly, this was as much Kurōbei's personal attempt to manipulate events as was Kuranosuke's midnight visit to Mataemon. The two Elders were now opposed not only in public, but clandestinely as well. That opposition was soon to end.

◆ ◆ ◆

By now, Kuranosuke, Kurōbei, and the rest of the command group must have become inured to the daily arrival of emissaries and couriers, but the arrival of the next two, on the morning of the 28th, seems to have made an impact greater than any previous visits. Toda Uneme-no-Kami had dispatched his kinsman Toda Gengobei and his Inspector General Uemura Shichirōemon to transmit to Akō the orders of the Shogun's Council of Elders. These men had been on the road for ten days. The news they carried was nothing not already known, but their rank and the size of their entourage—thirty-three men—commanded respect; in addition, they bore a copy of a directive from the Duty Elder, Tsuchiya Sagami-no-Kami, to Toda Uneme-no-Kami:

> *Concerning the matter of Akō in the province of Harima: Wakizaka Awaji-no-Kami and Kinoshita Higo-no-Kami will be sent to accept the domain's surrender. You are to inform the kinsmen of Takumi that the surrender will take place sometime in the middle of this coming month, and, of course, you will also inform the vassals of Takumi now resident in Akō. Please be advised that two official Inspectors will also be dispatched. And, as previously mentioned, you are to take particular pains to command the vassals and everyone resident in the domain to comport themselves in a seemly manner. Herewith the foregoing,*

> THIRD MONTH, 17TH DAY   *Tsuchiya Sagami-no-Kami*
> To: Toda Uneme-no-Kami Dono

P.S. Awaji-no-Kami will also garrison the castle.

Yet was this alone enough to generate the new sense of resolve that we see in Kuranosuke and those of his faction? I doubt it. I would venture instead that it was Toda Gengobei and Uemura Shichirōemon who finally confirmed beyond a doubt that Kira was still alive. They certainly would have known the truth, and Kuranosuke's actions from this day forward clearly presuppose his own knowledge of the truth. The evidence is circumstantial, but persuasive.

◆ ◆ ◆

The meetings of which we have already heard so much had continued through the 26th and 27th, producing no more agreement than before. But on the 28th, there seems to have been a new sense of purpose among the participants, a sense that the time for dithering was past, that now something must be decided. As before, we have no record of who said what at this meeting. But Muro Kyūsō has left us an imaginative reconstruction of it, based upon reports from Sugimoto Yoshichika in Edo. And Horibe Yasubei has recorded what he was told when he arrived in Akō. The climax we know directly from the protagonist himself. As Kyūsō and Yasubei tell it, then, the story goes something like this:

Kuranosuke began the discussion: "We all know that our present predicament was caused by the outrage committed by our lord in the palace. We know, too, that he did what he did because Kira had heaped intolerable abuse upon him. Yet not only did he fail in his attempt to kill Kira, but Kira was pardoned and set free. It is our duty, therefore, to vindicate our lord's wrath, for if we do not, we shall never be able to show our faces anywhere in the realm. How are we to do our duty, though, if we simply abandon the castle built by the founder of this house and disperse to the four corners of the land? Rather, we must make it the place where we die. Yet to die defending the castle is to defy the powers that be. It may be better that we make known our grievances to the officials who come to take possession of the castle, commit seppuku at the main gate of the castle, and through our death entreat the authorities properly to punish Kira."

Kurōbei responded, "Kuranosuke is utterly mistaken. In the first place, to shut oneself up in the castle and demand that Kira be punished is no entreaty; it is a threat. It is venting one's personal wrath upon constituted authority, and that will do Daigaku Dono no good whatever. What we must do is disperse immediately, hand over the castle to the officials, and only then humbly submit our entreaty."

Kuranosuke, of course, disagreed: "This sounds to me like someone who knows no shame and is afraid to die. The reinstatement of Daigaku Dono is a mere pretext, which he uses in order to abandon the castle and escape with his skin intact. What is the rest of the world going to make of that?"

But before Kurōbei could reenter the fray, another actor made his appearance. And here we leave behind Kyūsō and Yasubei's reconstructed colloquy. The speaker himself, Hara Sōemon, will tell us what he said.

"I worked very closely with Kuranosuke," Sōemon said. "We talked everything over together, and we were in complete agreement. But this Kurōbei always had some objection to anything Kuranosuke might say. Finally, I just couldn't listen to any more of it, so I told him: 'This is a terrible waste of time, repeating these same arguments day after day and reaching no agreement. You take a different view of the situation than Kuranosuke. It just so happens, though, that everyone else here agrees with him completely. If you have a different opinion, I see no point in your remaining here. So GET OUT—RIGHT NOW!'"

Sōemon, we are told, "was normally very placid, a man of few words, mild-mannered, and polite; but when the occasion called for it, his gaze could be as ferocious as that of an angry dragon." He seems to have struck genuine fear in Kurōbei, who without another word stood and hurried out of the room, followed by about ten others who had sided with him.

Kuranosuke and his cohort were now free to act as they thought right.

✦ ✦ ✦

What Kuranosuke and his cohort thought right was nothing rash, but a well-reasoned choice. They would first of all write to inform the official Inspectors of the situation they could expect to encounter upon their arrival in Akō, and have this letter carried to Edo by two vassals of respectable lineage and rank. Kuranosuke's letter is considered a masterpiece of its kind. In the most compliant and reasonable tones, it leaves no doubt about the intractability of the problem that the Inspectors will have to deal with in Akō:

> On this the occasion of the thoughtless transgression for which Takumi was commanded to commit seppuku, and for which his castle and lands were declared forfeit, we his liegemen do humbly bow in submission. Likewise do we submit, with all respect, to the directives issued on that day by Suzuki Gozaemon Sama to the Elders of this house resident in Edo, as well as to the subsequent instructions of Tsuchiya Sagami-no-Kami Sama to Toda Uneme-no-Kami Dono and Asano Mino-no-Kami. Hitherto, however, we had been given to believe that Takumi had been commanded to commit seppuku in consequence of the death of Kōzuke-no-Suke Sama. From subsequent reports, we now realize that Kōzuke-no-Suke Sama did not die.
>
> Now, the samurai of this house are a rough-hewn and rustic lot, utterly single-minded in their devotion to their liege lord. Having no understanding of the niceties of the law, they protest that they cannot surrender the castle and lands of their lord knowing that his enemy remains alive and well. We the Elders and senior officers have on several occasions attempted to reason with them, but these stubborn rustics will not be persuaded by our counsel. At this juncture, we the Elders find it all but impossible to placate them, and so, despite our scruples, we are forced to appeal to you. By no means do we petition for the punishment of Kōzuke-no-Suke Sama. We should be most grateful, however, if you gentlemen could kindly suggest some rationale by which we might win the acquiescence of the vassals of this house. Were we not to mention this matter until

your arrival within the domain, it might well prove an obstacle to the surrender of the castle. Herewith the foregoing,

THIRD MONTH, 29TH DAY

*On behalf of the vassals of
Asano Takumi-no-Kami
Ōishi Kuranosuke [monogram]*

To: Araki Jūzaemon Sama
Sakakibara Uneme Sama

The men selected to carry this letter to Edo were Tagawa Kuzaemon, a Company Commander of Foot Soldiers enfeoffed at 400 *koku*, and Tsukioka Jiemon, Commander of the Vanguard enfeoffed at 300 *koku*. The next step would depend upon the response that these two would bring back from Edo.

I am well aware that we were in disgrace with
His Lordship.

The bearers of bad tidings and dire warnings were not the only early arrivals in Akō. On the 23rd Day, only four days after news of the Catastrophe had arrived, travelers on the road into town might have been startled to see a sight that had once been common, but now was almost never to be seen. Five men, who were far from well dressed, came marching down from Takatori Pass. On their backs, they bore luggage boxes with bulging sides, built to contain a full suit of battle armor and a helmet. On their shoulders leant 9-foot lances, fully sheathed of course. We know very little about these men beyond their names—Okano Jidayū, Nakamura Yatanojō, Ōoka Seikurō, Izeki Tokubei, and Izeki Monzaemon—and that a few years earlier, they had been dismissed from service in the Akō Corps of Vassals for reasons unknown. To anyone who saw them now, they would surely have conjured up images of Osaka seventy-some years earlier, when heavily armed ronin were flocking to the castle in their thousands, eager for the chance to fight again—perhaps to make a name, or even a fortune, for themselves; but if not, at least to die from something more interesting than old age.

The secret agents from Okayama had already reported rumors of a plot to defend Akō Castle to the death. They would have heard people saying that musket balls were being molded (the smoke was from burning documents), that rice was being laid in for a siege (it was being portioned out to the vassals), that gunpowder was being shifted out of storage and into the castle (it was still under guard in a bunker deep in the foothills)—all of which they duly reported to Okayama. The same rumors must have traveled eastward with equal speed to the village of Kameyama, on the southern outskirts of Himeji. Okano Jidayū had a daughter who was married to a samurai in the service of the lord of Himeji, Honda Nakatsukasa. The other four men may have settled there simply because Kameyama lay within the fief of the old Pure Land temple Hontokuji, a less restrictive place for a ronin to live than in a domain ruled by a daimyo.

But Okano Jidayū had more reason than just rumor to round up his old comrades. His kinsman Hara Sōemon, when he had changed litters and bearers in Himeji on the last leg of his journey from Edo, had sent Jidayū a short note, which read: "There has been trouble in Edo involving Takumi-no-Kami Dono. I am now on my way to Akō. Send your son Tōhachi to me just as soon as you can."

◆ ◆ ◆

Tōhachi left for Akō early the next morning, the 20th, and returned on the 21st. Immediately after his son's return, Jidayū paid a visit to his son-in-law, Sasakawa Tadaemon, in Himeji. The Honda house, Tadaemon told him, had heard from Edo that Kira was very much alive and had been absolved of any blame for the quarrel in Edo Castle. That probably was what Sōemon wanted to know, and it was all Jidayū needed to know. His former lord had been punished unjustly, and that was ample reason to resist the confiscation of his castle in Akō. For Jidayū and his comrades, their old domain's misfortune was a welcome opportunity—an opportunity to fight and die, which seems to be precisely what these five ronin had in mind.

When they arrived in Akō, they went not to the castle or to the home of Kuranosuke, as some accounts claim. They first called on Jidayū's kinsmen. Hara Sōemon's first wife had been an aunt of Jidayū, and Jidayū's own wife was a younger sister of Okuno Shōgen. Both men ranked high in the Corps of Vassals and wielded considerable influence with Kuranosuke. Sōemon was a Company Commander of Foot Soldiers; Shōgen, a Commander of Mounted Samurai. For a ronin of questionable repute, their intercession could be crucial.

"I am well aware that we were in disgrace with His Lordship," Jidayū began. "But by no means have we forgotten how beholden we are for his sustenance, both of ourselves and of our forebears. And now we hear that our honored lord was made to commit seppuku, while his enemy is but lightly wounded and still lives. They claim, of course, that he was justly punished, 'in complete accord with the law of the land.' But as his vassals, we cannot simply let it go at that. If you should decide to defend the castle and demand that Daigaku Dono succeed as head of this house, or if they will not accede to this and you think it proper to commit seppuku when the Inspectors arrive, we are, in either case, fully prepared to join you."

There could be no doubting the sincerity of their offer. If Akō Castle was to be defended, there would be no fortunes of war to be garnered from it. For the besieged, defeat was certain; an honorable death, either in battle or by suicide, was the only reward that could be hoped for. Sōemon went directly to Kuranosuke to relay the proposal of Jidayū and his four comrades. Kuranosuke replied with equal sincerity: "I'm quite heartened by the depth of your devotion. But we're still not certain whether Kōzuke is dead or alive. Besides which, our foot soldiers are in a rebellious mood. If we don't proceed with great care, we'll end up accomplishing nothing."

This Jidayū could not accept. He knew better than Kuranosuke, he thought, what the facts of the matter were: "Surely something can be done to calm the foot soldiers. We hear from Himeji that Kōzuke Dono still lives; about *that*, there can be no doubt. The Honda have written confirmation, a letter from Edo that states not only that he has been pardoned, but that His Highness commands him to take care to recover completely. And so all the daimyo—even the Three Cadet Houses and the Council of Elders—have been sending messengers of condolence to inquire after his health and wish him well. Honda Nakatsukasa Dono, too, has sent a messenger; they've written to Himeji with all the details. We've got to meet and make plans immediately. First, we clear all outsiders out of the castle. Then move the gunpowder out of storage and into the ten turrets of the castle—and do it today. No more of these secret meetings; everyone of samurai rank must come to the castle and be allowed to express their opinions; then we can decide what to do."

Kuranosuke replied, "I have received your message and appreciate all your suggestions. I agree, too, that these matters must be carefully discussed. As for the gunpowder, we can move that anytime. I do wish I could meet with you, but just now, here in the castle, I'm in no position to discuss anything with outsiders. We plan to send someone to Edo to investigate whether Kōzuke is dead or alive, and on that basis decide what to do next. For the time being, you should return to Kameyama, and once we've reached a decision, we'll send word to you."

Kuranosuke let them down easily, not refusing them outright, yet reminding them gently that they, too, were now outsiders. At least three years had passed since Jidayū and his comrades had left the Asano Corps of Vassals. If Kuranosuke were to admit them to his number, it was certain that he would be accused of recruiting ronin to rebel against the Shogunate.

What Jidayū made of this oblique refusal he does not say, but his subsequent behavior suggests that he did not take kindly to it. Nor did he leave Akō immediately, as Kuranosuke urged him to do, for he was still there on the 27th to meet the first of the men to arrive from Edo: Muramatsu Kihei and his son Sandayū.

♦ ♦ ♦

The story of Kihei and Sandayū is so impossibly melodramatic that I wouldn't even mention it, were it not for the source. But Ochiai Yozaemon, that most reliable of reporters, tells us that he heard it directly from Kuranosuke. We have no choice but to accept it as one of those truths that sound suspiciously like fiction.

Muramatsu Kihei was one of the lowest-ranking of the samurai stationed permanently in Edo, not even enfeoffed, but paid a mere 20 koku and rations for five. He had just turned sixty and had two sons: his heir, Sandayū, aged twenty-seven; and a second son, Masaemon, who had been fortunate enough to find a place in the service of Ogasawara Nagato-no-Kami. When the Catastrophe struck, Kihei decided that his duty now lay in Akō. Once the mansion in Teppōzu was surrendered and he had moved his family out of their quarters there, he prepared to leave.

To his son Sandayū, Kihei said, "You have never been the recipient of any sustenance from His Lordship, so this doesn't concern you; you must stay here and care for your aged mother." Whereupon Kihei set out alone, bound for Akō, 155 leagues (388 miles, 620 kilometers) away.

But Sandayū worried how the old man would fare, all alone, on such a long journey, and before long came to the conclusion that, even if he owed no debt of fealty to any overlord, it was still his duty to be a filial son. So he set off at a run in pursuit of his father. Down through Shinagawa and over the Rokugō River into Kawasaki he ran, until at last he caught up with Kihei in Kanagawa, the third post station on the Eastern Sea Road.

I expect the same arguments were rehearsed there as when Kihei had announced his departure. But Sandayū had made up his mind. He packed their two suits of armor into a single bundle, and for the next ten or eleven days, father and son took turns bearing the load, until they reached the turnoff at the village of Kuga, just 3 leagues from the castle in Akō.

Here Kihei told his son, "You've more than fulfilled your filial duty now. You really must go back and look after your mother."

"Mother has nothing to worry about," Sandayū replied. "Masaemon has a secure position with Ogasawara Nagato-no-Kami. Now that I've come this far, why should I turn back? Please, I beg you, *please*—let me stay with you. That's all I ask."

Both men were still in tears when they reached Kuranosuke's home. "What's this?" Kuranosuke exclaimed. "Father and son? You've both come together?"

I'm surprised that Kuranosuke even recognized them. Kihei had been born in Edo, and ever since he had succeeded his father, he had been stationed permanently in Edo. He was an Akō samurai who had never before been to Akō.

"The upper mansion was surrendered, and I had yet even to *see* our castle," Kihei said. "As beholden as I am, I felt that I must at least see it before it was lost."

Such is the story as Kuranosuke told it, but his was not the only tearful encounter with the Muramatsu that day.

By sheer chance, just as he was leaving the home of one Kamishima

Yasuke, on the west edge of town, Okano Jidayū happened upon Kihei and Sandayū. Kihei turned to his son and said, "Remember what I told you in Edo? That I hadn't seen Jidayū Dono in years, but he was sure to come back to Akō now? And look! Just as I said!" Jidayū grasped Kihei's hands, and the two men wept as they lamented what a terrible stroke of fate this was and how they hated to part. But Jidayū was on his way to the quayside, where he would board the next ship bound for Shikama and sail home on the evening tide.

♦ ♦ ♦

By now, the town was overrun with merchants from other domains, "hundreds of them"—even Jidayū noticed. Most samurai families would already have disposed of whatever belongings they intended to sell—even their horses, if any of them owned one—but the possessions of the domain itself were only now being put up for sale. These were the items that the biggest merchants had their eyes on. The weaponry inherited from the previous lords, the Ikeda, would of course remain with the castle; and the rice stored in the castle in case of siege would, by custom, be given to the daimyo charged with enforcing the confiscation, as token recompense for his expenditures and efforts. Any goods considered the property of the domain, however, they themselves were permitted to liquidate.

The castle's kitchen utensils had gone five days earlier, on the 22nd— the cooking pots, kettles, crocks, bowls, and the like. And on the day after Jidayū's departure, the weapons, armor, and saddlery were put out to tender. This must have been quite an arsenal, for Nozaki Rokudayū sent to Okayama a list of sixty-some major items—230 suits of lancer's armor, 150 lances, 8,000 arrows, 1,000 matchlock fuses, 126 musket cases, 20 saddles, and much, much more—all of which went to a single buyer, one Tachiya Shōbei from Osaka, who bid 15 *kan* in silver for the lot. It is interesting to note, however, that no muskets appear in Rokudayū's list; the Akō musketeers were allowed to keep the weapons they had been issued, an act of generosity that the authorities either failed to notice or decided to condone.

A few days later, seventeen of the domain's ships were sold to a "local buyer" for 17 *kan*. And another ship of 80 koku burden, less than three years old, and built of camphor laurel, went to another buyer for 2 *kan*, 4 or 5 *momme*. The same day, the Superintendent of Construction put his department's store of lumber and bamboo out to tender, and that was sold two days later, on the 4th, price unknown.

❖ ❖ ❖

It is not likely that these goods fetched anything like a fair market price; their buyers' only aim was to turn a quick profit. But the money raised was nonetheless a welcome windfall, for it allowed Kuranosuke to begin paying the vassals a severance allowance. Some of the senior officers had already taken their allowances in rice, but now the middling to lower ranks could be paid in cash—and the main house in Hiroshima could be told that there would be no need to borrow from it.

These severance allowances, too, had been a bone of contention between Kuranosuke and Kurōbei. The financial expert did not oppose such a disbursement, for he, too, would benefit from it, but he argued strongly that the allowance should be in direct proportion to the enfeoffment of the individual—perhaps as much as 24 *ryō* in gold per 100 koku of enfeoffment. Kuranosuke, however, felt that the lower in rank a man was, the greater a fraction of his stipend he should receive; this would not make any of them well off, but for the lowest it might at least make the difference between poverty and beggary. It took Hara Sōemon's implied threat of lethal violence to settle the argument. But once Kurōbei and his cohort had scurried from that room, the proportion could be reversed from direct to inverse.

Everyone enfeoffed at 500 koku or more would be given 10 *ryō* in gold per 100 koku of enfeoffment; those enfeoffed at 400 koku and below, 13, 15, or 18 *ryō*, depending upon the level of their income. Those lower still were paid at a flat rate ranging from 10 *ryō* for unmounted samurai to 3 *ryō* for musketeers and 2 *ryō* for lancers. Even at this reduced ratio, Kuranosuke still would have been entitled to 150 *ryō*; he declined to take any of it.

Ah, what unforeseen turns life can take!
Here I am strutting about just like a puppet in
one of those plays about the wars of ages past.

As we have seen, when Hayami Tōzaemon and Kayano Sanpei uncoiled themselves from their express conveyances at the Honjin in Fushimi, they had to linger a bit longer than usual, in order to write a brief summary of the bad tidings they bore, which Ōtsukaya Koemon, proprietor of the inn, then delivered to the Akō Liaison Officer in Kyoto. Koemon's messenger knew the route well: 2 leagues (5 miles, 8 kilometers) and a bit up the Fushimi Road; left at Gojō, across the bridge and into the city; four blocks straight west, then right on Mushanokōji; four blocks more to the north, then left on Bukkōji, the street named for the huge temple complex that occupied four full city blocks. There, opposite the far end of the temple wall, stood the modest gateway to the Kyoto residence of the Akō Liaison Officer, Onodera Jūnai. It was not an imposing structure; it did not even face the street, but was built on rented land that had once been the common courtyard of the houses that faced outward around the block.

◆ ◆ ◆

A Liaison Officer in Kyoto was nowhere near as consequential an official as a Liaison Officer in Edo. Indeed, many domains did not maintain a representative in the old capital. Some years earlier, however, the Asano cadet house had been granted the privilege of financing and supervising the construction of new ramparts at the Shogun's castle at Nijō in Kyoto. At the same time, partly as a necessity and partly as token recompense, Akō was granted permission to maintain a "Kyoto residence." This honor was not granted indiscriminately. Far too many disturbances of the peace had begun in the connivance of an ambitious warlord with greedy court nobles, who in return for promises of future consideration would intercede to obtain imperial "legitimation" for the depredations of their benefactors. The founder of the Tokugawa Shogunate knew the practice well and explicitly prohibited all daimyo from passing through the old capital on their journeys to and from Edo. Their route to the west could no longer lead through the Eastern Hills to the Third Avenue Bridge. They were now required to leave the Eastern Sea Road at Oiwake and veer southwest to Fushimi, which previously, except for a brief period of dominion as a castle town, had been notable mainly for its ancient shrine devoted to the Fox Deity and the more worldly entertainments that occupied pilgrims who were not at their devotions. Fushimi was now a center of strategic importance, where a Shogunal Magistrate, in command of a sizable force of men-at-arms, kept daily watch on the comings and goings in and about the town and reported anything he deemed either significant or suspicious directly to the Council of Elders.

◆ ◆ ◆

And so the duties of Akō's Liaison Officer in Kyoto were more those of a procurement officer than a diplomat. Jūnai would, of course, transmit any items of rumor or intelligence that might be of interest to domain officialdom. And he might occasionally be called upon to represent the domain if litigation involving its borders or its people should be brought before the court of the Shogunal Deputy for Kyoto. He would also oversee the exchange of silver from the sale of rice in Osaka for the gold coinage required in the east. But it was the perpetual round of gift giving, the indispensable lubricant of diplomacy in Edo, that loomed largest in Jūnai's attention. Despite the growth of the Shogun's capital over the previous century, Kyoto remained the center of the production of luxury goods—fine fabrics, brocades, clothing, ceramics, lacquerware, paintings, implements of the tea ceremony—a constant supply of which had to be selected, ordered, paid for, packaged, and transported. These were the tasks that constituted the main duties of Jūnai and his wife, O-Tan. And there could hardly have been a team better suited, both to their work and to the refined ambiance of the old capital, than this attractive, talented, and utterly devoted couple. Jūnai has been described as a living exemplar of the ideal of his age, a master of both literary and military arts. He was a gifted poet, a student and friend of the great Confucian scholars Itō Jinsai and his son Tōgai, and a deadly accomplished lancer—skills of which we shall see convincing evidence. O-Tan is described in even more extravagant terms by her poetry teacher Konze Keian, who thought her the "Murasaki Shikibu of our time," a woman whose talent ranked with that of the author of *The Tale of Genji*. How, we cannot but wonder, did such extraordinary people emerge from the ranks of a remote rural domain such as Akō? Of O-Tan's forebears we know almost nothing, but Jūnai's we can trace in some detail.

◆ ◆ ◆

Jūnai, as we shall see, never lost sight of his ancestral origins in the Onodera of Senboku in the northern province of Dewa. Like the Ōishi, this branch of the Fujiwara clan traced its origins to the near-legendary Hidesato; like many other local lords of long standing, they took their name from a village, Onodera, in the northeastern province of Shimotsuke, where they maintained a small fortress. And there they might have stayed, had not Onodera Zenji-no-Tarō, one of the first traceable Onodera ancestors, decided in 1180 to forsake his allegiance to the Heike, far off in the capital, and join forces with Minamoto no Yoritomo, who was raising an army in the Eastlands. In 1189, after fighting with apparent distinction the length and breadth of the land, the Onodera were rewarded with an appointment as Resident Intendants of the Okachi district in the Senboku region. Thenceforth, they no longer were mere local lords, but had become a regional power. And throughout that age of almost constant civil war, they continued to hold their own against the Tozawa and the Akita to the north, the Andō to the northwest, and, above all, the Mogami to the south.

Then, toward the end of the sixteenth century, it all fell apart. The last lord of Senboku, Onodera Tōtōmi-no-Kami Yoshimichi, in a series of schemes so asinine as to be almost unbelievable, set completely at naught the accomplishments of his long line of forebears. On the eve of the battle of Sekigahara, Yoshimichi pledged his support to Tokugawa Ieyasu. But when he heard that Ieyasu had appointed Mogami Yoshimitsu as leader of all forces in the north, Yoshimichi baulked at serving under his old enemy. In a fit of pique, he ignored Ieyasu's call to arms. He failed to see that this was not just another regional conflict, but a battle for national hegemony and that his inaction would place him on the side of the vanquished. By the time that fundamental fact dawned upon him, it was too late. Ieyasu had triumphed at Sekigahara. That portion of Senboku that the Onodera still possessed was declared forfeit, Yoshimichi was banished for life to the province of Iwami on a subsistence stipend of 300 koku, and there he remained until his death at the age of eighty.

Fortunately, this did not mean the total demise of the House of Onodera. The family tree had many branches, and Jūnai's branch had already departed Senboku. We catch sight of them sporadically—in the Eastlands, in Kyoto, in Ise. But it is not until the age of Jūnai's grandfather Jūdayū that the line of descent can be traced clearly and unbroken. During the battle of Sekigahara, Jūdayū had fought with Ieyasu's rearguard in the fortress at Anonotsu. They were vastly outnumbered, and their fort was razed, but they had accomplished their mission of delaying the enemy. Jūdayū must somehow have managed to escape, for when he next appears in the genealogical record, he has become a vassal of Asano Nagashige, first in Makabe and then in Nagashige's new domain in Kasama, where both lord and vassal died in 1632. His son Onodera Matahachi served the new Lord Naganao, first in Kasama, where Jūnai was born, and then in Akō. Thereafter, Matahachi was succeeded by his son, who by now was in his fortieth year and had assumed the name of his great-grandfather, Onodera Jūnai. As the third generation in an unbroken succession of service, it was Jūnai who established the Onodera as one of the few families of hereditary vassals of the House of Asano. And when we consider the folly that brought about the ruin of the once-great House of Onodera, we can see why Onodera Jūnai was so determined to bring honor not only to himself but to the clan as well.

✦ ✦ ✦

What Jūnai and O-Tan thought and did after receiving the messages forwarded from Fushimi is nowhere recorded. There would, of course, have been the initial shock, then the dreadful realization of what this meant in terms of their own lives, then the bewilderment about what they might do next, and finally the enormous effort to overcome the inertia of desolation and begin to carry on anew. The first hint of their feelings does not appear until five days later, when O-Tan wrote to her friend O-Riku, the wife of Ōishi Kuranosuke, partly on business but mostly about how the Catastrophe had affected her and her husband:

> *I have no idea whether this will ever reach you, but I shall write nonetheless. Are you well? What with everything that has happened, we are both utterly devastated. I'm so bewildered that I'm at a loss to do anything but weep. Yet when I think of all that has befallen His Lordship, it does at least make me forget that we may soon go hungry; already we're feeling the pinch. Before long, we shall have to start packing. Where will you go? I suppose you'll move to Himeji? We've decided we'll stay right here. Rather than rush off elsewhere, I think that for the time being we'll move somewhere in the lower part of Kyoto. Well, I'm sure you can imagine what a shock this has been. I expect it is the same for you.*
>
> ITEM. *I have received the 19 momme, 9 bu in silver to pay for the goods ordered. I shall send payment for the dyeing of the obi immediately. I went yesterday to pick them up. With all best wishes,*

> THIRD MONTH, 24TH DAY   *Jūnai, his wife*
> To: Ōishi Sama,
> The honored lady of his house

> *P.S. I can imagine only too well what tumult there must be. We've put most of our affairs in order here and dismissed some of the servants, but what a great pity it all is. I feel utterly helpless. Now that this has befallen us, I wonder if we shall ever see each other again. I am hoping that Chūzaemon Sama will come up to the capital. Please do*

keep me posted. If we were to go our separate ways and lose touch with each other, I should miss you more than ever. I write on the off-chance that this may reach you. Please give my best to the children and to the young master.

In the meantime, Jūnai seems to have decided that his duty was to return to Akō, report to the Chief Elder, Ōishi Kuranosuke, and stand ready to follow his orders. Since for a samurai, duty must take precedence over any personal or familial considerations, he told neither his wife nor his mother that he was leaving. One of his men is said to have suggested that he at least report his departure to the Shogunal Deputy in Kyoto, but Jūnai rejected his suggestion. "The Asano cadet house no longer exists," he said, "which means that I am no longer a Liaison Officer, and thus no longer under any obligation to the Kyoto Deputy. Besides, if I report my movements, I might then be commanded to stay put—which would render me useless in this emergency." His preparations were simple. He took only his armor and helmet, a lance, and a change of clothing. I presume that his manservant, Kyūemon, went with him to bear the load. When he left Kyoto is not recorded, but he himself reports that he arrived in Akō on the 3rd Day of the Fourth Month. The two cities are 41 leagues apart, about 100 miles (160 kilometers) in modern measure. Jūnai could walk no faster than whoever was carrying his luggage trunk; to arrive on the 3rd, he probably would have left Kyoto on the 1st. On the 7th, four days after his arrival, he wrote to his cousin Onodera Jūbei, a Deputy in the office of the City Magistrate of Kyoto:

Item. With this letter, I send you my most respectful greetings. I've heard from no one since my departure. Is all well with you there?

Item. I expect that you will have heard what has happened here from others in neighboring provinces. Rumor must be rife in the capital as well. Since by now this is fait accompli, I see no reason to keep any deep secrets from you; still, it may be best not to mention any of this to others.

Item. *Having heard that Kōzuke-no-Suke Dono is still alive, these stubborn rustic warriors, whose only thought is for their liege lord, refuse to accept that there might be some justification for the way His Lordship's case was handled. Nor will they agree, under any circumstances, to surrender the castle and disperse. And so the house Elders have dispatched two emissaries—Tagawa Kuzaemon and Tsukioka Jiemon—to explain this situation to the Inspectors in Edo. They did not go so far as to demand that Kōzuke-no-Suke Dono be commanded to commit seppuku, but requested only that the authorities provide us with some rationale that might persuade the samurai of this house to cooperate. If this is forthcoming, I understand, the Elders will then command the men to obey. We expect these two men to arrive in Edo on the 5th of this month and to return as soon as possible thereafter. . . .*

Item. *I arrived here on the evening of the 3rd. I then went directly to Kuranosuke's home and spoke to him personally. "I am of low rank," I told him, "but our family has been a beneficiary of this noble house for over a hundred years. If there is any plan of action you are determined upon, kindly allow me to offer you my humble participation in it, whatever it may be." He accepted. That same day, the Samurai Commander Okuno Shōgen and one or two of the Vanguard Commanders had come to his residence to offer the same. Apparently, several others of like mind have come to Kuranosuke to make similar offers.*

Such has been Kuranosuke's performance that the entire Corps of Vassals is deeply impressed. They seem to place themselves entirely at his disposal. Even the young men show not the slightest resistance, but come every day, all day, to the castle, where they do whatever they are told without the least complaint and do their work with great dispatch.

My, but these are strange times that have been visited upon us, and this a strange letter that I write to you. Although I tell you that all of us, high and low, feel this way simply because we have heard that Kōzuke-no-Suke Dono still lives, it may nonetheless sound as though, in our zeal, we denigrate the Shogunate. A favorable response from the authorities would put a stop to all of this, but every one of us has come equipped with a full suit of armor, a lance, and a change of clothes, including a white robe, in our luggage trunks. I've not told my aged mother and my wife what I intend to do. They may well know, of course, from all that they see. But if I should die in the course of what goes on here, I beg your kind assistance on their behalf. I leave everything in your hands.

ITEM. *We bear no malice whatever toward the Shogunate. It is not as some worm that cannot bear to give up the tiny hole he inhabits that we defend this castle. Neither have we any quarrel with Wakizaka Dono. It is simply that each and every one of us is prepared to die in this castle. If my wife thinks of sending someone to plead with me, though I hate to trouble you, I would ask that you read this letter to her with care. She is not the sort of woman to be excessively alarmed by such things; that I know, so please tell her exactly what I say. I ask this because I would feel very bad if she were later to feel any resentment toward me.*

Herewith these faltering words, written hastily in the dead of night. To be burnt upon reading.

FOURTH MONTH, 7TH DAY   *Onodera Jūnai*
To: Onodera Jūbei Sama

P.S. Concerning our family's honor, you may rest assured that I shall do nothing to demean the good name of this house.

O-Tan certainly did deduce what Jūnai was up to "from all that she could see," for she wrote to him on both the 6th and the 7th, even before Jūnai had written to his cousin Jūbei. Unfortunately, neither these nor any other of her letters to him survive; Jūnai simply was in no position to preserve them. But O-Tan did keep Jūnai's reply, and this does survive:

Your letters of the 6th and the 7th arrived together last night. I was pleased to hear that Mother is getting on well. Please take special care to serve her tasty meals morning and evening. I was particularly pleased to hear that all is well with you and O-Iyo. I daresay events here must be very worrying for you. I can understand only too well how you must feel.

Item. *Kuzaemon and Jiemon are expected to return from Edo within a day or two. It looks as though our next move will depend upon whatever news they bring. As for myself? Our family, as you know, though low in rank, has lived comfortably for the past hundred years on the beneficence of Their Lordships. For the present Takumi Dono, I feel no particular affection, but I do feel that it is my duty to repay our debt of the past hundred years to this line of lords. My efforts may count for little, but there are many branches of the House of Onodera throughout this land of Japan. Were I not to act with resolve at a time like this, it would disgrace our own family and besmirch the good name of the entire clan. I am determined, therefore, that when the time comes, I shall die with dignity. It is not that I forget my aged mother or that I do not cherish my wife and children; it is simply that I must give up my life to do my duty as a warrior. I trust that I can count on you to understand that this duty is ineluctable and that you are not to grieve for me. Mother hasn't much longer to live; I hope that whatever happens, I shall be able to see her through to the end. And after all these years that you have looked after me, I'm not the slightest bit worried that you could go wrong. I know there's no need even to mention this, but—please do take care of everything and everyone after I am gone. What little money and what few possessions we have will not last indefinitely. There is Mother to look after; and if you should live to an old age, your resources may well run out, and then you shall die of starvation. That, too, is ineluctable. O-Iyo is betrothed, but again and again we have put off the marriage, thinking that there would be time enough after she recovered from her illness—and now this has happened, and she remains unmarried. We hardly dare say, "Well here she is, marry her now"; nor is the other party likely to volunteer to have her. She shall just have to survive as best she can with you and spend her days watching the world go by.*

Item. *Ah, what unforeseen turns life can take! Here I am strutting about just like a puppet in one of those plays about the wars of ages past. Now that my own life has become as precarious as the flame of a lamp in the wind, or a dewdrop about to fall from the tip of a leaf, I haven't a thought for any of the things I once desired so deeply. My mind has become as pure as ice. This disaster has at least freed me from the grip of worldly ambition.*

Item. *Even knowing that Kuzaemon and Jiemon will soon return, I can't begin to predict how sympathetic to our cause the present regime is likely to be. If they temporize, the vassals are not likely to accept it. I doubt that things will go as we would wish. One way or another, we shall end up dying. Or is it just possible—that one chance in a million—that I might survive and be able to see you again?*

Item. *It distresses me every time I think how difficult it will be for you, as a woman, to find a place where you can live. It would be best, I think, if you were to place yourself in the hands of friends who are sympathetic to your problem. . . .*

Item. *Please give my very best regards to Keian Dono. I haven't been in touch with him, as this is no time to be sending letters off hither and yon. Be sure to discuss matters with him and follow his advice.*

Item. *They say that the Inspectors are to arrive on the 13th. The castle is to be surrendered on the 18th. These dates may be altered one way or the other.*

Item. *I am sending you 10 ryō in gold pieces. Please accept it. Chōbei has come to the castle to fetch his daughter, and I've asked him to take it to you. It is to help you make ends meet. I'll send you more later. I don't need even a single copper here. I know there's no need to say this, but you mustn't trust anyone with even the smallest sum of money. If you once let this out of your own hands, you'll have nothing whatever to live on. You must be absolutely firm in this. The other things I'm sending are as in the attached note. I ask all of the same of O-Iyo. Respectfully,*

FOURTH MONTH, 10TH DAY   *Jūnai*
To: O-Tan Dono

*P.S. I have received various things that you sent. Tell Hanzaburō
and Roku that I ask them to serve you well.*

These are long letters, but worth reading in their entirety, for their
author was one of the most intelligent and thoughtful of the Akō ronin,
and the scenes and states of mind he describes are far more nuanced
than those found in other sources. It is telling, too, that once they knew
for certain that Kira lived and a date had been set for the surrender
of the castle, Jūnai remained pessimistic that the surrender would be
accomplished without a fight to the death.

Even so, when he placed himself at Kuranosuke's disposal,
Kuranosuke immediately decided that the Liaison Officer from Kyoto
should serve as a Liaison Officer in Akō; thenceforth, Jūnai was to
handle all relations between the domain and the Inspectors who would
supervise the surrender of castle and lands, the Deputies who would
govern the domain during the interregnum, and the several emissaries
sent by their Asano kinsmen. His first task would be to find and furnish
accommodation for these men before they arrived—despite his convic-
tion that none of this would take place peacefully.

CHAPTER 25

*I appreciate the purport of your command,
but I cannot guarantee our compliance.*

Onodera Jūnai was no alarmist. The extreme pessimism that permeates his letter to O-Tan is genuine, but there was little evidence of it when he wrote to his cousin Jūbei three days earlier. Something seems to have happened in that interval that made a deep impression on Jūnai. I suspect that it was the arrival of a delegation dispatched from Edo by Asano Aki-no-Kami Tsunanaga, lord of the Asano main house in Hiroshima.

When rumors of a movement to defend Akō Castle against confiscation reached Edo, the Council of Elders was quick to act. The Elders knew full well that the case of Takumi-no-Kami had been judged unfairly; they also knew that there was no reversing that judgment. And so the closest relatives of Takumi-no-Kami—Toda Uneme-no-Kami and Asano Aki-no-Kami—were warned that this rebellion must *not* take place; both houses knew that if they failed to prevent it, the consequences for themselves would be severe, perhaps even disastrous.

The Toda had already sent a delegation, from Edo via Ōgaki, led by Toda Gonzaemon, with a suite of thirty-three attendants of various ranks. But on the 9th, the day before Jūnai wrote to his wife, a much grander entourage arrived—more than a hundred men, perhaps many more—led by Inoue Dan'emon, Adjutant to Asano Aki-no-Kami. Dan'emon went first to the lodgings of the Toda delegation, where Gonzaemon assured him that they had been well received by the command group in Akō, their only cause for concern being that Uneme-no-Kami had ordered the Akō samurai to vacate their homes by the 15th, but so far there had been no sign of any movement. Dan'emon then proceeded to his own lodgings, whither he summoned Kuranosuke and six other senior officers. As the domain's official host to both delegations, Jūnai may have been present at the first meeting, and he almost certainly was at the second.

Dan'emon's report of his colloquy with Kuranosuke survives: he first assured the Akō samurai that Aki-no-Kami could understand only too well how distressed they must feel at the consequences of their lord's thoughtless transgression, but that until the officials appointed to take possession of the domain arrived, everyone was to behave with due propriety, and that they were then to surrender the castle and lands immediately and without resistance.

Kuranosuke replied, "We are very grateful for His Lordship's kind consideration, and we appreciate fully the purport of his command. We have already received a number of messengers from Uneme-no-Kami Dono, who has kindly sent written instructions with them as well. Asano Tosa-no-Kami Sama, too, has dispatched two envoys from Miyoshi, Tokunaga Mataemon and Uchida Magoemon, both bearing written instructions. All of them command us, just as Aki-no-Kami Sama does, to remain calm and behave with due propriety. And so when I say *only* that I appreciate the purport of His Lordship's command, that is because at first we did not know whether Kōzuke-no-Suke Dono was alive or dead. But when we looked into the matter, we learnt not only that he was alive and well, but that his wounds were healing rapidly. The young samurai of this domain, rough rustics that they are, find this unacceptable and will not listen to reason. We have therefore sent two of our Company Commanders, Tagawa Kuzaemon and Tsukioka Jiemon, to Uneme-no-Kami Dono, traveling night and day, in the hope that they may be vouchsafed some rationale that will persuade our men to obey our orders. We have also told our emissaries that they should call on the Inspectors who will be coming here and ask the same of them—even if they should encounter them only en route. And thus, until our men return, I cannot guarantee our compliance with His Lordship's command.

Dan'emon responded, "I understand your situation entirely, and I expect that when Uneme-no-Kami takes up your request with the

Inspectors, they will issue instructions of some sort. But what concerns Aki-no-Kami just now is this: if the surrender of the castle is delayed, this will seem an affront to authority; and still worse, evidence of strong hostility in the aftermath of Takumi-no-Kami Sama's death, which could be disastrous for every branch of this house. Such hostility would seem the ultimate in bad faith and disloyalty. Once again, I would remind you: Takumi-no-Kami Sama behaved with utter disregard for his presence in the palace and the augustness of the occasion, for which he was punished in strict accord with the law of the land. Concerning this, there can be no argument. Still, if by some chance surrender of the castle is to be delayed, and you plan to act as you contemplate, then please do keep us advised of your intentions. This is what we would ask of you."

Kuranosuke said, "I appreciate greatly your meticulous explanation of His Lordship's concerns, and I shall transmit them to the others."

It is not hard to see why such a conversation should dampen any hopes that Jūnai may have had for a peaceful resolution to this impasse. Neither Dan'emon nor Kuranosuke uttered a single uncivil word, and I doubt that either even raised his voice; yet neither retreated even slightly from his initial position.

◆ ◆ ◆

And if this were not enough, on the same day four samurai from Tatsuno, leading a detail of about thirty men, came into town and, uninvited, entered and inspected the homes of several townsmen. The domain of Tatsuno had given no notice of this intrusion, much less requested permission. They had simply taken it for granted that their appointment as enforcers of the confiscation of the domain was license to do as they pleased. The Okayama agent who reported this incident noted that Kuranosuke was infuriated, but he did not know what ensued thereafter. Much worse was soon to come.

◆ ◆ ◆

Two days later, on the morning of the 11th, the two men whose return from Edo everyone had so anxiously awaited, Tagawa Kuzaemon and Tsukioka Jiemon, arrived back in Akō. They had made the round trip in good time, but had completely botched their mission. The letter that Kuranosuke had so carefully crafted was never seen by the Inspectors to whom it was addressed. The Inspectors had left on the morning of the 2nd; Tagawa and Tsukioka had arrived in Edo late at night on the 4th. They must have passed each other on the road sometime on the 3rd, probably in the vicinity of Fujisawa. Tagawa and Tsukioka had been warned that they might cross paths, and if they did they should present their letter then and there, on the road; but deprived of sleep for four straight days, they probably had not been alert enough to recognize the Inspectors' entourage.

What happened when they reached Edo is not entirely clear. Both Muro Kyūsō and Horibe Yasubei maintain that before Tagawa and Tsukioka left Akō, they were instructed *not* to inform either of the Edo Elders of their mission. Yet where else could they have gone when they arrived in the small hours of the morning? What they seem to have done is gone straight to Iida-machi, just a short walk from the old Asano Upper Mansion, to the home of Yasui Hikoemon, the former Edo Elder of the Akō domain. Hikoemon, in turn, decided that this was a matter of sufficient importance to be taken to Toda Uneme-no-Kami's Elder in Edo, which is exactly what they had been commanded to do in the first place. What Kuranosuke intended, of course, was that Uneme-no-Kami would then arrange for them to meet with the Inspectors to whom they would present their letter, and that the intercession of a daimyo, presumably, would strengthen their appeal. Just when they learned that the Inspectors had already left Edo is not known. But neither does it matter, for it appears that Uneme-no-Kami was so appalled by the contents of the letter that he probably would never have permitted it to be taken to the Inspectors. "There is no need for you to appeal to the Inspectors," Toda's Elder told them. "If you do, they are certain to report it to their superiors, and that could work to the disadvantage of Daigaku Dono." Instead, Tagawa and Tsukioka were sent back to Akō with the following letter and a memorandum of some strongly worded warnings to be delivered verbally:

> *According to the letter sent hither with Tagawa Kuzaemon and Tsukioka Jiemon, the vassals of your house are crude rustics who*

have no appreciation of the situation here in Edo. As each and every one of you knows, however, Takumi always fulfilled his duties with the greatest respect for officialdom. It is thus as a duty to their lord that Takumi's vassals must vacate the domain with all speed, surrender the castle without delay, and do so in a manner that accords with Takumi's own unswerving attitude of respect for authority. Needless to say, it is a matter of supreme importance that you obey all subsequent directives, and that you withdraw speedily and peacefully. The foregoing is to be understood and complied with by the entire Corps of Vassals.

YEAR OF THE SERPENT, FOURTH MONTH, 5TH DAY

Toda Uneme no Kami [sealed in black]

To: Asano Takumi, his
Elders
Samurai Commanders
Adjutants
Inspectors
Corps of Vassals

P.S. The foregoing matters were explained at the outset to those vassals stationed here in Edo.

The letter itself contains nothing new. As Uneme-no-Kami himself says, he has already said the same to the vassals in Edo. And in Akō, any number of couriers had come, carrying much the same message. What *was* new, however, was a brief sentence in Uneme-no-Kami's verbal instructions, delivered by his intermediary Nakagawa Jingobei when he handed the letter to Tagawa and Tsukioka. Jingobei told them: "Uneme Dono is being held responsible for you. But if the castle is surrendered, he will not be considered culpable. So you must not ignore the instructions that Uneme-no-Kami Dono has been at such pains to convey to you."

Which is to say that if the castle should *not* be surrendered, the Shogunate will consider Uneme-no-Kami at fault—which for a major daimyo could be disastrous. As we shall see, this stricture carried great weight.

✦ ✦ ✦

Almost two years later, some of the men who were present described the return of Tagawa and Tsukioka in almost precisely the same terms. They quoted the letter almost verbatim and gave particular emphasis to Uneme-no-Kami's warning that he was "being held responsible for you." And then they went a step further and told us what happened next:

> When Tagawa and Tsukioka told him their verbal orders, Kuranosuke was left with no other choice. He summoned the fifty-four men who had signed the pact and asked their opinions. They all agreed that the situation was hopeless, and replied that they would now do whatever Kuranosuke thought best. And thus it was decided that they would vacate their homes and surrender the castle.

But who were these fifty-four men, and what was this pact they had signed? And *now*—are they just giving up? Or do they have something more in mind? Something beyond vacating their homes and surrendering the castle? The undercover agents from Okayama may help us answer these questions.

Should a man
take his own life.

On the 12th Day of the Fourth Month, an undercover agent in Akō, Nozaki Rokudayū, sent the following report to his superiors in Okayama:

Item. On the 11th, Ōishi Kuranosuke came to the castle and summoned the Samurai Commanders, Company Commanders, and other senior samurai, to whom he said: "I have resolved that when the envoys arrive, I shall explain to them our griev- ances, then commit hara-kiri, and die. Those of you who are of like mind, I would ask to sign this with your monogram. Those of you who do not agree are free to do as you please." Kuranosuke then produced a Go'ō Hōin, which he signed and sealed with the blood print of this thumb, and then passed it to the others. Okuno Shōgen then said, "I agree completely," and immediately signed with his monogram. Thereafter, five more men—Shindō Genshirō, Oyama Gengozaemon, Hara Sōemon, Kawamura Denbei, and Miki Dan'emon—all signed in succession. Kuranosuke then asked, "Would you now discuss this with the men under your command, and if any of them are of like mind, ask them to affix their mono- grams to this document." Those who signed were later called to the castle, and Kuranosuke said to them, "Very well! Now we shall all die together." In total, twenty-nine men signed. A separate list of their names is attached.

Item. After the completion of this pledge, Tsukioka Jiemon, Tagawa Kuzaemon, Tanaka Gon'emon, and Yamamoto Sarokurō arrived back in Akō by express conveyance bearing letters from Asano Aki-no-Kami and Toda Uneme-no-Kami that they handed over to Kuranosuke and that commanded that the castle be surrendered without objection, warned that any unruly behavior would be damaging to the cause of Asano Daigaku Dono, and noted several other ways in which an attitude of loyalty was called for. Kuranosuke then called the samurai who had signed the aforementioned pledge to his home, and showed them the letters he had received from Aki-no-Kami Dono and Uneme-no-Kami Dono; following a discussion of the matter, they decided to surrender the castle.

The above is what I have heard. Herewith the foregoing.

FOURTH MONTH, 12TH DAY   *Nozaki Rokudayū*

To: Tsuda Sagenta Sama

Fujioka Kan'emon Sama

I know that to many of my friends, this seems a totally futile gesture, a meaningless and useless waste of life. But to Kuranosuke and his comrades, it was nothing of the sort. To them, it made perfect sense, for in their day, suicide was still regarded as an extreme but effective means of revenge. The principle had been articulated clearly and unequivocally more than 150 years earlier by Daté Tanemune: "Should a man take his own life, leaving behind a statement of his grievance, the enemy named in his posthumous statement shall himself be put to death."

◆ ◆ ◆

This is precisely what Kuranosuke proposed to do. When the Inspectors from Edo arrived in Akō, he would give them a copy of the letter that Tagawa and Tsukioka should have shown them and explain its contents verbally, noting in particular that under the Principle of Equal Punishment, Kira should have been sentenced to death along with Takumi-no-Kami. What his emissaries failed to do, Kuranosuke himself would do. Then, after the peaceful surrender of the castle, should the Inspectors offer them no satisfaction of their grievance, the signatories to the pact would commit seppuku—and hope that then the Shogunate would be forced to honor its obligation to execute Kira

Kōzuke-no-Suke.

A solution to the problem of Kira's survival was now in place. Time would tell whether it would be necessary to resort to it. In the meantime, the surrender of the castle could be guaranteed; and the remainder of the plan need be mentioned to no one not already a party to it. Kuranosuke wrote to Uneme-no-Kami's Elder in Edo:

> *With this missive, we tender you our most respectful greetings. Concerning the surrender of the castle: we are humbly in receipt of the letter kindly sent to us by Uneme-no-Kami Sama and carried hither by Tanaka Gon'emon, Tagawa Kuzaemon, and Tsukioka Jiemon, and also the subsequent letter presented to us by Toda Gonzaemon Dono. We are most grateful that you have taken so much trouble to convey your commands to us, and we hereby agree to abide by them; likewise do we agree with all respect to abide by the verbal commands conveyed to us by Kuzaemon and Jiemon. We have explained these in full detail to the Corp of Vassals, who agree to obey and to disperse. Very shortly, we shall, as commanded, surrender the castle. We have already communicated our acceptance to Toda Gonzaemon Dono, but we beg your kind intercession on our behalf whenever it may be convenient for you. With all due respect,*

FOURTH MONTH, 12TH DAY   *Ōno Kurōbei [monogram]*

                                     Ōishi Kuranosuke [monogram]

To: Nakagawa Jingobei,
via his entourage

Officially, Ōno Kurōbei was still an Elder of the House of Asano. But ever since he had been shamed into fleeing from the discussion of severance allowances, Kurōbei's word had carried no weight in deliberations of domain policy. He must have burnt inwardly with resentment, and particularly toward Hara Sōemon. Alas, resentment proved the undoing of him. Once the Akō Currency Exchange had completed the redemption of the domain's paper money, it became clear that a few of those employed in the process had been unable to resist helping themselves to some of the silver they were handling. This revelation was too great a temptation for Kurōbei. The Officer in Charge of the Currency Exchange was Okajima Yasoemon, the younger brother of Kurōbei's nemesis Hara Sōemon. Kurōbei should have remained discreetly silent, but instead he went about defaming Yasoemon for having failed to prevent this misappropriation, suggesting even that he might be "one more fox from the same hole." This was an insult that no samurai could abide, and word of it soon reached Yasoemon. His response was entirely predictable.

On the evening of the same day—probably the 12th—Yasoemon announced himself at the gate to the Ōno residence and demanded to speak with Kurōbei. No one acknowledged his presence or opened the gate. And so Yasoemon took it upon himself to force open the wicket and proceed to the doorway that opened into the family's sitting room. There, again, he announced himself: "I have business with the man, and I wish to see him." And again, he was denied entry. "What does this mean?" he demanded. "I have come because I have business with the man concerning which I must see him, and I'll not leave until I do." A voice from within offered various excuses, finally claiming that Kurōbei had gone to the home of his younger brother. This may well have been true. He could easily have slipped out from a rear gate and made his way across the moat to his brother's place while Yasoemon was still at the front of the house. Yasoemon was not going to force his way into another man's home, but before he left, he made sure that there could be no doubt why he was there: "At the castle today, Kurōbei Dono claimed that I have misappropriated funds from the Currency Exchange. This is the reason I have come here. So make sure that he understands this."

At this point in the story, the facts of the matter grow scarce. Too much happened too fast, and those concerned wanted none of it to be known. All we can say for certain is that Ōno Kurōbei feared for his life, and for that reason, he fled in the night. Whether in women's palanquins or by boat from a jetty at the rear of the house, he and his son Gun'emon absconded to Shinhama at the tip of the point on the far shore of the Great River. In their haste, they either forgot, or purposely left behind, Gun'emon's baby daughter. The usual explanation is that they were afraid that the child would cry and give them away. But whatever the truth of the matter, the little girl was left behind with her nursemaid, who had no idea what to do with her. I don't think that anyone knows what eventually became of her.

The next day, Kurōbei wrote, not to Kuranosuke but to an unnamed staff officer, to report that he had suddenly fallen seriously ill and had retreated to a "nearby village" to recuperate. His "recuperation" regimen was to take passage in a ship sailing from Shinhama, bound for the Kyoto region.

Kuranosuke would surely have been relieved to be rid of this thorn in his side. Kurōbei's flight was nonetheless a criminal offense that he had to deal with according to proper procedures. The Inspectors from Edo, who would soon be lodged in the village of Ikaruga, had to be informed and asked to approve the appointment of a new Elder to take the place of Kurōbei. The Inspectors, of course, approved, and Okuno Shōgen was appointed to fill the opening. Shōgen was a natural choice. He was a Samurai Commander descended from one of the oldest families of Akō vassals, and he was enfeoffed at 1,000 *koku*. Just as important, however, he was the only man of that rank to side with Kuranosuke; all the others had been supporters of Kurōbei. Kuranosuke could now count on his second-in-command to work with him rather than against him.

Kuranosuke also sent Kataoka Gengoemon to the home of Kurōbei's younger brother Itō Goemon, first to ask where Kurōbei had gone, and then to request that he inform his brother that he would be in breach of the law should he leave the domain without permission prior to the surrender of the castle. For an ordinary samurai, this would pose no problem; but for an Elder of the house, responsible for the fulfillment of countless duties and obligations to the authorities, his departure was a serious offense. Goemon, of course, professed total ignorance of his brother's intentions, movements, or whereabouts. There was no point in pressing the man further, but Gengoemon felt confident that his message would make its way to Kurōbei before too long.

Finally, there were the contents of the house from which Kurōbei and his son were soon to be evicted. They had already arranged for their possessions to be put in storage with two Akō merchants, Ōtsuya Jūemon and Kiya Shōbei. Kuranosuke did not interfere with these arrangements, but he assigned a detail of foot soldiers to stand guard over the goods—particularly, the weapons and other military gear—to prevent pilferage; once everything was safely locked away, he had it impounded as the property of a fugitive, not to be released without official permission.

The 12th had been a busy day in Akō, full of unexpected events and a major shift in the structure of power within the domain. As the Corps of Vassals prepared to disperse, however, Kurōbei's name quickly disappeared from recorded discourse, and we hear nothing more of him until months later.

CHAPTER
27

*I no longer have the
authority to punish them.*

Ōno Kurōbei was not the only miscreant who had to be dealt with in
the last days of the Akō Corps of Vassals, and the quality of justice
meted out was, to say the least, uneven.

The best known case is that of the Hagiwara brothers, Hyōsuke
and Gizaemon, who were enfeoffed at 150 and 100 koku, respectively,
but were known to possess considerable independent means. In short,
they were two of a very rare breed, wealthy samurai. What the source of
their wealth was is not known, but among their possessions were two
large cannon, probably handed down in the family since the wars of
ages past, but a major burden to a family about to be evicted and forced
to move. The Hagiwara brothers made a perfectly reasonable decision:
they would sell their cannon. The sale probably would have attracted no
more attention than the sale of a horse or a suit of armor—except that
their buyer turned out to be no other than Wakizaka Awaji-no-Kami,
lord of the neighboring domain of Tatsuno, who had been assigned to
enforce the confiscation of the castle and lands of Takumi-no-Kami. To
some of the hot-headed young samurai in Akō, this was tantamount to
selling arms to the enemy. What the brothers had done was certainly no
crime; it wasn't even mildly immoral; it was just bad judgment. But the
foot soldiers of the domain (of all people) were determined to punish
them as traitors. They would wait until the hundredth-day obsequies
for Takumi-no-Kami to be held at the Asano family temple, Kagakuji.
The Hagiwara were certain to be in town for that event, at which time
the foot soldiers would seize Hyōsuke and Gizaemon, strip them naked,

batter them to death with staves (so as not to sully their swords on such scum), and make off with whatever of their worldly goods they could lay their hands on. To Kuranosuke, this seemed a classic case of making a mountain of a molehill. He secretly summoned Hyōsuke and Gizaemon to his home, escorted them to Shinhama, and helped them to escape by ship. And thereafter, he gave strict orders to the young samurai and foot soldiers that there was to be no more nonsense of this sort.

And then there was the Tea Monk in charge of the supply room in Edo, Taguchi Sōen, who for years had been enriching himself from the procurement of candles and writing paper, and now had decided to come to Akō to see what he might accomplish there. His reputation had preceded him, however, and when Ōtaka Gengo, leading a detail of five foot soldiers, encountered Sōen wandering about in the castle, he asked him what he might be doing there. "I've just come from Edo," Sōen replied. "I just had to have one last look at the castle." The foot soldiers knew what to make of this. "Good-for-nothing wretch," they said, and then seized him and extracted his paper fold from within his robe. When they opened it, they found that it contained five gold pieces. Five soldiers, five gold pieces. They took one each and sent Sōen fleeing from the domain.

◆ ◆ ◆

But it was the villagers, the peasants who labored to produce the bulk of the wealth of the domain, yet were allowed to keep so little of it, who were most in need of justice. For these people, who could never legally leave their villages, this was a moment to be seized, a rare chance for the settling of old scores. And given the way villages were governed in the Genroku era, their grievances were most likely to be with their village Headman or with the Rural Overseer who supervised a network of village Headmen. For as long as there were no disturbances of the peace or open acts of rebellion, officialdom in Akō was content to leave governance of the countryside to these Headmen. A few samurai were stationed in strategic locations, mostly to keep an eye on the progress of the rice crop and to estimate the yield upon which the rate of taxation for the current year would be based. Once that rate was established, it was up to the Headman to collect the stipulated amount from the peasants of his village and deliver it to the storehouses in the castle town. This made the Headman the most powerful figure in any peasant's life. A benevolent Headman could negotiate a rate of taxation that would keep the villagers from the brink of starvation for the coming year; a greedy one could connive to predict an unrealistic level of yield, to the distress of the villagers, but to the benefit of domain officials—and himself. A benevolent Headman could lend a peasant the cash he needed, on favorable terms, to buy seed rice after a bad year; a selfish one could foreclose an unpaid loan and take the peasant's fields as his own. A very benevolent Headman might even teach the children of his village to read and write; but, alas, Headmen of *this* sort were in very short supply.

And so there came a daily stream of peasants to the office of Sassa Kozaemon, the District Deputy, most of whom were there to lodge complaints against the abuses of their Headmen. Now, they seemed to think, they could hope to obtain the justice that they had been loath to sue for while the old powers remained in control.

From Uné, the villagers brought two Rural Overseers, Yasobei and Moemon, securely bound and quite literally in tow. For years, the farmers claimed, these two had been "fattening their own bellies" by skimming the rice they claimed to be submitting as taxes. Sassa Kozaemon examined the evidence, interrogated the suspects, and came to the conclusion that they were indeed guilty as charged. "But as an outgoing official," he told the villagers, "I no longer have the authority to punish them. You'll just have to deal with them yourselves, as you see fit." Yasobei and Moemon were lucky. They were driven from their villages with a warning never to show their faces there again on pain of death.

Elsewhere, the villagers did not even bother to seek official justice. In the northern reaches of the domain, 10 leagues (25 miles, 40 kilometers) from the castle, there stood a string of five villages in a long valley presided over by Yashiro Magobei, the Rural Overseer in Akamatsu. This man had been in the habit of adding a surcharge of a measure and a half on every koku of tax rice. But contrary to what he claimed, this surcharge was never passed on to the domain; he kept it for himself. The peasants decided that the time had come to pay themselves back. They took possession of their Overseer's fields, and then broke into his house and looted it. What might have happened next we shall never know, for at that point Magobei set fire to his house, slit open his belly with a sword, and died in a pool of his own blood as the flames rose around him and his entire family.

And so it went throughout the domain. Across the river, in the salt flats, three Headmen—Matashirō, Chōzaemon, and Shōemon—had been embezzling funds that they claimed to have given out in loans. In Osaki, two Headmen and an Elder of the village were driven out by the peasants. In Shinden, it was Matabei and in Hongō it was Rokurōemon who were sent packing. In Higashi-Uné, Yosozaemon drowned himself in the Nachi River before the peasants could lay hands on him. In the far northern district of Sayo, Hikozaemon took his own life when he saw that the peasants were heading toward his home.

For a time, it must have seemed that there was some justice in the world, some hope for a better life under a new lord. A futile hope no doubt, but at least the peasants managed to rid themselves of some old evils before any new ones could be inflicted upon them.

CHAPTER
28

Won't you, just this once, trust me?
I promise that I won't let you down.

Akō, Fourth Month, 14th Day

Precisely one month had passed, almost to the hour, since the death of Asano Takumi-no-Kami. The sun had only just dropped beneath the rim of the hills that lay to the west of Akō, separating it from the neighboring domain of Okayama. As the three travelers emerged from the last turn of Takatori Pass, there was still enough light to see the whole of the narrow plain below and the river that wound through it down to the castle that was their destination. It would not have been a familiar sight to any of them. None of them had been born to the service of Takumi-no-Kami; none of them had ever lived here. Horibe Yasubei, Takada Gunbei, and Okuda Magodayū were new men and had been stationed permanently in Edo from the time they had joined the Asano Corps of Vassals.

A month earlier, the farmers who were gathering up their tools and baskets at the end of the day might have paused to wonder who these travelers might be. Now they took no notice; there had been a constant stream of unfamiliar faces on the road that skirted their fields this past month. In the meantime, there was the barley to be brought in and paddies to be tilled, repaired, and filled with water in time for planting in just a few days; a new lord in the castle would change none of *that*. The three men hurried past and soon were but small figures in the distance, nearing the river crossing at the Turtle's Shell.

The journey from Edo to Akō normally took seventeen days. Yasubei, Gunbei, and Magodayū had covered the distance in ten. They were weary from long days on the road. They were unkempt, and their clothes were soiled. But they did not pause to look for lodging. They went directly to the home of Ōishi Kuranosuke. And even though they had arrived unannounced—and this was the last night that Kuranosuke would sleep in his home—he had them ushered into his reception room and came out to meet them immediately. Yasubei's greetings were minimal; he came directly to the point of their visit: "As long as Kōzuke-no-Suke is alive, we shall never dare show our faces again if we abandon this castle. We've only one choice now: we must defend it to the death, and die with its timbers as our pillow."

Kuranosuke listened attentively to all their arguments and allowed them to present their case in full before saying anything against it. He knew from the start, however, what his response would be: "As you may know, there are those of us here who agree that justice must be done, and we've discussed the matter among ourselves at some length. We sent Tagawa Kuzaemon and Tsukioka Jiemon with a letter of entreaty to the Inspectors. But the Inspectors had already left Edo, so they went straight to Yasui Hikoemon and Fujii Hikoshirō and told them everything. Those two, in turn, told Uneme-no-Kami Dono and Daigaku Dono, and the next thing we knew we were inundated with letters from both, commanding us to surrender the castle in good order. We told Tagawa and Tsukioka before they left that they weren't to breathe a word of this to the Elders in Edo. But now that they've spread it about, we don't dare defend the castle. The Edo Elders are in constant touch with Daigaku Dono; to the Military Tribunal, it would look as though we did it on his orders. And that would be the end of him; it might even mean the end of the Asano cadet line as a whole. For which we would be guilty of gross disloyalty. But if we forgo defending the castle, he may yet be reinstated. So we've decided that we'll not defend the castle; instead, we'll surrender it without protest, and then wait to see whether they restore him to a position of honor."

Yasubei and his comrades could not even consider accepting this argument: "There is no way that we can do that! We simply cannot give up the castle while Kōzuke-no-Suke Dono is still alive. How could we look anyone in the face, anywhere, while we can still see the enemy of our lord? Until they grant our request for an honorable settlement, there is no way we can surrender the castle and disperse without a protest. If we do, it will look as though there isn't a man worthy of the name in this whole Corps of Vassals. It will heap shame even upon generations to come. If our request is not granted, then we dare not disperse, even if it means that we must die of starvation while we wait."

"You're quite right, of course," Kuranosuke said. "But we've all promised Uneme-no-Kami Dono and Daigaku Dono that we would obey their orders. We can't very well go back on our word. That would leave Uneme-no-Kami Dono in the lurch, which would never do."

The three men had set out long before dawn that morning. Now it was nearing midnight, and they had yet to find a place to lodge. Weariness and disappointment were wearing down their resolve. There was no point in arguing further. After a few polite words of parting, they picked up their swords and left.

♦ ♦ ♦

Perhaps they had anticipated Kuranosuke's rebuff, or perhaps the weight of the long day had dulled their sense of outrage, but they seem to have felt no anger toward Kuranosuke as they walked through the darkness of the Third Perimeter, across the moat, and out into the streets of the town.

"It's Kuranosuke's duty, I suppose," one of three shadowy figures said. "As an Elder, he has to be concerned for the preservation of the Asano house. I suppose that's why he made that promise to Uneme-no-Kami Dono."

They walked on in silence, and then another spoke: "We'll have to leave Kuranosuke out of this—work something out with the others. I've heard that Okuno Shōgen believes in our cause. Let's talk to him first."

Before they slept that night, it been decided. Their next step would be to approach Shōgen. With his support, the entire group might be won over to their view. Then Kuranosuke, too, might feel compelled to forgo the lesser duty to his lord's kinsmen for the greater duty of defending the castle. That, surely, would exonerate him in the eyes of Uneme-no-Kami.

Akō, Fourth Month, 15th Day

Defending the castle was the last thing on most people's minds the next morning. The 15th was the date by which all samurai housing had to be vacated, but many samurai had remained in their homes until the last possible moment and were now in the throes of clearing and cleaning them before the deadline.

Kuranosuke was better prepared than most. His family steward, Seno'o Magozaemon, had procured a small plot of land just beyond the Hachiman Shrine in the village of Osaki, on the far side of the river. There, Kuranosuke had built a small cottage into which his family would move today and which would house them while he completed all the paperwork required upon the surrender of the castle. Since he was no longer the Chief Elder of a daimyo domain, Kuranosuke no longer traveled by palanquin, but the loss of that perquisite seemed not to trouble him. Before long, he would become a familiar figure on the road, followed everywhere by his old manservant, Hachisuke. Leaving home immediately after breakfast, he would cross the bridge and traverse the long, narrow islet that divided the river, enter the enceinte at the Eastern Portal, cross the main bridge into town, and proceed to the temple Enrinji, whither the administrative offices of the domain had been moved. The walk was refreshing, he told everyone, and good for his health.

◆ ◆ ◆

Yasubei, Gunbei, and Magodayū must have been among the first to use the new offices at Enrinji, for that is where they invited Okuno Shōgen to meet them. The Samurai Commander listened carefully to all their arguments, but in the end his response was short and unequivocal: "We've already discussed this with Kuranosuke and reached a decision. It would be impossible now, whatever the merits of your arguments, to break this promise, desert Kuranosuke, and launch some new scheme."

Although they tried every way they could think of to dissuade him, Shōgen remained firm. But there still remained the Company Commanders. They were lower in rank, and the men they led were not fully fledged samurai, but they were nonetheless men of some consequence in the domain. With their support, the others might still be won over; then Shōgen and Kuranosuke, too, would have no choice but to join them in defending the castle.

Kawamura Denbei, Shindō Genshirō, Hara Sōemon, and Oyama Gengoemon were invited to the temple, and Yasubei, Gunbei, and Magodayū again did their best to persuade them; but they, too, were as one in their opinion: "We've made a promise to Uneme-no-Kami Dono. And having done so, it is impossible for us to defend the castle. Besides which, we're committed to supporting Daigaku Dono. So there simply is no way that we can go along with your scheme. Kuranosuke, and all of us for that matter, have a responsibility to Daigaku Dono. And if he is not reinstated now, and in such a way that he can show his face among his peers again, our responsibility does not end; we remain bound by it into the future."

And so ended their hope of defending of the castle. Yasubei, Gunbei, and Magodayū remained fervent in their belief that it was the right thing to do, but they were not fanatics who had lost all grasp of reality. The Company Commanders were immovable in their commitment. And if the Company Commanders could not be won over, there was no point in trying to persuade the rank and file. The three men from Edo were alone. But they had the good sense to see their position and accept it—for the time being, at least—with good grace. They thanked the Company Commanders for coming and acknowledged the virtue of their position. They would go directly to Kuranosuke, they said, and offer him their support.

◆ ◆ ◆

Kuranosuke took care not to hurt or belittle the feelings of the three men when they told him that they had given up their plan. Only a few days before, he himself had entertained similar thoughts and had been forced to abandon them. As they were about to part, however, Kuranosuke said, "You say that you've come all the way from Edo intending to follow me. So won't you, just this once, trust me? I promise that I won't let you down. And I'll keep that promise on into the future."

"Then we'll take you at your word," Yasubei said, and the three men left and returned to their lodgings.

✦ ✦ ✦

Yasubei, Magodayū, and Gunbei stayed in Akō until the transfer of the
castle on the 19th, and on the evening of the 20th, Kuranosuke wrote to
all three of them, sending a separate copy to each:

> *I understand that you'll be leaving in a day or two. I am deeply*
> *touched by your good will in coming so far on this occasion, and*
> *I keenly regret that the chaotic state of affairs here has prevented*
> *me from spending more time with you. This is most unfortunate.*
> *Herewith the foregoing,*
>
> FOURTH MONTH, 20TH DAY   *Ōishi Kuranosuke*
>
> *P.S. When you depart, I shall make a particular point of coming to*
> *see you off.*

On the 22nd, true to his word, Kuranosuke came to see the three
men off. They exchanged farewell toasts, made tentative plans to meet
again, and once more Kuranosuke thanked them—repeatedly and profusely—for coming. Then Yasubei, Magodayū, and Gunbei set out on
the road back to Edo.

CHAPTER
29

*What Kuranosuke says
is perfectly reasonable.*

Akō, Fourth Month, 18th Day
This was the last day, the day on which the Inspectors and Resident Deputies were to conduct their final inspection of the castle and its grounds before the official surrender on the morrow. The guards at every gate knelt in deep obeisance as the officials from Edo passed within the ramparts for the first time since their arrival. Kuranosuke and a suite of senior officers greeted them at the drawbridge that spanned the inner moat. Tanaka Seibei, an Adjutant, and Mase Kyūdayū, the Inspector General, showed them around the grounds of the Second Perimeter, after which three men of the Akō Inspectorate guided them through the streets and residences in the Third Perimeter. And finally, Kuranosuke and Okuno Shōgen escorted them to the mansion in the Main Perimeter. When they were seated in the Gold Room, once the innermost sitting room, tea was served.

Kuranosuke took this opportunity to tell the officials what was uppermost in his mind: "Now that Takumi-no-Kami's castle and lands have been declared forfeit, we his Corps of Vassals assure you that they will be surrendered to you with no hindrance or delay. Various of Takumi's kinsmen have been at pains to urge us on several occasions to create no disturbance of any sort. And, indeed, we make no objection whatever to Takumi's punishment for his offense. We are greatly grieved, however, by the dissolution of this line of the Asano house, which for generation upon generation has been honored by the favor of the House of Tokugawa, since the time of the late Danjō Nagamasa, who fought at the side of Lord Ieyasu even before the establishment of this illustrious regime. As you know, Takumi's younger brother Daigaku has been sentenced to Domiciliary Confinement, and our Corps of Vassals appears reluctant to disperse without knowing what this gentleman's fate will be upon his release. I too, I must say, find this most unfortunate; presumptuous though it is of me to say so, I expect that you yourselves must understand how we feel. I would entreat you, therefore, that Daigaku be restored to a condition wherein he can once again serve with honor."

Total silence. Not one of the four officials so much as nodded or spoke a word of acknowledgment. Kuranosuke stood and led the way to their next object of inspection, the Grand Reception Room. Along the way, he watched for an opportune moment and spoke again: "As I said before, our Corps of Vassals is most reluctant to disperse. I do hope that you will be so kind as to take note of this."

Again, total silence. The Grand Reception Room was duly inspected; whereupon the party moved on to other hallways, other rooms, until the entire mansion had been officially scrutinized. Finally, when they had reached the end of their tour, in the vast vestibule just within the entryway, tea and refreshments were again served. This time, Kuranosuke was watching every nuance of expression on the faces of his guests in the hope of judging just the right moment to broach this seemingly delicate subject one more time.

"I do apologize for repeating myself," he began, his head bowed, his voice soft and almost plaintive, "but as I've said, our Corps of Vassals is in complete accord with Takumi's punishment for his crime; they've protested to me on countless occasions, though, how reluctant they are to disperse without knowing what is to become of Daigaku. Quite frankly, I think they have a point."

At this moment, Ishihara Shinzaemon turned to Araki Jūzaemon and said, "What Kuranosuke says is perfectly reasonable. It seems to me that there would be no harm in mentioning this when you return to Edo." This was actually rather brave of Shinzaemon. As one of the administrators who would remain behind in Akō until a new lord was appointed, he was the inferior of Jūzaemon, who would return to Edo as soon as the formalities of the surrender were over. Shinzaemon need not have risked irritating his superior and possibly receiving an unfavorable report upon his return. He spoke up nonetheless, and to good effect.

"Quite so," Jūzaemon said. "I can see that, in the main, Kuranosuke is right."

Kuranosuke said, "Your kind words embolden me to beg of you that, through your good offices, Daigaku might be released and restored to a condition in which he can perform his duties with no shame whatever in the presence of all his peers—for which, I know, our Corps of Vassals would be extremely grateful and much relieved." At which point, according to one report, his eyes welled with tears.

"For my own part," Jūzaemon replied, "I would be willing to take up the matter with the Council of Elders, after we return to Edo. But, Uneme Dono, how do you feel about it?"

"Absolutely," his colleague said. "I quite agree."

"Then you may inform your vassals that as soon as we arrive in Edo, we shall present your case in full detail, just as you have now explained it to us."

Kuranosuke bowed in acquiescence and said, "I am most grateful to you both." The party then moved on and completed their inspection with a tour of the now vacant samurai residences.

I have always wondered why no one ever mentions that the same Inspectors posted a great signboard before this castle enumerating the Laws of the Land that would now apply in Akō—the first provision of which read:

QUARRELING AND CONTENTION OF ALL SORTS ARE PROHIBITED. SHOULD THERE BE ANY WHO VIOLATE THIS PROHIBITION, BOTH PARTIES SHALL BE PUT TO DEATH. FOR ANY ACCOMPLICES, THE CONSEQUENCES SHALL BE SEVERE.

Surely, the irony of this message cannot have been lost on *everyone*.

♦ ♦ ♦

Outside the town, much larger movements were afoot. All the roads leading into Akō had by now been cleared, smoothed, cleaned, and swept in preparation not only for the officials from Edo, but for the approach of the two armies, from Tatsuno on the east and Ashimori on the west. Today, except for the occasional courier, they were virtually empty. All traffic by merchants, farmers, travelers—anyone who could not prove that they were on official business—had been halted.

◆ ◆ ◆

Kinoshita Higo-no-Kami had come back from Edo with only a small personal suite and was now lodged in the Honjin at Uné, where he awaited the arrival of his main force, coming up from his domain in Ashimori. Wakizaka Awaji-no-Kami, however, had already returned to his domain, and he now set out from Tatsuno in command of his full force in the early hours of the 18th. They marched south to the junction with the Southern Mountain Road, where they turned west. By midday, they had reached the post town of Katashima, where they stopped to refresh themselves and their horses. They then moved on to the hamlet of Kuga, where the column left the highway and veered south on the mountain by-road to Akō, the last leg of their journey. At the Hour of the Ram (ca. 2:00 P.M.), they emerged from Takatori Pass and wound their way down onto the plain. There they halted and set up camp in the cedar grove outside the village of Kōya. Again, the troops needed water, and their horses fodder. But this was no post town; the peasants of Kōya had little enough for their own needs and certainly no surplus to supply an army on the move.

A messenger who had been sent into town returned with the news that the hour of transfer had yet to be decided. He was misinformed, but Awaji-no-Kami sent the man back with a message to the Inspectors informing them of his arrival, and then gave the order to form up once more and advance. There was nothing to be gained by waiting indefinitely in a grove of evergreens. By the Hour of the Monkey (ca. 4:00 P.M.), the Wakizaka force stood at the Nakamura Bridge, just across the river from the Eastern Portal to the castle town. It was here that the trouble began.

The commander of the guard on duty at the gate immediately sent word to Kuranosuke of the impending incursion. Kuranosuke, in turn, sent Hara Sōemon to remonstrate with the senior officers of the

Wakizaka force. They were in violation of their agreement with the Inspectors from Edo, he told them: "The transfer of the castle is to take place on the morrow at the Hour of the Dragon [8:00 A.M.]; your men are not to enter the town until sunrise, at precisely the Hour of the Hare [6:00 A.M.]. Their premature intrusion is unacceptable. It would be much appreciated, therefore, if you would take note of the time and the date, and perform your duties as originally agreed."

This was not an argument that could carry much weight with an army of 3,500 men, who had been on the move since before dawn and were now exhausted, hungry, thirsty, and not at all inclined to be put off by the protests of those they had come to disenfeoff. At first, a few bands of rowdy foot soldiers crossed the bridge, forced their way through the enceinte, and broke into some of the houses of the townspeople, demanding food, water, and saké. Soon thereafter, someone seems to have decided that it would be better for the entire force to advance, although in a more orderly fashion. By early evening, the streets of the commoners' quarter were filled with armed men and their equipment, and Wakizaka Awaji-no-Kami had established his command post directly before the main gate of the castle.

♦ ♦ ♦

On the same evening, Kinoshita Higo-no-Kami was still forming up his force to move in from the west. His men had been resting in Nishi Uné throughout the day, but now they had a hard night's march ahead of them, over 3 leagues (7.5 miles, 12 kilometers) of winding mountain roads and through the narrow defile at Inochi Pass. Nor would there be much rest at the end of the route. They would halt between the villages of Ōtsu and Shinden, await the signal to enter the town, and then take up positions outside the rear gate of the castle.

♦ ♦ ♦

What the Inspectors—whose orders the Wakizaka had flagrantly defied—thought of all this is not recorded. We do know, though, that in the midst of all this commotion in the town, they again summoned Kuranosuke to their lodgings.

"We were deeply impressed this morning," they told him, "first of all by your entreaty in the castle, but also by the thoroughness and care with which the castle, the roads, the bridges, the weapons, the village registers, and such have been put in order. So we've decided that we'll send a report of this by courier, in advance of our return. We are also prepared to issue passes to all vassals, so they may travel wherever they choose to live. For those who wish to move to Edo, we'll also issue passes for their women. And if there are those who wish to settle in this region, their requests, too, will be granted."

In the castle, their speech had been curt and formal, as befitted their position and the occasion; but now, back at their lodgings and out of the public eye, the Inspectors were not only polite but almost genial. Kuranosuke, against all odds, had negotiated a highly advantageous settlement with them—and ended up being treated as a friend as well. In return for a promise that his "rough-hewn and rustic" warriors would neither resist the surrender nor commit mass suicide thereafter—a bluff that Kuranosuke could never have made good on—the Inspectors agreed to present to the Elders in Edo Kuranosuke's case for the reinstatement of Asano Daigaku and the restoration of his honor, which could be accomplished only by the punishment of Kira. It was a masterful stroke of negotiation.

◆ ◆ ◆

Kuranosuke was now free to return to the castle and make his final round of the gates and guard posts. The sight of the Wakizaka force, crowding the town and arrayed before the main gate, infuriated him. But at least Kinoshita Higo-no-Kami had followed the orders of the Inspectors, halting his force well short of the Saltsheds Gate until the appointed hour. Kuranosuke could still enter the castle at the postern without having to endure the stares of an enemy.

His first task was to ensure that all the gates were shut tight and bolted and that all posts were fully manned and on the alert. Then, as twilight dimmed and darkness fell, he ordered that watch fires be lit in every turret of the castle. A foot soldier from the small Asano branch house in Iehara, who happened to be in Akō that day, reported that this had exactly the effect that Kuranosuke hoped it would. The command group of the Wakizaka force was taken totally by surprise and made to wonder whether its heedless intrusion was about to provoke an armed response. Kuranosuke had no intention of doing anything so rash, but the Wakizaka had heard all the rumors about defending the castle and committing mass suicide. Now they were forced to remain awake throughout the night, in readiness for an attack. Besides which, the outraged townspeople were refusing to sell them saké, or even to supply them with cold water. After a long hard day, it would be a long sleepless night.

♦ ♦ ♦

When Kuranosuke had completed his circuit of the castle grounds—checking that none of the men on duty were asleep, that the gates were secure, and that there was no danger of fire—he returned to the main gate, climbed the stairs of the turret, and surveyed the scene below. The Wakizaka forces were arrayed in good order, with their command post immediately before the gate. For a time, Kuranosuke looked out silently, calculating their numbers, scrutinizing their formations, assessing their degree of discipline, and noting their banners and lanterns.

"Someone out there knows a bit about military matters," he said at last. A faint smile crossed his face as he turned to the senior officers accompanying him: "A hundred twenty years ago, a formation that well ordered would have won the battle. But nowadays—at least in my humble opinion—you can't hope to take a castle with brave men alone. Castles are armed with cannon. One musket can kill one man, and only at fairly close range. But a cannon can target an entire unit, nearly 1 league distant. We could blow that whole formation away with one blast. And if we were really determined to oppose them, we could line up a battery and blow their whole force to bits. All this bravado just makes the Wakizaka look foolish. We promised them that we'd open the gates tomorrow morning at the Hour of the Hare. What they should be doing now is resting their men and their horses at a safe distance. Then, at dawn, send out a party to check the mood and the layout of the castle. And when the gates open, make directly for them, by a route that avoids our fields of fire. But anyone who moves up in the middle of the night, exhausts his men and horses, and makes a target of himself camping directly under the walls of the castle—as a battle commander, that man is a fool."

+ + +

The gates remained manned and the watch fires tended, yet not a sound issued from within the castle. A state of high alert was maintained throughout the night, so that the Wakizaka had no choice but to remain equally alert, lest they be taken by surprise in a night attack. Kuranosuke was determined to make them pay for breaking their word. No one in the castle slept that night, but at least they had the satisfaction of knowing that those outside the walls would be as weary as they were when day dawned.

CHAPTER
30

*I could never address him as just
"Kuranosuke."*

Akō, Fourth Month, 19th Day

There cannot be many moments in life when one resents the dawning of a perfectly beautiful day, yet I do wonder whether the very beauty of the morning of the 19th might not have struck Kuranosuke as somehow discordant—welcome at almost any other time, but cruelly incongruous given the task that he had to perform that day. Just about everyone who was there remarked what a lovely day it was when the castle in Akō was surrendered.

◆ ◆ ◆

The time officially decreed for the surrender of the castle was the midpoint of the Hour of the Hare (6:00 A.M.). The Wakizaka forces were already arrayed before the main gate, and by the end of the Hour of the Ox (3:00 A.M.), the Kinoshita force had begun to move into the town to take up their positions at the postern, the Saltsheds Gate.

Within the walls, too, preparations were under way. Every one of the twelve gates was to be manned by a detail proportionate to its importance, led by a man of commensurate rank, who held the keys to that gate. At the main gate, Kawamura Denbei commanded a squad leader, five foot soldiers, and two guardsmen. At the Saltsheds Gate, Yashima Sōzaemon commanded a unit of equal size. And likewise with Hara Sōemon at the gate to the Second Perimeter and Fujii Hikoshirō at the gate to the Central Perimeter. All the other gates were guarded by only two or three foot soldiers and a guardsman. In the Central Perimeter, however, where the final act of surrender would take place, both Elders, Ōishi Kuranosuke and Okuno Shōgen, with a suite of eleven enfeoffed samurai, waited for the two daimyo to whom they would surrender.

As the appointed hour approached, Wakizaka Awaji-no-Kami strode out from his command post and mounted his horse, followed by the two Resident Deputies, also mounted. At the main gate, Araki Jūzaemon, the Senior Inspector, rode to the head of the column and at a stately pace led the way across the bridge.

At the same moment, the doors of both the main gate and the Saltsheds Gate swung open, and the two columns made a direct route through the Third Perimeter—the one due south and the other due east—to the gate of the Second Perimeter, where they converged. There the two daimyo, the Inspectors, and the Resident Deputies dismounted. Araki Jūzaemon called out in a loud voice: "I rejoice to report that transfer of the castle has been completed." Whereupon the entire group proceeded on foot to the Central Perimeter.

Kuranosuke and Shōgen had come out on the graveled path to meet them and escort them to the Grand Reception Room of the mansion, where Awaji-no-Kami, Higo-no-Kami, and their senior officers were seated on the veranda. Two samurai carrying their Certificate of Appointment as Confiscators-in-Chief, which bore the black-ink seal of the Shogun, then carried this august document to the seat of highest honor in the Upper Chamber of the central hall, the seat where the Shogun himself would have sat, had he been present.

The surrender itself could not have been simpler. Kuranosuke and Shōgen, who had waited respectfully in the vestibule, were called into the presence of the two daimyo. Kuranosuke spoke first: "With all due respect, we hereby surrender this castle." To which Araki Jūzaemon replied with equal solemnity, "We are particularly pleased that you have managed this transfer in so meticulous a manner."

"Kuranosuke!" At this point, Wakizaka Awaji-no-Kami spoke for the first time in the course of these proceedings: "Kuranosuke. We can imagine only too well how all of this must make you feel. We want you to know, though, that the fine condition in which you leave the roads and bridges of Takumi's domain—not to mention his castle—does not pass unnoticed. We are impressed, too, by the great care that you have devoted to the weaponry that will remain here."

How Kuranosuke responded to this praise—which can have brought him little joy—is not recorded. We are told only that he and Shōgen then withdrew from the palace and made their way out of the castle grounds through the nearest exit, the Shimizu Gate, which opened behind the warehouses at the river's edge. There they waited while the guard details at all twelve gates were being relieved, one after another, by men from the occupying force. Once the Asano force had departed the castle for the last time, they made their way together through the town to the Asano family temple, Kagakuji. A great many tears were shed among the group that gathered there, it is said; but Kuranosuke and Hara Sōemon sat stock still and betrayed no emotion—like the dragon, as one writer put it, that lies submerged until the time is right to break the surface and ascend to the heavens.

Back in the castle, the new custodians must have been feeling more relieved than celebratory to have accomplished their mission without having to mount a siege. But Wakizaka Awaji-no-Kami had decided that there should be a banquet and had brought his kitchen staff along to provide it. They had had to work through the night somewhere out in the town, as the palace kitchens were not available to them until a short time earlier. Somehow they had managed, though, and a repast of several courses, to be served on three lacquered trays, was carried to the castle in great lidded luggage boxes borne by four men each. The full menu survives in the Wakizaka archives, but I'll not go into detail, except to say that they at least had the good taste not to celebrate their success with saké.

Finally, the two daimyo composed their joint report to officialdom in Edo:

> *With this missive, we send you our most respectful greetings. We trust that this finds His Highness in the best of health and spirits. We two, together with Araki Jūzaemon and Sakakibara Uneme, on this, the 19th day, at the midpoint of the Hour of the Hare, have taken possession, without demur, of the castle in Akō in the province*

of Harima, and have posted guards in all appropriate locations. Awaji-no-Kami intends to remain here today in order to make garrison assignments and attend to other matters; he will depart for his domain on the morrow. Higo-no-Kami will set out for his domain today.

Our Certificate of Appointment, sealed in black, has been returned to Jūzaemon and Uneme, who will report all details to you. In the interim, we proffer this humble missive. With the greatest respect,

FOURTH MONTH, 19TH DAY   *Kinoshita Higo-no-Kami Kinsada*
                               Wakizaka Awaji-no-Kami Yasuteru
To: The Council of Elders et al.

By the midpoint of the Hour of the Serpent (10:00 A.M.), it was all over, and those who were free to leave began to do so. Most of them we hear no more of, but Inoue Dan'emon, Adjutant to the lord of Hiroshima, took the trouble to report not only to his lord but also to the Hiroshima cadet house in Miyoshi. This report was, of course, forwarded to Yōzei'in, the widow of Takumi-no-Kami, and thus passed through the hands of her Chamberlain, Ochiai Yozaemon, who noted down one of the more interesting episodes from it in his archives.

◆ ◆ ◆

Dan'emon had no part in the surrender. His mission was simply to ensure that the surrender take place. And so, once it had taken place, he hurried to the lodging of the senior Inspector, Araki Jūzaemon.

"We are very pleased that the transfer was completed so smoothly," Jūzaemon told him. "I expect, though, that this has been very trying for all of your people."

"This is a question that I'm very reluctant to ask," Dan'emon said, "but what has been your impression of all that you've seen in the course of the transfer? I ask because, as you know, Ōno Kurōbei fell ill and was unable to participate, which meant that Kuranosuke had to manage everything on his own. For us, this has been a great worry, lest anything go wrong. When I return to Edo, I shall have to submit a complete report to Aki-no-Kami, and I should like to set his mind at ease on this score."

"I can tell you precisely what I myself intend to report," said Jūzaemon, "that the samurai who executed the surrender behaved impeccably and that I was particularly impressed by the meticulous judgment with which Kuranosuke handled every detail—the castle, the men under his command, everything. Despite all the confusion, his performance left naught to be desired. When you return to Edo, you are most welcome to report, in the most favorable terms, what I have just said."

Thereafter, Dan'emon called on Sakakibara Uneme Dono, who said, "Ah, we meet again—and you've been so kind as to come to me before I've had a chance to go and greet you! You may be sure that it will count for a great deal that the surrender of the castle today went so smoothly. And the way Kuranosuke, in the midst of all this turmoil, managed every detail—within the castle, with the samurai of the house, and in every other respect—was flawless. It was a noble tribute, both to the late Takumi Dono and to the entire Asano clan. I trust that you will report every detail of this to Aki-no-Kami Dono when you return to Edo. I expect, too, that you yourself will return much relieved."

Good news was by no means the only thing that Dan'emon hoped to carry back to Edo. After speaking to the Inspectors, he sought out Shindō Genshirō in his new lodgings in town.

"The entire Asano clan is, of course, delighted that the castle has been surrendered, as am I as well," Dan'emon said. "But rumors have spread even to neighboring domains that the castle was to be defended against a siege. Could you give me the names of those pledged to participate in this? I should like to let Aki-no-Kami know who the loyal ones were."

"No, I'm afraid I cannot," Genshirō told him. "Defending the castle was considered a crime. How can I reveal who was a party to it? Or reveal who agreed to commit suicide in the castle? Kuranosuke has kept a record. All I can do is pass on your request to him."

Genshirō kept his word; he went to Kuranosuke and told him precisely what Inoue Dan'emon had asked. Kuranosuke never hesitated. He took up his brush, wrote a complete list of the fifty-seven men pledged to commit suicide in the castle, inscribed it with an oath swearing to its truth, signed it, sealed it with his blood print, and handed it to Genshirō.

"Give this to Dan'emon," he said. Kuranosuke saw nothing that they need be ashamed of.

◆ ◆ ◆

At some point after Dan'emon had returned to Edo, he was discussing matters with the Hiroshima Elders Tōshima Yasuzaemon and Terao Shōzaemon; once they had dealt with the business at hand, he went on to talk about his experiences in Akō.

"Kuranosuke himself told me this," Dan'emon said. "He knew that if by some chance he should *not* surrender the castle, and if the members of his pact were to commit suicide, I could never return to Edo alive. Yet nothing that he did can be faulted. It was plain to see: he is a most extraordinary man. Indeed, I could never address him as just 'Kuranosuke'; I would feel rude not to call him 'Kuranosuke Dono.' He is a man of such great refinement and dignity." Somehow word of this conversation, too, reached the Miyoshi house, and Ochiai Yozaemon duly recorded it.

◆ ◆ ◆

When the first lot of severance allowances were distributed on the 5th Day of the Fourth Month, many samurai were then free to leave Akō, but not all of them. There was a great deal of winding-down to be done in preparation for the transfer of the domain, business that could be put in order only by the men who had been handling it. The overall leadership of the two Elders was required, of course—which is why Ōno Kurōbei was considered a criminal when he absconded. For similar reasons, the Samurai Commanders and Company Commanders, too, were required to remain on duty. And likewise with several lesser officials. Sugiura Tadasuke, the Officer in Charge of River Transport, had to ensure the cooperation of the boatmen who carried produce downstream from the villages and supplies back upstream. Inoue Denpachi, Superintendant of Construction, had to put the lumber stocks in order and oversee the sale of them. Yatō Chōsuke, the Superintendant of Finance, was the only man who could bring all the account books up to date. And even those who manned the guard posts, both in the castle and in the borderland villages, could not be allowed to leave their posts until they were relieved.

But after the surrender, new people garrisoned the castle, kept order in town, and guarded the borders. It was a different sort of work that had to be done now, work with brush, ink, and paper. There were reams of lists, documents, and ledgers to be submitted—some to the Inspectors from Edo, whose main concern was the castle and its equipment, and some to the Resident Deputies, who would remain in Akō and whose concern was the day-to-day governance of the domain. Now it was the men who made the rounds of the countryside, the men who kept the maps of the region up to date, the men who maintained the population registers (and made sure that there were no Christians in the domain) who were to remain in Akō—and also, of course, men who wrote a clean, clear hand in which they would make fair copies of all the documents being prepared. To the Inspectors, they submitted lists of weapons that would remain in the castle, reckonings of rice in the storehouses, rosters of the Corps of Vassals and other stipendiaries, inventories of portable fittings in the samurai houses, catalogues of horses and oxen in each of the villages—even a list of dogs living in the castle grounds arranged by the colors of their coats. To the Resident Deputies, they submitted village registers, population records, water-use regulations, prison records, maps, firearms registration records, and accounts of unpaid taxes.

+ + +

There is nothing very interesting to be said about the administrative work that remained after the surrender of the castle, but there was a touching beginning to it all. Mimura Jirōzaemon was one of the lowest-ranking samurai in Akō. In fact, some people questioned whether he was a samurai at all. Mimura himself would vigorously dispute that imputation. He could prove beyond doubt that he was a great-grandson of Mimura Bizen, a warrior of old whose fame lived on, at least in the western provinces. But in rosters of the Akō Corps of Vassals, Mimura is described as either the "Saké Officer" or a "Kitchen Official." He described his experience of that month of paperwork in a letter to his cousin Nonomura Heitazaemon in Okayama:

Ōishi Kuranosuke Dono, on the 16th Day of the Fourth Month of this Year of the Serpent, moved to the temple Enrinji, and in the Seventh Hour [4:00–6:00 A.M.], at dawn on that day, he summoned me to his sitting room. "I know," he said, "that you are one of the most poorly paid of our many vassals; yet you have served this house since the time of your father with a strong sense of fealty and have remained fiercely devoted to your duty. There is no need for me to tell you this, I know; but, alas, there are many samurai in the service of this house, and many others who have been its beneficiaries, who have behaved with unspeakable selfishness. You, however, have been so unswerving in your loyalty and so deeply devoted that, I swear, you put even me to shame. Truly, Jirōza, you are the one who always does exactly what I ask." That he should speak so kindly and so considerately to someone as lowly as me, that I found myself there in his presence and he did not reject me—I felt so very grateful. But my eyes filled with tears, and I was unable to utter a single word in reply.

Jirōzaemon was the first man summoned, and he remained at Kuranosuke's beck and call throughout the entire task, nor was he ever far from him thereafter.

*The walk to and from the temple
is bracing and good for my health.*

The paperwork would drag on for another month and more, but before
it could begin, there were logistical matters to be attended to. More
than thirty men would be working in the temple, many of whom would
have to lodge there as well, now that they had been evicted from their
homes. To accommodate them, both the Hall of Burnt Offerings and
the Reception Hall were requisitioned. Enrinji was not a rich temple, so
before the work began, Kuranosuke saw to it that the tatami mats were
resurfaced, the shōji re-papered, and the sliding doors replaced—probably at the expense of the Shogunate.

Once work was under way, though, the most immediate task was
the issue of checkpoint passes to the women who required them. Any
women traveling to Edo had to pass through two of the strictest checkpoints in the land, Arai and Hakone on the Eastern Sea Road. Any
women from Akō wishing to make that journey were fully entitled to
do so, but a pass signed by the Inspectors alone would not suffice to
ensure their passage. Their passes had to bear the seal of Matsudaira
Kii-no-Kami, the Shogunal Deputy in Kyoto. This would take time;
but the applications were sent to Kyoto immediately, and the passes
were returned from the Shogunal Deputy to Araki Jūzaemon by the 5th
Day of the Fifth Month.

Some of the men, too, felt that they required rental permits, especially if they planned to live in Kyoto, a city somewhat inhospitable to
ronin. One of these documents survives, that issued to Kaiga Yazaemon,

assuring potential landlords that he was a bona fide Akō ronin who was entitled to rent lodging in any location under whatever terms were mutually agreeable. The signatures of the Inspectors were sufficient to validate these permits.

Among the more routine tasks, the documents to be submitted to the Inspectors had to take precedence, as these officials were planning to leave Akō on the 11th of the month. But as always in an under-taking of this magnitude, there were last-minute hitches. It turned out, for instance, that a floor plan of the mansion in the Main Perimeter could not be found. Perhaps none had ever been made. This meant that Kuranosuke had to request permission from the new custodians of the castle to escort a detail of four carpenters through the build-ings so they could measure all the rooms and draw up the requisite plan. The Wakizaka were not keen to agree to this, but in the end the Inspectors lent their weight to the request, and the interlopers were allowed within, under the watchful eye of a Wakizaka samurai who accompanied them everywhere.

Moreover, someone had neglected to retrieve the Sectarian Registry Records from the turret at the Saltsheds Gate, where they were stored. Again, the reluctant cooperation of the new custodians had to be sought.

Yet none of these hitches seems to have upset Kuranosuke, as we can see from a letter to his father-in-law, Ishizuka Gengobei, written the day before the Inspectors were to leave Akō:

> I have perused the letter that, once again, you have been at such pains to write. We are most grateful for all the delicacies that you send us, which are so rare in these parts—two salted bream, one salted salmon, three dried cod, a tub of bream sushi, a jar of pickled fish, 120 skewered gudgeons. I shall ensure that these treasures find their way into our meals straightaway and call the whole family together so that all may enjoy them. I am delighted, too, to hear that all of you there are well and remain in robust health.
>
> Here, most of our official business has been completed without delay, and we shall soon be able to submit the village registers. You can

imagine, I am sure, how pleased I am that everything has gone so smoothly. Mohei will give you all the details when he returns. . . .

On the evening of the 7th, I, too, moved to our retreat in the village of Osaki. I leave home after breakfast, at about the Fifth Hour [8:00 a.m.], and return midway through the Seventh [5:00 p.m.]. The walk to and from the temple is bracing and good for my health.

I understand that the Shogunate is to pay us for this work in rice rations, for which I am grateful. This has been a major undertaking, as you yourself said it would be. In recompense, we are to receive one lump sum for the duration of the stay of the Inspectors, from the 19th of the Fourth Month to the 10th of this month. I am to receive a year's rations for twenty-nine men, plus a supplement of 3 koku. Those enfeoffed at 100 to 200 koku will receive rations for seven men, and those below that level will be paid in proportion to their enfeoffment or stipend. . . . In the meantime, we remain hard at work. Mohei will tell you all the details. The reason I must remain here for such a long time is that when we submit the account books, registers, and such, I must inspect and then sign all of them with my monogram. At that time a courier will come and inquiries will be made. That there should be no unfavorable reports is, as you say, the least we can do for the reputation of Takumi-no-Kami. That, of course, is our wish as well.

I do not yet know where we shall live. At the very least, though, I feel that we cannot go on living in temporary lodgings in Osaki.

Now that our daughter has recovered from her fever, you may rest assured that the entire family is well. I will be in touch with further details soon. . . . With great respect,

FIFTH MONTH, 10TH DAY   *Ōishi Kuranosuke*
To: Gengobei Sama

Eventually, however, all the documents, registers, and accounts required by the Inspectors were submitted to them on time, and they were able to leave on the 11th as planned. No record remains of Kuranosuke's parting with them, but he refers indirectly to the occasion in a report that he wrote later the same day, addressed to two vassals of Asano Mino-no-Kami and Asano Sahyōe:

> *With this missive, I send you my most respectful greetings. Reluctant though I am to be so forward as to inquire, I trust that everyone in the houses of Mino-no-Kami Sama and Sahyōe Sama is enjoying good health.*
>
> *Item. We completed the surrender of the castle on the 19th of this past Fourth Month, and the Corps of Vassals has dispersed. Even so, it distresses me to see how uneasy our vassals remain, having dispersed without knowing what is to be the fate of Daigaku Sama. Even after he serves out his sentence and is set free, there will remain the matter of his honor. Our Corps of Vassals, one and all, hope that he will be restored to a condition in which he can serve without shame in the presence of his peers. When the Inspectors arrived and they were inspecting the interior of the castle, I explained this to them, and they promised that they would report the substance of what I said when they returned to Edo. And when I went to bid them farewell prior to their departure today, this proved a good opportunity, and they agreed in every detail with what I had said previously. I have asked that they convey all the details of what we had discussed to the Council of Elders. The Corps of Vassals has accepted this in good grace. And the Inspectors have cordially asked that I pass word of it on to those who remain in this region.*
>
> *Item. The account books, maps, and such that the Inspectors commanded us to prepare have all been completed and submitted in good order. The documents concerning the villages, to be submitted to the Resident Deputies, will be completed within the next day or two. Then, if there are no further requests, all our work will be done, and we shall be free to depart this region. May we ask that you pass word of this on when you have the opportunity? We shall keep you posted of any further details.*

Item. May we ask, too, that if you learn anything concerning the fate of Daigaku Sama, for better or for worse, you inform us immediately? Since we no longer have any reliable contacts in Edo, this is a considerable worry for us. If you write to me in care of Ōtsukaya Koemon in Fushimi, your letters will be delivered immediately. I shall alert Koemon and ask that he get in touch with me without delay. Hereafter, I shall keep a low profile and not inquire after you directly. That I shall do through Inoue Goemon. Respectfully,

FIFTH MONTH, 11TH DAY   *Kuranosuke*
To: Sugiura Tōbei Sama
Maeda Ichiemon Sama

Kuranosuke himself, as well as two or three of his closest associates, would have to remain at work in the temple for another ten days or so, but as the end drew near for the others, he decided that a celebration was called for. This is how Mimura Jirōzaemon describes it in a letter to Nonomura Heitazaemon:

Until the 18th of the Fifth Month of this year, when all the account books and registers were at last completed, he continued to work as hard as ever. And then, for all who had remained behind, both greater and lesser, and even for us lowly sorts, Kuranosuke ordered a magnificent fish dinner to celebrate the completion of our task. Thereafter, he summoned everyone of samurai rank individually to his sitting room, thanked them for their efforts, and paid them their wages. The others were commended and paid as a group by Tanaka Seibei in the Reception Hall. I, however, was treated as a samurai and summoned by name into his presence in his sitting room. He said, "I've witnessed—and with great satisfaction—your many acts of kindness toward everyone here, as well as the diligence with which you have worked, day and night. I truly wish that I could continue to offer you a living; but in my present condition, I can give you only this small token of my appreciation. But come what may, I do hope to see you prosper." He then gave me my wages with his own hands. I felt so unworthy of his kind words and so grateful that I was quite unable to thank him properly. I had to ask Masé Kyūdayū to thank him on my behalf.

This is by no means the last we shall see of Jirōzaemon.

CHAPTER

32

*If the conditions of his release are not such
as to preserve his honor, we feel that it will be all but
impossible for him to perform his duties.*

Akō, Fifth Month, 12th Day

The day after the Inspectors left Akō to return to Edo, well before all his administrative work had been completed, Kuranosuke embarked upon a new project—although many people, including his own comrades, seem to have misunderstood his motives and thought it a newer sort of project than in fact it was. The Reinstatement Movement, it is often called. That is not a misnomer, but it fails to tell the whole story.

Kuranosuke did indeed wish to bring about the reinstatement of Takumi-no-Kami's heir, Asano Daigaku, as head of a newly restored Asano cadet house—but only under the conditions set out in his plea to the Inspectors during their pre-surrender inspection of the castle. There is no mistaking what he meant; he used the same phrase again and again: Daigaku must be restored to "a condition in which he can perform his duties with no shame whatever in the presence of all his peers." It is a fine-sounding phrase, but how could it be achieved?

It takes but a moment's reflection to realize that Asano Daigaku could never "perform his duties with no shame" as long as his brother's enemy, Kira Kōzuke-no-Suke, was still alive. But how was Kuranosuke to deal with that intractable fact? For the moment, the problem lay in the hands of the Shogunate. In return for Kuranosuke's promise to surrender the castle peaceably, without resort to siege warfare or mass suicide, the Inspectors had promised to take the matter to the highest levels of power in the Shogunate: the Council of Elders and the Junior Council.

It was not that Kuranosuke mistrusted the Inspectors, but he did feel that they would stand a greater chance of success if he could convince others in high places to add their support to the cause of Asano Daigaku. Hence his Reinstatement Movement. His first move was to write to an eminent cleric, Fumon'in Gisan, now the Abbot of Rokuharamitsuji, a major temple in Kyoto, but formerly the Superior of Enrinji in Akō— the very temple in which Kuranosuke sat as he wrote:

> I take the liberty to address this brief missive to you, having heard, to my delight, that you are in the best of health.
>
> Item. The Corps of Vassals was recently persuaded to surrender Akō Castle without delay, although this was accomplished only after repeated warnings from Asano Aki-no-Kami and Toda Uneme-no-Kami that this must be done without fail. His Lordship's younger brother Daigaku was sentenced to Domiciliary Confinement, and the Corps of Vassals, having no news of what was to become of him, was reluctant to disperse. This made matters difficult for me, and our men are still quite upset, which, I think, is only to be expected. I write to entreat you, therefore, to intercede with officials in Edo to have Daigaku released from Domiciliary Confinement, and then restored to a condition in which he can serve with honor among his peers. Were this to happen, then our Corps of Vassals would rest easy. And thus, although I am extremely reluctant to mention this, I should like to ask you to travel to Edo and present our case in a favorable light to officialdom there. I understand that you have for long been on familiar terms with Goji'in, and I should like to ask that you take up this matter with him. . . . There is no one else of whom I can ask this. But knowing how kind you have been over the years, even to the men of our Corps of Vassals, I nonetheless make

bold to request this of you. Onerous a task though it is, I pray that you will be so good as to acquiesce. Hara Sōemon and Okamoto Jirōzaemon will acquaint you with the details of the matter when they meet with you.

FIFTH MONTH, 12TH DAY   *Ōishi Kuranosuke*
To: Fumon'in Sama,
via his fellow disciples

P.S. I should by rights come to call upon you myself, but our task here remains unfinished and I do not yet know when we shall complete the work. Fortunately, however, Sōemon and Jirōzaemon are free to come up to you and will be sure to tell you all that you need to know. Herewith the foregoing.

Fumon'in never saw this letter. Kuranosuke had commissioned Hara Sōemon and Okamoto Jirōzaemon to carry the missive to Kyoto; shortly thereafter, he sent Yūkai, the current Superior of Enrinji, to join them. But at Rokuharamitsuji, they were told that the Abbot was out of town and was not expected to return anytime soon. Yūkai then decided that he himself must undertake the mission to Edo, and Sōemon sent word of their misfortune to Kuranosuke.

The sequence of events that followed is not entirely clear, but in the meantime, Kuranosuke seems somehow to have heard that the lords of both Hiroshima and Miyoshi would soon arrive in Osaka, on their journey home after a year of attendance in Edo. Sōemon and Jirōzaemon were already in Kyoto, an easy day's distance from Osaka. Kuranosuke quickly drafted a letter to the lord of Hiroshima and sent it by courier to Sōemon in Kyoto, with instructions that he present it to His Lordship. The next morning, Sōemon and Jirōzaemon boarded the Yodo riverboat for the trip downstream and were waiting in Osaka when the two daimyo processions arrived. Once Asano Aki-no-Kami and his suite were settled in their lodgings, Sōemon and Jirōzaemon sought out Toshima Yasuzaemon and Terao Shōzaemon, the two Hiroshima Elders traveling with their lord. This is the request that they asked the Elders to transmit to him:

Prior to the recent surrender of Akō Castle, Tosa-no-Kami Sama had written to us via courier, and Asano Aki-no-Kami Sama and Toda Uneme-no-Kami, too, sent successive emissaries. Once the commands conveyed by these emissaries were explained to the Corps of Vassals, they were persuaded to execute the transfer of the castle without delay and then disperse. But not since Daigaku Dono was sentenced to Domiciliary Confinement has the Corps of Vassals heard anything of what is to become of him; thus they were still somewhat perturbed when they dispersed. We have heard that Kōzuke-no-Suke Dono has been relieved of office; but as long as he remains alive, it is difficult to predict when Daigaku Dono will be released. Still, Domiciliary Confinement does have its limits; when he is released, we expect that it will prove difficult for him to perform his duties, unless certain conditions are fulfilled. Given which, the Corps of Vassals is deeply concerned about what will transpire when he is released. And thus, as long as no favorable judgment is forthcoming, we would ask that, to whatever extent you can, you acquaint your contacts among Shogunate officials with our concerns, so that when Daigaku Dono is released his honor may be preserved. Just recently, when the Shogunal Inspectors were making their rounds of the castle and grounds, they were advised of these matters, whereupon they promised to mention them to their superiors upon their return to Edo. Thereafter, when we bade farewell to them upon their departure, this being a good opportunity to mention the matter again, they confirmed that they felt the concerns of the Corps of Vassals to be perfectly reasonable. Of course, it is difficult to say what may come of all this, but if both Inspectors report all that they have said they would, and if you were to add your voice to theirs, then full details of the matter should reach the ears of the Council of Elders.

The two Hiroshima Elders were not even mildly sympathetic to Kuranosuke's request. A note attached to this letter says that they told Sōemon that they couldn't possibly do as Kuranosuke asked, since in the coming year they would be in Hiroshima and not in Edo. How, then, could they do all the running about that would be required?

Sōemon, having just suffered a rather rude rebuff, was more point-edly specific when he spoke with Ōkubo Gendayū, Tosa-no-Kami's Adjutant: "Just for the record, let me be clear what our thoughts on the matter are: we can see why the Hiroshima Elders might find it awkward to approach the authorities directly just now. But in the final analysis, we do not believe that censure from the Shogunate would be so severe that they need fear the downfall of the entire clan. They needn't approach those officials in person; we ask only that our case be presented in a way that will make those they approach, whoever they may be, well disposed toward us and that our kinfolk help us only in ways that take into con-sideration the concerns of everyone in the clan. It is hard to say when Daigaku Dono will be released from Domiciliary Confinement, but if the conditions of his release are not such as to preserve his honor, we feel that it will be all but impossible for him to perform his duties."

There is no record of the reactions of the Miyoshi people to Sōemon's polite but firmly worded argument. But having heard what he had to say, they would at least be aware that doing nothing at all was not an accept-able option, at least as far as Kuranosuke and Sōemon were concerned.

◆ ◆ ◆

It was at this same time—on the 11th, to be precise, the day the Inspectors departed and the day before Kuranosuke composed his letter to Fumon'in—that Kuranosuke first noticed a swelling above the elbow on his left arm, a skin infection that was to grow into a large, painful, and ultimately disabling carbuncle. At first, it seemed only a minor ailment, and Kuranosuke could not bring himself to take time off to recuperate. One understands why. The 21st, the day the Inspectors had specified as the terminus of their work, was but ten days off, and only a few of Kuranosuke's colleagues remained behind to help him finish it. That delay proved to be a mistake. The work was finished, but the very next day, the 22nd, Kuranosuke's carbuncle flared up again with a vengeance. The poison had not fully dissipated, and now it festered and spread so rapidly and painfully that Kuranosuke soon found it dif-ficult to extend his arm. He had no choice now but to lie down and seek medical attention.

On the 4th Day of the Sixth Month,
I myself took possession of these funds.

Akō, Sixth Month, 4th Day

The deadline had been met. All the maps, village registers, account books, and other documents required by the Inspectors and Resident Deputies had been submitted on time. But that was by no means the last of the work to be done. There remained the unpleasant task of collecting unpaid debts—debts that were unrelated to agricultural income and thus were the property of the departing regime. By far the greatest of these was the money lent to salt merchants to cover operating costs until their next shipments could be sent to market. Since the Eleventh Month of the previous year, a total of 317 *kan*, 216 *momme*, 4 *rin* in silver had been lent. But being astute businessmen, the recipients of these funds could see that their creditors no longer had any power to enforce payment—and that the creditors themselves would soon disappear. It is hardly a surprise, therefore, that efforts to recover this investment—vigorously pursued, it is said—yielded only 33 *kan*, 200 *momme*, or about 570 *ryō* in gold. Barely 10 percent of what was owed. In his account book, Kuranosuke noted, "On the 4th Day of the Sixth Month, I myself took possession of these funds." Over the next few months, we shall see what he did with them.

◆ ◆ ◆

Now everyone was free to leave. Yatō Chōsuke, the Superintendent of Finance and the only person with the knowledge and skills to put the domain's accounts in order (though he had received only 20 koku per year for doing so), could take his wife and son and three daughters to Osaka, where they had decided to settle. Yoshida Chūzaemon, who had governed more than one-quarter of the Asano enfeoffment as District Deputy of Katō and Kasai, decided that he would move back to Katō; by now, he knew more people there than in Kyoto, Edo, or even Akō.

Kuranosuke himself was unable to move anywhere. By the time he had vacated the "offices" in the temple, the pain in his arm, which until now he had neglected, had grown so great that he could only retreat to his cottage in Osaki and rest until the infection abated. Kuranosuke knew, though, that his wife, O-Riku, had long had her heart set upon seeing the Tenjin Festival in Osaka on the way to their new home. To deprive her of this one pleasure in what had seemed an endless succession of tragedies would be just too cruel. He could not accompany the family himself, but somehow Kuranosuke arranged for O-Riku and the children to sail for Osaka around the middle of the Sixth Month. He would join them later, after the pain of his carbuncle had subsided sufficiently for him to travel.

All that we know of this episode, we know from a manuscript by a young man we shall never meet again, Fujie Heisuke Tadayasu. Heisuke was the son of a town doctor in Akō, a boy whose brilliance as a scholar of Chinese had caused Kuranosuke to employ him to teach the rudiments of reading classical Chinese to his eldest son. Heisuke was only three years older than Matsunojō, but the combination worked well, and the two boys became close friends. Before the Catastrophe, Heisuke had gone to Kyoto to study under Itō Jinsai and his son Tōgai at their Kogidō Academy on Horikawa Avenue; but he and Matsunojō were to meet again, quite unexpectedly. In this manuscript, *Tōkyakumon*, Heisuke writes: "The Ōishi family, one and all, are moving to the capital. In the Sixth Month, I went to Osaka, where quite by chance I encountered their young heir. And so, I joined them for the Tenjin Festival. The entire city was lit with lanterns, and we hired a boat from which to watch the festivities on the river. We spent that entire night together, and at dawn we parted."

They certainly chose the best way to enjoy the festivities. Preparations for and preliminaries of the festival had been under way for at least a month, but the climax of the celebration took place on the night of the 25th of the Sixth Month on the Yodo River. From dusk until dawn, there was—and still is—a seemingly endless procession of boats, all of them aglow with lanterns and with banners of all shades fluttering in the light, propelled by long ranks of men in matching costume rowing in perfect unison. From some, there rang the clangorous rhythm of a high-pitched gong in time with the furious beat of a deep bass drum—what the locals still call *donjiri-bayashi*. While from the banks of the river, there arose a succession of starbursts, lighting both sky and water with a stunning array of fiery color. All of this to accompany a stately circuit of the river by the deity enshrined in the Osaka Tenmangū—the spirit of that great but wronged scholar Sugawara no Michizane—who would then be welcomed back by yet another boat bearing greater than life-size dancing dolls. O-Riku and her children would have seen, and felt, all of this from within the very heart of it, an experience that they would not soon have forgotten and that might help them forget, for the space of a night at least, the anxiety and distress with which they must now live.

After their dawn parting with Fujie Heisuke, none of the Ōishi ever again saw their companion for the night. Heisuke returned to Kyoto to continue his studies at the Kogidō Academy, and in later years he would find employment with the House of Wakizaka as a resident Confucian scholar of the Tatsuno domain. He not only survived without setback the disenfeoffment of the Asano, but gained a career with the daimyo who had enforced the confiscation of their domain. We'll not encounter Fujie again in this narrative. But fifty years later, when a monument to Takumi-no-Kami was to be erected at the temple Kagakuji in Akō, it was Fujie Yūyō, as he was by then known, who was asked to compose the inscription.

Akō, Sixth Month, 24th Day

This was to be Kuranosuke's last full day in Akō. It was also the hundredth day since the seppuku of Asano Takumi-no-Kami. And so, since he was still in town, Kuranosuke arranged that quiet memorial rites be performed at Kagakuji, the Asano family temple in Akō. It is not known how many members of the old Corps of Vassals still lived in the region and which of them came to the temple; but under the circumstances, it must have been a subdued affair.

On the evening tide of the next day, the very time the festivities on the river in Osaka were beginning, Kuranosuke boarded a ship at Shinhama, at the tip of the peninsula opposite the castle, and set sail for Osaka. Katashima Shin'enshi waxes sentimental as he imagines the scene:

> As he looked back, the empty castle, towering in the mist against the limitless expanse of blue sea, brought tears to his eyes. When his lamented lord had set out to the east for the last time in his life and the brocade hawsers of his great ship were cast off, the oars of katsura and the rudder of magnolia sang under the moonlight as they were fixed to the gunwales. But now, as Kuranosuke consigned himself to this lonely craft, streams of tears clouded his vision, and he could hardly distinguish Suma from Akashi as they rowed past Muko, Wada Misaki, and into the harbor of Osaka.

Kuranosuke never saw Akō again. He and his family arrived in Yamashina on the 28th.

Edo, Late Sixth–Early Seventh Month
I doubt that Kuranosuke gave much thought to all the activity that he had set in motion in Edo until he was reasonably well settled in Yamashina. But a great deal had been going on there while he was on the move.

Precisely when Yūkai, the Superior of Enrinji, arrived in Edo is not recorded. His trip had not been easy. The rainy season had begun, roads were muddy, rivers were impassable, and everything was more expensive: lodging, porterage, ferrying. He would, however, have reached his destination by the time Kuranosuke left Akō, for on the 1st Day of the Seventh Month and again on the 10th he wrote to report what he had been doing. Neither of these letters survives, but we know something of their content from Kuranosuke's reply to them.

In Edo, Yūkai had lodged at the Kyōshōin, one of that row of fourteen small chapels on either side of the steep stone stairway leading up to Atago Shrine. The Superior was a monk whom he had known for many years, since they had been acolytes together, and thus was a man he could confide in and ask to help him make contact with the influential people he wished to entreat. Kyōshōin proved to be a worthy friend. It was he who arranged for Yūkai to meet both Ryūkō, the Abbot of Goji'in, and Kai'i, the Abbot of Gokokuji. The two clerics must have been bribed liberally, for they "responded favorably" to Yūkai's plea that Asano Daigaku be released from confinement and restored to honorable service. Neither man had any direct influence upon affairs of state, but it was well known that, despite their notoriety for avarice, they enjoyed the devotion of the Shogun's mother, Keishōin—toward whom the Shogun was almost abnormally filial. A word in the ear of Ryūkō or Kai'i, if he could be persuaded to pass it on, might thus be whispered to the Shogun by his own mother. Such was the hope of many petitioners, and like most petitioners, Yūkai received nothing more for his efforts (and investment) than a bit of kindly worded but disingenuous sympathy.

Kuranosuke had also suggested that Yūkai might attempt to contact Yanagisawa Dewa-no-Kami, the Shogun's Chief Adjutant:

> Dr. Uemura Yōsen has heard of a quick way to make contact that he told me of recently. He says that if you solicit the intercession of Yanagisawa's Elder, Hiraoka Uemon, and his Adjutant, Toyohara Gon'emon, they will bring the matter to the attention of Yanagisawa Sama. The elder brothers of these two, Hiraoka Ichiemon and Toyohara Michinosuke, are both employed in the Shogunate's Bureau of Finance. I'm told that it might be well to seek the good offices of these men first. Please give the idea some thought and discuss it with Kyōshōin. I expect that it might cost a bit to attempt this, but I trust you to make whatever arrangements seem appropriate. If you need more money, please let me know.

Whether Yūkai ever did attempt to approach Yanagisawa is not known. But the conditions demanded by Kuranosuke made it all but impossible for Yūkai to extract agreement from anyone but the Shogun himself. Kuranosuke wrote:

As I told you in Akō, I have not so much as hinted that Daigaku Sama be granted early release from Domiciliary Confinement. What I request is that his release, whenever it may be, be granted under conditions of honor such that he need feel no shame before any of his peers. For however exalted a position he may be restored to, as long as Kira remains in office and might serve alongside Daigaku Sama, then the standing of Daigaku Sama can never be one of honor. . . . This poses problems, I know . . . , for there is no way we can request that Kira and his son be dealt with harshly. Nor, for that matter, is it likely they ever will be dealt with harshly. Of that, I am well aware. But if father and son should be relieved of official duties, and Daigaku Sama should be pardoned, he might then move freely in society with his honor intact. But if ever they were to serve together, he could not do so without shame before his peers. Please keep this point firmly in mind and discuss it carefully with Kyōshōin. Our own hopes are based entirely upon this possibility. Whatever may transpire, however, it seems to me that Kira Dono's own safety depends entirely upon what becomes of Daigaku Sama. Were Kira's people to ponder this point, I should think that they, too, would agree.

How I wish that I could know Kuranosuke's private thoughts as he wrote this message. Did he really believe that Daigaku "might move freely in society" if only Kira and his son were "relieved of official duties"? Or, when he spoke of "Kira Dono's own safety," was he beginning to think that only the death of Kira Kōzuke-no-Suke could vindicate the honor of Asano Daigaku?

CHAPTER
34

*This is not the Genshirō
we knew in Akō.*

For many Akō samurai, the scattering of the clan had meant the breaking
of old ties, the destruction of delicate webs of friendship and mutual
assistance, the pain of building new lives in much reduced circumstances. For Shindō Genshirō, a Company Commander of Musketeers
and enfeoffed at 400 koku, it was quite the opposite. Once Genshirō
was free to leave Akō, he had moved to the village of Nishinoyama in
Yamashina, a comfortable valley just over the Eastern Hills from the
old capital; there, he found himself received not as an outsider but as
lord of the manor. He was thus in a position to invite his cousin Ōishi
Kuranosuke to move his family to the same village. Two months later,
Kuranosuke did just that.

How all of this was arranged is not clear. As we have seen, Kuranosuke
wrote to his adopted son, Ōnishibō Kaku'un, Superior of the small
temple Ōnishibō, just south of Kyoto, asking for advice on where a
ronin might live in that vicinity. Nothing more of their correspondence
survives, but it seems reasonable to assume that Kaku'un, Genshirō, and
Kuranosuke conferred further, eventually settling upon Yamashina as
the solution to Kuranosuke's problem.

But how was it that Shindō Genshirō found himself in such an
advantageous position? As we know, the Shindō had for long been in the
service of the great regental House of Konoe, and the entire Yamashina
Valley had once been an estate of the Konoe. But the genealogies that
might have told us how this portion of the Konoe estate passed into
the hands of its stewards, the Shindō, were destroyed during Oda

Nobunaga's march on Kyoto in 1568. We are left with little more than legend to fill this gap in our knowledge. Yet not all legends are entirely false; some may contain grains of truth passed down orally through successive generations, embroidered perhaps, but not so drastically as to make fictions of them. Here, for example, is what Katashima Shin'enshi was told when he sought an answer to the same question, sometime in the early eighteenth century:

> *Shindō Genshirō had for generations been related to the family of Kuranosuke, and his forebears had once been enfeoffed with the village of Nishinoyama in the province of Yamashiro, the district of Yamashina. When he was preparing to move there upon leaving Akō, he informed Kuranosuke of this, saying that he would go thither first and seek permission to retire there—whereupon something strange took place.*
>
> *Within this village of Nishinoyama in the province of Yamashiro, there is one place of particular antiquity. There are peasants who live there, but the place has no overlord, it pays no yearly tax, and the villagers refer to it with great respect as "the Manor House." Tradition has it (so say the village Elders) that during the reign of the GoDaigo Emperor, a warrior on the imperial side constructed a fortress there in which he himself dwelt and that this man was extremely respectful of the deities. On the west, he fervently worshipped Kōjin; on the south, Kumano Gongen; on the north, Inari Daimyōjin; and atop the hill, Atago Gongen. Thereafter, he fought against Ashikaga Takauji, and perished. The distant descendant of this brave defender of the valley was the warrior Shindō Genshirō, who served Asano Takumi-no-Kami, the castellan of Akō. Thus it was that the villagers, whose gratitude had never waned, still looked up to the Shindō as lords of that region and said that if their lord should again appear, there would surely be some sign.*
>
> *Now, at about that time, a man who lived in the capital at Ichijō Fuda-no-Tsuji was vouchsafed a miraculous dream that directed him to this mountain village, as a result of which he acquired something*

~ 285 ~

of great value. The man kept this a deep secret, yet word of his good fortune was somehow noised about, and great numbers of people began coming to Yamashina to pray for a miracle of their own.

In this region, on a low hill, there stood a pine grove—deep, still, and melancholy—and in this pine grove were a great many foxes' burrows. The supplicants who came here believed that if they put offerings of food in these burrows and the foxes came out and ate them, their pleas would be granted. Thus it was that a monthly festival day was established, and the place was given the name Inarizuka; the hustle and bustle there was like that at the Fourth or Fifth Avenue Crossroads. Since for several hundred years no one had lived here and the old shrine's observances had long since lapsed, the villagers were saying that an omen of this sort could be no ordinary occurrence, that this was a certain sign that the lord of this place would return. Whereupon the Catastrophe befell Asano Takumi-no-Kami, and to everyone's astonishment, Shindō Genshirō came to live in Yamashina.

The arrival of Genshirō did not, of course, mean that his peasants would again deliver up one-third or one-half of their crop to their lord. That, under the new regime, was no longer the system. But their welcome was genuine, and it is no legend that upon his arrival, Genshirō was considered the rightful owner of a considerable expanse of land in this "place of particular antiquity," including the hill that was home to that multitude of miracle-working foxes. Not exactly an estate, but sufficient to bring him a modest income without undue exertion. And when Genshirō broached the subject of his maternal cousin Ōishi Kuranosuke, the assembled Elders and Headman were quick to assure him that the same favors would gladly be extended to his worthy relative. All that would be required was a letter vouching for the good character of this gentleman and confirming that he was not a clandestine believer in any troublesome alien superstition—that is, Christianity. The letter survives:

DECLARATION OF GUARANTEE

On this present occasion, Ōishi Kuranosuke, a ronin of the domain of Akō in the province of Harima, he being a kinsman of mine, is to move to this village under my auspices. He is a trustworthy man. Even so, in the unlikely event of any difficulty involving the said Kuranosuke, I declare that I myself shall settle the matter with all speed, so as to cause no inconvenience whatever to the village. Needless to say, I shall countenance no extravagance on his part. The family have for generations been adherents of the Zen sect. A Temple Declaration to this effect shall be duly filed. For future reference, I hereby guarantee the foregoing.

GENROKU 14, YEAR OF THE SERPENT, SEVENTH MONTH

Signed and sealed: Shindō Genshirō

To: Village Headman
   Tahei Dono
Village Elders
   Gorōemon Dono
   Shōemon Dono
   Tokuemon Dono
   Kyūemon Dono
   Gen'emon Dono
   all other villagers

Thus was the way prepared for the arrival of Kuranosuke.

✦ ✦ ✦

Kuranosuke and his family could not have lingered long in Osaka, for only two days after his arrival in that city, they had already reached Yamashina. The Yodo riverboat would have taken them upstream as far as Fushimi, and there they halted briefly. Kuranosuke wished to thank Ōtsukaya Koemon, proprietor of the Honjin, for all his help over the past few months, and to collect any mail that had been delivered to him there. One letter that was waiting pleased him particularly. The letter itself does not survive, but the gist of it is unambiguous. Araki Jūzaemon was unsure where Kuranosuke had moved after leaving Akō, but he wished to let him know that "after returning to Edo, when the Council of Elders was in session, I had the opportunity to tell them in full detail what you requested of us in Akō. You may rest assured that their response was favorable." One could wish for a more detailed report, but perhaps Araki himself was unable to be more specific.

◆ ◆ ◆

Sixteen days were to pass after Kuranosuke's arrival before we hear anything further from him. Others had been in touch, but he had been too weary and unwell to reply. Finally, however, on the 13th Day of the Seventh Month, he answered a letter from his father-in-law, Ishizuka Gengobei, Chief Elder of the Kyōgoku house in Toyooka. In it, he described, better than any historian could hope to do, his new life as a ronin. It is worth quoting at length:

> I have perused your letter of the 7th of this month, which arrived via courier on the 11th, the day before yesterday. I am extremely pleased to hear that, despite the dreadful lingering heat of summer, you remain in robust health and that all in your household are well. Our voyage was trouble-free, and my family and I arrived here in Yamashina on the 28th of last month. With the help of people Genshirō sent from the village, all has gone smoothly, just as you said it would; so you may rest assured that we are now comfortably settled.
>
> You were so kind as to inquire after my abscess. It is still far from well. The pain is no longer quite so severe, but I still cannot extend the arm. And the pustules have yet to drain. The doctors in Akō told me that because the poison had spread to the muscles, it would prove difficult to flex them, and that before the pustules burst, I should go as quickly as possible to take the waters at the hot springs in Arima. But seeing how serious the infection had become, I instead consulted the surgeon Yamamoto Jotetsu, whose expertise is held in high repute here, as well as His Lordship's internal-medicine specialist, my close

friend Terai Genkei. Both men, after careful examination, tell me that it is not likely to heal quickly. Previously, I had been applying the ointment cold; but this, they say, only encourages the muscle to contract. If I were to apply the ointment warm, however, it would do no harm, and I should soon be able to flex the muscle. There is no need to take the waters, the surgeon told me; and rather than trying to extend the arm, it would be more beneficial to bend it. Before I came here, the swelling had abated a bit, but now it seems to have spread. In Akō, the poison had grown active, and so from the 21st of the Fifth Month until I arrived here, I ate nothing but a few pickles morning and evening. Both doctors now tell me, however, that the poison is no longer active, so I can eat anything I like, and I may drink saké as well. Jotetsu himself offered me a drink, which I downed straightaway and immediately felt vastly better for it. Astonished though I am to say this, you need worry no longer about my health.

Item. We have truly enjoyed savoring the two magnificent varieties of sea bream and other seasonal delicacies that you were so kind as to send us. We are most grateful to you for them. Being a ronin, I had resigned myself to having but one kind of pickle day in and day out. A number of my old comrades and friends who now live in Kyoto and Fushimi from time to time come to visit, some of them from more than 2 leagues away. When they do, I like to offer them something to eat. We still have a bit of the salt fish that we brought from Akō, and we do our best to eke it out with one thing and another. But that will soon be depleted, which would have left us rather badly deprived. But now, thanks to this wondrous bounty of your good will, we are able to treat all of our guests from Kyoto. . . .

Being as far from Kyoto as we are, there is hardly anything one can buy here. No peddlers come to Yamashina. Even for tofu, or any of the seasonal vegetables, such as eggplant, we have to send someone all the way to Kyoto, which is a great bother. And there are no fish of any sort. It's really terribly inconvenient. Still, it is the perfect place for a ronin to live, they say.

Genshirō knows the region well and especially this place where we are living. He arrived here before us and has arranged for someone to supply us with eggplants and all sorts of garden vegetables, which provides us with just about everything we need to cook with. His family for generations has owned quite a lot of land around here— rice paddies, garden fields, mountain timberland. And so he is also able to supply us with firewood.

There are a great many rural samurai living here. The village Headman and the village Elders are all descended from Genshirō's forebears, and there are several tens of people who go by the name Shindō and claim membership in the clan. Genshirō is the quite the lord of the manor in these parts—our undisputed local daimyo. On one of the mountains he owns, there is a great foxes' lair, which for some reason has become very popular with Inari worshippers in recent years. Tens of thousands of them have come from Kyoto and its suburbs; it's become one of the most popular of all the Inari shrines. Numbers have fallen off a bit since last year, but even now not a day goes by but what ten or twenty pilgrims turn up. Naturally, we find all this rather amusing . . . , so do please share the story with your wife and family. "This is not the Genshirō we knew in Akō," we chuckle among ourselves.

We've not been terribly well off of late and don't have the means to buy much land around here without resort to borrowing. . . . But be that as it may, I have purchased a small house, which comes with a few rice paddies and an extensive bamboo grove. The interior isn't at all cramped, but the house itself is not in the best of condition and needs to be refurbished in order to make it livable. For one thing, the lack of a barrack block is terribly inconvenient, for I've no place to house my retainers. A while ago, I undertook to build a small barracks, thinking that would be no problem since this is a private dwelling. But then I found that in order to erect any additional buildings, one must apply to the Resident Shogunal Deputy, which was an exasperating process. This region comes under the jurisdiction of Kobori Jin'emon Dono. Eventually, my application was approved and work has begun. I'm inconvenienced, too, by the lack of a storehouse.

Item. We had intended to send your courier back immediately, but he was taken ill en route, and after arriving here was stricken with stomach pangs. We insisted, therefore, that he rest here for a time. He will leave today. We are most grateful for your kindness in sending the man such a great distance bearing gifts for us.

Item. There is a great deal more I wish I could tell you. But of late . . . I've been having dizzy spells, after which I feel unsteady on my feet, so much so that I've not even been able to write a letter. I've been depressed and listless, too, which the doctors say may in part be due to the heat. And so I've been resting in order to recover from all these ailments and have only now got around to writing this letter. I hope you'll forgive me if at times it seems incomprehensible. . . . Most respectfully,

SEVENTH MONTH, 13TH DAY   *Ōishi Kuranosuke [monogram]*

To: Gengobei Sama,

in reply

Katashima Shin'enshi's version of the move from Akō to Yamashina certainly retains some of the embroidery of long tradition. But Kuranosuke himself, who would never see what Shin'enshi wrote, corroborates a good deal of it.

CHAPTER

35

*I think that you three may have misunderstood
the thrust of what I was saying in Akō.*

Three days after the surrender of Akō Castle, on the 22nd Day of
the Fourth Month, when Horibe Yasubei, Takada Gunbei, and Okuda
Magodayū left Akō to return to Edo, Kuranosuke came personally to
the Eastern Portal to see them off. He thanked them for having taken
the trouble to travel so far, told them how touched he had been by
their thoughtfulness and devotion, apologized for having been unable
to spend more time with them, made tentative plans to meet again
in Edo, and finally, with an agreeable exchange of pleasantries, bade
them farewell. The three men must have sensed that Kuranosuke's
warm reception and good humor had been genuine, for Yasubei
wrote to his father Yahei that "everything went just as we three had
hoped it would." All had not gone quite as they had hoped, but when
Kuranosuke and Yasubei parted, each thought that he understood the
other and that they had reached mutual agreement. Both would have
to revise their opinions.

♦ ♦ ♦

When Yasubei, Gunbei, and Magodayū left Edo for Akō, they made
the (normally) seventeen-day trip in ten day days; that was about as
fast as it could be done on foot, given that anyone who walks must also
sleep. On their return, they took twenty-four days, stopping in Fushimi,
Hachiman, Kyoto, and Nara along the way. They were not sightseeing.
They were visiting old comrades who had moved to these places, discussing their plans with them, and trying to recruit them to their cause.

Nothing of what they said or were told is recorded, but shortly after they arrived back in Edo, on the 16th of the Fifth Month, they began—as they saw it—to put their plans into action.

✦ ✦ ✦

In Yasubei's first letter to Kuranosuke, written on the 19th, only three days after his return, we see the first signs of misunderstanding between the two. Yasubei clearly expected Kuranosuke not simply to visit Edo, but to move there, most likely for the purpose of leading an attack on Kira. Yasubei did sometimes seem to hear only what he wished to hear, but this time his hopes were not based entirely upon wishful thinking. In Akō, when Kuranosuke had pleaded with Yasubei to trust him, he did say that there were no limiting conditions on his promises. We know, too, that Kuranosuke himself wished to visit Edo as soon as possible, if only to thank the Inspector Araki Jūzaemon for having presented his petition to the Council of Elders. But Yasubei could not have known that Kuranosuke now suffered from a carbuncle so severely infected that he could travel nowhere. Thus it was that Yasubei wrote:

> . . . Have you any thoughts where you will lodge when you come to Edo? If you've made no arrangements before you arrive, you can stay with us for a day or two. Please let us know what your travel dates will be. After the first day or two, once we've found lodging for you, all will go well. We wait in the hope that you will come just as soon as possible and trust that you will arrive in time for the memorial rites next month.
>
> Shall we get together the things that you'll be needing in your daily life here? Just let us know; we'll obtain whatever you think you'll need. I know that there's no need say this, but you mustn't hesitate to tell us what to do. If you find that you have to postpone your departure, one of us could come to you, as we have much that we wish to tell you. Please let us know all the details in your reply.

Almost a month was to pass before Kuranosuke even saw this letter. Yasubei and his comrades had sent it by commercial courier, addressed in care of Ōtsukaya Koemon in Fushimi. Normally, the letter would have been delivered about six days later, by which time, Yasubei thought, Kuranosuke would either have reached or been en route to Yamashina. But Kuranosuke was still in Akō, and even Koemon had no idea when he would arrive in Fushimi. Once he learnt that Kuranosuke was too ill to leave Akō, however, Koemon forwarded Yasubei's letter to him there.

In the meantime, Yasubei, Gunbei, and Magodayū were left waiting for a reply that never came. They would not have expected an immediate reply, of course; mail could move no faster than a courier could run, and it was a run of 125 leagues (312.5 miles, 500 kilometers) from Edo to Fushimi. By the time half a month had passed, though, their expectations had begun to rise, only to be dashed, day after day. Finally, on the 18th of the Sixth Month, a full month after he and his comrades had written, Yasubei decided to approach Kuranosuke by another route. Oyama Gengoemon, Commander of the Corps of Pages, was an uncle of Kuranosuke. But Yasubei also considered Gengoemon to be a close friend with whom he could talk more frankly than with the Chief Elder. If Gengoemon could be persuaded to intercede with Kuranosuke, some action might result. After the requisite pleasantries, Yasubei came straight to the point:

> We hear all manner of interesting news here, but for us it is just day after dull day as long as we have no idea when any of you will be coming to Edo. . . . I sincerely hope that you will be firm and make up your minds to act.
>
> We understand that at the hundredth-day memorial rites, Ochiai Yozaemon will be sent to represent Her Ladyship the Widow. . . . Yet even if they chant 1,000 or 10,000 scrolls of scripture, I doubt that His Lordship will be much pleased by it. Our late lord must be utterly exasperated by all these equivocating creatures. . . . We have been running about inquiring of one person after another, but so far have found no more than four or five who feel as we do. Most of the others are extremely cautious; they want to wait for a decision from on high, and see what is to become of Kobiki-chō. They have

to adapt, they say, and try to make a living. Some of them are such smooth talkers that they make us feel like beggars, these old hands. There is no point in approaching any of them again. . . .

Some of those who previously disagreed with Kuranosuke, though, may by now have acquired a bit of courage, so we should discuss the matter with them again. For I doubt that we can achieve our goal with only a small force. If all you want to do is die in the Kira mansion, then there is no need to make any plans at all. But we want something more than that; we want to lay to rest our late lord's rage. . . .

We shall send a copy of this letter to Kuranosuke together with our jointly signed letters. We await your early reply to our letter of the 19th of last month. Respectfully,

SIXTH MONTH 18TH DAY *Horibe Yasubei [monogram]*
To: Oyama Gengoemon Sama

Edo, Sixth Month, 24th Day

On the same day that Kuranosuke had arranged quiet memorial rites at the temple Kagakuji in Akō, Yasubei, Gunbei, and Magodayū attended the hundredth-day rites at Sengakuji, where Takumi-no-Kami was actually buried. They made the customary contribution to the temple, knelt patiently through the chanting of the sutras (in which they obviously placed little faith), and offered incense at the altar; but once the rites in the main hall were completed, they proceeded up the path to the newly erected gravestone and did what they had come to do. They first made deep obeisance, and then proclaimed aloud: "We men of resolve have now roused ourselves to action and are determined, just as soon as we possibly can, to sever the head of Kōzuke-no-Suke and present it to Your Lordship upon this very gravestone. This we are pledged to do." Then, once more, they made deep obeisance.

And having done so, the first "action" to which they roused themselves was to visit the former Edo Elder of the domain, Yasui Hikoemon. At the time of the Catastrophe, Hikoemon had refused even to discuss the matter with them. But if now they could win him to their cause, others who had hesitated might then follow the lead of their superior. As they had hoped, their messenger returned, saying, "Yes, do come, whenever you please."

This was their first meeting since returning from Akō, Yasubei tells us, so there was a bit of greeting and gossip to be got through before they could come to the point. But finally, Yasubei said: "Now then—our late lord has cast away the noble house established by his grandfather; indeed, he has cast away his very life, which normally one would not trade for the entire realm. Yet just when he was about to vent his wrath, he was thwarted and then made to commit seppuku. As his vassals, we find this intolerable. We have already discussed the matter with those in Akō; now we would urge you to join us. If you do, this will strengthen the resolve of some of the others stationed in Edo, and they most likely will follow your orders."

"Quite so!" Hikoemon replied. "I feel exactly as you do. You are absolutely right. By all the gods of Japan, I swear that you're the very first men I've yet encountered to show such firm resolve. When the time comes, I'll be with you. But rumor has it, you know, that Daigaku Dono will be treated with considerable favor. People in the service of Yanagisawa Sama say that it's most unlikely he'll be dealt with harshly and that they want us to know that he is behaving with exemplary discretion during his confinement. I know that I'm only saying what's been said any number of times, from antiquity onward; but if the Asano house can be reinstated—the house of our late lord's grand-father—that surely will give His Lordship greater cause for joy than the sight of the head of Kōzuke-no-Suke. For the moment, I think, it would be best to wait until we see what the fate of Daigaku Dono will be."

"If our late lord had prized the noble house of his grandfather so highly, surely he would never even have attempted to vent his wrath," Yasubei said. "But instead, he chose to abandon even his life. We reckon that it would please him immensely to see the head of Kōzuke-no-Suke. You, of all people, as well as the rest of us who look to His Late Lordship as our lord and master, are bound to his service forever. It makes no sense whatever to reinstate the house under Daigaku Dono while we can still see the enemy of our lord with our own eyes. If we could ask His Lordship, we're certain that he would say that Daigaku Dono should join us. And Daigaku Dono would surely agree; they're related by blood, after all. As a bannerman, though, he's still duty-bound to the Shogun; he'd be a traitor if he joined us. But he'd certainly want us, as direct vassals of his brother, to do the deed. No, on this point you are mistaken. You might give the matter a bit more thought before you make up your mind."

Hikoemon hesitated before he answered: "This is not something that you should talk yourselves into recklessly, in a fit of passion."

"Of the three of us," Yasubei shot back, "I am the youngest. I expect that when you speak of 'a fit of passion' you do so with reference to me—impertinent though it is of me to say so. So let me tell you my present thoughts on the matter: that the enemy of one's lord is far more to be detested than the enemy of one's parent. Indeed, I would go so far as to say that I would cut off the head of my father if commanded to do so by my lord. There is no greater service that any of us can render to our lord than to take the head of Kōzuke-no-Suke just as soon as we possibly can, present it to him at his grave, and in that way dispel the wrath that lingers on after His Lordship's death. If you can commit yourself to this course of action, then we are prepared to follow your orders in every particular. This is what we have come to tell you."

Hikoemon, however, said nothing to commit himself. Instead, he cleverly deflected Yasubei's challenge: "We hear that Kōzuke-no-Suke maintains very tight security. That worries me. But we must discuss this again soon, so think it through very carefully. It's good that you've a group of people prepared to go through with this."

The four men parted amiably, and Yasubei, at least, claims that he was "delighted that, on the whole, Hikoemon seemed to agree with us." He was in for a rude surprise. Shortly thereafter, he encountered Isogai Jūrōzaemon, one of the former Page Boys who had cut off his topknot when Takumi-no-Kami was buried. Yasubei knew that Jūrōzaemon, too, was bent upon killing Kira; he had said as much in Akō when he refused to join Kuranosuke's pact. So Yasubei saw no harm in telling him of their meeting with Yasui Hikoemon; he may even have hoped that their "success" would persuade Jūrōzaemon to join their group. But Jūrōzaemon, too, had encountered Hikoemon in the meantime, from whom he had heard a rather different version of that meeting.

"That's not what he told me," Jūrōzaemon said. "He said, 'Those three are planning a vendetta. I thought about it for some time after they left, but—they're out of their minds. If they're burning with such zeal, they should leave the rest of us alone and attack the man themselves, just the three of them. It's outrageous, trying to force others to join them.'"

"I never realized that he was such a coward," Yasubei said. "How can he—someone as deeply indebted as he is to our late lord; who was raised up to be an Elder of the house—how can he say such a thing, while we three, all of us new vassals, are prepared to do our duty and throw away a hundred years of life for the sake of our lord? Does the man know no shame? Is he that craven a coward?"

Thereafter, Yasubei, Gunbei, and Magodayū severed all relations with Yasui Hikoemon.

◆ ◆ ◆

A few days after arriving in Yamashina, Kuranosuke sent a brief note acknowledging receipt of Yasubei's long-delayed letter, and on the 13th of the Seventh Month, he composed a long and thoughtful response to it:

> Item. *I have read Yasubei Dono's letter to Gengoemon. Considering what he writes therein, I think that you three may have misunderstood the thrust of what I was saying in Akō. As I said when we met, I am convinced that, in the present situation, our deliberations must be premised entirely upon the outcome of Daigaku Sama's case. As long as that remains an unknown, no matter what we ourselves may think best, we must strive with all our might to do whatever best serves his cause. This is no time to be concocting schemes just to please ourselves. I have discussed this with everyone in Akō, and all of them share this opinion. And so, at present, and until we know what his fate will be, I am exploring every possible way in which we*

might benefit Daigaku Sama. Even were you to come here, I would tell you the same and ask your assistance in doing so.

If a great many men from Akō were now to go to Edo, far from benefiting Daigaku Sama, it would only damage his cause. This is something we discussed countless times in Akō, and in the end we decided that only I, Sōemon, and one other man would go. We would pay our respects at Sengakuji, and I would inquire whether the request I made of the Inspectors when they were in Akō had been transmitted to the Council of Elders and, if possible, request that it be acted upon. Immediately thereafter, I would come back here. For me to remain too long in Edo could prove troublesome for Daigaku Sama. For if anything were to transpire that made it impossible for me to come back to Edo thereafter, that would be disastrous. . . . And now that we have heard that Araki Jūzaemon Dono has told Asano Mino-no-Kami Dono that he has conveyed my request to the Council of Elders and the Junior Council of Elders, and that their response was favorable, it seems best that I delay my visit a bit longer. As I mentioned previously, the abscess is still painful, and I'm unable to extend my left arm. I'm currently being treated here, both surgically and with medication, and still need to convalesce. It's difficult to predict how long it will take to heal, so with one thing and another, I must postpone my visit.

Item. You were saying previously that it would be best if we were to proceed to Edo in groups of about twenty; but at this point in time, it would quite wrong to assemble such a large force. I have already made this clear to the men in Akō as well as those living in other provinces, so until I tell them otherwise, it is unlikely that there will be any movement to Edo in large numbers, except for those who have private business there. For better or for worse, that is what we must resign ourselves to until we learn the outcome of Daigaku Sama's case. . . . At this point in time, I have no other plan; at no moment throughout the day do I contemplate any course of action other than to do my very best by Daigaku Sama. Gengoemon, Genshirō, and my other kin are in agreement with me, as are all the others here.

Gengoemon was quite shocked by the letter from Yasubei Dono. He himself will write in greater detail concerning this. Respectfully,

SEVENTH MONTH, 13TH DAY   *Ōishi Kuranosuke [monogram]*

To: Takada Gunbei
Horibe Yasubei
Okuda Magodayū

P.S. Please inform those in Edo with whom you are in contact of the foregoing, and that it is best that we now bide our time. . . . Herewith the foregoing.

And so the scene was set for a vigorous—although never acrimonious—struggle of wills between two men, very different in nature but agreed that the wrong done to their liege lord must be righted, each man trying to persuade the other that his was the right way to go about it: Yasubei, single-mindedly focused upon immediate attack and decapitation of Kira Kōzuke-no-Suke; and Kuranosuke, determined to wait and see whether the Shogunate would act upon the agreement that he had reached with the Inspectors—even though he must have suspected that in the end he, too, would be forced to act. Over the next few months, until Yasubei and Kuranosuke could meet again, this was to be an epistolary struggle. Fortunately for us, Yasubei was careful to preserve copies of every letter that passed between them. He knew from the start that they would be making history.

CHAPTER
36

*They're telling Takumi's men,
"Kill him!"*

In the northernmost outskirts of Kyoto, on a site long linked with the House of Asano, there stands a small chapel, the Zuikōin. Most passers-by take no notice of its dull earthen walls and the three low roofs within, for they have no notion of how much history they conceal.

Ten centuries ago, legend has it, a minor but devoted retainer of the Seiwa Emperor, now known only as Asano no Sukune, buried the placenta of his newborn sovereign here. On the site, he then built a small shrine at which the august imperial relic might be worshipped and dedicated it to Inari, the fox-messenger of the gods. Logically enough, people began calling the shrine the "Asano Inari"; and in one of those near-miraculous accidents of history, it continued to be maintained and its relic worshipped long after its builder had passed away.

Nearly 750 years later, when Toyotomi Hideyoshi began building his great palace in the north of the city, the Asano Inari was still there; and by another curious accident, the land on which the little shrine stood was allotted to Hideyoshi's brother-in-law Asano Nagamasa. Asano no Sukune was in no way related to the line of Asano Nagamasa. Their names are pronounced alike, but the characters with which they are written differ totally. Even so, Nagamasa thought the coincidence a happy one, perhaps even auspicious. He adopted the shrine as the guardian deity of his new villa, and before long, people were writing "Asano Inari" with Nagamasa's name instead of Sukune's.

But how swiftly fortunes could change in those years of constant warfare. Hardly a decade later, Hideyoshi was dead, his palace demolished, and with it the mansions of his retainers that clustered about it. The Asano Inari, one account tells us, was for years so overgrown with brambles that it "became the lair of foxes"—live foxes, not the supernatural sort sent by the gods.

Sometime after the battle of Sekigahara, however, the site of Nagamasa's villa in Kyoto passed into the hands of Yamazaki Samanosuke Iemori, lord of Wakasa Castle in Inaba, who decided to build a Zen temple there, where his remains might one day be interred and prayers offered for his repose in the afterlife. A monk, Takuho Sōrin, was summoned from the nearby monastery Daitokuji to serve as Superior, and the new temple was named Zuikōin (Chapel of the Gleam of Good Omen), this pleasant appellation being drawn from its patron's posthumous name. But the advent of the Yamazaki was by no means the end of the Asano connection.

Takuho lived for another sixty-one years after the battle of Sekigahara, during which time he buried and conferred the merit of his prayers and devotions upon four generations of the Yamazaki house: Iemori, Ieharu, Toshiie, and (Toranosuke) Haruyori. Alas, he outlived them all. The boy Haruyori died suddenly, without heir, bringing an end to the Wakasa branch of the Yamazaki line. For the last four years of his life, Takuho was left destitute, with no patron, no parishioners, and no support from his home temple, Daitokuji. After his death, Zuikōin was left uninhabited, while the Yamazaki graves disappeared into the newly resurgent thicket. Had it not been for the Asano, the temple might have gone totally to ruin.

+ + +

As chance would have it, however, a second cousin of the late Haruyori had become the consort of Asano Inaba-no-Kami Nagaharu, lord of the Asano cadet house in Miyoshi; this lady, O-Ishi by name, took it upon herself to restore the chapel of her Yamazaki ancestors. Her first cousin, a Zen monk named Yōho Sōton, was summoned to be the second Superior of Zuikōin. And when the daughter of O-Ishi was married to Asano Takumi-no-Kami, she continued the patronage resumed by her mother. The third Superior, Reigaku Sōshū, was a cousin of Lady

Asano; while for yet another cousin, Kai Shuso, a small hermitage, the Shūsuian, was built in a corner of the temple grounds. The now ancient Asano Inari Shrine was refurbished and enclosed within its own fence of pointed red palings. And most importantly, the temple was supported by Takumi-no-Kami with a benefice of 100 koku per year. Thus it was that by the time of the Catastrophe, the Zuikōin was devoted as much to the posthumous welfare of Asano ancestors as to that of the Yamazaki line—and, of course, to prayers for good fortune in battle, should the need for such luck ever arise.

Quite naturally, the Zuikōin was Kuranosuke's first destination after his arrival in Yamashina, for one of the first tasks on his agenda was to arrange for the erection of a memorial to Takumi-no-Kami. He had already disbursed 100 ryō of the funds that he had brought from Akō to purchase a plot of timberland for the temple—a small mountain, in fact—to finance prayers and devotions for his late lord in perpetuity.

Once he had recovered sufficiently from his carbuncle, he spent two or three days with Kai Shuso in his hermitage while details of the memorial were worked out. It was then, Katashima Shin'enshi tells us, that Kuranosuke came to see that the chapel and its hermitage were ideally situated for clandestine meetings of the ronin. Their gatherings to mourn their late lord on the 14th of every month would arouse no suspicion, and the compound was well protected from prying eyes and ears. There were no dwellings of any consequence nearby. To the north, it bordered the fields and groves of Murasakino, while to the west were the pines and bamboo thickets sheltering the way station of the Imamiya Shrine, used but once or twice a year at festival time:

> *The path was overgrown with weeds, hiding any trace of people's passage. A solitary gate set in the wall, cutting it off from this world of dust, was the only entrance. . . . The grounds were thick with trees and rampant vines; brambles obscured all sign of human habitation. Apart from the moan of the wind in the treetops and the beat of driven rain against the gate, the only sounds were the hoot of the owl and the plaintive cry of the cuckoo. The ronin rejoiced that it was so perfect a place and met here often.*

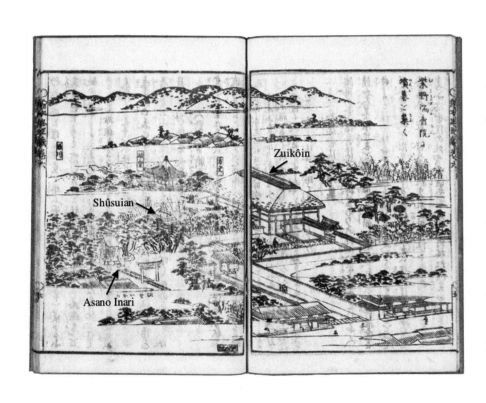

figure 12
Zuikōin. (*Edo meisho zue*, 1834–1836)

I doubt that the site was quite as desolate as Shin'enshi would have us believe, but it was indeed well isolated from the attention of the world; the neighborhood was better known for the pine tree across the street that legend claimed was a manifestation of Michizane, returned to Kyoto after his death in Kyushu. And the temple did indeed become the regular meeting place of the ronin. On the 14th Day of the Eighth Month, the memorial was dedicated, and a court cap and robe worn by Takumi-no-Kami were buried at its base. All the ronin within traveling distance of the capital gathered there for the rite, the first of a long series of monthly meetings at which the future of so many of them would be decided.

◆ ◆ ◆

What with moving his family to a new home in a new province, arranging matters at Zuikōin, and establishing contact with everyone in the Kyoto region, Kuranosuke was kept busier than he wished to be in his present weakened condition. Still, it would not do to lose touch with Edo. Yasubei, Gunbei, and Magodayū—the Edo Three—were now his only former comrades there with whom he was still in correspondence. He had nothing new to tell them, but just to keep that link alive, he wrote again on the 22nd of the Seventh Month. He still could not extend his arm, he told them, and he regretted the recent mix-up of their mail. But that aside, he continued to think it unwise that he travel to Edo just now or that they come to Kyoto. This was no time to be rushing things or pushing one's personal preferences: "Once we know what is to become of Daigaku Sama, we will call everyone together and discuss what is to be done."

This bland and rather repetitive missive seems not to have sat well with Yasubei. He took it not as a well-meant assurance that he had not been forgotten, but as evidence that Kuranosuke might be lapsing into indecision and temporizing, perhaps even going back on the promise he had made in Akō. His reply is signed only by Yasubei himself. Gunbei and Magodayū may well have agreed with everything he had to say, but Yasubei seems to have been determined to impress upon Kuranosuke just how firmly he believed that there was only one honorable way to settle this matter—to kill Kira Kōzuke-no-Suke. That must be the goal of all that they did, and it must be done now:

Item. *I gather that you have read my letter to Gengoemon Dono, for in your letter you state that you find it upsetting. We here find it most unpleasant that we must ignore the presence of Kōzuke-no-Suke Dono before our very eyes. And the more we three discuss it, the more difficult it is to endure. This is what we would like to impress upon you. And since Gengoemon Dono has always been so sympathetic to our cause, we wanted to let him know how firmly resolved we are to exact the satisfaction of His Lordship's wrath just as soon as we possibly can. . . . Say what we will, however, our goal will not be easily accomplished, and we find it mortifying that we are not free simply to do as honor dictates. You say that once you know the disposition of Daigaku's case, you will tell us what you have in mind. We look forward to hearing your thoughts, and unpleasant though the passing months and days will be, we shall await that moment.*

Item. *You state, too, that what you told us in Akō and what we think here seem to you to differ. In my humble estimation, however, it appears that the difference you perceive is rather more a discrepancy between your original thoughts and your present opinion. From the very start, our aim has never been anything other than to dispel His Lordship's rage against Kōzuke-no-Suke. . . . And it seemed to us that your intentions were no different from ours . . . , which is why we have sent letter after letter urging that you hasten to make up your mind.*

Item. *Rumor here has it that Daigaku Dono's case will be decided very favorably. But even if he is granted a fief comprising all of Japan, and India besides, he'll still not be able to overlook the continued existence of Kōzuke; so it's hard to see what good a pardon of any sort will do him.*

Edo, Eighth Month, 19th Day

News traveled fast in Edo. Despite the strict prohibition of any publication even remotely resembling a modern newspaper, people knew
a great deal about what was going on in their city. Through networks
of friends; through domainal Liaison Officers, who were constantly
in touch with their contacts in officialdom and their counterparts in
other military houses; through the gossip of lowly menials who were
so often within earshot of their superiors—through myriad chan-
nels—people knew.

It is no surprise, then, that Yasubei and his comrades were quick to
learn that the Council of Elders was on the verge of commanding Kira
to surrender his mansion within the outer ramparts of the castle and
move to Honjo, on the far side of the Sumida River.

The most likely instigator of this command was Hachisuka Hida-
no-Kami Takashige, who occupied the mansion immediately adjacent
to Kira's. As castellan of Tomita in the province of Awa, a middling
domain rated at 50,000 koku, Hida-no-Kami did not rank among
the grandest of lords. But as head of a branch of the great House of
Hachisuka, whose domains comprised two entire provinces, Awa and
Awaji, he had the attention of the Council of Elders when he com-
plained of a threat to the safety of his neighborhood. Like so many
who knew that justice had not been done, Hida-no-Kami was convinced that his neighbor would soon be attacked and assassinated,
and he worried lest the violence spill over onto his own side of the
wall. Ever since Takumi-no-Kami had been made to take his own
life and Kira had gone free, Hida-no-Kami had kept his samurai on
full alert, night and day. By now, they—and their lord—were weary
of this imposition (as they saw it). His complaint, everyone agreed,
was meant as a tacit request that this nuisance be moved elsewhere in
the city. The Elders, too, took it as such and complied. On the same
day that Yasubei reported this news to Kuranosuke, a directive from
the Council of Elders was delivered to the Kira household, ordering
them to vacate the mansion at Gofukubashi and move to a residence in
Honjō that for the past three years had been occupied by another bannerman of the Shogun, Matsudaira Noborinosuke. This intelligence,

Yasubei reported in passing, came to them directly from a Liaison Officer in the Hachisuka house.

The reaction of the Kira household is not recorded. But one of Kira's nephews had a story to tell of his own response to the news. Mizuno Hayato-no-Kami, lord and castellan of Matsumoto in the province of Shinano (65,000 koku), was married to a half-sister of Kira's wife.

Like many lords of his stature, he maintained a personal entourage of the sort that had come to be called a Circle of Talkers; like all absolute rulers, he could never be sure whether his vassals were telling him the truth as they actually saw it, or telling him what they thought was most likely to please their lord. Thus the need for men whom he could talk to and who were not afraid to talk back—intelligent men, usually of low rank, known for their frankness and even bluntness, men who had nothing to gain by being otherwise. The practice had arisen in wartime, not only from the need for reliable intelligence, but from the more practical need to keep their commander awake in time of danger. In those days, the group would be made up of battle-hardened old warriors, men wise in military stratagems, as well as falconers, intelligencers, masters of linked verse and ceremonial tea, and even the occasional scholar. One of Hayato-no-Kami's favorites was a blind masseur who attended him at the end of every day. This was the man whom His Lordship relied upon for an unvarnished analysis of each day's news.

"Well, what do you make of Kōzuke?" Hayato asked. "Being forced to move . . ."

"It's a command from on high," the blind man said.

"A command?"

"Yes. They're telling Takumi's men, 'Kill him!' Discreetly, of course."

"That's it, isn't it?" Hayato replied. "You're absolutely right!"

Now it is most unlikely that anyone in the Shogunate had any intention of encouraging anyone to kill Kira. Yet it was Hayato-no-Kami himself who told this tale to his friends—quite unconcerned that they should know how little love he felt for his esteemed uncle.

◆ ◆ ◆

How this story reached Yasubei, we do not know. But the Edo Three, of course, agreed with the blind masseur and lost no time in writing to Kuranosuke to point out what a boon this move would be to a would-be assassin. Nor was it only one blind man, they insisted; all of Edo had their eyes upon them and were expecting them to act:

Item. *We understand fully your desire to await the decision of the fate of Daigaku Sama. We know, too, that you have good reasons for this. Yet even if we do await the decision of his fate, we shall still be beholden thereafter to carry out our late lord's intentions. . . . Once Daigaku Sama was granted his own enfeoffment and was established independently in his own right, he became a mere sibling of our lord. We, and everyone else, look to His Late Lordship as our liege lord. As his vassals, it is to him that we owe our utmost loyalty. Our late lord gave up not only his own life, which no one would exchange even for rule of the entire realm, but also the noble house handed down to him from the generation of his grandfather. For his vassals to ignore the continued existence of our lord's enemy, and insist that we lavish all our attention upon the independently enfeoffed Daigaku Sama, smacks more of safeguarding our own lives than of exacting the satisfaction of His Lordship's wrath, does it not? What all the lords in this city of Edo, lesser and greater alike, and even the Shogun's own bannermen are saying is this: "Takumi-no-Kami Dono is descended in a noble house of long standing; it is most unlikely that there should be no samurai who will do their duty by him; surely these men will not disregard the continued existence of their lord's enemy."*

Item. *"Even if Daigaku Sama were to be restored to the domain of Akō at its full 50,000 koku—indeed, even if he were to be granted a domain of 1 million koku—he still could never hold his head up among his peers after seeing his own brother being made to commit seppuku."* This is what all of Edo is saying.

Item. *"Takumi Dono's vassals will never be able to endure the presence of their lord's enemy. If they would just cut down Kōzuke, then Daigaku Dono would be able to serve with his peers on a footing of honor. But if they kill Kira after Daigaku is released from Domiciliary Confinement, then it will be assumed that they did so on Daigaku Donos orders. That will not stand him in good stead. Even if his vassals turn out to be cowards, Daigaku Dono himself will surely attack Kōzuke's mansion." This is what all the lords and bannermen are saying. And when His Lordship's distant kin hear this, even they say: "Daigaku Sama could never defy his superiors like that. but surely Takumi's vassals will not stand for it."*

But somewhere along its long route, this letter seems to have gone astray. Yasubei would have addressed it to Kuranosuke in care of Ōtsukaya Koemon in Fushimi, and Koemon would have sent one of his own men to carry it up the road to Yamashina. Normally, that would have taken about ten days, perhaps even less. Kuranosuke tells us, however—and we have no reason to doubt him—that their letter did not arrive until the 29th Day of the Ninth Month, forty days after it was written. Forty days in which Yasubei, Gunbei, and Magodayū were left to wonder why their news had prompted no response from their Chief Elder. And even longer for Kuranosuke to wonder why the Edo Three had lapsed into silence. Both parties reacted to their uncertainty in the same way.

Kuranosuke still was not well enough to travel to Edo himself, but he summoned Hara Sōemon from Osaka and asked him to go in his place, both to assess the present situation there and to persuade the Edo Three to proceed with caution and do nothing rash. And shortly thereafter, so as to lend even more urgency and authority to his word, he sent his cousin Shindō Genshirō on the same mission.

In Edo, Yasubei, Gunbei, and Magodayū decided that they must travel to Yamashina and deal with Kuranosuke face to face—"argue their case and urge him to make up his mind." Yet even as they were preparing to depart, a note arrived announcing the imminent arrival of Hara Sōemon and, shortly thereafter, the arrival of Shindō Genshirō.

To their own astonishment, though, the new arrivals found themselves so much in agreement with the Edo Three that instead of trying to placate them, they decided that they must summon Kuranosuke to Edo. On the 9th, Sōemon and Genshirō dispatched a joint letter, via commercial courier, that they insisted must reach Yamashina within six days. It did.

Traveling in the opposite direction was Kuranosuke's response to that long-delayed letter from Yasubei, Gunbei, and Magodayū, which he had written in total ignorance of all that was going on in Edo. By then, events had overtaken just about everything that he had to say:

> Item. *I understand fully the devotion that you feel toward our late lord. And although I find it difficult to accept the distinction, I recognize that there may be some justice in your view of Daigaku Sama as a mere sibling. Why, then, do we now find ourselves at odds with each other? As I have said on previous occasions, we must consider the origins of our difference. Had we acted hastily, for reasons of our own, none of this would now be troubling us. What really matters, though, is that we accomplish our original purpose. Yet can we claim that that purpose is to push our personal priorities so forcefully that we bring about even the downfall of the succession? It is only to be expected that others will criticize us for one thing or another. If we renounce personal motives, however, and focus upon the fundamentals, then the criticism of others, it seems to me, is nothing we need worry very much about. To me, it seems best that we await the disposition of the case, and then respond according to whether it be favorable or unfavorable. I am only too well aware that the chance of a favorable outcome is hardly one in ten thousand; still, that possibility is the reason I have continued to wait until now. If, despite the odds, Daigaku Sama should be restored to a position of honor among his peers, would not this please even our late lord? But if the outcome should be otherwise and his honor should not be restored, then, I am sure, His Lordship's anger will be even more intense than ours; and you and I shall find ourselves comrades in a common cause. . . .*
>
> Item. *There is no need for you to remind me that Daigaku Sama cannot be restored to a position of honor among his peers as long as nothing is done about Kira. My thoughts on all that this entails would be difficult to explain in an epistolary conversation of this sort, but I have discussed the matter with all of you previously, so I*

expect that you already know what I think.

Katashima Shin'enshi has described Kuranosuke as "a gentle and generous man, yet staunchly resolute and coolly courageous." This eloquent reply to that insistent, almost accusatory missive from the Edo Three exemplifies beautifully both aspects of his character. He reasons with them in the most even-tempered terms, yet does not retreat even slightly from his previous position. By the 15th Day of the Tenth Month, however, when the letter from Hara Sōemon and Shindō Genshirō arrived, he could see that this letter was now totally irrelevant. By the 20th, Kuranosuke was on the road to Edo.

*We are determined to do all in our
power not to exceed this deadline.*

For seven months now, Yasubei, Gunbei, and Magodayū had persevered in virtual isolation. And by the beginning of the Tenth Month, they were still the Edo Three—but still no more than three. Now, however, with this migration from Kyoto that Kuranosuke had set in motion, it began to look as though a larger group might be about to take shape.

When Kuranosuke asked Hara Sōemon to go to Edo in his stead, he sent along two other men to accompany him: Ushioda Matanojō and Nakamura Kansuke, both former members of the Akō Horse Guards, mature men from the middle ranks of the Corps of Vassals. Both had stayed in Akō after the surrender of the castle to help Kuranosuke with the administrative chores that remained, Matanojō having long been the keeper of maps, and Kansuke being a skilled calligrapher. Now, with Sōemon, they were to represent Kuranosuke in Edo and attempt to persuade the Edo Three to refrain from any rash action until the time was right.

As Yasubei tells it, when he and his comrades first called upon their visitors and reiterated what they had been telling Kuranosuke, all three of the men from Kyoto voiced complete agreement with them, and thereafter their sense of accord only deepened. Finally, it was decided, they would all go to see the sights in Kamakura, and while there pray at the Hachiman Shrine that they might "get their hands on" the enemy of their late lord and proffer a pledge of their determination to do so. They would set out on the 7th Day of the Tenth Month, they agreed— whereupon, they received further notice from Kyoto that Kuranosuke's cousin Shindō Genshirō, accompanied by Ōtaka Gengo, would be arriving in Edo on that very day. Their excursion to Kamakura was, of course, canceled, and Genshirō did indeed arrive, although a day late, on the 8th.

Ōtaka Gengo had not been keen to travel in the company of Genshirō —or "Genshi," as he rather rudely called him in a letter to Sōemon's brother. Once in Edo, though, Gengo fell in immediately with the six men who welcomed him; even Genshirō, hardly a man prone to enthusiasms, joined in the general mood of amicable harmony—the upshot of which was unanimous agreement that they must urge Kuranosuke to come to Edo immediately.

Thus it was that only one day after the arrival of Genshirō and Gengo, at midday on the 9th of the Tenth Month, these eight men sent a joint letter to Kuranosuke by relay courier, which they were assured would reach him by the 15th. The letter does not survive, but it must have arrived on time, and it must have been mightily, perhaps even frighteningly persuasive, for "with only four or five days to prepare himself," Kuranosuke set out from Kyoto on the 20th Day of the Tenth Month.

♦ ♦ ♦

In Edo, while they waited, discussions went on, the gatherings rotating from one man's home to another to another, in the course of which, quite naturally, nuances of opinion began to emerge. No outright disagreement divided them, but Yasubei began to think of some of his new comrades as the "stronger" men—Ushioda Matanojō, Nakamura Kansuke, Ōtaka Gengo, and a new member of the group, Takebayashi Tadashichi, who had moved back to Edo in the summer but only recently had made contact with the Edo Three. No disparaging mention is made of the older men, Hara Sōemon and Shindō Genshirō, but lest any division develop after such a satisfying sense of unity had been achieved, Yasubei, Gunbei, and Magodayū thought it best to revive their plan for an excursion to Kamakura—and to compose a pledge to be signed by all and offered up at the Hachiman Shrine:

Item. *When our late lord, in order to exact the satisfaction of his wrath, forsook the noble house handed down since the generation of his grandfather, as well as his very life, which one would hardly exchange even for rule over the entire realm, he then failed to accomplish his desired goal. This most regrettable of events, we, his vassals, find it impossible to ignore. Given which, despite certain differences of opinion among those devoted to the cause and delays resulting therefrom, we are agreed that the Way of Loyalty demands that by the Third Month of the coming year, on or about the anniversary of our lord's death, we shall die in an attack upon his enemy's residence. We are determined to do all in our power not to exceed this deadline, as well as to exact the satisfaction of His Lordship's wrath. Having determined upon this, let there be no departure therefrom. Should there be any who contravene this pledge, may they not escape the punishment of our late lord. Herewith this oath, as above,*

TENTH MONTH, 29TH DAY
　　　　　　　　　　　　　Okuda Magodayū
　　　　　　　　　　　　　Horibe Yasubei
　　　　　　　　　　　　　Takada Gunbei

The Edo Three were hoping that their new comrades would affix their monograms to this oath, thus binding them to rally those in the capital region when they returned. But they declined.

"We need hardly mention," they said, "that your strength of purpose is plain to see. We, too, wish that here and now we might present you with a pledge sworn before the gods. As it happens, though, Kuranosuke, and probably a number of others, will soon be arriving; if these men are of the opinion that we should proceed at a more measured pace, we should discuss the matter with them, exchange pledges, assemble the others, and then vindicate His Lordship's wrath. We feel, therefore, that this matter should be left until then."

There was nothing for it now but to wait.

◆ ◆ ◆

Yasubei, Gunbei, and Magodayū had indeed persevered for months in isolation, but not because they were the only Akō ronin in Edo who were keen to see "justice" done to Kira. Some of the men who, at the very outset, had refused to join forces with Yasubei were still in Edo. They had refused the man, but not the mission; although they were now out of touch with the mainstream, they were still just as eager as Yasubei to attack their common enemy. One of these men was Maebara Isuke.

Isuke, like Ōtaka Gengo and Takebayashi Tadashichi, was a member of that lowly cohort of samurai, the Mid-Corps of Pages. The nomenclature is misleading. The Mid-Corps was "mid-" not because its members were middle-ranking, but because their place in the hierarchy was midway between proper mounted samurai and those who did not rank as samurai at all. Maebara Isuke received a stipend of 10 koku plus rations for three men per year, probably not enough to support a family. Although he was nearly forty, there is no record of his having married, which probably explains why, after the Catastrophe, he did not return to Akō. His parents were dead, his relatives scattered; he had no family to return to. Instead, he used what little cash he had—probably his severance allowance plus the money given to him to finance his return "home"—to buy odd bits of silk and cotton. To this stock, he added some garments of his own, which he unstitched for the material, and then set himself up as a dealer in remnants. At first, he moved to Tomizawa-chō, near the used-clothing market. But when he heard that Kira had been commanded to move to Honjo, Isuke moved his "shop" to Aioi-chō, immediately opposite the southwest corner of the property that Kira had been allotted, where he could "watch what went on in the abode of the enemy." He even managed to get work as a day laborer with the contractor hired to renovate the residence, and in that way was able to inspect the interior as well. As far as we know, Isuke did all of this on his own initiative, consulting no one else, with no larger plan to guide him.

We shall meet a few more of these resourceful Mid-Corps men as time passes and they begin to make contact with Kuranosuke and Yasubei.

CHAPTER
38

Kazuemon! You're said to be a brilliant swordsman.
Let's see you cut down one of these swallows.

When Kuranosuke set out for Edo, he was accompanied by the senior
members of the command group—Okuno Shōgen, Kawamura Denbei,
Okamoto Jirōzaemon, and Nakamura Sei'emon—and probably the personal retainers of each. They left Kyoto on the 20th Day of the Tenth
Month and arrived in Edo on the 3rd of the Eleventh Month. And
when they arrived, they lodged not at an inn, but in Mita with Maekawa
Chūdayū, an employment agent for day laborers who had long been a
contractor to the Asano house and who remained a loyal friend. The
very next morning, Yasubei, Gunbei, and Magodayū called there and left
convinced—as was Yasubei's habit—that Kuranosuke agreed completely
with them. In their delight, they arranged to have a cask of saké sent to
him; on the 8th, Kuranosuke wrote to thank them and invite them to a
meeting to be held on the 10th at Maekawa Chūdayū's home.

Two rooms were required to accommodate everyone in attendance.
In the main room were the most senior men: Kuranosuke, of course,
Okuno Shōgen, Kawamura Denbei, Shindō Genshirō, Hara Sōemon,
and Okamoto Jirōzaemon. And in the anteroom were Ushioda Matanojō,
Nakamura Kansuke, Ōtaka Gengo, Nakamura Sei'emon, Takebayashi
Tadashichi, and another newcomer, Katsuda Shinzaemon. Yasubei did
not say where he and Gunbei and Magodayū sat, but it must have been
at the juncture of the two rooms, for, at least as he described it, his was
the principal voice in the meeting.

He began, "Given that we have already agreed that we should take
action in the Third Month of the coming year, we must now discuss

how we shall go about it. To go on waiting, thinking that whatever we do presupposes knowing the fate of Daigaku Sama, seems to us to pin everything on Daigaku Sama while neglecting the proprieties of relations between lord and vassal. Even if Daigaku Sama is dealt with favorably, we ourselves cannot ignore the continued presence of Kōzuke-no-Suke Dono. But if we dispel His Lordship's wrath while Daigaku Sama is still in Domiciliary Confinement, then when he is released, he will be able to face his peers on a footing of honor, and we shall have upheld the proprieties of relations between lord and vassal."

Whatever Yasubei thought Kuranosuke had told them at their first meeting, Kuranosuke was not prepared to swallow this formulation of it: "I see no reason we need limit ourselves to the Third Month. If an appropriate opportunity presents itself prior to the Third Month, then that must be the moment when we all band together. There remains, however, one crucial matter concerning which I still wish to know the outcome."

That "one crucial matter" was, of course, the outcome of the case of Asano Daigaku. But Yasubei had already thought of a way around that obstacle: "We don't really see why deciding upon a date should be a problem. The Third Month corresponds roughly to the first anniversary of His Lordship's death. Daigaku Sama may even have been pardoned by then, which would satisfy your wish to show respect for the authorities and await their decision. . . . If perchance we still lack certain knowledge, even by the Third Month, we can postpone the action a month or two and focus our efforts upon working out the strategy of our attack. But if we fail to settle upon a deadline, everyone will remain in a state of uncertainty, and our planning will be half-baked and ineffectual. In short, it just makes good sense to aim for the Third Month."

Kuranosuke seems to have been unwilling to push back any harder. As Katashima Shin'enshi imagines it, "He smiled faintly as he gave in to the forceful arguments of the three samurai." His reply: "Well, in that case, you had better come to Kyoto as soon as possible in the New Year. We'll need the benefit of your thinking when we make our plans."

To which Shindō Genshirō added, "If great numbers of us are seen to be gathering here in Edo, rumors will spread through the city very quickly. I think that it would be very difficult for all of us to assemble here. We should meet in Kyoto and work out everything there—at Maruyama or Ryōzen or somewhere else up in the hills."

The lower-ranking men in the anteroom must have found it difficult to hear precisely what was being said in the main room, for as the meeting was breaking up, they rushed up around the Edo Three.

"Is it settled, then?" they asked. "Have they agreed upon the Third Month of next year?"

"They have indeed," Yasubei answered. "We should hear from them before then how they plan to proceed; once we do, we'll discuss and decide all the details. They want the three of us to go Kyoto next year, to work all that out." Matanojō, Gengo, and Kansuke agreed: this was just what they had been hoping for.

♦ ♦ ♦

Kuranosuke would remain in Edo for twenty days, only one of which was given over to this meeting. But we have only the sketchiest knowledge of what he did with the rest of his time in the city. Yasubei does at least tell us that Kuranosuke called upon the Inspectors Araki Jūzaemon and Sakakibara Uneme, probably to thank them for having transmitted his entreaty to the Council of Elders and the Junior Council, and to request their continued support—but nothing more. He makes no mention of any further meetings with the Edo Three.

Ogawa Tsunemitsu, too, mentions Kuranosuke's visits to the Inspectors and says also that he paid his respects at the grave of Takumi-no-Kami at Sengakuji and made a courtesy call upon the widow, Yōzei'in. It would almost certainly have been on the 14th, the date of his lord's death, that he went to Sengakuji. His visit to the widow is undated, but a rather charming vignette of it survives from later sources. Kuranosuke seems to have had a reputation for being exceptionally sensitive to the cold. And so, in anticipation of his visit, the widow herself sewed a nightcap of violet silken crêpe for him, which he wore to bed regularly thereafter.

Although no record of it survives, it is hard to imagine that Kuranosuke would have gone all the way to Edo and not paid his respects to Asano Aki-no-Kami, lord of the Asano main house in Hiroshima, or that he would have neglected to visit his relatives Asano Mino-no-Kami and Asano Sahyōe. If for no other reason, this would have been too good an opportunity to renew his pleas for their support of his efforts to have the legacy of Takumi-no-Kami reinstated under his heir, Asano Daigaku.

✦ ✦ ✦

Whatever Kuranosuke did do while in Edo, the tale most often told of that visit—his rehabilitation of Fuwa Kazuemon—is totally fictional. It is true that Kazuemon required rehabilitation. He was the son of Okano Jidayū, whom we have already encountered, fully equipped to fight to the death in Akō Castle. Like his father, Kazuemon had been dismissed in disgrace from the Akō Corps of Vassals at least two or three years earlier. As a ronin, he should never have been admitted to the group of those pledged to the cause. But shortly after Kuranosuke's visit to Edo, Kazuemon's name begins to appear among those who are legitimate members of the pact. How did this happen? There is no evidence that Kuranosuke had anything whatever to do with Kazuemon's return to the fold. But in the absence of evidence, a beautiful legend was created, according to which Kazuemon, despite his ill fame, retained undiminished affection for his late lord, as well as a deep sense of his own indebtedness to him. And so, when he heard that Kuranosuke was in Edo, he went to him and, in the most abject fashion, begged forgiveness for his past transgressions and pleaded to be restored to the good graces of his comrades so that he might join them in their struggle for justice. "It is not within my power to pardon someone His Lordship has punished," Kuranosuke told him; but, then, His Lordship was no longer living. After a long and thoughtful pause, Kuranosuke said, "Come see me tomorrow morning."

The next morning was the morning of the 14th, when Kuranosuke was to pay his respects at the grave of Takumi-no-Kami at Sengakuji. He took Kazuemon with him, and as they knelt at the grave, he implored their lord to forgive Kazuemon so that he might join those pledged to dispel His Lordship's wrath against Kira Kōzuke-no-Suke. Kuranosuke then prostrated himself, and moments later when he arose, he turned to Kazuemon and told him that His Lordship had reinstated him at a stipend of 100 koku. From that moment forward—so the story goes—Fuwa Kazuemon was a proper member of the pact.

◆ ◆ ◆

So who was this man, and what was it about him that should inspire so elaborate a legend?

Fuwa Kazuemon was descended in a line that traced its service to the Asano house back to those days of endemic warfare when Asano Nagamasa rose to become one of the great powers of the land. Thus Kazuemon and his father, although not of high rank, were, in terms of long service, among the senior vassals of the house. They seem also to have been some of the worst behaved of the Asano vassals. What the father did to merit dismissal we do not know; but Kazuemon's dismissal was the direct result of his passion for swordplay.

A typically gilded version of the story tells a tale of virtue spurned. Asano Takumi-no-Kami, accompanied by an entourage of his vassals, was aboard a boat, heading for Atago, a spot of great beauty a few leagues upriver from Akō Castle. Perhaps under the influence of an excess of saké, His Lordship taunted Kazuemon: "Kazuemon! You're said to be a brilliant swordsman. Let's see you cut down one of these swallows."

Kazuemon bowed in assent and made his way to the prow of the boat—where for some time he stood stock-still. Takumi grew impatient and shouted: "Well, we're waiting!"

No response from Kazuemon and no movement. Then suddenly, there was a glint of steel—so fleeting that no one saw the source. By the time their eyes caught up with the action, Kazuemon was slowly slipping his sword back into its sheath, and a tiny wing tinged with blood was fluttering down like a crimson maple leaf and floating past the moving boat. Kazuemon had done his duty, but after prostrating himself before his lord, he turned to the senior officers who were sitting beside him and tendered his resignation from the Akō Corps of Vassals. He could not disobey a direct order, he protested, but his skill with the sword was no party amusement; it was meant to be used only in defending the life of his lord. His injured pride thus forced him to become a ronin. A beautiful story; but, alas, the truth of the matter is quite different.

Kazuemon was indeed a brilliant swordsman, and one of the ways he developed his skill was through the grisly practice of "blade testing"—which is to say, the "testing" of one's sword not on stalks of bamboo or bundles of straw, but on real human bodies. Early in the Edo period, this was accomplished simply by cutting down some unsuspecting pedestrian on a dark street corner, a practice known as *tsujikiri*. But as law and order came to the cities, *tsujikiri* was severely curtailed, and the testing of blades was transferred to the execution ground, where it was known as *suemonokiri*. Strictly speaking, one was supposed to entrust one's sword to the executioner, who for a small fee would test it on the neck of a criminal and provide the owner with a written report. But with the right connections—usually through one's teacher of swordsmanship—one could do one's own "testing," and slice up the bodies of these criminals oneself. Yet one source tells us that Kazuemon—as late as the Genroku era—still went out "night after night" for practice on passers-by—so often that His Lordship eventually commanded that he not be sent to Edo anymore but remain permanently in Akō. There were nowhere near as many executions—or opportunities for anonymous killing—in a provincial castle town as in the roaring metropolis of Edo. But Kazuemon seems to have found other ways of maintaining his skills.

He would go to the graveyard at night and dig up newly buried bodies to practice on. On one occasion, the mother of a Palace Usher, a Tea Monk, had died. Kazuemon did not know who had been buried, and when he found that it was an old woman, whose body he thought useless for his purposes, he cut her up in a rage and scattered the pieces all about the place. The next morning, the monks of the temple discovered the remains of Kazuemon's rampage and reported it to the Tea Monk. He rushed to the scene, but having no idea who might have done it, he could do nothing but put things in order and leave. He was bitterly angry and wanted to investigate, but had no clue where to start. Later, a rumor spread among the samurai that it was Kazuemon, and when it transpired that the Tea Monk, too, suspected this possibility, the domain Inspectors reported the incident to Takumi-no-Kami. Since there was no proof, it was difficult to mount an official investigation. But the voice of rumor was growing clamorous. And so, on other pretexts, Kazuemon was dismissed. In secret, he was given traveling money and sent away as a ronin.

Other versions of this story, and other entirely different stories, abound. But these episodes seem to be the most that can be said of Kazuemon without venturing into the realm of fantasy. It can be reported with complete certainty, though, that however Kazuemon managed to insinuate himself into the pact, Kuranosuke did nothing to exclude him, and eventually must have accepted a written pledge from him. Ogawa Tsunemitsu reckons that Kuranosuke relented in the case of Kazuemon because he was a warrior of such rare courage, skill, and daring. As we shall see, he was right.

◆ ◆ ◆

Anticlimactic though it is, there is one unquestionably true case of Kuranosuke welcoming a new member to the pact during his sojourn in Edo. Maebara Isuke, who was eking out a living by selling remnants of fabric and working as a day laborer—and was now living within sight of the rear gate of the mansion that Kira would soon inhabit—sought out Kuranosuke and submitted a pledge to him shortly before his return to Kyoto. Isuke, too, in a less flamboyant way, would prove to be a stalwart of the group.

◆ ◆ ◆

Kuranosuke set out from Edo on the 23rd Day of the Eleventh Month. Hara Sōemon and Ōtaka Gengo remained behind with 70 ryō in gold that Kuranosuke had given them to buy a house in Mita. They would need a place for the group to lodge in months to come.

CHAPTER

39

To leave things to a careless crew of slipshod carpenters . . . is not at all the way to proceed.

When Kuranosuke returned to Yamashina on the 5th Day of the last month of the year of the Catastrophe, he was met by a series of three shocks. The first saddened him, the second forced him to abandon some of his options for action, and the third sobered him. By the time that month was over, the world would seem a more difficult place for him to persist in his plans. But persist he would.

Osaka, Eleventh Month, 6th Day

Hashimoto Heizaemon was but a youth of eighteen. Only two or three years earlier, he had succeeded to a place in the unit of Horse Guards commanded by Okabayashi Mokunosuke. When news of the Catastrophe reached Akō, he was among the first to pledge his allegiance to Kuranosuke. And that is all we know of his past. What happened to him after the Corps of Vassals dispersed may seem an old story, but is nonetheless a tragic story.

Heizaemon seems to have moved to Osaka, where he began frequenting a teahouse, the Awajiya, in the New Quarter near the Shijimigawa River. What happened next is only what happened to many other young men, for whom there was no other way that they could meet young women before a marriage had been arranged for them. And like some of those others, Heizaemon fell in love—with a girl, probably his own age, named O-Hatsu. It could never have been anything but an impossible love. Heizaemon was a ronin, with no income and only as much money as he possessed when he had left Akō. O-Hatsu was a prostitute, whom he could never meet without payment and who was indentured to the Awajiya, probably for ten years. Their love could last only as long as Heizaemon's money lasted. When that ran out, they decided to do as others in their predicament had done. They would die together.

In the Seventh Hour (ca. 4:00 a.m.) of the 6th—three days after Kuranosuke arrived in Edo—they slipped out of the Awajiya, probably with great difficulty, and somewhere nearby, probably at a temple or shrine, Heizaemon stabbed O-Hatsu and then himself. Fortunately, they both died. O-Hatsu had been Heizaemon's first love, and his last.

Word of the tragedy somehow reached a relative, Sassa Kozaemon, a former Company Commander who was living in Kyoto. Kozaemon immediately wrote to Hayami Tōzaemon, a member of the same unit of Horse Guards as Heizaemon, who was then living in Osaka. Tōzaemon had been one of that first pair of messengers who had carried news of the Catastrophe from Edo to Akō. Now, in response to Kozaemon's request, he went to the Awajiya, collected Heizaemon's body, and had it returned to his next of kin (identity unknown) in Aburanokōji, Kyoto.

Kuranosuke would have known nothing of this sad episode until he returned to Yamashina a month later, on the 5th Day of the Twelfth Month.

Edo, Twelfth Month, 11th Day

A bit of news leaked out of Edo Castle today that caused great alarm to Yasubei, Gunbei, and Magodayū. The Council of Elders had granted the petition of Kira Kōzuke-no-Suke that he be allowed to retire and that his son Kira Sahei succeed him as head of the house and as a Master of Court Protocol. To most people, this would have signified very little; to the Edo Three, it meant that there was no longer any hope that Kira would be punished, that justice would be done.

Yasubei, Gunbei, and Magodayū carried the news immediately to Hara Sōemon and Ōtaka Gengo, who were still in Edo. As far as they were concerned, they said, there was no longer any reason to wait.

"Quite right!" Sōemon said. "So you three must travel to Kyoto in the New Year. We'll get everyone in the region together, talk things over, and make our plans. Then we'll all come back to Edo in the spring."

Sōemon also thought that he and Gengo should set out for Kyoto immediately and carry the news personally to Kuranosuke. But Gengo was ill, and Sōemon was unwilling to leave him behind. He would have to write instead.

Two days later, on the 13th, Kira gave up his mansion within the outer ramparts and moved across the river to Honjo. At the same time, his wife moved to the Uesugi Lower Mansion in Shirogane for the duration of the renovations to their new home. Kira's retirement and Sahei's succession were now complete.

Sōemon dispatched his letter via commercial courier on the 15th, and Kuranosuke received his second shock of the month on the 23rd. Unfortunately, Sōemon's letter no longer survives, but its force must have been great. Kuranosuke mulled the matter for a day, and on the 25th, he wrote three letters, all of them very different in tone from those he had written thus far.

His first letter is addressed to Terai Genkei, Takumi-no-Kami's personal physician, who now lived just over the Eastern Hills in Kyoto. Parts of this text are illegible; it was not well preserved in the archives of the Zuikōin. It is clear, though, that Kuranosuke spoke to Genkei very directly, as a friend and as a confidant whom he could trust. This he could do because the letter would be delivered by Genkei's son Gentatsu, and thus would not be seen by anyone whom he would not wish to see it. After thanking Genkei for some medicine that he had sent, and inquiring after the eye ailment his son was suffering, Kuranosuke continued:

> Item. *In a letter from Edo sent on the 15th, news came that there is no change in Kobiki-chō and that on the 11th of this month, Kira was granted permission, on the most favorable terms, both to retire and to pass on his position without encumbrance. I am not sure how best to deal with this. We now have no choice, though, but to make up our minds and act. Gentatsu will explain the details to you. The Edo Three will be coming to Kyoto toward the end of the First*

Month, at which time we will discuss the matter and decide what to do. Hara is still en route from Edo. When he arrives in the coming year, I expect that we will then begin to move.

LAST MONTH OF THE YEAR, 25TH DAY   *Ōishi Kuranosuke*

[monogram]

To: Terai Genkei Sama

Kuranosuke's next two letters, likewise inspired by the news of Kira's retirement, were addressed to the Edo Three and to Yasubei's father, Horibe Yahei. In both of them, he wrote in a manner sharply contrasting with that of his letter to Genkei. He couched both letters entirely in metaphor. The attack that they were contemplating is a "building project"; the participants in the attack are the "carpenters"; and the message is that the carpenters must not be so hasty and slipshod that they erect a structure, only to have it collapse. But before they do anything, they must make contact with the "sawyer," Asano Daigaku, and consult his opinion. Why Kuranosuke chose to express himself in such a strained manner is hard to imagine. Perhaps he meant to soften the stringency of his warnings with a touch of humor, or to avoid speaking too directly in a letter that could fall into the wrong hands. Or was it simply an irresistible train of associations with Kobiki-chō, the "Sawyer's Quarter," home of Asano Daigaku, that sprang into his mind? Whatever his reasons, the results were not what he intended. Both Yahei and the Edo Three replied in terms that made clear their anger and exasperation. First, to the Edo Three, Kuranosuke wrote:

The year is nearly at an end, and thus, in the coming year, we must discuss our project carefully, considering all its merits and demerits. I worry, though, lest we act too hastily, like a crew of slipshod carpenters. We must pay close attention to the lay of the land and the foundations, discuss everything thoroughly, and then assemble and erect the uprights. But since at present we lack suitable materials, whatever we might construct would be unsound, which would not only invite criticism, but reflect badly upon our client. We must plan this building calmly and carefully in order to forestall even the least disparagement of it. I say the same at every opportunity to the carpenters in this region. If we proceed rashly, I fear that we shall end up with a building constructed of inferior timber. And even with the best timber we can lay hands on, I worry lest we fail to build with sufficient care.

But the most thoroughgoing exposition of his views (and his metaphor) he directed to Horibe Yahei. Until now, Kuranosuke had not corresponded with Yahei. But before his retirement, Yahei had been the Edo Liaison Officer of the Akō domain; he knew the city and those who governed it well. Kuranosuke knew, too, that as Yasubei's adoptive father, Yahei was the silent but influential partner of the Edo Three. To Yahei, Kuranosuke wrote:

I take the liberty of addressing this brief missive to you. It was a great delight to see you after such a long while on my recent visit. The bitter cold continues. I hope to hear that you and yours remain well. All of us, high and low, managed to return safely, without delay en route.

Item. I heard the day before yesterday the joyous news that on the 11th, the gentleman in question was granted permission to retire and to pass on to his heir his position as head of house. This certainly is most auspicious. If what we hear is true, this is one matter now settled. I hardly think we need watch and wait any longer. But what do you think? I should like very much to hear your thoughts on the matter, as well as those of your comrades.

Item. If we are now to undertake a building project, we shall need to ascertain how things stand with the sawyer. To begin building without word from the sawyer will never do. Is the sawyer's enthusiasm for the project ten times that of our own, or is he displeased with the project? Until we know this, nothing can be settled. You yourself being an accomplished builder, I hope that you will make known your views on all aspects of the project and provide detailed supervision of the work. I hope to hear, too, what the three carpenters, and also the other men, have in mind.

Item. *As I have said before, if, at last, we are to undertake this construction project, we must begin by examining the lay of the land with extreme care, and as we build make sure that all the timbers and pillars, without exception, are of sufficient strength. To leave things to a careless crew of slipshod carpenters, who in their haste begrudge the time and effort to do the job properly, is not at all the way to proceed. Care, care, and more care must be taken in calculating the number of day laborers to be employed and, above all, in assessing the merits and demerits of the site. Only when this has been done to the best of our ability should work begin. But what are your thoughts on the matter?*

Item. *If the old gentleman in retirement willfully refuses to entertain our request and cooperate with us, then I plan to apply directly to his son, the young lord. I would prefer, of course, to take up the matter with the retired gentleman and would find it most regrettable should he persist in keeping to himself. But there is nothing we ourselves can do about this; so if he is not amenable to our proposal, then we shall take up the matter directly with the young lord. In any case, I mean to spare no expense on our construction project, and thus I think it of great importance that we exercise the utmost care as we build, starting from the ground up. Whatever our crew of clumsy carpenters is to do, they should first consult with the supervisors of the project. I do hope that you will be able to make our clumsy carpenters grasp this point, for it is of prime importance.*

Item. *The plan is for our three carpenters to come to Kyoto in the New Year to discuss the project, prior to which it is of first importance that you confer with them and apprise them of the merits and demerits of the plan. I trust that you will agree. I say the same at every opportunity to the carpenters in this region. I await hearing in detail your thoughts on the matter at your earliest convenience. Respectfully,*

TWELFTH MONTH, 25TH DAY   *Ōishi Kuranosuke [monogram]*
To: Horibe Yahei Sama

~ 329 ~

Despite all the circumlocution, Kira's retirement with official sanction clearly forced Kuranosuke to abandon certain of his previous schemes. He could no longer entertain even the faintest hope of an honorable disposition of the case of Asano Daigaku. He could no longer consider any resolution to the problem other than to attack and kill Kira. His concerns had now narrowed to the meticulous planning and precise execution of that attack. But even these concessions would seem too lukewarm a response to those fired with a sense of the urgency of this moment.

CHAPTER
40

Monogram not affixed
because of illness.

The third in the series of shocks that greeted Kuranosuke upon his return from Edo probably took place shortly before he heard of Kira's retirement and wrote his "clumsy carpenter" letters. For on a letter from the Edo Three, dated the 27th Day of the Twelfth Month, a part of the signature read: "Takada Gunbei (monogram not affixed because of illness)." This was subterfuge. Gunbei had, in fact, defected.

◆ ◆ ◆

Like Horibe Yasubei and Okuda Magodayū, Takada Gunbei was a new man—recruited in Edo and stationed in Edo. All three were members of the Edo Horse Guards, and all three were disciples of Horiuchi Gendazaemon, that great proponent of "long weapons." And since the Catastrophe, the three had been further united by their belief that only the death of Kira could right the injustice to their lord. So what had happened to break this bond?

Whether we can ever know the whole truth remains a question. Yasubei has recorded what he knew of the story, for which he, in turn, depended upon what Gunbei told him. It is a firsthand account, but the account of a man who was anything but disinterested. External evidence corroborates some of what Gunbei said, but the question of his motives must remain open. Given these cautions, this is what we are told.

◆ ◆ ◆

Gunbei had held a tenuous position in the service of Ogasawara

Sado-no-Kami, but had been recommended to Takumi-no-Kami a few years earlier by Toda Yamashiro-no-Kami. He cut a fine figure, it was said, and had a great many friends in the service of various bannermen—which made a good impression when he was assigned to guard duty at the Sakurada Gate. Gunbei was able to bow and greet by name each bannerman who passed, and this, of course, redounded to the credit of Takumi-no-Kami.

The source of Gunbei's problem was an uncle in his father's line named Uchida Saburōemon, who himself had been the victim of an injustice. Saburōemon's father had been a bannerman, but was judged guilty by relationship and thus disenfeoffed, because his elder brother was suspected of being in league with the banished daimyo Ōkubo Tadachika. Never mind that the charges against Ōkubo were false to begin with; never mind that Saburōemon's father was guilty of nothing more than being related to a suspect; never mind that Saburōemon had not even been born at the time. The damage done to them all was long lasting. Saburōemon's father died unreprieved, and Saburōemon himself was denied his birthright until pardoned in an amnesty when he was sixty-seven years old—eighty-five years after the crime that had never been committed. In 1700, Saburōemon was at long last made a bannerman and assigned to the Reserve Force; on the 1st Day of the Twelfth Month of the present year (1701), he was granted his first audience with the Shogun, awarded a stipend of 110 bales, and assigned to a unit commanded by Murakoshi Iyo-no-Kami. In short, Saburōemon was an old man who had never married because he could never afford to marry, and thus had no heir to inherit his belatedly attained position. It was entirely natural that he should offer the opportunity of adoption to his talented nephew Takada Gunbei, now a ronin.

It was only days after his audience with the Shogun, probably about the time Kuranosuke arrived back in Yamashina, that Saburōemon enlisted his close friend Hashizume Shinpachi as his intermediary and sent him to convey to Gunbei his desire to adopt him. Gunbei said, "There is a small matter with which I'm occupied at the moment, but I'll give you an answer shortly." He told Shinpachi nothing further; but thereafter, he asked his elder brother, a ronin named Takada Yagobei, to go to Saburōemon and tell him that "owing to unavoidable circumstances, he would be unable to accept his proposal." But Saburōbei was, as Yasubei himself put it, "a stubborn old man, enamored of his own opinions and incapable of listening to reason." His face flushed with shock and anger.

"Circumstances? What sort of circumstances? I don't get it. Do his objections have something to do with his having served Takumi-no-Kami? If so, then there's no problem at all. Once I adopt him, he will succeed to my position in the service of the Shogun; I don't see any problem with that." Saburōbei clearly did not understand. And Yagobei, not being thoughtful enough to skirt the issue, blurted out everything that the Edo Three had been planning.

"That's a preposterous notion," Saburōbei said. "It would constitute open defiance of a legally rendered judgment of the Shogunate. If that's what he means to do, he'll get our entire family into trouble. Apparently, he doesn't care what sort of suffering he causes his kinfolk. That's unforgiveable! In the first place, any scheme involving five persons or more is bound to be construed as seditious conspiracy. If Gunbei refuses to do as I ask, that will mean the end of my lineage. If they go through with this, there's hardly a chance that I would escape implication; it's dead certain that the entire house would be abolished. Besides which, I've already told my commander, Iyo-no-Kami, about Gunbei, and I've told him that I have no other close relatives whom I can adopt. This may, in some way, reflect badly upon me, but I'll have to report Gunbei and see to it that he is punished first.

Gunbei's uncle may have been a bit of a crank, but on this point of law he was absolutely correct. Any band of five or more men was almost certain to be regarded as being up to no good. To the modern mind, that may seem obsessively suspicious, especially in the midst of the Great Peace, which lasted for nearly three hundred years. But peace does not just happen. There had been incidents enough over the previous century to prove that rebellion was not a thing of the past. The Shogunate was taking no chances; it was determined to keep the peace. It decreed, therefore, that banding together was to be punished by death, as was the swearing of oaths that invariably preceded it. And it was clear that

Yasubei, Gunbei, and Magodayū were in violation of this law. They were already sworn members of Kuranosuke's pact, which they had signed and sealed in blood in Akō, and they were actively attempting to recruit other members of the Edo contingent of the Akō house to join their cause. Saburōemon had good reason to be alarmed. He had tasted the bitter fruits of guilt by relation, and he knew the law.

But to Gunbei, his uncle seemed totally unreasonable, for he had put him in an untenable position. And so he went immediately to Magodayū and Yasubei, both of whom agreed about what he should do.

"You must get in touch immediately and talk this over with him," they said. "A man as hidebound and angry as he is will soon be telling everyone. And if he does that, then none of us will be able to do what we mean to do. This is simply a 'small sacrifice for the greater good.' In due time, we will explain it carefully to our comrades. For now, though, we'll keep it to ourselves. You, too, must say nothing, for if you do, it is sure to be noised about. Just agree to accept his offer as quickly as you can."

"Very well," Gunbei said. "I'll send Saburōemon a reply that will satisfy him, after which I know what I must do."

"That's right," Yasubei said, "there is nothing for it but for you to kill yourself."

"I'm resigned to that," Gunbei said. "I have no intention of remaining alive after you've accomplished our mission; I'll just have to feign insanity and commit suicide. There's no rush, though, so please don't mention this to anyone. Nor do I see any need to tell our comrades in the capital region until you go to Kyoto next spring. In the meantime, when you write, you can tell them I'm unable to sign because I'm ill."

♦ ♦ ♦

Eventually, though, Yasubei and Magobei did tell their comrades in the capital. The illness excuse soon wore thin. Everyone they wrote to expressed deep concern for Gunbei's health, and they had no explanation to offer. And so finally, in the postscript of a letter to Ōtaka Gengo, they told him the truth, and then asked:

Please discuss this letter with Yamashina, and also Hara, Ushioda,
and Nakamura. This is a subject that we two find extremely diffi-
cult to bring up. How fickle the human heart can be! There are
countless tales passed down from times past of those who take the
wrong road, who desert their duty to their lord and defect to the
enemy, cowards who flee death only to suffer the penalty of death.
Here, it seems, we have another such example before our very eyes.

But Gengo, Sōemon, and the others in Kyoto seemed less shocked than
sympathetic to Gunbei:

Item. We have pondered carefully each and every point of your
letter, as well as the separate sheet describing the case of Takada
Gunbei Dono. As you say, this is indeed most unfortunate, but we
can well imagine how painful it must have been for Gunbei Dono.
He could hardly have done anything else. We've been discussing the
matter here, so I'll tell you what we think.

Item. There is really no reason that Yagobei should not have told
Uchida Saburōemon Dono what he did; it was perfectly natural that
he should do so. But under the circumstances, Saburōemon Dono's
outrageous response was quite uncalled for. He was utterly thought-
less of Gunbei Dono's honor, and he ought also to have shown some
consideration for your good selves. Still, we agree with what both of
you said in reply to Gunbei Dono. The upshot of our discussions
here was that if Gunbei Dono were now to feign derangement and
commit suicide, that would only let the other party know how seri-
ous our intentions are, and thus would serve no purpose whatever.
Gunbei is, of course, concerned above all to uphold his honor. But
that would only shock and anger the other party all the more, and
thus expose us, which would make it all but impossible to accom-
plish our mission. Our most pressing concern is the trouble this could
cause our entire group. Everyone is well aware that Gunbei Dono's
devotion to the cause has always been beyond question. In the pres-
ent situation, he should follow Uchida Dono's wishes and go about

his work as though nothing at all were amiss. If in the meantime he were to keep his ears open for any intelligence he might glean and pass that on secretly, he could be of great help to us. Once we have accomplished our mission, Gunbei can do as he wishes—feign derangement or whatever. This would do us no harm and would satisfy Gunbei without his having to be disloyal. I have shown your letter to everyone in Yamashina, and after discussing it, they, too, came to the same conclusions.

Item. As for what Uchida Dono said about seditious conspiracy, we here do not agree. If one solicits help from outside and forms a group on that basis, then five or even three members might suffice to constitute a conspiratorial band. But when a Corps of Vassals sets out to execute the will of their lord, after his death, even if there be several hundred of them, what cause has anyone to call that a conspiracy? The Inspectorate has already been informed that our Corps of Vassals is not content. Of course, there is no need to remind you two any of this; I mention it only in passing.

Item. Considering Gunbei's devotion to the cause from the very start, we haven't the least intention of breaking off relations with him. It will be up to you two to make Gunbei Dono understand that the greatest act of loyalty he can now perform is to preserve the safety of our secret.

Item. We were reluctant to omit Gunbei Dono's name from this letter, but since it is omitted from your previous letters, we decided to do so.

But did Takada Gunbei ever actually commit suicide? Or, for that matter, did Uchida Saburōemon ever actually adopt Gunbei? We know only two things for certain, neither of which answers either of these questions for certain.

As we shall see, Gunbei was still alive, and seemingly in good spirits, one year later; but whether by then he was the adopted son of Saburōemon, no one mentions. The official Kansei Genealogies reports that ten years later, just before Saburōemon died, he was granted permission to adopt a young man named Takezawa. What might this signify? It could be that Gunbei kept both of his promises: that he became the adopted son of Saburōemon, and then feigned insanity and took his own life, thus vindicating his honor and forcing his adoptive father to find another heir. Yet it could just as well be that he absconded and never kept either promise.

We shall never know.

PART II

Year of the Horse

Genroku 15 (1702)

CHAPTER

41

We fail to understand why you still feel
such concern for Kobiki-chō.

This year would be different, concerning that there was no question.
The only questions now were: How different? And how soon? The por-
tents were not in agreement, nor among those involved was there yet
any unanimity.

◆ ◆ ◆

We know that when Kuranosuke left Akō, he took with him the pledges
of fifty-four men who had committed themselves to his cause. None of
these pledges survive, so we have no precise knowledge of what these
men were promising to do—or even if they all signed a single document,
attached to a Go'ō Hōin, such as the undercover agent from Okayama
described. Whatever they signed, though, defense of the castle, mass
suicide, or both must have been at the core of what they agreed to.

Now, however, Kuranosuke was bent upon a new and different
course of action. In Edo, he had agreed to lead an attack on the Kira
mansion with the aim of taking the head of Kōzuke-no-Suke. Yet
almost immediately, the number of those pledged to follow him began
to swell. Shortly after their return to Kyoto, Ushioda Matanojō and
Nakamura Kansuke wrote to the Edo Three that "a number of young
people who previously showed no interest have one after another come
to join us." And Ochiai Yozaemon reports that even some of those who
had not submitted pledges the previous spring in Akō now came to
Kuranosuke and promised that "they would follow his lead no matter
what he should command."

Who were these new recruits? Some were men who had been in Edo, Kyoto, or Osaka when the castle in Akō was about to be surrendered; some were younger sons still living at home, who were not yet members of the Corps of Vassals; some were samurai whose commanders had not signed pledges, and thus they themselves could not sign without seeming insubordinate. Some were no doubt sincere in swearing allegiance to Kuranosuke, even if it did mean following him to their death. But rumor had it that the retirement of Kira, followed shortly thereafter by the restoration of Asano Mino-no-Kami to the right of audience, was a sign that the reinstatement of the Asano house was imminent. The pledges of some of these new men may simply have been a ploy: those who pledged their loyalty now, they reckoned, would be the first to be recalled to the new Corps of Vassals. Only time would tell which of the 130 signatories to the pact would remain loyal at year's end.

◆ ◆ ◆

Although the number bespeaks expansion, Kuranosuke was at the same time narrowing his options. On the 11th Day of the New Year, he wrote to Yūkai, Superior of the temple Enrinji in Akō: "If there are matters that Your Reverence might wish to discuss further, you must not hesitate to let us know, for you are most welcome to come to the capital at any time. Now, however, it is unlikely that there will be more business of that sort. And thus it is hard to say when I shall have the pleasure of seeing you again."

"Business of that sort," of course, refers to Kuranosuke's efforts to enlist the aid of the Abbots of Goji'in and Gokokuji in his attempt to influence officialdom in Edo in Asano Daigaku's favor. Despite the wily Ryūkō's "favorable response," it was now clear that any further expenditure would procure only more polite but empty assurances. The project had already consumed sixty-five gold pieces. There was no further need to subject Yūkai to the rigors of a journey from Akō to Edo and back in the service of that futile scheme.

◆ ◆ ◆

Anyone reading the signs could have seen that Kuranosuke was not simply changing his plans; the fundamental attitudes upon which he had based those plans were changing as well. It was nothing he discussed with anyone, at least not that we know of, but an observer of the way he lived his life would have seen those signs.

It had begun in the middle of the previous month, shortly after the Shogunate had granted permission for Kira to retire and for his son to succeed him. Kuranosuke's eldest son, Matsunojō, was now in his fourteenth year, and on the 15th Day of the Twelfth Month, his father had allowed him to celebrate his majority. Thenceforth, he would no longer be known as Matsunojō; he would be Ōishi Chikara. He was now an adult, free to make his own choices in life. The choices to be made were momentous.

At about the same time, it became clear that Kuranosuke's wife, O-Riku, was again pregnant, with a child who probably would be born in the Seventh Month. By the middle of the First Month of the New Year, Kuranosuke had already arranged that O-Riku would leave Yamashina and return to the home of her father, Ishizuka Gengobei, in Toyooka. The correspondence describing this plan no longer survives; we know of it only through a later letter from Kuranosuke acknowledging Gengobei's agreement to his plan:

> I am very grateful that you agree to take my wife under your care. . . . She is in good health, but we do not have the best of physicians here in Yamashina; and then there is the worry of her recovery after she gives birth. It seems imperative, therefore, that I send her to you in the Third or Fourth Month. I am concerned, too, about the journey; and so, if you could send your man Kumode Yoshizō, I will send a young samurai and my son Chikara to accompany them. I expect that she will give birth in the Seventh Month. There is still time, but I think that she should set out sometime within the next month or two.

With Kuranosuke's younger son, Kichinoshin, already in Toyooka; his younger daughter, Ruri, living with Genshirō; and his wife and elder daughter, Kū, preparing to leave, he and Chikara would soon be the only members of the Ōishi family left in Yamashina. Chikara, in his first major decision as an adult, chose to remain with his father.

In a certain sense, Kuranosuke, too, was becoming a new man. From about this time, he began signing some of his letters with a new name, Ikeda Kyūemon. The name was not a random choice. Kuranosuke's mother was a daughter of Ikeda Dewa, Chief Elder of the great Okayama domain; and Kuranosuke's great-great-grandfather had been Ōishi Kyūemon. Combining his mother's surname and his great-great-grandfather's given name, Kuranosuke forged an identity the sources of which anyone in the family would have recognized. Outside the family, it was a protective nom de guerre that shrouded his movements in at least a shadow of secrecy.

♦ ♦ ♦

Yet despite all these signs of change, quite visible to those in the capital region, the men in Edo were now more impatient and disgruntled than ever. Kuranosuke's "clumsy carpenter" letters had arrived there on the 17th of the First Month. On the 26th, nine days later and still more than a little irate, both Yasubei and Yahei replied. On behalf of himself and Magodayū, Yasubei wrote:

> Your letter of the 25th of the Last Month of last year was deliv-
> ered to Takada Gunbei on the 17th of this First Month, and we
> have perused it. We are very pleased to hear that you are in good
> health.
>
> Item. I believe that our letter of the 27th of this past Twelfth Month
> will have reached you by now. As we said therein, we have finally
> ascertained the gentleman's whereabouts and have verified this intel-
> ligence through various reliable sources. But if you think that means
> you can stay put, that you've got him in hand until you decide to
> come down here, you're going to be sorely disappointed. . . . We, too,
> after all, are keen to succeed in this venture; we propose nothing
> reckless. But if you refuse to listen, no matter what we say, we are
> helpless to do anything. Throughout the Third Month, the gentle-
> man in question will definitely be in Honjo. Takebayashi, too, has

Year of the Horse

heard that he is in residence there; he should arrive in Kyoto any day now, so do ask him to tell you about it.

Item. You should consider more carefully whether to discuss the matter with Kobiki-chō. If you reveal your plans to him, we expect that he will attempt to prevent all of us from acting. . . . So we see little advantage in discussing the matter with him, and the disadvantages should be obvious.

Item. Now that this particular matter has been settled and there is no further need for postponement, we fail to understand why you still feel such concern for Kobiki-chō. . . . You postpone; you refuse to recognize the merit of a good plan; when we express our irritation, you only think us reckless; and when we propose a plan of action, you won't have it. In the meantime, we approach the first anniversary of our lord's death, and still you propose no plan of action, but only counsel us to exercise "care, care, and more care," while we haven't the least idea what goes on in your mind. From last year on into this New Year—we swear by all the honored gods of Japan—we've done nothing but formulate plans and gather intelligence while you offer us no response of any substance, but tell us only that all action must be delayed.

Item. If you are content to vent His Lordship's wrath upon the heir of his enemy, how are we not to be upset by this? We are upset because we consider the retired gentleman himself our first priority. For those whose minds are occupied with run-of-the-mill concerns—even here in Edo—it may make no difference. But there are those of us who are insatiably intent upon the business at hand, who have forgone all attempts to earn a living, and have made this task our first concern, so much so that now we are finding it difficult to make ends meet. For us, it has been a long wait. If ultimately the chance to attain our goal should come within our grasp, no matter how low we may sink, we'll not complain. But we do worry lest we all plunge to the depths of poverty before anything worth waiting for should materialize.

Item. We expect that you have every intention of listening to

~ 345 ~

Yahei's opinions and giving them due consideration and that your choice of which recommendations to adopt will be based upon their individual merits. It is for you to consider and decide what is to be done, and it is for us to follow your orders. Those who disobey your orders, no matter how many there be, shall be dismissed, and only those devoted to the cause shall be invited to participate. For in no other way can a venture of this magnitude succeed. Knowing as we do that if you yourself decide to act, more than half the Corps of Vassals will follow you, it would be deplorable if you were to squander the devotion of so many others. Some strength of charac- ter on your part could inspire even those who now show no hint of bravery; yet day after day, you spend all your time just pondering the matter. This is too pathetic for words. What with one thing and another, well over half a year has passed; before long, it will be a whole year. . . . Our late lord behaved thoughtlessly and was punished for his transgression in full accordance with the law. His lot of a warrior's fortune was exhausted. As his vassals, we now have no choice but to die in his stead. Neither repute nor personal gain has anything whatever to do with it. It is simply that the desire to kill Kira and his son permeates us to the very marrow of our bones. There are those of us who, without the slightest compunc- tion, are determined to strike immediately, and we are keen to offer ourselves up to you.

All of the foregoing we swear by the all the honored gods of Japan to be the truth.

FIRST MONTH, 26TH DAY *Horibe Yasubei [monogram]*
Okuda Magodayū [monogram]
To: Ōishi Kuranosuke Sama

The same day, Yasubei's father, Yahei, also wrote—less passionately perhaps, but no less frankly:

In my first letter to you, I scrupulously refrained from saying a single word about the business at hand. Last year, when Shindō and Hara came to call, I expected that they would remark how firm my resolve had remained from the very outset; but not at all; they marveled only at how old I have grown. Well, I decided, if that is where I stand, I will follow the old proverb, "Ask no questions, give no answers," and tell them nothing whatever. You yourself, exalted personage that you are, hardly noticed me on the two occasions I went to call upon you, and so I left having accomplished nothing.

As I mentioned briefly at the time, to be constantly changing your mind is futile and a needless source of pain. No matter if there are those who differ with you, you should not depart from your chosen path, but command strictly in accordance with what you think is right. Whatever plan you may formulate, I shall not oppose it. Neither has my son, at this moment, the slightest intention of altering his allegiance. If these delays continue for much longer, however, it is hard to see how he will be able to make ends meet. But even if the struggle comes hilt-to-hilt, he'll not turn against you like Takada. I do not mean to be praising myself, but that much I can say on my own behalf. I trust that you will understand. Most respectfully,

FIRST MONTH, 26TH DAY   *Horibe Yahei [monogram]*

To: Ōishi Kuranosuke Sama

Both Yasubei and Yahei were effusive in their professions of constancy and allegiance to Kuranosuke. I sometimes wonder, though: Was there ever more misunderstanding or greater mistrust among the members of Kuranosuke's pact than in this First Month of the Year of the Horse? It was not simply that Yasubei and Yahei seem not to have grasped the subtlety and humor of Kuranosuke's "clumsy carpenter" metaphor or that Kuranosuke seems not to have realized how profound a sense of urgency Kira's retirement had aroused in them. Now there were also new signatories to the pact, some genuinely committed to the cause, and some only pretending to be, probably in the hope of securing a place for themselves in a reconstituted House of Asano. But who were the ones he could trust? And then there were men like Hara Sōemon, a staunch ally of Kuranosuke from the very start, who in Edo found himself beginning to lean toward the views of the more radical faction there—as did some of the others who had just returned to Kyoto from Edo: Ōtaka Gengo, Ushioda Matanojō, and Nakamura Kansuke. If these differences could not be straightened out, the pact itself was in danger of dissolution. No one wanted it to break up; but the danger was real, and not everyone saw it.

CHAPTER
42

Now I find myself trapped between loyalty
to my lord and filial devotion to my father.

With the breakup and scattering of the Akō Corps of Vassals, the prospects for Kayano Sanpei were nowhere near as bleak as were those for
some of his comrades. His family was again settled in its home valley
on the Westlands Highroad. More than a hundred years had passed
since the Kayano were lords of the Kayano Valley, but they were still
paid the honor due its oldest family. And his father, Shichirōzaemon,
still managed those lands for their present lord, the bannerman Ōshima
Ise-no-Kami. In short, Kayano Sanpei had a prosperous and welcoming
home to return to. He was guaranteed not only a comfortable life but
also a future to which he could look forward. For Ise-no-Kami was
the benefactor not only of his father but of the Kayano sons as well.
Riemon, the eldest, had already entered the service of the Ōshima and
was now living in Nagasaki, where he had gone when Ise-no-Kami had
been appointed Shogunal Magistrate of that city. Sanpei, the youngest,
had also been provided for. In his thirteenth year, on the recommendation of Ōshima Ise-no-Kami, he had been taken into the service of the
Asano house as a Page Boy to Takumi-no-Kami, and later had been
promoted to the Mid-Corps of Pages. Now, since the Catastrophe, Ise-
no-Kami had been casting about for a new position for the young man
while in the meantime, he was prepared to take Sanpei into his own
service until a suitable new post could be found.

And so, after the surrender of the castle in Akō, Sanpei was free to
return to the Kayano Valley and relax from the harrowing tensions of
the past month. He was, of course, still in mourning for his mother,

whose funeral cortege he had chanced to encounter en route from Edo
to Akō. On the 27th of the Sixth Month, at her hundredth-day memorial rites, Sanpei composed a moving haiku in his mother's honor:

> mijikayo ya / hyaku no yumeji o / kachiwatashi
> How short the nights; and now she has trod this
> road of dreams a hundred times.

Beyond this, we know very little of how Sanpei spent his days. In
Akō, he was one of the fifty-four who had signed and sealed with his
blood print the pledge attached to the Goʻō Hōin, still in Kuranosuke's
possession. He was therefore invited to, and attended, the hundredth-
day memorial rites for Takumi-no-Kami at the Zuikōin in Kyoto. And
he speaks of spending "thirty to forty days in a place called Kawabe in
Mino," the home province of the Ōshima house—doing what, we have
no idea.

Sanpei's only other known activity was an excursion to the temple
Katsunoʻodera in Minō with his friend Ōtaka Gengo, sometime in the
Ninth Month of the previous year. Sanpei and Gengo were but two
of a number of Akō samurai who were aficionados and practitioners
of haikai poetry, and both were enrolled as disciples of the Edo haikai
master Mizuma Sentoku. And like all haikai poets, they had haikai
names with which they identified themselves in their personae as poets.
Gengo went by the name Shiyō, and Sanpei by the name Kensen. These
names were not mere affectation. Often they were an indication of the
school to which the bearer belonged, and they facilitated the mixing of
classes and ranks. Freed from the names that marked them as high or
low, samurai or merchant, artisan or farmer, under their haikai names,
men—and occasionally women—could mingle as equals in their love
of poetry. Thus when Gengo and Sanpei traveled to Katsunoʻodera—
just a short distance to the north of the Kayano Valley—they went as
Shiyō and Kensen, for their purpose was not simply to see the sights,
admire the autumn leaves, and marvel at the wonderfully tall, thin Minō
Waterfall, but to seek inspiration for the composition of haikai.

Gengo later published the poems they exchanged when he arrived at Sanpei's home in the Kayano Valley:

When I called upon Kensen, who had returned to the land:

kabe o hau / momen no mushi no / momiji kana
Beneath autumn leaves, a cotton weevil crawling along the wall.
SHIYŌ

aki kaze ya / ingen mame no / tsue no ato
Autumn winds arise as your string bean of a staff
leaves behind its tracks.
KENSEN

And Gengo recorded his impressions of the temple and the waterfall:

We went to Katsuno'odera, and there in the south towered the main gate, its plaque inscribed "Ōchōzan" glistening in the sunlight that shone down through the clouds. Twenty-three rows of monastic cells crowned in glossy tiles. Twin peaks rising in lonely desolation. Men raking through the leaves, alongside the monkeys, gathering wild chestnuts. Enchanting, is it not?

mizuhiki o / nusa ni mushiru ya / katsuno'o yama
Is that slim white cord strung out as a talisman?
Katsunō Mountain.

Gengo gently likened the slim line of the waterfall as it streams down from the crest to a talisman of twisted white paper, hung there to protect the mountain from malign forces.

It would be more interesting, though, to know what he and Sanpei discussed when they were not waxing poetical. They would not yet have heard the news of Kira's retirement, but Kuranosuke was by then settled in Yamashina and had established contact with everyone in the capital region. Both Gengo and Sanpei were sworn members of his pact; they would surely have had much to say to each other about Daigaku, Kira, and what was to be done. And Sanpei himself tells us that he later met with Yoshida Chūzaemon and Chikamatsu Kanroku, and made concrete plans to travel in their company to Edo.

As his departure date approached, however, a problem arose. It was probably early in the First Month of the New Year when Sanpei, quite properly, decided that he must inform his father of his plans. He would by then have known of Ōshima Ise-no-Kami's offer of employment and his father's ready acceptance of it. He did not, however, feel free to reveal that he was bent upon vendetta, with the result that his father, vehemently but understandably, opposed his departure for Edo. Sanpei himself tells us no more than this; what passed between father and son in this confrontation must thus be left to the imagination. Ogawa Tsunemitsu says that "someone told him" that Shichirōzaemon "hadn't the slightest knowledge of military matters, but only of agriculture, commerce, profit and loss." I find that hard to believe of a man who held his military lineage in such high regard.

As Katashima Shin'enshi imagines it, however, Sanpei told his father that he and his friends meant to seek positions in the service of other daimyo in Edo, and asked him for the severance allowance that he had received when he left Akō. To which his father replied: "You say you're going to the Kantō to seek new employment? In these times, when there is hardly any place in the world for a warrior, I find that unthinkable. Even the most accomplished of warriors can hardly make a name for themselves these days; they are just swallowed up in the welter of the city. This government has so long neglected military preparedness that an upright man like yourself, unfamiliar with the ways of the world, will find that your virtue puts you at a disadvantage. You mustn't waste the money that your late lord left you on fruitless wandering, only to return home weary and empty-handed. That is just too dismal a prospect."

At this point, Sanpei must have realized that given how little his father knew, his argument was entirely reasonable, and the only way he could persuade him to think otherwise was to tell him the whole truth—which he felt his pledge to Kuranosuke prevented.

How many days passed after this confrontation we do not know.

Sanpei had decided, however, that he would act on the 14th, the day of the month upon which Asano Takumi-no-Kami had died. The evening of the 13th, he spent in the main house, chatting cheerfully with his father and his elder brother's wife, O-Yuri, who was now the mistress of the house. When the night grew late, he returned to his room in the gatehouse, lit a lamp, sat down at his desk, and wrote two letters, one addressed to Ōishi Kuranosuke and one to his father, both of which he left lying on his desk. The letter to Kuranosuke read:

> *Having spoken last year with Yoshida Chūzaemon and Chikamatsu Kanroku, I was expecting to proceed to Edo in the spring of this year. But my father, Shichirōzaemon, was unaware of my intentions and vehemently restrained me. Had I told him what I meant to do, I expect that he would have been delighted. But in the pledge I submitted to you, I swore not to reveal our plans even to my own parents. Now I find myself trapped between loyalty to my lord and filial devotion to my father. I shall therefore commit suicide.*
>
> *As I shall not write separately to Yoshida and Chikamatsu, may I ask you to inform them as well? With great respect,*
>
> FIRST MONTH, 13TH DAY *Kayano Sanpei Shigezane [monogram]*
> To: Ōishi Kuranosuke Sama

To his father, Sanpei wrote:

> *Last year, when my late lord served as official host to the Imperial Envoys, for reasons unknown he became angry with Kira Kōzuke-no-Suke and attacked him in the palace with his sword. At the time, he was restrained by others who were in attendance and was prevented from accomplishing his purpose. So pitiable were his feelings when he ended his life that we his vassals found this impossible to bear, and so last year when the domain of Akō was declared forfeit, those of us who were of like mind swore an oath among ourselves. As we made our plans, however, I realized, to my chagrin, that if I were to depart without taking proper leave, I should later be thought*

figure 13
The gatehouse to the Kayano family homestead. The room just beyond
the gateway is where Sanpei lived and died. (Photo by Jojo2000)

negligent and unfilial. I therefore returned home to take leave of you. That you should restrain me was entirely reasonable, and for that I am most grateful. But I found it impossible to reveal the oath I had sworn and thus have ended up in defiance of you. If I now follow your dictates, I shall be guilty of disloyalty to my lord. And if I am loyal and go against your wishes, I shall be guilty of unfilial behavior. I shall therefore commit suicide.

Would you please forward the letter I have left behind to Ōishi Kuranosuke in Yamashina? Those whom I was to accompany will probably come calling as well. I had hoped to be able to take leave of them, but there was no time. Would you kindly tell them, too, what I have said?

FIRST MONTH, 14TH DAY   *Kayano Sanpei*

To: Shichirōzaemon Sama

When the day began to show faint signs of dawning, Sanpei unsheathed his short sword, a blade 9.5 inches long forged by Mizuta Kunishige of the province of Bitchū. He then bared his abdomen and with his fingers sought the lowest rib on his left side. Just beneath it, he drove in the blade and drew it slowly across to the right. There was no one in whom he felt he could confide, no one he could ask to strike off his head when the pain of his wound had robbed him of the strength to cut further. He fell forward, sprawled in anguish until the flow of blood gradually drained the last of his life.

♦ ♦ ♦

The gatehouse of the Kayano homestead still stands, facing the Westlands Highroad, and the Kayano family still farm the few fields that remain to them. If you call at the main house, Shichirōzaemon's present-day descendants will gladly show you the very room in which Sanpei lived his last days, and in which he died.

CHAPTER
43

For the time being, then,
we must give in to these senior officers.

On the 9th Day of the First Month, when Hara Sōemon and Ōtaka Gengo finally arrived back in Kyoto, they went immediately to Kuranosuke's home in Yamashina to tell him their news from Edo. This was to be the first of five meetings, spread over the next month or so, that came to be known as the Yamashina meetings. No record survives of the arguments and counter-arguments exchanged at these meetings, other than sketchy summaries in the correspondence of Sōemon and Gengo. As we shall see, neither man was pleased with the way things went. Yet from the outpourings of their displeasure, we can at least reconstruct some of the schemes that were debated and the attitudes that aroused their ire.

♦ ♦ ♦

Two days later, on the 11th, Kuranosuke called the senior members of the pact together at his home—Shindō Genshiro, Oyama Gengoemon, Okamoto Jirōzaemon, and Onodera Jūnai—and he asked Sōemon and Gengo to tell these men exactly what they had told him upon their return from Edo. And, again, on the 14th, the same group gathered to attend the memorial rites for Takumi-no-Kami at Zuikōin, after which they all retreated to the home of their late lord's personal physician, Terai Genkei, where they continued their discussion. Ōtaka Gengo recorded his impressions of these meetings in a letter to the Edo Three:

> On the 11th, everyone gathered in Yamashina—Shindō, Oyama,
> Okamoto, Onodera, and even Yatō Emoshichi, who by chance

happened to turn up just then. Sōemon told them everything that had happened while we were in Edo—beginning, middle, and end. He told them what you three were thinking, what he and I thought; he omitted nothing. And everyone agreed that this was the moment that all our preparations had been leading up to; that, just as you say, we need concern ourselves no further with the fate of Kobiki-chō; that there was nothing more to deter us; that this was it, the final act in this great drama.

But then we met again on the 14th at the home of Terai Genkei, that being a perfect place to confer clandestinely. There we went on to discuss plans for Edo. The general consensus was that the retirement of the other party meant that this was the end of the line, but somehow they could not reach a firm decision to act immediately. It was all just too terribly half-baked; an enormous disappointment. We were pleased, though, that at least they were able to agree we should not put it off any later than this autumn. . . .

I don't know if you three are aware of it, but we've certainly noticed: that Oyama is utterly useless. Sōu and I were just appalled. Perhaps this can happen to anyone in times like this. You can trust a man one day, but not the next. . . . I understand that you've had a valiant-sounding letter from him. I hardly know what to make of that. I think the man is two-faced. At our meeting on the 14th, and also on the 11th, he was more evasive than Okamoto. He's a contemptible creature, in any number of ways. Sōu has quite given up on him.

It has been decided to dispatch Yoshida Chūzaemon and Chikamatsu Kanroku to Edo. This is an excellent development. I know nothing whatever of Chūzaemon's opinions. But I spoke to Kanroku again today. He's a rock-solid dependable man and entirely in agreement with us. Magodayū Dono should by all means discuss matters with him when he arrives. These, I think, will be the first two to go, and apart from you three, I've no word of any others.

After the meeting at Genkei's home, Sōemon, too, wrote to the Edo Three:

> *Since coming here, I've talked with the Yamashina group. But with so many differing opinions, I found it all rather perplexing, and so I decided to leave and go back to Osaka. I'll stay away for a while, and then talk everything over with them again. Ever since news of the retirement reached here last winter, everyone appears to be growing more restless. I hear, too, that many of the younger men are beginning to make preparations. But I can see that their opinions are at odds with our own in several respects. This will have to be handled with care.*
>
> *As I have said all along: if things seem not to be progressing smoothly, and we are the only ones who can make up our minds to act, then given what I know of what people here think, I see no chance that they are going to cast their lot with us. And if the Yamashina group does not participate, I doubt that anything can come of this. These deliberations must be handled with great finesse.*

Sōemon and Gengo were not the only ones aware of the problem. Even Kuranosuke took it upon himself to entreat the understanding of the Edo Three for the difficulty of his situation:

> *These people here say that, if no absolutely perfect opportunity presents itself, they simply will not take part in this operation. You tell us in your recent letter that you have reliable sources of information there; that is excellent. Yet even so, having discussed the matter directly with these senior officers, I know that unless we postpone this until we can be absolutely certain, they are not likely to assent, and nothing will come of it. For the time being, then, we must give in to these senior officers, and then come up with an absolutely foolproof plan that they will be willing to participate in.*

If Kuranosuke genuinely agreed with Sōemon, Gengo, and the Edo Three, then why did he bother to coddle these contrary senior officers?

Probably for two reasons: without them, and the men who still followed their lead, he might not be able to muster enough men to mount a successful attack; and if there were to be an attack, the more senior men who participated, the more powerful an act of protest it would seem. Two of those men, moreover, were his own kin: his cousin Shindō Genshiro and his uncle Oyama Gengoemon.

♦ ♦ ♦

In the meantime, Sōemon decided that he would not return to Yamashina for further discussions, as he had said he would. Whatever Kuranosuke thought of his senior officers, Sōemon was fed up with them. "Strange to say," he wrote,

> these people who now do nothing but warm their own hands and criticize everyone else are the same timorous lot who, since the Third Month last year, have been flailing about in a frenzy of fright trying to save their own skins. . . . Just when it looked as though things were going to happen fast, objections began to arise out of nowhere, among them the notion that we simply must put this off until the Sixth or Seventh Month. And Yamashina went along with them.

Instead of meeting with those people again, Sōemon wrote a nine-page letter to Kuranosuke and asked Gengo to deliver it. Unfortunately, this letter does not survive. We know of it only from a letter that Gengo wrote to the Edo Three in which he summarized Sōemon's arguments and Kuranosuke's response:

> Hara wrote a detailed letter to Yamashina, and yesterday, the 2nd, I carried it thither. While there, I, too, read it. It was nine pages long, and in it he expounded his own views in great detail. But given that our original aims have not changed substantially since we left Akō, he said, in discussions either among ourselves or with others, there remain only two alternatives as to how we should proceed. I will describe these below.

The first alternative was Sōemon's understanding of Kuranosuke's opinion: that they dare not attack until the case of Asano Daigaku had been decided. Sōemon granted that there were good reasons for wishing to wait. Yet, he objected, if Daigaku should then be granted even a small enfeoffment, it would be impossible to mount an attack on Kira, as that would jeopardize Daigaku's position. And merely to take vows and become monks would not suffice to vindicate their wrath. Their only remaining option would be suicide, which might demonstrate their anger, but certainly would not even the score between Takumi-no-Kami and Kira.

The second alternative was Sōemon's own idea of what they should do: that they recognize that Daigaku's case had already been decided when Kira was granted permission to retire and his son allowed to inherit. They should thus give up waiting and devote themselves wholly to the satisfaction of their resentment. They should proceed to Edo in the Third Month, attack, kill Kira, and take his head. And if in the meantime, the Uesugi should decide to remove Kira from Edo to the safety of their domain in Yonezawa, they should pursue him and attack en route.

Kuranosuke responded on the spot, and Gengo summarized his reaction:

> Last winter in Edo, it was decided that our deadline should be the first anniversary of His Lordship's death, and I agreed. Yet in subsequent discussions, we failed to reach any firm conclusions. . . . And then, just when we seemed about to reach a conclusion, we heard news of Kira's retirement, and that raised new questions about Kobiki-chō. His fate then became a known quantity, but it still seemed best to await the decision of his case before executing our plan. We do not know when that might happen, but I do not intend to wait indefinitely. As a rule, Domiciliary Confinement lasts over a span of three calendar years before one is released. That is not a long way off, and so I would like, above all, to wait until then, so as not to leave that matter weighing on my mind. But once the third anniversary of His Lordship's death is past, and Asano Aki-no-Kami

has returned to Hiroshima, there will be no further reason to delay. If at that point there is still no solution in sight, that will be the time to see the matter through.

If in the meantime, Kobiki-chō is granted an enfeoffment upon his release, Sōu says that we would not then be able to satisfy our grievance against the other party; but I fail to understand this. No matter how great an enfeoffment he may be granted, if the other party is still alive, no grant will suffice to restore Kobiki-chō's honor. It would be better to be disinherited than to succeed to a tainted legacy, so this need not deter us from exacting revenge, even after seeing his case through to its conclusion.

While all this quibbling and caviling was going on in Kyoto, movements of a more significant sort were taking shape in the castle town of Miki in the district of Katō in the eastern reaches of the province of Harima. Yoshida Chūzaemon, the former District Deputy for both Katō and Kasai—and thus the steward of more than one-quarter of the Akō enfeoffment—had moved back to the region that had become his home, where he awaited the call from Kuranosuke. That call now came. Whatever course of action the senior officers would force upon the group in the short term, Kuranosuke wanted a man he could trust for the long haul to take charge of things in Edo. Not simply someone who would "pacify" the Edo Three, but who would lead the longer-term effort there until Kuranosuke himself could move his base to Edo.

Chūzaemon would not go alone. Apart from his duties as District Deputy, Chūzaemon was a Company Commander of Foot Soldiers, one member of which was a man he had taken into his home as a boy, raised, and then inducted into his company as a fully fledged vassal of Takumi-no-Kami. Terasaka Kichiemon Nobuyuki was now in his thirty-eighth year and had proved himself a retainer of unquestioned competence and loyalty. Kichiemon would accompany Chūzaemon to Edo. He would also keep a record of what they did, which is invaluable to us now.

At first light on the 25th Day of the First Month, Chūzaemon and Kichiemon set out from Miki, bound not for Kyoto but Osaka. Chūzaemon seems to have known that Hara Sōemon would give him a more accurate description of the state of things than anyone in Kyoto. He arrived in Osaka on the 26th, spent the day with Sōemon, and then moved on to Sumizome just north of Fushimi, where he visited a kinsman who was the Superior of a Nichiren temple there. Finally, he continued on to Yamashina, where he arrived on the 28th. He and Kuranosuke had a long and leisurely talk, and thereafter, there were repeated meetings at the homes of Onodera Jūnai and Oyama Gengoemon. In the end, Chūzaemon told Kuranosuke: "You ask me to go to Edo and take charge there. I will do that. But before I go, I must be certain that I can assure people there that everyone here remains committed to the pledges that they swore this past year."

"Of course," Kuranosuke said, and he dispatched a circular to everyone living within reach of the capital summoning them to a meeting at his home on the 10th Day of the Second Month. He made a particular point of asking Hara Sōemon to be present.

The meeting was only a partial success. There was general agreement that Chūzaemon should proceed to Edo, and that Chikamatsu Kanroku should join him as his aide. But again, it proved impossible to agree upon a deadline for action. And since some of the participants still had not arrived, it was decided that they would meet again on the 15th. This was to be their final meeting, the one that would come to be known as *the* Yamashina meeting. This is what Hara Sōemon told Yasubei and Magodayū about it:

> On the 13th, they all arrived in Kyoto, and on the 15th we met again. Everyone agreed, as we had on the 10th, that Yoshida and Chikamatsu would depart for Edo on the 21st. Having reached this decision, we several times pressed them to consider the need for speed, but our leader remained reluctant to break his commitment. Yet it was not as though he had no good reasons for his opinion, and by delaying for what ultimately amounts to but a short while, we shall avoid a breach of our fundamental duty of fealty. To desert the leader whom we have followed ever since we left Akō, to walk away without a word, just because we want to do this our own way, simply would not be right. So we decided to go along with him. . . . Now that

all of us, albeit reluctantly, have accepted this decision, we ask that
you, too, should acquiesce.

Sōemon's letter was co-signed by Ōtaka Gengo, Ushioda Matanojō, and
Nakamura Kansuke, which no doubt made it that much more persuasive. Kuranosuke, too, felt that he owed his men in Edo an explanation,
and he wrote the very next day, addressing his letter not only to Yasubei
and Magodayū but to Yahei as well—and signed it for the first time
with his nom de guerre, Ikeda Kyūemon:

> *As you so rightly say, in one sense the way is now open; and yet,*
> *I have held from the very start that we dare not abandon Kobiki-*
> *chō; and I still feel that to break our commitment would not be*
> *right. No matter how often I mull the matter, I simply cannot bring*
> *myself to do that. . . . Once Kobiki-chō is released from Domiciliary*
> *Confinement, however, I will come immediately to Edo, state our*
> *views to him, and if we are in agreement, press forward with our*
> *plan and go willingly to my death under his command. At the*
> *moment, I have no way of knowing how Kobiki-chō feels about this,*
> *but surely he must feel as we do. If we were now to abandon him*
> *with no notification and break our commitment, it simply would*
> *not be right.*

Yoshida Chūzaemon carried both letters to Edo. Yasubei and his
father, Yahei, and Magodayū and his son Sadaemon read them together.
In their reply, they said simply that they could understand how Sōemon
felt, that they agreed with him, that they could see there was some justification for Kuranosuke's opinion, and they would do as they were
asked. But in his personal record, which he kept to himself until months
later, Yasubei lamented:

> *Everyone in the capital has decided that they agree with Kuranosuke.*
> *We've told them what we think, but can't seem to convince them to*
> *join us. If only six or seven of us attack the mansion, there's not*
> *a chance we could succeed. Rather than clearing our good names,*

we would only be thought fools. We'll not abandon our plan, but we will have to endure the unendurable and suffer all manner of shame while we await the right moment. That, too, can be a form of courage.

For the time being, at least, a schism had been avoided.

*The vassals are very angry and keen to
wreak revenge upon the other party.*

Kuranosuke was determined not to break his commitment. He would
not move against Kira Kōzuke-no-Suke until the Council of Elders
had officially decided the case of Asano Daigaku. As Kuranosuke saw
it, his commitment was not simply to the reinstatement of the Asano
cadet house under Daigaku, but to the Council of Elders and, by exten-
sion, the Shogun. In return for the peaceful surrender of Akō Castle,
Kuranosuke had tendered a request, through the official Inspectors, for
the restoration of the honor of Daigaku—which could be accomplished
only by applying of the Principle of Equal Punishment to Kira. But now
that the Elders had granted Kira permission to retire with honor and
pass on his patrimony, it was all but impossible that they would decide
to punish him. Indeed, the council *could* not decide to punish Kira; the
Shogun would not allow it. The Elders now had no choice but to disregard Kuranosuke's request, despite having told the Inspectors that
they thought it reasonable. All of this Kuranosuke knew perfectly well;
even so, he would wait. He would wait until Daigaku was released from
Domiciliary Confinement and until the Council of Elders, openly and
officially, evaded granting what Kuranosuke had requested in return for
the surrender of Akō Castle. He would not retreat from the moral high
ground that he now held. And while he was waiting, he would let certain
people know, in subtle ways, that once he could no longer be accused of
breaking his commitment to await that decision, he was determined to
seek satisfaction in his own way.

✦ ✦ ✦

In the latter days of the Third Month, well after Kira had retired and his son had succeeded him, and about a month and a half after the last of the Yamashina meetings, Kuranosuke somehow learnt when the procession of Asano Aki-no-Kami would be passing through the capital region on the way from Hiroshima to Edo. He knew, too, that once it had left Fushimi, the next stop for the night would be in Ishibe, two post stations beyond Ōtsu. And so, on the morning of the 23rd Day of the Third Month, he set out on the Fushimi Road, which passed only a short distance from his home; crossed over Meeting Slope Hill; and proceeded down through Ōtsu to the southern shore of Lake Biwa, over the Seta River, and on to the post town of Ishibe—a distance of nearly 10 leagues (25 miles, 40 kilometers). There he met with Terao Shōzaemon and Toshima Yasuzaemon, the two Hiroshima Elders who were traveling with Asano Aki-no-Kami. No record of their conversation survives, but Kuranosuke did leave behind a memorandum of the main points that he wished to make so that the Elders would overlook nothing when they passed his message on to their lord:

> As I said last summer when His Lordship passed through Osaka, when Takumi Dono was punished, the other party, Kōzuke Dono, was permitted to remain alive, which the members of our Corps of Vassals found most upsetting. In Akō, we were fully determined to commit suicide; but out of respect for the repeated commands of Aki-no-Kami Sama and Toda Uneme-no-Kami Dono, we agreed among ourselves that since Daigaku had been sentenced to Domiciliary Confinement, it would be an act of insolence toward this noble house to take our lives before we knew what his fate was to be. We had no choice then but to disperse, but by no means did we abandon our dismay. Since this past summer, various of our men have come to me, complaining of one thing and another. And now, toward the end of this past year, Kōzuke Dono has been granted permission to retire and pass on his patrimony, which means that Daigaku can no longer serve with honor. Given which, the vassals

are very angry and keen to wreak revenge upon the other party. But because it would not be in Daigaku's interest for us to do anything rash in the present state of affairs, I am doing my best to pacify them and convince them to postpone any action until after he is pardoned. Now, if Daigaku were to succeed as the new head this house, and he should be restored to a position in which he can serve with honor, I am sure that our Corps of Vassals would be totally placated. I would humbly beg, therefore, that His Lordship lend his good will to the cause of the restoration of Daigaku. Needless to say, I do not by any means make this request in the hope that, if all does go well for Daigaku, our Corps of Vassals will in any way benefit from it. I would be most grateful if, when an appropriate occasion presents itself, you could bring the foregoing to His Lordship's attention.

THIRD MONTH   *Ōishi Kuranosuke*

The wording of his request is extremely polite, but his message is clear: matters have reached a state where only a daimyo of the stature of the lord of Hiroshima can bring sufficient influence to bear upon the Shogunate to prevent an act of revenge.

But Kuranosuke had never before met the two Elders, Terao and Toshima. To what extent he could trust these men to convey a convincing report of his plea to their lord he could not have known. He certainly was acquainted, though, with Aki-no-Kami's Adjutant, Inoue Dan'emon, from their association in Akō prior to the surrender of the castle. We know, too, that the two men had great respect for each other. It may well have been in the hope of finding a more sympathetic confidant of Aki-no-Kami that, immediately after his return to Yamashina, Kuranosuke wrote to Dan'emon. His kinsman Shindō Sebei, he said, had passed on Dan'emon's greetings to him in Fushimi, and his meeting with the two Elders in Ishibe had gone well. They were receptive to his request, they promised to relay it to His Lordship at their first opportunity, and they had passed the time amiably with him. But now that Kira had been granted unconditional permission to retire, and it was unlikely that Daigaku would be restored to a position of honor, the problem had grown acute:

I have urged our vassals to wait until we know how the case of Daigaku shall be decided. But even if he is pardoned and released from Domiciliary Confinement, yet not restored to a position of honor in which he can serve without shame, it will be all but impossible to restrain them. I have written out a summary of my argument and presented it to the two Elders. "Once a decision has been rendered, there is nothing further that I can do," I told them as they read my summary, "and thus I hope that before he is pardoned, a suitable solution can be arranged with good speed." As they took receipt of the summary, they promised that they would relate the details of it to His Lordship verbally. This was the first time I had met these gentlemen, but I was extremely grateful for their cordial reception, and particularly all that they told me of His Lordship's good will since times past. Which made me hope all the more that the prestige of everyone in this great house may yet bring about a favorable outcome to this affair. I look forward to hearing from you. Most respectfully,

THIRD MONTH, 27TH DAY   *Ōishi Kuranosuke [monogram]*
To: Inoue Dan'emon Sama, via his entourage

Almost a month later, Kuranosuke made a somewhat longer excursion, this time to Ōgaki, the seat of Toda Uneme-no-Kami, 27 leagues from Kyoto. With him went his former Kyoto Liaison Officer, Onodera Jūnai. Their mission was the same as that of Kuranosuke's previous excursion, to persuade a powerful (and closely related) daimyo to urge the Shogunate to do something that it hadn't the slightest intention of doing: to apply the Principle of Equal Punishment to Kira.

Kuranosuke had hoped to meet with the Chief Elder of the Toda house, Toda Gonzaemon. The two men knew each other from their association in Akō, where Gonzaemon had been sent to ensure compliance with Uneme-no-Kami's repeated directives to surrender the castle. And Jūnai had seen to the needs of the entire contingent from Ōgaki during their sojourn. But as luck would have it, Gonzaemon was away from Ōgaki when Kuranosuke and Jūnai arrived, and it was not known when he would return. And so they decided to wait, and in one sense it turned out to be a very productive wait.

Kuranosuke was a skilled amateur painter and Jūnai, a poet of some note. With time on their hands, they decided to while it away by pooling their talents. Kuranosuke painted a chilling scene of five white herons standing in a marsh or river while a winter wind ruffles their feathers; at the edge Jūnai wrote:

rei no rakugaki gomen
ichi ni san shi gowa ashima ni mietaru wa
sora ni shirarenu yuki no shirasagi

With apologies for my habitual scribble
What is it we see there among the river reeds?
One, two, three, four, five—a veritable blizzard of snowy white herons.
HIDEKAZU

♦ ♦ ♦

Kuranosuke's painting with Jūnai's inscription upon it somehow came into the possession of the lord of Ōgaki, Toda Uneme-no-Kami. Kuranosuke was never granted an audience with Uneme-no-Kami, but the mounting of his painting—which survives in excellent condition—is embroidered with a long row of circles of nine stars, the well-known family crest of the House of Toda. Did Kuranosuke and Jūnai intend to present their work to Uneme-no-Kami? Or did they just leave it behind with no recipient in mind? Whatever their intentions, they eventually decided that they could wait no longer for Toda Gonzaemon to return, and instead left a letter with Kano Jibuemon, another man whom they knew from his visits to Akō as the bearer of stern injunctions from Uneme-no-Kami.

It is not a letter that differs in any significant way from those addressed to the Elders and Adjutant of the main house in Hiroshima, but it clearly states the crucial point: that "if Daigaku Dono is released on unfavorable terms, that will by no means settle the matter."

♦ ♦ ♦

figure 14
Ōishi Kuranosuke's painting of five herons.
The poem was composed and inscribed by Onodera Jūnai. (1702)

Kuranosuke's last effort of this sort is the one we know the least about. After writing to Yūkai, Superior of the temple Enrinji in Akō, and telling him that there would be no further need for him to intercede with the ecclesiastical establishment in Edo, he seems to have decided to send the monk on another mission to Edo. Who Yūkai met with, what he asked of them, and what their responses were are nowhere recorded. Neither does any of the relevant correspondence survive. We know only that Yūkai arrived in Edo on the 24th of the Fifth Month and left on the 13th of the Sixth Month. Concerning his mission, however, Terasaka Kichiemon, the foot soldier who accompanied Yoshida Chūzaemon to Edo, makes a brief but possibly significant comment: "Fifth Month, 25th Day. Yūkai Hōin, Superior of the Enrinji in Akō, has come to make confidential inquiries among his fellow disciples in the great temples of Edo—by which I mean inquiries concerning the true state of the Kira house and what is being said in governmental circles."

If we can take this comment at face value, then Yūkai may have been sent on this trip as much—perhaps even more—to gather intelligence among his ecclesiastical brethren as to influence the judgment of Asano Daigaku. The world to which Yūkai belonged was a world to which the Akō samurai in Edo had no access. What he could learn there might prove to be of great use to Kuranosuke and other members of the command group when finally they began to make concrete plans.

◆ ◆ ◆

What, then, are we to make of all this activity on Kuranosuke's part—all of it subsequent to the retirement of Kira, which even Kuranosuke realized was the end of all hope that Kira might yet be punished, thus restoring the honor of Asano Daigaku? Why would he, at this point, continue to urge the Toda and the Asano main house to intercede with the Shogunate on behalf of Daigaku? He would surely have known that they would do no such thing and that even if they did, it would do no good.

Kuranosuke was not a dreamer. His reasons must lie deeper than surface appearances would suggest. For my own part, I find it tempting to think that his entreaties to the Toda and the Hiroshima main house are not to be taken as genuine pleas for action on their part, but subtle warnings that their inaction will have consequences that they might wish to avoid. Likewise with Yūkai's sojourn in Edo. To a casual observer, it might appear that he was there for much the same reasons as before; Kichiemon regarded it as something quite different.

As Kuranosuke said in his letter to Terai Genkei toward the end of the previous year, "We have no choice now but to make up our minds and act." This is precisely what Kuranosuke was doing. He had made up his mind that he would not break his commitment, but when the Shogunate broke its commitment, he would act.

takebayashi / sosen wa tora mo / sunda kuni
Takebayashi: his forebears come from a
land where tigers once dwelt.

Takebayashi Tadashichi was in Edo at the time of the Catastrophe, but soon thereafter returned to Akō, where he pledged himself to Kuranosuke's pact. After the surrender of the castle, he made his way back to Edo, and we hear nothing further of him until he turned up as one of that group of lower-ranking samurai who listened in the anteroom while Kuranosuke met with Yasubei, Gunbei, and Magodayū in Mita. Now that events had taken a new turn, however, we need to know more about Tadashichi, for he was a man with an extraordinary history, and we shall be meeting him often further on in the story.

◆ ◆ ◆

People are always shocked, or at least dubious, when I tell them that Tadashichi was descended of Chinese stock—and proud of it. Some simply refuse to believe it. But Japan was more cosmopolitan in those days than it is now—indeed, aggressively so. And the records leave no room for doubt: Tadashichi's grandfather not only was Chinese, but was descended in the sixty-first generation from the great Chinese sage Mencius.

It all goes back to the Keichō Campaign, Toyotomi Hideyoshi's second attempt to conquer Korea, which would open the way, or so he hoped, to the conquest of Ming China. The Ming, of course, had no intention of waiting for him to arrive on their borders, and so when word of the broken truce reached them early in the year 1597, they again sent a large force to the aid of the Koreans. One column, some 3,000 mounted warriors led by Deputy Commander Yang Yüan, arrived in the walled city of Namwŏn, in the southwest of the Korean Peninsula, in the middle of the Sixth Month and set about strengthening its defenses. Yang also summoned the Korean Military Commander of the province, Yi Bok-nam, to his assistance. Yi led another 1,400 warriors to Namwŏn. This confluence of forces was to change totally the lives of two people on the periphery of the action. Meng Erh-k'uan was a physician attached to the Ming army, but, presumably because his medical ministrations were not in great demand before the battle began, he was assigned to serve as guardian to the young son of the Korean commander.

When word reached Namwŏn that the Japanese Army of the Left was approaching, some 56,000 strong, much of the civilian population fled, and the Korean Military Commander, Yi Bok-nam, urged a strategic withdrawal to a mountain fastness north of the city. But the Chinese Deputy Commander, Yang Yüan, would not hear of it; the walled city must be defended: 800 soldiers were to man the ramparts; 1,200 were to secure the city streets; and another 1,000 stood ready to be sent wherever they were most needed.

When the Japanese arrived on the 13th Day of the Eighth Month and surrounded the city, it quickly became obvious with whom the advantage lay. Not only were the defenders outnumbered by about fourteen to one, but their firearms were vastly inferior to those of the Japanese, who pelted them with highly effective fire, while in the meantime constructing siege equipment. The 14th was a forced hiatus for everyone. It rained so ferociously and thundered so vociferously that the monk Keinen—a literary-minded cleric in the service of the Shimazu— thought that it called to mind the night described in *The Tales of Ise* when a demon devours a young court lady in one gulp. He even wrote a poem about it:

> *nasake naku furishiboritaru ame ya somo*
> *oni hitokuchi o omoi koso yare*
> Will this rain that pours down so heartlessly be as
> bad as on *that* night?

For it does indeed call to mind that demon's single gulp.

Those within the city could see that much worse was now in store for them, for on the 15th, preparations were again in train to breach the walls of Namwŏn. Yang Yüan seems to have decided that against such odds, a negotiated settlement would be preferable to a fight to the death; but Konishi Yukinaga would settle for nothing less than immediate surrender and the opening of all the gates to the city, terms that Yang was unable to accept. Negotiations went no further. Although they say that Yang did gain some satisfaction from the successes of his cavalrymen, whose sallies drove the enemy back from only a few of their forward positions.

The next day, the 16th, chaos reigned within the walls. The Chinese cavalrymen were seen whispering to one another and furtively saddling their horses. Everyone knew what was on their minds, and some began to make preparations of their own. In the midst of all this, Yi Bok-nam, the Korean Military Commander, somehow contrived the successful escape and flight of his young son and the boy's guardian, Meng Erh-k'uan, who was to send up a smoke signal once they had reached safety in the mountains. That done, Yi settled down to wait. But it was not until dusk that the barrage began. For an hour or more, the south wall was battered by massed artillery, and no sooner had that ended than a great roar arose from the enemy camp as the soldiers rushed forward with their scaling ladders and firing platforms. Before long, the moat had been filled, and the enemy warriors were clambering up to the tops of the walls. Then they were in the city, and the gates were thrown open. And the massacre began. Yang Yüan seems to have been taken by surprise while trying to catch a few winks of sleep. He leapt from his bed, ran to his horse without even bothering to dress properly, and somehow managed to make a clean escape. Some seemed to think that this had all been prearranged during his "negotiations" with the Japanese, for virtually all of his cavalrymen were cut down in their attempt to escape. Only Yi Bok-nam and his remaining contingent of 117 Koreans held their ground. All were slaughtered.

In the morning, our monk in the Shimazu entourage, as he looked out from the city walls, remarked that "the roadside was strewn with more corpses than there are grains of sand." Again, he was moved to poetry:

nanmon no shiro o tachiide mite areba
me mo aterarenu fuzei narikeri
As I set out from the walled city of Namwŏn and gaze about me,
I'm unable to rest my eyes upon the sights I see.

A more precise report claims that 3,726 heads were taken, in addition to which there were those who had only their noses removed—in some cases, while still alive.

Neither, as it turned out, did Yi's son and his Chinese guardian escape. They were spotted by men in the service of Asonuma Bungo-no-Kami Motohide, one of Mōri Terumoto's commanders. Yet miraculously, amid the frenzy of wanton killing, they were spared. Perhaps, as the Mōri household records suggest, this was because the boy carried a tufted lance emblazoned with the motto "Dragons and Tigers of the House of Yi," which identified him as a scion of that royal line. Whatever the reason, their case was referred to Mōri Terumoto himself, who had established his command post on the island of Iki. Terumoto commanded that they be sent back to Japan and appointed Asonuma Shinjirō and Naganuma Kurōzaemon as their "retainers." The child was seven, and Meng was twenty-six.

The boy was entrusted to the care of the Asonuma house, where he was to be raised in a manner befitting his royal lineage. Thus for the next three years, at least, he would have lived with the Asonuma in their home fortress on Mount Tokonoyama, a few leagues to the east of Hiroshima, or perhaps in Hiroshima itself, if the Asonuma maintained a mansion there. Thus far, I expect, the boy's guardian would have remained with him. And there he might well have stayed, were it not for the battle of Sekigahara in the Ninth Month of 1600, which wrought such disastrous consequences for the Mōri and their vassals.

Mōri Terumoto had thoughtlessly allowed himself to be lured to Osaka and appointed the figurehead commander-in-chief of the anti-Tokugawa Western Army, led by Ishida Mitsunari. During the battle,

Terumoto never left the Western Perimeter of Osaka Castle, and a wise senior vassal managed to prevent the Mōri force from being committed against the Tokugawa. But in the post-defeat reckoning, Terumoto paid for his misjudgment with the loss of six provinces, including Aki, where his home castle in Hiroshima stood, leaving him only Suō and Nagato at the far western tip of Honshū. For three years, he was detained in Fushimi, and only in 1603 was he allowed to return to the west, this time to a far lesser fortress in the town of Hagi.

It was in the same year that his young Korean prisoner, now thirteen, was permitted to celebrate his majority, on which occasion Terumoto graciously granted him the use of a character from his own name. Henceforth, the boy would be known as Rinoie Motohiro, and to support him in his new condition as a Mōri vassal, he was granted a fief rated at 100 koku in the district of Kumage, the village of Katsuma. By one of those strange ironies of history, the Hachiman Shrine where Hideyoshi had stopped to pray for victory in his conquest of Korea now lay within territory ruled by a captured scion of Korean royalty.

From this time forward, the new House of Rinoie remains a constant presence in the records and registers of the Mōri. Motohiro married, and thereafter, until the Meiji Revolution, the firstborn sons of his line were appointed to the powerful Advisory Council of the Mōri house, and the younger sons to the Great Guard or the Corps of Attendant Physicians.

But not a word is said in any of the records about Meng Erh-k'uan and his relationship with the young Motohiro. They may well have been parted after the move to Hagi. The boy, after all, being descended in a branch of Korean royalty, was an ornament to the Mōri Corps of Vassals, while his rescuer, despite his illustrious ancestry, was but another medical officer. The severe economies forced upon the Mori by the loss of their vast territories may well have made it impossible to support the Chinese physician any longer.

In retrospect, we realize that at some point after his arrival, Meng decided to adopt a more Japanese-sounding name. His home in China was Wu-lin, which in Japanese is pronounced "Takebayashi," and he took that as his surname. And as a given name, he called himself Jian, which would immediately mark him as a medical man. Thus renamed,

Takebayashi Jian embarked upon a new career in a new country. Some say that he practiced medicine in Hagi and taught the medical arts to the children of Rinoie Motohiro. Some say that he found employment elsewhere in the province of Nagato. And some say that he migrated to Edo.

The one thing that we know for certain is that he eventually entered the service of the Asano, who had become the new lords of Hiroshima in 1619. A genealogy in the possession of his present-day descendants in Hiroshima states that in 1643, after years of "service" in the province of Nagato, Takebayashi Jian was made a vassal of the Asano house. And on the island of Miyajima in Hiroshima Bay, there stands a stone monument upon which is inscribed a poem in Chinese, "Depicting the Beauties of Mount Misen." This poem is dated the 3rd Day, First Month, 1645; its signature reads, "Composed by Shih-erh, descended in the sixty-first generation from that sage of the land of Tsou who was second only to Confucius"; and it is sealed with a double circle that encloses archaic characters that read "Takebayashi." A beautiful rubbing of this inscription was later reproduced in an illustrated gaz-etteer of Miyajima, the compiler of which further explains: "Shih-erh was a descendant of Mencius from the district of Wu-lin in Kwang-chou, China. In the latter days of the Ming dynasty, he settled in Japan and took the name Takebayashi Jian. As everyone knows, his great-grandson [grandson] was Takebayashi Tadashichi, who was a member of the Loyal League of Akō. Many of his descendants still reside in this domain." After forty-five years in obscurity, Meng Erh-k'uan reemerges under the name of Takebayashi Jian, very much alive and still—or again—in Hiroshima.

The next two generations of the Takebayashi line are far easier to trace. Some remained in the service of the Asano main house in Hiroshima, while others were assigned to the new cadet branch in Akō; some retained the name Takebayashi, while others adopted the name of Jian's wife's family, the Watanabe. All of them, though, are clearly identifiable. Tadashichi's father, Watanabe Hei'emon, as the second son of Takebayashi Jian, was assigned to service in Akō and took the family name of his mother. Hei'emon's first son, Tadashichi's elder brother, was named Han'emon. Tadashichi, the second son, reverted to his grandfather's name and retained his Chinese clan name: throughout life, his full name would remain Takebayashi Tadashichi Mō Takashige.

Although a younger son, he was made a member of the Mid-Corps of Pages, for which he was paid 15 *ryō* per year plus rations for three retainers. Of his life as a vassal of Takumi-no-Kami, we know virtually nothing, until he accompanied His Lordship to Edo in the summer of Genroku 13 (1700), the year before the Catastrophe.

*Private valor is a
small man's valor.*

Knowing what we know of the ancestry of Takebayashi Tadashichi, it comes as no surprise that filial devotion to his parents was a matter of supreme importance to this distant descendant of Mencius. And at this particular moment, at about the time of the Yamashina meetings, it was a matter that was causing him great anxiety. His mother and father, who still lived in Akō, were very old and very ill. Tadashichi's elder brother, Watanabe Han'emon, was there to care for them. But Tadashichi nonetheless felt guilty to be 155 leagues (387.5 miles, 620 kilometers) away, where he could be of no help whatever. While there was still time, he decided, he must travel to Akō one last time and do what he could to comfort them. But Edo to Akō is a journey of several days, not only long and lonely but often difficult for a lone traveler in need of accommodation. Such, at any rate, was Fuwa Kazuemon's stated reason for volunteering to go along with Tadashichi. And so on the 18th of the Second Month, the two men set out, bound for Akō by way of Yamashina, where they would call upon Kuranosuke; Osaka, where they would visit Hara Sōemon and Ōtaka Gengo; and Kameyama, where Kazuemon's father, Okano Jidayū, still lived. It was to be an eventful journey.

◆ ◆ ◆

Tadashichi seems to have been known among his contemporaries not only for his ancestry but also for his temper. Ogawa Tsunemitsu describes him succinctly: "He is utterly fearless, and being of mature years is extremely strong-willed. In conversation, he tends to be short tempered and roughly spoken, as a result of which Hara Sōemon is always saying to him, 'Now just calm down; let's take it easy.'" But without the even-tempered patience of Sōemon to restrain him, a discussion with Tadashichi could apparently become quite volatile.

On the 28th or 29th of the Second Month, Tadashichi and Kazuemon arrived in Yamashina and went directly to Kuranosuke's home. We know very little of this meeting, but Ōtaka Gengo tells us that Kuranosuke first told Tadashichi about the Yamashina meetings—that a consensus had been reached to wait until the case of Asano Daigaku had been decided and that Yoshida Chūzaemon and Chikamatsu Kanroku had gone to Edo and persuaded Horibe Yasubei and Okuda Magodayū to abide by this decision. But when Kuranosuke told him that even Gengo and Nakamura Kansuke had agreed to wait, Tadashichi was furious. "Those cowards!" he exclaimed. "Well, there's no need now to go to Osaka and talk to *them*. I'm going straight to Akō from here." What else passed between Tadashichi, Kazuemon, and Kuranosuke is not recorded, but whatever it was alarmed Kuranosuke sufficiently that he wrote to Okuno Shōgen in Kameyama, warning him that the two men were bent upon some wild scheme and he should be prepared to counter it when they passed through.

In the meantime, Kazuemon seems to have calmed Tadashichi a bit, and they continued their journey to Osaka as planned. Gengo was in Ōtsu when they arrived, but when he returned the next day, Tadashichi reviled him mercilessly.

"You're a coward! A coward from head to toe!" he said. "I suspected as much from the start; but you always spoke so smoothly, and I believed you. Well now your mask has fallen off—just as I suspected!"

Gengo found this hard to take, but he remained as calm as he could: "I can quite understand why you might think this, but it's nothing that calls for such abuse. There are good reasons for what I've done; my intentions haven't changed in the slightest. Kuranosuke Dono is firm and determined, and he has set a definite deadline. If you'll listen quietly, I'll tell you all the details. And if you still think that I am wrong, I will side with you here on the spot, head for Edo without a moment's delay, and lay down my life with you. So let me tell you how this decision was reached."

But when Gengo said that, Tadashichi fairly exploded. "Tears came to his eyes," Gengo said, "and he wouldn't listen to a word I said. There was nothing I could do about it; we parted in anger."

◆ ◆ ◆

Kuranosuke's letter to Okuno Shōgen does not survive, and there is no record of anything that Tadashichi and Kazuemon said to Hara Sōemon in Osaka. A memoir recently discovered in the temple where Kazuemon's sister once lived, however, describes a plan of action that Kazuemon proposed to his father, Okano Jidayū, in Kameyama—perhaps the same plan that they proposed, unsuccessfully, to Kuranosuke and Sōemon. Here is what Kazuemon said:

> In the last month of last year and the First Month of this year, Kira has gone to the temple Kan'ōji in Yanaka. He travels in a woman's palanquin and is attended by four or five maidservants. Half a block to the rear, they are followed by about ten samurai. When they reach the temple, the palanquin is carried in at the entrance to the kitchens. The maidservants go to a nearby teahouse; only the samurai go in with him. This must be Kira. The two of us, together with four or five of the others in Edo, could do it. Two or three of us attack the palanquin, while the others fight off the samurai. We think that we could kill him easily, but no one else agrees with us. What do you think?

Jidayū had an interesting answer: "No; at this stage, you should not do it. You are right, of course, that this is, almost certainly, Kira; and with only two or three men, you *could* kill him. But if you do, then all the efforts of Kuranosuke and the other members of the pact will have been in vain. . . . It would be a private victory, but private valor is a small man's valor. Your comrades would not appreciate it."

Tadashichi protested that Kira was an old man and might die of natural causes while they were waiting for Kuranosuke to act—and then what? But Jidayū simply reminded him that death is no respecter of age. Even Kira's young son might die before they had a chance to kill him. They would just have to chance it, and hope that their luck did not run out.

As far as we know, that was the end of Tadashichi and Kazuemon's scheme to kill Kira on their own. They stayed in Kameyama for another four or five days, resting from the rigors of their journey, and then took their leave and parted. Tadashichi continued westward to his parents' home in Akō, and Kazuemon went north to Himeji and on through the mountains to Sasayama and the temple Sōgenji, where his elder sister lived.

◆ ◆ ◆

We may not know what Tadashichi told Sōemon when they met in Osaka, but we know very well what Sōemon made of it—and it is rather surprising. In a long letter written about a month later, Sōemon proposed a plan of his own to Yasubei and Magodayū. Sōemon seems to have thought that to attack Kira *after* Daigaku's case had been decided could only harm Daigaku. And even if Kuranosuke did not participate, he would still be forced to commit suicide to preserve his honor. His suicide might then be considered in breach of the law against *junshi*. In attempting to preserve his honor, he could instead be denounced as dying a dog's death. An entirely different approach was required. "Given which," Soemon said, "I have a plan."

> I've said nothing whatever about this to Genshirō or the others. I've kept it entirely to myself; but this is a notion I must discuss carefully with you two, so here it is. As I hinted last year, we should secretly break off from the Kyoto group and execute this plan by ourselves. If Kuranosuke Dono and most of the other Kyoto people are excluded, then Kobiki-chō can hardly be blamed for anything. We'll cause him no trouble.
>
> Tadashichi arrived here recently, and his resolve remains as firm as ever. This time, too, he urged me to break away and join forces with him. But to break away now, after discussing matters so thoroughly

only a short while ago, would mean deserting those with whom we have just reached agreement. Yet, as I said, if taking action against the other party could be harmful to Kobiki-chō, and committing suicide would serve only to express our personal feelings, then it might be better to execute our plan with only a small number of participants. With all the leaders leaning their heads toward Kobiki-chō, those of us who attack will be seen as a separate group. Those who agreed to do as decided at Yamashina are not likely to be implicated in any way, for they will not be abandoning the cause of Daigaku. I think that we should select a group of about fourteen or fifteen men. It should put the other party at ease, too, if we give the appearance of patience.

When Tadashichi was here a while ago, I thought that I might tell him, but whatever you tell these young people can so easily leak out. And this particular plan must be kept a secret of the highest order if it is to succeed. Even those of our own group must be scrutinized very carefully before we tell them. When Tadashichi said, "I just can't accept this thing that you've agreed to," I answered, "I have another plan, so don't be so impatient. It will all come clear by the Fifth or Sixth Month. Just remain calm until then."

What do you think of this? If you are of like mind, then reply and let me know. There is no need to discuss this point by point in writing. I don't think that we should be discussing anything as secret as this in letters. Just let me know by the way you write whether you think this appropriate or not.

Yasubei and Magodayū wrote back in a manner every bit as ambiguous as that recommended by Sōemon: "We have both read with great care the thoughts that you kindly convey to us and find them quite to the point. Truly, we feel, we could wish for nothing better. Since there is no need to answer each and every point you make in your letter, we think it best that we meet to discuss the matter further. We fervently hope, therefore, that we may await your coming to Edo in the Seventh Month."

A bit later, Kuranosuke, too, felt the need to write, although in a tone entirely different from that of Sōemon. And this time, he addressed his words not only to Yasubei and Magodayū, but also to Yasubei's father, Yahei, and Magodayū's son Sadaemon:

> *I am sure that the delays have been wearisome for you, but it is for the best that you remain steadfast until I come to Edo and join you there. It is but a few more months now, and if anyone acts rashly in the meantime, our past plans will all come to naught. That would be ruinous for Kobiki-chō. Indeed, at this point, it would constitute an act of disloyalty to our honored lord. Our time will come, and distant though it may seem, it is for the best that you endure the long wait patiently until the Third Month next year. I hear that there are those in Edo who criticize me for the repeated delays and call me a liar, but there is nothing I can do about that. As I have said time and again, I have persevered in this commitment ever since we left Akō. If we wait until the Third Month next year and there is still no judgment forthcoming, then I see no need to wait any longer than that. I know that there is no need to tell you this, but recently Takebayashi Tadashichi came to Kyoto, and said, "I was told you had something in mind, but this is hardly what I expected. Do it now, by all means!" But I had to refuse him. The Third Month is but a short time away; I find it strange that he should not accept the decision that was made here. What do you people think?*

The four men replied, reassuringly, honestly, but by no means barring the way for a change of plans:

> *We can well imagine how anxiously you must await a judgment in the case of Kobiki-chō. And thus we quite understand the concerns that you express in your letter. You tell us that Takebayashi Tadashichi recently came to Kyoto and spoke his mind to you. You are absolutely right to feel that there should be no rash action at this time. And surely there shall be no rash action. For even if we were discussing some plan of action, we would certainly let you know*

what we were doing. This past spring, disappointed though we were,
we responded as requested and undertook no unannounced action in
opposition; so please bear this in mind.

Takebayashi Tadashichi and Fuwa Kazuemon may have failed to persuade anyone that an attack at the temple Kan'ōji was a good idea; but they had set a great deal else in motion. After they returned to Edo, on the 12th Day of the Sixth Month, they again met with the "four or five men" who were to join them in this scheme, and this time swore mutual solidarity with ceremonial cups of saké at a teahouse in Asakusa. Those present were Takebayashi Tadashichi, Kurahashi Densuke, Maebara Isuke, Katsuda Shinzaemon, Sugino Jūheiji, and Fuwa Kazuemon. What they discussed or decided is not recorded, but we see at least that Kazuemon, despite being a ronin, had by now managed to gain acceptance as a peripheral member of the pact.

Three days later, on the 15th, Horibe Yasubei put the final touches to the collection of correspondence and comment that we have been reading and delivered the completed volume to his friend Hosoi Kōtaku (1658–1735), now a ronin, but a brilliant scholar of Chinese who until recently had been a vassal of the Shogun's Chief Adjutant, Yanagisawa Mino-no-Kami. Kōtaku was one of those rare men who was a consummate master of many arts, only one of which was the sword. He and Yasubei had become friends because both men were senior disciples of Horiuchi Gendazaemon. Yasubei knew that Kōtaku was a man whom he could trust to preserve the record of his struggle to enforce the Principle of Equal Punishment.

On the 16th, Yasubei walked to Shiba Matsumoto-chō, where he told Yoshida Chūzaemon and Chikamatsu Kanroku that he would soon be leaving for Kyoto. What he intended to do there he did not reveal, but early on the morning of the 18th, Yasubei left Edo, and twelve days later, on the 29th Day of the Sixth Month, he arrived in Kyoto.

As we shall see, unforeseen events were about to overtake everyone's plans. But at the moment, despite Okano Jidayū's wise warning to his son, it was beginning to look as though Kuranosuke's efforts actually would be rendered vain, that he would soon be left behind by those who had lost patience with his highly principled but overlong persistence in keeping his "commitment."

CHAPTER
47

Through the evening mist, a pale glow
from the window where Yūgiri waits.

I can't imagine anyone passing through the town of Fushimi without pausing to visit the Fushimi Inari Shrine. It is just too grand a sight to miss. A whole mountainside dotted with beautifully crafted, vermilion-enameled sacral structures, the paths between them spanned with long rows of vermilion torii, all set against a luxuriant background of deep-green forest. I doubt, though, that many who do visit the shrine ever make their way up to the peak of Mount Inari. If you do, though, and if you look carefully, you will find an interesting object that has nothing to do with the shrine. Just beyond the Little Swordsmith's Shrine, a narrow path branches off from the main circuit, and at that juncture, lying among a bed of leaves, is a fallen granite signpost of the sort once used to mark partings of the ways at highway intersections throughout the land. The signpost reads:

STRAIGHT AHEAD TO YAMASHINA. ŌISHI HOMESTEAD, 10 *CHŌ*

And, indeed, if you follow that path through the pines, about half a mile down the eastern slope of Mount Inari, you will emerge in the Yamashina Valley just a short distance from a rather large commemorative stone that marks the site of Ōishi Kuranosuke's home after he left Akō and moved to the village of Nishinoyama.

But why should anyone take the trouble to erect a carved granite signpost on a disused path, showing the way from the top of Mount Inari to the site of Kuranosuke's old home? Many people still visit that site, but no one I know has ever gone there via this roundabout route. I found it all a bit puzzling at first, but I've now come to think that the signpost itself is commemorative, that it was erected not to show sightseers the way to Kuranosuke's home, but to mark a path that Kuranosuke himself used to travel.

Travel where? It is well known that in the summer of Genroku 15 (1702), Kuranosuke began to frequent the brothels in Fushimi's pleasure quarter, Shumoku-machi. And if you look at a map of the region, it is plain to see that the path marked by that signpost—up Mount Inari and down through the shrine to the Fushimi Highroad—is the most direct route from Kuranosuke's home to Shumoku-machi. I possess no proof, but I suspect that whoever erected that granite signpost did so as a memorial to a man whom he admired, whom he thought must have passed this way many times. And it may well be that Kuranosuke did pass this way on some of his evening escapades.

◆ ◆ ◆

Much has been written about this period in Kuranosuke's life, very little of it based upon sound evidence. The most common notion is that Kuranosuke's "debauchery" was in fact a ruse meant to deceive spies sent from Edo by Kira and the Uesugi. According to this theory, the spies would observe Kuranosuke disporting himself disgracefully and report that he showed no sign of any interest in avenging his late lord, thus putting his enemies off the scent and causing them to relax their vigil. But no contemporary sources make any mention of such spying, and Kuranosuke himself never hinted that he thought himself spied upon. In point of fact, Kuranosuke was probably less virtuous than proponents of the spy theory wish to think him, but more typical of his time than his detractors care to admit. All we can do is review what we do know with some certainty and draw our own conclusions.

◆ ◆ ◆

As we know, Kuranosuke's wife, O-Riku, was pregnant with her fifth child, and "in the Third or Fourth Month" was to return to her father's home in Toyooka, where she would have better medical and postnatal

figure 15
A rubbing of the granite signpost that marks the way from Fushimi Inari Shrine
to the Yamashina Valley. (Rubbing by author, mounting by Liza Dalby)

care than would be available to her in Yamashina. It is generally assumed that Kuranosuke's excursions to Shumoku-machi began after her departure, probably early in the Fourth Month. But what do we know of the details of those excursions? "Wine, women, and song" is the modern phrase used to sum up activity of this sort, and it is certain that Kuranosuke indulged in all three of these. But beyond this, specifics are hard to come by.

Some writers speak as though he made the rounds of all the pleasure quarters in the capital, Shimabara and Gion as well as in Shumoku-machi. But the only direct evidence that we possess suggests that it was the Sasaya in Fushimi that he visited most often. Reminiscing much later, the Confucian scholar and physician Tachibana Nankei (1753–1805) writes:

> When I first came to live in Fushimi, the Sasaya, which Kuranosuke frequented, was the largest house in Shumoku-machi. It still remained as it had been in Ōishi's day, a large building that brought to mind thoughts of what it must once have been. The master, Sei'emon, was an old man in his seventies. He was a devotee of haikai and went by the nom de plume of Arisuke. I knew him well. Sei'emon's mother remembered Ōishi well from her younger days. They still possessed letters from him in the house. Ōishi's nom de plume was Uki, and all his letters were signed "Uki." There are also several letters from some of the other ronin who came to enjoy themselves there. Sei'emon used to tell me all manner of fascinating stories every time I saw him. The woman with whom Ōishi disported himself was called Yūgiri. They also had a koto that Ōishi had given to this Yūgiri, as well as an inkstone of Chinese manufacture. And the panels above the doors of the second-story rooms were carved to depict the mountains on Kuranosuke's route from Yamashina to Fushimi. . . . The old Sasaya was an enormous house. The stairway to the second story was 9 feet wide, so broad that three or four people abreast, carrying trays of food and drink, could ascend it together. When I first moved to Fushimi, it was all still intact.

Some of the letters that Nankei mentions still survive, most of them addressed to the mistress of the house, who at that time must have been Sei'emon's mother. It would have been one of the duties of this lady to write regularly to her customers, urging them to return, to which end she kept a list of the addresses of the ronin among their replies. Here, for example, is one of Kuranosuke's replies to her:

How very fondly I perused your kind missive. First of all, let me say that on our recent visit, although so long delayed, I was utterly delighted to find your hospitality quite as warm as ever. When I left, it was in the dark of night, and I was unable to take proper leave of you, which even now I greatly regret. I do hope that all remains as well with you as ever. My return was uneventful and swift and not the least bit troublesome. You really needn't have worried on my behalf. I had hoped ever so much that I might come again soon and enjoy your hospitality; but, alas, things have not gone as I would wish of late. I should like to tell you all about it, but must write in haste. Hence this all too brief reply. Sincerely,

FIFTH MONTH, 11TH DAY   *Uki*

To: Sasaya
On-Umoji Sama,
with respect

How often Kuranosuke made these excursions alone we have no idea. But it is obvious from these letters that he often met other members of the pact at the Sasaya, and that even his manservant, Kasemura Kōshichi, accompanied him. Here is a typical letter from Ōtaka Gengo, almost businesslike in tone:

I take the liberty of sending my man with this message to you. I am, above all, pleased to hear, from your recent letter, that you remain as well as ever. But regarding our appointment for tomorrow, the 11th or the 12th: just this morning, a visitor from the country arrived, making it impossible for me to come either tomorrow or the next day. I have sent word explaining the circumstances to Kado Sama. Might I ask you to be so kind as to postpone our visit until the 14th or 15th? It is most unfortunate that this has arisen so very suddenly. But I have informed the others that even though I shall not be able to attend, they should still enjoy themselves. Having happened previously as well, it is most unfortunate this should happen again.

Shiyō

To: Sasaya
On-Uchi Sama

P.S. Should this be possible, I beg your indulgence. But if you are busy, I certainly do not insist. Sincerely,

Nor, apparently, was Kuranosuke quite as regular a customer as he is thought to have been:

Your recent letter I have perused carefully and longingly. How splendid to hear that you remain well. As you say, far too much time has passed, and I do hope to see you soon. I am very pleased that you have been so forbearing. Since last time, I have been burdened with a steady stream of ineluctable tasks, which inevitably, but unfortunately, have kept us apart. I do hope to come again soon, but that must be as circumstances dictate. I am delighted that Bugyō Dono remains as well as when I last saw him. I have been far too long-winded.

EIGHTH MONTH, 11TH DAY   *U*
To: On-Uchi Sama,
with respect

P.S. I have heard from Bugyō Dono concerning the 15th. It will be the night of that justly famed full moon, which I quite long to view. But my plans are unsettled, and I cannot now say for certain whether I shall be free. If things go well in the interim, I shall come, for I look forward with delight to enjoying your hospitality once more. Sincerely,

But lest it seem that the mistress of the house was the only lady with whom Kuranosuke and his comrades were concerned, Ōtaka Gengo has left us a series of five verses that he inscribed, probably in a state of inebriation, on a "broken-down folding screen." Each verse incorporates the name of one of the girls of the Sasaya:

> *yūgiri ya / hitomachi mado no / usuakari*
> Through the evening mist, a pale glow from the window
> where Yūgiri waits.

> *yoshino ikani / shiroi kosode wa / yamazakura*
> How so, Yoshino, that your robe gleams as white
> as the mountain cherry?

> *takahashi ya / takai tokoro no / yūsuzumi*
> Ah, Takahashi! To enjoy the evening cool from
> the heights of your room.

> *kaze kaoru / ame no tamoto ya / awatsu toki*
> Fragrant is the breeze, when Kaoru's
> sleeves flutter as she flees the rain.

> *hatsune to ya / ichibandate no / hototogisu*
> Hatsune we call her—always the first of the songbirds to sing.

The Mito scholar Aoyama Enkō says that Kuranosuke, as a young man, was fond of composing lyrics to be sung as "little songs" (*kouta*). None of these early compositions survive, but one of his later songs, composed while he was frequenting the Sasaya, not only survives but seems to have become moderately famous. It was probably based upon his experiences in Shumoku-machi:

Satogeshiki	**Hon chōshi**
Views of the Quarter	Standard tuning

> *fukete kuruwa no yosooi mireba,*
> As night falls, I gaze out upon the splendors of the quarter,

yoi no tomoshibi uchisomukine no,
Then turn my back upon those eventide lights; and there, where I lie,
yume no hana sae chirasu arashi no sasoi-kite,
I'm swept away in that storm that scatters even the blossoms that
bloom in dreams.

neya o tsuredasu tsurebito onoko,
Her man, her partner for the night, she leads from her bedchamber.
yoso no saraba mo nao aware nite,
Now, even the farewells of others seem touching;
uchi mo nakado o akuru shinonome,
As the pale glow of dawn illumines the inner door
okuru sugata no hitoeobi
Where she stands, her summer sash loosely tied, seeing him off.

tokete hodokete nemidaregami no
Smoothing, straightening her sleep-tangled hair
tsuge no, tsuge no ogushi mo,
With her boxwood, her little boxwood comb,
sasuga namida no harahara sode ni,
Yes, tears stream down upon her sleeves,
koborete sode ni,
Spill over onto her sleeves.
tsuyu no yosuga no yasashiki tsutome,
Her scant support, is this sweetly rendered service.
koborete sode ni,
. . . Spill over onto her sleeves,
tsuraki yosuga no UKIzutome. (Uki = Kuranosuke)
Her painful support, is this dismal service—that she renders *me*.

And that is about as much as we know for certain about Kuranosuke in
Shumoku-machi. There are a few more letters, a couple more songs, and
a charming saké cup that he designed. But no more; for whatever else
went on, it does not seem to have alarmed the members of his pact or
even moved them to comment upon it. They did not hesitate to berate

him for his reluctance to launch an immediate attack on Kira, but, as we have seen, some of his most stalwart comrades actually joined him at the Sasaya. This is not to say, though, that no one disapproved of his behavior. Ochiai Yozaemon writes:

> *Kuranosuke was by nature a very lively man. And thus in the course of his outings and excursions in the capital, he engaged in some rather unsavory activities. And he threw money about in a profligate manner. His cousin Shindō Genshirō and his uncle Oyama Gengozaemon, both gentlemen of the old school, found this most distressing and remonstrated with him severely. "It is very important that you keep in good health, for you have no idea what ordeals you may yet encounter," they told him. "And you will be needing a great deal of money as well. Really, your behavior of late has been most unbecoming."*

Nor were Genshirō and Gengozaemon content merely to remonstrate. They decided to fight fire with fire. Again, we know nothing of how their scheme was executed, but we know for certain, from Kuranosuke himself, that it was executed.

In brief, there seems to have been a dealer in second-hand wares in the back streets of Teramachi Nijō whose daughter was regarded in the neighborhood as something of a beauty. Typical of those in his trade, Nimonjiya Jirōzaemon probably harbored fantasies of selling goods of scant worth at great price to unsuspecting buyers, thereby enriching himself with minimal effort. And after many years in this trade, it was perhaps natural that he should be willing to offer his nineteen-year-old daughter as a "companion" to the erstwhile Chief Elder of an attaindered daimyo. There would be the immediate recompense of a few gold pieces. But even more tempting, perhaps, was the hope of future benefit from a "connection" with this eminent family. The eminent family was, it was true, in embarrassed circumstances at the moment. But if the clan should be restored, and if in the meantime his daughter should bear a son whose name would be Ōishi. . . . Yes, this was an opportunity of an alliance that a dealer in second-hand wares could hardly dream of in the normal course of things.

How his kinsmen arranged this with Kuranosuke, and what O-Karu—for that was the girl's name—thought of her father's bargain are not recorded. Before very long, O-Karu was pregnant, but as far as we know, her presence did nothing to deter Kuranosuke from his visits to Shumoku-machi.

48

*You are to take him to your domain
and settle him there.*

There had been no warning whatever. It came as a complete surprise to everyone, and a total shock.

◆ ◆ ◆

On the 18th Day of the Seventh Month, at the height of a long stretch of the "lingering heat" of early autumn, a messenger from the Duty Elder, Abe Bungo-no-Kami, arrived at the Sakurada mansion of the Hiroshima main house. Aki-no-Kami was requested to dispatch one of his vassals in connection with an item of official business, the nature of which was not stated. When Akashi Kichidayū, the Edo Liaison Officer of the Hiroshima house, presented himself as directed, an Adjutant handed him a directive, signed by the full Council of Elders, that read: "Asano Daigaku is to be released from Domiciliary Confinement. You are to take him to your domain and settle him there. Be apprised as well that Daigaku himself will be informed of the foregoing." The execution of the transfer, the Adjutant said, would be supervised by the Duty Officer of the Junior Council, Katō Etchū-no-Kami. With that, Kichidayū was dismissed. He gathered his entourage and returned to report to Aki-no-Kami.

◆ ◆ ◆

At about the same time, Asano Daigaku was summoned to the official residence of Katō Etchū-no-Kami, whither he was escorted by his cousin Asano Sahyōe. There he was read the same directive. He was also told that he would not be permitted to return to his own home, but was to proceed directly to the Hiroshima Upper Mansion in Sakurada, where he arrived just before the sounding of the Seventh Hour (4:00 P.M.). At nightfall, a detail was sent to fetch his wife and infant daughter, who were to accompany him to Hiroshima. He would be allowed to take about half of his retainers with him; the others were dismissed and told that they were free to do as they pleased.

While preparations for the long journey were being made, the family would occupy the house opposite the main mansion within the Sakurada estate. They would be waited upon by a considerable contingent of Aki-no-Kami's samurai, and the guard at the gate and the entry hall of their new residence would be strengthened. Their meals, too, would be prepared for them in the kitchens of the main mansion. That first evening, they were served a feast that filled two trays—two soups, six side dishes, and two varieties of fish. Thereafter, however, at their own request, this was reduced to a single tray at the main meal plus a light supper in the evening.

◆ ◆ ◆

This was not the disposition of the case that anyone had anticipated, and Aki-no-Kami felt the need for further clarification. And so on the 19th, Akashi Kichidayū was sent back to the residence of Bungo-no-Kami.

"Daigaku has been fully pardoned upon his release from Domiciliary Confinement," an official told Kichidayū, "and he has *not* been remanded to custody. There is no need for you to request further instruction about what you may or may not do, nor to ask permission for anything whatever; you may treat him just as generously as you wish. Bungo-no-Kami Sama has instructed me to ensure that you understand that he is not to be treated as though he were under strict supervision. Although previously he was sentenced to confinement, that was necessary only because he had been adopted as a son by Naganori. 'Be sure that you tell Kichidayū that,' Bungo-no-Kami Sama told me."

And yet it was apparent that Daigaku was *not* free to live anywhere other than in Hiroshima. There were those who chose to see it—a bit hopefully, it seems to me—as an act of kindness, intended to spare

Daigaku Dono the privations of life as a ronin. Or was it simply a geographical stratagem, meant to keep Daigaku out of the same city as Kira? However you interpret it, this was an unprecedented judgment, and not to anyone's liking. Still, it was Daigaku's duty, that same day, to make the rounds of the mansions of all the Elders, thanking them for his pardon and their provision for his family.

That done, there remained the practical business of preparing for their journey. For Aki-no-Kami, this began with a series of gifts for Daigaku, his wife, and his daughter—mostly clothing and fabrics, but more practically, books to dispel the boredom of long days in a palanquin, toys for the little girl, and even gifts for Daigaku's six vassals and his wife's maidservants. Most practical of all, though, was a present of 100 *ryō* in gold to make up the shortfall in revenue from the fief that Daigaku no longer possessed.

✦ ✦ ✦

Yoshida Chūzaemon and Chikamatsu Kanroku had arrived in Edo five months earlier and were soon to be relieved by Onodera Jūnai and Oyama Gengoemon. Their present plan was to leave Edo on the 25th of the Seventh Month, in preparation for which they had already vacated their rooms in Shiba Matsumoto-chō and taken temporary lodging in Shin Kōjimachi, where they told the landlord that they were ronin from Mimasaka. But then on the 18th, just seven days before they were to leave, Chūzaemon somehow learnt of Asano Daigaku's "pardon." This changed everything. The Council of Elders had spoken, and far from restoring the honor of Asano Daigaku, they had simply shifted the place of his detention from Edo to Hiroshima. And Kira remained free; the Shogunate had no intention of subjecting him to the Principle of Equal Punishment. There was nothing more to wait for; the time had come to act.

That day, Chūzaemon wrote a quick letter explaining the situation to his younger brother Kaiga Yazaemon in Kyoto and sent it by express courier. It arrived in Kyoto on the 22nd, and Yazaemon immediately carried the missive to Kuranosuke in Yamashina. Kuranosuke did not hesitate. He summoned Yokogawa Kanpei, a very low-ranking samurai, and insisted that he leave for Edo the same day by express conveyance.

The message that Kanpei carried was a simple one: "Wait! Wait until the rest of us come from Kyoto. Do not attack before we arrive."

Two days later, on the 24th, another letter from Chūzaemon arrived, urging those members of the pact in the capital region to settle their wives and children as quickly as they could and come to Edo. Kuranosuke had already taken this task in hand.

◆ ◆ ◆

Before dawn on the 29th, Asano Daigaku, his family, and his few remaining vassals and servants set out from Edo, traveling along the Eastern Sea Road, turning off at Miya onto the Mino Highroad, and thence to the Middle Mountain Road—a route that would take them through the castle town of Ōgaki, seat of his cousin Toda Uneme-no-Kami, a welcome respite on their way to Fushimi. This was no meager entourage of twenty or even thirty people. Asano Daigaku's personal party must have seemed but a small contingent in the midst of the force that Aki-no-Kami sent to escort, serve, and guard them. The procession was led by Amano Heizaemon Kiyoyuki, Commander of the Hiroshima Great Guard, twenty members of which accompanied him. Tōge Han'emon Yukitaka led twenty-four of his company of archers. In addition, there were two members of the Edo Horse Guards, nine dismounted samurai, and thirty-seven long lancers. There was as well a considerable service staff: a doctor, a chef and his provisioners, kitchen people, and servitors, as well as two Tea Monks—a total of more than 130 men. The Hiroshima house would not be seen as stinting in their provision for the heir to their cadet house.

◆ ◆ ◆

On the 2nd Day of the Eighth Month, a fleet of thirteen ships and four escorting vessels sent from Hiroshima arrived in Osaka, where they would meet, and to some extent replace, the procession from Edo. Normally, such a force would have sailed under the command of Ueki Kozaemon, the Maritime Officer of the domain, but on this occasion, someone seems to have decided that matters other than maritime must take precedence. Ueki was reported ill and replaced by the Forestry

Officer Shindō Hachirōemon, who happened also to be an uncle of Shindō Genshirō and thus was related to Kuranosuke as well. And with Hachirōemon went Oki Gondayū, an Elder of the Hiroshima house. Senior officers in Hiroshima would have seen as clearly as anyone that the nature of Asano Daigaku's "pardon" left the Akō ronin—at least those who still cared—little choice but to take the punishment of Kira into their own hands. This was a complication that they were keen to prevent. The mission of Hachirōemon, the uncle, was plainly to persuade; that of Gondayū, the Elder, to apply the pressure of rank in the name of the lord of Hiroshima. Daigaku had left Edo only three days earlier; another ten days would pass before he arrived in Fushimi. There was time aplenty to travel upriver and discuss this matter with Genshirō and Kuranosuke in Yamashina.

◆ ◆ ◆

At first, their efforts met with no success whatever. Hachirōemon and Gondayū were received politely, but neither Genshirō nor Kuranosuke would admit to any plotting of any sort. Finally, however, Hachirōemon went alone to his nephew Genshirō.

"Everyone here seems to behave as though something out of the ordinary were afoot," he said. "Clearly, you've decided to embark upon a scheme of some sort. Yet when I asked you confidentially the other day, you pretended this wasn't so. I just don't understand what you're up to. We're related by blood; we bear the same surname; we should be able to talk these things over. If what you tell me seems right, I'll support you; if it seems something I can't accept, I'll do my best to discourage you. But you must see how helpless this secrecy of yours makes me feel." He spoke with great earnestness of how unfortunate a situation this was, which moved Genshirō to reply sympathetically.

"Everything you say is entirely reasonable, but I'm troubled about what I should do. It is not that I wish to hide anything from you; but I worry what the consequences for you might be if we should break the law, and thereafter Aki-no-Kami should learn that someone in his service knew all about it. It was out of concern for you that I declined to discuss the matter. But the situation is thus-and-so," Genshirō said, and told him in a general way all that had been planned.

Hachirōemon heard him out, and then said, "Indeed! And quite right all of you are to feel as you do. But the time is not right. Aki-no-Kami Sama, too, feels that this could create a scandal of enormous proportions. 'Stop and think!' That is what he would say, I'm sure. Besides which, with Kira's people so much on their guard, what if you should fail? That would be ignominious. Give this up, by all means; that is what I would advise. But if everyone is still bound and determined to go through with it, then at least wait for the right moment." Hachirōemon did all he could to calm and dissuade him. Finally, Genshirō agreed and told Kuranosuke, Shōgen, Denbei, and Gengoemon all about it. Hachirōemon and Gondayū had at least succeeded in complicating the issue for everyone before they returned to Hiroshima.

✦ ✦ ✦

On the 13th Day of the Eighth Month, Asano Daigaku and his party arrived in Fushimi, and Shindō Hachirōemon was waiting there to greet them. Kuranosuke, however, sent his apologies, saying that he was ill and unable to get about just then. He was perfectly healthy, of course, but thought it best not to meet Daigaku lest that implicate him in the subsequent activities of the signatories to the pact.

The next day, they boarded the Yodo riverboat for Osaka, where they arrived early in the evening. On the 15th and 16th, while the ships were being loaded, they lodged there, and with the morning tide on the 17th, set sail for Hiroshima. Four days later, on the 20th, they arrived at the port of Ondo and rested in a teahouse there; on the 21st, the party boarded river boats, which took them the rest of the way to the city. There they were moved into a house commandeered from one of the Hiroshima Heralds, and fêted exactly as they had been in Edo, so that again they had to request simpler fare. On the 22nd, word of their safe arrival was sent to Aki-no-Kami in Edo. Of the subsequent life in Hiroshima of Asano Daigaku and his family, we know almost nothing.

*Those fools in Edo think of nothing but
rushing to their death.*

Kuranosuke had first learnt of Daigaku's "pardon" on the 22nd of the Seventh Month, only five days after the judgment had been rendered in Edo. Within about the same number of days, he had written to everyone within a reasonable distance of Kyoto, and he had reserved a room where they could meet inconspicuously, in the Jūami Chapel of the temple An'yōji.

A "chapel" I call it, but actually it was more like a restaurant than a temple. Originally, of course, it was genuinely a chapel; but An'yōji is situated in one of the most beautiful valleys of the Eastern Hills, at the foot of Mount Maruyama. Here, the hills at first rise slowly enough to be terraced for rice, and then more sharply; the temple is situated just high enough to look down over the fields and command a stunning panorama of the city beyond. At the rear, the site is sheltered by the sharp rise of the mountains, down from which flows a gentle brook that wanders pleasantly between the chapels and waters the fields below. And so as time passed, and the monks began to realize that their location could be a rich source of income, their interests, as well as their activities, gradually shifted from religion to hospitality, to the rental of rooms and the provision of food and drink. The Six Ami, as the chapels came to be known, became a favorite venue for worldly gatherings of all sorts. Jūami, in particular, became famous as a meeting place for the wives of the richest men in Kyoto, who would gather there to show off their finery, each hoping to put all the others to shame. On one such occasion, an Elder of the Silver Guild hired the great artist Ogata Kōrin to stage-manage the entrance of his wife. Kōrin, brilliantly, turned the tables on everyone and dressed the man's wife entirely in black, but arrayed every one of her attendants in the most luxurious fabrics money could buy. A meeting at Jūami would be costly, but a few ronin would attract no undue attention.

According to the only surviving report of this meeting, nineteen men gathered at Jūami on the morning of the 28th:

Ōishi Kuranosuke	Ōishi Chikara	Hara Sōemon
Onodera Jūnai	Onodera Kōemon	Masé Kyūdayū
Masé Magokurō	Horibe Yasubei	Ushioda Matanojō
Ōtaka Gengo	Takebayashi Tadashichi	Nakamura Kansuke
Kaiga Yazaemon	Ōishi Magoshirō	Fuwa Kazuemon
Yatō Emoshichi	Okamoto Jirōzaemon	Ōishi Sezaemon
Mimura Jirōzaemon		

The list is telling. For one thing, it reveals that, whatever danger of schism there had been, the pact was now intact. Horibe Yasubei, Hara Sōemon, Ōtaka Gengo, and Takebayashi Tadashichi—all of whom had hoped to muster a splinter group and mount an independent attack— were among those present at Maruyama. Okuda Magodayu had sent the news to Yasubei at about the same time that Chūzaemon wrote to his brother Yazaemon, whereupon Yasubei, Sōemon, and the others seem to have concluded that Kuranosuke would now have no choice but vendetta and decided to rejoin him.

The list also betrays a potential for further fracture. The nineteen men present at Jūami represented only about half of those living in the Kansai region. Why the other twenty or so did not attend we do not know. Some, no doubt, had perfectly good reasons. Notice had been short; some would have had other commitments. And then there was the weather. For ten days running, it had been fine. But in the afternoon of the previous day, rain had set in, and by the morning of the meeting, a strong wind had arisen as well. Not a good day for travel. Even so, the absence of Shindō Genshirō and Oyama Gengoemon does rouse suspicion. From the time of the Catastrophe, both had been active as senior members of the command group, both were closely related to

figure 16
The Maruyama meeting at the Jūami Chapel. (*Ehon Chūshingura,*
Waseda University Library, Tokyo)

Kuranosuke, and both lived within easy distance of Jūami. One wonders whether Kuranosuke suspected ulterior motives in their absence.

♦ ♦ ♦

Kuranosuke took his seat at the head of the room and began by asking if anyone had any opinion that he wished to express. No one responded. A bit of desultory talk followed, while everyone waited for Kuranosuke to state his own thoughts. But Kuranosuke, as always, was slow, if not reluctant, to come to the point. Finally, the oldest member of the group, Masé Kyūdayū, spoke: "I received a letter recently from Horibe Yahei. He is growing very impatient with our endless deliberations here in the capital. He is nearly eighty, he says, and doesn't expect to live much longer. If he should die (or 'rot,' as he puts it) before we attend to this matter, that, for him, would be the ultimate disgrace. He would prefer, he says, to break into the Kira mansion and be cut down in the garden— even if he has to do it alone, even if it does mean letting the enemy make a plaything of his head. Then, at least, he shall have done his duty as a true vassal, and when he meets his lord down below, he'll not be greeted with silent contempt. I must say, I know how he feels. I am sixty-two this year. If we can't count on the help of you younger men, then I would rather die with Yahei than do nothing at all."

The next to speak was Kyūdayū's cousin Onodera Jūnai, and he did so with characteristic understatement and brevity: "I am in complete agreement with Kyūdayū. I should consider it an honor to accompany my old friends and fellow vassals on the Mountain Road to Death. So whenever you're ready, let's get started."

Now it was the turn of a younger man, Horibe Yasubei, to speak: "The point upon which I have differed with you gentlemen, is that I've always thought we could best accomplish our mission with a group of about ten of the strongest and nimblest of our men. It has proved extremely difficult to ascertain Kira's movements. But if we divide these men into two groups of five, they could lie in wait inconspicuously along the streets leading out from the castle. When Kira's entourage appears, we attack with full force and take his head. And thereafter, of our own free will, commit seppuku. Or even with only one group of five men, we could still storm the Kira mansion. If we're lucky and we get Kira, that would be superb. But even if we fail to get him and are killed in the attempt, we would at least have done what we've been wanting to do these last few years. But never mind all that. We've seen what the Council of Elders decided to do with Daigaku Dono. We should now join forces, lay our plans, and kill the man. I, for one, don't want to waste another day getting started."

All eyes were now on Kuranosuke. And when finally he broke silence, he spoke with the old sharpness that some of them hadn't heard since the surrender of the castle: "Gentlemen, I can only say that I am deeply moved. Your loyalty, your courage, your sincerity—you are one and all beyond compare. This past year, I've felt that I must take the long view in planning our strategy, lest we miss the best opportunity to prove our fidelity. This has meant that I've often had to dampen your enthusiasm and force you to delay. But now that the fate of Daigaku Dono has been decided, there is no need to delay even one more day. By the end of the Ninth Month, I shall have wound up all our business here in the capital, and I shall set out for Edo early in the Tenth Month. Those of you who precede me should by all means spend your time there gathering intelligence, but you must not make any move against the enemy. I know that some of you have thought my caution cowardly and were planning to part company with me. Yet even though I myself should be thought a disloyal coward, if I can fulfill my duty of fealty and clear the name of our late lord, then I care nothing for what the rest of the world may think of me. Besides which, as Sun-tze says, 'Those who plan carefully triumph, whereas those who plan insufficiently triumph not; much less do those who plan not at all.' I only hope that my delays while waiting to learn the fate of Daigaku Dono will have served to sharpen your zeal for the task that lies before us. For the time is now come for us to demonstrate our fidelity."

If there was any single moment when the matter was decided, this was it. The mood of the room changed instantly. Saké cups were brought forth and passed around, whereupon Onodera Jūnai—surely the most austerely dignified member of the group—began beating out a rhythm with his hands, and then chanted in haunting tones Minamoto no

Yorimitsu's exhortation to his fellow warriors of seven centuries past:

> *Dreary are these long rains of spring,*
> *Dreary are these long rains of spring,*
> *When of a lonely evening one lies and listens*
> *As jewel-like droplets fall from ferns along the eaves.*
> *But nay, my boon companions, one and all:*
> *Let us take these cups and drink as we converse.*
> *A band of warriors are we;*
> *We drink with comrades we can trust!*

And then Hara Sōemon took his turn—now a man of fifty-five, but still remembered for his skill at Nō dance when a Page Boy to Takumi-no-Kami Naganao, two generations earlier. Sōemon rose, snapped open his fan, and commenced the "Men's Dance" that accompanies the climactic scene from the tale of the revenge of the Soga brothers:

> *From beneath their fluttering sleeves,*
>   (He stamps out a strong beat with his feet)
> *From beneath their fluttering sleeves,*
> *The brothers' eyes meet, tearfully acknowledging that*
> *Their bond between mother and sons is at an end.*
> *Lest they be late for the hunt, they bid her sad farewell.*
>   (He kneels and bows his head)
> *They must seize this chance on the hunting ground in Fujino,*
> *And there wreak revenge upon their enemy of these many years.*
>   (He spreads his fan and raises it high)
> *This smoke from flames of rage within their breasts:*
> *At last cleared by winds that roar down from Mount Fuji.*
> *The light of the moon shines clean and pure,*
> *Just as their names shall live on as exemplars of filial sons.*
>   (He tosses his right sleeve over his head and stamps
>   a final beat)

It was in a much-altered mood that these nineteen men left Jūami.

Gravity had taken the place of impatience, but there was also a suppressed buoyancy at knowing the road that now lay before them, which they would soon travel together.

All told, the day's festivities—the venue, the service, the food, the drink—cost an entire gold piece, which Mimura Jirōzaemon, still serving in his lowly function as Prefect of Provisions, paid to the monks who managed Jūami. The receipt, which he would later submit to the widow of Takumi-no-Kami, Kuranosuke filed in his account book. He also took Ushioda Matanojō aside and told him that he must carry the news of their decision to Chūzaemon and the others in Edo. Matanojō and Yasubei left early the next morning, the 29th.

◆ ◆ ◆

So goes the story in the only account of the meeting at Jūami that has been handed down to us. And we've no reason to doubt that something like this gathering did take place—indeed, *must* have taken place. An entry in Kuranosuke's account book, albeit undated, clearly states: "1 gold piece. Costs of a meeting at Maruyama; 19 men; paid by Mimura Jirōzaemon; receipt in hand." But there may well have been more to it than *just* this. The reporter is Katashima Shin'enshi, who could never have concocted the story out of pure imagination. Yet none of the people whom Shin'enshi interviewed would have been present at the meeting, not even Terai Genkei, Kai Shuso, or Ōnishibō Kaku'un; their knowledge, in this case, was at best secondhand. And we know from another very reliable reporter that at roughly the same time, there arose serious cause for alarm that threatened to destroy the newly formed consensus of the meeting. Ochiai Yozaemon, Chamberlain to Lady Asano, and certainly no sensation monger, has left us a detailed description of it. This is what he says:

◆ ◆ ◆

Just as they were preparing to leave for Edo, a snippet of news from Fushimi, a mere 3 leagues south of Kyoto, sent a wave of shock through the members of the pact. The Shogunate's Magistrate in Fushimi, Takebe Masanobu, had learnt of the plot and had reported it not only to his superiors in Edo, but, even worse, to his kinsman Kira Kōzuke-no-Suke.

How could such a thing have happened? Apparently, it was the result of a series of disconnected coincidences. A certain young man happened to be in the service of Takebe because he was born in Hayashida, a village that lay within Takebe's fief. And this young man happened to marry a girl from Akō, the daughter of Kasuya Kanzaemon. It was a typical marriage of neighbors; Hayashida was located only a short distance from Akō. Moreover, this young man happened now to be in Fushimi, because Takebe, his liege lord, had been appointed the Shogunate's Magistrate in Fushimi, and the young man was stationed there in his service. And, finally, when the domain of Akō was declared forfeit, his wife's father, Kasuya Kanzaemon, now a ronin, had come to Fushimi to live with his daughter and son-in-law. This is what set the scene for some very damaging family gossip.

Kasuya Kanzaemon was not present at Jūami, but he had submitted a pledge to Kuranosuke and thus must have known that vendetta had been decided upon. He must have thought, too, that he could speak in confidence within the family and trust his daughter's husband not to betray him. He was wrong; the young man seems to have repeated what his father-in-law had told him among his colleagues in the Magistrates office.

Before long, rumors were spreading of ronin gathering furtively in the Kyoto–Fushimi region and selling off their possessions; reports from Edo were reaching Kuranosuke that security at the Kira mansion had grown particularly strict; and, most worrying of all, it was said that word had gone out from the Shogunate to the several checkpoint barriers that ronin were to be interrogated with particular severity, and that any members of the Akō group proceeding toward Edo were to be arrested and bound.

With these and other such rumors rampant, everyone was uneasy. Okuno Shōgen, Shindō Genshirō, Oyama Gengoemon, Kawamura Denbei—all the highest-ranking members of the pact—were grumbling: "If these rumors are true, and we proceed to Edo despite them, we shall only disgrace ourselves. Even if we arrive without incident, these rumors will spread to Edo; and if security at the Kira mansion is as strict as they say, it is highly unlikely that we shall succeed in attaining our goal. We should postpone the attack until next spring."

In principle, Kuranosuke agreed. Just this once, he said, he would delay his departure. But first, he would write to those already in Edo.

None of this correspondence survives. But Ochiai Yozaemon tells us that when Kuranosuke wrote to say that everyone in Kyoto now thought that they should postpone the attack, those in Edo met, discussed the matter, and decided: "This is not the way to go. None of us here have encountered any problems en route. And if the enemy's security is strict, well, so be it; every one of us is fully prepared to die in battle. This is no time to dither." The young men, too, were very angry and would not accept this new proposal from Kyoto. And so Yoshida Chūzaemon and Horibe Yahei wrote to Kuranosuke, saying, "What you say makes good sense, but we are old men; we don't know whether we will even be alive next spring. If you fail to come to Edo now, then while you quibble over what you should do, we here will go ahead and do what we've been wanting to do." When their reply reached Kuranosuke, he grew more impatient than ever. He refused to listen to anything more that Genshirō had to say. Come what may, he said, he would go to Edo.

Genshirō and Gengoemon reacted very peevishly: "Those fools in Edo think of nothing but rushing to their death. They are swayed by every little rumor they hear and haven't a thought for their all-important duty of fealty. If they insist upon staging their great attack immediately after the release of Daigaku Sama, then there's no telling what may befall them along the way—even in a city as large as Edo. Given which, this man they're so determined to kill is certain to escape. We here," they argued, in complete disagreement with Kuranosuke, "We here should wait until the present commotion quietens down, and then, one by one, make our way to Edo. But you people—Kuranosuke and all the rest of you—have bungled everything you've attempted to do so far, and now you're about to destroy even the good name of this noble house." Genshirō was so ruthlessly persistent in pushing his own point of view that it created considerable friction within the group.

When and where this confrontation took place is not recorded. But we do know that on the 7th Day of Intercalary Eighth Month, more than a month after the meeting at Maruyama, another meeting was held somewhere in Kyoto that apparently aroused the ire of several members of the command group. The next day, Shindō Genshirō wrote to Kuranosuke, in care of Terai Genkei:

MEMORANDUM OF VERBAL DECLARATION

My personal convictions concerning this endeavor force me to withhold my participation. I trust that you will honor me with your understanding. As your kinsman, and as the beneficiary of your particular favor, I cannot but regret that we differ as we do. In the end, however, yours is not a decision to which I can assent with whole heart, and thus differ we must. Herewith the foregoing.

INTERCALARY EIGHTH MONTH, 8TH DAY   *Shindō Genshirō*
To: Ōishi Kuranosuke Sama

Two days later, Kuranosuke's uncle, Oyama Gengozaemon wrote:

VERBAL DECLARATION

Until recently, I have remained a staunch ally of everyone pledged to this pact, but your present opinions on this matter now differ from my own. And thus, regrettable though it be, I must part company with you and act in accord with my own convictions. I trust that you will understand. For your information, herewith the foregoing.

INTERCALARY EIGHTH MONTH, 10TH DAY   *Oyama Gengozaemon*
To: Ōishi Kuranosuke Sama

Kuranosuke was later to deplore how few high-ranking officers of the domain were willing to join him, but these two rejections hurt the most. Both Shindō and Oyama were senior officers and close kinsmen. *Their* defection he could not accept without demur. But Kuranosuke must have felt that another face-to-face confrontation could only end in still deeper disagreement. And so he decided to appeal to his kinsmen through an intermediary, the former personal physician to Takumi-no-Kami, Terai Genkei.

The letters that Kuranosuke entrusted to Genkei do not survive. But both replies to them do. Genshirō was "most grateful" that Kuranosuke had "not simply abandoned him but has been so kind as to send Genkei to explain his views.... But as I said to Genkei, I part company with you not over any larger issue.... I simply cannot concur with your decision [not to delay]." Gengozaemon replied in a similar vein. He was "particularly pleased by and grateful for your deep consideration and detailed clarification . . . but the differences between your intentions and my convictions remain insurmountable." Their refusal could not have been more polite, or more final.

◆ ◆ ◆

In the end, the consensus of Jūami survived, but with a much shakier foothold than on the 28th of the Seventh Month. Attack was still the plan. But if the attack was to succeed, considerable shoring up of the pact would be necessary. Kuranosuke now needed to know for certain who was with him and who was not.

CHAPTER
50

*We hereby pledge ourselves humbly
and irrevocably to the accomplishment of the purpose
lately discussed and agreed upon with you.*

Ushioda Matanojō and Horibe Yasubei wasted no time on their journey
to Edo. Kuranosuke had given them their orders after the meeting on the
28th at Maruyama. Early the next morning, in Yamashina, he gave them
eight gold pieces, 1 *bu*, and a bit of silver to cover the expenses of a round
trip, and they set off directly from there. Midway, in Hamamatsu, they
encountered the entourage of Asano Daigaku en route to Hiroshima,
but skirted the procession in silence. On the 10th of the Eighth Month,
they arrived in Edo, a journey of only eleven days, a full day quicker than
the usual twelve.

On the morning of the 11th, they visited Yoshida Chūzaemon in his
new lodgings in Shin-Kōjimachi, 6-Chome. Chūzaemon immediately
wrote a circular letter to those members of the group whom he felt he
could trust and told them to meet on the morrow at the Imadobashi
Bridge, just below the Seitensha Shrine in Asakusa, where the Sanyabori
Canal flows into the Sumida River. Who was included in this group and
who was left out, we do not know. There must have been more than just
a handful of men, though, for they rented two pleasure craft upon which
they drifted up and down the river, gunwale-to-gunwale, throughout
the day and into the night, ostensibly enjoying the cooling sea breeze
and the light of the moon, but probably laying plans for their attack.
Terasaka Kichiemon tells us that at one point, the boatmen were put
ashore and told to take a break at a nearby refreshment stand; there were
crucial matters to be discussed that were not for the ears of strangers.

Beyond that, however, all that survives from this long day are two poems by Kanzaki Yogorō:

> *onaji kokoro naru hitobito o izanai,*
> *hachigatsu jūninichi sumidagawa no shōyō ni makarite*
> *tori no na no miyako no sora mo wasurekeri*
> *sumidagawara ni sumu tsuki o mite*
> When on the 12th Day of the Eighth Month, having invited
> friends of like mind, we drifted down the Sumida River.
> Those distant skies, which gave the Capital Bird its name,
> we quite forget,
> as we gaze at the moon that lights the banks of the Sumida.

> *getsuzen no tomo*
> *teru tsuki no madoka naru ma ni madoi suru*
> *hito no kokoro no oku mo kumoraji*
> Viewing the moon with friends
> Under the spell of its brilliant light on this night when the moon is full,
> likewise unclouded are the depths of the hearts of these men.

Five days later, on the 17th, Matanojō set out on his return trip to Kyoto. With him, he carried not only the news of all that he had seen and heard in Edo, but also a letter from old Horibe Yahei. He had been given a full report, Yahei wrote: Matanojō and Yasubei had told him of the meeting in Kyoto and of Kuranosuke's decisive call to action, by which he was "extremely pleased."

◆ ◆ ◆

Elsewhere, however, the news of Maruyama and Kuranosuke's call to arms was received more with alarm than with pleasure, and a stream of "broken promises" began to trickle in. Yamagami Yasuzaemon "cannot agree" with Kuranosuke and thus "cannot accompany him." Tagawa Kuzaemon "has convictions of his own" and thus cannot see his way clear to go to Edo. Hirano Hanbei asks that he "kindly be excluded on this occasion and left behind." The Iguchi brothers are "caught up in affairs" from which they find it difficult to extricate themselves. Tagi Tarōzaemon has heard that "everyone will soon be going to Edo," but since he, too, has "convictions of his own" he will not be joining them.

On the far shore of the Inland Sea, in Marugame, four former Akō samurai who received their call from Kuranosuke were so terrified of its consequences that two of them, bearing letters from their comrades, boarded a ship bound for Shikama. From there, they went first to see Okuno Shōgen in Kameyama. What they told him is recorded in some detail:

> We've just received word via courier from Yamashina that all signatories to the pact are to make their way down to Edo, where shortly we're to fight our way into Kōzuke's residence. But do they really think that we can succeed in killing Kōzuke? For if we do break in and then fail to kill him, we'll have accomplished nothing. Besides which, we'll be charged with conspiracy, for which everyone in our families will be punished and Daigaku Dono will have to commit seppuku. This is why all of us here in Sanuki think it best to give up this outrageous scheme. Not to do so would be to act in total disregard of our wives and children. On this occasion, we shall refrain from participation. If an appropriate occasion should arise, then we may join in, but this time we'll not be going to Edo. Thus we ask that the monograms with which we signed our pledges be returned, which is why we have come here from across the sea.

"Yamashina has always said that no one who disagrees with him need go to Edo," Shōgen replied. "You are perfectly free to do as you wish."

So they hurried on to Yamashina, where they begged Kuranosuke to cut out and return their monograms and blood prints from the pledge they had signed. Their pleas were so desperate they are almost comical. Sakayori Sakuemon wrote:

> Since this spring, I've been able to walk only about 5 to 7 chō with the help of a cane; yet I was determined, when the time came, to march at least as far as Kira's gate. Now, however, I hear that Daigaku

Sama has been pardoned and his honor restored, so that we vassals no longer dare raise any objection. . . . We know, too, that if we break the law, that will be seen not as loyalty but perfidy, for which even our kinsmen and their families would be punished. Since all of us are of such low rank that we only ever stood guard at the roadside when His Lordship went forth, I now have the gravest doubts about participating in this undertaking. . . . What is more, I have lately been suffering from severe diarrhea.

And Nagasawa Rokurōemon wrote:

Yesterday when I called at your home you were out; thus, unfortunately, I shall not have the honor of meeting with you personally, for since last night I have suffered from stomach pangs so severe that I am unable to walk. . . . I hear alarming reports that you have now decided to embark upon a venture of some sort. . . . But, as I said this spring when I affixed my monogram to the pledge, I had my doubts even then; and thus I shall not be able to accompany you to Edo. I would ask, therefore, that you cut out and return my monogram from that document.

Kuranosuke did not refuse them. It was only natural that there were many such signatories to the pact. They had pledged themselves to Kuranosuke for no deeper reason than the faint hope that they might be recalled to service, if ever Daigaku were reinstated. The thought that they might be called upon to sacrifice their lives—either in battle or as punishment—had never crossed their minds. Now they were being asked to do just that. There was no point in trying to change their minds, but their pleas made Kuranosuke realize that he now needed to know for certain who was willing to fight and who just wanted his job back.

✦ ✦ ✦

These two pleas were dated the 15th Day of the Eighth Month. A few days later, on the 21st, after discussing the matter with a few of the men he trusted most, Kuranosuke called the Kyoto group together to discuss

what should be done. What they decided was that the best test of anyone's devotion to the cause would be to return his pledge and watch his
reaction. The two men assigned this task were Kaiga Yazaemon and
Ōtaka Gengo. This is how Yazaemon himself described what they did:

> After the first defections, Kuranosuke and the rest of us began to
> wonder how many more members of our group might drop out.
> Discussing this among ourselves, we decided that we would cut out
> the signatures from the pledge documents and return them; anyone
> who was pleased with this and wished to withdraw, we would permit
> to do so. We two would make the rounds of every signatory to the
> pact living in Kyoto, Osaka, Akō, and elsewhere in the province of
> Harima. This is what we were to say: "Upon inquiring into the fate
> of Daigaku Dono, Kuranosuke finds that he has been taken into the
> custody of the Hiroshima main house. Given which, there is nothing
> more we can do. We shall have to abandon the plan we have so long
> been determined upon. You must now devote yourselves to making a
> living and caring for your wives and children. You are free to do as
> you please." We would then return their signature and blood print.
> Those whose allegiance was divided would be pleased by this and
> withdraw, whereas those who remained devoted to the cause would
> call Kuranosuke a coward and heap abuse upon us. We would then set
> their minds at rest and retain them in the group. It took about twenty
> days to complete this task. In the meantime, all those still devoted to
> the cause went to Kyoto to meet personally with Kuranosuke.

That is a fair—and firsthand—summary of what took place. Yet,
as with all subtle stratagems, a closer examination reveals intriguing
nuances. Here, in Kuranosuke's written instructions to Yazaemon and
Gengo, is what he told them they were to say about *him* when they made
their rounds:

> As I said yesterday, you are to describe me as cowardly. But not too
> cowardly. For if you exaggerate, no one will believe you; they'll only
> think that you're up to something. It's particularly important that

you be careful about this with those in Kyoto. This will anger some
of them, who will say that I'm always talking about my firm commit-
ment, but they've never been able to depend upon me. You will have
to deal very carefully with each individual. You can tell them I have
been meaning to bring this up once Daigaku Dono has been pardoned
and restored to a position of honor, but that until then it would be
pointless. And so none of them should expect anything of me in the
meantime. I expect that they'll find this a bit suspicious. So if anyone
asks the reason you are returning his pledge, tell him that you don't
know the details, but that Kuranosuke seems to think rumors are
rampant that we're rounding up a large group and are bent upon some
scheme, for which we are certain to be apprehended and punished. He
may have some other plan in mind; but whatever he ends up doing,
we have to return the pledges. He certainly hopes that you will all be
well and that you will succeed in whatever it is you yourselves hope
to do. But with so much going on, and with rumors about us growing
steadily more troublesome, for the moment, we have no choice but to
give up our plan to attack. Tell them this as though you really mean
it—and that if they wish, they can go to Edo and there await a more
opportune moment; or, alternatively, they can seek other employment.
In short, they are free to do as they please. Just be a bit vague and
claim no knowledge of detail. . . . Those who assent to this, you should
ask for a receipt in their own hand, and then return their monograms.
But if anyone refuses, you mustn't insist.

The night boat for Osaka sailed on the 24th with Yazaemon and
Gengo aboard.

✦ ✦ ✦

What, then, were these pledges that Yazaemon and Gengo were setting
out to return? We have heard mention of them since the earliest days
of the Catastrophe. But unfortunately, only one of them still survives.
It is well worth examining as a guide to what the others may have been.

As you see, there are two components to the document. On the left is
a talisman of the sort known as Goʾō Hōin (The Treasured Seal of the

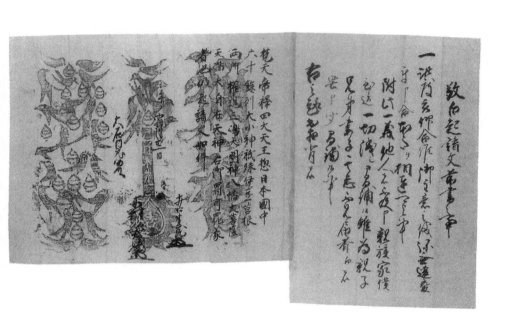

figure 17
One of the pledges submitted to Kuranosuke.
(Akō Municipal Museum of History)

Ox King of Kumano), upon which are depicted seventy-five crows, the messengers of this deity. Originally, these sheets were sold as all-purpose charms to ward off evil and bring good fortune that people would post on the doors to their homes or at the sluice that irrigated their rice seedlings. But because the deity of Kumano was known for his severity in the punishment of liars, these talismans also came to be used for the swearing of oaths. A great many survive bearing promises—sometimes written on the reverse of the sheet, sometimes on a separate sheet—to fight on the side of a neighboring warrior or to relinquish the rights to a certain piece of land. In this case, a sheet of blank paper was pasted to the right-hand edge of the talisman, upon which the pledge itself is written, and on the front of the talisman is written a daunting anathema clause, followed by the signatures of the men submitting the pledge:

> We hereby pledge ourselves humbly and irrevocably to the accomplishment of the purpose lately discussed and agreed upon with you. Further: we shall not so much as mention this matter to any outsiders, or even to our kinfolk or servants. Neither shall we reveal anything whatever to anyone of whose devotion to the cause we are uncertain, be they our parents, our brothers and sisters, our wives, or our children. Should we act in breach of any of the foregoing,

[the following written on the talisman itself]

> then may there be visited upon us all the punitive wrath of Brahma and Indra; the Four Heavenly Kings; all the deities, both greater and lesser, in the sixty-some provinces of Japan; and, in particular, the Avatars of both Izu and Hakone, Mishima Daimyōjin, Hachiman Dai-Bosatsu, and Tenjin the Almighty of the Tenman Shrine. Thus do we swear!

YEAR OF THE HORSE [1702], FOURTH MONTH, 21ST DAY

> Iguchi Hanzō [monogram, sealed in blood]
> Kimura Magoemon [monogram, sealed in blood]

To: Ōishi Kuranosuke Dono

We note first of all how vague is the description of *what* is being pledged: "the accomplishment of the purpose lately discussed." There is good reason for such extreme indirection; the swearing of oaths was rightly associated with the formation of rebellious factions and thus was illegal. A promise was one thing; an oath was another. If it was unnecessary to state what was being promised or sworn, it was wiser, and safer, not to state it.

But were all the pledges now being returned of the same sort? No doubt, some were, but others could not have been. The undercover agents from Okayama reported that Kuranosuke inscribed his pledge on the same sort of talisman from Kumano, but the number of signatures would have been far greater—sixty-some according to one count. Which is why some of the defectors now spoke of "cutting out" their signatures and blood prints.

◆ ◆ ◆

When Yazaemon and Gengo left Yamashina with this bundle of pledges, they went first to Osaka, made the rounds there, and then boarded a ship bound for Akō, where a number of their comrades had settled in the surrounding villages. From there, they made their way back east through the provinces of Harima and Settsu and on to Kyoto. Yet as far as I can tell, only one anecdote of their experiences on this journey has been recorded.

Early in Intercalary Eighth Month, Yazaemon and Gengo arrived in the village of Kameyama, just south of Himeji, where Fuwa Kazuemon was staying with his father's family. "Our plan to assemble in Edo has been exposed," they told Kazuemon, "which makes it all but impossible for our mission to succeed now. Besides which, the Shogunate is investigating, and if it discovers our pact, there is no telling what might happen. So we've cut out everyone's monograms and we're returning them." Kazuemon immediately saw through their pretense. To him, it was obvious that this was a test, so he took his signature and his blood print, and then said, "Kuranosuke Dono is absolutely right to do this; it's the perfect plan. But here is my response." Whereupon he set fire to the paper he had just been handed, swirled the ashes in a cup of water, and drank it down. Yazaemon and Gengo clapped their hands in delight. Kazuemon had taken his written pledge and transformed it into something even more binding: a libation to the gods. Here was one man determined to remain in the pact.

By the time Yazaemon and Gengo returned to Kyoto, fewer than 60 of the original 120 and more still stood by their promise to Kuranosuke. The time had now come for the faithful few to assemble and make their way to Edo.

CHAPTER
51

*Not all of them were
cowards.*

The winnowing process was not as simple as it may at first appear. The stories of the faithless seem to attract the most immediate interest, but there were others who did not participate for perfectly legitimate, even honorable, reasons. As Ochiai Yozaemon says, "When Kuranosuke was preparing to leave Kyoto, more than sixty men broke with him; but not all of them were cowards. Some genuinely thought that he might fail; and if he did, they would make a second attempt." Yozaemon might have added that there were others who wished to participate but were not permitted to do so, and still others who were deterred by force of circumstances.

The most forceful of those circumstances was poverty. People nowadays find it hard to comprehend how incredibly poor some ronin were and how stubbornly proud they could be, despite their poverty. They could not farm. They had no idea how to manage a business. Their bows, arrows, horses, lances, and swords were of no use to them. They had no choice but to sell off, bit by bit, their weapons, their equestrian gear, their clothing, and even the household furnishings they had accumulated over the years, and use the proceeds to feed themselves and their families from day to day. But as the proverb says, "If all you do is sit and eat, eventually even a mountain gets eaten up." Few people now living have ever known such men. I can tell you a story, though, that I know to be true, that will give you some idea of what these men were like. It took place one spring in the Tenmei era, the 1780s.

A vagrant samurai, holding the hand of his six- or seven-year-old son, arrived at the Ryōgoku Bridge. His clothes were totally in tatters, but he still bore one of his swords. His son, too, was clad in only a single layer, likewise in rags. It was still very cold, and the child could not stop shivering. Besides which, they looked as though neither of them had eaten anything in two or three days. It was heartrending to see the boy, in all innocence, say, "Daddy, I want something to eat." The father, tears in his eyes, comforted him, saying, "I'll get you something to eat, very soon now." In a shop just this side of the bridge, there was a tall pile of sweet potatoes. Seeing this, the child burst into tears, crying, "I want to eat one; I want to eat one." It was a pitiful sight, for there was nothing the man could do but try to console the boy.

An outcaste sandal repairman sitting at the head of the bridge could no longer endure to look on in silence. "This is terribly impertinent of me," he said, "but, I too, have children. I know how this honored child of yours must feel, and I should like very much indeed to offer him one of those potatoes. If you have no objection, please do let me give him one." And he held out a coin. The ronin, with tears in his eyes, said, "Oh my; I am deeply grateful for your kindness. I lack words with which to thank you, but I shall accept with gratitude." Whereupon he purchased potatoes enough that the boy might eat his fill, while he gazed at him, weeping tears of joy. Then he returned to the outcaste, still weeping, and thanked him profusely: "As you see, I've let him eat his fill. My gratitude to you is so great that even in death I shall never forget." He then took his leave and turned back to the bridge. When he was about halfway across, he picked up the child and flung him into the river. And before anyone could ask what was going on, he himself leapt in.

Here was a warrior who, like a hawk, "even if it meant death, would never make off with an ear of rice." But his compassion as a parent led him, out of love for his child, to accept the charity of an outcaste and allow the boy to eat his fill one last time in this life.

◆ ◆ ◆

Most of the lower-ranking samurai in Akō found themselves in similar straits. Their stipends had never been sufficient to allow them to save, and their severance allowances were meager. Once what little cash they had was exhausted, they had no choice but to begin selling off their weapons, furnishings, clothing, and whatever other valuables they might have possessed. Thereafter, many had to seek other means of supporting their families, a choice that usually meant giving up their status as samurai and becoming either farmers or townsmen. What became of these men, we have no idea. But for those who felt strongly enough to sign a pledge to Kuranosuke, this was not an option. A few, like Maebara Isuke, who had never been able to marry, managed to remain faithful to the cause by selling remnants, fruit, fan papers, or whatever they could while they kept an eye on the Kira mansion. Others probably would have dropped out of the pact, were it not for the generosity of a more fortunate member of their group.

Sugino Jūheiji was a nephew of the notorious Hagiwara brothers, wealthy to begin with and wealthier still after the sale of their two cannon to the Wakizaka house. In some fashion, Jūheiji's branch of the family had shared in the Hagiwara fortunes, and Jūheiji, although he had since severed relations with them, is said to have possessed personal savings of more than 1,000 gold pieces. For four hundred and some days now, Jūheiji had been parceling out this gold to his less fortunate colleagues. By the time Kuranosuke was preparing to leave Kyoto, more than a hundred people (if you count wives and children and aged parents) were living on Jūheiji's largess; but his "mountain" was nearly eaten up. With no means of earning a livelihood, how were they now to support their families, much less pursue their cause? It is all very well to talk of those heroes of antiquity who smeared their bodies with lacquer in lieu of clothing and sucked on bits of charcoal for nourishment, but to these men, it made more sense simply to do what they were determined to do with no further delay. The press of poverty gave new urgency to the call for immediate action. It must also have been the last straw for some who were not cowards, but who felt that they could hold out no longer and thus, however reluctantly, accepted the return of their pledges.

◆ ◆ ◆

There were also some who were more thoughtful, for whom life did not seem to be simply a matter of doing what was easiest or most convenient. We know, for example, that Watanabe Han'emon, still living in Akō, not only discussed the matter with Kaiga Yazaemon and Ōtaka Gengo when they offered to return his pledge, but also took the trouble to describe his situation in writing. Han'emon's letter does not survive, but it appears that he was torn between participating in the attack and caring for his old and ailing parents—the classic conflict between fealty and filiality. This we know from the response of his younger brother, Takebayashi Tadashichi, to whom Gengo showed Han'emon's letter upon his return to Kyoto. Tadashichi wrote to his brother:

> I have read your letter to Gengo and am most distressed to learn that Father's health grows steadily worse, that his sight is failing, that he feels listless, and furthermore sees little chance of recovery. It will not be long now before we act. I wish there were time to come down and visit you so we could discuss these things. But I have orders from Yamashina and must depart for Edo today, the 11th. Our dear mother being as ill as she is, I fear that my concern for her may prove a hindrance to me hereafter. . . . What I would ask of you, since you are now out of employment, is that you give up participating in our present endeavor. For if Father should die, Mother would be left all alone. You should place her in the care of Tan'emon, sell off our weapons and equipment, and set aside the proceeds for her benefit. Have O-Natsu go into service, and then let come what may. After I am dead, you can work out among yourselves what to do next. I think it best, though, that one of we two brothers remains behind, for filial reasons, and sees this through. But if you do not agree, then if you first do whatever will cause you no regrets and then commit seppuku, we shall still consider you one of our number. I, too, would like to remain behind and care for Mother in her illness, but I served Takumi-no-Kami since I was a boy and thus am deeply beholden to him. I trust that you will bear this in mind. If Father were to die, leaving Mother all alone, and we were both to abandon her and die for the cause of fealty, this might pass in the world at large as loyalty; but we could hardly be called filial. . . . If Father is still alive, kindly

tell him about this. And please tell Mother in such a way that it will not distress her. Most respectfully,

INTERCALARY EIGHTH MONTH, 11TH DAY   *Takebayashi Tadashichi*
                                                      [monogram]

To: Watanabe Han'emon

P.S. If, as I suggest, you place Mother in the care of Tan'emon, and there are no further concerns to detain you, then once you hear of my death, you may commit seppuku. But if, after my death, it appears that Mother may be punished by the authorities, then you must kill her. Please give your most careful thought to these matters.

There may well have been others, too, who like Watanabe Han'emon would genuinely have preferred to honor their pledges, were it not for dire familial circumstances, such as those in which Han'emon found himself.

✦ ✦ ✦

And then there is the example of a would-be participant who had to be dissuaded by Kuranosuke himself. Takumi-no-Kami's personal physician, who had been recruited to service in the Asano house less than two years earlier, had apparently stated several times his desire to participate in the attack as a battlefield medical officer. Yet despite the extraordinary degree of trust that everyone placed in him, Kuranosuke and others of the command group decided that he should not accompany them to Edo. For the record, Kuranosuke wrote:

I take the liberty to address you via this brief missive. The matter of your wishes, which you yourself have mentioned on various occasions, has been brought to my attention. They are most admirable, and I am deeply touched by them. Yet having discussed the matter with the senior members of the group, I feel that it would be inappropriate for you to accompany us on this journey. I know that it will come as a disappointment to be thwarted in your good intentions. The functions in which we serve, however, differ fundamentally. Were you to make common cause with us, there might be those who claim that we coerced you—which would be unfortunate for all concerned. It goes without saying that medical officers are required on the battlefield. But this, after all, is no battlefield. I think it only proper, therefore, that you remain behind. I swear to you that in saying this, I in no way mean to disparage your offer of life and limb. Whatever may become of us all, public opinion thereafter is bound to be divided. You being the one person who knows best what we have been up to these past several months, I would entreat you, above all else, to take particular pains to make the truth known when the time comes. To this end, it is of crucial importance that you agree to remain behind. Okuno Shōgen has recently arrived and spoken of you. He, too, asks that I convey to you his earnest desire of your concurrence in this matter. And, of course, Sōemon, Denbei, Gengozaemon, Genshirō, and Jūnai have said the same when they discussed the matter with you. Respectfully,

EIGHTH MONTH, 6TH DAY   *Ōishi Kuranosuke*

To: Terai Genkei Sama

Kuranosuke had long been concerned that no one think that he coerced anyone to participate or that he recruited outsiders to his cause. But in this letter, he reveals a new concern: that there remain a reliable living witness to what he and his comrades had done.

*His will of iron
simply melted.*

That long street that runs the full length of the eastern half of Kyoto, the one we still call Temple Street, was once far truer to its name than it is today. If you look at a Genroku-era map, you will see that it was then lined with temples—more than a hundred of them, in an unbroken stretch from the northernmost limits of the city to the southernmost. Perhaps the biggest of them all, though, was the temple Kinrenji, known popularly as the Shijō Hall of Worship, because it occupied a huge block just above Shijō Avenue between Temple Street and Kawaramachi. "Perhaps," I say, because Kinrenji no longer exists, but one thing we know for certain about it is that Kuranosuke lodged there for more than two months, between leaving Yamashina and setting out for Edo. Like all great temples, Kinrenji was surrounded by a cluster of chapels and hermitages, one of which, Bairin'an (Plum Grove Hermitage), seems in some way to have been connected with the Shindō and the Ōishi houses. It was to this pleasantly named cloister that Kuranosuke removed himself. But how so? Katashima Shin'enshi seems to have been the only contemporary even to mention the move:

> Since Asano Daigaku had been banished to Hiroshima, and Akō Castle had been granted to Nagai Iga-no-Kami Naotaka, not a few of those who for a time had feigned loyalty in the hope of Daigaku's reinstatement, now deserted the cause. But the forty-some whose resolve remained rock solid no longer had any doubts to deter them, and seemed utterly determined upon death in the cause of justice.

And so, Kuranosuke, saying that he would soon depart for Bizen, whither his maternal kinsman Ikeda Genba had invited him to come and live, bequeathed his property in Yamashina to the Yawata monk Shōsan; on the 1st Day of the Intercalary Eighth Month, he left Yamashina for temporary quarters that he had rented in Bairin'an in Shijō.

But what, then, became of his young mistress, O-Karu, who a few months hence would bear his child? In the absence of evidence, stories abound—all of them pure melodrama. I expect that Kuranosuke returned her to her father, Nimonjiya Jirōzaemon, generously rewarded I would hope; but what became of her thereafter, no one knows.

Shin'enshi also mentions the visits of a silk merchant and clothier, Kikuya Yahei, long a supplier to the Akō cadet house. Kikuya, he says, is the one who made the black surcoat and shirt of chain mail that Kuranosuke would later wear—and may have done the same for some of the other ronin.

This would also have been the time when Kuranosuke was selling off various of his possessions that he no longer needed, the proceeds of which he would distribute among the ronin who were destitute. He must have realized a substantial sum from these transactions, for one of the defectors, Hirano Hanbei, is said to have absconded with thirty gold pieces that he filched from Kuranosuke, and then "hid himself away in the backstreets of Kyoto."

Even so, funds were running low, and Kuranosuke decided that he must try to top up the war chest further with loans—loans, alas, that could never be paid back. To this end, he approached three of his cousins: Ikeda Sahyōe and Ikeda Shichirōbei in Bizen, and Shindō Chikugo-no-Kami, Steward to the Konoe regental house in Kyoto. Chikugo-no-Kami seems to have refused him, but Kuranosuke was later to write that "Sahyōe and Shichirōbei have been extremely gracious in their response to my request for loans, and I want them to know how grateful I am." Both men were sons of sisters of Kuranosuke's mother, and thus, like Kuranosuke, grandsons of Ikeda Dewa Yoshinari. Both sent him a hundred gold pieces.

◆ ◆ ◆

Matters of this sort were not Kuranosuke's principal purpose in Shijō, however. Attending to them simply cleared the way for him to assemble his attack force before he himself left for Edo. To those who still remained members of the pact, he wrote that word had come from Edo that the time was right and that they should now make their way east in groups of two or three at their earliest convenience. When they passed through Kyoto, Kuranosuke would give each of them three gold pieces to cover the costs of his journey. On the 18th, four men left Kameyama as instructed: Fuwa Kazuemon, Yoshida Sawaemon, Masé Magokurō, and Takebayashi Tadashichi; they arrived in Edo on the 2nd Day of the Ninth Month. A few days later, Kuranosuke gave Senba Saburōbei twenty-one gold pieces to be divided among seven travelers: Saburōbei himself, Hazama Jujirō, Okajima Yasoemon, Tanaka Riheiji, Yatō Emoshichi, Suzuta Jūhachi, and Nakamura Sei'emon. And so it went, on through the Ninth Month and into the early days of the Tenth. Yet even after the return of the pledges, the mustering of the faithful did not proceed as smoothly as Kuranosuke had hoped it might.

◆ ◆ ◆

In Kameyama, Kuranosuke was counting on Okuno Shōgen to serve as his right hand, just as he had in Akō when Ōno Kurobei had absconded and Shōgen stepped into his place and took on all the responsibilities of an Elder. Shōgen not only was a distant relative of Kuranosuke, but had been the only Samurai Commander to side with Kuranosuke from the very start. Now he was the senior officer in the region west of Kyoto, and Kuranosuke was relying upon him to mobilize those living not only in Kameyama but in Akō, Katō, and Kasai as well. But when Shōgen received his call to action from Kuranosuke, he seems to have had second thoughts. Instead of preparing to leave, he called together a group that included his kinsmen and friends, ronin, and even the retired doctor Kumode Genzui, to whom he elaborated his most recent thoughts on this matter. And since everyone in Kameyama agreed with him (so he says), he decided that he would try to convince Kuranosuke as well.

◆ ◆ ◆

On the 21st of Intercalary Eighth Month, Okuno Shōgen and Kawamura Denbei set out for Kyoto to remonstrate with Kuranosuke at Bairin'an.

"Are you absolutely certain that, if you rush off to Edo now, you'll be able to kill Kōzuke?" Shōgen asked. "And why must *everyone* go with you?"

"I can't say for certain that we'll succeed in killing Kōzuke," Kuranosuke replied. "But our people in Edo tell us that the time is right. Besides which, our men everywhere are finding it more and more difficult to make ends meet; some are close to starvation. All the while we've been putting this off, our numbers have steadily dwindled. So rather than see good men die in misery, I've decided that it is better to die fighting within the gates of Kōzuke's mansion. That is why I'm now mustering everyone."

"If you just storm the place, you won't succeed," Shōgen responded. "To die a dog's death now, after the humiliation we suffered last year in Akō—not only would that make life difficult for Daigaku Dono, but we all would be considered guilty of seditious conspiracy, which would implicate our families as well. If you're prepared to accept the consequences, I suppose that's no objection; and if you accomplish your mission, you'll be satisfied. But if all you do is die a dog's death and end up incriminating everyone else, that would be stupid. Last year, we should never have surrendered the castle, but instead we dispersed, and the disgrace of that earned us the scorn of the world. If all we do now is, one after another, make our way to Edo, there is no way we'll escape more of the same. So instead, once all of us are there, you and I, with no thought for our own lives, should reiterate our entreaty. And since we shall do so forcefully—directly to the Duty Elder—we shall be deemed in breach of the law and punished for it. For us, that will be that. But those who remain can then break into Kōzuke's mansion and kill him. If we do it that way, we'll have done everything we want to do and have no cause for regret. We'll have stated our case in advance, and once we've done that, attack will be our only choice. We'll have vindicated our own honor, and no one else will be punished. So please, let us do it *that* way."

"At this stage," Kuranosuke said, "I couldn't possibly propose such a thing to the others. If you can't go along with us, you'll just have to withdraw."

"I'm afraid that I can't agree with you," Shōgen said. "This time, I shall be forced to withdraw. But my determination is not the slightest bit diminished. You are certain to fail; I shall take up the cause thereafter."

Shōgen and Denbei stayed in Kyoto and Osaka for twenty days and more, hoping that some of the others might side with them. But since no one would agree to a change at this late stage, eventually they left.

Kuranosuke found it quite upsetting that someone as high-ranking as Shōgen should defect.

"We can still do what we want to do," the others told him, "even if only twenty of us remain."

"That's not the problem," Kuranosuke said. "When it's all over, and word gets out that there were no senior vassals in the pact, it will leave a bad impression of our late lord. It will look as though his leaders were worthless, and that will be a great pity."

◆ ◆ ◆

The defection of Okuno Shōgen leaves us with some unanswerable questions: Why, in the first place, would someone who had shown such strength of purpose and such unwavering support of Kuranosuke for such a long time change his mind so completely at the last minute? And did he really think that lodging a renewed entreaty with the Council of Elders would exempt the families of the attackers from punishment? Or was he just concocting an excuse that would help him escape certain death? We shall never know, but Kanzaki Yōgoro sums up his opinion rather poetically: "His will of iron simply melted, and then drained away in a pool of perfidious mire."

◆ ◆ ◆

Now, however, Kuranosuke could proceed with the principal purpose of his move to Shijō. His role was no longer that of a Chief Elder governing his lord's domain in the glory days of the Great Peace; he had become the commander of a clandestine attack force, bent upon disturbing the peace in a major way.

CHAPTER

53

━━━━━━

Chill mist rising from the
River Kamo shrouds my heart.

For those who had pledged their loyalty to Kuranosuke from the very start, it had been a long wait, almost a year and a half for some; even for those who had not signed on until after the surrender of the castle, it was more than a year. Now there would be no more waiting. Many had dropped out along the way, but those who remained pledged to the cause now faced a test far more severe than the return of the pledges. To keep the promise of their pledges, they must now set out on a journey that, sooner or later, could end only in death. Prior to which they willingly had to submit to what probably would be the most emotionally wrenching experience of their lives: they must part with parents, wives, children, kinfolk, friends—knowing that their partings would be permanent and, even for those most fervently devoted to the cause, painful.

◆ ◆ ◆

Yatō Emoshichi was one of the youngest members of the pact, only sixteen at the time of the Catastrophe. He and his father, Yatō Chōsuke, were among the first to pledge themselves to the defense of the castle and then to commit seppuku in protest. And after the failure of those schemes, Chōsuke was one of the few whom Kuranosuke asked to remain behind to help prepare the accounts for submission to the Shogunal Inspectors—and for the funds that Kuranosuke was now using to finance the attack on Kira. But Chōsuke was not a well man, and after the Corps of Vassals dispersed and he moved his family to Osaka, he was stricken with a severe case of what is now thought to have been intestinal typhoid. He had "great hopes" on behalf of his late lord, he wrote to a friend in Akō, "but now those hopes have come to naught. I have told my son Kamenojō, 'It will not be long now before I die, and after I die you must assume my ambitions.' My son is no less fervid than I, and even bolder. He is keen to fulfill my ambitions, he says. On that score, at least, I shall die with no regrets."

And in the postscript to another letter, he wrote: "My son Kamenojō will celebrate his majority, take the name Emoshichi, and will no doubt go to Edo while I lie ill. Death, I know, is the normal fate of a warrior, and yet I cannot help feeling a certain regret, for which, alas, I am a bit ashamed."

◆ ◆ ◆

Emoshichi, as we have seen, did indeed take his father's place at the meeting at Jūami, in Maruyama, and probably at other gatherings as well. But Chōsuke finally died on the 15th Day of the Eighth Month of Genroku 15 (1702), which left Emoshichi with the additional task of settling his mother and three younger sisters before he could leave for Edo. Fortunately, an arrangement had been made. While the family was still living in Akō, his mother's sister had married a samurai in the service of Matsudaira Yamato-no-Kami, then the lord of the neighboring domain of Himeji. In the meantime, however, Yamato-no-Kami had been transferred from Himeji to Shirakawa, far to the north of Edo. It would be a very long trip, but Emoshichi's mother and sisters could go to live with his aunt and uncle. Somehow, they scraped together the money and set out shortly after the funeral for Chōsuke. They never made it. Unbelievable though it seems, both Emoshichi and his mother were unaware that all women must present a checkpoint pass at every checkpoint, or they would not be permitted to proceed. Emoshichi was young and had never traveled before. And for some reason, no one had mentioned this crucial fact to them. When they arrived at Arai, a notoriously strict checkpoint, they were turned back. They had no choice but to return to Osaka and no money to attempt the trip again.

It could not have been too much later, probably in the latter days of the Intercalary Eighth Month, that Emoshichi set out for Edo in the group led by Senba Saburōbei. They arrived there on the 7th of the Ninth Month. Emoshichi would never know what became of his mother and three sisters.

◆ ◆ ◆

Ōtaka Gengo is a name familiar to us by now. He accompanied Kuranosuke on his first trip to Edo and remained behind with Hara Sōemon to arrange the purchase of a house in Mita. After his return to Kyoto, he participated in all the meetings at Yamashina and Zuikōin and Jūami. With Kaiga Yazaemon, he made the rounds of all the signatories to the pact, offering to return their pledges as a test of their sincerity. And apart from all this, he was a poet of sufficient repute to have published a volume of his own *haikai*. Now we are to see another side of this versatile man.

After the surrender of the castle, when Gengo moved to Kyoto, his widowed mother, Teiryū, seems to have moved there with him. She had many relatives in the region. Onodera Jūnai and Okano Kin'emon were her younger brothers. Jūnai's adopted heir was her younger son. Masé Kyūdayū was her cousin. Hara Sōemon was related to her late husband. Now all these men were about to leave for Edo. "You can imagine how I would feel living all alone in the capital," she said. It was time for Gengo to take his mother back to Akō and settle her there. Toward the end of the Intercalary Eighth Month, they left Kyoto, and Gengo remained in Akō until the 4th of the Ninth Month.

I would like very much to know what passed between Gengo and his mother in the course of those few days, for when he left Akō, he left behind a long letter explaining why he felt that he had to do what he was about to do. Had his mother taken him to task for going off and leaving her alone in the world? Had she been trying to persuade him to stay behind with her in Akō? This is what he wrote:

> Item. *My decision to go to Edo on this occasion, as I have explained*
> *to you previously, is due entirely to my desire to redress*
> *His Lordship's wrath and to cleanse the stain on the honor of his*

noble house. Moreover, in keeping with the Way of the Samurai, I mean to abandon my life in the cause of fealty, and in so doing bring glory to the name of our forebears. Of course, there are a great many other vassals, some of whom were infinitely more favored samurai than I. To me, our lord showed no particular consideration. My lot has been that of a commonplace man, and thus I've tended to think of loyalty in a commonplace way; while in the meantime, I've done my best to care for you as long as you may live. I doubt that anyone could fault me on either score. Yet even now I cannot forget, even for an instant, those times I waited upon him, however ineptly, and was privileged to look upon his noble visage morning and night. That he should have failed to slay the enemy upon whom he was so determined to vent his wrath—wrath so great that he was willing to cast away his very life and dismiss from his thoughts all the claims of his ancestral house—only to die such a dismal death. His luck had run out, one might say, yet how infinitely pitiable nonetheless. Whenever I think how he must have felt at that time, presumptuous though it be to do so, it pierces me to the marrow. It leaves me never a day, never even a moment, of peace. To be sure, he was short-tempered and behaved with utter disregard for the occasion and the place, for which His Highness the Shogun was sorely outraged and commanded that he be executed. But those are matters that lie beyond our power, nor have we any reason whatever for resentment against

His Highness. That is why we surrendered the castle without protest, for with

His Highness himself we have no quarrel. Nonetheless,

His Lordship was not deranged; he attacked Kōzuke-no-Suke Dono because he bore a grudge against him. That man, therefore, is clearly his enemy. And in the Way of the Warrior, since time immemorial, be it in China or in our own land, it is unheard of that an enemy who has angered one's lord so grievously as to cause him to cast away his own life should be left to live in peace. By rights, we should have attacked our enemy straightaway. But

Daigaku Sama was in Domiciliary Confinement at the time, and we

were still hoping that once released, he might possibly be designated to succeed
His Lordship, even if at a much smaller enfeoffment, and that Kōzuke-no-Suke, too, might somehow be dealt with. And if Daigaku Sama were to be restored to a position of honor and respect among his peers, then despite all that has befallen
His Lordship, the house would be saved. We ourselves would then enter holy orders, or else take our own lives, thus allaying
His Lordship's wrath. We wasted months of precious time on this assumption—only to see Daigaku Sama banished to Hiroshima. His release from Domiciliary Confinement was only nominal. Of course, after some months have passed, he may well be allowed to take his place in the world again; yet even so,
His Lordship's line is now come to an end. To delay any longer while we worry what else might happen would only be cowardice. That is not the Way of a Warrior. There are those who insist that we should stake our lives on a plea to
His Highness, entreating him to punish the other party and to restore Daigaku Sama to the fullness of his place in the world; and if our appeal is not accepted, we can then attack our opponent. There is some merit in this argument, but I do not think it right that we resort to such convoluted tactics. Moreover, if once we submit a petition and it is rejected, an attack on our enemy would then constitute an affront to
His Highness. An outrage of that sort would work to the detriment not only of Daigaku Sama but of the entire clan as well. My sole aim, therefore, is to redress His Lordship's wrath.

Item. As I have said repeatedly above, our purpose is but to act in accord with the Way of the Warrior and to wreak revenge upon the enemy of our lord. We bear no enmity whatever against
His Highness. But if, for whatever reasons, this should be regarded as tantamount to enmity against
His Highness, and our parents and wives and children are to be

punished for it, we shall be powerless to help. In the unlikely event that this should happen, pray do as you have always said you would do: accept it in good grace, and obey the directives from

On High in every particular. But by no means are you rashly to take your own life. This you must understand. It would be most regrettable, and a worry to us as well, if you were to behave foolishly, as most women would, making a great display of your grief. But, of course, you have long been prepared for this; indeed, your resolve has been a source of strength and encouragement to us all: a blessing in this life and a joy in lives to come. What more, really, could we brothers wish for than to be so favored by fortune as samurai? You mustn't worry how things will turn out. I am thirty-one, Kōemon is twenty-seven, and Kujūrō [later Okano Kin'emon] is twenty-three; every one of us is at the peak of his strength. We shall accomplish our mission with ease, and set at rest the feelings of our

Late Lord; and with that as a present for King Enma to take with us to the netherworld, you may rest assured that we shall get our golden ticket to Paradise. Just take care to keep well; and come what may, let it come when it will. In these your waning years, with so little time remaining, life is bound to be lonely, and there will be few to whom you can turn for help. When I think of you having to endure the passing months and days, it saddens me horribly; but that, too, is beyond our power. One hears of those who, in defiance of their lord's command, carry away their parents and hide them deep in the mountains or far afield—or of those who, for the sake of

Their Lord, take the lives of their parents. There are times when such things are unavoidable in the course of performing one's duty. But you, of course, are not ignorant of such matters; I've let my brush run away with itself. Please remind Kujūrō's mother and his sister O-Chiyo of these things from time to time, and be of support to one another so that you shall not grieve foolishly over us. How fortunate that you've already taken vows! When all of this is over, I

*trust that the diligence of your devotions to the Buddha will lighten
your cares and sorrows, so that your mind will never stray from
thoughts of lives to come. And if you are left to live in peace, please
go to the temple on the appropriate days and pray for us. All else
aside, the walk will be good for your health. And be sure to talk
this over with Nanny so she will accept it with due resignation.
Respectfully,*

GENROKU 15, MIZUNOE UMA   *Ōtaka Gengo*

NINTH MONTH, 5TH DAY
To my honored mother,
proffered herewith

It was Nanny, Gengo's nursemaid of thirty years earlier, whom his
mother, Teiryū, went to live with. Gengo returned to Kyoto, and shortly
thereafter left for Edo.

◆ ◆ ◆

It could not have been too much later that Ōishi Chikara left Kyoto,
together with Masé Kyūdayū, Ōishi Sezaemon, Onodera Kōemon,
Kayano Wasuke, Yano Isuke, and also one of Kuranosuke's most
trusted family retainers, Kasemura Kōshichi. On the face of it, this
was nothing out of the ordinary. But should you pause to wonder
why Chikara did not travel with his father, Kuranosuke, you will find
there was an interesting reason. As one of the ronin later explained,
"Kuranosuke sent his son and heir, Chikara, ahead as a hostage to
those waiting in Edo." There is no evidence that this was expected,
much less demanded, of him. But Kuranosuke may well have sensed
that, after so many delays and last-minute changes, there were those
who still doubted that he would actually come to Edo, possibly
even those who themselves would not move until he did. Now, with
Chikara safely within the fold, there could be no doubt that his father
would follow.

◆ ◆ ◆

Surely, the most emotional of all partings was that of Onodera Jūnai, the former Kyoto Liaison Officer, and his wife O-Tan. I know that the expression did not exist in their day, but I can think of no other way to describe them as a couple than to say, anachronistically, that they were deeply in love. Jūnai was sixty; O-Tan was fifty. They were childless, but had adopted Ōtaka Gengo's younger brother, Kōemon, who was to marry O-Tan's younger sister O-Iyo and carry on the line. Were it not for the Catastrophe, few people would have known what a rare couple Jūnai and O-Tan were, but disaster and separation were forcing them to articulate feelings that otherwise would have been expressed more privately and subtly. We have already seen Jūnai's letters, written when he expected to die in the siege of Akō Castle, and we shall see more of them as this story progresses. But the emotions of their parting when Jūnai left Kyoto for Edo are captured most poignantly in the poems that he sent back to O-Tan along the way.

We do not know precisely the date of Jūnai's departure, but since he preceded Kuranosuke and traveled in the company of Kuranosuke's family steward, Seno'o Magozaemon, perhaps intending to arrange accommodation for Kuranosuke and his party, we can probably assume that they departed on the 5th or 6th Day of the Tenth Month. We know, too, that on the night before his departure, Jūnai visited the Horikawa Academy to take leave of the scholars under whom he had studied there, Itō Jinsai and his son Tōgai.

Jūnai's first poem suggests that O-Tan may have accompanied him to the head of the Sanjō Bridge on the morning of his departure:

genroku jūgo-nen no fuyu
miyako o tachite azuma ni kudaru tote
nakiwakare kesa uchiwataru kamogawa no
mizu no kemuri wa mune ni tachisou

Winter, Genroku 15

Upon leaving the capital to set out for the Eastlands
As we part in tears this morning, and I turn to stride across the bridge,
chill mist rising from the River Kamo shrouds my heart.

ausaka o koshite
tachikaeri mata ausaka to tanomaneba
tague ya semashi shide no yamagoe
On crossing the pass at Ausaka
Not daring hope I might turn back from
Meeting Slope to see you once more,
would that I might cross with you this pass on the road to death.

shiga no ura nite
furusato ni kakute ya hito no suminuran
hitori samukeki shiga no uramatsu
Along the lakeside at Shiga
In the city, once our old home, there must be one who now lives like this,
waiting, alone and cold, like the lone pine upon this shore.

miyako no sora yōyō tōzakaru ni
furusato no kokoroate naru ōbie no
yama mo kakururu ato no shirakumo
As skies over the capital gradually fade into the distance
Even great Mount Hie, that landmark
that shows us where our old home lies,
now stands far behind us, its every trace hidden in white cloud.

hi ni hi ni shigure furikereba
wakareyuku omoi no kumo no tachisou ya
kyō mo shigururu azumaji no sora
As wintry rains fall day after day
Is it that clouds of grief at our parting follow me on the road east?
Today, again, cold winter rain falls from the skies above.

tokorodokoro ni yomu uta no naka ni
yoriyori ni miyako ni kaeru tabibito no
kazu ni morenan mi no yukue kana
From among poems composed here and there along the way
Such is my destiny, that I'll not likely be among those travelers

who now and again pass on their return to the capital.

> *wasure'enu miyako no tomo no omokage ni*
> *michi yuku hito o taguete zo miru*
> The likeness of my love in the capital, so unforgettable,
> I fancy I see in the faces of passing travelers.

◆ ◆ ◆

Kuranosuke would be the last to leave. His departure date was set for the 7th of the Tenth Month, after all the others traveling from the west had passed through Kyoto and he had disbursed the money they would need to make their journey. His companions would be Ushioda Matanojō, Chikamatsu Kanroku, Hayami Tōzaemon, Suganoya Hannojō, and Mimura Jirōzaemon. Kuranosuke's family retainer Muroi Saroku would be with them, too, as would Chikamatsu Kanroku's man Jinzaburō. If any of the others were attended by servants, the group could well have grown to ten men or more.

But Kuranosuke's own preparations had been in train since at least the end of the previous month, among which was the unpleasant, and probably saddening, task of divorcing his wife, O-Riku. The process was simple enough, but it forced him to write in his own hand a letter that he would much rather not have written:

> *With this missive, I send you my most respectful greetings. It will give me great pleasure if it finds all of you in good health. I myself remain as ever.*
>
> *Item. As I intimated to you some time ago, I have been finding it steadily more difficult financially to reside in the capital region. And since, moreover, I have certain plans, I shall in the near future betake myself to the countryside, where I expect I shall remain for some time. In this connection, I am reluctant to leave my wife in her present state; in consequence of which, I hereby return her to you. This declaration implies no disapproval either of you or of my wife, but is made entirely of my own volition. I shall leave instructions*

that this be forwarded to you by courier from Mount Hachiman
upon my departure. Most humbly and respectfully,

TENTH MONTH, 1ST DAY   *Ōishi Kuranosuke [monogram]*

[in another hand:] Arrived on the 27th from Ōnishibō
To: Ishizuka Gengobei Sama
Ishizuka Uemon Sama,
via their entourage

As he said, he held nothing against O-Riku herself; this was an essential precaution for her own protection. For after their attack on the Kira mansion—whether successful or unsuccessful—it was entirely possible that the Council of Elders or the Shogun would decide to punish not only the perpetrators, but all members of their families as well. It was of crucial importance that O-Riku no longer be Kuranosuke's wife—but surely disheartening to have to make her so.

♦ ♦ ♦

Thanks to Tachibana Nankei, we know, too, that there were other women whom Kuranosuke felt he must take leave of—in particular, those at the Sasaya in Shumoku-machi. "Just before Ōishi was to leave for Edo," Nankei writes, "he was very drunk and wrote a verse on the boards of the ceiling describing his emotions. His words remained on that ceiling, as clear as if the ink were still wet." This is the verse—written in Chinese—that Nankei saw:

> *Once more tonight, I meet with this lady of pleasure,*
> *And aimlessly, we while away the hours.*
> *But on the morrow? Ah, there's the pity!*
> *With a sudden wave of her sleeve, I fear, she'll be gone.*
> *After which, one may linger no longer in this floating world.*
> *Never a second night may one pass here.*

Nankei's account inspired several paintings and prints depicting this scene.

figure 18
Kuranosuke writing a poem on the ceiling of the Sasaya. (Private collection)

✦ ✦ ✦

A day or two before the 7th, Kuranosuke gave up his lodgings in the Bairin'an and moved to an inn on the city side of the Sanjō Bridge, where early in the morning of the day of their departure, the entire company gathered.

Later in the day it would rain, but at dawn on the 7th, the clouds were still moving in from the west and hadn't yet obscured the sky. A few patches of pale blue still remained as the last farewells were being said and the party began moving toward the bridge.

✦ ✦ ✦

The Sanjō Bridge is so famous that we tend to think it must be grand. It is not. And it was even less so in Genroku. It was only as broad as need be to accommodate pedestrian traffic; the oxcarts had to leave the street and cross at the ford on the riverbed below. In length, the bridge is barely a hundred paces from end to end. But as a dividing line between city and country, capital and provincial, it was as formidable as a great mountain or a vast sea. You feel it the moment that you set foot on the planking.

The river is not in full flood this time of year, but the autumn rains keep the flow quick and lively. Somehow, the stones seem almost as carefully placed as in a garden, and on each stone of any size stands a white heron. Some crane their necks in search of unsuspecting fish; some hunch up against the weather, their feathers all disheveled; some stroke the glistening stream with one foot as though to make it move faster and bring them a meal a bit quicker. And in the midst of them all stands a lone blue heron, balanced on one leg and lord of his own rocky islet that still sprouts a few withering reeds. His head is pulled down, his feathers are fluffed, making him look as though he is sound asleep and utterly oblivious. But his smaller cousins know that he is not and give him the extra space, in every direction, that his rank and size demand.

Once across the bridge, travelers seem to sense that they have entered a different world. Their pace grows more purposeful as they touch terra firma again and stride off between the inns that line this stretch of the avenue. Before long, they come to the Shirakawa, a lovely shallow stream that cuts diagonally beneath the road, pebbles glistening under the ripples, long strands of water weed on either side "swaying as a woman's hair sways," as the poets used to say. Over one bank hangs a persimmon tree, heavy with orange fruit and all but bare of its tawny leaves; from the other, a slender pine reaches out as though to touch it. Here, to the right of the road, is where mountains begin to loom in the near distance, steamy mists still filling their narrow defiles, houses and temples with walled gardens nestling at their base.

This wasn't the best of days for our travelers to be viewing the foliage in its autumnal splendor. I don't suppose that anyone mentioned it, but every time I walk this way myself, I can't help thinking they must have known that this probably was the last time they would see such a display. Perhaps the last autumn they would see anywhere. There were the flaming reds and scarlets of the maples, of course, brilliant even under a cloudy sky, as was the glowing gold of the ginkgos, some of them still not quite at their peak; here and there, in contrast, were the late camellias, covered with red and white buds, some already beginning to bloom. Then in moments when the sun burst through a gap in the clouds, it would set alight the russet of the last remaining cherries, the reddening yellow of the zelkova, the greenish-yellow of the beeches, the pale beige of the oaks—all the more subtle shades of "the brocade of autumn" (those ancient poets again). And all along the route, one would hear the patient, deliberate scratch, scratch, scratch of bamboo brooms sweeping up the now rapidly falling leaves—always the task of the early-rising old folks of the household—and with the sound came the scent of fragrant smoke from the little fires that returned the leaves to earth.

A bit farther on, there rises the graceful curve of the roof of the Imperial Temple Shōren'in, and framing it, the thick limbs of massive camphor laurels; even in Genroku, they would have been at least six hundred years old and forty paces broad. And just beyond is the place where, centuries earlier, the Little Swordsmith from Sanjō forged his miraculous blade with the help of Inari Daimyōjin and his band of foxes. A commemorative plaque still marks the site.

Here the road starts rising; then it veers sharply southeast, and just as sharply back east again, as it enters Awataguchi Pass. If anyone still accompanied the travelers, this is where they would have parted company. The city can no longer be seen; the valley narrows as it deepens. Steep banks line both sides of the way as it winds over the Eastern Hills, into Yamashina, and onward to Lake Biwa. Kuranosuke and his companions were climbing now. This was no longer Kyoto. They were on the road to Edo. Kuranosuke was not often moved to versification, but somewhere along this stretch he composed this:

azuma e kudarite
tou hito ni kataru kotoba no nakariseba
mi wa musashino no tsuyu to kotaen
On setting forth for the Eastlands
Should words fail me when I am asked, then I can only answer:
As dew upon Musashi Moor, thus shall I myself be.

figure 19
The Sanjō Bridge. (*Ise sangū meisho zue*, 1797)

*Nails hammered from a
distance never hold firm.*

Little is recorded of anyone's journey east. Jūnai wrote to O-Tan,
lamenting the loss of so many old friends:

> *edo ni itarite taenureba furuki tomo no*
> *nokoreru wa sukunashi*
> *makura karu yukari no kusa mo karehatete*
> *shimo no okifusu musashino no hara*
> Arriving in Edo, only to find that defections
> have left so few of our comrades of yore.
> That grass of comradeship we once cut for pillows, the Murasaki,
> withers away now that frost falls upon Musashi Moor.

Kuranosuke and his son Chikara, of course, traveled incognito.
Kuranosuke had adopted the surname of his grandfather Ikeda Dewa
as his nom de guerre, and Chikara chose the name of a senior retainer
of Ikeda Dewa, calling himself Kakei Sanai. And since Chikara was
posing as a young man proceeding to Edo in connection with a law
suit, Kuranosuke changed his own name yet again to Kakei Gorōbei,
posing as the boy's uncle and guardian. Yet despite the dire rumors of
increased security that so alarmed his ranking kinsmen, the ruse seems
to have worked supremely well, gaining both parties unquestioned passage through the checkpoints at Arai and Hakone—and it is there, at
Hakone, that their narrative can resume.

◆ ◆ ◆

The first step in Kuranosuke's preparation for action was to enlist the aid of otherworldly powers—at least those that dwelt along the road to Edo. Once he had passed the checkpoint at Hakone, Kuranosuke's first stop was at the Hakone Gongen Shrine, where he made obeisance to the resident deity, long held in high regard by the warrior clans of the Eastlands. From there, it was but a short distance to the graves of the Soga brothers, still revered for avenging the murder of their father five hundred years earlier. As a talisman, Kuranosuke plucked a small clump of moss from one of the graves, wrapped it in paper, affixed his vermillion seal to it, and thereafter, it is said, carried it with him wherever he went.

Their route then led down the steep slope and onward to Edo. But since it was just a short jaunt on a side road to Kamakura, site of the Tsurugaoka Hachiman Shrine, it must have seemed an opportune chance to entreat the support of this most powerful of all warrior deities; and thus arrangements had been made in advance for Yoshida Chūzaemon to come from Edo and meet Kuranosuke there. Both men arrived on schedule, on the 21st of the Tenth Month, and stayed for three days, deep in consultation. On the 25th, they left, spent the night in Kawasaki, and the next day walked 1 league up the Rokugō River to the village of Hirama, where Kuranosuke was to lodge.

We have already met Karube Gohei, the farmer from Hirama who once supplied vegetables to the Asano kitchens and fodder for Tominomori Suke'emon's horse. We have seen, too, that after the Catastrophe, Gohei offered Suke'emon and his family a place to live in Hirama, which Suke'emon accepted. Suke'emon's son Chōtarō was born on the Karube farmstead, and the family stayed there for some months. After a year or so, however, Suke'emon and his family decided to move back into the city, but they did not sever their connection with Karube Gohei. It was arranged that when Kuranosuke arrived, he would lodge in the same cottage that had housed Suke'emon. A local carpenter, Watanabe Kiemon, was hired to refurbish the place, and Kuranosuke wrote to Suke'emon, thanking him profusely for all he had done.

Once he and Chūzaemon had arrived in Hirama, Kuranosuke seems to have settled in almost immediately. Although everyone else had already arrived, there could be no definitive planning without Kuranosuke, and so every day, two or three men would come out from Edo to see him, each with a different problem to be solved. Kuranosuke quickly decided that he must issue a set of general orders to be distributed to everyone:

Item. *I have decided that I shall lodge in the village of Hirama. Here is where I shall discuss all matters with members of our pact.*

Item. *When we attack, we shall wear black. Your sash should be knotted on the right-hand side. Be sure to secure your loincloth so that it does not come loose. We shall also wear breeches, leggings, and straw sandals.*

Item. *Marks of identification and passwords will be discussed later.*

Item. *Everyone is free to choose whatever weapons he uses best. Some, however, will be asked to arm themselves with lances and battle bows. This will be discussed.*

Item. *Now that everyone has safely arrived here, we must remain constantly on our guard. The requisite weapons and equipment must be assembled, so that we shall be prepared to attack whenever the chance arises. And we must be careful not to speak unnecessarily of these matters to others, even among our own kinfolk.*

Item. *Since we have agreed to accomplish our mission as a group, even if one encounters our enemy on the street and would be able to kill him, one must not do so. He is not the enemy of any one of us, but of all of us.*

Item. *In order to accomplish our mission, we must not attack recklessly, without being absolutely certain of our enemy's whereabouts, which means that there may be delays of several days. Lest our people run short of food during this time, it is most important that we not spend irresponsibly on clothing, eating, or entertainments. It is by no means our aim simply to storm the enemy's mansion in the heat of rage, without a thought for whether we find him or not.*

Item. *When members of our group gather together, we must be careful what we say and what we do. If we are neglectful, word of our intentions could reach the other party. We must be extremely circumspect.*

Item. *The object of our endeavor, of course, is Kōzuke-no-Suke and his son Sahei. But if everyone concentrates upon these two alone, paying no attention to anyone else, these two might contrive to elude us. When we attack, we must take great care to let no one, man or woman, escape. We must assign battle stations carefully throughout the property, guarding with special care the main gate, rear gate, and New Gate. We must also note whether there might be places where they could escape over the walls, and position our forces accordingly.*

Item. *Our opponent probably has more than a hundred men under his command. But we have more than fifty, all of us determined to fight to the death. If each of us takes on two or three of the enemy, we can easily triumph.*

Item. *I think that we should now, as a group, swear a new oath and reaffirm unequivocally our determination. We shall discuss the wording of this oath in the near future. These are ideas jotted down at random as they occurred to me. If you have further thoughts, please do not hesitate to let me know. We shall refine these plans in the course of further discussion. Herewith the foregoing.*

For Kuranosuke, the question was no longer, Shall we? It was now, *How* and *when* shall we? He clearly knew that as a combat commander, it would be one of his first tasks to learn as much as he could about the enemy, while keeping the enemy ignorant of himself and his intentions. In all that this involved, he could call upon the considerable expertise of his senior officers.

It was the most senior of these men, apparently, who first responded to Kuranosuke's call for further thoughts. Horibe Yahei, although now in his seventy-sixth year, remained a formidable figure. His age, far from deterring him, made him only the keener to attack, lest he die of natural causes while he waited for others to make up their minds. And as the retired Edo Liaison Officer, his knowledge of officialdom, daimyo, and their politics was invaluable. But the first of Yahei's further thoughts was of a very practical sort:

> Your own base in the region is too distant, so you must immediately establish good communications with all other locales, and then select a new base somewhere not too far from the vicinity in question. If you are not in constant secure contact with the stalwarts of the group, things are bound to go wrong. I am particularly worried about the behavior of the young men. Nails hammered from a distance never hold firm. If you do not regularly make the rounds of their lodgings, they will end up doing whatever they please.
>
> I understand your concern lest your base of operations stand out too conspicuously, but I do not share that concern. If we were planning this a year or two in advance, it might make sense to remain at a distance; but acting in haste as we are, with only one or two months lead time, excessive caution may only cause failure. It should be easy enough to remain inconspicuous. But if we are too cautious, delay will follow delay, and the whole thing may come to naught. That is my greatest worry.

This was a thought that Kuranosuke would take seriously. What his own experience was, of trying to plan and manage so delicate an operation from beyond the Rokugō River in Hirama, he does not say. But it could not have been very long after his arrival that Kuranosuke decided that Yahei was right. On the 5th Day of the Eleventh Month, after only ten days at the Karube farmstead, he left Hirama and moved to rooms at the rear of the Oyamaya in Nihonbashi Koku-chō. The move was not haphazard. The Oyamaya was what was known as a litigant's inn, a highly specialized hostel that provided not only convenient lodging for those come to Edo in connection with legal matters, but also assistance in preparing the documents that a litigant must submit to the court. Kuranosuke's son, still posing as Kakei Sanai, a young litigant who had come to Edo on unstated business, had moved into the Oyamaya only a few days previously. Kuranosuke himself could thus continue to pose as Kakei Gorōbei when he moved in with him. And their joint (though fictitious) legal concerns would serve as plausible cover for all the comings and goings of those who came to consult Kuranosuke. Now the action could begin in earnest.

♦ ♦ ♦

None of Onodera Jūnai's letters to his wife, O-Tan, written en route from Kyoto to Edo, survive. But once Jūnai was settled in temporary lodgings, even before he moved in with Kuranosuke, he wrote her one of the most revealing and moving of all the letters that survive. It is a very long letter, and parts of it deal with matters that he can only hint at. But the passages in which he describes his feelings for O-Tan are deeply affecting:

> Item. *I take this opportunity to address a quick word to you. Are you well? I've received no letters and worry constantly about you. You may rest assured that all of us here are in the best of health. Kōemon, Gengo, Kyūdayū, and Kansuke are all well.*
>
> Item. *Are you still living in the same place? I've even been wondering if you'd found it too lonely there and moved elsewhere. I find myself imagining, as if I could actually see it, how the house, without my things lying all about, has come to seem larger, yet ever more empty and barren, and how fewer and fewer callers come and life for you grows lonely. We've both resigned ourselves to this from of yore, but now we must take care not to let self-pity get the better of us. Just do your best to stay strong, and don't let your health deteriorate.*
>
> Item. *Did you get your money back from your brother Tōbei? You must insist on taking it back. If you don't get it back now, you'll lose it. I'm sure that he must have received both principal and interest from Tōsuke by now. You must be very careful not to let anyone take advantage of you.*

Item. *The forty-ninth-day observances of Mother's death would have taken place on the 28th or 29th; but we are in hiding here, so I did not go to the temple. I cherished her memory in the privacy of my solitary thoughts, and then, as a small remembrance, I went to see Kyūdayū, Kansuke, and Magokurō, who are sharing lodgings, and we drank to her and talked of her at their place. You and I would have been of one mind in remembering her that day, for I expect that you went to the temple, as we planned in Kyoto, and made offerings there on her behalf.*

Item. *Are you managing somehow to get by for the time being and keep your spirits up as best you can? Have you been able to do as you wished, contrary to what you'd previously feared? Of course, we've never known what the future might hold; still, I can well imagine that my departure could make things turn out different from what we had thought. But I've had no letters and heard nothing.*

Item. *I've not been in touch with any of our family here, but I did send word to Haikata Kihei Dono that I would like to talk to him about your future and ask his help on your behalf. I told him that I would be glad go to his place, but he wrote back saying that since I had broken off with Tōbei Dono, he would not be willing to meet me. So we never met. Tōbei, I'm sure, must have told him everything; and that, I expect, is what made him refuse. . . . What a useless pair of brothers they are! Feeling as they do, and given what is about to happen here, they are not likely to care much what becomes of you. With that much less that you can depend upon, it is of the utmost importance that you strive with all your might to make your own way in the world when I am gone. As time passes and their anger cools, I hope that they may be less inclined to abandon you, but that is nothing we can predict. You will just have to act in accord with the way things go there.*

Item. *Yesterday afternoon, toward evening, when no one was about and I was writing a bit more to send you, your letters of the 15th and 16th were delivered from Mino-ya. They told the man I sent yesterday that they didn't know my address and were waiting for someone to come and pick them up. So now I have news of all the details up to the 16th. It is a wonderful feeling, almost as though I were with you and could see you again. I unrolled and reread them over and over. But you say that the pain on the lower left side of your chest has returned, just as before; that you can't sleep lying on your left side, and that your pulse is weak. You were quite right to get some medicine from Keian Dono. It's almost certainly caused by mental strain. But no matter how you may despair, you mustn't let your health deteriorate. You'll have little enough to support yourself as it is, which is why it is vital that you strive to stay healthy so that somehow you can manage to get by. Don't encourage your illness; take your medicine regularly. I'm terribly worried lest you should will yourself to grow steadily worse.*

Item. You are too good to me—to have gone to the temple on the 14th and promptly sponsored a meal for the monks. I am delighted, too, that Mother's stone will be placed properly just next to O-Iyo's grave.

Item. You say that, contrary to what we expected, you feel power-less and at a loss what to do and that by day you feel distracted, and by night you lie awake turning over in your mind one thought after another. I know exactly how you feel; it's the same with me here. It would be utterly mistaken to say that we are of two minds in this respect. As you say, every passing day seems to grow more depressing. Our ups and downs are so unpredictable, they say, that if we once fully grasp this principle, misfortune may prove to be the seed of our awakening to the True Way. In a general way, I can see what they mean. Yet it's a thought unlikely to inspire either credence or consolation, unless you encounter some sympathetic soul whose counsel and encouragement can spark that awakening. I find myself recalling all that we did in the past, dwelling longingly, the whole day through, upon every detail of the way things once were; there seems no end to it. All we two can do is force ourselves to think that "this is how it must be"—these lives we lead and these feelings that beset us—in the hope that that will distract us as long as we yet have life, and inspire us not to forget each other. A dismal thought.

Item. *It was very discerning, I think, that you should single out
my "Ausaka" poem as the most moving. But your poems! I am so
deeply touched by them. Unable to staunch the flow of tears, yet
worrying all the while whether others might see or hear me, I chant
them over and over again, trying my best to swallow my sobs. . . .
In the present state of things, you must not abandon your poetry,
but continue ceaselessly to write. Whenever you have a moment,
copy them out and send them to me. On the road, even when I was
utterly exhausted, with nothing else to occupy my mind, I could
still ponder drafts of poems. But since I've arrived here, I encounter five, six, seven, or more of my comrades every day, and they
are constantly coming and going. I've hardly a moment to think
of anything else. With never a quiet moment to spend alone, it
is impossible to think a poem through properly. Everything I see,
everything I hear, sets me to thinking how things must be with you,
and imagining how straitened and lonely your life must be now. . . .
My brush cannot begin to express all that I am thinking, all that I
would wish to say.*

Item. *We live from day to day here. The young men are particularly
keen; they seem so full of energy! We older men—Chūzaemon,
Sōemon, Kyūdayū, and myself—are responsible for planning
everything. On the 1st, Kōemon and some of the younger men
seem to have gone to the theater to see the new season's Kabuki.
With none of their relatives about, they get to do whatever they
please. The young men are terribly solicitous of us "oldsters," as
they call us; they even serve us our meals morning and evening.
The young men gave me a name, too—Senboku Jūan—because
they think that I look like a doctor. They rush about doing everything they can for me, and call me "Jūan Sama, Jūan Sama." I
could pass the days drinking saké and nibbling on snacks without
ever having to exert myself. But already the sleeves of my kimono
are beginning to fray, and the hem is a bit tattered; with no one
to turn to for help, I just tell myself, "Well, it won't be that much
longer," and let it go at that. I had to ask Kōemon to sew up a
seam in the lining. The nights are so cold that we have to wear*

layer upon layer of clothing. By day, we fold them up and put them away, and save our best for when we really need them. When I left, you were urging me to "take one more garment"; now I'm wishing that I had taken it. I'm at least content, though, that father and son are respectably dressed.

Item. I recently went to a poulterer to buy a wild goose for our group's dinner. They were such exceptionally fine birds, and so very cheap, that I bought another, which I've packed in salt and miso and will send to you. I hope that you'll find it a rare treat. I'll give some to Kōemon, too. But do eat it as soon as you can. It is lightly salted, so don't leave it for long without salt, but plunge it directly into boiling water and save the broth. With some daikon, ginkgo nuts, and a light miso, it makes a lovely soup. You could ask Tōsuke to make it for you and treat him to some. Or when Keian calls to take your pulse, you could offer him some soup and saké. Do with it whatever seems best to you under the circumstances there.

Item. I am going to move to Chikara Dono's lodgings. They are not in the neighborhood where I've been staying until now, and they're some distance from where Kōemon is staying. So far I've been in rather good health, so you can put your mind at rest on that score. The most important thing is that you carry on with strength and resignation. It is only natural that you should wish to know what happens and when. But rest assured that you will hear immediately when something happens. I shall be writing to you again. There are so many people about that it's taken any number of attempts to write this letter. Please let me know how all goes with you there. Herewith the foregoing,

ELEVENTH MONTH, 3RD DAY *Senboku [Onodera] Matashirō [Jūnai]*
To: O-Tan Dono

*In embarking upon this attack,
we do so fully prepared to die.*

If you look at a list of the places where the ronin lodged, and compare it with a map of Edo, it looks as though they were scattered about the city in a totally random manner—Kuranosuke, Jūnai, and Chikara in Nihonbashi; Chūzaemon, Sōemon, and Suke'emon on the far side of the castle in Kōjimachi; others across the river in Honjo and Fukagawa; still others farther afield in Hatchōbori and Shiba. No doubt, it was a random matter where some of them ended up: friends moving in with friends who had already found a place, and others seeking accommodation nearby. But the process was not entirely random. We have already seen how Kuranosuke and his son purposely lodged in a litigant's inn. And the ronin themselves tell us that they "rented two large rooms to be used as meeting places, in Hayashi-chō at the Second Bridge." Even before Kuranosuke arrived, Horibe Yasubei had moved out of his adoptive family's home and into one of these large spaces, where he posed as a teacher of swordsmanship. "And every evening," they tell us, "we would gather in this meeting place and discuss what we had learnt that day."

At one of these meetings, Kuranosuke told them of something that he had heard: "It is rumored that there might be a force held in readiness to come from the Uesugi mansion. So if we attack, but then can't find him and kill him immediately, it is possible that reinforcements from the Uesugi might come in the meantime. We can easily cope with Kōzuke-no-Suke's vassals, but it would be humiliating to be attacked by massive reinforcements and die a dog's death, all for nothing. If those rumors are true, I think that we should prepare to defend ourselves with lances, halberds, mallets, and the like."

In short, there were unknowns still to be investigated.

◆ ◆ ◆

A good start had already been made. Even before Kira moved to Honjo, Kanzaki Yogorō had opened a fruit and vegetable shop opposite the guardhouse on the southwestern corner of the property. Then Maebara Isuke, who had been dealing in fabric remnants in Tomizawa-chō, moved in with him. Together, they were able to keep almost constant watch on the comings and goings from Kira's rear gate. Isuke seems also to have found work as a day laborer with the contractor who was renovating the house for Kira; but once Kira had moved in, Yogorō found it impossible to gain entry posing as a peddler. Yet whenever there was warning of a fire, or even just heavy wind, both men would make that their excuse to climb to the roof, pretend to search the horizon for smoke or flames, and in the process look down into the Kira property and take note of what was where and the general layout of the place. Once, in the midst of a rainstorm, Yogorō saw a man's palanquin emerge from the rear gate surrounded by a considerable entourage. He followed it all the way to the Uesugi mansion, but was unable to ascertain whether or not it carried Kira.

There are fragmentary reports of other, more successful, attempts to gain entry, all from firsthand sources, but unfortunately lacking in detail. In the spring of the year, before Kuranosuke's arrival, there had been a spate of rumors of new defenses being constructed. A new storehouse had been built, said to hide an escape tunnel leading under the wall to a neighboring mansion. It was said, too, that all local help had been dismissed and replaced by people from Kira's fief in Mikawa, and that a barrier of thick bamboo, too strong to be bashed down, had been built separating the entire mansion from the barrack blocks. But a young man named Mōri Koheita somehow managed to find work as a servant to an Elder of the Kira house, and in the course of delivering a letter for this man was able to see that no such barrier existed. Perhaps the same was true of the tunnel?

In the meantime, the more prosaic but no less important work of learning the lay of the land had begun. A map was made of the entire neighborhood, from the block beyond the Kira mansion to the Ryōgoku Bridge, and all the relevant dimensions and distances were paced out— the length and breadth of the Kira property, the width of the streets, the distance to the gate of the Temple of the Unknown Dead, the area of the square at the head of the bridge—information that everyone would need in case of a counterattack.

By the beginning of the Eleventh Month, about the time of Kuranosuke's arrival in the city, a system of surveillance had been established. Four teams of young men took it in turns to patrol every night the two main routes between the Kira mansion in Honjo and the Uesugi mansion in Sakurada—as ceaseless, one writer says, as "the turning of a waterwheel." Others kept a constant eye on traffic into and out of the Uesugi mansion as well as the middle mansion in Shirogane, where Kira's wife had moved for the duration of the renovations in Honjo, and Kira himself was said to spend a good bit of time.

And lest all this patrolling and surveillance alert the enemy, Yoshida Chūzaemon laid down some fairly strict rules meant to prevent the young men from attracting undue attention and missing their enemy entirely. For night patrols, he told them, evening until midnight was the best time. But from midnight through the Eighth and Seventh Hours (2:00–6:00 A.M.), one must take great care, until the streets began to fill again. This was particularly true in Honjo, which was out of the way and little frequented at night. And there must be no patrolling at all in the immediate vicinity of the Kira mansion, for one was sure to be spotted by guards at the gates and in the corner guardhouse. Neither must there be any arguing or quarrelling.

◆ ◆ ◆

Shortly after Kuranosuke's arrival, on both the 7th and 8th of the Eleventh Month, the "old men"—Kuranosuke, Chūzaemon, and Sōemon—met at the home of Horibe Yahei, the oldest of the old men, where "with great care and attention to detail, they drew up a battle plan." The result was a Memorandum of Instructions, probably meant to supplement the set of general orders that Kuranosuke had issued from Hirama:

Item. *When the date is decided, everyone will proceed with all stealth to the three previously appointed locations.*

Item. *Our mustering place shall be the rental rooms at Hayashi-chō, 2-Chōme.*

Item. *We shall set out at precisely the previously appointed hour.*

Item. *When the enemy's head is taken, circumstances permitting, the body will be stripped of an outer robe in which the head will be wrapped.*

Item. *Should Inspectors arrive, they are to be greeted as follows: "We hope that we may be allowed to bear this head to the grave of our Late Lord. If this is not to be permitted, we bow to the inevitable. We are most reluctant, however, to discard unceremoniously the head of so eminent a personage. Might we therefore, with your permission, return it to the mansion? We shall do as you direct in this matter." If all goes as planned, we shall take the head to Sengakuji and present it at His Lordship's grave.*

Item. *If the son's head is severed, it need not be taken with us, but may be discarded.*

Item. *It is most important that every effort be made to take our wounded with us when we withdraw, even if they must be carried on our shoulders. If any are too severely wounded to be transported, we shall do them the honor of removing their heads ourselves before we leave.*

Item. *The signal that we have taken the heads of father and son will be repeated blasts of the whistle.*

Item. *The place of withdrawal is to be the Temple of the Unknown Dead, Ekōin. If we are not permitted entry to the temple grounds, we shall assemble in the square at the eastern end of the Ryōgoku Bridge.*

Item. *If, in the course of withdrawal, we are challenged by forces dispatched from neighboring houses, we shall state truthfully the* facts of the matter: "We have absolutely no intention of fleeing or hiding. We plan to withdraw to the Temple of the Unknown Dead, where we shall await the arrival of official Inspectors, to whom we shall explain all the details of the matter. If you doubt our intentions, we should be pleased to have you accompany us to the temple. None of our number shall attempt to escape."

Item. If we are beset by pursuers from the Kira house, we shall stand our ground calmly and do battle with them.

Item. Should official Inspectors arrive during the battle, the main gate is not to be opened. One man is to go out through the wicket and greet them politely. If the battle is still under way, we shall greet them only after our mission has been accomplished. They are to be told the truth: "We have just dispatched the gentleman we sought. As soon as the survivors have been assembled, everyone will emerge, at which time it is our intention to submit to your orders. None of our number has any intention of attempting to escape."

Item. Should the Inspectors wish to enter and survey the scene, and command us to open the gate, then say to them: "The attack force is still deployed in several positions around the property. We fear that if you were to enter now, there could be an accident. The gates will be opened momentarily, and you will then be able to see everything." The gate is to remain firmly shut; under no circumstances should it be opened.

Item. We shall depart from the rear gate.

Item. It need hardly be added that in embarking upon this attack, we do so fully prepared to die. The foregoing mention of our withdrawal is merely for your information when the time comes. To embark upon an attack with a head full of plans for retreat can only give rise to fear and cowardice. Even if we must retreat, it is nonetheless crucial that we do so in the same stalwart spirit with which we attack. It goes without saying that everyone must fight with all his heart and might.

In retrospect, we know that by the time their preparations were well under way, the ronin also possessed a detailed and professionally drafted plan of the Kira property, which included a complete floor plan of the mansion itself. What we do not know is how such a detailed plan was obtained. A scattering of references to it survives, but only with a great deal of speculation can we connect these as a coherent whole.

Ten months earlier, on the 30th of the First Month, Horibe Yasubei wrote to Ōtaka Gengo that "we have managed to obtain a plan of the property." And Terasaka Kichiemon, who arrived in Edo with Yoshida Chūzaemon on the 5th of the Third Month, wrote, "We obtained a plan of the property through a confidential connection with a certain person, but it was a plan of the house of the previous occupant, and after it was transferred to [Kira], he altered the interior." Still later, we read that "we managed to obtain two plans of the Kōzuke Dono property, one old and one new. . . ." And last of all, in a letter dated simply "Tenth Month, 11th Day," Ushioda Matanojō informed Ōishi Mujin that "I have finally obtained a copy of the plan we discussed yesterday, which I send for your inspection. Kindly peruse it at your leisure . . . and burn it when you are finished."

What, then, are we to make of these fragments? The last of them contains two clues that may be useful. The writer of this letter, Ushioda Matanojō, was both a member of the Horse Guards and the Officer in Charge of Maps. Which is to say, he must have been an accomplished draftsman, and thus was the logical person to prepare a fair copy of the final revision of the plan. It may also be significant that Matanojō sent the copy mentioned in his letter not to Kuranosuke, but to Ōishi Mujin; old Mujin (whom we shall get to know better in the next chapter) had a brother-in-law, Ōta Kahei, in the service of Matsudaira Noborinosuke, the previous inhabitant of the Kira property. Could it be that Mujin was the "confidential connection" and Ōta Kahei was the "certain person" from whom he obtained a copy of the "old plan"? That, thereafter, a "new plan" was acquired showing the alterations that Kira had commissioned? And that Ushioda Matanojō, combining the old and new plans, and incorporating the fruits of observation and measurement, drafted a working plan drawn precisely to scale?

Whatever the history of this final version—a copy of which survives

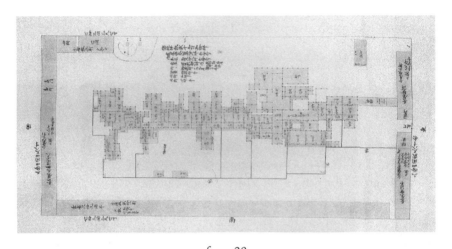

figure 20
A floor plan of the mansion of Kira Kōzuke-no-Suke, possibly drafted by Ushioda Matanojō. (Collection of Tominomori Fujio, Akō Municipal Museum of History)

figure 20a
Planning the attack. (*Ehon Chūshingura*, Waseda University Library, Tokyo)

with the descendants of Tominomori Suke'emon—this was what the ronin studied when they planned the grouping and placement of their forces and formulated the strategy of their attack.

♦ ♦ ♦

The entire force had now assembled in Edo; bit by bit, intelligence was being gathered; battle plans were taking shape; the lay of the land and the layout of the house that would become the battlefield were now known. There remained, however, one crucial yet intractable unknown: the whereabouts of their enemy, Kira Kōzuke-no-Suke. No date for an attack could be decided until that was known. To attack an empty house and die a dog's death in the process was not an acceptable reward for these months of endeavor, deliberation, and deprivation. Yet despite their best efforts, the ronin had so far failed to ascertain when Kira would be in Honjo or at the Uesugi mansion in Sakurada or anywhere else. It was only with the help of people we have yet to meet that they began to move toward a solution to this problem.

CHAPTER
56

*I think it would be best not to
question these men too insistently.*

To sort out the connections among the people we are about to meet, we must first look to the past—to begin with, the distant past, and then the more recent past.

The reader may recall that Shimo, the mother of Ōishi Yoshikatsu, the first Kuranosuke, was in fact a "misplaced seed," an illegitimate child of the highest-ranking nobleman in the land, Konoe Sakihisa, courtier of the First Rank and Prime Minister to the Emperor. As an infant, she had been given to Lord Sakihisa's steward, Shindō Chikugo-no-Kami, to raise; and once Shimo was grown, Shindō arranged for her to be married to his kinsman Ōishi Kyūemon. To their great credit, members of the House of Konoe never forgot their inadvertent relationship with the Ōishi.

More recently, the reader may also recall that just prior to the Catastrophe, Kuranosuke sent a rather pessimistic New Year's greeting to his elderly kinsman in Edo, Ōishi Mujin. Mujin was, of course, the old man's retirement name; by the fifteenth year of Genroku (1702), he had been living in retirement for a very long time. For thirty-six years earlier, in Kanbun 6 (1666), he had resigned in protest from the Akō Corps of Vassals.

Ōishi Gozaemon—as was his name then—was the son of a Samurai Daishō, the commander of a battle group of fully fledged mounted samurai, who held that position because he had taken the head of one of the enemy at the siege of Osaka Castle. But just before Gozaemon was to inherit his father's position, he discovered that domain officials had decided to divide his father's 450 koku between himself and his younger brother, each to be recompensed at 225 koku per year. And neither he nor his brother was to be notified of the change until the moment of its enactment the following morning. A more docile spirit might have swallowed his resentment, told himself that 225 koku was a respectable salary, and reported to the castle as commanded. Gozaemon was made of tougher stuff. He knew that if he first accepted the position and *then* resigned it, *his* 225 koku would forever be lost to the family. The only way to keep the post intact and in the family would be to resign *before* it was split and flee that very night. The authorities would then be forced to appoint his younger brother to succeed their father—at the full 450 koku. Thus, on the night of the 2nd Day of the Ninth Month, Gozaemon and his wife fled Akō.

How Gozaemon and his family survived those early years of his life as a ronin, we do not know. But at some point, probably when his two sons were nearing their majority, the Konoe came to their aid. A Konoe daughter had recently married the lord of the Tsugaru house, and through that connection they were able to arrange a position for Mujin's elder son, Gōemon Yoshimaro, in the Tsugaru Corps of Vassals. His younger son, they invited to serve their own house in Kyoto, and it was Konoe Motohiro himself who gave the boy the name by which we now know him: Mitsuhira.

And so, in Genroku 15, Mujin was living in Honjo, a short distance from the Tsugaru Upper Mansion, where his elder son was employed, and, quite fortuitously, an equally short distance from the Kira mansion. Mitsuhira, too, was at home in Honjo, having returned to Edo three or four years earlier.

✦ ✦ ✦

With these people and their histories in mind, then, let us shift our attention to Kyoto, where fate had for some time been at work on behalf of the ronin, through people whom none of them had ever met.

The first of these people was an old tea master, Yamada Sōhen. In his youth, Sōhen had studied under Sen Sōtan, the grandson of Sen no Rikyū. And through that lineage, Sōhen had come to the attention of

Ogasawara Sado-no-Kami, then the Shogunal Deputy in Kyoto. When Sado-no-Kami was recalled to Edo in Genroku 10 (1697) and raised to the Council of Elders, he insisted that Sōhen accompany him. Thus, under Ogasawara patronage, Sōhen became the first exponent of the Sen school of tea in the new capital of Edo. He built his hermitage to the east of the Sumida River, at First Bridge, Quay's End in Honjo, and through his patron, as well as his illustrious lineage, he soon acquired a sizable following. Whether Kira had known Sōhen before he, too, moved across the river, we do not know. But when he was ordered to move to Honjo, the property assigned to him turned out to be barely five minutes' walk from Sōhen's hermitage. Kira had long been a devotee of ceremonial tea, and particularly that of the school of Sen Sōtan. Now that he had so much more time on his hands, it was only natural that he should befriend his new neighbor Sōhen.

The second of fate's instruments was another migrant from the old capital to the new, Hakura Itsuki, a young scholar still struggling to make a name for himself in Edo. Itsuki was the second son of an old priestly family attached to the ancient Inari Shrine in Fushimi. In Genroku 10, he had entered the service of the Prince-Abbot of the Imperial Temple Myōhōin, who, as it happened, was well acquainted with Kira. But two years later, an old family connection, the former Minister of the Right Oinomikado Tsunemitsu, offered Itsuki a place in his entourage when he was appointed Imperial Emissary to the memorial services commemorating the fiftieth anniversary of the death of the third Shogun, Iemitsu. Itsuki apparently thought that his chances of making his way in the world would be better in Edo than in Kyoto or Fushimi, and Tsunemitsu's patronage would cover the costs of his journey there. Having arrived in Edo in the Fourth Month of Genroku 13 (1700), Itsuki requested Lord Tsunemitsu's permission to remain there rather than return to the old capital. Tsunemitsu not only granted his request, but asked an old acquaintance of his, the rich timber merchant Nakajima Gorōsaku, to look after the young scholar. Gorōsaku provided Itsuki with rent-free quarters in his establishment at Sanjikkenbori, near Kyōbashi.

Thus it was that this rich merchant became yet another instrument of the fate of the ronin. How old Gorōsaku was in 1702, we have no idea. It seems likely, though, that he was advanced in years, as he was no longer as active in business as he had once been. Neither do we know how he happened to be acquainted with so eminent a court noble as Tsunemitsu. But we have it directly from Horibe Yahei—who as former Edo Liaison Officer would know more of such matters than most—that Tsunemitsu himself did indeed intercede with Gorōsaku on Itsuki's behalf.

And so by the time Kuranosuke arrived in Edo, Kira's tenuous earlier connections with both Yamada Sōhen and Hakura Itsuki had matured, if not into discipleship, at least into association of a more familiar sort. Sōhen was a frequent guest at Kira's tea gatherings, and Itsuki probably taught Kira something of court lore and poetry. And Nakajima Gorōsaku had become a disciple of both Sōhen and Itsuki.

◆ ◆ ◆

None of this would have had any relevance for Kuranosuke and the ronin, however, were it not for the mediation of Ōishi Mitsuhira. Through his connection with the Konoe and his sojourn in Kyoto, Itsuki was a familiar name to him—and he may have known of Sōhen as well. Mitsuhira seems not to have been a devotee of tea, but he must have been one of Itsuki's first students in Edo, for he had been attending his lectures over the past three years, and in this way had come to know Itsuki's patron Gorōsaku. Horibe Yahei describes their relationship in some detail:

> They are not exceptionally close friends; but Mitsuhira has become a sort of cousin to Gorōsaku. . . .In this connection, he sometimes visits Gorōsaku's home, and four or five times has been treated to meals there. From time to time, he also meets Gorōsaku in lectures at Itsuki's place. As a result, both Gorōsaku and Itsuki know that Mitsuhira is related to a number of the members of the Asano house, and both have often had things to say about Boku-ichi [Kira]. But it is hard to judge what people are really thinking, so Mitsuhira pretends that this is of little concern to him, telling them that everyone from Akō is now scattered hither and yon; that he is no longer in touch with them, even by letter; and that he has heard that no one

cares much about the matter anymore.

Then, around the 2nd or 3rd of the Eleventh Month, when Mitsuhira chanced to meet Gorōsaku, he remarked, "You must be invited to quite a few tea gatherings this time of year."

"Indeed I am," Gorōsaku replied. "But one of them is rather unusual. I've been contacted by Kira Dono and invited to one of his tea gatherings. The date isn't set yet, but I expect that it will be in the near future. This is something I never expected." Then on the 6th, when Mitsuhira attended a lecture at Itsuki's place, Gorōsaku told him, "I'll be going to a gathering at Kira Dono's this evening."

Two days later, on the 8th, Mitsuhira went again to Hakura Itsuki's place, but Gorōsaku wasn't there; so he asked Itsuki, "Did Gorōsaku actually go to Kira Dono on the 6th?"

"Yes," Itsuki replied, "he went to a gathering on the evening of the 6th, in Kira's private tea room. Kira himself performed the ceremony, he said. But just outside the tea room, he could see four or five samurai, all of them armed with two swords. In the anteroom, too, there were a few samurai—which shows the level of security that Kira maintains. After the tea ceremony, their host accompanied them to a small sitting room, where they were served light refreshments. Gorōsaku said to him, 'You must find it lonely, living all alone like this.' Kira said, 'Yes, but I often go to stay with my son Danjō. Danjō's mansion is very spacious, which is a comfort. But hereafter, do come and visit me whenever you like.' It was still light when the refreshments were finished, Gorōsaku said, so he must have returned at about sundown. But I didn't ask him any more about it."

There was more, though, and at some point Itsuki passed it on to Mitsuhira. Kira had been ill of late, he said, and for that reason had let his hair hang down instead of tying it back. And the construction of the tea room was very shoddy. None of the structural damage and none of the patches where plaster had fallen off the walls had been repaired. There were even corners that hadn't been cleaned. "If he means this to be his permanent residence, one would expect it to be in a bit better repair," Gorōsaku had said.

For his own part, Itsuki said, "I've met Kira Dono and previously frequented his mansion, but the things people say about him are so unflattering that I began to have doubts about frequenting his place and lately have refrained from visiting him. But his Elder Matsubara Tachū is a student of mine, so I am still in touch through him."

All of this gave Mitsuhira a rather adventurous idea: "His love of tea is genuine, and his invitation to Gorōsaku seems sincere. If only we could get Gorōsaku to invite him to his place for an 'Evening's Converse,' and he were to travel there incognito. That would be ideal." The "Evening's Converse" that Mitsuhira referred to is, of course, one of the seven styles of tea, held on a wintry evening around a glowing hearth in a room lit by candlelight. The season, the time of day, the ambience, would indeed be ideal—either to waylay him en route or to take him unawares in the comfort of a warm room. But nothing ever came of Mitsuhira's idea. Perhaps he himself had second thoughts on the matter, for later he remarked, "I think it would be best not to question these men too insistently about the layout of the mansion and whether Kira is in residence there. For if suddenly we start asking questions, and these men should form an unfavorable opinion of us, it could work to our detriment, and we could lose our advantage." This was a totally unsuspected and potentially rich mine of information that would have to be worked with great care.

CHAPTER
57

*In our attack . . . no distinctions shall be made
between greater and lesser feats of arms. He who takes
the head of Kōzuke-no-Suke or his son shall be
considered the equal of he who merely stands guard.*

Uesugi Danjō Daihitsu, Kira's natural son, had been ill since the summer
of this year, on through the autumn, and into the winter, yet still he
showed no sign of improvement. His father was, of course, concerned
for his health, and thus was absent from Honjo far more often than he
might otherwise have been, sometimes spending day and night at the
Uesugi mansion in Sakurada. Then, too, there were Kira's tea engage-
ments, some of which took him here and there at irregular intervals, and
some of which he himself hosted at home. For Kuranosuke, these unpredictable movements were serious impediments to his planning. Some of
the young men were irrationally keen to attack immediately, no matter
what. Kuranosuke, of course, insisted that they wait until they could be
absolutely certain that their enemy was in residence—despite all the
complications and delays. But there were also those whose courage had
begun to wane now that they were parted from their families and far
from home. Two or three of them had already absconded in the early
days of the Eleventh Month and fled back west.

Kuranosuke seems to have realized that wait-and-see was no longer
a practical plan. If he could ascertain with absolute certainty the date
of the next tea gathering that Kira was to hold at his home, he could
set a date for the attack with absolute certainty that their enemy would
be present. But he could not just sit back and wait for this news to
come to him; he would have to pursue it. He needed to penetrate the tea

~ 476 ~

network and manipulate it from within. With the help of their newly acquired connections, Hakura Itsuki and Yamada Sōhen, this should now be possible.

It was decided that Ōtaka Gengo would be the one to infiltrate the tea clique. Gengo was by no means a practiced hand at ceremonial tea, but he had studied the art in the Kansai and was a highly skilled *haikai* poet. He should be quite convincing in the role of a cultured townsman. And so Gengo was outfitted as a well-to-do merchant from Osaka, Wakuya Shinbei, and introduced to Yamada Sōhen—probably by Nakajima Gorōsaku—as a would-be disciple. Fortunately, Sōhen agreed to teach him.

Gengo immediately ceased all other activity and devoted himself entirely to the practice of tea and making himself useful to Sōhen. Once he felt that he had earned the old man's confidence, he said to him, "You must see great variety in the people you know and teach. Whom would you say are the most accomplished practitioners these days?"

"Who are the best?" Sōhen replied. "Well, Kira Kōzuke-no-Suke Dono is exceptionally skilled. He is retired now and holds a great many more gatherings than before, some of which I attend."

Gengo refrained from further comment for a time, but then, almost as an aside, he said, "I wish I might sometime watch Kōzuke-no-Suke Sama's technique, if only from afar, from an anteroom."

"There might one day be a chance," Sōhen said. This was a chance that never materialized, but Gengo's quest for an indisputable date continued. And before long, he learned that the next gathering at the Kōzuke mansion would be on the 23rd of the Eleventh Month. But then, this was postponed until the 5th of the Twelfth Month. By what process Gengo discovered these dates, we are not told. But at last there was a date.

◆ ◆ ◆

Now that a date could be set, Kuranosuke turned to one of his final chores—accounting for his use of the funds that he had taken possession of just before he left Akō. By the middle of the Eleventh Month, all these "remaining funds" had been exhausted, and the ronin were reduced to living entirely on their own resources. As we have seen, Kuranosuke had borrowed at least 200 *ryō* in gold from his kinsmen in Bizen; Sugino Jūheiji and Chikamatsu Kanroku were sharing what was left of their personal savings; and Yoshida Chūzaemon and his younger brother Kaiga Yazaemon had "borrowed" 100 *ryō* from a benevolent merchant in Kyoto, Wataya Zen'emon. But the wait for Daigaku's "pardon" had gone on far longer than anticipated. Kuranosuke now prepared a box that he would fill with all the documents that he had preserved and prepared over the past several months and that he would submit to Ochiai Yozaemon, Chamberlain to Yōzei'in, thus demonstrating his probity as a trustee to his late lord's widow.

First of all, he inserted the account book that he himself had been keeping since his departure from Akō and, with it, a sealed pouch containing all the receipts for funds that he had disbursed. The account book is the only item of the contents of the box that survives, but a list of the other documents remains in the Asano temple Kagakuji, from which we know that copies of many of the lost documents are still to be found in a large dossier labeled *The Surrender of Akō Castle.* Some of these documents are duplicates of accounts submitted to the Inspectors, which Yōzei'in would never have seen and which would verify the sources and amounts of income, as well as the uses to which these funds had been put. Kuranosuke was particularly concerned that she see these records, as ninety of the gold pieces that he had taken to Yamashina were from a fund of interest on loans that had accrued to her. Originally, Kuranosuke had not intended to spend her money; but now that he had, he wished to assure her that it had been spent responsibly. In addition to these accounts, there was a variety of other materials: the deed to the mountain that had been donated to Zuikōin, documents accounting for income and weaponry that were the property of Asano Daigaku, copies of applications for checkpoint passes for women of the domain—a total of sixteen items in all.

Finally, on the last day of the Eleventh Month, Kuranosuke wrote and added to the other papers in the box a letter addressed to Ochiai Yozaemon. None of this material would be sent until the eve of the attack, of course, lest somehow the plot be compromised. But everything was now in readiness to be delivered. Kuranosuke wrote:

> *With this brief missive, I take the liberty to convey to you my most respectful greetings. Above all, I delight to think that Yōzei'in Sama enjoys ever increasing good health and spirits. I can well imagine how distressing she must find the removal of Daigaku Sama to Hiroshima. That was a matter quite beyond our control. Since then, I have purposely refrained from asking after him, even by letter. I am pleased, though, that all remains well with your good self as you carry on with your duties.*
>
> *Item. As I mentioned when we met last winter, the uses to which I have put the funds that I assumed control of last spring in Akō, and have since used to further our cause, are recorded in detail in the enclosed account books. From the 19th of the Third Month of last year, all such disbursements—in gold, silver, or rice—were verified and recorded by our Financial Officer Yatō Chōsuke, and are accompanied by receipts signed by their recipients. All of these I hereby enclose and submit to you.*
>
> *Item. Those funds that remained I myself took possession of on the 4th Day of the Sixth Month, carried them with me to Yamashina, disbursed them bit by bit, and recorded their use in an account book. Not the slightest portion of them was used to cover any of my personal expenses. Kindly check the account book carefully against the receipts, all of which are enclosed with it. If all seems in order, might I ask that you bring these details to the attention of Yōzei'in Sama whenever you have an opportunity? I also submit to you various other documents, as I promised I would do last year. By rights, I should submit these to Daigaku Sama as well, but purposely have refrained from doing so. If in your opinion it would be best to apprise Hiroshima of their contents, then I beg to avail myself of your good offices in doing so.*
>
> *Item. Among the aforementioned funds were some 5 kanme [= 90 ryō] of interest on money belonging to Yōzei'in Sama that had been collected in Akō. As I said when we met last winter, if Daigaku Sama*

had been free, I should by rights have reported this and returned the money to him; but since he now has been removed to Hiroshima, I have not done so. Moreover, I have since disbursed this money to make up deficiencies in the funding of our cause. Reluctant though I am to do so, might I trouble you to seek Her Ladyship's acquiescence to my appropriation of these funds, regarding them as a grant to be distributed among all concerned? Details of these expenditures are recorded in the account book; if you will kindly compare them with the accounts kept by Chōsuke, you will see clearly to what uses they have been put.

Item. In addition to the accounts and receipts, I submit documents of various other sorts, such as maps and plans, that I have thought might be of some use. Kindly consult the list of these materials that accompanies them.

Item. Concerning the mountain that was donated to Zuikōin: Just after we left Kyoto, I heard word of some malfeasance that had gone on there. I have known since last year that the Superior of the temple is an untrustworthy monk. But the Master of Shūsuian, the hermitage within the temple grounds, is scrupulously honest; since it is his desire to husband the mountain well so that it may remain a resource for the temple in years to come, I have entreated him earnestly to do so. Even if the Superior himself should ask for the deed to the mountain, sending it to him would surely result in further malfeasance. for which reason you should exercise great caution in this matter. I would appreciate it if Tosa-no-Kami's Liaison Officer in Kyoto could be made cognizant of our problem with this mountain, and he were now and again to mention the matter to both the Superior and the Master of Shūsuian, Kaishuso. I mention this to you as I am deeply desirous that the mountain remain the property of the temple in order to cover the funerary expenses of our late lord in perpetuity.

Item. Concerning the possessions of Ōno Kurōbei: as I said last winter, this is a matter that should be brought to the attention of Daigaku Sama and should be subject to his approval; but as things *stand now, we've no possibility of consulting him. Besides which, now that a new castellan has been assigned to Akō, the matter can no longer be left unattended to. As luck would have it, however, I have heard from a representative of the Interim Intendant in Akō that Kurōbei has submitted a petition, through an intermediary, that he be allowed to reclaim his possessions because he is financially hard-pressed. I immediately replied that his petition should be granted as requested. I have collected the documents that detail the particulars of this matter and submit these to you as well.*

Item. Might I ask that you dispatch without fail the enclosed paper-wrapped parcel to Inoue Dan'emon Dono. It will apprise him of matters concerning funds and weapons belonging to Daigaku Sama. I send these copies of the relevant documents so that he may peruse them. As I am no longer resident in Kyoto, it will not be necessary to reply to this letter.

ELEVENTH MONTH, 29TH DAY   *Ōishi Kuranosuke [monogram]*

To: Ochiai Yozaemon Sama,
via his entourage

There was unfinished business that Kuranosuke had left behind in Kyoto, too. But that he would have to persuade others to handle in his stead. One of those he was depending upon was the monk Shōsan, the guardian and mentor of his adopted son, Ōnishibō Kaku'un, who was training to become the Superior of a small temple on Otokoyama in Yawata. These are some of Kuranosuke's last requests to Shōsan:

Item. How goes it with the Yamashina property? If the business at hand here is resolved this month, the conveyance may not yet be complete. We must keep close watch on that transaction.

Item. What have the turncoats been saying against us? I can imagine only too well what sort of brave nonsense Oyama, Shindō, and their ilk have been noising about. Although it is of no significance, I would be interested to hear what they are up to. My departure must be widely known there by now.

Item. *There is the matter of the pregnancy of Nijō [Nimonjiya O-Karu], concerning which I have asked Genkei's assistance. If the child is delivered safely, Genkei is to send O-Karu a bit of money, no matter where she may be. And lest the child grow up in abject poverty, I would ask you to give it your kind attention as well. I've also written to Ōnishibō about this. For if the child should grow up to be a prostitute, whether male or female [yarō, hakujin, nado], that would be tragic. This is a worry that I could do without just now, but it does trouble me somewhat and distracts my attention from our cause. Thus my entreaty to you.*

Item. *Since our arrival, I've had hardly a moment to myself, nor has there been a day I've been able to pass at leisure. The amusements and sights of the city are of no interest to me. My mind is focused ever and entirely upon the people who have come here with me. I am totally resigned to whatever judgment King Enma may pass upon me, although even in the midst of the bustle, I feel an occasional twinge of wistful longing for Kyoto.*

◆ ◆ ◆

The entire force was now assembled in Edo, but scattered around the city as they were, they had yet to meet one another as a single group. Some had not seen some of the others since they left Akō. And some may not have known one another very well even before the Catastrophe. If they were to attack on the 5th Day of the Twelfth Month, it was time for a meeting, a convocation of all fifty-some men who remained members of the pact:

On the 2nd Day of the Twelfth Month, all members of our pact gathered at a large teahouse in front of the Fukagawa Hachiman Shrine. We told the proprietor that, with the year drawing to a close, we had decided to form a mutual aid society, and so today we had to get together and discuss the matter, which was why all of us were

there. We talked things over the whole day long, and at nightfall we
all went home.

Fukagawa is nowadays a rather lively locale, an unlikely place for fur-
tive meetings. But in Genroku, Toda Mosui says, Fukagawa Hachiman
was a little-frequented shrine, so remote from the city and distant from
the castle that the area failed to prosper. For which reason, he says, the
authorities relaxed their enforcement of regulations and allowed the
building of many teahouses, completely filling the two or three blocks
in front of the shrine. They then turned a blind eye when these estab-
lishments began to keep a number of women for the delectation of
worshippers at the shrine. In Genroku 15, therefore, only four years
after the completion of the Eitaibashi Bridge (1698), a teahouse at
Fukagawa Hachiman would have been an out-of-the-way venue, not at
all conspicuous to prying eyes.

◆ ◆ ◆

What went on at this daylong meeting—who said what, and about
what—is not recorded. The general purpose of it, though, is not hard
to surmise. With an attack in the offing, the overall plan of battle, the
memorandum of which we have already seen, would have to be reviewed
and discussed. It was also emended in small but important ways. Since
much of the fighting would take place indoors, all lances should be cut
to about 9 feet in length. Sword hilts should be wrapped in cotton or
flat cord to ensure a better grip. Everyone should carry smelling salts,
styptic powder, rice balls, and a small sum of money. And to these,
Horibe Yasubei added a precaution based on his own experience at
Takadanobaba: everyone's sash should be threaded with a length of fine
chain, for if one's sash should be cut—as Yasubei's was—one loses one's
swords and one's clothing comes undone.

Less practical, but no less important, however, was the swearing of
the new oath mentioned by Kuranosuke in his original general orders
issued from Hirama. A draft of this had been prepared by Horibe Yahei
and refined in the course of the two-day meeting of the "old men":

Item. *We the samurai who are determined to kill and take the heads of Kira Kōzuke-no-Suke and his son Sahei, hated enemies of Reikōin [Takumi-no-Kami] Sama, having reached agreement among ourselves, and having purged our ranks of those cowards who refuse to join us on this occasion—we who have decided that we shall fight to the death, now call upon the honored spirit of our late lord to be our witness.*

Item. *In our attack upon the Kōzuke mansion, no distinctions shall be made between greater and lesser feats of arms. He who takes the head of Kōzuke-no-Suke or his son shall be considered the equal of he who merely stands guard. Thus must no one voice a preference for assignment to any particular group or duty. The entire group shall act as a single unit; no one shall express the slightest discontent, no matter what duty or function he may be assigned.*

Item. *In expressing their personal opinions, individual members of the group must bear no grudges against any of the others, or speak in an obstructive or disruptive manner. Everyone must work together constructively. Even those who may previously have entertained feelings of discontent must in this operation help and look after one another, and strive for total victory.*

Item. *Once we have succeeded in taking the heads of Kōzuke-no-Suke and his son, no one must think of fleeing to save his own life. As we have previously agreed, we are not to scatter hither and yon. Even if some are wounded, we must help them to assemble at the appointed place. Should there be those who fail to observe these four provisions, the entire operation could fail; they shall thus be considered as cowardly as those refused to join us.*

As an oath sworn before the gods,

Once Kuranosuke had read aloud these four provisions to which everyone must swear, one by one, each of the ronin signed his name, added his monogram, and then drew his short sword 1 or 2 inches out of its scabbard, slit his left thumb lightly on the blade, and affixed his blood print to the oath. At this point, there were fifty signatures. When everyone parted, they were expecting to meet again and attack three days hence.

CHAPTER
58

Life is short, and we all must die; I shall just be
ending my life a bit sooner than expected.

Matters that we would now call "political" would not have concerned
most of the ronin who were preparing to attack. But the same could not
be said of Kuranosuke and perhaps some of the other "old men" who
would lead them. Ōtaka Gengo had somehow ascertained that Kira
would definitely be having guests for tea on the evening of the 5th Day
of the Twelfth Month, and the entire force had been alerted; they were
to attack in the small hours of that night.

But then news had come from an unnamed source that the Shogun, on
that very day, would be paying a visit to the home of his Chief Adjutant,
Yanagisawa Mino-no-Kami. To most of the ronin, this was no news at
all. Kuranosuke, however—as a former Chief Elder, for whom "politics"
had been the stuff of everyday life—could see that an attack on the 5th
might not be considered a mere coincidence, that it could be taken as an
intentional affront to the Shogun who had decreed that Kira would not
be punished. Kuranosuke had on several occasions stated clearly that
the object of their enmity was Kira alone, not the Shogunate. Now, he
felt, he dared not act in opposition to that stance. At the last minute, he
called off that night's attack. Indeed, it must have been on the very day
of the attack that he canceled it, for in a letter dated the 5th, Kayano
Wasuke had already written to his kinsmen in Tsuyama:

> *I write to tell you that about fifty of us, under the leadership of*
> *Ōishi Kuranosuke, are about to slay the enemy of our lord. Were*
> *I to miss this chance, it would stain the honor of our entire family,*

and in particular reflect badly upon Takejirō and my son Inokichi. I myself, of course, would be deemed no warrior at all. . . . Life is short, and we all must die; I shall just be ending my life a bit sooner than expected. And so, come what may, in keeping with this principle, early in the morning of the morrow we shall attack the Kira mansion. If luck is with me, and I die having fought a good fight, I shall consider myself fortunate.

Kaiga Yazaemon says that he and some of the older men could see that the young men would never abide this cancellation. The Shogun's social peregrinations were of no interest to them, and certainly no reason to give up their first sure chance of catching Kira at home. And so the older men persuaded Ōtaka Gengo to tell them that the tea gathering itself had been canceled. That was a mistake. It was only a matter of three or four days before the young men learnt that Gengo had lied to them, which made them even angrier at Kuranosuke for being "two-faced" than cancellation alone would have done. The integrity of the pact was not threatened, but now Kuranosuke had to deal with nearly fifty men on the verge of mutiny. Yazaemon says that he somehow managed to placate them, but I suspect that it was Hara Sōemon's air of calm authority that did it, rather than Kuranosuke's own powers of persuasion.

Sōemon had been sent to Yasubei's lodgings to deal with the matter, and he could hear the commotion even before he opened the door. Being an even-tempered man, Sōemon was always saying, "Now let's calm down and take it easy." When he entered the room, the men were shouting: "How long is this going to go on, all this dithering? Every day, there's a new excuse. When are they going to make up their minds?"

Sōemon responded with his usual, "Calm down now. Let's take it easy. . . ." Whereupon Fuwa Kazuemon burst forth with a satirical poem:

> *mi-uma yori hodo yō sen to korarete wa*
> *dosha kakerarete kaeru mototoki*
> From south-by-east he blows in to tell us,
> "Calm down, now; take it easy";

but back he goes, Mototoki, all the wind knocked out of him.

Even Sōemon himself had to laugh. For the moment at least, the situation was defused. And fortunately, not long thereafter, a new chance appeared in the offing.

✦ ✦ ✦

Two days later, on the 7th, Kuranosuke wrote to Ōishi Mitsuhira: "Will you be coming here today? I've heard from another source that there is to be a gathering sometime after the 10th. I'd like some verification of this. Might I ask you to inquire into the matter and let me know the details when I see you?"

From whom Kuranosuke heard this report, we do not know, but Katashima Shin'enshi relates a version of the episode that he heard. How reliable Shin'enshi's source was must remain a question, but this is what he was told.

Yokogawa Kanpei, who was lodging with Yasubei in Hayashi-chō at the time, had befriended an old monk who lived in the neighborhood. This monk was a great devotee of tea and had been a guest at the Kira mansion several times; but according to Shin'enshi, he was illiterate. And so he asked Kanpei to write a note accepting his most recent invitation. I suspect that Shin'enshi exaggerates a bit, calling the man illiterate; he could hardly have read his invitation if he were. But his eyesight may well have been failing. In any case, Kanpei not only wrote the acceptance, but was kind enough to deliver it to the Kira mansion himself. Following which, he immediately carried the news to Kuranosuke—of both the invitation and what he had seen when he delivered it.

Whatever the source of this report, though, no further news seems to have been forthcoming. Four days later, they still knew nothing definite, which moved Horibe Yahei, obviously in a state of some anxiety, to write to Mitsuhira on the 11th: "Now that the 5th has been postponed, has another date been decided upon? I'm very worried that it might even be tomorrow. I'd like to know by this evening, so if you can find out before then, difficult though that may be, please get word to me as soon as you can."

Yahei's letter produced no more information than Kuranosuke's had. But two days later, there were at last signs of movement. When Masé Kyūdayū visited Kuranosuke on the 13th, Kuranosuke told him that he had heard indirectly from Itsuki that there would be guests on the 14th. He then asked Kyūdayū to ask Mitsuhira to visit Itsuki and check whether the 14th was indeed the date. Kyūdayū decided that he would go to Itsuki himself. Itsuki told him that he thought the gathering was still on, but that he was not yet absolutely certain. Once he found out for certain, he said, he would let them know, probably first thing the next morning. Kyūdayū reported this not only to Kuranosuke, but also, by letter, to Mitsuhira's father, Ōishi Mujin. At this point, Kuranosuke began calling his cadre together.

♦ ♦ ♦

Early on the morning of the 13th, Yahei wrote again to Mitsuhira:

> *Yesterday when I called upon Kuranosuke, he asked me to send word that evening requesting that you be certain to come to him today. But I was busy in the evening and put it off. This is a little late, therefore, but please, by all means, do come to Ōishi's place today. There are certain matters that he wishes to discuss with you. I, too, shall be going immediately after breakfast. If you come early, I shall see you there. Herewith the foregoing.*

When Mitsuhira arrived at Kuranosuke's place, in response to both Yahei's request and Kyūdayū's letter to his father, he probably had with him a letter that he had just received from Hakura Itsuki. Most of this letter concerned matters entirely unrelated to the attack; but at the very end, following the date, there was a postscript that read: "As for the matter in question, I chanced to hear that it probably will take place on the 14th."

Kuranosuke now had a date. Itsuki's letter to Mitsuhira confirmed what Itsuki had told Kyūdayū. Itsuki still could not claim absolute certainty, but Mitsuhira would call at Sanjikkenbori the next morning in the hope that by then, he would know for certain.

✦ ✦ ✦

Tominomori Suke'emon was thus able to write to Ōishi Mujin: "I write in haste. As regards the confidential matter in question, we understand at last that there are to be guests on the morrow; but since we are still somewhat uncertain, we intend to await further word of Itsuki's efforts. Given which, would you kindly come to Kuranosuke's lodgings sometime after midday today? Herewith the foregoing."

Such were the goings on among the members of the command group. In the meantime, Kaiga Yazaemon tells us, the men who were going to fight this battle were just as busy. Even before the date was definite, Kuranosuke sent word that everyone should pay their rent and settle any outstanding bills by the 12th, and then tell their landlords that they had completed their business in Edo and would be returning to Kyoto on the 14th. If anyone lacked sufficient funds to do this, Kuranosuke said, they should let him know and he would make up the shortfall from a fund set aside for that purpose. And so, on the evening of the 13th, the younger men gathered at Yasubei's lodgings, pooled whatever money they had left, spent it on saké and snacks, and held a drinking party. They were bidding one another their last farewells in this life, they laughed. Some might die sooner, some later; but they would all meet again in the netherworld and report to their lord that they had exacted the satisfaction of his wrath.

✦ ✦ ✦

At about the same time, Kuranosuke summoned Chikamatsu Kanroku and his personal retainer, Jinzaburō, to Koku-chō. Jinzaburō was the son of the Headman of the village of Hiruta, Kanroku's ancestral home in the province of Ōmi, and he had proved himself a diligent and intelligent young man. Which probably is why Kuranosuke singled him out to deliver the box of documents that he had prepared as well as the letter that he had written on the 29th of the previous month. He was to take them to Ochiai Yōzaemon at the middle mansion of the Miyoshi cadet house, Kuranosuke told him. Yozaemon would know without being told what this meant and would inform Takumi-no-Kami's widow, Yōzei'in, that at last the time had come. Her late husband would soon be avenged.

◆ ◆ ◆

The morning of the 14th passed slowly while the ronin awaited confirmation of that evening's tea gathering. A little after midday, however, Mitsuhira arrived at Kuranosuke's lodgings with word that Kira definitely had returned to Honjo and would be entertaining guests that very evening. Shortly thereafter, Ōtaka Gengo, too, entered and announced that his mentor, the tea master Yamada Sōhen, had mentioned that he would be attending a gathering at the Kira mansion, probably that evening, but if not, then within the next two or three days. No more certain confirmation could be hoped for. It even seemed to some that fortune had been working with them in postponing the attack until now, for, of course, the 14th was the monthly memorial of their late lord's death. Success seemed assured.

*I am only too well aware of the depth of my sin
in subjecting you to this bitter hardship.*

Early in the morning of the 13th, a heavy bank of dark clouds began rolling in from the northwest. By daybreak, it was snowing, and the wind had turned bitter cold. There had been flurries two or three times earlier in the month, but now it snowed hard. If this were to keep up, it could prove difficult to get about on the morrow and very difficult to wield a sword with fingers stiff from cold. In their unheated tenements, the ronin found it almost as difficult to wield a writing brush, which is exactly what many of them were doing, in between last-minute preparations: writing to wives, children, parents, kinsmen, or friends; reminiscing; taking leave for the last time before the attack—and trying to explain why they were choosing to die and why they thought it right to do so, despite the difficulties it would create for those they were leaving behind.

✦ ✦ ✦

Kanzaki Yogorō must have been one of the more interesting of those fifty men gathered in Edo. This was the second time in his life that he had become a ronin. He had inherited his father's position as a vassal of Mori Mimasaka-no-Kami in the domain of Tsuyama. But when Mimasaka-no-Kami died without heir, the domain was, of course, declared forfeit. Yogorō, however, somehow managed to find a position in Akō, although at a stipend of only five gold pieces and rations for three per year. Yet it was he whom Kuranosuke dispatched to Edo after the Yamashina meetings, and he who, on his own initiative, opened a small shop opposite the Kira property even before Kira himself had moved there. Added to this, he was one of the most talented and prolific composers of poetry in the group. With his partner Maebara Isuke, he is also the author of a scathing critique of some of his fellow ronin, *Sekijō meiden*. And he was a great, and appreciative, drinker besides. I like to think that we can see something of the depth of the man in his farewell letters. To his kinsman Tōgorō, he wrote:

> *The time of our attack draws near, and I fear that I shall not have the chance to raise another cup with you. Saké is dreadfully expensive here, and as a ronin I find it difficult to drink as much as I would like to. That is my only regret. But at least my comrades take pity on me and keep me supplied, so there is never a day when I haven't a saké cup in my hand. Vast and limitless are the virtues of saké, in every way imaginable. You are fortunate to have so many close kinfolk, and I pray that you shall never know hardship. Kindly take this as my parting wish for you.*

And to his wife, O-Katsu:

> *I'm very sorry to hear that you worry so about me that you feel all choked up. And I truly appreciate your saying that there isn't a moment when you forget me. But please try to put yourself in my place and do your best for Mother. It is not right for the wife of a samurai to be this way. Please do try to get hold of yourself. I miss you terribly, too, but it is my duty as a warrior to do this.*

Chikamatsu Kanroku was quite as filial as any of his comrades, but neither of his parents still lived. His mother had died thirty years earlier and his father, seventeen. So he wrote to the woman who had raised him in their stead, his old nursemaid. The letter is also addressed to the nursemaid's son Sakubei, who probably was born at about the same time as Kanroku, and thus would have grown up with him, almost as a brother.

When I was very young, I lost my mother, and you were kind enough to raise me until I had grown up. Even now, I am certain that your devotion and your sincerity far exceed that of the usual nursemaid. With this brush alone, I could never express the full extent of my gratitude. I had hoped to be able to care for you throughout your lifetime, but to my great misfortune, I have become a ronin. I hope you can accept that this, as with everything in life, was my fate, determined in a previous existence. To Sakubei, I would say: "Look after your mother well, and I shall be both pleased and grateful to you."

Kimura Okaemon, the Officer in Charge of Maps and Plans, had been one of those required to remain behind with Kuranosuke after the surrender of the castle, in order to produce the documents needed for submission to the Inspectors from Edo. Thereafter, he and his wife and children moved to a village in the district of Katō. They were anything but well off, for Okaemon's letters reveal that he had sold his armor to a samurai in the nearby castle town of Ono, and he had asked to be paid in rice for other possessions that he had been forced to sell. Yet despite his family's poverty, he answered Kuranosuke's call to Edo. To his wife, O-Tomé, who was by then settled in Osaka, he wrote on the night before the canceled attack:

As I have told you in confidence, Ōishi Kuranosuke and the others have gathered here in order to kill His Lordship's enemy Kira Kōzuke-no-Suke, and I have agreed to join them. About fifty of us will attack a daimyo mansion, and we are thus, one and all, resigned to death. We are very keen to take the heads of Kira Dono and his son. I worry, though, that you will be upset when you hear that I have died. Yet anyone born into a samurai house, even a woman, must accept that such things may happen; so you must not, under any circumstances, lament this. I am forty-six, not of an age you could call young. I could just as well die of illness. But I would far prefer to perish in the service of my liege lord. And yet—and yet, I do know what hardship this will create for you in caring for O-Saké and O-Mino. . . . As for yourself, as I have said already, after I die, you should remarry immediately. If you decide to start calling yourself a widow, I shall be very upset, even though I lie beneath the grass. If you find a suitable match, then you must by all means marry just as soon as fifty days have passed. And if there is no suitable partner, then you could go into service, either in Akō or among the townspeople where you are now, and work while you wait to hear of an opportunity to marry.

Each and every one of the fifty men participating in this attack is certain to die. Ōtaka Gengo leaves behind his aged mother; his brother Onodera Kōemon and his nephew Kin'emon will die with him. Hazama Kihei and his two sons will all die together. Masé Kyūdayū, too, will die with his son. As will other parents die with their children. I, at least, will die alone, which should cause far less grief than in other quarters. Many young men will die, too, some only eighteen or nineteen or in their twenties. Your own grief will be light, so you mustn't be too upset. My brother Gen'emon says that he will not let you down, so be strong and don't let yourself go to pieces. Comport yourself in such a way that people will say, "Okaemon gave his life in the service of his liege lord, and his wife, too, behaved with great dignity and composure."

Okano Kin'emon was the son of Onodera Jūnai's younger brother and until recently had been named Kujūrō. After the dispersal of the Corps of Vassals, the family had moved to the village of Tai, in the countryside to the north of Akō, where Kin'emon the elder had died only three months earlier, at the age of forty-eight. Kujūrō then assumed his father's name, Kin'emon, and his father's place as a signatory of the pact. From Edo, he wrote to his mother:

The time has now come when all of us who have joined together are about to die. From the time I left home, I was resigned to the fact that I should never return again. That I had decided long ago; yet the memory of you, Mother, I nonetheless find a great deterrent on the road to death. Even so, please try very hard to think of this as the way a samurai must be and do not lament it too deeply. This is the way it has been since ages past and is nothing to grieve over. Those of us in this family who together will give our lives for our lord consider this a filial tribute to our mothers. I do worry, though, what sort of impression you will make when you hear what has become of us. You must resign yourself to the fact that such is the way things are in this dismal world. I am only too well aware of the depth of my sin in subjecting you to this bitter hardship—we whom fate has somehow brought together as parent and child.

Hazama Jūjirō seems to have been a great friend of Takebayashi Tadashichi, which may explain why his last letter should be addressed to Tadashichi's elder brother, Watanabe Han'emon, who remained in Akō to care for his ill and aged parents. Jūjirō told him about his life in Edo; his anger at those who defected after wasting the money spent on their trips to Edo; how he and Tadashichi managed to see a good bit of each other, despite living nearly 2 leagues apart; and then concluded:

I do wish that I could get together with you one more time and tell you all about our troubles and tribulations here, but I shall just have to entreat you, most earnestly, to look after everyone there for me in my absence. For my own part, I've enjoyed myself in Shimabara, Yoshiwara, and Fushimi—one night in each place—so I've no regrets to leave behind me in this world. But I do greatly pity my poor woman there in Akō.

There are many more such letters, but with these as a sample, we can leave the last word to Kuranosuke. If he wrote to any members of his family in Toyooka, those letters do not survive. His last surviving letter, written on the day of the attack, is addressed to Terai Genkei, and his chief concern, as always, was that the stories told after the vendetta—and after their death—be true:

Item. I am delighted to say that we have decided upon the early-morning hours of this present night to execute our secret mission. I am sure that Gentatsu will tell you everything that happens hereafter. We are very grateful for his kindness in staying so long with us and attending to all our medical needs. . . .

Item. For your diversion, I enclose a copy of the manifesto we intend to leave behind for the perusal of those who come to investigate. As a courtesy to the authorities, in keeping with the custom of this noble house, and since several of our number are higher-ranking officers, I have thought it best for our reputation to produce such a manifesto. I send as well a list of assignments for the attack, as I expect that you will be curious about these matters. I also send a separate list ranking everyone according to the degree of their devotion over this past year. As you suggested some time ago, everyone is listed by name, in the order that I have assigned them for their fidelity and their contribution to the cause. As I said, these are materials you will be able to use. I understand that Jūnai has given you a copy of the text written by Kanzaki Yogorō and Maebara Isuke. We have read it, but have our doubts about it. In the first place, it is full of errors. And their more irresponsible claims will be of no use to you.

Item. I am extremely grateful for your friendship over the years and your devotion on this particular occasion. How very unfortunate that it must end like this. My son Chikara, too, asks that I convey his best wishes to you.

TWELFTH MONTH, 14TH DAY   *Ōishi Kuranosuke [monogram]*
To: Terai Genkei Sama,
via his entourage

✦ ✦ ✦

Tominomori Suke'emon was writing no letters. His wife, and now his infant son, had remained with him since the Catastrophe, when the family moved first to Karube Gohei's farmstead in Hirama, and then back into the city, in Kōjimachi.

Suke'emon was out in the snow, on his way to Honjo for his nightly check on the Kira mansion. Few faces were visible under the umbrellas and hats and shawls. His own features must have been visible, though, for as he was crossing the Ryōgoku Bridge, a man passing at his elbow suddenly wheeled and called out, "Shunban!" This was the nom de plume with which Suke'emon signed his *haikai* verses, and the man who uttered it was Kuwaoka Teisa, a leader of the *haikai* circle to which Suke'emon had belonged when he was stationed in Edo.

"Shunban! You're back in Edo? Good to see you!" The two men immediately fell to chatting, oblivious of the snow swirling about them. Teisa told Suke'emon of his recent trip to Kyoto, and Suke'emon said, "I've composed a verse about the hail. Tell me what you think of it.

tonde iru / te ni mo tomaranu / arare kana
Bounding in it comes, yet no hand can hold it: the hail.

It seemed rather an untimely verse for the middle of a snowstorm, Teisa thought; but, then, it hadn't been composed right there, on the spot. It was a fine effort, he told Suke'emon. There followed talk of Gengo and other members of the circle, as well as other verses. And then the two men parted—perhaps with a promise to meet again at a later date.

CHAPTER
60

$\blacksquare\!\!\!\blacksquare\!\!\!\blacksquare\!\!\!\!-\!\!\!\!-\!\!\!\!-\!\!\!\!-\!\!\!\!-\!\!\!\!-\!\!\!\!-$

This is our last chance to share our feelings for each other.

Even on the day before the attack, final confirmation had not been received. But the date now seemed certain enough that they felt it foolish to put off preparing themselves, only to be caught short of time when final confirmation did come. Each man's priorities differed a bit from those of every other man; but Kuranosuke, who was responsible for all the men under his command, felt that the time had come to send his two his personal retainers, who would not be participating in the attack, back home to Akō. Kasemura Kōshichi had come to Edo with Chikara, and Muroi Saroku had come with Kuranosuke. They had shared in all the hardships since the Catastrophe; they were privy to all the plotting and planning; they had served Kuranosuke, and many of the other men, tirelessly. Now it was time to bid them farewell. And since they would be passing through Kyoto on their way home, both Kuranosuke and Onodera Jūnai asked them to carry their last letters to Jūnai's wife, O-Tan. This is what Kuranosuke wrote:

> *Having given my retainers Saroku and Kōshichi leave to return to the capital, I take this opportunity to write to you.*
>
> *It has been bitterly cold here. I hear news of you regularly from your letters to Jūnai and am glad to know that you are well. Jūnai is lodging with me now and is in good health. It is a great delight to be spending day and night with him, chatting away at our ease. You are not to fret about us, for we want for nothing. I can imagine only too well, though, what a worry it must be for you, as time stretches*

on day after day. I'll just tell you a bit of what goes on here.

It troubles me that, since our arrival, we've been delayed so much longer than I had expected. Still, preparations are now well in hand. I'm pleased that in that respect, things have turned out quite differently from what I had expected when we were in Kyoto. Within a short while, the matter should be resolved to our satisfaction. You may rest assured that nothing further remains to be attended to. It won't be much longer now.

As I've said before, when I think how many men of Jūnai's family are now prepared to die for loyalty, and what a reputation their devotion is bound to make for them in ages to come—well, I am very envious. My own family are a great bunch of cowards. There is only myself and my son and a single kinsman, Sezaemon. It is shameful. And only a few days ago, on the 3rd, my retainer Magozaemon absconded. Just when I was thinking, with some pleasure, what a credit it was to us that even so low-ranking a man as he should join us, he does this utterly disgraceful thing. But then, it is nothing unusual, for the high in rank as well as the low.

I must also inform you that Kōemon Dono and Gengo Dono are well and thriving. The moment approaches inexorably, yet we pass the days in idleness, having no notion whatever whether it will be the end of this year or the beginning of the New Year. Already the merrymakers are making their rounds, reminding me that the year is coming to an end. Sometimes, Jūnai and I just burst out laughing at ourselves—at what a truly bizarre situation we find ourselves in.

I used to come and visit you so often in Kyoto, and you would cook for me; now all of that seems like a dream from long, long ago. I grew so accustomed to living there that now I tend to talk only of things in the capital, which makes both of us smile with nostalgia— and regret.

I can't resist the amusing thought that these two men I'm sending home are my Oniō and Dōzaburō, as faithful to us as those men of old were to the Soga brothers. Right up until the present moment, they have served us unfailingly, day and night, with never a thought for themselves. Their devotion has been extraordinary, far out of proportion with their rank. Of lowly station they may be, but as different from Magozaemon as are clouds different from mud. It seems a terrible pity that this must happen to such dependable people. When I heard that Saroku would be calling upon you, I wanted to let you know that Jūnai is in good health, and also to bid you farewell. I expect that by the time this reaches you, there'll be no point in replying. Sincerely,

TWELFTH MONTH, 10TH DAY   *Ōishi Kuranosuke*
To the wife of Jūnai Sama,
proffered with respect

P.S. You must take particular care to keep in good health. And you're not to worry about Jūnai Dono. We are together constantly, drinking saké and whatnot. Every day is a delight; we're actually having a very good time. Saroku will tell you all about it. Yours sincerely,

I can't help but wonder whether O-Tan found Kuranosuke's letter anywhere near as heartening as he obviously intended it to be. To be reminded that so many of her closest male relatives were soon to die, and to be assured that Kuranosuke and her husband were "actually having a very good time," might well have seemed cold comfort to someone as lonely and bereft as O-Tan. Her husband's letter—also carried by Saroku and Kōshichi—offers no more cause for optimism than Kuranosuke's, but at least is free from any well-meant attempt at jollity:

I take this opportunity to address a quick word to you. My recent letters must have reached you by now, so I expect that you'll be waiting and wondering, "Has it happened yet? Has it happened yet?" I can imagine only too well how that must feel. But the time has now come, and barring some unforeseen disaster, there will be no further change of plans. The deed should be done before these next three days are out.

Item. All the effort that we have expended and the hardships that we have endured over these past two years are about to bear fruit; and now that that moment has arrived, it inspires us all the more with satisfaction and delight. Of course, the other party, too, will be prepared. The outcome will depend upon whose portion of a warrior's good fortune is greater. As I've said before, no matter what sort of punishment the authorities may mete out to us—even if they expose our dead bodies in public—you are not to feel the slightest regret or distress. To display to the warriors of the world the bodies of men who have died for the sake of loyalty should, in fact, be an inspiration to everyone. Nothing could give us greater satisfaction. These being our own sentiments on the matter, you must not harbor even the slightest anxiety on our account. You can set your mind at ease. And knowing as I do how much in accord with us you have been all along, I am quite certain that you'll not disgrace yourself, no matter what sort of suffering may chance to come your way. And should it be your lot to escape punishment, I know that you possess the intelligence to make your way through life in one way or another. My mind is completely at rest on that score. At this point, I have no more regrets; I can set forth into battle in good spirits. I do hope that you, too, can find some small satisfaction in this. We are not alone in this present predicament, and it is such an extraordinary sequence of events that has brought things to this pass, thus causing you all this misery, that it seems to me fruitless to fret whether it might be caused by bad karma from some time past. This is simply an inexorable stroke of fate, and we've both no choice but to accept it as such.

Item. Your first notification that matters here have been settled will come to you from Genkei. Be very sure to keep in mind all that I've told you of late when you hear reports of what other people are saying. Whatever you deem suitable you may pass on in appropriate form to everyone: to Jūbei, of course, and Kanezawa Dono, as well as Tōsuke and O-Roku, and Wataya Zen'emon. I've purposely refrained from telling Jūbei. I've never talked with him about this or written to him since coming to Edo. He may think this unfriendly of me; but afterward, do urge him, very earnestly, to consider the reasons for my reticence and forgive me, for I can never thank him *enough for his continued concern, which has been far greater than I deserve. If it should happen that you escape punishment, I must ask you to take care of this matter for me. I've not been in touch with any other members of the family either, so please be sure to tell them all that I've said. None of it can injure my honor as a warrior, so please put your mind at rest and pass all of this on to others in the family. You yourself should speak to Jūbei.*

Item. I would ask you, too, to have a care for Teiryū Sama and O-Chiyo. You may tell Teiryū Sama everything that I've said in my letters. The time draws near. Here, of course, is where everyone comes to discuss plans and preparations. With so many people about, I finally had to retreat upstairs before dawn, just to write this letter. I haven't been able to write to anyone else. I'll have to ask you to contact Keian Dono and Saihōji Ryōkenbō and, of course, Ekōin Sama. I'll be sending my luggage in the next day or two. Circumstances permitting, I'll also write again, and I'll send you some poems that I've composed as well as some poem strips. I hope that you'll find some consolation in reading them. Already this place is alive with people. I'll have to put my brush away. From here on, I must leave everything in your hands. Sincerely,

LAST MONTH OF THE YEAR, 12TH DAY   *Onodera Jūnai*
To: O-Tan Dono

P.S. I'm certain that after we're gone, someone in Kyoto will write an account of this incident. Even here, there are already rumors to this effect. For us, there could be no greater satisfaction than to leave behind our names in writing for future generations throughout the land. I hope that you, too, might find some pleasure in reading such a thing, and at the very least you might treasure it as a memorial to your own name. But there'll be no word before we carry out our mission here. Herewith the foregoing.

Jūnai was probably able to give this next short note to Saroku and Kōshichi just before their departure on the same day:

My letter of the 11th should have reached you via Genkei by now. Our plans remain as described therein. There's nothing further to add—except that I think constantly about you in Kyoto. I've packed a luggage box with my night robe, two layers of bedding, a surcoat, and several small items; written up the bill of lading, and shipped it to you in care of Mino-ya Tahei. I've also sent a poem strip. Ōishi Chikara is now in his fifteenth year; he is 5 feet, 9 inches tall, and of character and conduct to match. He's so exceptional that I've asked him to inscribe a poem strip for you. He writes a fine hand. Kōemon and Kin'emon are equally impressive, so set your mind at rest on their account. Barring some unforeseen disaster, I shall write again. Sincerely,

TWELFTH MONTH, 13TH DAY   *Jūnai*
To: O-Tan Dono

The poem strip inscribed by Ōishi Chikara:

> *au toki wa kataritsukusu to omoitomo*
> *wakare to nareba nokoru koto no ha*
> When we were still together,
> I thought I must have told you all; and yet,
> now that we are parted, there remains so much more to say.

Saroku and Kōshichi were gone by now. This last note to O-Tan, written only hours before the attack, would be carried to her by the merchant Mino-ya Tahei:

Item. You've entrusted two gold pieces to Mino-ya Tahei with instructions that I should take receipt of them here. But I no longer need any money, so I'm returning them. You can pick them up from Tahei in Kyoto. You are far too good to me.

Item. My, but your poems are touching; I am just awash in tears. They are so heart-rending. As for the rest, this is a time of frantic preparation, so I'm unable to tell you about it in any detail. Do please

*understand. At his shop, Tahei said that he would be leaving tomor-
row morning for Kyoto. I expect that before long, you'll know what
has happened. This is our last chance to share our feelings for each
other. Please don't worry about us here. Herewith the foregoing,*

TWELFTH MONTH, 14TH DAY   *Jūnai*
To: O-Tan Dono,
in reply

*P.S. Just as I was about to write this, I received your letter from
Mino-ya. All is well. Sincerely,*

P.P.S. My farewell poem:

> *wasureme ya momo ni amareru toshi o hete*
> *tsukaeshi yoyo no kimi ga nasake o*

Could I ever forget? The kindness of the lords we've served, age upon age,
in a line now reaching back more than a hundred years.

CHAPTER
61

I wonder where we'll be
this time tomorrow.

At this point, we must renew our acquaintance with a man whom we met briefly in a previous chapter, Satō Jōemon. Jōemon, the reader may recall, was Horibe Yasubei's cousin, and the two men had been close friends—"just like brothers," as Yasubei put it—since their boyhood in the hinterlands of Echigo. Both men had been born samurai, but neither had any prospect of employment as samurai. Had they remained where they were, they, or their children, probably would have ended up as peasants.

Jōemon was the first to leave Echigo and seek his fortune in the great city of Edo. There he had found a place in the entourage of a bannerman, Suwa Iki-no-Kami, just before Suwa was appointed City Magistrate of Nagasaki. It was not a permanent position, but Jōemon had proved his worth as a samurai while stationed in Nagasaki, and thus was assured of honorable employment until a better opportunity should arise—and he was certainly better off than back in the village of Ushizaki.

Jōemon, you may also recall, was the first to encourage Yasubei to leave Togashira and move to Edo. It was likewise he who introduced Yasubei to his teacher of swordsmanship, Horiuchi Gendazaemon—which, in turn, led to Yasubei's fame as the hero of Takadanobaba, his adoption by Horibe Yahei, and ultimately his appointment to the Akō Horse Guards.

While all the travails described in the last several chapters were in train, we have seen nothing of Jōemon. But he was always there in the background, in constant touch with his cousin Yasubei, and thus fully aware of all that had transpired and all the plans that were being laid. Now we must look to Jōemon to continue that story, for fortunately, he has described in some detail all that he saw and heard on the day and night of the attack on the Kira mansion—a time when everyone else involved was far too busy to be writing anything.

◆ ◆ ◆

Jōemon had heard from someone (he doesn't say who) that the attack was to take place very soon. And so, despite the blizzard that had been blowing since early in the morning of the 13th, he trudged through the snow to the lodgings of Horibe Yahei in Yonezawa-chō. But Yahei was not at home; he was with Kuranosuke in Koku-chō just then. And if the rumor that Jōemon had heard was true, it made little sense for him to continue across the Ryōgoku Bridge to Yasubei's place, only to find that he, too, was in Koku-chō—no, not in this storm. Jōemon left a note, saying that he would call again tomorrow, and turned back to the training hall of his martial arts master in Koishikawa. Gendazaemon might have heard what was up. Yet he, too, was out, and Jōemon was by now exhausted. He could go no farther; he would spend the night there, sleeping as best he could on the polished planks of the practice floor.

◆ ◆ ◆

The 14th dawned bright and clear, as different as could be from the day before. The city was covered with a thick blanket of snow; but the cold front that had come with the snow remained, and the surface was neither slippery nor slushy but crunchy—almost as firm underfoot as a dry street.

After leaving the training hall, Jōemon went first to Kōjimachi to discuss the matter with Hara Sōemon, after which he "borrowed" a servant from Sōemon and set out again for Yahei's place. Quite a crowd had gathered there by now, but when Yahei saw that Jōemon had arrived, he took him aside and told him that the attack was to take place that night, in the small hours of the morning.

"Superb!" Jōemon said. "I'm just delighted. If you go on postponing it day after day, the perfect chance will never come." Yahei then called his wife over, and told her that it probably was best that they say nothing beforehand to their servants. He would let her know when she could tell them.

Jōemon now realized that he would not be returning home that night, so he wrote a note to the Adjutant of his benefactor, Suwa Iki-no-Kami, explaining his extended absence. He could not tell the truth, of course, so he concocted a total fiction: he had gone to visit his boyhood friend, only to find that his friend's mother was dangerously ill, and he did not wish to leave her side until she showed signs of recovery. Later, he would have to confess the truth; but by then, he hoped, he would have such a heroic tale to tell that everyone would forgive him. He also wrote a note to the younger brother of his teacher, asking him to pass on news of the attack to Gendazaemon. And to the borrowed servant, he gave a note to take home to Sōemon (after delivering the other two notes), expressing his delight that the weather would be so perfect tonight.

The rest of that afternoon, Jōemon made himself useful in various ways. Yasubei was now here with Yahei, but he needed to get word to some of the people across the river in Hayashi-chō; Jōemon offered to carry his messages, so Yasubei could stay with Yahei. There was a note for Sugino Jūheiji, who lived next door, and another note for Yasubei's long-time comrade Okuda Magodayū. Then, after he left Hayashi-chō, Jōemon went to the Hachiman Shrine in Fukagawa. The wives of Yasubei and Yahei had asked him to offer prayers in their stead for the success of tonight's attack. Magodayū walked part of the way there with him. He and Jōemon were fellow disciples of Horiuchi Gendazaemon, and they had much to discuss.

When Jōemon returned to Yahei's place in Yonezawa-chō, Yasubei and Kurahashi Densuke were calculating how much rent they still owed on the Hayashi-chō rooms, so they asked Jōemon to write a suitably formal-sounding statement that they could leave behind there. What Jōemon wrote does not survive; he tells us only that he wrote it on an unfolded sheet of fine paper. But I expect that it resembled the statement that Yasubei's neighbor, Jūheiji, had just left for his landlord:

We hope tonight to accomplish our aim of avenging the grievance of our late lord Takumi-no-Kami. I have been fortunate beyond my due to have lived so comfortably in these rented quarters of late. I wish that I might express my gratitude to you in person, but given the nature of the occasion, I must refrain from doing so. I trust that the accounting that I tender under separate cover will meet with your approval.

TWELFTH MONTH, 14TH DAY   *Sugino Jūheiji*
To my landlord, Chōjūrō Dono

Once all of this was done, Yasubei came downstairs and asked Jōemon to sit with him. For a time they talked of nothing in particular; then Yasubei paused.

"We'll get him! We'll take his head! I'm certain of it! But I wonder where we'll be this time tomorrow."

"And so may it be!" said Jōemon.

"At this time tomorrow," Yasubei said it again. "At this time tomorrow, we should all be able to relax."

"He seemed determined to leave nothing unsaid," Jōemon wrote. "He spoke as though he were able to see into the future."

◆ ◆ ◆

At the same time, on the far side of the river, last-minute precautions were being taken. Ōtaka Gengo had by then heard that Yamada Sōhen, his tea master, would definitely be attending a gathering at the Kira mansion that night, and so he stopped in again at Quay's End, probably in the hope of verifying that report. What he said or asked is not recorded, but it would have seemed suspicious if he had simply asked Sōhen his plans for the evening. Perhaps the subject was never mentioned. But after leaving, Gengo watched the house from a discreet distance until Sōhen left, and then followed until he could see him enter at the rear gate of the Kira mansion.

From their shop on the corner, Kanzaki Yogorō and Maebara Isuke were watching the same gate and were able to ascertain that guests were indeed arriving. They could not identify them, but there was now no question but that Kira would have to be there to receive them.

I am always mildly amused to think how astonished those guests must have been the next morning, when they realized that the "Forgetting the Old Year" gathering that they had attended would make this a year that would never be forgotten.

✦ ✦ ✦

In Koku-chō, as the sun fell low in the sky, Kuranosuke and Jūnai boarded town litters and left Oyamaya for the last time. They were on their way to Yahei's rooms in Yonezawa-chō, which was to be their final meeting place before everyone mustered on the far side of the river to dress for the attack. By sundown, Jōemon tells us, all the following people had arrived and filed up the stairs: Ōishi Kuranosuke, Ōishi Chikara, Yoshida Chūzaemon, Onodera Jūnai, Ushioda Matanojō, Chikamatsu Kanroku, Ōishi Sezaemon, Hayami Tōzaemon, Suganoya Hannojō, Fuwa Kazuemon, Kurahashi Densuke, Sugino Jūheiji, Masé Kyūdayū, Yoshida Sawaemon, and Terasaka Kichiemon. Jōemon remained below, helping out in the kitchen and serving soup, snacks, saké, and the like. In the course of which he said to Yahei, "I've never had the honor of meeting Kuranosuke; I'd like to make his acquaintance."

"Of course," Yahei said. "What with all the help you've given us, we really must include you. Just wait here. I'll call you from upstairs when there's a convenient moment." And soon thereafter, Yahei did call, and Jōemon went up.

"This is my son Yasubei's cousin, Satō Jōemon," Yahei said to the group. "Allow me to introduce you to him. He has known of our plans from the very start, so please do feel that you can be at your ease with him. He is our friend." Kuranosuke came over and greeted him, as did Hara Sōemon, Yoshida Chūzaemon, Masé Kyūdayū, Onodera Jūnai, and everyone else there. Then Jūnai spoke for them all: "We very much appreciate your thoughtfulness in coming to see us off tonight. We're quite heartened by it." To which Jōemon replied, "Then might I drink with you?" Kuranosuke held out a box of saké cups and said, "Here, take one of these." Jōemon seemed a bit flustered, but then said, "No, what I meant was, may I *share* a cup with you?" Whereupon Kuranosuke immediately passed his own cup to Jōemon and filled it for him. Before long, Jōemon had exchanged cups with everyone in the room. Then someone started to chant, and the others joined in; it was the climactic scene of the Nō play *Tsuna*:

> *Tsuna, undaunted, raising his sword, shouts,*
> *"Know you not that you desecrate Imperial Domain?*
> *For that you'll not escape the wrath of the Heavens."*
> *Whereupon Tsuna attacks. The demon, brandishing a bar of steel,*
> *Shouts "Ei ya!" as it strikes back;*
> *But leaping at the demon, Tsuna deals it a deadly blow.*
> *Though wounded, the demon moves to grapple with him again,*
> *Yet now the sweep of Tsuna's blade severs its arm.*
> *The demon seems at first to falter, then mounts the wall beside the*
> *   gate,*
> *And flees into the heavens above, taking cover in a bank of black*
> *   cloud.*
> *Faintly comes its cry, "I'll await my chance! I'll get you yet!"*
> *Now more to be feared than the famed demon itself,*
> *Tsuna brings yet greater fame to his own name!*

The scene sounds like an incipient drunken carousal—but it wasn't. Some men went downstairs and began to prepare themselves, and others left for Honjō to do the same. Only Kuranosuke, Sōemon, Chūzaemon, and Jūnai remained upstairs. Yahei's wife brought up some slices of sword beans that she had pickled in miso, for which Kuranosuke thanked her profusely. And then Jōemon asked a question that, to his surprise, amused everyone greatly. He had from time to time heard people mention a man named Oyama Gengozaemon Dono. "What has become of him?" Jōemon asked. Kuranosuke turned to Hara Sōemon, and his face broke out in a grin, almost a laugh.

"He had important business to attend to in Kyoto," Sōemon said with a smile, "so he wasn't able to come here with us."

"Disgusting!" Kuranosuke muttered, whereupon they changed the subject and began chatting in leisurely fashion again.

When the time bell tolled the midpoint of the Fourth Hour (11:00 P.M.), everyone said it was time to move on to Honjo.

"It's bitterly cold tonight," Jōemon said, "and the saké we drank earlier must have worn off by now; let me offer you a little more before we go." Everyone assented with good will, so Jōemon brought saké and cups down from upstairs. "You can pour us all a cup of that!" they said.

They all had their gear wrapped in bundles and ready to go. Yasubei was the first to leave, and Jōemon said to him, "Shouldn't you have a servant carry that for you?"

"Normally I would," Yasubei said, "but tonight no one is taking a servant with him." And then he added, "But be sure that *you* stay close by me tonight." Jōemon promised that he would follow along directly.

♦ ♦ ♦

Then, just as everyone was about to depart, who should show up but the two sons of Ōishi Mujin: Gōemon, the vassal of Tsugaru Etchū-no-Kami, and his younger brother, Mitsuhira. They had an important message to transmit, they said, so Jōemon showed them in.

"Just now Hakura Itsuki came to us. He said that he had heard about tonight's plan and had come to tell us there would be guests staying overnight with the other party. What if someone should cut down one of the guests by mistake? It might be better to put off the attack until tomorrow, Itsuki thinks, and so he came to tell us this confidentially. Our old father told us that we should at least come and let you know, which is what brings us here now."

"How on earth did word of this leak out?" Kuranosuke asked. "This is very suspicious."

"We questioned him quite closely concerning this," the brothers said, "but all he would say was that he had heard it from a source who need cause you no worries." Everyone thought this very strange. Did he have a friend who knew? And what if, by some long chance, *they* too should know?

Jōemon decided that he would make bold to offer an opinion: "I know that it is impertinent of me to interfere, but I wonder if this isn't actually *good* news? If there are guests staying over tonight, that should mean that Kira Dono is certain to be at home. No matter how many guests there may be, you needn't worry the least bit about them. Just kill them all."

"Indeed! Quite so!" Kuranosuke agreed. To Jōemon's surprise, everyone seemed quite pleased with his suggestion and decided that they should gather nonetheless at the appointed place. As they left, Jōemon wished each of them great success.

When everyone else had gone, Jōemon left with the two Ōishi brothers. Someone had forgotten his bundle and left it at Yahei's place, so Jōemon took it with him to Hayashi-chō. As they parted along the way, the Ōishi brothers promised that they would turn up again in the morning.

CHAPTER
62

*One must not live beneath the same heaven
as the enemy of one's lord or one's father.*

By midnight, just about all the ronin had gathered at Jūheiji's and Yasubei's rooms in Tokuemon-chō and Hayashi-chō. Some of the younger men, more eager than thoughtful, had turned up far too early, in the Seventh Hour (4:00 P.M.). Fortunately, a few senior men were there, too, and told them to break up into small groups, go to a teahouse where they would not be conspicuous, and come back after it was completely dark. Some of the older men, coming from Horibe Yahei's place, had stopped along the way for a bowl of soba at the Kamedaya and were only just arriving.

Old Ōishi Mujin was there, too, fully armed and wearing arm guards and a sword belt that he had received years earlier as a gift from Asano Naganao, but had never before had a chance to use. Mujin had asked his friend Yahei to let him to join in the attack, but Yahei would not hear of it. "That would be foolish," Yahei told him. "You're associated with the Tsugaru house now. You could ruin your son's career if you came with us. It makes no sense whatever." Tonight, Mujin would have to be content to lead one column to the main gate of the Kira mansion—even though the men he would lead there knew the way perfectly well. The old would-be warrior had been too willing and helpful an ally to deny him that small part in the action.

◆ ◆ ◆

In the kitchen at Yasubei's place, Satō Jōemon was hard at work on a stalk of bamboo. This was a fairly substantial stalk that would be driven into the earth before the main entrance to the Kira mansion and would hold a letter box containing the manifesto that the ronin would leave behind for the benefit of any investigators who might follow. The lower end of the stalk, Jōemon had shaved to a sharp point, and the upper end, he sliced partway down the middle so that it could be spread apart to grasp the letter box. The box itself—which seems miraculously to have survived—was long and thin and decorated with a seasonally appropriate painting of a sprig of sasanqua camellia. The manifesto it contained read:

DECLARATION OF THE VASSALS OF ASANO TAKUMI

In the Third Month of this past year, Takumi, while serving as official host to the Imperial Envoys, conceived a grievance against Kira Kōzuke-no-Suke Dono. Whereupon, driven by the force of circumstances, he drew his sword and attacked His Lordship in the palace. For this outrage, perpetrated in disregard of both the occasion and the venue, he was commanded to commit seppuku, and his domain in Akō was decreed forfeit. To this, even we his vassals fully acquiesced. In compliance with the commands of the Shogunal Envoys, we surrendered his castle and lands and disbanded forthwith. On the occasion of the aforementioned quarrel, however, there was a gentleman present who restrained Takumi, and thus he failed to kill Kōzuke-no-Suke Dono. The mortification that this must have caused him in those last hours of his life is more than we his vassals can endure. Loath though we be to harbor enmity against a Master of Court Protocol of such illustrious lineage, neither can we ignore the fact that one must not live beneath the same heaven as the enemy of one's lord or one's father. And so today, we make bold to intrude upon the residence of Kōzuke-no-Suke Dono, which we do only by way of settling this grievance on behalf of our late lord. Should there be those who come to investigate following our demise, we beg that you peruse the foregoing.

Given herewith as above,

GENROKU 15 [1702], TWELFTH MONTH, ____ DAY
Vassals of Asano Takumi-no-Kami
Ōishi Kuranosuke
(and forty-six others)

This document has a fascinating history. In its original incarnation, it was written by Horibe Yahei, probably toward the end of the Eleventh Month, to leave behind for his kinsmen, explaining in a general way why he and his comrades were about to do what they later did. But at some point, probably prior to the attack planned for the 5th Day of the Twelfth Month, it must have been decided that it would be best to leave behind at the scene of the attack a statement of the motives and intentions of the ronin. Since Yahei had already drafted just such a statement, it was easy to adapt his personal declaration for use by the entire group.

The story of how this document was adapted is well known. Yahei wished to add a sentence, citing the ancient Confucian classic, the *Book of Rites*, claiming that "a vassal must never live beneath the same heaven as the enemy of his lord." But, alas, in the *Book of Rites* version of this principle, it is the enemy of one's father with whom one must not coexist. And so Yahei decided that he would ask the advice of his friend Hosoi Kōtaku, a Confucian scholar. Kōtaku told him that when one is embarked upon matters of great moment, one need not trouble oneself over mere words. Yahei thus altered his text to read "lord or father."

But was it all quite as simple as that? Few people outside the immediate circle of the pact knew as much about their plot as Kōtaku. For one thing, he was a fellow disciple of the swordsman Horiuchi Gendazaemon, and through that connection knew not only Yahei and Yasubei but a number of other Akō ronin as well. We have seen, too, that when Yasubei left Edo for Kyoto, it was Kōtaku to whom he entrusted copies of his entire correspondence with Kuranosuke and other members of the pact. Everything that Yasubei knew, Kōtaku knew. Yet he was also a deeply learned scholar of Confucianism, which Yasubei and Yahei were not. He would know, therefore, that the sentence that reads "lord or father" was not Yahei's adaptation from the *Book of Rites*, but a direct quotation from a more recent work, the *Collected Works of Chu-hsi*. Which is to say, it is far more likely that Kōtaku himself suggested the addition of that entire sentence, rather than that Yahei asked Kōtaku's advice concerning a sentence of his own—that it was Kōtaku who added the indispensable element of moral justification to this document.

Whatever the history of the text, however, there were by this time several copies of it. Kuranosuke, Chūzaemon, Sōemon, Kyūdayū, Jūnai, Suke'emon—all carried a copy. And copies had also been sent to Terai Genkei in Kyoto and Ochiai Yozaemon in the household of Yōzei'in. But there were now only forty-seven men left to sign it.

Jōemon took the copy that he had been given, asked Kuranosuke to enter the date in the blank space, folded it, wrapped it, placed it in the letter box, and secured the cord in a neat bowknot. He then spread the split in the bamboo stalk, placed the box between the two halves, and tied it in place. It was now ready to be erected, with a few taps of a mallet, at the main entrance to the Kira mansion.

◆ ◆ ◆

Once Jōemon had finished his carpentry project, he turned to more mundane tasks. Yahei's wife had suggested that he take the leftover sword beans that she had pickled and give them to the men at Yasubei's place. Jōemon told Yasubei that the beans were from his mother, and immediately the young men swarmed around. "What's that?" they said. "Something good to eat? Well, we'll have some of those!" In no time at all, they were gone. Then Okuda Magodayū came over and began joking with Jōemon, as did a number of the young men as well. In the midst of which, Muramatsu Kihei quietly handed Jōemon a piece of paper and said, "Would you pass this on to our mentor?" meaning Horiuchi Gendazaemon. "There are many things I'd like to write and tell him; but if anything should go wrong, I'd be sorry not to get this to him at least. So please . . ." Jōemon slipped the sheet into the breast of his kimono without looking at it. The next morning, he discovered that it was Kihei's farewell poem:

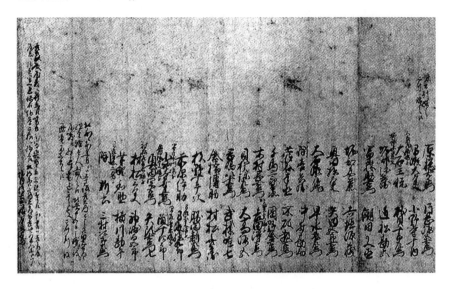

inochi ni mo kaenu hitotsu o ushinawaba
igekakuretemo koko o nogaren
Should I miss this one chance, which I would not trade even for life itself,
run and hide though I may, could I ever escape the shame?

When the Honjo time bell tolled the Eighth Hour (2:00 A.M.),
Jōemon told Yasubei, "I'm going back to Yonezawa-chō and bid farewell
to Yahei, and then come back here."

"No," Yasubei said, "stay here until everyone has left, so you can check
for any danger of fire. You can bid farewell to Yahei at Yogorō's place.
That's where we're supposed to meet him."

"But if anything should go wrong," Jōemon said, "that would be
dreadful. Yahei may need help. It's only the Eighth Hour. I can go to
Yonezawa-chō and still get back here in time."

"All right, then, go ahead," Yasubei said. Jōemon bundled Yasubei's
bedding into a basket and gave it to a servant to carry. The sheath of
Yasubei's great sword was lying there, too. Yasubei would not be taking
that; Jōemon carried it away himself.

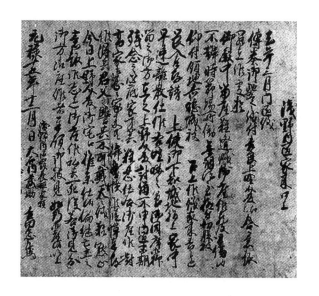

❖ ❖ ❖

By now, nearly everyone was in the final stages of changing into battle gear. They were not totally uniformed, but uniform enough to give the impression they sought. A group of forty-seven armed men marching through the streets in the early hours of the morning could hardly expect to be regarded as normal. But if they could contrive to look something like a fire brigade from one of the lordly mansions, they probably could reach their destination without being subject to undue scrutiny.

In the first place, they all wore shirts of chain mail, and some even wore mail that would cover their thighs. Their under-robes were not uniform, but over them, everyone wore breeches that were loose at the thighs and tight about the calves, as well as straw traveling sandals that tied at the ankles to keep them from coming loose. Over the shirts and breeches, all the ronin wore a uniform hip-length surcoat of black, the cuffs of which were lined with broad bands of plain white muslin, for easy identification in the dark. Most also wore standard quilted fire hats with a neck guard trailing down at the back, buttoning over the mouth and chin, with a metal crown inside to make it as protective as a battle helmet. A few, Kuranosuke among them, had specially made fire helmets of thick leather. At their waists—as Yasubei had recommended—they wore specially made sashes of white muslin twisted about fine chain that they tied in a firm knot, so it could not be cut loose in combat. The sashes they used not only to secure their swords, but also to hang accessories from—rice balls, smelling salts, styptic powder, and the like. Less visibly, everyone had a small name tag sewn to his surcoat, and carried a child's "Chinaman's whistle" for signaling. To complete the impression of a fire brigade, they agreed to carry their lances at an angle over their shoulders, resembling the long-handled billhooks that real firemen used to pull down burning buildings. The mallets and crowbars and ladders that some carried of course enhanced the disguise.

♦ ♦ ♦

Then it was time. The Honjo time bell, just across the bridge on the banks of the Crosswise Canal, tolled thrice to alert any early-morning listeners. Then more slowly—one, two, three, four, five, six, seven. It was midway through the Hour of the Tiger (ca. 4:00 A.M.), the coldest time of night, when everyone sleeps most soundly. It had been agreed that they would wait for the bell to toll seven times, let a few moments pass, and then emerge from their meeting place. But the young men were so keen to be off that they slid open the doors and pushed out into the street while the bell was still ringing. At first, they formed up in two columns marching abreast.

"Now remember! The password is *yama* [mountain], and the countersign is *kawa* [river]. If someone challenges you with "mountain," you answer "river," and then you'll be safe. Now let's move."

They set out straight along the south side of the Vertical Canal, for five blocks, until they reached the Second Bridge, where they crossed to the north side of the canal, then on toward the river for three more blocks, where they turned right into Aioi-chō, which brought them out at Yogoro and Isuke's shop, immediately across from the guardhouse at the corner of the Kira mansion. Here they met their first challenge.

+ + +

In all samurai districts, it was the responsibility of the residents to maintain guardhouses at regular intervals so as to keep order in the streets outside their walls. These "corner guardhouses" were staffed by samurai from the houses of the neighborhood association, and one of them was located at the southeast corner of the Kira property. Who was on duty that night, we do not know. Neither do we have a firsthand report of what took place there when the ronin approached. But Tōjō Shusetsu, a doctor in the house of Mizuno Kenmotsu, tells us what he heard from one of the ronin later that year.

When they reached the guardhouse, the guard emerged, but the ronin approached him with lowered lances, and someone said, "We have our reasons for being here," and then, thrusting forward the blade of his lance: "But you weren't intending to raise an alarm, were you?" When he saw this, the guard said, "I beg your pardon, gentlemen, most humbly. Please forgive me."

"Very well then, go back inside, shut your door, and bolt it." There were a few passersby, but no one was so foolish as to stop and ask what was going on.

+ + +

Here, too, was the parting of the ways for the two columns. The one turned to the right, heading for the main gate; the other, to the left and the rear gate.

CHAPTER
63

They should have left earlier,
he knew.

Jōemon did not return in time to see Yasubei off, as he had promised he would. He was still with old Yahei when the two columns set out from Hayashi-chō.

"We agreed that we'd set out at the Seventh Hour [4:00 A.M.]," Yahei said. "So after everyone left, I lay down and took a nap." He was up now, though, and at his writing desk when Jōemon arrived.

"What's that?" Jōemon asked.

"It's a sketch of our gravestones," Yahei said. "If my son and I die, I'd like you to collect our bodies and have them sent to our family temple, Seishōji. I'll note down our posthumous names, too."

"In Hayashi-chō, everyone seemed ready to go. Shouldn't you, too, prepare yourself? I'll take these notes with me, without fail, just as you ask."

"Please do," Yahei said, and quickly finished writing them. Very calmly, he dressed, gathered all the things that he had been given to take with him, and made ready to leave.

"I came here just to bid you farewell," Jōemon said, "so I'll be going back to Hayashi-chō now."

"When the bell strikes seven, I'll be leaving, too," Yahei said. "I'd like you to go with me. So wait here just a little longer."

"If you'll be leaving on the stroke of seven, then all right, I'll wait." In the meantime, Jōemon readied everything that they would be needing, and gave some things to Yahei's manservant Tokubei, who would be coming with them. Then the bell began to toll.

"Well, let's be off," Jōemon said. They should have left earlier, he knew.

◆ ◆ ◆

The night was as near perfect as they could hope for. The sky was clear, and the moon only one day short of full. With a fresh fall of snow on every roof and on the surface of the street, their way was lit almost as brightly as at midday. There would be no need for torches or lanterns, which could attract attention or even start fires. The night was crisp and bitter cold, though, which would make movement less precise, but could also deter any insomniac who might be tempted to slip out of bed to see who the passing footsteps belonged to—and having seen, report it.

◆ ◆ ◆

As the right-hand column silently strode the length of the long south wall of the Kira mansion, heading for the main gate on the east, Ōtaka Gengo and Hazama Jūjirō signaled to each other with a nod, and then split off from the group. From a fire watchtower about halfway along that street, they deftly commandeered the two ladders that rested against it, then rejoined their column. It was not that ladders had been forgotten. Lists of the equipment that the ronin had laid in say they had eight ladders with them. But Gengo and Jūjirō were keen to be those honored as "First over the Wall"—a truly great accomplishment in the days of siege warfare, and a title that still had a ring of glory in the minds of peacetime warriors. To be first over the wall tonight would demand no bravery in the face of enemy archery or musket fire; the honor would go to whoever had a ladder in his hands and was the first to put it in place. Gengo and Jūjirō had been planning ahead, and their plan succeeded.

The Kira mansion was flanked on three sides by barrack blocks, which formed the outer walls of the property and in which Kira's vassals were quartered. The main gate, in the eastern wall, was tall and strong, but the gaps between the gate and the barracks on either side were filled by roofed walls that were much lower than either the gate or the buildings. It was against those walls that Gengo and Jūjirō placed their ladders and began climbing—"up and up," as the playwright put it, "as lightly as spiders"—followed by Yoshida Sawaemon, Okajima

Yasoemon, and all the others. It all happened so fast that at one point, someone had to warn them to slow their pace a bit; too many men on a ladder could break it.

The roofs on the walls were still slippery with snow, and there were no ladders on the inside. The attackers had to jump down. At first, Yokogawa Kanpei thought that he might get a foothold on a wooden wall of the barracks, and slow his descent that way. But if he should slip in that awkward position, he could be injured worse than if he jumped. So jump he did, directly from the edge of the roof. Some tried to break their fall with the hafts of their lances, and Hara Sōemon landed badly and turned his ankle. But everyone went over the top. The gate was never opened, for they were just as determined that no one should get out as they were to get in.

The gate was, of course, guarded, and the guards were immediately aroused, first by the commotion of the climbers, and then by the apparition of several men clad in black and armed for battle. All three of the guards emerged at once and were quickly overpowered. One was cut down by a sword and died on the spot. Another, Mori Han'emon, took the thrust of a lance, fell, and began crawling away toward the stables, where he, too, later died. The third man, Nakazato Jin'emon, was unharmed; the ronin would be needing him later as a witness. He was bound tightly and told that if he cooperated, he would later be released—a promise that was kept.

Once over the wall, their first task was to regroup. Kuranosuke would stay at the gate and make that his command post. If their attack was reported and Inspectors should arrive while it was still in progress, this was where they would come; and it was Kuranosuke who would have to explain what was going on and deter them from entering. With him in the command group were Hara Sōemon and Masé Kyūdayū.

Another group of four men would position themselves along the east wall between the main gate and the small New Gate at the north end of it. Their job would be to prevent anyone from escaping through the gates and fight off anyone who might emerge from the mansion or the barracks. Okano Kin'emon asked specifically that he be assigned duty there, where he would have ample room to wield his cruciform lance—a heavy weapon with three blades at the tip. "This is the weapon for me," he said. "I'll fight out in the open where I can take on the lot of them." And according to his uncle Onodera Jūnai, he did indeed fell every man who challenged him.

Two more groups of three men each would spread out along the east end of the south wall, between the barracks and the fences around the mansion gardens. Most of Kira's men would be asleep in their quarters here, but if any of them should be so foolish as to emerge, they had to be stopped. One member of this group, Hayami Tōzaemon, was a highly skilled archer who decided that he could best contribute to this mission by climbing to the roof of the mansion itself and shooting down at any door that looked about to open.

Finally, there were three more groups of three men each who were to storm the mansion from the front entrance and begin the room-by-room search for Kira Kōzuke-no-Suke. Once the surrounding areas had been secured, these nine men could move in at their end of the long residence.

♦ ♦ ♦

The rear gate was a different matter. There were no conveniently low walls that could be easily scaled with ladders. But the gate itself was far less substantial a structure than the main gate. The doors were not hinged, but sliding, and thus had to be of lighter construction. It had not passed unnoticed that the planking of this gate was of much thinner timber. Ladders were brought, but abandoned. Sugino Jūheiji and Mimura Jirōzaemon stepped up and, with a shout of "Ei, ya!" began splintering those thin planks with the huge hardwood mallets they carried. In they went, followed by all the rest. A foot soldier who was on guard came out and was killed; two others were bound and gagged. Then these men, too, had to regroup.

The nominal commander was Ōishi Chikara, but the actual commander was Yoshida Chūzaemon, with two other "old men," Onodera Jūnai and Hazama Kihei, in his command group.

Between the barracks and the mansion were three groups of three or four men each, and three more groups of three and four that would break into this end of the residence. The concentration was stronger here because the rear of the mansion was where Kira, now retired, would reside. His son and heir would inhabit the more public spaces, within the main gate. But the rear was where the man they sought would most likely be found.

♦ ♦ ♦

While all of this was going on, Yahei and Jōemon were just crossing the Ryōgoku Bridge. Whereupon Bungorō, Yahei's wife's younger brother, came running after them. Jōemon turned and asked, "What's the matter?"

"Yahei dropped his Chinaman's whistle. Here it is."

"That's good of you," Jōemon told him, and handed it to Yahei. Then Jōemon asked Yahei, "Is there anything you want to say to me before we part? Any messages?"

"No, I have no last words for anyone. But messages? You could tell my friend Nakane—he's in the service of Kuze Izumo-no-Kami—that my son has turned out to be the very finest of all the young men in this group. He'll know how pleased I am. He's a man of discernment, so I expect he'll take delight in this, too."

Yahei was an old man, and he recently had developed an abscess on his leg. The pain had gradually eased, but he still found it difficult to walk. They made their way slowly over the Ryōgoku Bridge to Kanzaki Yogorō's place. The lamps there were still lit, but there was no one in sight. The clothes that the ronin had changed out of, and the bowls and trays that they had used to prepare food, were scattered all about.

"It looks as if they have already left for the attack," Jōemon said.

"Let's just look inside," Yahei said.

"I doubt there's any need for that," Jōemon said; but just to be sure, they went in and looked about. There was no one there; they were too late. Jōemon grasped Yahei's arm and set out for the main gate of the Kira mansion. At the guardhouse on the corner, there were six or seven men who looked like townsmen standing around. When they saw Jōemon and Yahei coming, the guard ducked back into the guardhouse, and the townsmen ran off to their houses in the neighborhood. Some of them even lost their sandals and left them behind, which Jōemon and

Yahei found hilarious.

At the mansion of Makino Ichigaku, opposite the main gate of the Kira mansion, two or three men had come out onto the street. In order to avoid them, Jōemon stopped short of the gate, removed the sheath from Yahei's lance, helped him remove the coat he had worn on the way there, and gave these to his manservant. He then went with Yahei to the gate. He took the oaken cane that Yahei had been using and was about to leave when Yahei called out and Jōemon turned back.

"The gate won't open," he said. "There's no way I can get in." When he looked about, wondering what they might do, Jōemon noticed that two ladders were propped on either side of the gate; they looked as though they had been used to get in. When Jōemon told Yahei, he said, "I'll climb the ladder." It was dangerous for such an old man; he could easily slip, but there was no other way. Jōemon had Tokubei push Yahei up from behind while he steadied the ladder at the bottom. When Yahei had climbed the ladder onto the roof, someone called out, "Who's there?"

"It's me, Yahei," he replied. Some of the men who were already within came over to the roof where he sat, and when Tokubei grasped him and lowered him, Ōtaka Gengo rested his great sword against the wall, and then reached up from below to catch him and break his fall.

Then from within came a voice asking, "Is the manifesto out there?" When Jōemon looked about, he found the bamboo stalk and letter box that he himself had fashioned standing next to the barred window of the guardhouse. So he picked it up and flung it over the wall into the courtyard. "Got it!" the voice replied. But just as he was about to leave, one of the samurai standing outside Makino Ichigaku's gate came over.

"Just what's going on here?" he said.

"I have no idea," Jōemon replied.

"Well it looks to me as though you were with that man who just went in."

But Jōemon said only, "I just have no idea." He wasn't questioned any further. When Yahei's man, Tokubei, came down from the roof, however, three more men came over from Makino's gate.

"Then who is *he*?" one of them shouted. "And what's he doing climbing over the roof into someone's mansion in the middle of the night?"

"It's nothing at all," Jōemon said. "He just had something he had to do up there." They started raising a ruckus about how "strange" it all was, so Jōemon called out twice, "Tokubei! Tokubei!" and the three samurai left. Tokubei hurried down, and they left together and went back to the corner by the rear gate.

"You go over to Yasubei's place," Jōemon told him, "and make sure that no fires are still lit. Then take Yasubei's man with you, go back to Yonezawa-chō, and tell them that I'll be staying here." Alone now, Jōemon went to have a look at the rear gate. It had been bashed open with mallets, and in front of it two mallets and two ladders lay scattered about. Inside the gate, someone wearing a black surcoat with white sleeve markings stood guard, his lance upright and at the ready. Jōemon set out to make a circuit of the block and have a look at the neighboring mansions.

kirimusubu tachi no shita koso jigoku nare
fumikomite miyo soko wa gokuraku
Beneath the blades of two swords joined in battle,
yes that is where hell is;
But close in on your man and you'll see!
There you'll find heaven.

Some of the fiercest fighting that night took place immediately after the ronin broke in at the two entrances to the Kira mansion. Their battle plan—as best they could plan anything in such unfamiliar surroundings—was for the two groups to move toward each other through that long labyrinth of small rooms, systematically eliminating all resistance as they went; and once they met, they would begin a room-by-room search for the man they had come to kill. In the meantime, the ronin in the open spaces between the barracks and the mansion were to prevent anyone in those barracks from rushing to the aid of those within the mansion.

But a warrior knows that few battle plans survive contact with the enemy. The search for Kira was no exception. Very little went as planned; much was improvised. Even firsthand reports of the fighting suffer from the fragmentation and chaos that everyone there felt. It is left to the reader to piece together these bits and pieces in as coherent a whole as one can. That is not a fruitless endeavor.

✦ ✦ ✦

Once the twenty-three men at the main gate had regrouped and were moving into position, Hazama Jūjirō grabbed the lantern in the guardhouse and ran up to the entryway, where he proclaimed in a loud voice:

"We are the vassals of Asano Takumi-no-Kami, come to avenge our late lord; come out and fight!" There was not a sound from within. At that point, someone began bashing down the door (although no one says who was wielding the mallet at this end of the house), and those assigned to clear the house rushed in. There they found what appeared to be the bedding of three guards who had been on night watch, but no one was in sight. Yokogawa Kanpei, who should have remained on duty at the gate, began stamping his feet on the floorboards and shouting in a manner that he later admitted was a bit excessive: "I am a vassal of Asano Takumi-no-Kami. I've come this far in search of Kōzuke-no-Suke, but none of you come out to fight. Are you afraid for your lives? Sahei Dono, you're the young lord—come out and fight like a man! You vassals, aren't you going to challenge us?"

With forty-seven men bellowing at both ends of the house and along the barrack blocks, some of them calling out to a (nonexistent) "company of fifty" or "company of a hundred," the shocked defenders at first thought that there must be a vast number of attackers.

Within the house, it was not long before the challenge of the ronin was answered. When they stepped up from the floorboards of the entryway onto the tatami mats of the reception chamber, four or five samurai on duty there met them with drawn swords. The defenders were instantly cut down. This must have been where Hazama Jūjirō broke his cruciform lance, for the next morning, the body of Shingai Yashichirō was found there, his chest and abdomen torn open by the triple-bladed head of that lance, still stuck in the congealing gore of his wound, the shattered haft lying alongside him. Just beyond was the narrow Lance Room, so named because it contained a rack of fourteen lances. Jūjirō grabbed one for himself, cut the haft to a more usable length, and then destroyed all the others.

By now, word was spreading through the house that there were intruders, and as the ronin moved on to the adjacent Envoys' Room, more defenders came out from the inner rooms. They were at a dreadful disadvantage. This was something that they had long anticipated, but twenty-two months had passed and they had grown careless. Still, they quickly grabbed their swords and, rubbing the sleep from their eyes, ran into the fray. Most were cut down with the single stroke of a sword or felled with one thrust of a lance. Those who were immobilized were left as they were, while the ronin moved on to attack those who had not yet joined battle. As Hara Sōemon later said, "Some may only have been wounded, and some half-dead. It was difficult to tell in the dark." As long as they were out of action, it did not matter. The ronin had agreed beforehand that anyone who made no attempt to hinder them could be ignored.

In the alcove of the Envoys' Room was another weapons rack, this one containing seven bows, their quivers full of arrows. Onodera Kōemon was quick to notice this, despite the dim light and deep shadows. He sliced every bowstring and cracked every arrow before moving on. A stroke of good judgment, as there were reputed to be some skilled archers in the Kira household.

From the Envoys' Room onward, the path narrowed, down a long boarded corridor that opened into a small anteroom adjacent to the main reception rooms. Yada Gorōemon was the last of his squad to head down this passage, and as he passed through the doorway into the anteroom, he was attacked from behind by a man who had been lurking in the shadows. Gorōemon was, of course, wearing mail, and the blow did not injure him. He simply wheeled and felled his assailant with one stroke. The man fell back onto a metal charcoal brazier; Goroemon struck him again, angrily, and the blow cut the man's body in two. But his blade struck the brazier and broke 5 or 6 inches from the tip. Gorōemon threw it down, picked up the dead man's sword, and moved on.

◆ ◆ ◆

At the rear gate, three foot soldiers were standing guard, and one of them, Ōkōchi Rokurōemon, demanded, "Who's there?"

"There's a fire in the house; open the gate," one of the ronin said. Rokurōemon looked out from the guard room and saw what looked to be men dressed in firefighting gear; but there was no sign of fire, so he refused to open up. That was when they battered down the gate and rushed in.

"I fought back with my sword," Rokurōemon said, "but was wounded."

Nine days later, he died. The other two who did not resist were bound and gagged, lest they shout and raise the alarm.

A moment later, a far more consequential gentleman emerged. Matsubara Tachū, an Elder of the Kira house and a disciple of Hakura Itsuki, lived in private quarters immediately adjacent to the rear gate.

"I heard someone saying that there was a fire," he later explained, "so I went out immediately to see what was the matter, whereupon I was shot at by archers, hit by an arrow, and struck a blow with a sword. A great many men came rushing at me, and one of them knocked me flat with the mallet that they had used to break open the gate. I was in such pain that I couldn't fight back. . . . I know nothing of what went on elsewhere. This much I know only because my quarters are next to the gate." Matsubara, too, later died of his wounds.

In the meantime, Sugino Jūheiji and Mimura Jirōzaemon ran on ahead with their demolition mallets. The retired gentleman's apartments had their own inner gate, and beyond that was his entryway, the door to which was, of course, barred this time of night. These barriers, too, had to be battered down to make way for the ten men who would clear this end of the mansion. This was the sector where they were most likely to corner the man they sought.

The command group at the rear gate was made up of Yoshida Chūzaemon, Onodera Jūnai, and Masé Kyūdayū and was nominally led by Kuranosuke's fifteen-year-old son, Ōishi Chikara. With a large, irreparable hole in one panel of the gate, it was crucial that this exit be carefully guarded. But once security had been ensured—as Jōemon saw that it had—the three older men were free to investigate the nooks and crannies of this corner of the property.

Jūnai and Kihei were standing in front of the barrack block to the right of the gate when two men rushed out at them. Jūnai killed the first with a single thrust of his lance, and Kihei felled the second. Kihei then stayed behind to keep watch at the gate, while Jūnai moved toward a rear door in the north wall, meaning to call out to the men on the far side of the wall who were guarding the mansion of Tsuchiya Chikara. Just then, however, two more of the enemy came at him, and he felled them both. Kataoka Gengoemon saw him kill the first one and shouted,

"Jūnai Dono, well done!" The other kill, Ōishi Sezaemon saw. As that man fell, Jūnai could hear him invoking the name of the Buddha Amida. "The sins of my old age, I suppose I must call them," he later wrote to his wife. "All committed with the lance; I never laid a hand on the hilt of my sword."

＊ ＊ ＊

The layout of the rooms at this end of the house was rather different from that of the more formal rooms within the main gate; it was a different lot of people here, too. The boarded floor just within the entryway was hardly wider than a veranda, and there was only one tatami-matted room beyond it in which to receive callers. To move any farther forward took one into the kitchens—a board-floored room where serving trays were prepared and an earthen-floored space where all the cutting, washing, and cooking took place. The living spaces of the retired gentleman's apartments were off to the right. They were nowhere near as spacious as those of his son, who was now head of the house; but they did include two rooms, each with a small central hearth, for the practice of ceremonial tea. Here is where Kira would have entertained his guests earlier in the evening.

Once Mimura Jirōzaemon had battered down the thin doors to the entryway and the men behind him burst in, they moved directly forward into the kitchens, where they were confronted by a rather motley lot of men.

Three menials were already up, lighting the fires in the great hearth next to the rear door. Taken totally by surprise, they just dropped everything and fled, each in a different direction, "like the hatchlings of a spider." They were no threat, and no one pursued them. But then Yokogawa Kanpei grabbed a firebrand from the hearth and leapt back up to the raised floor. There cowered several men, cornered with nowhere to flee. But Kanpei, remembering what Kuranosuke had said about caution with fire, threw the firebrand back under the kettle.

The problem of lighting was solved more efficiently by Isogai Jūrōzaemon, who grabbed hold of one of the men whom Kanpei's firebrand had revealed.

"Who are you?" Jūrōzaemon demanded.

"I'm in charge of confections and candles," the man answered.

"Then take me to where you keep your confections and candles." The man wisely did not hesitate. And when he slid open the cupboard door, they found not only candles but also lanterns in which they could use the candles to light the house. Apparently, the ronin also helped themselves to Kira's confections, and were seen nibbling on them as they lit the lanterns and distributed them.

The descriptions one reads of those early moments in the kitchens give the impression that the ronin were almost as confused as the men they caught there by surprise—and that a bit of needless killing went on in that part of the house. One reason was that Fuwa Kazuemon, who had been assigned to a detail guarding the outside area between the barracks and the mansion, abandoned his post and went into the house through the rear entrance. There was no action out of doors, he said, and action is what he had come for.

One story has it that just as Kazuemon was coming from the reception room into the kitchens, he spotted a man cowering beneath some shelves. "Who are you?" Kazuemon demanded.

"I'm only a rear vassal. Pray spare my life," the man said. Kazuemon came closer and saw that he was wearing two swords and was dressed in silk.

"You don't look like a rear vassal to me."

"I beg you!"

"All right," said Kazuemon, "tell me where Kōzuke-no-Suke Dono is, and I'll spare you."

"But I told you. I'm only a rear vassal. I know nothing at all."

"Insolent fool!" Kazuemon shouted. He drew and, with only one hand, brought the sword down on the man's head so hard that it split in two.

Another ronin who was watching said, "There's a man who's been training for a long time! I doubt that I could do that, even with the finest Masamune blade, even if I held it with both hands and cut straight down."

This is the sort of story that sounds totally fictitious—yet even the

Uesugi house records tell us that the man's name was Torii Riemon, and that his head was indeed split down the middle.

One further report does not reflect well upon Kazuemon: a little serving boy, his pate shaved like a monk, unarmed and frightened out of his wits, was running about screaming, "Don't kill me; don't kill me." Kazuemon cut him down, again showing everyone what he could do with just one hand. The boy was Suzuki Shōchiku.

And so, by the time the rear gate detail moved on toward the center of the mansion, a great deal of blood had been shed in the kitchens, and a number of men still lay there, dead or dying.

◆ ◆ ◆

Outside, between the mansion and the barracks, the six squads assigned to that area took up their positions and proclaimed themselves vassals of Asano Takumi-no-Kami come to avenge their late lord. Hara Sōemon, despite his sprained ankle, seems then to have made a circuit of the mansion, checking their disposition, for he was later able to say, "Once we had surrounded the entire property, we called out, 'Is there no one who'll challenge us?' but the samurai in the barracks would not come out. Eventually, two or three did emerge, and we felled them with our lances, as I recall. Whether they lived or died was impossible to tell in the pre-dawn darkness."

Onodera Jūnai had good reason for wishing to call out to the men on the far side of the rear wall, just before he was attacked. This wall was all that separated Kira from his two neighbors to the north, Tsuchiya Chikara and Honda Magotarō. No record survives of deliberations in the Honda household, but both houses reacted in the same way. They raised a number of large bright lanterns, bearing their family crests, on tall poles at the very edge of the wall. Even at the time, this was taken by some as a sign of their support for the Akō ronin, but it was no such thing. They intended neither to abet the attack nor to come to the aid of Kira. A report in the hand of Takenaka Suke'emon, Chief Elder to Tsuchiya Chikara, reveals that they had been expecting just such an attack and had made plans well in advance. Lanterns would be raised. Samurai of the household would stand in readiness at the wall, armed with lances or the weapons of their choice. Tsuchiya Dono himself, armed with a lacquered bow and hunting arrows and attended by his lance bearers, would command from the center, seated upon his folding battlefield stool. "If anyone comes over the wall, shoot him," he told his men. Their aim was personal protection and nothing more. If any of the violence should spill over the wall, they were prepared to defend themselves; if not, they would simply remain in readiness.

From what he could see on his side of the wall, Onodera Jūnai felt that the neighbors were owed an explanation. And so, after he had disposed of his last assailant, Jūnai, joined now by Kataoka Gengoemon and Hara Sōemon, approached the wall and called out. Their exact words are not recorded, but they identified themselves by name, explained the nature of their mission, apologized for the commotion they would create, and asked their neighbors, as fellow samurai, not to interfere. To which, Tsuchiya Chikara tersely communicated his agreement.

We must note, however, that Tsuchiya Chikara was not just another high-ranking bannerman. The observant reader may have noticed that he bore the same surname as Tsuchiya Sagami-no-Kami, a member of the Shogun's Council of Elders. And contrary to what one might expect, Tsuchiya Chikara, the bannerman, was the head of the main branch of the Tsuchiya house, and Sagami-no-Kami, the Elder, headed the cadet house. It was only natural, therefore, that the bannerman should send one of his vassals to his junior kinsman, the Elder, bearing this message: "The vassals of Takumi-no-Kami Dono have just mounted a night attack on the mansion of Kira Sahei. It sounds as though there are a great many of them. I have gone out to the boundary between us and am observing from there. For the present, I dispatch this initial notification and will send further details as soon as I am able." The consequences of this "initial notification," as we shall see, will be of great importance.

◆ ◆ ◆

The men who were inside the barracks that night tell a different, yet nonetheless revealing, story of their experiences. These were men who were being asked by senior officers of Kira's natural son, Uesugi Danjō, to justify their failure to act. Here is what two of them had to say:

As they burst in, they made a great commotion, shouting "Fire, fire!" They quickly secured all the doors to the barracks, with men bearing lances and halberds at each. Those who were startled into coming out by the shouts of "fire" were mowed down, their heads chopped off neatly, one after another after another, some with barely a moment to chant the name of the Buddha before they died. No one got out undetected. Those of us who escaped with our lives—though only barely—could look out through the cracks in the doors and see four or five men with lances and halberds at every door, men roving through the property, and even men on the roof with bows shooting battle arrows, never missing a beat. They were inescapable.

A great many men, I don't know how many, forced their way into the property. They were right at the door to the room we were in; we could not get out. I have no idea how many there were. Nor have I any idea how those three men who were killed managed to get out.

Both men exaggerated the number of ronin patrolling the area. Nor were any of the ronin armed with halberds. What we should really like to know, though, is whether any of Kira's men were physically, rather than psychologically, prevented from joining battle. We know that the ronin guarding the area between the mansion and the barracks carried a good supply of crampons—the oversize staples used by builders to join pillars to crossbeams and crossbeams to rafters. They also carried the metal hammers that they would need to pound the crampons into place. And if they did pound a crampon across the crack between a door and its jamb, the only way anyone inside could get out would be to destroy the door. But did they ever use these crampons? There is no mention of any use of them by those on the outside, but here is what one man on the inside said: "Last night, midway through the Eighth Hour [ca. 3:00 A.M.], a great many men broke in through the rear gate, saying that there was a fire. We went out to face them, but the first man out was felled by a lance, and we retreated straightaway into our quarters. They then secured the doors from the outside and prevented us from going out again."

Perhaps some of the doors were hammered shut. Still, a very few of Kira's men did manage to get out, but their success was short-lived. Here is what happened to one of them:

> *Kobayashi Heihachi, a man of about thirty, a very skilled swords-man, and known for his great courage, had been sent by the Uesugi to guard Kira. At the time of the attack, he was in his quarters in the barracks. But because all doorways were under close guard, he could not get to the main house. Then he heard one of the attackers command, "Anyone who flees, let him go; and spare any women, children, or menials." So Heihachi disguised himself as a menial and ran out the door, pretending to flee. He zigzagged across the open space and somehow made it to the house. There he fought fero-ciously, but in the end was surrounded by a great many ronin, was wounded in several places, and fell.*

While all this was going on, two Elders of the Kira house, hiding in one of the rooms in the barracks that lined the south wall, conceived a craven but clever plan of escape that seems not to have occurred to anyone else. Sōda Magobei and Saitō Kunai, instead of just staying put and awaiting their fate or attempting to flee through the door, began breaking open a hole in the outer wall of their room. How they accom-plished it without attracting anyone's attention, we have no idea. But renovations were still under way, and we have seen how in places light could leak through the bamboo lath that faced the street. It may not have been terribly difficult to open an escape passage through a wall so thin and poorly constructed.

Having made their escape, Magobei and Kunai did not flee far. Almost directly across the street was the shop of Karakasaya San'emon, an umbrella maker. The front room of this man's establishment was by day used by the neighborhood watchmen; but at this time of night, it was empty. San'emon opened up the watch room and let the two Kira Elders hide there until the ronin had left. Thereafter, Magobei and Kunai would return to their duties, but their flight did not go unnoticed in the neighborhood.

It's still warm!
He's only just left here.

So far, the battle had been a series of unanticipated collisions, from which the ronin seem always to have emerged the victors. When the two forces—one from the main gate, one from the rear—converged somewhere near the center of the mansion, they could see that the operation had been a total success, far beyond their expectations—but an empty success. The enemy, surprised and without armor, was defeated; all power to resist had been crushed. Yet the man whose head they sought still eluded them. In the midst of all this violence, Kira's men had somehow managed to spirit him away and hide him without any of the attackers catching even a glimpse of them. At this point, a new battle began, for which a more focused plan of action would be needed if they were to accomplish anything more than the defeat of Kira's vassals.

Just how organized and focused the search that ensued was is hard to tell from the reports that survive. What we do know for certain, though, is that it began in Kira's own quarters, that it involved a great deal of smashing and bashing of doors and panels and walls, and that after the house had been searched three times, end to end, many of the ronin were ready to give up.

◆ ◆ ◆

They began by grabbing one of the foot soldiers whom they had bound and gagged at the rear gate, and demanding that he show them which rooms Kira himself inhabited and that he do so quietly. The man did as he was told. Mimura Jirōzaemon stepped up again, battered down the door with his mallet, and everyone else burst in behind him. But the lantern they carried revealed only an empty bed, scattered bedclothes, and a sword still in its rack. Now what? While the others were bemoaning their lack of luck, however, Yokogawa Kanpei had the presence of mind to kneel down and slip his hand under the quilt.

"It's still warm!" he said. "He's only just left here. Let's hurry!"

Everyone's spirits seemed revived by that news, and they all rushed off, each group in a different direction.

Just as they were leaving, Kayano Wasuke caught sight of a writing box in a corner. He turned back, ground some ink, and on the paper of a panel at one side of the room, he wrote in large, bold characters, "We, the vassals of Asano Takumi-no-Kami, forty-seven young men under Ōishi Kuranosuke, have fought our way this far, only to find that Kōzuke-no-Suke Dono will not honor us with his presence." Wasuke's effort was not wasted. Ochiai Yozaemon tells us that this panel was later stripped from its frame and mounted as a hanging scroll—and that he knows the bannerman who is now its owner.

The dangerous task of investigating Kōzuke-no-Suke's toilet fell to Yokogawa Kanpei. The corridor leading to it was too narrow for more than one man to pass. It was only 3 or 4 yards long, but to Kanpei it felt more like 12 or 14 yards. There might well have been one of the enemy lurking in there. But when he kicked the door open, there was no one. He thrust his lance through the thin panels of the ceiling, and then bent down and peered into the hole. No one there either. Kanpei was so relieved that he burst out laughing.

The progress of the other groups as they made their way back through the rooms that they had just cleared was marked by the thump of mallets and the crack and snap of timbers and doors as they were forced open with crowbars or knocked off their hinges.

At the front of the house, they again searched the reception rooms, the anteroom, the corridor, the Envoys' Room, the Lance Room, the entryway. And at the rear, the tea rooms, the sitting room, the upper rooms above the tea rooms, everywhere. They even broke into the storerooms and split open the storage chests. Wherever they thought something looked suspicious, they broke through the floor and probed under the veranda. Kira was nowhere to be found.

At this point, some of the ronin began to drift despondently out of the house, where they told their comrades on guard there that they had failed to find their man. They did not get much sympathy.

"Then you're not doing it right," their comrades shouted angrily. "Not one person has come out of that house since we've been here. So how *could* he have escaped? You'd better get back in there and do a *really* thorough search."

Back in the house, someone had grabbed hold of another bound foot soldier and asked him—more gently this time, they say—"Have you no idea where Kōzuke-no-Suke might have fled?"

"None at all," the man said. "But it's possible that he's hiding in the kitchen of his Elder Saitō Kunai, in the barracks. He sometimes goes there."

In response to this, another ronin insisted that they start going through the barracks, room by room, and search for him there. But Kuranosuke said, "No. It's a simple matter to search the barracks. First you should search the house again as carefully as you can. If it turns out that he's not there, then you can sweep through the barracks. It's a waste of time doing it the other way around." Kuranosuke was right, although not necessarily for the reason he gave. Saitō Kunai's quarters must have been where he and Sōda Magobei had broken out through the wall. If the ronin had found their escape route, they probably would have assumed that Kōzuke-no-Suke had gone with them—a false assumption that might have driven them to despair and made them quit.

◆ ◆ ◆

All the while this exasperating search was under way, there were continued but sporadic outbursts of combat. Two of these seem to have involved a rather remarkable man, Yamayoshi Shinpachi, aged thirty-two. Shinpachi was a low-ranking but hereditary vassal of the Uesugi house, the son of a member of the Fifty Horse Troop. Ten years earlier, he had been sent from Yonezawa to Edo, at a stipend of only three gold pieces per year, to serve in the Corps of Pages attached to Kōzuke-no-Suke's heir, Kira Sahei. Shinpachi took his duties seriously, not only in the diligence with which he served his young lord, but also in perfecting his skills as a swordsman—both qualities that he was to display on the night of the attack.

Like everyone else that night, Shinpachi was awakened by a great commotion, which he at first thought was caused by fire, and then discovered was an attack by ronin bent upon vendetta. His first duty, he knew, was to protect his lord, Kira Sahei. But no sooner had he thrown open the door to his room in the barracks, intending to run to the mansion, than he found himself face to face with the sharp end of a lance. He immediately ducked back and slammed the door.

After a time—how long a time we have no idea—Shinpachi could see that the lancers who had confronted him previously had moved on and, for the moment at least, the way was clear. He grabbed his sword, which lay at the side of his bed; ran across the open space; and vaulted the bamboo fence into the garden in front of Kira Sahei's sitting room. There he encountered three ronin—probably the squad made up of Chikamatsu Kanroku, Ōtaka Gengo, and Hazama Jūjirō. Shinpachi first took on Kanroku, whom he wounded on a finger and a thigh; then he managed to land two very solid blows on the top of Kanroku's head. The metal crown in Kanroku's fire helmet saved him from any injury; but when Shinpachi tried one last time to split that crown, Kanroku found his head reeling from the impact. Thrown onto the defensive, he tried to withdraw toward his comrades, but he stumbled on a stone and fell into the garden pond. Shinpachi might well have finished him off there, but just then Jujirō came at him with his lance. Shinpachi managed at least to deflect the blade so that it failed to penetrate his side; then the third ronin slashed down the side of his face with the tip of his sword, a wound from which the blood poured out. Shinpachi fell, unconscious. Kanroku escaped—wet and chilled to the bone, but still very much alive. "The Fortunes of War must have been with me," he said later. The three ronin moved on, continuing their search for Kira and leaving Shinpachi sprawled in Sahei's garden.

◆ ◆ ◆

At some point, though—again, we've no idea when—Shinpachi regained consciousness, roused himself, and even more miraculously managed to find his lord, Sahei. Everyone remarks what a big man Shinpachi was and how strong. He would have to have been to carry on as well as he did after that first clash in the garden. But there he was: his head bound up tightly with a strip torn from his own robe; still in possession of his sword; and ministering to Sahei Dono, who was wounded in two or three places himself—on his forehead, his arm, and his chest.

It must have been just then that Fuwa Kazuemon entered the room, saw that the young man was dressed more splendidly than the average samurai, and concluded correctly that this was Kira Sahei. Sahei met his challenge, and Kazuemon said that he fought well, cutting his kimono in two places and striking his arm guard. But then Kazuemon closed with the youth and dealt him a blow that cut deeply from his right shoulder down across his rib cage. Sahei dropped his halberd, turned, and fled. At that point, Shinpachi leapt into the breach to cover Sahei's retreat. Kazuemon described Shinpachi as particularly skilled, but he was too severely wounded to hold out against a swordsman as formidable as Kazuemon. Before long he fell again, and Kazuemon left him for dead. As we shall see, Shinpachi and Sahei somehow found each other again, and Shinpachi would rescue the youth from further harm. But there is no contemporary record of that.

◆ ◆ ◆

By now, the house had been searched end to end, room by room, three times over. The interior looked as though it had been struck by a storm of extraordinary violence. Not a single door remained standing; the floors were littered with the splintered remains of panels, furnishings, and the contents of storage spaces; the walls were splattered with blood. But not a sign of Kira Kōzuke-no-Suke or the slightest hint of where he might be found.

For the first time since he came over the wall, Kuranosuke left the main gate, wandered over to the entryway, and sat down. One of his men came over to him and said, "We simply can't find Kōzuke Dono. We'll have to give up, and commit seppuku."

"I know," Kuranosuke said. "It's a horrible waste, after all we've been through. But we may have run out of luck; we may have attacked when he was out."

"But what about that samurai we tied up?" someone said. "Ask him."

So they dragged the man out again and questioned him: "Was Kōzuke Dono definitely here in this house this evening? Tell us exactly what you know. If you lie to us, even the least little bit, we'll kill you, right here and now."

"Indeed he was," the man said, "he was here in this house. No mistake about it! If you'll just search a little more carefully...."

"Then we've got to search this house one more time—very carefully," Kuranosuke said. "Dying is the easy way out. But if we fail, well, then we may have to call everyone here and commit seppuku together."

Even coming from Ochiai Yozaemon, who is the least likely reporter to fabricate or even embroider the truth, it is hard to believe that Kuranosuke would consider seppuku. But the ronin themselves tell us much the same story.

◆ ◆ ◆

On the far side of the rear wall, Tsuchiya Chikara could hear everyone at the rear gate "so clearly that it was as though he could reach out and grasp them."

"He seems to have escaped," one of them said. "We've searched everywhere, but we just can't find him."

Then he heard a voice that he recognized as that of Yoshida Chūzaemon: "Well, that's no reason to panic. If we don't find him, we'll keep on searching, even if it takes all day tomorrow. Just stay calm and search *carefully*."

There was no talk of seppuku at the west end of the mansion.

That's a dreadful commotion in there. Is there something amiss?

Tsuchiya Chikara was not the only person keeping watch on the Kira mansion from outside the walls.

The one man almost everyone has heard of was the proprietor of the tofu shop in Aioi-chō, just across from the south wall of the Kira property. Tōfu-ya (the only name we know him by), awakened by the commotion, ascertained correctly who the attackers were and, having done so, set out for Sakurada, where he presented himself at the East Gate to the Uesugi Upper Mansion, midway through the Seventh Hour (ca. 5:00 A.M.). About 150 vassals of Asano Takumi had attacked the Honjo mansion, he told them. The place was in tumult, but he had come immediately to report the matter before investigating any further. Some of the men he recognized, he said; they had been living in the neighborhood. And with that, Tōfu-ya left.

Back in Honjo, we presume that old Ōishi Mujin was still standing outside the main gate and that his son Mitsuhira remained somewhere in the vicinity of the rear gate. The doctor Terai Gentatsu and his assistant Shinsuke certainly would have been nearby, ready to treat any of the ronin who might be wounded. And Chikamatsu Kanroku's personal retainer, Jinzaburō—who had delivered Kuranosuke's last letter and a box of documents to Ochiai Yozaemon the night before—was waiting there with a good supply of mandarin oranges to pass out to the ronin when they emerged. Farther away, in Fukagawa, Hosoi Kōtaku tells us that he climbed to the rooftop of his house and there maintained a frigid vigil throughout the night, watching for smoke on the horizon to the north and hoping that he would not see any. He was assuming that the ronin, if they failed to find and kill Kira, would set fire to his mansion and burn him out.

＊ ＊ ＊

It is a man we have already met, however, Yasubei's cousin Satō Jōemon, who has left us the most detailed description of what went on outside the walls while all hell was breaking loose within.

After Jōemon had sent old Yahei's manservant, Tokubei, back to Yonezawa-chō, he himself set out to make a circuit of the block, past the rear gate of the Kira mansion and then around the corner past the mansions of Tsuchiya Chikara and Honda Magotarō. At the next corner, he turned again, back toward the main gate of the Kira mansion. There were still two samurai standing across the street at the gate of Makino Ichigaku.

"He's the one who was here before," one of them muttered. He must have recognized the crest on Jōemon's coat. Jōemon pretended not to notice and walked right on past.

By now, both neighbors to the north of Kira had raised tall lanterns at the wall. From within, Jōemon could hear the shouts and clash of sword fighting. One man would call out, and another would answer, "Right!" "There must be fifty men hiding in there." "Well just make sure you get anyone who comes out." "Aren't any of you coming out? Now's the time. Come out and fight."

As Jōemon continued around again toward the rear gate, he could hear the whispers of people in the commoners' houses. No one was asleep; they were all hiding and peeping out through the cracks.

Then a man who appeared to be the neighborhood watchman came by on his rounds, making a great racket with his staff, to which were attached multiple metal rings that jangled whenever the butt end struck the ground. Jōemon approached him and asked, "What's all the noise in this mansion?"

"Oh, it's that night attack."

"Night attack?" Jōemon replied. "And what might *that* be?"

"Asano Dono's men have broken in," the watchman said. "A while ago, they came to the rear gate here—every one of them armed with lances and halberds, blades bare and unsheathed. Then they battered down the gate. The neighborhood people, of course, wondered what was up and came out to see. 'Back in your houses! Back in your houses!' they said. 'This is nothing you commoners need concern yourselves with. If you hang about here and get in the way, we'll just have to cut you down.' So they all ran home. They're a frightful lot. This is a nasty business."

That's an interesting story, Jōemon thought, as he turned and started back toward the main gate. As he rounded the corner by the guardhouse, he could hear voices coming from the second story above Kira's tea rooms. Then from below, someone called out, "Who's that?" "Mountain," the password, was the answer.

About midway down the south wall, Jōemon could see a hole where the paneling had been cut or broken. But then he encountered three men coming from the opposite direction who looked like fishmongers, bearing baskets full of fish. Jōemon spoke to them: "What can be the cause of all the commotion in this mansion?"

"Yes, what *can* it be?" one the fishmongers said. "I suppose it could be spring cleaning." "Of course," Jōemon agreed. "This *is* the season." Then the paneling seemed to break again.

"What can *that* be?" Jōemon said.

"It looks like someone making his escape," the fishmonger said. A very big hole had been bashed out through the paneling, and it made a dreadful crack.

It occurred to Jōemon that Kōzuke Dono and his son may have been hiding in the barracks and were making their escape under cover of the commotion within; so he positioned himself unobtrusively, where, if necessary, he could go to the rear gate and tell someone. It was already past the midpoint of the Seventh Hour (5:00 A.M.). The moon was setting and had fallen below the roof line, making the night a bit darker.

Just then, two men whom he had met at Yahei's rooms in Yonezawa-chō happened by, the younger brother of his mentor Horiuchi Gendazaemon and a senior disciple named Sakitama. Jōemon recognized the crest on their coats and spoke to them: "So you've come back?"

"Yes. What time did they attack?"

"It was some time ago," Jōemon said. "Some men have broken out from within the barracks, so I've stationed myself here; but you should go around to the main gate and have a look there." They both went off in that direction, and Jōemon turned back toward the rear gate. On the way, he again encountered the three fishmongers.

"One more fellow has just come out of the hole," they said. "But don't bother with them; just let them go."

"Oh, I'm not worried about any of them," Jōemon said, trying his best to sound unconcerned.

The man who had just escaped from the barracks headed slowly east along the wall. As Jōemon moved slowly along behind him, Horiuchi and Sakitama, who by now had made a complete circuit of the block, came up behind him. Jōemon spoke softly to them: "A man has just broken out of the barracks, and I am following him. So pretend that you don't know me and head up toward the main gate again."

Jōemon continued to follow the man, and when they reached the corner, Jōemon said casually, "You're very fortunate that the weather is so good. Where will you be going from here?" For a while the man just stood still, and then he turned about and headed back in the opposite direction. Again, Jōemon followed him. Then he stopped, and so Jōemon stopped and said as though to himself, "Whatever can be the cause of so much commotion in there?" The man just stood still, looking down at his feet. Jōemon, too, stood there, pretending not to notice him. The man was trembling terribly. He was wearing two swords and a striped surcoat. Jōemon didn't think that he could be Kōzuke Dono, but wondered if he might be Kira's son Sahei, and so continued to follow him. When the man came to the corner, he went up to the guardhouse and said, "Something strange is going on in the mansion."

"What can it be?" the guardsman replied. "It's a dreadful commotion." At a glance, they appeared to be acquaintances.

"It's bitterly cold," the man said. "Could you let me come in?"

"Yes, do come in," the guard replied, and opened the door for him. From their conversation, Jōemon realized that the man could not possibly be Kira, father or son; he must be just a cowardly vassal. Jōemon paid him no further attention. Looking out from within the guardhouse, the guard and the unknown man seemed to regard Jōemon with suspicion, so he simply pretended not to notice.

Then Horiuchi and Sakitama came around again. Since Kanzaki Yogorō's place was just across the street, Jōemon took them there and showed it to them; then the three of them went back to the main gate.

For a while they listened, but could hear nothing. This made them a bit uneasy. Horiuchi and Sakitama thought that they should return to the rear gate and check there, and they left to do so.

Just then, a great many men carrying lanterns came out from the gate of the Makino mansion. They spoke brashly of going somewhere to report this, and how they were going to dispatch a courier. Then one of them came over to the main gate of the Kira mansion and in a loud voice demanded, "Open up! Open up!" A voice from within answered, "Who is it?"

"That's a dreadful commotion in there. Is there something amiss?"

"There's nothing amiss in here."

"We are vassals of Makino Ichigaku, and we intend to report this!"

But again, "There's nothing amiss in here."

None of the guards who had been stationed at Kira's main gate were still there—only Kuranosuke and the members of his command group. Makino's vassals were left with nothing to report.

◆ ◆ ◆

Suddenly, the silence from within was broken. It sounded to Jōemon like someone questioning a man, but he couldn't make out what either of them was saying. Then another long silence, followed by the shrill signal of a Chinaman's whistle. Then another, from a different direction, and another. Jōemon knew what that meant.

We have just beheaded your lord, Kōzuke-no-Suke Dono!
Will none of you come out to avenge him?

The tumult of battle had died down. Now and again, the silence was broken by the crack of a splintering door or panel, a name called, a muttered curse. Between them were long stretches so quiet that you might think everyone had left.

Chūzaemon had just returned to his post after lecturing his disheartened men. His exhortation to calm, deliberate, and even more extensive searching did not sit well with some of the younger samurai. Rather than go crawling about above the ceilings and below the floors, they grumbled, "Let's just set fire to it and burn the whole house down." A totally unreasonable notion, but understandable as an expression of their extreme disappointment.

Chūzaemon himself was alone now, pacing his assigned sector yet again. Fortunately, he was the sort of man who remained perpetually alert. In the midst of a raging battle, someone once said of him, he might grab a cup of water to slake his thirst; the next day, he could tell you which kiln that cup had been fired in and describe the pattern on it. If anyone else had been patrolling that stretch of 30 or 40 yards at the northwest corner of the house for an hour or more in the bitter cold, he might have been too distracted by the pain in his fingertips and toes to notice the faint whispers that seemed every now and again to rise to the level of audibility. Chūzaemon noticed.

He was passing a reed screen that he had passed countless times earlier in the night and that he thought hid the entrance to a toilet. But this time, hearing what seemed to be the sound of voices within, he paused, listened for a moment, and then beckoned silently to a group of his men standing nearby. At first, they tried the door, found it barred, and then battered it down. It turned out to be a storeroom that opened in two directions. The outside door came to ground level, whereas the other entrance, from the raised floor of the kitchen, was only 3 feet high. One of the men hiding there darted up into the kitchen and made his escape. But those who remained began hurling anything that they could lay their hands on—a barrage of cups, plates, bowls, charcoal, kindling, and firewood came flying out the door. Then one of the men emerged, his weapon drawn; he fought ferociously and well, but only briefly, before he was felled. Then came another, who was likewise felled.

It was dark and almost impossible to see into the depths of the room, but they sensed that another man was still there. Hazama Jūjirō stepped in, leveled his lance, and thrust it into the gloom. It struck flesh. Jūjirō yanked his weapon back, and after it came a staggering figure, flailing about frantically, and uselessly, with a short sword. Takebayashi Tadashichi sprang forward, and with one hard stroke of his sword cut deep into the man's shoulder where it joins the neck. The carotid artery spewed forth a great spray, followed by steadily slower surges. The figure fell forward on his knees and then his face, dead.

But *who* was dead? They immediately assumed that it must be Kira Kōzuke-no-Suke. But could they be certain? When they dragged his body farther into the open, they could see that he was an old man wearing a white night robe and that his pate was not shaved.

"Look for his scar," someone said. "He was wounded on the forehead." But Jūjirō had wounded him on his face, as well as on his hands and thighs. There was too much blood to distinguish a scar in this light.

"Then look on his back. He was wounded there, too." Tadashichi rolled the body over, thrust his sword down the gap at the neck, and ripped the robe open. There was the other scar, clearly to be seen.

Fuwa Kazuemon came running up just then. "Get some water," he said. "I'll wash the blood from his face." That done, Kazuemon brought his lantern closer; now they could see the thin line of a scar on the man's forehead, just above his eyebrow. They could also see that he wore an elegantly fashioned talisman about his neck that no ordinary person could afford. This could only be Kira Kōzuke-no-Suke.

By this time, Kuranosuke had come down from the main gate, and as commander of the force, he administered the ceremonial coup de grâce, thrusting his sword down through Kira's neck. This detail is sometimes questioned, but later inspection of Kuranosuke's sword revealed that it was blood-stained along the first foot of the blade, and the tip had chipped when it struck rock or frozen earth. Kuranosuke then called to Jūjirō. It was he who had drawn first blood; he would thus be granted the privilege of severing the head. He did so with a single stroke.

One final step remained. They carried the head back to the main gate, where old Yahei still stood guard over the foot soldier whom they had bound when they first came over the walls.

"Do you know this head?" they asked

Tears flowed from the man's eyes, we are told, as he said, "That is My Lord Kōzuke-no-Suke Dono. Unmistakably."

The signal to assemble could now be sounded. One blast of the Chinaman's whistle called forth another and then still others from all corners of the property. It had been agreed that they would muster in the open space before the rear gate, and once everyone had gathered there, they allowed themselves a cry of victory: "Ei, Ei," cried the commander; "Oooh!" answered the warriors. "Ei, Ei, Oooh! Ei, Ei, Oooh!" Their "Whale Wave" was perhaps less vociferous than after a battle fought by hundreds or thousands. But they were no less elated. The young men strode about, triumphantly shouting, "We have just beheaded your lord, Kōzuke-no-Suke Dono! Will none of you come out to avenge him?" No one emerged.

The head was then wrapped in a white sleeve torn from the dead man's robe and lashed to the haft of a lance. Kuranosuke affixed his seal to the fabric, as well as to the talisman and paper fold that would accompany the head as further proof of its identity. Yoshida Chūzaemon took out his copy of the manifesto and from it called the names of all forty-seven men who had signed it. No one was missing. Finally, the three men who had spoken to Tsuchiya Chikara—Jūnai, Gengoemon, and Sōemon—returned to the rear wall and once again identified themselves. This time, they reported the successful beheading of Kira

Kōzuke-no-Suke, apologized for the disturbance, and thanked the Tsuchiya for their forbearance.

As the company began to form itself into a column and wind its way toward the rear gate, Hayami Tōzemon noticed a low door, sheltered by a sloping roof of cedar shingles, and cracked open about 1 foot. This would be the quarters of one of the Elders of the house. Inside, a low light shone, not the light of a lamp but the flickering flame of a candle. Tōzaemon decided that he would give whoever was within one last chance to prove himself a warrior and not a coward: "I am Hayami Tōzaemon! Whoever you are, come out and fight!"

Total silence. The occupant, Matsubara Tachū, was already mortally wounded, but Tōzaemon would not have known that. He reached back to his quiver, notched an arrow, drew, and shot; then he drew and shot again. Both arrows struck hard and loud, but no other sound came from within. The column moved again, issuing quietly into the street. Some of the men were already planning their next battle.

♦ ♦ ♦

There was no doubt in anyone's mind that there would be another battle and that it would be fought against a force sent from Sakurada by Kira's natural son, Uesugi Danjō. The ronin bore no grudge against the Uesugi. Their object in fighting such a battle would be simply to clear the way to Sengakuji, where they would present the head of Kira Kōzuke-no-Suke at the grave of their late lord, after which they would surrender themselves to the Shogunate. The great question, though, was where and when that battle would be fought. If news of their attack had reached the Uesugi rapidly, the force from Sakurada might come at any moment. They must establish a good defensive position as soon as possible. Ekōin (Temple of the Unknown Dead) was only a short walk away. Within its walls, they could rest until they were forced to fight again; and when the Uesugi arrived, it would serve as a sort of urban fort. The temple Ekōin was their first destination.

♦ ♦ ♦

As the column emerged from the grounds of the mansion and swung left into the street, they were greeted joyously by some of those who had waited through the cold night while the ronin fought. Jinzaburō was there with his great basket of mandarin oranges. Satō Jōemon, of course, sought out his cousin Yasubei and Yasubei's father, Yahei.

"It was much easier than we expected," Yasubei said. He was carrying both Yahei's lance and his own great sword; they were heavy, so he passed them to Jōemon to carry. The day had only faintly begun to dawn.

Jōemon took Yahei's arm as they walked to the corner and turned toward the Ryōgoku Bridge. "Quite different from when I led you to the attack, isn't it? You must be quite relaxed now."

"Indeed, indeed!" Yahei said. "When we went to Yogorō's place and saw that everyone had left, and I was late, I was terribly worried whether we would make it." Then they encountered Kuranosuke, and Jōemon told him how delighted he was that they had succeeded.

"I'm sure you can imagine how pleased we feel," Kuranosuke said.

◆ ◆ ◆

They walked the length of Aioi-chō; turned right into the broad, open approaches to the Ryōgoku Bridge; and there most of them waited for further orders while the command group proceeded down the avenue that led to the temple gate. If the Uesugi should arrive now, it would be better to meet them in the open than in the confines of a narrow street. But there was as yet no sign of any counterattack; most of the ronin fell to desultory conversation.

Hazama Jūjirō was carrying the head of Kōzuke Dono, Jōemon recalled, and offered to show it to him. Jōemon seems to have assumed that it was Jūjirō who had killed Kira, and said, "You must be very proud of your accomplishment." But their chat was cut short when another ronin came over and spoke to Jōemon.

"I'd like to ask a favor of you."

"May I ask who you are?" Jōemon said.

"I'm Tominomori Suke'emon."

"Ah! So you are Suke'emon Dono? I'll gladly do anything for you that I can."

"Then may I ask you to take these to my family?" he said, and began removing his sleeve markers. But while Jōemon was waiting for him to do that, another ronin came up from behind him, tugged at his sleeve, and said, "I'd like to have a word with you."

"What is it?" Jōemon asked. "And who are you?"

"I'm Takebayashi Tadashichi. Could you come over here with me for a moment?" He led Jōemon back to where Hazama Jūjirō was standing.

"Jūjirō Dono!" Tadashichi shouted at him angrily. "I know we agreed from the start that there would be no ranking of merit. But this is something people are going to be talking about long after we're dead. So let's get the story straight. *You* cut off the head of a dead man, a man *I* killed with this sword. See how it's bent here? It was dark in there, and I hit something with it. It still won't slip all the way into the sheath. Anyhow, I'm sick to death of hearing you run off at the mouth like some imbecile!" Then turning to Jōemon, he added, "And I want *you* to remember this."

"I shall indeed," Jōemon replied. "You must be very proud of what you've done, and I can understand how you feel."

By this time, Tominomori Suke'emon had come back, and he handed his sleeve markers to Jōemon: "Thank you for doing this. I'm sorry that I didn't get to meet you sooner."

✦ ✦ ✦

At this point, I cannot resist repeating a tale that I suspect is at least in part fanciful, but that was making the rounds in Edo almost immediately after the attack. It was told by Sakaya Jūbei, the proprietor of a saké shop at the approaches to the Ryōgoku Bridge, where the ronin were awaiting further word from their leaders.

Jūbei was just opening the shutters of his shop when a great number of men, quite unknown to him and smeared with blood, appeared, saying to one another, "Danjō's men are certain to come after us. Four or five of those with the strongest legs had better take the head to the grave as quickly as possible. The rest of us will stay and fight to the death against Danjō."

"What *is* this?" Jūbei wondered. But just when he had decided that he had better shut his shop again, five or six ronin forced their way in and said, "Could you give us a cup of hot water for this man? He's wounded." When Jūbei told them that he hadn't boiled any water yet, they said, "That's too bad; he's utterly exhausted. But give us a cup of saké instead." Jūbei was then forced to tell them that he was forbidden by law to serve seated customers.

"Well, we've just broken some of the strictest laws in the land, so what do we care about one more little law? Here," one of them said, tossing him a paper fold, "this should cover the cost of your saké." Then they took a whole keg from the shop, split the lid with the butt end of a lance, and started serving it out in Jūbei's teacups. "Sakaya!" one of them called. "Lend us your inkstone." Jūbei did as he was asked, and the man wrote on a piece of paper produced from within his coat:

> yama o nuku / chikara mo orete / yuki no matsu
> Even the pine, with its power to split a mountain,
> snaps under the snow.
> ŌTAKA GENGO

Then they all ran off. Jūbei picked up the paper fold that one of the men had tossed at him, and in it were two gold pieces. They were wrapped in paper that was sealed with paste and upon which was written, "Genroku 15, Year of the Horse, Twelfth Month, 15th Day. This money is to buy drinks for those who dispose of the body of Ōtaka Gengo, vassal of Asano Takumi-no-Kami Naganori, after he dies in battle."

◆ ◆ ◆

The command group had now returned from the temple, but the news was not good. The ronin would not be admitted to the Temple of the Unknown Dead. At first, the monk on watch at the gate had told them that it was too early, that they did not open the gate until dawn. But then he had run to the Superior of the temple, who ruled that no one bearing unsheathed assault weapons and clad in armor would be allowed within the gate at any time. Since they chose not to force their way in, they now had no choice but to proceed to their lord's grave as best they could and hope they would not, somewhere en route, be forced to fight their way to Sengakuji.

figure 22
Nagayasu Gasan's painting of the ronin withdrawing from Honjo.
(Akō Municipal Museum of History)

One way to avoid that fight, of course, would be to go by boat. But the boatmen proved no more cooperative than the monks. For much the same reasons, and likewise fearing the wrath of the Shogunate, they too refused. The ronin decided that they would array themselves in a battle formation suitable for city streets and set out straightaway. When they began to move, the formation looked roughly like this:

⊙ ⊙ ⊙   Three lancers

⊙   Kira's head

⊙ ⊙ ⊙ ⊙

⊙   Ōishi Chikara

⊙

⊙   ⊙

⊙⊙ ⊙⊙   The wounded

⊙⊙   Old Horibe Yahei

⊙   ⊙

⊙ ⊙ ⊙ ⊙

⊙   Ōishi Kuranosuke

⊙ ⊙ ⊙ ⊙ ⊙ ⊙ ⊙

⊙ ⊙ ⊙ ⊙

CHAPTER
68

*These brave men, their blood now running hot,
were left to gnaw at their own navels.*

Shortly after Tōfu-ya arrived at the East Gate, imparted his news, and departed, a foot soldier from Honjo, Maruyama Sei'emon, arrived at the main gate of the Uesugi Upper Mansion in Sakurada. He brought the same news: the Kira mansion, at that very moment, was under attack. Everyone had long been aware that such a thing *might* happen, but the actual fact nonetheless took them by surprise. They must act; that they knew. But they had no prearranged plan of action. Their own records reflect clearly the confusion in the Uesugi household on the morning of the 15th.

◆ ◆ ◆

Their first move, mentioned only in passing, was to dispatch three men from Sakurada to Honjo at first light—Fukazawa Han'emon, a Liaison Officer; Katagiri Rokurōzaemon, an Adjutant; and Yamashita Yogodayū, a Herald. Their mission was to survey the situation at the Kira mansion and report back. In the meantime, provisional preparations would be made for a subsequent expedition.

Only the first faint gray of dawn had begun to appear when Nomoto Chūzaemon, an Usher to Lord Uesugi Tsunanori, was awakened in his quarters by a messenger from the Captain of the Night Watch in the Great Hall. It was still too dark to read the note.

"A strange hour for a message from the Great Hall," he thought. "I need a lamp." But none was lit. He went to the garden side of the room,

~ 560 ~

slid open the panel to the veranda, and tilted the paper to catch what little light there was. It was enough. He threw the paper aside, and turned to his manservant: "There's no time to change; I'll go as I am. But get out a full set of formal wear, and follow me as quickly as you can." With that, he rushed out the door, across the courtyard to the mansion, and into the Middle Hall. Already a crowd was gathering. By now, he noted, dawn had come.

The first detail had already departed, and there seems to have been some quibbling over who should be included in the next. Those slated for duty that day thought that they should be the ones, and those who were off duty disagreed. Nomoto thought them all quite ridiculous.

"This is no time to be splitting hairs over who is on watch and who not. I'm going to go straightaway." But Mori Kenmotsu, Commander of the Corps of Pages, was not having it.

"Not so fast!" Mori said. "Nobody's going until we can check this out. It's no good charging in there when you've no knowledge of what's waiting for you."

"Well, then get moving and check things out," Nomoto snapped, and strode back to his quarters to make ready to leave. But while he was there, someone seems to have pointed out that the three men who had gone on ahead could not possibly report back in so short a time. Honjo was too far away. And so the others departed without Nomoto, who was left to catch up as quickly as he could.

◆ ◆ ◆

Just when in the course of all this confusion Uesugi Danjō was informed that his father was under attack, no one mentions. It may well have been after both the first and second details had left Sakurada. Danjō had been seriously ill since the summer. His ailment is never specified, but it was grave enough to keep him bedridden. His men may have hesitated to disturb him so early in the morning. But when they did break the news, they told him that the vassals of Asano Takumi-no-Kami Naganori, several tens of them, had surrounded the Honjo mansion and launched an attack against it; with the darkness of the night and the suddenness of the attack, Kira's men had lost the advantage, and their lord had been forced to commit suicide—so they said.

When His Lordship heard this, he was aghast and commanded that his forces make haste to attack the assailants. Seven units were to be sent to Honjo immediately: three troops of mounted Horse Guards, supported by numerous samurai and foot soldiers. Upon their arrival, His Lordship added, they were to cut down every one of the assailants, none excepted. But while the logistics of assembling this force were being discussed, word arrived from Honjo that the attackers were gone. But gone where? It would not do to send a great force running hither and yon through the city in search of them. Should they first dispatch five or six men, each in a different direction, and try to discover the destination of the ronin? Before anything at all could be done, however, an Usher came to announce that Kira's colleague Hatakeyama Shimōsa-no-Kami had just arrived.

"I expect that you may intend to deploy a force in response to this morning's fracas," he began. "But you would be ill-advised to disturb the peace of Edo in this age of tranquility. The miscreants will be punished without delay by the authorities. Under no circumstances are you to retaliate." Such was the command of the Council of Elders, he explained.

"But how am I to abandon the Way of Filial Duty and force these men of mine to go empty-handed?" His Lordship protested. Yet to disobey a command of the Shogunate was nothing to be undertaken lightly. In the end, he commanded his samurai and soldiers to stand down—"and these brave men, their blood now running hot, were left to gnaw at their own navels."

This all sounds fairly straightforward, but if you stop to consider the question of timing, you may wonder how it was that the Council of Elders managed to thwart a counterattack by the Uesugi before it even started. The details are nowhere recorded, but they are not difficult to work out. Tsuchiya Chikara, Kira's neighbor to the north, sent news of the attack to his kinsman Tsuchiya Sagami-no-Kami while it was still in progress. Sagami-no-Kami would immediately have notified his fellow Elders. They would have met, composed their injunction, and sent Hatakeyama Shimōsa-no-Kami to Sakurada well before the Uesugi were sufficiently organized to counterattack. Shimōsa-no-Kami was their chosen emissary not only because he was a colleague of Kira, but also because he was related by marriage to the Uesugi.

+ + +

One has to wonder, too, just how keen the House of Uesugi was to avenge the father of their adopted lord. Nothing of this sort is ever mentioned in the official records of the house or even in the correspondence of the Uesugi vassals. But Tōjō Shusetsu, of the Mizuno house, reports some of the rumors that were current in Edo at the time. According to one report, Danjō later in the day insisted that a force be sent to Sengakuji to attack and kill the ronin, whereupon his own Elders told him: "Kira Dono may be your natural father, but this is not his house. For you, Danjō Dono, his is now a different house. You were adopted to lead *this* house. And that matter in no way concerns this house, so you had best abandon your scheme."

Tōjō also reports that Nagao Gonshirō, Chief Elder of the Uesugi house in Yonezawa, was outraged to learn that His Lordship's mad battle plan had not been nipped in the bud, but allowed to progress almost to the point of execution. It could have meant the demise of the House of Uesugi. Nagao immediately left Yonezawa, and when he arrived in Edo, refused even to lodge in the Sakurada mansion.

"What are these Edo Elders up to?" he fumed. "They should be petitioning the Shogunate for a change of lords."

+ + +

When the detail from Sakurada finally arrived in Honjo, they found the entire Kira mansion in a shambles. Every gate, every door, every shoji, panel, and partition had been smashed to smithereens. The ceilings, floors, folding screens, and storage boxes were riddled with holes pierced by probing lances. Bedding, clothing, and accessories were scattered everywhere. Every wall of every room was splattered with blood, and the floors smeared.

Nomoto Chūzaemon entered at the rear gate, proceeded to the quarters of Kira the elder, and from there walked the length of the long narrow mansion. In Kōzuke-no-Suke's bedchamber, he found Kira's

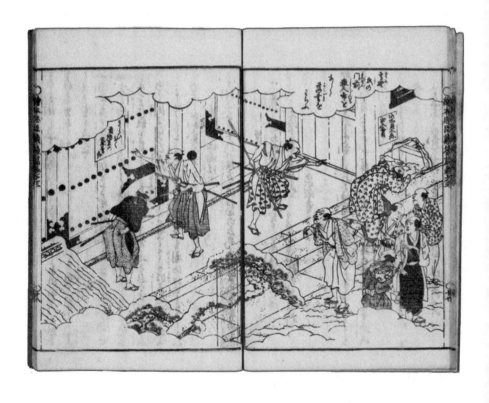

figure 23
Neighbors laughing at the hole in Kira's wall.
(*Ehon Chūshingura*, Waseda University Library, Tokyo)

adopted son Sahei, bloodied and severely wounded, but still alive. The two men with him told Nomoto that he had lain alone here until only a short time before.

Farther along, Nomoto had to step over the bodies of the dead and wounded sprawled in "obscene postures." It was "beyond description," he tells us. At the rear of the house, in the food-preparation rooms, he found two more dead bodies—as well as a jumble of discarded equipment: lances, axes, arm guards, mallets, and the like.

Moving on to the anteroom of Sahei's bedchamber, Nomoto came upon two men sprawled across the floor, both of whom *looked* dead; but then one turned his head and identified himself as Yamayoshi Shinpachi. The other said nothing. "They looked like two corpses sharing a single pillow," Nomoto remarks.

In the hallway leading to the reception rooms, he stepped around the body of someone he knew well, Sudō Yoichiemon. And as he entered the anteroom, he came upon a heartrending scene: "I found Shimizu Dan'emon, badly wounded and propped up against the wall. His father was there with him. In my medicine kit, I had a bit of ginseng and five bits of smelling salts. 'Here,' I said, 'you can use this when he loses consciousness' (which he was doing frequently). I emptied the kit and gave it all to his father before I left."

In the main kitchens, Nomoto found two more bodies, and in the main hall, another two. When he reached the main entryway, he saw that still more dead and wounded lay outside. For whatever reasons, he decided not to investigate further.

What time of day Nomoto and his colleagues made this tour, he does not say; it must have been about midday or earlier, for he recalls that the two official Inspectors, Abe Shikibu and Sugita Gozaemon, arrived to conduct their investigation just after the Eighth Hour (2:00 P.M.). They questioned all the wounded who were conscious and recorded their statements. They then gathered all the weapons, tools, and equipment that the ronin had abandoned, and made a detailed inventory of them. Among the castoffs were several name tags, one of which read: "Ōishi Kuranosuke, vassal of Asano Takumi-no-Kami," and on the reverse side, "Twelfth Month, 14th Day, killed in action."

✦ ✦ ✦

It was not until late that afternoon, however, that anyone in the Kira mansion would be given the medical attention he needed. By that time, those bleeding men had been lying in pain for at least twelve hours. Again, medical attention came in the form of Kurisaki Dōyū, the surgeon who had ministered to Kira himself in the castle almost two years earlier.

The initial request for Dōyū's services came directly from the Kira household. It must have been an alarmingly garbled request, as Dōyū's first response was to refuse on the grounds that he was not equipped to deal with such carnage. Thereafter, however, a second request came from the Uesugi, whose standing in the hierarchy of warrior houses made it all but impossible for Dōyū to refuse again. He knew now that there were at least seventeen seriously wounded patients awaiting his attention, and he went prepared for a long session of surgery. Seven of his disciples accompanied him.

Immediately after he arrived, Dōyū himself attended to Kira's adopted son, Sahei. He describes his condition as follows: "The son, Sahei, had one wound, 7 inches long, starting at his lower rib cage, where it cut into the ribs, and reaching across his back. On his forehead, there were two or three more wounds, each about 3 inches long." This case alone was going to take a good deal more cleansing, stitching, and dressing than the boy's father had required. And there were sixteen more injured men still waiting. Yamayoshi Shinpachi, Dōyū says, had sustained eight wounds. And nine other men bore heavy wounds of various sorts.

Once Dōyū had treated Sahei, he examined the others, undertaking the most critical cases himself and assigning the rest to one or another of his disciples, intermittently instructing each how he should treat his patient. Dōyū completed his own share of the work by about the Fourth Hour (10:00 P.M.), but his disciples were unable to leave until early the next morning. It was a long night.

Nomoto Chūzaemon had been assigned to stand watch throughout the night in Honjo, but at the Eighth Hour (2:00 A.M.), he was sent as a courier from Kira Sahei to Sakurada bearing the message that Sahei wished to arrange the return of the head of his father.

+ + +

Strange to say, though, no one from the Uesugi house mentioned the hole in the south wall of the barracks through which Sōda Magobei and Saitō Kunai escaped, but the hole did not pass unnoticed. One of the wits in the neighborhood had that very morning posted a notice next to it that read, "This entrance reserved for the exclusive use of the Elders of the house."

This doesn't mean that no one is coming.
It means that they know where we are going.

If only they had known! It would have made everything so much easier. But there was no way the ronin could have known that the Council of Elders had warned the Uesugi not to retaliate, on pain of dire but unstated consequences—and that the Uesugi, having had their enfeoffment slashed twice already, could imagine only too well what those consequences might be. And so the ronin set out from Honjo fully prepared to be attacked somewhere between there and the temple Sengakuji in Takanawa.

Nor were the Uesugi their only worry. The 14th may have been an auspicious day on which to sever the head of their lord's enemy, but the 15th was a day of general audience at Edo Castle. The main streets of the city would be bustling with the processions of daimyo and bannermen. It would not do to cross paths with any of them, as menacingly armed and bloodied as they were. They would have to move through the back streets and avoid the thoroughfares as much as possible. It would be a long, hard trek. The distance was great; everyone was weary; and some were disabled by wounds or just old age.

✦ ✦ ✦

It is often thought that the ronin must have crossed the river on the Ryōgoku Bridge, but not so. That would have taken them into streets that would soon be filling with traffic bound for the castle. Instead, they stayed on the east side of the river, crossing the canal at the First Bridge and heading down the street that runs behind a long row of boathouses, where the Shogun's great warship, the *Atake Maru*, was once moored. It must have been obvious even then that it would be impossible to maintain a tight formation all the way to Takanawa. By the time they had passed the boathouses, some men were already falling behind, so they halted and hired town litters to carry those who could not keep up. Then they continued along that route, following the river downstream, past the Great New Bridge, through Fukagawa, and on to the Eitai Bridge.

◆ ◆ ◆

Perhaps some of you have seen the print by Suzuki Harunobu—one of his less than decent ones, I'm afraid, but a thing of beauty nonetheless—the print depicting two lovers gazing down from a window at the top of a brothel in Fukagawa, enjoying the snowy dawn riverscape, while enjoying each other. (It is always hard to tell with Harunobu's women—they are so blasé—though I suspect that this woman is enjoying the scene more than the man.) Well, as it happens, the street by the riverbank that the couple overlooks is the very one that the ronin were tramping along this morning. And whenever I see that print, I cannot but wonder what it might have done to the pleasure of those two if instead of a few boats and early-rising tradesmen, they had seen a procession of blood-stained warriors carrying a severed head.

◆ ◆ ◆

The Eitai Bridge was the last chance for the ronin to cross to the opposite shore before the river widened into an estuary too broad to be spanned by bridges. They crossed and immediately turned left into Reiganjima, still following the river as closely as possible. Kuranosuke, they say, would regularly drop out of his protected position, fall back to the rear of the column, and do his best to tighten the formation before resuming his place.

This is where we first catch a closer glimpse of the ronin, chatting to one another as they make their way through the city. A certain townsman, whose name has never been known, apparently a collector of snippets of lore, recorded bits and pieces of conversation overheard by residents of Reiganjima when the ronin were skirting the huge mansion of Matsudaira Echizen-no-Kami. This is what he tells us they were saying:

> "I'm utterly exhausted. I didn't do all that much. I shouldn't feel this worn out."

> "It's because you're relaxed now. That's when it hits you."

> "When I stepped into the entryway, one of those guys was hiding behind a door on the left. He drew his sword and came at me something ferocious. I was fighting back as hard as I could, but I just couldn't get past him. But it was dark, and he tripped and fell. Then I was able to kill him and move on. But he's the one who gave me this wound."

> There was an old man named Yahei. He had given his sword to a servant to carry and was walking with a bamboo staff. As he passed, he said, "Even on level ground, my legs are a bit wobbly. But up on that rooftop this morning—I can't imagine how I managed that. I must have made a dreadful spectacle of myself."

> "Far from it! You were steadier then than you are now. Many of the younger men didn't do as well as you. They didn't all come over the rooftop, you know. But doesn't your wound hurt?"

> "Not at all, but I'm utterly exhausted."

Immediately after crossing the Inari Bridge, they turned right and followed the street that runs alongside the Hatchōbori Canal. This was their old neighborhood, just around the corner from the former Asano Upper Mansion in Teppōzu. On this street lived many of the shopkeepers who had once provided for the day-to-day needs of the Asano vassals. Their old tofu maker, Hishiya Sanjūrō, had come out and offered some of them tea. And another, Ōshimaya Hachirōbei, was just rising as the procession passed his shop. By the time he had opened his shutters, most of the ronin were already out of sight. But as he stepped out into the street, broom in hand, the first thing he saw was two samurai in firefighting gear. To his amazement, one of them looked straight at him and in a hearty voice called him by name.

"Hachirōbei! A good morning to you!" Only then did he realize that it was Tominomori Suke'emon. The only words that Hachirōbei could get out were, "But, what . . . ?" Suke'emon was in high spirits and went right on talking.

"We've been wanting to do this for ages, and last night, finally, we did it! We're just delighted." The bearers of the head had by then turned the next corner, but Hachirōbei had heard enough gossip in past months to guess what it was they had done.

"But look," Suke'emon continued, "I wonder if I can ask a favor of you. You know my mother and my wife? They're living in Kōjimachi now, just next to the Tenjin Shrine. I'd be terribly grateful if you could run over there and tell them we've done it." Hachirōbei still hadn't said a word. Not to Suke'emon or to anyone in his house. He just dropped his broom and set off at a trot in the direction of Kōjimachi, which was on the far side of the castle, at least an hour away from Hatchōbori. Suke'emon had to shout after him: "Hachirōbei, wait!" He pulled off his fire helmet and tossed it to the shopkeeper: "Take this to them, too—as a souvenir."

In Kōjimachi, when Hachirōbei broke the news to Suke'emon's mother and wife, both women were overjoyed.

"Did Suke'emon fight well?" his mother asked. "Did you have a look at his swords for us?"

Hachirōbei was nonplussed. "I'm afraid not," he replied. In fact, he had no idea why he *should* have looked at them. "I was so shocked when he told me what they'd done, I just started running."

"Well that's a shopkeeper for you," the mother muttered, "but I'd feel a lot better if you had checked his swords before you came." Hachirōbei could hardly believe that this was a woman talking. But when he turned to Suke'emon's wife, who at first had seemed so thrilled, he saw that she was weeping.

◆ ◆ ◆

Once the ronin had rounded the corner and walked a short way along the Prince-Abbot's Canal, those at the head of the procession halted, just opposite their old home, the mansion in Teppōzu, which was now inhabited by Sakai Yugei Dono. It was a landmark that everyone knew, so they had agreed that those in the lead would pause there and wait for the stragglers to catch up before moving on. The presence of such an outlandish group attracted the attention of those on guard at the gate, of course, and before long one of them approached the ronin.

"Judging from appearances," the man said, "you would seem to have been up to something quite out of the ordinary. But I fail to see why you should halt just here. I shall have to detain you until you explain yourselves."

"We are ronin formerly in the service of Asano Takumi-no-Kami," they said. "This morning, we killed and took the head of Kōzuke-no-Suke, a mission from which we are now returning. This place was formerly the mansion of Takumi, so we've decided to wait here for the slower men to catch up with us. We have already reported to the Duty Inspector General, and we shall proceed from here to Sengakuji, the mortuary temple of Takumi-no-Kami. So, you see, there is no need for you to detain us." The guard agreed and allowed them to pass.

◆ ◆ ◆

From Teppōzu, they moved on to the great Honganji temple, two borders of which they traversed before arriving at the Shiodome Bridge. There stood the upper mansion of Okudaira Mimasaka-no-Kami, and there, too, their passage aroused alarm. Sakurai Sōemon, the Duty Inspector that morning, described it:

> On the night of the 14th, forty-seven vassals of Asano Takumi-no-Kami Dono broke into the mansion of Kira Kōzuke-no-Suke Dono and had their way with him. On the morning of the 15th, sometime after the Sixth Hour [ca. 6:00 A.M.], they passed by our gate. At the time, a menial came in saying that a group of men who had perpetrated a vendetta were just in front of the gate, whereupon I rushed out and saw about twenty vassals of Takumi-no-Kami Dono, armed with unsheathed lances and halberds. Their blades were wrapped in

*scraps of white cotton, and they were all carrying their own weap-
ons. All of them were wearing black half-length surcoats. There was
blood on their lances, halberds, swords, and other gear. Two of them
were wounded, one on the left hand and the other on his thigh. The
head was wrapped in a piece of white material and was suspended
from the haft of a halberd that was borne by two men. It was a
bizarre sight. I'd never even heard of, much less seen, any such thing
passing our gate. But there they were, and I could not but wonder
what was up, so I went out and accosted them.*

*"You gentlemen present a most unusual appearance. May I ask
where you are from and where you've been fighting?"*

*They answered: "We are vassals of Asano Takumi-no-Kami. As
you may already know, we broke into the residence of Kira Kōzuke-
no-Suke last night, and exacted the satisfaction of him that we've so
long desired. We're now in possession of his head."*

"May I ask where you're bound for?" I said.

*"The temple called Sengakuji in Shiba is Takumi-no-Kami's mortu-
ary temple; we're on our way there to offer the head at his grave."*

Sakurai, too, invited the ronin to carry on. And when they had
crossed Shiodome Bridge, they again halted. Here, instead of joining
the thoroughfare that led to the Eastern Sea Road, they would take
the narrow street that ran parallel to it. But first there was an important matter to be seen to. Here, Yoshida Chūzaemon and Tominomori
Suke'emon would part company with the procession. They would then
make their way through the maze of mansions that gave this sector of
the city the nickname "Daimyo Lane" and on to the official residence of
Sengoku Hōki-no-Kami, the Duty Inspector General for the Twelfth
Month. There they would turn themselves in, report what they and
their comrades had done that night, and await the consequences.

While the column was halted, Kuranosuke also sent someone
to hire a town litter for Chikamatsu Kanroku, who was finding it
increasingly difficult to walk because of the wound in his thigh. This

may also be where old Yahei was told that he, too, might ride the rest of the way. As we have seen, he was still on foot in Reiganjima, but by now he had walked more than half the distance; that was enough for a man of his age.

Some of the men seem to have grown hopeful: having come this far unmolested, they thought, it was unlikely that the Uesugi would pursue them farther. Kuranosuke disagreed.

"This doesn't mean that no one is coming," he said. "It means that they know where we are going. They have three hundred men on fire watch at Zōjōji. All they have to do is wait until we pass." Before long, they would have to pass the Great Gate of that temple; but for the moment they could continue to avoid the highway.

◆ ◆ ◆

The mansions of three major daimyo stood in a row on the narrow street that the ronin were about to enter: Wakizaka Awaji-no-Kami, Matsudaira (Daté) Mutsu-no-Kami, and Matsudaira Higo-no-Kami. These properties being as large as they were, each had its own corner guardhouse that the daimyo themselves were required to man. It was almost inevitable that the procession should be stopped at one of them. Some accounts say that they were stopped at all three. That is not impossible, but only their parley with the vassals of Matsudaira Mutsu-no-Kami has found its way into the written record.

One of the men from the guardhouse signaled the column to halt while another ran into the mansion. Immediately thereafter, a man in full formal wear came out of the gate and asked them to explain themselves. Once again, Kuranosuke explained that they had just killed the enemy of their late lord, that they were on their way to Sengakuji, and that they had already informed the Inspector General. The man in formal wear then, almost apologetically, offered them an explanation of his own.

"These corner guardhouses are required by Shogunal ordinance to detain anyone of suspicious appearance. But since you explain yourselves totally to our satisfaction, you are free to pass." Kuranosuke thanked the man, and then asked if he might trouble him for a drink of water.

"You must be very tired," the man said. "Shall I call for a town litter to carry you?"

"No, no thank you," Kuranosuke replied. "I'm by no means too tired to walk."

◆ ◆ ◆

Just beyond these three daimyo mansions, the road they were traveling was blocked by an unbridged waterway, and the ronin were forced to veer right and finally to turn onto the main thoroughfare. This would be the most dangerous leg of their journey. If they could travel it unchallenged, it would take them directly to the temple Sengakuji. But only four blocks farther on was the gate to the great Shogunal Temple Zōjōji, where three hundred or more warriors of the House of Uesugi might be lying in ambush. Added to which, it was a street certain to be taken by various of the daimyo houses en route to the castle on this day of general audience. There was nothing for it but to move out, keep a tight formation, and remain alert.

◆ ◆ ◆

Their presence in the neighborhood did not go unnoticed. But in one case at least—which they would never know of—the results were more humorous than damaging to anyone.

It had been an unexpectedly quiet morning at the upper mansion of Hisamatsu Oki-no-Kami. Normally, on the 15th, the house would have resounded with activity from before dawn in preparation for His Lordship's progress to the castle. But today, His Lordship was laid low with illness and confined to his bed. A messenger had been sent to the Duty Elder bearing his apologies, and now everyone was waiting quietly for the command to stand down. In the duty room, the lower-ranking samurai were talking, quietly, about nothing in particular. Then the door slid open a crack. Shimomura Suke'emon, the overseer of the kitchens, looked in and asked Haga Seidayū if he might speak to him outside for just a moment.

"There's a tradesman in the kitchen," he said. "It's Gohei, the man who supplies us with firewood and charcoal. He says that he's seen a huge band of heavily armed men. About two hundred of them. They're wearing armor, and they're armed with lances and halberds and bows and arrows. Their blades are covered with blood, and they're carrying a head on the end of a lance. When Gohei saw them, they were passing the mansion of Matsudaira Mutsu-no-Kami, heading in the direction of Shiba. The rumor is that they're ronin of the house of Asano Takumi-no-Kami. At least that's what Gohei says."

Seidayū seems almost to have relished this bizarre bit of news. He sent Shimomura to fetch Gohei; questioned the man thoroughly, although he had nothing more to tell than he had already told; and then told him to wait in the provisioner's room. He then returned to his colleagues in the duty room and proceeded to lecture them on the importance of military preparedness, a virtue of which he considered himself a shining exemplar. His attempts to rouse them to action produced no reaction.

"It was ever thus," Seidayū spluttered. "The signs of trouble are plain to see, and no one pays any attention. Even when disaster is well on its way, no one takes it seriously. But if the seeds of trouble are there before one's very eyes, and a daimyo fails to respond, then there's no escaping the censure that's bound to follow. Now, I say that we should send out observers to monitor the situation, and we should warn our men at the middle and lower mansions. That's the least we can do."

Seidayū's comrades remained unimpressed. Some of them looked away and said nothing. Some of them smiled wryly at one another. And some of them shook their heads as though to say, "There goes Seidayū, preaching again." To Seidayū, their indifference only demonstrated how right he was.

"As I'd expect," he said. "But this is no idle nonsense; what I'm talking about is nothing less than the honor of this noble house." He left the room and sent for his own men, a young retainer and a menial. He had them wrap up his firefighting gear and stow his armor in a luggage box, and then he mounted the observation platform, the view from which seemed to him somehow unsettling. And in that state, one presumes, he awaited the impending disaster that would never come. We shall get to know this man better further on in our tale.

♦ ♦ ♦

Having turned onto the main thoroughfare, to everyone's astonishment they traveled the first four blocks without the slightest sign of opposition anywhere within the vast temple complex. And on they went: three more blocks to the Kanasugi Bridge, around the bend at Moto Shiba, and down that long stretch, past Signpost Corner, until they reached the Mita Hachiman Shrine. And there they were greeted by, of all people, Takada Gunbei. No one would speak to him.

Finally, Horibe Yahei told him, "Well, we've done it, just as we intended. We've killed Kōzuke-no-Suke Dono, and we're taking his head to Sengakuji. So what do you make of that!"

"My, my," Gunbei replied. "You must all be very pleased. I myself have just been to Mita Hachiman to pray for your success." No one said another word to him, and the column moved on.

♦ ♦ ♦

By now, the column that had been formed up with such care in Honjo was strung out, straggling, and exhausted. The sense of threat had relaxed, and the weariest of the men were no longer even trying to keep up. But, strange to say, we have an astonishingly accurate idea of what these people looked like just then. A samurai named Sakakibara, in the service of the Kutsuki house, just happened to be at the Shiba Shinmei Shrine that morning when the ronin passed. To our good fortune, the scene so moved him that he sketched it—and quite competently.

♦ ♦ ♦

Any traveler who rises before dawn to begin his journey down the Eastern Sea Road will understand perfectly why the print artists of Edo always depicted Takanawa at sunrise. As you head out of town to the south, the hills on your right push the road closer and closer to the sea, until suddenly, at Takanawa, you find yourself walking almost at the water's edge. With no more walls or warehouses to block the view, your gaze inevitably shifts seaward. The view is superb, and if you pause to watch the sun rise out of the sea, you will have seen that scene at its best.

At first, sea and sky are uniformly black, with no visible line to set them apart. Then slowly they separate as the sky turns a pale gray. Colors become dimly distinguishable, and as the sky gradually lightens and blues, waves begin to show on the dark sea. Then that thin line starts to glow, at first a deep maroon, almost like a bruise, and then a red that grows iridescent, spreads across the whole horizon, and rises like fiery mist. Slowly, though, that red band begins to pale; then it contracts, rounds, and grows intense at its center, until finally it sends up a ball of red fire surrounded by a hazy aura that sits for a moment on the horizon. When finally that ball slips free, it is so brilliant and blood red that it appears to be dripping with wet lacquer. And as it arches over the sea, it casts long paths of dazzling red in every direction, looking exactly like those sixteen broad red rays on the ensign of a warship—for this is exactly what a seaman on the first dogwatch sees as he looks out from the bridge of a ship at dawn. And it is precisely what the artists portray. If there is mist in the air to soften the glow, you can watch for just a moment more as it turns brighter and brighter and then begins to rise, growing whiter, smaller, and vastly more intense as it moves upward. The display doesn't last long, but as it fades, warmth comes, the tips of the waves sparkle, and white sails in the offing billow as they catch the morning breeze and begin to move.

I like to imagine that it was just about then, when the sun was fully risen and spreading its broad rays across the rippled surface of the sea, that that ragged procession of blood-spattered, bizarrely clad, heavily armed ronin, followed by a motley crowd of sightseers, rounded the bend in the road and hove into view. This must have been one of the few moments in the history of Takanawa when a spectacle on the road proved a stronger attraction than the sunrise. As the procession turned in at the front gate to Sengakuji, no one was looking toward the sea; it would be far more interesting to follow the ronin into the temple.

figure 24
**An eyewitness's sketch of three of the ronin straggling past the Shiba Shinmei
Shrine on their way to Sengakuji (1702.12.15).**

CHAPTER
70

We're afraid . . .
that we're a rather unsightly pair.

It would not have taken Chūzaemon and Suke'emon long to wend their way from Shiodome to Atagoshita. Neither man was disabled, neither more exhausted than anyone else, nor was there any delay along the way. They probably would have arrived at the gate to Sengoku Hōki-no-Kami's official residence even before their comrades had emerged from the backstreets onto the main thoroughfare.

When they reached the gate of Hōki-no-Kami's mansion, they announced themselves as having come to report a matter of importance to the Duty Inspector General. Their appearance must have been convincing, for the guard took them at their word. They were admitted; but rather than proceed to the main entryway, they went around to the informal entrance and made their presence known there, whereupon an Usher, Kuwana Buzaemon, emerged. He was struck by their strange garb, but nonetheless greeted them politely: "And what might your business be?"

"We are Yoshida Chūzaemon and Tominomori Suke'emon, former vassals of Asano Takumi-no-Kami. As you may know, Kira Kōzuke-no-Suke was our late lord's enemy; last night, we broke into Kōzuke Dono's mansion, killed him, and took his head. Our comrades have taken the head to the temple Sengakuji in Takanawa, and we have come here to report what we have done. We now await your instructions. If you wish to question us, you need only summon everyone here. Our names are all listed in this document." They then presented the copy of the manifesto that they had brought with them. Buzaemon took it directly to Hōki-no-Kami.

It was a day of general audience, and Hōki-no-Kami would soon be

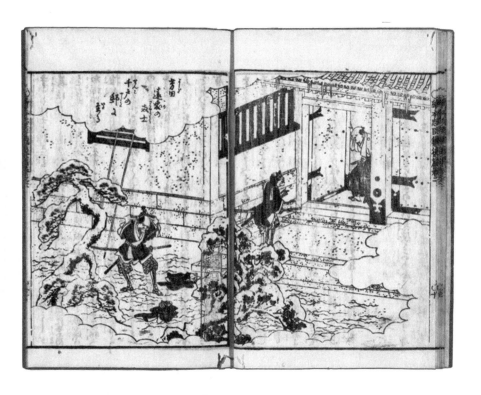

figure 25
Yoshida Chūzaemon and Tominomori Suke'emon reporting to the
Duty Inspector General, Sengoku Hōki-no-Kami.
(*Ehon Chūshingura*, Waseda University Library, Tokyo)

~ *581* ~

leaving for the castle. But the Fifth Hour (ca. 7:00 A.M.) had not yet rung, and he came to the doorway immediately, still dressed informally in trousers and surcoat, swords in his sash, and accompanied by two of his Adjutants.

"You gentlemen are the two ronin formerly in the service of Asano Takumi-no-Kami?"

"We are, and we are most grateful that you grant us an audience on such short notice."

"And you have killed Kōzuke?"

"We have taken Kōzuke-no-Suke Dono's head."

"I have read your statement," Hōki-no-Kami said, "and I must say, your conduct has been in every way exemplary. I shall soon be going to the castle and will make a full report to the Council of Elders. In the meantime, please do take off your sandals, come in, and rest while you wait. You're welcome, too, to rearrange your clothing in any way that will make you feel more comfortable."

Hōki-no-Kami seems also to have noticed that Chūzaemon was favoring his left hand. Chūzaemon explained that it was a minor wound on his middle finger, but that he expected that it would heal quickly.

"It may be a minor wound," Hōki-no-Kami said, "but take care not to aggravate it." He then went within.

The two men were shown to the courtyard of the reception rooms, where they were provided with warm water with which to wash their feet.

"You're very kind indeed," they said, bowing deeply to their hosts. "We're afraid, though, that we're a rather unsightly pair." As Chūzaemon slipped his arms out of his sleeves and untied his obi, the guard in the anteroom withdrew out of politeness. And when Chūzaemon had re-tied his sash, he reached into his sleeve, took out a rice ball, and handed it to the serving boy.

"Might I ask you throw out this foul thing? It was good to have had them last night when I was running out of strength, but. . . ."

Chūzaemon had graying hair, which he had left untied; while Suke'emon, as became a younger man, had shaved his pate and tied his hair back in a whisk.

The two men were then shown into the anteroom, where they were served a meal, after which another of Hōki-no-Kami's men, Inoue Man'emon, came with two scribes in his company. He asked Chūzaemon and Suke'emon to describe in greater detail the events of the previous night. When Hōki-no-Kami left for the castle, he took the transcript of this conversation with him.

◆ ◆ ◆

On his way to the castle, Sengoku Hōki-no-Kami stopped first at the official residence of Inaba Tango-no-Kami, Duty Officer of the Council of Elders for the Twelfth Month. Thereafter, at the castle, he reported to the full Council of Elders. We are told that at that meeting, Abe Bungo-no-Kami, the senior member of the council, said, "It is cause for rejoicing throughout the land that such staunchly loyal samurai still exist." The Shogun, too, is said to have been impressed. "*Appare no mono ja,*" he said: "Fantastic—those fellows!" Whatever else went on, the upshot of it was that the ronin, for the time being, would be placed in the custody of four daimyo houses: Hosokawa, Hisamatsu, Mōri, and Mizuno.

Hisamatsu Oki-no-Kami was ill and thus not present at the general audience. But as soon as the ceremonies of the day were completed, Hosokawa Etchū-no-Kami, Mōri Kai-no-Kami, and Mizuno Kenmotsu were summoned to the Pine Gallery. (One wonders if any of them remarked that this was where the vendetta had begun.) There they were told that they had been assigned to take a number of Asano ronin into their custody—seventeen men in the Hosokawa house, and ten each in the other three houses. They were each to send a force immediately to Sengakuji to fetch their detainees; prior to that, they were to send word of their intentions to the temple, lest the ronin be alarmed at their arrival and mistake them for the Uesugi. Needless to say, there were questions:

HOSOKAWA *and* MŌRI: *Should we ourselves go?*

HŌKI-NO-KAMI: *That will not be necessary. You may send your vassals.*

HOSOKAWA: *Shall I send an Adjutant?*

HŌKI: *Whatever you wish.*

HOSOKAWA: *Will it be acceptable if the palanquins are not new?*

HŌKI: *Perfectly. You may use women's palanquins, too, if you wish.*

MŌRI: *Should the palanquins be covered with netting?*

HŌKI: *They may be locked, they may be covered with cord or rope netting, or not covered at all. Whatever you wish.*

HOSOKAWA: *What sort of quarters are they to be held in?*

HŌKI: *Any sort you wish. They may be quartered in one room, or you may divide them and house them in two or three locations. Concerning which: in which of your mansions do you intend to quarter them?*

HOSOKAWA: *The mansion in Mita [Takanawa] is closest to Sengakuji. I'd prefer to keep them there. Our upper mansion is too small.*

MŌRI: *I'll keep them in the Azabu mansion. It's a bit farther from the temple than Lord Hosokawa's mansion, so my men will be arriving a bit later than his.*

To Hisamatsu Oki-no-Kami, the Duty Elder wrote:

> Ten vassals of Asano Takumi-no-Kami shall for the time being be entrusted to your custody. Since these men are now at the temple Sengakuji in Shiba, you are to send your men there to fetch them. Sengoku Hōki-no-Kami, Suzuki Gengoemon, and Mizuno Kozaemon will themselves go to the temple; you are therefore to instruct your men to leave command of all matters to them.
>
> TWELFTH MONTH, 15TH DAY   *Inaba Tango-no-Kami*
>   *Masamichi [monogram]*
>
> To: Hisamatsu Oki-no-Kami Dono

All four daimyo houses began immediately to mobilize the forces that would be sent to Sengakuji and to prepare their mansions to accommodate the detainees.

+ + +

On a freezing morning in a cold house, there is no greater pleasure than to bundle up for a brief walk to the neighborhood bathhouse, there to throw off the weight of winter clothing for a long soak in a hot tub. And that is precisely what Kuwaoka Teisa decided to do early on that bitter-cold morning of the 15th. Hot the bath was, no doubt, but the soak was far from long. For it was in the bath that Teisa first heard the news of the night before. Even before he entered the steaming room, he could hear the hubbub from within. As he scrubbed, he began to piece together the details. And by the time he had slipped into the water, he found himself as excited as everyone else in the room. The most extraordinary thing had happened. A band of warriors, former vassals of the House of Asano in Akō, had broken into the Kira mansion in Honjo. They had slaughtered several of Kira's men. Then they had cut off His Lordship's head and carried it away to . . .

Bounding in it comes . . .

The snatches of gossip echoing around him no longer held Teisa's full attention; in another corner of his mind, memories were forcing their way back to the surface—memories of his meeting with Suke'emon on the bridge three days earlier and memories of Suke'emon's verse:

yet no hand can hold it . . .

So *that* was what he meant! Taken in *that* sense, it was an extraordinary verse and more timely than Teisa ever could have imagined:

Bounding in they come,
Yet no hand can stop them;
Like hard-driving hail.

Curious though he was, Teisa could wait to hear no more. He rose from the tub, hurriedly dried and dressed himself, and, without returning home, set off at brisk pace for Takanawa.

+ + +

On the highway, not far from the outer gate to the temple, Teisa spotted what he was looking for—a saké dealer. Without slowing his pace, he strode up to the shopkeeper and said, "I'd like to have a keg of saké delivered—immediately, please, to the temple. I'll go with you." Then he reached into the folds of his kimono and . . . His purse! He had left it at home. He had taken only enough money for the bath, and now he hadn't a single copper on him. And in a neighborhood where no one knew him. But he couldn't let that be the ruin of his plan. He explained his mission to the shopkeeper, as well as the reason for his temporary embarrassment. And as he talked, he untied the cords of his cloak, drew his arms from the sleeves, and began folding it carefully. Although in color and cut it was a sober garment, the material and the tailoring were obviously beyond the means of a young teacher of poetry. It was a gift from a lord of some note who patronized Teisa, and it bore the lord's crest in proof of their relationship.

"I'll come back in a day or two to pay you," Teisa said, handing over the cloak. "In the meantime, you can keep this as security." It took only a few moments to write the appropriate note, attach it to the keg, and load the gift on a cart. A shivering Teisa and his handsome gift soon rounded the corner and were rolling up the slope toward the temple.

+ + +

The middle gate of Sengakuji had long since been shut and bolted against the crowds. By the time Teisa arrived, it was further barred by a contingent of guardsmen dispatched from the castle. Teisa was not deterred. He strode up to the gate and called out: "Tominomori Dono, are you there? Ōtaka Dono, are you in there? Come have a drink! I've brought a little something for you and your comrades. Are you there?" He might as well have shouted at a mountain. His friends were far beyond earshot, nor could they have come to the gate, even had they known Teisa was there.

But his shouts did not go unheeded. Just as Teisa was resigning himself to a patient wait, in the hope that some unforeseen opportunity might present itself, a guardsman, who seemed to recognize him, approached. Teisa perhaps expected a threatening scowl and a warning, but the samurai smiled and spoke softly, almost conspiratorially.

"Why don't you just leave it there? It will not go undelivered, I'm sure." Teisa immediately grasped the guard's meaning. He himself was not the only one who thought that the men inside the gate deserved hearty congratulations.

◆ ◆ ◆

To Teisa, despite the loss of his cloak, the walk from the temple to his home in Shiba Zaimoku-chō seemed nowhere near as chilly as it had when he was fully clad. The morning had been bright, sunny, and frigid; but now the wind had shifted, and a cloudy bank of warm, damp air was moving in from the sea. The snows of the past few days were beginning to melt. Yet the instant that Teisa took notice of this welcome change, he broke out in a cold sweat. The cloak! It bore the crest of his patron. Useful though that had been as security, it was also proof of the daimyo's identity. By now, the shopkeeper would have told the tale of his well-tailored but impecunious customer several times over. Ripples of that rumor could easily reach the ears of His Lordship's vassals; when it did, he knew what they were bound to think—that he held the generosity of his patron in such low esteem that he had pawned a crested cloak, once worn by His Lordship himself, to buy saké. That was far from the whole truth, but rumor does not trade in subtle details. If his honor was not to be permanently impugned, there was only one thing to do. He must confess before he was compromised—if it were not too late already. At the next corner, Teisa turned off the highway and hurried toward His Lordship's mansion.

◆ ◆ ◆

Teisa's unexpected call at the mansion of his patron went far better than he had any right to expect. He had won the race against rumor.

Although it was a day of general audience, His Lordship had already returned from the castle. And he was willing to receive Teisa immediately. Best of all, though, he found Teisa's tale of the bathhouse and the cloak and the saké vastly amusing; he even praised the poet for his fidelity to his friends. Everyone was happy now. Teisa's integrity was intact. His Lordship had a new story with which to regale his own circle of friends, of the part played by his very own cloak in the rapidly expanding saga of the Akō vendetta. He rewarded Teisa with twelve reassuring syllables:

> nanigoto mo naki / nowake ato
> With no harm whatever done
> the wild storm is past.

For long, Teisa thought it his duty to cap his gift with another five syllables, to make it a proper 5-7-5; but he could never think of a line that he liked. Years later, his young colleague Katsukatsubō asked him, "Why don't you just leave it—a twelve-syllable verse? It says it all. If you tack on something extraneous, you'll only ruin it." Teisa was persuaded. And when Katsukatsubō died in 1764, his disciples remembered and gave the posthumous collection of their own teacher's verse the title *The Storm Past*.

◆ ◆ ◆

In the castle, the Inspectorate were making their own plans for the transfer of the ronin—from Sengakuji to the residence of Sengoku Hōki-no-Kami, then on to the daimyo houses of their detention. Those charged with the direct supervision of the move, however, seemed to think it a mission fraught with danger, and their discussions were by chance overheard by some of the Elders. Asked to explain why they thought this so dangerous, Suzuki Gengoemon and Mizuno Kozaemon told the Elders: "Once the Kira clan, and especially the Uesugi, learn that the ronin have gone to Sengakuji, they are not likely to overlook it. They are sure to lie in wait for them and ambush them en route. We assure you nonetheless that we are prepared to die in the discharge of this duty."

The Elders could see that the Inspectors had good reason for their apprehension and thought it prudent to alter their present plan. The Uesugi had been warned against reprisal, but would they obey? Yet if the ronin were to make their way from Sengakuji to Atagoshita unescorted, and if they were then to be ambushed, they would not yet have come under the jurisdiction of the Shogunate. No one from the Inspectorate and none of the men from the four daimyo houses would be involved in the ensuing combat. It was immediately decided that the daimyo should withdraw their forces from Sengakukji and station them instead in the vicinity of the official residence of Sengoku Hōki-no-Kami. To Hisamatsu Oki-no-Kami (and probably the other three daimyo as well), they wrote:

> *Although originally you were commanded to take custody of the aforementioned vassals of Asano Takumi at Sengakuji, Inaba Tango-no-Kami Sama now commands us to hand them over to you at the residence of Sengoku Hōki-no-Kami Dono. You shall therefore send your men instead to the residence of Sengoku Hōki-no-Kami Dono. Herewith the foregoing,*

TWELFTH MONTH, 15TH DAY

> *Mizuno Kozaemon*
> *Suzuki Gengoemon*
> *Sengoku Hōki-no-Kami*

To: Hisamatsu Oki-no-Kami Dono

Sengoku Hōki-no-Kami returned to his official residence, commanded his kitchen staff to prepare food for fifty men, and then met again with Chūzaemon and Suke'emon.

"I intend to summon everyone here for questioning," he told them. "I'm concerned, though, that Kuranosuke might baulk at this, considering the danger involved. I should like, therefore, to send him a letter from you two."

That letter no longer survives, but it was delivered to Sengakuji by three Deputy Inspectors who arrived there at about the Eighth Hour (2:00 P.M.). All was now in readiness. Unfortunately, however, word of this sudden change failed to reach any of the daimyo in time for them to alter their own plans. Four formidable forces were already on the march to Sengakuji.

CHAPTER
71

It was like nothing ever seen before;
a veritable battlefield.

It would be a busy day for the Inspectors. Not only had they to arrange the transit of the ronin from Sengakuji to the mansion of Hōki-no-Kami, but they also had to send a detail to Honjo to investigate the scene of the attack and take the testimony of those who had survived it or witnessed it. One way and another, their entire force would be fully occupied today.

It was just past the Eighth Hour (2:00 P.M.) when the Inspectors Abe Shikibu and Sugita Gozaemon, accompanied by four Deputy Inspectors and six Sub-Inspectors, arrived at the Kira mansion in Honjo. We have already seen something of the chaos that they encountered there; but one of the Uesugi reports sums up the state of things quite succinctly:

> _Throughout the house, in every room, the shoji, the folding screens, the sliding doors, the tatami mats had all been smashed and hacked and slashed with the blades of swords, halberds, and lances. The bodies of the dead and wounded lay sprawled every which way. There was hardly any place one could step, and the floors were so soaked with blood that everyone had to wear sandals just to walk through the house. It was like nothing ever seen before; a veritable battlefield._

The Inspectors, however, seem to have concerned themselves less with damage to life and property than with the details of what had happened. Their report is thus a compilation of statements and lists—beginning with the report from Kira Sahei, which had been carried by Kasuya Heima to the Duty Elder Inaba Tango-no-Kami:

> Last night, midway through the Eighth Hour [2:00 A.M.], the vassals of Takumi-no-Kami fought their way into my residence and killed Kōzuke-no-Suke. I fought back and was wounded. Fourteen or fifteen of my vassals were killed. Some of the assailants were severely wounded, but subsequently they withdrew and left none of their dead behind. As this all happened very suddenly, I send only this interim verbal report.

Perhaps those to whom this report was submitted already knew enough of the facts to recognize the mendacity of it. And if contemporary rumor is to be believed, they did not hesitate to let Kasuya Heima know that they knew—although in the politest manner possible, of course. After inquiring how many wounds Sahei had sustained, and whether they were serious or slight, it is said that they asked Heima, "And how is it that you were so fortunate as to escape?" Heima's embarrassingly lame excuse was, "I was off duty last night." Everyone, they say, was much amused, and the story quickly made the rounds of the city.

◆ ◆ ◆

In Honjo, the Inspectors first called at the residences of Kira's three samurai neighbors and took their depositions.

Tsuchiya Chikara told them that he had been awakened by a great commotion in the Kira mansion that he at first thought must be a fire, but then realized was an altercation of some sort. He mustered his vassals, and they secured their own property against assault. A while later, Kataoka Gengoemon, Onodera Jūnai, and Hara Sōemon called over the wall to tell him that they had taken revenge upon their lord's enemy, Kira Kōzuke-no-Suke. Forty or fifty of them then filed out the rear gate, but it was still dark and Tsuchiya could not see them clearly.

Makino Ichigaku, who lived opposite Kira's main gate, was away on garrison duty at Sunpu Castle in Suruga. His vassal Mogi Tōdayu told the Inspectors that they had at first thought there must be a fire, but then they heard a great deal of shouting just inside Kira's gate, and had no idea what it was all about. Eventually, things quietened down, and they paid it no further attention.

Honda Magotarō, an Elder of the house of Matsudaira Hyōbu Taifu, like Tsuchiya Chikara, shared Kira's north wall; but he, too, was absent from Edo. His vassal Magara Kandayū said that, like everyone else, they had thought there must be a fire, but then things quietened down, and they still had no idea what had happened.

◆ ◆ ◆

The Inspectors, of course, ignored the commoners whose homes lined the other two sides of the Kira property—and who probably would have had more of interest to tell than had their samurai neighbors. Instead, they went into the Kira mansion, where all remained much as the ronin had left it after taking Kira's head, the dead and the wounded still lying there, "sprawled every which way." The task was probably shared by all twelve men from the Inspectorate. But one by one, they recorded a brief statement from everyone still alive and conscious. For many of them, this must almost have been a record of their last words, for about half the men questioned died of their wounds soon thereafter.

Most of the wounded had little more to say than that they were on duty that night, either in the room adjacent to the vestibule or in the anteroom to Sahei Dono's bedchamber, and that they were taken totally by surprise by a large number of men armed with both swords and lances. Yamayoshi Shinpachi, however, described how he managed to make his way past the enemy, from the barracks to the mansion: "I was in my quarters when someone said there was a fire. When I went out, I encountered men armed with lances and swords. I fought my way past them and made it as far as His Lordship's quarters. The intruders were there, too, and I fought against them and was wounded. But my wounds were severe, and I fell, unable to fight."

Matsubara Tachū, whom we met previously in the course of the battle, said, "I heard someone saying there was fire. My quarters are just next to the rear gate, so I went out immediately to see what was the matter, whereupon I was shot at by archers and hit by an arrow. A great number of men came rushing at me, and one of them struck me down with the mallet he had used to break open the gate. I was in such pain that I could not fight back." Later in the day, he died.

+ + +

There were also a great many more men who had not joined battle at all. The Inspectors did not bother to take their testimony individually. Some said that they had been wounded, and others claimed that they had been forcibly confined to their rooms and could not get out. Probably none of them was telling the truth. The Inspectors made no comment, but their names are duly listed, along with a list of those who simply absconded. And finally, there is a list of all the things discarded or dropped by the ronin before they left: a copy of the manifesto, a lance, five arrows, two axes, a mallet, twenty-three name tags, a whistle, and more.

+ + +

Attached to these lists is the most interesting part of the report, a "letter" in which the Inspectors offer some of their own observations on what they have seen and heard. Parts of it simply describe the progress of the attack, from mounting the walls at the main gate to departing from the rear. But a few passages are worth noting:

> Item. *When Sahei was attacked in his apartments, he defended himself with his halberd and was wounded in two places. Blood streamed into his eyes, and for a time he lost consciousness. He was concerned about Kōzuke-no-Suke, but when he regained consciousness, his father had already been killed and the attackers were gone he knew not where.*
>
> Item. *The blade of Sahei's own halberd was nicked and smeared with blood, proving that he did actively join battle.*
>
> Item. *The wound on his forehead was about 2 inches long; that on his back about 6 inches long and very deep. But he appeared to be in good spirits.*

Item. Only the body of Kōzuke-no-Suke remained. His head was missing. He had wounds on the palms of both hands, on his left thigh, and in two places on his kneecaps. His vassals say that he fought back, but his sword is not nicked; and although there is blood on the blade, we doubt that he did actually fight back.

Item. When we questioned Kōzuke-no-Suke's vassals Saitō Kunai, Sōda Magobei, and Iwase Toneri, they said that they had wished to go out and fight, but there were three or four armed men outside every door, and if they had emerged they would have been killed. And so they remained within and did not know what had happened.

TWELFTH MONTH, 16TH DAY   *Abe Shikibu*

Sugita Gozaemon

✦ ✦ ✦

While the investigation next door continued, another caller was announced at the home of Tsuchiya Chikara. Rumors of the previous night's uproar had reached Tsuchiya's friend the scholar Arai Hakuseki, and he had come to hear a firsthand report of the incident. Tsuchiya, Hakuseki says, was pleased to oblige him. But there was also another man there, a ronin living on the patronage of Tsuchiya, who, a year or so earlier, had himself avenged the murder of his father—or was it his brother? This was a man who had seen the whole thing and could speak with the voice of experience. He said: "The calm deliberation with which they went about it was incomparable. Until they had killed Kōzuke-no-Suke, they were quite disciplined; but even thereafter, until the very end, their behavior was impeccable. They were extraordinary."

Hakuseki himself offers no comment on what he heard that day. Later, however, he met another friend, Muro Kyūsō, who seemed determined to make Hakuseki reveal his thoughts: "I am sure that the behavior of the forty-seven left naught to be desired," Kyūsō said. "But what do you make of Tsuchiya's behavior? As a fellow vassal of the Shogun, and a neighbor separated by only a wall, should he have let those forty-seven men just escape? In Kaga, that would not pass muster. But what do you people in Edo think?"

~ 595 ~

"Under the circumstances," Hakuseki said, "Tsuchiya would claim that there was nothing else he could do. But there are, I think, things that he *could* have done."

"Like what?" Kyūsō asked. "What exactly do *you* think he should have done?"

"Under the law," Hakuseki said, "one is permitted to kill the enemy of one's lord or one's father. Moreover, the other party did ask, as fellow samurai, that they be allowed to kill him. Tsuchiya, as their fellow samurai, cannot be faulted for doing as they asked. Yet when they sent their messengers the second time, he could have met with Yoshida or Ōishi and said, 'You have now accomplished your mission, and I am delighted that you have done so. And although I am the man's neighbor, since you declare him to be the enemy of your lord, I did nothing to prevent you from doing as you wished. But now, pray attend to what I have to ask. If, as a neighbor, I now simply allow you to withdraw, then subsequently I shall have no justification to offer for my own behavior. For I cannot, after all, be party to a vendetta. Might I ask, therefore, inconvenient though it may be, that one or two of your senior men remain here with me. I do not ask that all of you remain behind, nor would I wish to detain you. But if one or two of you could remain as security, then my honor will be preserved. If, perhance, you intend to flee somewhere to preserve your lives, there is nothing I can do about that. No one could say that I had been party to a plan of that sort. But since I have complied with your original request, kindly give some consideration to this request of mine. As you say, we fellow samurai must depend upon one another. If you should now just depart, for me that would be a loss of honor.'

"If Tsuchiya had said that," Hakuseki concluded, "a man of the caliber of Kuranosuke would surely have agreed. Tsuchiya could then have taken custody of two or three of them and told the rest that they might do as they please. That is what he should have done. And if, perchance, they had not agreed, but simply departed, no one could then have claimed that Tsuchiya Chikara was in the wrong."

◆ ◆ ◆

Yet whatever fine thoughts Arai Hakuseki had as to how his friend *should* have behaved, neither Tsuchiya nor the Inspectors who had come to investigate would have been much moved to hear them. Tsuchiya had done all within his power to defend his own property against possible incursion. The Inspectors found no fault with that, nor did anyone in the Shogunate to whom they reported voice any objection. And that was that. Case closed.

*There are fifty or sixty men at the gate—dressed very
strangely and armed with lances and halberds.*

The temple Sengakuji had three gates. The front gate faced directly upon
the highway, and although the guardhouse there was manned, it was not
a terribly substantial barrier—just a timber frame set in a simple fence,
left open most of the day. Beyond it stretched a long, gently stepped
slope, cut through high ground that rose on either side, leading up to
the middle gate. It was this gate that in Genroku served as the principal
entrance to the temple grounds, for at some point in the previous fifty
years, the much grander main gate had burnt, and all that remained of
it were twelve foundation stones. Within the middle gate, the way continued straight along an avenue lined with pines, and behind the pines
stood two rows of dormitories, six on either side. Three of these housed
the ordained monks of the temple, and the other nine, the more than
two hundred novices. Finally, passing between the foundation stones of
the burnt gate, one arrived at the central complex of temple buildings:
the main hall directly ahead, the Abbot's quarters adjoining it at the
rear, the kitchens and refectory at the right, and on the left a broad stone
stairway rising to the graveyard on the slopes of the surrounding hills.
Not only was Asano Takumi-no-Kami buried there, but also the late
lords of the Mōri, the Kutsuki, the Oda, the Ikeda, and several lesser
daimyo and bannermen. Sengakuji did not want for wealthy parishioners in those days.

As the young novice Hakumyō points out, Sengakuji was a training
temple for Zen monks, and hence observed strictly the ninety-day
periods of summer and winter retreat. The 15th Day of the Twelfth

Month being the precise midpoint of the winter retreat, there was to be a ceremonial offering of tea in the main hall that morning. Hakumyō himself had already finished his breakfast and taken his place there, when one of the warders from the gatehouse came in and asked to speak to the Bursar: "There are fifty or sixty men at the gate—dressed very strangely and armed with lances and halberds. They say that they are the vassals of Asano Takumi-no-Kami. Should we allow them to enter?"

The Bursar's reply was that he would have to ask the Abbot, and the Abbot, for his part, sent another monk to investigate further before making any decision. This seems not to have been a question to which anyone had a ready answer.

In the meantime, however, the ronin were not waiting patiently for permission to enter. They marched straight in; yet before they had gone very far, a knot of men began to form in the middle of their ranks, and the procession stalled. The center of attention in this knot, strange to say, was the foot soldier Terasaka Kichiemon, around whom were clustered the whole command group: Ōishi Kuranosuke, Hara Sōemon, Masé Kyūdayū, and Onodera Jūnai, as well as Kataoka Gengoemon and Horibe Yasubei. Kichiemon stood silent, staring at the ground, his face a mask of confusion and dejection.

"Temples are governed by laws of their own, you know," someone was saying. "If you once set foot inside that gate, you can't come out again. That means that you'll have violated the orders that Chūzaemon gave you. You don't want to do that, do you? You've got to hurry now; you're off to Harima."

Chūzaemon himself was not there, of course; and so far, his son Sawaemon and his brother Yazaemon had watched silently from the fringes. But now they, too, stepped in, tentatively to be sure, but taking Kichiemon's side.

"We understand what you're telling him, but wouldn't it be all right if he . . . ?" Kuranosuke would have none of it, but this time he spoke in more paternal tones.

"Come now, this is no time for discussion. You have your orders from Chūzaemon. You know that you'll regret it if you disobey him, and I'm sure that's not what you mean to do. So no more dithering; you've got to hurry. Of course you feel bad; we understand that. But you're not doing anything cowardly. Here!" From within his surcoat, Kuranosuke produced a small missive, wrapped in white paper, and held it out to Kichiemon. "Your name is on it, and we've all signed it: Chūzaemon, Sawaemon, everyone. If anyone doubts your word, this will prove that you're under orders. Now, you've got to get away and get there in a hurry. So take this!"

There was no way out now. Kichiemon took the manifesto, bowed deeply, and stepped back into the crowd as he watched his comrades disappear within the middle gate, followed by a surge of sightseers, who, for the moment at least, were quite free to go where he was not. But he did not immediately follow the rest of his orders. With some alteration to his conspicuous costume, no doubt, he hid himself somewhere in the neighborhood. There he would wait until he heard what was to happen to the others, before setting out on his journey west.

◆ ◆ ◆

It was just after the tolling of the Fifth Hour (ca. 8:00 A.M.), the monk Kaishū says, when he and his companions saw three men in strange garb, armed with unsheathed lances, approaching the middle gate. The monks were, of course, curious about who these men might be. But as they watched, their curiosity only grew, for next there hove into view two more men—the Hazama brothers—bearing a single lance between them from the haft of which hung an object that they could not identify. At this point, Kaishū decided that they had better find out what was going on. They approached the three men in the vanguard as they were about to enter the middle gate.

"May we ask where you gentlemen are from?" Kaishū said. "For we cannot without good reason allow you to enter the temple grounds clad in this outlandish fashion."

"We are vassals of Asano Takumi-no-Kami," they replied, "and in pursuance of our late lord's wishes, we have taken the head of Kira Kōzuke-no-Suke and brought it to His Lordship's grave here in the temple. We shall create no disturbance. You have nothing to worry about."

"Well in that case," Kaishū replied, "you have legitimate business here." Two monks were sent to the main hall to inform the Abbot, while the remaining forty-some ronin streamed in through the gate.

And following them came a large and noisy crowd of sightseers. The ronin urged the monks to shut the gate and keep the mob out, but so many of them had already entered that at first this seemed impossible. The problem was easily solved, however; twelve or thirteen of the blood-spattered ronin lowered their lances threateningly, whereupon the curiosity seekers turned and fled. But once all the ronin were within the compound and the gates had been shut, Kuranosuke commanded those who had not already done so to wrap the unsheathed blades of their weapons as a mark of respect in the presence of the Buddha. They then proceeded to the grave of Takumi-no-Kami.

◆ ◆ ◆

Strangely little is recorded of what actually took place at the grave, with the result that many stories of doubtful authenticity have been invented. All that we know for certain is that first, the head was unwrapped, and someone fetched a bucket of water with which to wash it. Then the blood-stained sleeve in which it had been carried was folded neatly and placed beneath it as a cushion on the second step of the stone surrounds of the grave. The head in place, all the ronin knelt and offered incense, the necessary equipment and materials having been borrowed from the temple. The first to do so was Hazama Jūjirō, he having been the first to draw blood and the actual taker of the head; then Ōishi Kuranosuke, as leader of the group, followed by the remaining forty-two men in the order of their rank. We know, too, that all the monks and novices of the Sengakuji—more than three hundred of them—went to watch. The winter-retreat observances seem to have been completely forgotten, but Hakumyō is adamant that the monks chanted no sutras for the occasion or in any way participated in the ceremony. As Kaishū says, the whole thing did not take very long, and as soon as they were finished, everyone went back to the temple, the ronin carrying the head with them.

◆ ◆ ◆

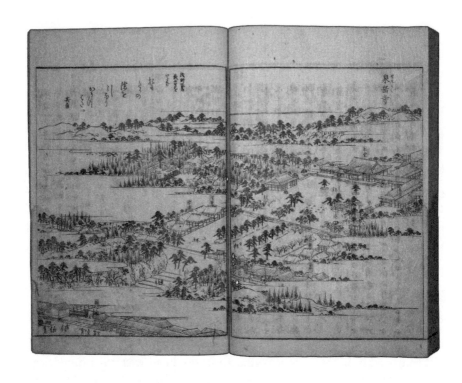

figure 26a
Sengakuji. (*Edo meisho zue*, 1834–1836)

figure 26b
Presenting Kira's head at Takumi-no-Kami's grave.
(*Ehon Chūshingura*, Waseda University Library, Tokyo)

figure 26c
The ronin in the student monks' dormitory at Sengakuji.
(*Ehon Chūshingura*, Waseda University Library, Tokyo)

It seems to have been an exhilarating morning for everyone at Sengakuji. The ronin first gathered in the reception rooms of the main hall, and the Abbot came out and greeted them warmly. They were, of course, parishioners of a sort, and Kuranosuke was known from previous meetings in connection with Asano family affairs. But for someone to whom the severing of heads is not supposed to be a matter of rejoicing, the Abbot came dangerously close to congratulating them on their accomplishment.

"You must be very pleased with what you've accomplished," he said.

"Quite so," Kuranosuke said. "Having waited as long as we have, nothing could please us more."

"Have you reported this to the officials?" the Abbot asked.

"We have. We've sent two of our men to Sengoku Hōki-no-Kami."

"In that case, I, too, must submit a report. But first, let me ensure that all of you will be comfortable," the Abbot said.

Thereafter, Kuranosuke, his son Chikara, and the senior members of the group were shown to the Abbot's private quarters, while the rest of the ronin were taken to one of the dormitories. The atmosphere there can only be described as boisterous.

The ronin were obviously enjoying their new status as heroes. Chikamatsu Kanroku had a nasty wound on his thigh, 6 or 7 inches long and very deep. One of the monks had summoned a doctor, who offered to attend to the gash. "No, no," said Kanroku; "it's only a scratch. Besides, we'll all be committing seppuku before the day is out, so what's the use of having our wounds bound up? Let it bleed!"

Mimura Jirōzaemon was telling everyone, "I'm really very lucky. Everyone congratulates me on it. I was assigned the demolition mallet. My job was to batter down doors, and apart from that, I had nothing else to do. But every time we'd bash our way into a room, I'd be the first one in; which meant that if anyone was hiding there, I'd be the first to get his head cut off. But I've survived without a scratch. I'm really very lucky."

Just then one of the warders on watch at the gatehouse came in and told the ronin that a man named Takada Gunbei wanted to present them with some saké.

"Why, that rat!" one of them said.

"No, this is a lucky break," said another. "Call him in, and we'll stomp the life out of him. We can't dirty our swords on such scum." Kuranosuke, who seems now to have rejoined the group, moved quickly to calm them.

"Come now," he said. "What good would that do—to trample someone like him?" He then told the monk from the gate, "Don't let him in. Just give him back his saké."

Apparently, Yasui Hikoemon, the former Edo Elder, also turned up at the front gate, dressed in full formal linens, as though he were still a man of consequence, which prompted Takebayashi Tadashichi to say, "Well wouldn't he make a nice meal? Let's roast him!" But, again, Kuranosuke's response was, "Just ignore him."

In the meantime, the young novices were busy serving bowls of steaming hot gruel, which the ronin consumed, they say, in great quantity with great enthusiasm—and in the course of which Kimura Okaemon struck up a conversation with young Hakumyō.

"How old are you?" he asked the boy.

"I'm nineteen."

"And where are you from?"

"I'm from Tosa."

Many of the men, Hakumyō noticed, still had name tags attached to the right shoulder of their coats, but Kimura Okaemon had also attached a tag to his left shoulder bearing a posthumous name, Eigaku Sōshun Shinji.

"May I ask who gave you your posthumous name?" Hakumyō asked.

"It was the Zen master Bankei," Okaemon told him, "back home in Harima."

Hakumyō had heard of Bankei, a renowned old monk of the Rinzai sect who had traveled the land and had sat at the feet of some of the greatest masters. And Kimura came from the same province as this venerable monk. This somehow encouraged Hakumyō to be a bit more forward.

"Might I ask you to write out your parting poem from last night for me? Or even an impromptu verse?" Okaemon assented, took out a sheet from his paper fold, and wrote:

omoiki ya waga mononofu no michi narade
kakaru minori no en ni au to wa
Would I ever have thought it? That but for the Way of the Warrior
I should never have forged this bond with the Law of the Buddha?

But just as Okaemon was signing his poem—"Kimura Sadayuki, aged
forty-five, Eigaku Sōshun Shinji"—a drop of blood fell on the paper,
from a wounded finger on his right hand.

"Oh, I'm sorry," Okaemon said. "I'll write that out again for you."

"No, no!" Hakumyō protested. "That drop of blood makes it even
more a treasure. Please! Let me keep it." And he did.

◆ ◆ ◆

All the while, at the front of the room, presiding over all this noisy good
cheer, was—The Head. Years later, Hakumyō would be at great pains
to deny reports that it was installed on the altar of the main hall. In
every Zen temple, he says, directly in front of the principal image, are
enshrined the tablets of both the incumbent Emperor and Shen Nung,
Lord of Fire, as well as a sacred talisman of the Sun Goddess. This
is a site of supplication for the welfare of the entire land. It would be
unthinkable to place anything so foul and polluted as a freshly severed
head on an altar of such purity. The head, he says, was relegated to a box
from the kitchens.

That is true, as we shall see, but it was not so politely packaged until
much later in the day. In the meantime, the head seems *not* to have been
thought too polluted to place on the altar of the dormitory where the
ronin were gathered—although it *had* been restored to its blood-stained
wrap and was not displayed in its "raw" state.

◆ ◆ ◆

Once the Abbot had welcomed his guests and seen to all their needs,
he had to excuse himself, in order to report the morning's events to the
Commissioner of Temples and Shrines, Abe Hida-no-Kami. But as he
was about to board his palanquin, he turned and spoke to Kuranosuke.

"Drinking is not normally permitted in this temple," he said, "but this is a special occasion, and you must be exhausted." He then instructed his monks to prepare saké, adding that if any problems should arise over this infringement of the rules, he would take full responsibility upon himself.

After they had eaten their fill, however, and drunk a fair bit besides, the ronin declined the offer of a hot bath, lest the Uesugi attack and they be caught with their guard down. Ultimately, though, exhaustion, abetted by a hearty breakfast and plenty of warm saké, had dulled their fervor, and by midday many of the ronin were sound asleep.

◆ ◆ ◆

Not long thereafter, however, their vigilance seemed vindicated. The temple had posted men in positions where they could observe from a distance any move against the temple. Well past noon, one of the warders on watch at the front gate came running to report that a large formation of samurai had arrived at the gate and were creating quite a commotion.

"We've been expecting them," Kuranosuke said. "Those will be Uesugi Danjō's men, come to counterattack." By now, the younger men had awakened and gathered in the courtyard outside the reception rooms, and Kuranosuke gave them their orders. He had obviously thought this through in advance.

"There are three streets that converge just outside the middle gate. We'll be at a terrible disadvantage if we meet the enemy there. But if we remain within the middle gate—with that as our shield, so to speak—and pick them off one at a time, we can put up a good fight. We'll shoot off a long arrow, let them know that we're here, and when they approach the gate, shoot them down until we run out of arrows." Everyone agreed that that was a sound plan. They began securing their coats of mail, retying their sandals, unwrapping their lance blades, and drawing their swords.

But then, it all turned out to be a false alarm. Another monk came running and told Kuranosuke that the commotion at the front gate was not caused by Uesugi Danjō and his men. They were men sent by Mizuno Kenmotsu, come to take custody of some of the ronin. And they were followed by Hosokawa Etchū-no-Kami, Hisamatsu Oki-no-Kami, and Mōri Kai-no-Kami. But then, just as suddenly as they had appeared, these hundreds of warriors vanished. Shortly thereafter, the reason for this strange sequence of events would become clear.

Early in the afternoon, the ronin were called again to the reception rooms in the main hall, to be questioned by three Deputy Inspectors: Furukawa Yaichiemon, Ichikawa Shinroku, and Matsunaga Kohachirō. This turned out to be a very cordial meeting. Once the matter of the missing member, Terasaka Kichiemon, had been explained, the Inspectors praised the ronin for their conduct and invited them to proceed at their leisure—fully armed and unescorted—to the mansion of the Duty Inspector General, Sengoku Hōki-no-Kami.

And before taking their leave, the Inspectors did the ronin the courtesy of asking if *they* had any questions. They did: Should they bring the severed head with them to the mansion of Hōki-no-Kami, or should they leave it behind? The question seems to have caught the Inspectors unprepared, for their answer was: "This is a matter we've not been authorized to decide, but we doubt that there should be any objection if you were to leave it here at the temple."

But before the band set out in obedience to their summons, the Abbot commanded that they be served another meal; and it was then that one of the ronin asked if they might borrow a box of some sort in which to stow the head. The monks were at a loss as to what they might use for this purpose, until someone remembered that the temple had recently received a gift of a jug of tea leaves. The box in which this jug had been delivered might be just the thing. In the meantime, however, the meal had been served, and everyone was busily eating by the time the box was finally produced. Kaishū's description of the scene is worth quoting:

> *Hazama Jūjirō was halfway through his meal, but he pushed his tray aside and went to retrieve the head from the altar. As he removed it from its wrapping, he said, "Have a look everyone! Last chance to see the head! See? His Lordship still has his scar." And as he spoke, he took the head in both hands and held it high for all to see. Then, with a thud, he flung it down into the box, crammed the blood-stained wrap in atop it, quickly tied up the cords, shoved the box*

to one side, and, with his now blood-smeared hands, picked up his chopsticks and returned to his meal.

Nor was Jūjirō the only one whose appetite was unimpaired by a bit of fresh blood. When the meal was finished, another round of saké was forthcoming, of which the ronin drank heartily. And when the monks apologized that they were unable to provide any of the usual snacks to serve with the saké, they were assured that this was no inconvenience at all.

"We don't need a thing to eat with it. Nothing makes quite so delicious an accompaniment as *this*," they said, and pointing to the box containing the head, they raised their cups and drank.

✦ ✦ ✦

It was shortly after the beginning of the Fifth Hour (8:00 P.M.) by the time the ronin had completed their preparations and fallen into formation for their march to Atagoshita. The older men, the wounded, and the injured would be carried in twelve town litters, surrounded by their comrades marching in battle formation, still on their guard against the Uesugi. But before they departed, Kuranosuke had one last word with the Abbot.

"I must apologize for imposing upon your hospitality so unexpectedly today; I hope that you won't think ill of us for this. I hope, too, that I may entrust this head to the safekeeping of your temple?" The Abbot accepted the head, and the ronin began moving toward the gate.

The head, in its box, was taken to the reception rooms of the main hall, where it was surrounded by an enclosure of folding screens. The monks took it in turns to guard it throughout the night. It was now the Abbot's turn to wonder what to do with this head.

*You've been extremely
kind to us today.*

Satō Jōemon, who had spent the entire night with the ronin—before, during, and after the attack—had not gone with them to Sengakuji. Okuda Magodayū had warned him that he might be suspected of complicity if he were seen with the ronin that morning, and he took that warning to heart. He went instead to Horibe Yahei's home in Yonezawa-chō, to tell the wives that Yahei and Yasubei were safe and sound and that the attack had been a success. After which he attempted to rest. But to no avail. There came a steady stream of relatives and friends bearing news of all sorts—in the course of which he learnt that the ronin had made their way to Sengakuji without mishap. In that case, he decided, he would go to the temple and meet them. He sent for Chikamatsu Kanroku's man Jinzaburō, and they set out together.

◆ ◆ ◆

The bank of balmy air that had rolled in from the sea while Kuwaoka Teisa was on his way home brought dark, heavy clouds with it as well as warmth. By the time Jōemon and Jinzaburō arrived in Takanawa, rain had begun to fall. But the shoreline was crowded with samurai who were creating considerable commotion, yet making no effort to take shelter. It was all quite puzzling. Jōemon went up to the guardhouse at the gate.

"Could you be so kind as to let me in?" he asked. "I have kinsmen in the temple." The monk on duty told him quite firmly that no one was to be admitted. Then a group of formally dressed men from the city arrived and showed the leaders of the samurai something that looked like an official document. Whereupon all the warriors who had lined the highway turned and marched off toward Edo, leaving not a one of their number behind. Only the sightseers remained.

"I simply couldn't work it out," Jōemon says. But then by chance, he caught sight of someone he knew, a man named Hirosawa who was the Liaison Officer for Matsudaira Sahyōe, lord of Akashi. Hirosawa was able to tell him why all the samurai had been there and why they had left so suddenly. But then, there was another spate of comings and goings. Two men on horseback, sent by the Commissioner of Temples and Shrines, rode up to the gate, dismounted, and went within; very shortly thereafter, they reappeared and rode back toward Edo. Then, as dusk was gathering, there came three Deputy Inspectors in full formal linens, attended by six Sub-Inspectors in surcoat and trousers. The rain was falling steadily by now, so these Inspectors had bloused up their trousers above the knee, removed their sandals, and were walking barefoot in the cold mud. Yet they were no less officious for all that. Once they had washed their feet and refitted their sandals, they demanded that all spectators be cleared away from the gate, allowing them to make a properly pompous entrance.

Jōemon still knew no more than what his friend Hirosawa had been able to tell him, so he walked up the road to the nearest corner guardhouse. But all the guards could tell him was, "They say it looks like seppuku." This Jōemon found terribly disturbing. It was already past the Seventh Hour (4:00 P.M.), but he decided that he would stay as far into the night as he had to, until the ronin themselves should emerge. He told Jinzaburō to keep an eye on the gate and went to sit in a tea shop while he waited.

It must have been early in the Sixth Hour (ca. 6:00–7:00 P.M.) when Jinzaburō came running.

"Right now!" he cried. "They're coming out of the gate right now! Come, have a look! It looks like they're carrying little banners."

Jōemon hurried back to the gate just as Yasubei was coming out, at the very head of the procession, his great sword unsheathed and at the ready.

"So you've come?" he said when he saw Jōemon.

"I've been here since before midday," Jōemon said. "But the gate was shut; there was nothing for it but to wait. Where are you going now?"

"We're going to Sengoku Hōki-no-Kami Dono."

"And then what?"

"Seppuku!" Yasubei said. "Seppuku!"

Behind Yasubei, the ronin marched quietly in two files. None of them had the sheaths for their lances, so they had wrapped the blades in their cotton sleeve markers, some of which had come loose and were waving in the breeze—which was why, in the dark, Jinzaburō thought that they looked like banners.

Following those on foot, the wounded and the old men were being carried in town litters: Chikamatsu Kanroku, Yokogawa Kanpei, Masé Kyūdayū, Kanzaki Yogorō, Hazama Kihei, Muramatsu Kihei, Horibe Yahei, Okuda Magodayu, and Kimura Okaemon. When Jōemon saw Magodayū, he said, "What are *you* doing, being carried? You're not wounded."

"I know," Magodayū said, "but I'm exhausted. I'm going to ride."

Finally, Jōemon found old Yahei's litter, and he walked alongside him the entire distance. They talked about the battle, Jōemon telling him what he had heard outside the walls and Yahei telling Jōemon how they had found and killed Kōzuke-no-Suke.

"And you yourself were not wounded?"

"Not a one of them came near the place where I was stationed," Yahei said.

"And how did Yasubei do?"

"I'd like to know myself," Yahei said. "But it doesn't seem right for me to ask in front of the others, so I've purposely avoided doing so."

"How many wounded and how many dead?" Jōemon asked.

"We killed sixteen or seventeen; I've no idea how many were wounded."

✦ ✦ ✦

The highway into which the ronin emerged was very different from when they had walked it early that morning. This stretch at least was not deserted, being the terminus of the Eastern Sea Road. But neither was it the bustling thoroughfare that it would have been on any other day at this hour. Earlier in the afternoon, a detail of Sub-Inspectors had walked the entire route from the temple to the official residence of the

Duty Inspector General, Sengoku Hōki-no-Kami. Their mission, quite simply, was to clear the field for battle and keep collateral damage to a minimum. They stopped at every precinct watchman's post and the corner guardhouse of every lordly mansion along the way. Where the route passed through residential wards, they went into the back alleys between the tenements. An "unusual procession" would pass their way, they told these people. Until it passed, they were to keep their streets clear of idle spectators and curiosity seekers, and ensure that the way was well lit. If they saw anyone carrying weapons, or anyone who looked at all suspicious, they were to report them immediately. By the time the ronin emerged from the temple and turned north to begin their march, lanterns lined the entire length of the route, armed men stood at every corner, and hardly a soul was to be seen on the streets. It must have looked like a festival to which no one had come.

At first, the procession remained on the Eastern Sea Road, from Takanawa through Mita, until it reached the old Signpost Corner. There the ronin veered left, off the highway, and into the street that leads in a long, perfectly straight line to the Akabane Bridge. They traveled the length of that street without incident, but once they had crossed the bridge, they came to a sudden halt in the square adjacent to the archery range.

"I'll go up ahead and see what the matter is," Jōemon told Yahei. And when he came back, he said, "They say that the lower mansion of Uesugi Danjō Dono is just up ahead on the left. Someone has gone up to investigate, and the command group is conferring. We'll have to be on the alert in this neighborhood." A moment or two later, Mimura Jirōzaemon came back to tell everyone being carried in litters that they, too, should be on guard. Then the column began to move again, although much more slowly now. At every side street and at every little bridge, they would stop until someone had shone a lantern into the shadows. But again they passed without incident.

◆ ◆ ◆

As they drew near their final destination, they sensed a subtle change in the atmosphere. The expectant silence that had prevailed so far, as though the city were holding its breath, was now suffused with the muffled murmur of a distant crowd. The last corner on their route was already in sight, perhaps 300 yards ahead. What they were hearing were the massed contingents of armed men sent by the four daimyo in whose custody the ronin were soon to be placed. Kuranosuke halted the column at Kurumazaka. By rights, there should be no danger in passing among those forces; their approach was expected. But then they were armed for battle, bearing unsheathed lances and bows and quivers full of arrows. Caution was called for. Kuranosuke sent Onodera Jūnai—a man well practiced in diplomacy—ahead to the gate of the Sengoku mansion to announce their arrival and seek instructions concerning their weapons.

"Our entire group has come, in response to your summons," Jūnai told the Deputy Inspectors stationed at the gate. "Our marching orders were that we should carry our assault weapons with us. We're reluctant to approach your gate armed in this fashion, but it would hardly do to discard these weapons in the street, either. We don't wish to do anything that might arouse hostility, so if you'll instruct us where you would like us to abandon our weapons, we'll gladly comply."

"Your concern is much appreciated," the Inspector replied, "but we've not the least objection to your bringing your weapons within the gate." Jūnai bowed in assent and returned to the formation.

As the column again began to move, the mood of the men seemed to rise. With every step, they advanced farther into a pocket from which there could be no escape. Yet surrounded by their several hundred heavily armed captors, neither was there any further chance of attack by their enemies. They had done their job and done it well. The battle was over now. By the time they rounded the corner and saw the gate, their wary silence was broken by bursts of laughter.

One of the older men strode up and announced, "We are ronin, formerly the vassals of Asano Takumi-no-Kami, reporting in compliance with your summons." The rest of the group hardly noticed. Some were stacking their lances and bows neatly against the wall; some were dropping them carelessly onto the street or even into the gutter. Their tight formation had disintegrated into small knots of elated men congratulating one another and sharing for the first time the fullness of their victory. Without saying as much, they were also bidding one another farewell, for none of them knew where they might now be bound for or if they would ever see one another again.

Jōemon helped Yahei out of his litter and took his arm to lead him to the gate. But Yahei stopped and pointed to his lance, which was tied to the roof of the litter.

"Take that with you," he said to Jōemon.

"No, I'd better not," Jōemon said. "They're collecting all the weapons over there." Then he heard someone calling his name: "Jōemon Dono! Jōemon Dono!" At first, he couldn't make out whether it was Jūemon or Jōemon who was being called. But it turned out that it was indeed he, and that Takebayashi Tadashichi was looking for him.

"There's something I need to talk to you about," Tadashichi said.

"What might it be?"

"In the course of all this," he said, "I've severed relations with all my relatives; now there is no one to collect and dispose of my body. I can see perfectly well that we are going to have to commit seppuku. And since we samurai must depend on one another, I'd like to ask you to attend to my body."

"I shall indeed do that," Jōemon told him. "Don't worry about a thing. I'll see that everything is properly taken care of."

"I'm very grateful for that—and much relieved," Tadashichi said. "Even if I had died in the attack, I would already have felt fulfilled. But having killed that man with my own hands, there's nothing further that I could wish for."

The Deputy Inspectors from the castle had by now ordered the gate unbolted and pushed one door of it ajar. The ronin were to enter one at a time, they told them, stating their family name and familiar name as they did.

◆ ◆ ◆

Among the crowd of those waiting at the gate of the Sengoku mansion was Haga Seidayū Tomohisa, a Deputy Inspector in the house of Hisamatsu Oki-no-Kami—the same Seidayū who had been haranguing his colleagues earlier in the day, when the procession of ronin had first been sighted.

It had been a long, cold, and wet wait; but as Seidayū watched the procession round the corner, he was surprised to see that the ronin were still clad as they had been when they mounted their attack on the Kira mansion—wearing chain mail, armored guards on their forearms and shins, got up to look rather like a fire brigade. Some of them were armed with bows and arrows, and some with lances and halberds, their blades bared for a battle that never began. When they reached the gate, they took off their helmets, cradled them under their arms, threw down their weapons, and one by one entered the gate, each of them checked by a Deputy Inspector and a Sub-Inspector.

Seidayū's curiosity was piqued. So he took advantage of the confusion to brazen his way through the gate, just before it was shut. By rights, he had no business there; his place was with the Hisamatsu formation. But the opportunity was too good to be missed, and he found it a simple matter to conceal himself among those who did have business there. Seidayū moved slowly through the crowd to a vantage directly opposite the vestibule. There he could watch the Sub-Inspectors as they took possession of the swords and personal effects of the ronin—fans, paper folds, even sleeve markers—asking each man's name as they did, and then writing out a tag to be attached to his possessions. He could see the ronin washing their feet in the tubs of warm water, drying them with the towels that had been provided, and then mounting the entry and moving into the reception rooms. Beyond that, however, they were too far in the distance for him to see clearly what went on, and his view was blocked by folding screens.

◆ ◆ ◆

Outside in the rain, the Sub-Inspectors began clearing the streets of everyone but the forces that had come to take custody of the ronin. Jōemon retreated to the back streets, but before long, he was shooed out of there, too. Now there was nowhere he could hide until his friends were taken into custody. So he left to return to Yonezawa-chō, where he could at least give the women news of Yahei and Yasubei. Only Terasaka Kichiemon remained somewhere in the vicinity. He had spoken to no one, revealed himself to no one. Nor did he ever mention where he hid when the streets were cleared. But he was determined that, before he set out for Harima, he would wait until Yoshida Chūzaemon should emerge and he could find out where his commander would be held.

◆ ◆ ◆

Once the gate had been shut and bolted, and all the ronin processed, their names were called in the order of their appearance on the manifesto submitted that morning by Chūzaemon and Suke'emon. They filed into the reception room and took their places, Kuranosuke in the first seat, Mimura Jirōzaemon in the last. The wounded were helped to their places by Deputy Inspectors and told that they might sit cross-legged rather than more formally on their knees. Once they were seated, all bowed low. Hōki-no-Kami then entered at the head of the room, attended by two Deputy Inspectors: Suzuki Gengoemon and Mizuno Kozaemon. The interrogation began:

HŌKI-NO-KAMI: *And you are Ōishi Kuranosuke?*

KURANOSUKE: *I am he.*

HŌKI: *For what reasons did you kill Kōzuke?*

KURANOSUKE: *Our reasons are as stated in the manifesto we submitted.*

HŌKI: *Your liege lord, in defiance of duly constituted authority, committed an outrage in the palace, for which he was punished in strict accordance with the law. You have no ground whatever for any grievance against the Shogunate. This affray, in which you have all taken part, is thus an offense of the most serious sort.*

KURANOSUKE: *Quite so. I assure you, though, that we bear no malice whatever toward the Shogunate. Yet the fact that Kōzuke-no-Suke Dono remained alive was, for us, our lord's vassals, a source of bitter rancor. And thus we broke into his residence and killed him. Whatever punishment may be meted out to us for this offense, we shall accept without the slightest resentment.*

HŌKI: *Were you normally resident in the domain or resident in this city?*

KURANOSUKE: *I was resident in the domain.*

HŌKI: *At what time of day did you proceed to the Kōzuke residence?*

KURANOSUKE *and* CHŪZAEMON: *It would have been after the Eighth Hour [2:00 A.M.] but before the Seventh [4:00 A.M.].*

Perhaps because Kuranosuke tended to be rather taciturn, Chūzaemon, too, seems to have answered some of these questions. From here on, however, the text indicates only that both spoke and does not distinguish who said what:

HŌKI: *Then it was a night attack. In which case, you must have been equipped with some sort of illumination. Did you carry lanterns? Or torches?*

KURANOSUKE *and* CHŪZAEMON: *Neither. The fire-prevention ordinances in the castle city are extremely strict. We all agreed that we would carry no lighting of any sort.*

HŌKI: *You must have found it awfully dark.*

KURANOSUKE *and* CHŪZAEMON: *The moonlight was exceptionally bright last night. None of us had any problem whatever.*

HŌKI: *This being a night attack, did you use passwords?*

KURANOSUKE *and* CHŪZAEMON: *We did. When one of us said "mountain," the other was to answer "river."*

HŌKI: *What were your marks of identification?*

KURANOSUKE *and* CHŪZAEMON: *We attached white cloth to our sleeves.*

HŌKI: *By what means did you gain entry to the premises?*

KURANOSUKE *and* CHŪZAEMON: *We battered down the gate.*

HŌKI: *What did you do for light when you were indoors?*

KURANOSUKE *and* CHŪZAEMON: *Once we had broken in, we*

figure 27
The ronin arriving at the mansion of the
Duty Inspector General, Sengoku Hōki-no-Kami.
(*Ehon Chūshingura*, Waseda University Library, Tokyo)

apprehended one of their men, secured his arms behind his back, and asked him where the candles were kept. Then we took out the container in which they were packed, and in this man's presence counted them. Taking the lamp from the entryway, we fought our way farther into the house, placing candles along the way as we went. We searched the bath and under the veranda, but Kōzuke-no-Suke was nowhere to be found.

HŌKI: *Did you enter his personal quarters?*

KURANOSUKE *and* CHŪZAEMON: *We entered what we took to be his quarters, but he was not to be found there. There was great deal of what appeared to be bedding scattered about in his anteroom. In the meantime, one of our men named Hazama Jūjirō proceeded to the charcoal storeroom. The door was shut, but he heard voices within. With the butt of his lance, he broke down the door, whereupon a man with a sword emerged and put up an extraordinary fight; but we surrounded him and cut him down. We then shot into the room with a battle bow.*

HŌKI: *And that was the end of it?*

KURANOSUKE *and* CHŪZAEMON (both smiling): *Well, not quite. They also flung charcoal and teacups and saucers and plates at us—all manner of things. And then another man emerged, fighting as he came. Hazama Jūjirō brought a candle, and when we looked inside, there was a man sitting on a storage case. He wore a brown outer robe and a white under-robe secured with the sash of a night robe. "Surely this could not be Kōzuke-no-Suke Dono?" we thought. Everyone gathered around, wondering who it might be. "Tell us where your lord is," we said. "If you don't talk, we'll make you talk." He said nothing. And so Takebayashi Tadashichi struck him above the right eye with the point of his lance.*

HŌKI: *So none of you knew what Kōzuke Dono looked like?*

KURANOSUKE: *No one knew what Kōzuke-no-Suke's face looked like, but we reckoned that anyone wearing a white under-robe would not be a retainer; when we parted his hair with a comb, we found a scar about 5 inches in length. This we took to be the wound inflicted by our lord in the Third Month of the previous year. We were still uncertain, however, and so we removed his talisman and paper fold and wrapped them in the white robe with his head, secured it with his sash, and took it to the man we had bound up at the outset. We asked him, repeatedly, whether this was Kōzuke's head. He said that it was indeed his lord's honored head.*

HŌKI: *Did you wound Sahei?*

KURANOSUKE and CHŪZAEMON: *We have no idea. We never saw anyone who looked like he might be Sahei Dono. We bore no grudge against him, and we had agreed beforehand that we needn't attack him. Of course, if he had challenged us, that would have been a different matter.*

HŌKI: *Approximately how many men did you kill? Were there any who fought back?*

KURANOSUKE and CHŪZAEMON: *I think that we killed about fourteen or fifteen. It was dark, and Kōzuke-no-Suke Sama's men came at us one after another. We held our ground. Four or five of our men would take on each one as he came and kill him. Later, we made the rounds of all the barrack buildings, calling for anyone with the courage to come out and fight. No one came out. We were very careful not to start any fires. We went through all the rooms, pouring water on every fire and extinguishing the lamps. We collected all the candles, counted them to be sure that we hadn't missed any, and poured water over them. The Inspectors, I am sure, will find all in order. A hole had been opened in the wall. We suspect that someone escaped through it. Thereafter, we opened the gate. We were certain that Sahei Sama's men would pursue us, and we planned to await them at the gate to the Temple of the Unknown Dead. But no one came. We asked two or three times that the gate be opened, so we could await orders from the authorities there, but they wouldn't open it. We were reluctant to wait there on the thoroughfare, and so we had no choice but to make our way to Sengakuji . . .*

HŌKI: *Then there is nothing further that we need ask. You may now proceed to the houses of your custodians.*

Suzuki Gengoemon and Mizuno Kozaemon bowed to their superior officer; then Kōzaemon addressed the ronin: "Takumi-no-Kami was fortunate to have had such exemplary retainers. What a pity that it must come to this, just when you have served him so well." The other officials present murmured their agreement, while the ronin remained with their heads bowed.

As they filed out of the reception room, Chūzaemon and Suke'emon stepped aside briefly to speak to Inoue Man'emon.

"You've been extremely kind to us today. We're very grateful, and we shall never forget it."

*I am well aware, of course, how unnecessary it was to
send so many samurai to escort you here.*

They had been on the move since midday. They had marched from
Daimyo Lane down to Takanawa, only to be told that they must turn
around and march all the way back to Atagoshita. And the rain had not
let up since it began sprinkling early in the afternoon. Now, well into the
night, the assembled forces of all four daimyo houses were arrayed in
close proximity to the mansion of the Duty Inspector General, Sengoku
Hōki-no-Kami, waiting in the pouring rain to be called to the gate, each
to take custody of its assigned quota of Akō ronin. The ronin themselves
had not arrived until the Fifth Hour (8:00 P.M.), and even then no one
had any idea how long it would take the Inspectors to process and interrogate them. But at least no one could get any more thoroughly soaked
than he was already. The cold, wet, wearisome wait would continue.

◆ ◆ ◆

It was past the Fourth Hour (10:00 P.M.) before there were any signs of
further activity within the gate to the Sengoku mansion. Haga Seidayū,
who had slipped in uninvited before the gates were shut, was still loi-
tering in the vestibule and could see what no one out on the streets
could see.

The interrogation concluded, Seidayū says, one of the Inspectors
strode out of the reception rooms into the vestibule and called out, "The
Elders of Hosokawa Etchū-no-Kami Dono, please." In response to his
summons, two gentlemen in full formal linens and one in surcoat and
breeches came forward. (Seidayū tells us that he thought them terribly

overdressed for the occasion—indeed, unbecomingly so.) Miyake Tōbei, the Traveling Elder; Kamata Gunnosuke, the Chief Adjutant; and Horiuchi Heihachi, the Edo Liaison Officer, were shown into the presence of Sengoku Hōki-no-Kami, who said simply, "Please be advised that we entrust these seventeen men to your custody," and handed them a list of their names. Kuranosuke seems to have expressed polite reservations whether they deserved the privilege of transport in palanquins.

"Some of your men are old, and some are wounded," he was told. "It is best that they be escorted in this way." The true reason, of course, was security; but a decent degree of decorum was maintained by both sides.

Outside the gates, those waiting were told that they might now send in the seventeen palanquins and the men who would bear them. One by one, as the names of the ronin were read out, a palanquin would be carried to the edge of the entry; as each man boarded, he was carried out the gate and down the street to the gate of the upper mansion of Hosokawa Izumi-no-Kami, where their escorts waited. Their palanquins were neither locked nor shrouded in netting, and they were told that they might open the windows if they wished. Once all seventeen conveyances were aligned in proper order, their escorts began to fall into formation.

At the head of the procession were two large lanterns bearing the nine-star crest of the House of Hosokawa, followed by three senior officers on horseback—Horiuchi Heihachi, Kamata Gunnosuke, and Hirano Kurōemon—the first attended by four foot soldiers bearing hand-held lanterns, the second by eight foot soldiers, and the last by ten foot soldiers and their commander. Then came the first of the palanquins, preceded by two crested lanterns and escorted by ten foot soldiers and two dismounted samurai, six men on either side, and followed by a large lantern mounted on a tall shaft. The remaining sixteen palanquins were similarly escorted, except that they were preceded by only a single mounted samurai.

Following the palanquins came two pairs of long luggage boxes, each guarded by four foot soldiers and followed by two dismounted samurai. Then, finally, a rear guard of three mounted samurai, followed by the column's commander, the Elder Miyake Tōbei; and to see them off the

Liaison Officer of Hosokawa Izumi-no-Kami, Shibasaki Koemon. Both dignitaries were mounted and preceded by large, crested lanterns.

The whole procession comprised more than 750 men; although they were the first to leave the mansion of Sengoku Hōki-no-Kami, they had the greatest distance to travel and thus would be the last to reach their final destination.

✦ ✦ ✦

As soon as the last of the seventeen disappeared through the gate, there came the call, "The Elders of Matsudaira [Hisamatsu] Oki-no-Kami Dono, please." Two Samurai Commanders, Okuda Jirōdayū and Tsukuda Kyūbei, came forward, dressed in breeches and surcoats secured by a sash in which they bore their swords. Both men apologized. Owing to the sudden change of venue, they said, they had been unable to change into attire more suitable for an audience with the Inspector General. The names of ten ronin were then called; they came to the main entry and were there handed over to the custody of the Hisamatsu house.

Haga Seidaiyū thought that the samurai assigned to escort the ronin should have searched them more thoroughly, lest they have daggers secreted in the folds of their garments; but under the circumstances, he just nodded in assent and let them pass. One by one, the ronin boarded their palanquins and were carried out into the street.

The procession of the Hisamatsu was, of course, less magnificent than that of the Hosokawa. They had only ten ronin in their custody, and theirs was a far lesser domain. Even so, with only three hundred men, they managed to give the impression that they maintained much stricter security over the men in their charge. In the van were four large crested lanterns, held high on long shafts, followed by a contingent of twenty foot soldiers and their commander; two more lanterns preceded the three senior officers on horseback. Then came the ten palanquins, each of which was preceded by two tall lanterns; escorted by a mounted samurai, a dismounted samurai, and ten foot soldiers armed with hard-wood staves; and carried by four bearers. Thereafter came the two Samurai Commanders who had served as representatives of the Elders of the House, preceded by four crested lanterns and followed by two columns of twenty liveried menials and two columns of ten foot soldiers. And last of all were the two Deputy Inspectors in overall charge of the procession, Miyahara Kyūdayū and Haga Seidayū.

The Hisamatsu at least did not have far to go. They would spend the rest of the night at their upper mansion, before escorting their charges to the middle mansion the next day. With only about three long blocks to travel from the Sengoku mansion, they were able reach their destination by about midnight.

Yet despite the short distance, Haga Seidayū was determined to practice what he had been preaching that morning about military preparedness. Just in case, in the course of that brief journey, they should be attacked by the Uesugi and he should be killed in action, he had prepared a full-size sheet of heavy paper upon which he wrote: "Haga Seidayū Tomohisa, vassal of Hisamatsu Oki-no-Kami Sadanao, in gratitude for generation upon generation of His Lordship's magnanimity, is determined to fight to the death. Genroku 15, Twelfth Month, 15th Day."

He then folded the sheet, wrapped it in waterproof oiled paper, tied it, and tucked it into his talisman. Whoever came upon the body of Seidayū would know that he had gone to his death that night fully prepared. And for the benefit of his descendants, he describes how much better prepared he was for the day's travails than were his comrades:

> The men sent with me on this mission are the sort who delight in fine foods, dress extravagantly, drink to excess, and have grown careless from living in an age of peace. They may be perfectly accustomed to the way we normally live nowadays. But on a cold day like today, soaked to the skin from midday until after midnight, they suffered horribly. I, however, because at all times I endeavor to exercise moderation, was not the least bit distressed. . . . I trust that my descendants will read this with care and take it to heart.

The procession entered the Hisamatsu Upper Mansion from the side gate, skirted the main entrance—from which His Lordship, Oki-no-Kami observed their arrival—and went on to the central barrack block. Each of the ronin was assigned a separate room, allowed to bathe, given three kimono, an obi, a loincloth, nightwear, bedding, a pillow, two hand towels, and a wrapping cloth. They were then treated to a sumptuous dinner served on two separate trays. Thereafter, one presumes, they wished only to sleep—while Haga Seidayū was left to lament that the war he had so fervently hoped for had never happened.

◆ ◆ ◆

I'll not describe the transfer and transport of the remaining nineteen ronin to the Mōri and Mizuno houses. The process was exactly the same as in the cases of the Hosokawa and Hisamatsu houses. And the formations in which they marched to their respective destinations, although not identical, were very similar to the formation of the Hisamatsu house—but with only 200 men from the Mōri, and 150 from the Mizuno. Their wait in the rain, however, was much longer. It was not until after midnight that the Mōri arrived in Azabu Higakubo and the Mizuno in Shiba.

◆ ◆ ◆

When the Hosokawa procession finally moved on from the mansion of Hosokawa Izumi-no-Kami, they at first followed the same route as the Hisamatsu column, passing the main gate of the Hisamatsu Upper Mansion (where they were observed clandestinely and with great interest) before turning south to that broad open expanse just above the temple Zōjōji. From there, passing through Mishima-chō, they turned right onto the Eastern Sea Road, which they followed for some distance until they reached the narrow, winding side road that rises to Isarago. They were almost home now. At the top of the hill, they turned left onto the road to Meguro and shortly thereafter entered the Meguro Gate of the Hosokawa Lower Mansion in Takanawa. The Eighth Hour (2:00 A.M.) had just tolled.

His Lordship Hosokawa Etchū-no-Kami had waited up through the night, and when the ronin were shown into the Actors' Room adjacent to the Nō stage, he came immediately and took a seat directly facing Kuranosuke.

"Each and every one of you has acted with consummate loyalty on this occasion," he said. "I am deeply impressed. And I am convinced that what you have done is precisely what the heavens destined you to do. That you should be entrusted to our care in this mansion is as great an honor as any military house could wish for. I hope that now you'll be able to relax and enjoy a highly deserved rest after all those months of privation and pain, not to mention your exertions of this past night. If there is anything whatever that we can do for you, please don't hesitate to let us know. We'll do our utmost to serve you in any way within our power.

"I am well aware, of course, how unnecessary it was to send so many samurai to escort you here. Indeed, it was rather foolish; but I trust you'll understand that we did so only for the sake of appearances in the eyes the authorities. The law also requires me to place a few of my vassals in your company. These men are by no means your guards. First and foremost, they are here to do whatever they can to assist you. So whatever you may need, don't hesitate to mention it to whoever happens to be on duty." And turning to his own men, he said, "Do all that you can for them, every one of you." The ronin were so choked with emotion that some nearly wept in the attempt to express their gratitude.

"Well, the night has grown late. Let's get these men something to eat as quickly as we can." With that, he left the room.

Immediately thereafter, his heir, Lord Naiki, a boy aged only thirteen, entered and said, in particularly friendly tones, "If there is anything you wish to say to my father, Etchū-no-Kami, but feel reticent to do so, you need only mention it to me." Then he, too, left the room.

◆ ◆ ◆

Terasaka Kichiemon had now seen all his comrades carried away and had overheard enough of what was being said to know where they were going. It was, at last, time for him to head out of town on the Eastern Sea Road, bound for the village of Kameyama in Harima.

◆ ◆ ◆

Jinzaburō had been there, too, lurking in the shadows and somehow evading the Sub-Inspectors who had gone about clearing the streets.

Finally, though, he decided that he must leave. The wait had been so long that it seemed to him the ronin were being kept in custody by Sengoku Hōki-no-Kami. He was alone now, with no place to go but back into the city. And off he went: back along the Eastern Sea Road to its starting point at Nihonbashi, then on through the wards of Kanda to the Sujichigai Gate, and across the outer moat and up the broad avenue leading to Ueno. High up ahead, he could just see the massive gate of the temple Kan'eiji, where the fourth Shogun, Ietsuna, was buried. But at the foot of the slope he veered left, following the path along the edge of the Shinobazu Pond—even in winter, a beautiful sight. The snow had melted from the tiled roofs and pines of the little island that held the Benten Shrine, but there were still piles of it by the gate to the causeway. It reminded Jinzaburō of the last time that he had passed here, toward the end of the snowstorm. Men pushing plows with all their might to clear the way, and then sweeping the path clean with their bamboo brooms; passers-by bundled up snugly, huddling under their umbrellas and, like himself, shuffling along as quickly as they could without slipping; snow-white herons winging their way to the far shore. At the pond's northern end, the road jogged sharply to the right, and then zigzagged up the slope to the temple Tennōji, opposite which stood Jinzaburō's destination—the much smaller temple Chōfukuji. This probably would be the last time he would walk this way. He and Kanroku had relinquished their lodgings in Kōjimachi the day before yesterday. There was no returning there. But Kanroku's brother Bunryō would put him up for a few days. Then he would have to make his way back to Hiruta, alone.

*An offering of
first fruits . . .*

The ronin had left Sengakuji too late in the day for the Abbot to do anything about the severed head that they had left in his care. Something
had to be done, however, before it became any more putrid. Whatever
that something might be, it could not be done without the consent of
the Commissioner of Temples and Shrines, Abe Hida-no-Kami. And
so at the Fourth Hour (7:00 A.M.) of the 16th Day, the Abbot set out
again for Daimyō Lane to request further instructions. Hida-no-Kami
received the Abbot immediately: "I must say, Your Reverence's handling
of all that has happened of late has been flawless. I am most impressed;
and I certainly shall tell my colleagues all about it."

"You are most gracious," the Abbot replied. "But there remains the
matter of Kōzuke-no-Suke Dono's severed head, which was entrusted
to me by Kuranosuke. I am quite at a loss what to do with it. It's a terrible burden to the monks who must guard it; I'd like to dispose of it as
soon as possible."

"My superiors have said nothing about this," Hida-no-Kami said. "I
would think, though, that it should be returned to Sahei. I understand
that Banshōin is Kōzuke's mortuary temple, and as it happens, a monk
from Banshōin is waiting here just now. Might I suggest that you meet
with him and arrange something?"

"I would be much obliged if we could resolve the matter right here
and now. I'll discuss it with Banshōin immediately." The Abbot rose,
went into the next room, and an agreement was quickly reached.

"If you will send it on, then," Banshōin said, "I shall advise Sahei

Dono in advance of your arrival." With a polite exchange of pleasantries, the Sengakuji Abbot left the mansion of Hida-no-Kami and returned to his temple.

✦ ✦ ✦

The delivery was to take place on the evening of that day and was entrusted to two monks: one named Sekishi, and the other Ichidon. Before they set out on their mission, the Abbot gave these men detailed instructions about how the matter should be handled: "I am appointing you two as my emissaries, to return the head of Kōzuke-no-Suke Dono to Sahei Dono. First of all, I would advise you to choose your route to the Kira mansion with great care. And when you announce yourselves at the gate, you must tell the intermediary that you will hand over the head only within the gate. If the intermediary nonetheless wishes to take delivery outside the gate, you must firmly refuse. If ultimately they *demand* delivery outside the gate, you may comply only after being given a written receipt bearing Sahei Dono's personal seal. And even within the gate, you must demand a receipt before handing over the head. This is not to be handled in a slipshod manner."

The box containing the head was then wrapped in waterproof paper and secured with twine to a pole, which would be borne by two servants. With it was sent an inventory and a statement:

MEMORANDUM

Item: *One severed head*

Item: *Two paper parcels: one containing a tissue paper fold and a talisman*
one containing the sheath of a lance

Kindly accept the aforementioned items. Herewith the foregoing,

TWELFTH MONTH, 16TH DAY   *Sengakuji*
To: Kira Sahei Dono

Statement

Our condolences on the occasion of this unfortunate incident involving Kōzuke Dono. With full approval of the appropriate officials, we hereby return the head that was entrusted to us by Kuranosuke.

So instructed and so laden, Sekishi and Ichidon set out for Honjo in the Fifth Hour (ca. 8:00 P.M.).

✦ ✦ ✦

Even under cover of darkness, however, the procession seems to have attracted a fair bit of attention. In Shiba and Tamachi, some were so bold as to approach the monks and ask what they were carrying, while others recognized immediately what it was and could be heard whispering about "the head of Kōzuke Dono."

It would have been at least two hours later when they reached the main gate of the Kira mansion and announced themselves. Whereupon commenced one of the most bizarre events in the whole process. At first, they were asked to wait outside for a moment; when they were finally admitted, they understood the reason for the delay. As the gates swung open, they saw that the entire length of the path leading from the gate to the vestibule was lined with samurai in full formal attire, together with thirty or forty foot soldiers and lesser retainers, all kneeling in attitudes of deep obeisance. And then the monks realized: the preparations that had kept them waiting were not for their benefit. The head that they bore represented the lord of the House of Kira, and the survivors of his household had been waiting expectantly to welcome him home.

At the entryway, the monks were met by a man of fifty-plus, also in formal attire, who greeted them with great deference and invited them into the house. The monks at first demurred.

"As you can see our feet are dirty, and there is only this one small matter to attend to. . . ." But the gentleman insisted, and they were led within—first through a narrow corridor, then through two sitting rooms, and finally into a third room—a room pervaded with a vile stench, which Sekishi and Ichidon found quite sickening. And in that room were seated two other monks: the Superior of the Banshōin and his attendant. Introductions were made and greetings exchanged, and Sōda Magobei, the gentleman who had first met them, identified himself and a companion as the Elders of Kōzuke-no-Suke's household. The monks read out their statement as instructed, and the Elders told them that they must go within and speak to Sahei. Shortly thereafter, one of them emerged and inquired how the receipt should be worded. The monks replied that they would leave the wording to the discretion of the Elders. Again, the Elder left the room. The head had remained all the while with Sekishi and Ichidon; when the Elders emerged once more from within, they asked if they might now take possession of it. The two monks handed over the box, still wrapped in waterproof paper.

"We would like to inspect the contents, please," the Elders said.

"You'll find everything intact," the monks replied, "still as sealed by Kuranosuke. We've brought it exactly as we received it, so do feel free to inspect it." The Elders produced candles, and four or five samurai were called in to cut the seal and lift the lid. As they gathered around and peered into the box, they could be heard whispering, "There's his wound." Then they replaced the lid and carried the box within. But a moment later, Sōda Magobei returned.

"I'm an old man and hard of hearing," he said, "and I'm afraid that I didn't catch all of your statement when you read it out before. Might I ask you to read it out again?" It was read again, slowly this time, while a scribe copied it down. Again Magobei left, but a moment later he reappeared, this time with a somewhat stranger request.

"I know nothing at all of events the other night," he said. "Would you be so kind as to tell me what all those men were saying while they were at your temple?" Sekishi and Ichidon replied simply that they, too, knew nothing.

Magobei then asked the Superior of the Banshōin to step out of the room with him, where he whispered something to the monk. A moment later, the Superior came back, obviously having been asked to see if he could pry any information out of Sekishi and Ichidon: "Surely it can't be that you've heard nothing at all about the night before last. Magobei has asked that you tell him whatever you do know."

"We really know nothing," they told him. "When the forty-six men arrived at Sengakuji, our Abbot commanded immediately that no one without good reason was to go near them; everything was to be handled as quietly as possible. Neither of us has even met them; we know nothing at all."

"Well, in that case," Banshōin asked, "did they by any chance bring an *extra* head to the temple? You see, they're missing a head, and they want me to question you about it." The Sengakuji monks' answer to this preposterous query was a derisive (and moderately learned) joke, playing on the fact that the word *yokei* ("extra" or "superfluous"), when written with different but homophonous characters (余計, 余慶), as it is used in the *I-ching*, can mean "the good fortune of a child owing to the virtue of his forebears."

"*Sate, sate, mezurashiki koto! Yokei to mōsu kotoba ni, kubi no yokei to mōsu wa, sate, sate, okashiki koto!*" Which we might translate as, "Well *that's* an odd one! Using the words 'good fortune' to describe a severed head. Very odd indeed!"

And before they could be importuned any further, the Sengakuji monks turned the tables on Banshōin, and asked a question of him: "That horrid smell in this room—what on earth could be causing it?"

There is no hint of evasion in Banshōin's reply.

"On the other side of those shoji," he said, pointing to the sliding doors, "lie all the dead bodies from the other night. You may have noticed that the rooms you passed through earlier were spread with thin mats. Well, the tatami beneath them are soaked with blood. That's what the horrid stench is from." No authorization for the burial of the bodies could be issued until the investigation had been officially closed, and so the dead lay rotting in the next room, awaiting this important piece of paper.

No sooner were the monks told this, than the door slid open again and trays of food were set before them—steaming bowls of rice porridge. You can imagine their reaction. At first, Ichidon and Sekishi protested politely that it was getting late, and it was a long walk back to their temple; so they had rather just take their receipt and be on their way. But the Kira Elders were having no polite refusals. The guests must eat. And so in the end, they did as good guests should.

As Sekishi put it, "The stench of blood mingled with the scent of steaming rice was simply appalling, but we forced ourselves to gulp it down." Only then, were they given their receipt for the head of Kira Kōzuke-no-Suke:

MEMORANDUM

Item: *Severed head, 1*

Item: *Paper parcel, 1*

The foregoing duly received. Herewith,

YEAR OF THE HORSE
TWELFTH MONTH, 16TH DAY   *Vassals of Kira Sahei*
                                      Sōda Magobei
                                       Saitō Kunai

To: Emissary monks from Sengakuji
Ichidon
Sekishi

Nothing is recorded of the monks' journey home, but one imagines that they found the crisp night air refreshing.

✦ ✦ ✦

On the following day, the 17th, Kira Kōzuke-no-Suke was buried—body and head reunited—at the Banshōin in Ushigome Kagurazaka. In later years, he had to share some of the limelight with Kurisaki Dōyū, the specialist in sword wounds who had treated him in Edo Castle, and the woodblock-print artist Utagawa Toyokuni. Still, on most maps of Edo large enough to show the Banshōin, Kira remains the main attraction of this temple's graveyard, for they all bear the notation: "Kira's grave here."

✦ ✦ ✦

That night, the neighborhood wits struck again, this time with poems pasted to the doors of Kira's main gate:

~ 635 ~

kubi to dō / banshōin e / nido ni kuru
Head and body: it takes him two trips to get to the Banshōin.

shōshō no kubi o ko'oke ni ireokite
tera yori sato e okuru hatsumono
The Lieutenant's head, painstakingly packed in a little wooden cask:
an offering of first fruits from the temple to his home.

*You are forbidden to discuss this
recent incident with them.*

How long would they now have to wait? And what was to come at the
end of that wait? There had been moments when the ronin could have
decided these matters for themselves—if they had all agreed to commit
seppuku together. But if they had decided to die in Honjo, they could
not have carried Kira's head to the grave of Takumi-no-Kami. And if
they had decided to die at Sengakuji, they would have not only discommoded their hosts, but also undercut the promises made by the two
men sent to Sengoku Hōki-no-Kami. Having turned themselves in to
the Shogunate, only the Shogunate could now decide the fate of the
ronin; and the Shogunate was nowhere near making up its mind on
that question.

The possibilities were numerous. The ronin could be commended for
their loyalty and set free—a solution that was certain to please public
opinion. Or they could be left in custody for a time, and then quietly
released. Or they could be banished to a distant island and left there
until the next amnesty. Or they could be allowed to commit seppuku,
the most honorable death for a samurai. Or, worst of all, they could be
bound and beheaded like common criminals. And, of course, there were
infinite variants and combinations of all these. It would take a great deal
of discussion and debate to decide the matter.

In the end, though, the final decision would have to be made by the
Shogun himself. But Tsunayoshi was a Shogun who considered himself
a believer in the rule of law. The established conventions would be followed, and only then would a decision be made. The Council of Elders

would seek precedents and weigh them; the Junior Council would probably do the same. The matter would certainly be on the agenda of the
Shogunal Tribunal, which met three times every month, on the 2nd, the
12th, and the 22nd. And like all decision makers, the Shogun could also
be influenced by the opinions of advisers. We shall catch glimpses of all
these processes along the way, but little more than glimpses; when the
end result is revealed, we shall be hard put to judge the weight any one
of them had in deciding the matter.

♦ ♦ ♦

In the meantime, the day-to-day lives of the ronin would be governed
by the spirit in which the four daimyo houses undertook their duties
as custodians. The custody of anyone detained by the Shogunate
demanded, by definition, a high level of security. At the same time, it
was important for the daimyo to know the attitudes of the Shogunate
in this particular case. Did the officials suspect that the ronin might
attempt to escape? Commit suicide? Harm their guardians? Or was officialdom inclined to indulge their prisoners? All the daimyo therefore
questioned the Council of Elders—sometimes in absurd detail—about
how they should treat the ronin. Should they be allowed to use twee-
zers? Should their hairdressers be permitted the use of scissors? Should
they be given paper, brush, and ink? And what about toothpicks? All the
daimyo were given the same answer: "Do as you please; they have committed no offense against the Shogunate, and they shall remain in your
custody only for the duration of our deliberations." This left infinite
leeway for variation, and vary they did.

As we have seen, Hosokawa Etchū-no-Kami could hardly have
greeted the seventeen men in his custody more warmly or with greater
sincerity. He traveled the considerable distance from his upper mansion in Daimyo Lane to his lower mansion in Takanawa through a cold,
wintry downpour; he waited up until after the Eighth Hour (2:00 A.M.)
for the ronin to arrive; he sat down among them on the same level, as
he praised them and assured them of their welcome. It should not in
the least detract from such great-heartedness to note that it may have
been easier for a daimyo of Etchū-no-Kami's stature—long a trusted

ally of the Tokugawa, enfeoffed at 540,000 koku, lord of an entire province—to be so magnanimous. His warmth does contrast, however, with the strictness of the other three daimyo, which seems to have grown in inverse proportion to their rank in the hierarchy of daimyo.

◆ ◆ ◆

At the Hosokawa mansion, two large rooms, adjoining each other, were allotted to the seventeen ronin. In the main room were quartered Ōishi Kuranosuke, Yoshida Chūzaemon, Hara Sōemon, Kataoka Gengoemon, Masé Kyūdayū, Onodera Jūnai, Horibe Yahei, Hazama Kihei, and Hayami Tōzaemon. In the anteroom, Isogai Jūrōzaemon, Chikamatsu Kanroku, Tominomori Suke'emon, Ushioda Matanojō, Akabane Genzō, Okuda Magodayū, Yada Gorōemon, and Ōishi Sezaemon. In overall charge of their detention was the Traveling Elder of the house, Miyake Tōbei. Tending to the immediate needs of the ronin were three men, serving in rotation: Horiuchi Den'emon, Hayashi Hyōsuke, and Murai Genbei. And in charge of the day and night guard details were Yagi Ichidayū and Yoshihiro Kazaemon.

Despite the obvious good will of the lord of his domain, the Hosokawa Elder Miyake Tōbei seems to have been determined to maintain strict segregation of the ronin from their hosts.

"You are forbidden to discuss this recent incident with them," he told the five men who would be in closest touch with the ronin. "Even if they themselves raise the subject, you're to give only a perfunctory reply and bring the conversation to an end. So keep this in mind, and go about your duties accordingly."

Fortunately, few of those under his command were inclined to obey Tōbei. Horiuchi Den'emon felt that to do so would contravene the Way of the Warrior. "This recent incident," he felt, must be one of the most remarkable acts of loyalty in history, and the telling of such tales to young people was one of the duties of a warrior. Den'emon took the chance of discussing the matter with his kinsman Horiuchi Heihachi, a Liaison Officer, and Hirano Kurōemon, a Commander of the Bodyguard. Both men not only agreed with him, but said they, too, wished to hear what the ronin had to say. The three of them decided, therefore, that they would ignore the Elder's orders. There would be too many men of high rank coming and going during the daylight hours. But that evening, after the ronin had finished their meal, seemed a good opportunity. Den'emon sent word to Heihachi and Kurōemon, and together they called Yoshida Chūzaemon and Hara Sōemon to a corner of the room and asked that they tell them all about "this recent incident." Thus began a conversation that would continue for the duration of their custody of the ronin, involving many others besides the original three, and that Den'emon would record in great detail. We shall be returning to this fascinating record repeatedly.

♦ ♦ ♦

When the ten ronin remanded to the custody of the Hisamatsu arrived in Atagoshita, their sojourn there would be for only one night. The rain had been unrelenting, and it was only a short walk to the upper mansion. But on the next day, the 16th, they again boarded palanquins and were transported—under guard of three hundred samurai, foot soldiers, and liveried menials—to the Hisamatsu Middle Mansion in Mita. And there again, they were confined to solitary rooms in a barrack block, with a guard detail of six men at each door—one samurai, one musketeer, two foot soldiers, and two menials. They were well fed, well provided for, and even given extra quilts and charcoal braziers to ward off the cold; but nine more days would pass before any of them saw any of the others again. Fortunately, however, word of their solitary confinement seems somehow to have reached the castle, and some sympathetic Inspector or Herald suggested to the Hisamatsu that they might instead house the ronin in two groups of five men each. Such a suggestion could hardly be ignored, so two of the barracks, of about twenty tatami mats each, were refurbished to allow the ronin the company of their comrades for the remainder of their detention. On the 25th Day of the Twelfth Month, they moved to their new quarters. In the No. 1 Block were Ōishi Chikara, Horibe Yasubei, Nakamura Kansuke, Kaiga Yazaemon, and Fuwa Kazuemon. In No. 2, Okano Kin'emon, Ōtaka Gengo, Suganoya Hannojō, Senba Saburōbei, and Kimura Okaemon. On the 27th, Okino-Kami sent two of his Elders to the middle mansion to greet the ronin on his behalf and apologize for his inability to do so in person, owing to his illness.

We have already met the man charged with the direct supervision of the ronin, Haga Seidayū Tomohisa. Seidayū is the man who harangued his superiors on the need for constant vigilance when Gohei, the charcoal man, came running to report his sighting of the ronin on their way to Sengakuji. It was likewise Seidayū who slipped stealthily into the vestibule at the mansion of Sengoku Hōki-no-Kami. And it was Seidayū who was hoping for a battle with the Uesugi once the ronin were safely ensconced in their palanquins. Like Horiuchi Den'emon, Seidayū would later record some of his conversations with the ronin; but unlike Den'emon, his interest in them lay mainly in military matters: he was keen to learn how they had planned and executed such a highly successful attack, and much of what they told him we have already had occasion to report.

♦ ♦ ♦

The experience of the ronin in the custody of the Mōri is yet another example of the difference that attitude can make. On the morning of the 15th, when all the daimyo resident in Edo were gathered in the castle, Hosokawa Etchū-no-Kami convened a meeting with Mōri Kai-no-Kami and Mizuno Kenmotsu (Matsudaira [Hisamatsu] Oki-no-Kami was ill and could not attend), immediately after they had been commanded to take custody of the Akō ronin. As lord of a domain more than ten times the size of those of the other two, it was the prerogative of Etchū-no-Kami to dictate the material conditions of custody that would prevail in all four houses, and at least attempt to insinuate upon his fellow daimyo his views of the way the ronin should be treated. For this reason, there was considerable uniformity in the meals that were served, the clothing and bedding that were given the ronin, and the frequency with which they were allowed to bathe. But Etchū-no-Kami seems to have left it to individual discretion how the ronin should be accommodated and how freely they should be allowed to communicate, both among themselves and with the outside world.

We have already seen how the Hisamatsu initially subjected their ronin to solitary confinement. In the Mōri house, a similar attitude prevailed. There, too, the ronin were divided into two groups and housed in two separate barracks, within which they were segregated from one another by folding screens. In the North Block were Okajima Yasoemon, Yoshida Sawaemon, Takebayashi Tadashichi, Kurahashi Densuke, and Muramatsu Kihei. In the South, Sugino Jūheiji, Katsuda Shinzaemon, Maebara Isuke, Hazama Shinroku, and Onodera Kōemon. Between the two barracks there was to be no communication, either verbal or written, and likewise between the ronin and anyone in the outside world. Enforcing this regimen was a guard detail of eighty-six samurai, foot soldiers, and menials, divided into two watches, night and day. In short, at the Mōri house, the ronin were treated as prisoners.

✦ ✦ ✦

The duty to provide security and the human disposition to benevolence combined in a curious way at the Mizuno house. The house took pride in its military heritage and was determined to uphold it. When you read the house records, it is eminently clear that the Mizuno meant to maintain the strictest possible security. Whether anyone actually believed this truly necessary is impossible to say. But they were the first to arrive at Sengakuji, despite having farther to travel than any of the other houses; even Haga Seidayū had to admit their superiority on that occasion. And when they took the ronin into custody, they were the only house already equipped to transport them in locked palanquins. Then, when finally they moved the ronin to longer-term quarters at the Mizuno Middle Mansion, the Mizuno built a double-layered fence of strong bamboo around those quarters that blocked even the main entry to the mansion, and could be entered only through two gates that were guarded day and night, where none but members of the Mizuno house were allowed to pass.

And yet, in the popular imagination, the Mizuno were seen as second only to the Hosokawa in their magnanimity to the ronin. As a satirical poem that was making the rounds at the time put it:

HOSOKAWA *no* MIZU *no nagare wa kiyokeredo*
*tada tai*KAI *no* OKI *zo nigoreru*
Pure are the WATERS that flow in the RIVULET,
yet foul the depths FAR OUT at SEA.

How so? In a purely material sense, the kimono the Mizuno provided
the ronin with, even on the first night of their detention, were of particularly fine silk and were lined rather than single layered. Then, too, they
were extremely solicitous of the men who were ill or had been injured
or wounded in the attack. Kaiga Yazaemon was suffering a recurrence
of his chronic chest pain; Yokogawa Kanpei was wounded on his left
thigh and one of his fingers; Okuda Sadaemon was wounded on the
middle finger of his right hand; and Kanzaki Yogorō had taken a bad
fall when he leapt from the roof at the main gate of the Kira mansion,
suffering contusion of his right wrist and both knees. All these men
were given immediate and continued medical care. And Yogorō—whom
we would now probably describe as an alcoholic—had particular reason
to be grateful. No one else in custody at the Mizuno house was allowed
to drink, but Yogorō was given a daily ration of saké—"for his injuries,"
they said. His Lordship Mizuno Kenmotsu, the day after the ronin were
moved into their new quarters at the middle mansion, traveled from
the upper mansion to greet them personally. In honor of the occasion,
Yogorō composed and presented to him a poem in Chinese "on being
overcome with emotion at the sight of his noble face."

Housed in their quarters were only nine men. Terasaka Kichiemon,
the tenth on the list, was by now far down the Eastern Sea Road, bound
for Harima. Those remaining were Hazama Jūjirō, Okuda Sadaemon,
Yatō Emoshichi, Muramatsu Sandayū, Masé Magokurō, Kayano
Wasuke, Kanzaki Yogorō, Yokogawa Kanpei, and Mimura Jirōzaemon.

◆ ◆ ◆

Unfortunately, there was no one like Horiuchi Den'emon in any of the
other three daimyo houses. Our knowledge of the daily lives of the
individual ronin while they were in custody will thus be limited mainly
to those in the Hosokawa house. We shall catch occasional glimpses

of those in the Hisamatsu, Mōri, and Mizuno houses, but no more. Den'emon's memoir, alas, will be our only window into this fascinating interlude in the lives of the ronin.

CHAPTER

77

———⚔———

I expect that we'll be seeing you
here for a long time to come.

When we left the ronin who were in custody at the Hosokawa Lower
Mansion, Horiuchi Den'emon and two of his colleagues were asking
Hara Sōemon and Yoshida Chūzaemon to tell them all about the "recent
incident," as the Elder Miyake Tōbei timidly described it. Den'emon did
not record the conversation that ensued, except to say that Sōemon
offered to write a summary of the attack that Den'emon and his comrades could show to anyone else who wished to know—and that Sōemon
worked on this document throughout the next day and into the night.

Thereafter, Den'emon says, as they talked with one another, everyone
began to relax, so much so, in fact, that Tominomori Suke'emon soon
felt free to ask Den'emon to tell them about himself. Which he seems to
have been happy to do:

"I was born into a family that has served the Hosokawa for many
generations. But I am the youngest son, and so at first I served in only
minor positions, although I have always accompanied His Lordship to
Edo. Gradually, I rose in rank and was granted a small fief; later still, I
was promoted to Company Commander. In recent years, as I've grown
older [he was then fifty-eight], I've been excused from attendance duties
and can live at my ease in the townhouse. Now, I've been assigned to
come and keep you gentlemen company. From the time I was young
until just a year or so ago, however, I served as guide for His Lordship's
palanquin, so I know the city of Edo and the streets of Kyoto and Osaka
quite well. When I was living in the upper mansion, I wasn't always able
to come and go as I pleased; but now that I'm living in the townhouse, I

can go anywhere I wish, with no restriction, day or night. So if there is anything I can do for any of you, I can assure you that Etchū-no-Kami would not be pleased if you were to refrain from asking me. I know what sort of men you are, and I swear by all the gods in Japan that I'll spare no effort to do my utmost for you. Of course, that goes for every one of you, so please tell all the others what I've said. It would be unseemly for me say that to everyone myself."

♦ ♦ ♦

As it happened, Suke'emon did have a request. "All seventeen of us have something we'd like to ask of you," he said. "It's just this: we probably shall be sentenced to be beheaded, and we hope it can be arranged that that at least be done in a decent location. Or if we should be so arrogant as to believe all that's being said about us, we could imagine that we might be allowed to commit seppuku—in which case, we might do that right here, in this mansion. But our families all belong to different sects, so we would ask that you not surrender our bodies to any monks or relatives who come to claim them. All seventeen of us wish to be buried together in a single hole in a vacant corner at Sengakuji. We'd be very grateful if you would keep that in mind when the time comes."

"A perfectly reasonable request," Den'emon said. "And if it does come to that, we'll do exactly as you say. But I doubt very much that will ever be necessary. I expect that we'll be seeing you here for a long time to come."

♦ ♦ ♦

Another evening, when Den'emon was talking with Suke'emon, Hara Sōemon heard his own name mentioned. He turned and asked, "What are you two talking about?"

"It's that night in Akō when you sent Ōno Kurōbei packing," Suke'emon replied.

"What!" Sōemon looked at Den'emon and laughed. "He's telling that dreadful story on me?"

"Don't worry, it won't go any further than me," Den'emon said. "But please, do tell what happened."

"Well, Suke'emon was there, too; I wasn't the only one," Sōemon began. "But in Akō, I worked very closely with Kuranosuke. We talked everything over together, and we were in complete agreement. But this Kurōbei always had some objection to anything that Kuranosuke might say. Finally, I just couldn't listen to any more of that, so I told him: 'You take a different view of the situation than Kuranosuke. It just so happens, though, that everyone else here agrees with him completely. If you have a different opinion, I see no point in your remaining here. So why don't you just get out—and be *quick* about it!' That's all there was to it. Kurōbei did just as I said. But if he hadn't, I'm afraid that I'd have killed him on the spot. And if I'd done that, we could never have done what we wanted to do. As I look back, I think I could hardly have been more foolish."

Suke'emon laughed. "Well, it didn't seem such a bad idea at the time."

◆ ◆ ◆

Yada Gorōemon called out, "Den'emon Dono! I hear that you're quite a connoisseur of weapons, that you have very good eye."

"Well, when I was young I did think myself a connoisseur; but more often than not, it turned out I was mistaken."

"Oh yes, I know how that feels," Gorōemon said. "I have a terrible eye. The sword I was using in this recent battle was a new blade, but it must have been flawed. It broke 6 or 7 inches from the tip. I had to throw it away and grab the sword of the man I'd just killed."

◆ ◆ ◆

Old Horibe Yahei told Den'emon, "I'm very grateful that you've been so kind to Isogai Jūrōzaemon. We older men feel very sorry for him. Most of us have served this house for a long time, over two or three generations of lords. I was a ronin when I was taken into service, three generations ago. Later I was granted a fiefdom, and under the last Takumi-no-Kami, I was made a Company Commander. Now, as you see, I am an old man and deeply indebted to these lords. I wasn't able to join in the fight; I only stood guard at the gate. But the young men all fought brilliantly."

"That's quite as it should be," Den'emon said, "that the young men fight and the older men guard the gates."

"But Jūrōzaemon has served only this last generation. When he was fourteen, I was able to arrange that he be summoned as a Page Boy. Since then, he has served for only ten years, and yet he is as devoted to the cause as any of the older men. On the morning after the attack, when we were about to cross the Shōgen Bridge on our way to the temple, Kuranosuke, and everyone else, urged him to go and bid farewell to his mother, who lived nearby. But for some reason he declined, probably out of modesty."

"That is truly deep devotion," Den'emon replied.

Later, when Den'emon was in the anteroom, he mentioned his conversation with Yahei to Jūrōzaemon. "Presumptuous of me though it is to say so, I was quite impressed by your modesty," Den'emon said.

"I'm sure that Yahei describes me much more favorably than I deserve," Jūrōzaemon said. "I was summoned to His Lordship's service when I was very young and was treated extraordinarily well. I rose steadily, and I was assigned very spacious quarters in Edo, so that even my old mother could come and live with me. I am no less indebted to His Lordship than are any of the older men. When we withdrew after the attack, Kuranosuke and the others did urge me to go and see Mother; but dressed as we were, it would have been too great a shock to the people in the place where she lives. Besides which, there was no telling what might have happened, even if I were gone for only a short while. So, for various reasons, I didn't go. I realize now, of course, I could easily have done so—but I don't regret my choice," he said, smiling as he spoke.

At this point, Tominomori Suke'emon joined in the conversation. "Sengoku Hōki-no-Kami was very impressed by him, too," he said. "When we were interrogated and he heard how Jūrōzaemon had got that menial to produce the candles, he remarked how unusual it was for a man so young to be so calm and unruffled in battle."

◆ ◆ ◆

All the weapons and personal possessions of the ronin had been gathered up at the Sengoku mansion and handed over to the Hosokawa Liaison Officer, Kagizaka Heibei. Now they had to be sorted out and put in order until it was decided what should be done with them.

Den'emon was one of those asked to inspect them. He recorded a few of his observations.

Kuranosuke's swords were *Sōshū mono*, forged in Sagami. On the blade of his long sword, there were bloodstains about 1 foot long, and a bit of the tip was chipped off. This must have been the sword with which he administered the coup de grâce. The sheaths of both swords were black lacquered, and the short sword was fitted with an old wooden handle on which was carved the word *chūgi* (loyalty).

Okuda Magodayū's great sword had a blade about 3 feet long, an unpatterned guard, and a hardwood haft about 19 or 20 inches long. Den'emon thought that it looked like a small halberd.

In Horibe Yahei's paper fold, there was a little bamboo whistle, the kind children play with. This was one of the signaling whistles. He seems also to have carried a small sword that he hid in the fold of his kimono. In Isogai Jūrōzaemon's paper fold, there was a koto plectrum. Den'emon would ask him about this later.

The hafts of all their lances had been cut down to about 9 feet, and the blades were of the larger sort, 9 or 10 inches long and more than 2 inches wide. All the blades were stained with blood, and most were missing their sheaths. Some were still wrapped in strips of white cotton taken from their sleeves, a few of which had names written on them.

Most of the ronin had wrapped the hafts of their swords with flat cotton cord, so as to give a better grip. It reminded Den'emon of stories that his father used to tell him about the battles in Shimabara, where some of the men had wrapped the hafts of their swords in cord.

Yoshida Chūzaemon told Den'emon that he had studied military science as a young man and had brought his baton of command with him to the attack. But he had kept it a secret from Kuranosuke. Would Den'emon please burn it when he found it? It had a black handle with a sword-blade motif embossed in gold. Den'emon felt that he had no right to burn it.

◆ ◆ ◆

On the 18th, only four days after the attack, the first news of repercussions in the outside world reached the men in the Hosokawa house.

An old man, Oyamada Ikkan, aged eighty-one, had killed himself. Years earlier, Oyamada Jūbei had been a member of the Akō Corps of Vassals, one of the Horse Guards, enfeoffed at 100 koku. But he had long since retired, changed his name to Ikkan, relinquished his post to his son Shōzaemon, and moved to Edo to live with his daughter and her husband. After the Catastrophe, Shōzaemon had joined the pact and had been living with Horibe Yasubei in Hayashi-chō. Ikkan thus knew all about the plan to kill Kira, and presumably approved of—perhaps even took pride in—his son's participation in it. What Ikkan did not know was that prior to the attack, on the 2nd night of the Twelfth Month, Shōzaemon had stolen a kimono and three gold pieces from Kataoka Gengoemon and absconded. And so when a peddler came by hawking lists of the Akō ronin, Ikkan bought one. At first, he must have been puzzled not to find his son's name among those of the ronin. How much he then learnt of his son's transgression and betrayal is not known. We know only that he was sufficiently shocked that he shut himself in his room; drove his long sword into his solar plexus, out his back, and into the wall; and then leant forward onto the upturned blade and died.

*If . . . these men should be punished severely,
this cannot but earn the derision of all under heaven.*

Discussion must have begun almost immediately, once word of the attack reached the castle. And opinion was divided from the very start. Many senior officers of the Shogunate—not to mention the Shogun himself—were deeply impressed, by both the deed itself and the consummate skill with which it had been planned and executed. They also saw, however, that the same deed could be considered highly illegal. For the time being, then, the ronin would be remanded in custody; advice would be sought; the Military Tribunal would be asked to submit an advisory opinion; debate would continue. And that, alas, is about as much as we can say for certain about the state of things in the castle, for not a word was ever recorded, or even leaked, of any of the many meetings that must have taken place.

♦ ♦ ♦

The earliest documented submission seems to be a memorial tendered by Hayashi Hōkō, Rector of the Shogunal Academy. This is a dense document, written in classical Chinese and replete with allusions to Chinese sources that only a savant would recognize. Fortunately, however, a contemporary took the trouble to summarize its substance in Japanese for those of us who find the original too abstruse:

> *I need hardly note that since time immemorial, in both China and Japan, it has been a fundamental precept of all humanity that no man can live beneath the heavens with the enemy of his lord or his father.*

In this instance, Ōishi Kuranosuke and other former Asano vassals have taken upon themselves the grievance of their late lord and killed Kira. In their execution of this deed, they offered no affront whatever to the Shogunate and have fulfilled to the utmost their duty as loyal vassals. For this, they deserve praise.

There are, nevertheless, those who object that these are lowly rear vassals who have willfully slain a high official of the Shogunate, or who claim that their banding together, brazenly brandishing unsheathed weapons within the capital city of the Shogun, constitutes gross disrespect. Yet if on these grounds these men should be punished severely, this cannot but earn the derision of all under heaven, and debase the Way of Loyalty.

This is not your humble servant's personal opinion; I state only what is to be found in the Greater Classics of the Sages. I trust, therefore, that this case will be considered with due care.

Whether Hayashi was asked his opinion or he offered it of his own accord is not recorded. It might have been either. The opinion of the Military Tribunal, however, was unquestionably requested by the Council of Elders.

◆ ◆ ◆

The tribunal met three times a month on days ending in the number 2. Their first meeting after the attack was thus on the 22nd of the Twelfth Month. The composition of this body varied, depending upon the importance of the matter under consideration. On this occasion, not only was the full membership present—all Commissioners of Temples and Shrines, Inspectors General, City Magistrates, and Superintendents of Finance—but they conducted their deliberations in the presence of the full Council of Elders. The day after their meeting, they submitted the following:

ADVISORY OPINION OF THE FULL TRIBUNAL

Rendered upon official request this 23rd Day, Twelfth Month, Genroku 15 [1702] in joint session with the Council of Elders, concerning the killing of Kira Kōzuke-no-Suke by the vassals of Asano Takumi, and the question of condign punishments in this case.

Kira Sahei: *Having conducted himself disgracefully, he ought at least to have taken his own life on the spot. This he failed to do. These are lapses that cannot be condoned. He should therefore be commanded to commit seppuku.*

The vassals of Kira Kōzuke-no-Suke: *Those of samurai rank who failed to join battle on this occasion should without exception be beheaded. Those who sustained wounds, however slight, should be remanded to the custody of their kin. Foot soldiers and lackeys should be banished from Edo.*

Uesugi Danjō Daihitsu and his son Minbu Dayū: *When the vassals of Asano Takumi withdrew from the mansion of Kōzuke-no-Suke and proceeded to Sengakuji, the Uesugi failed to avail themselves of this opportunity to retaliate. Since neither gentleman can offer any justification for his negligence, their punishment, whatever else may be decreed, should certainly include forfeiture of their domains.*

The vassals of Takumi: *Two ways of judging their deeds were debated:*

1. On the one hand, they took upon themselves the resolve of their late liege lord and, heedless of their own lives, broke into the mansion of Kōzuke-no-Suke and took his head. This, surely, was genuine loyalty. They acted in complete accord with the Military Code, which enjoins us to "cultivate the Civil and the Martial Arts, to practice Loyalty and Filial Piety, and to conduct ourselves with due Propriety."
2. On the other hand, they banded together in great numbers and, clad in armor and bearing assault weapons, perpetrated an act of violence. Had they refrained from acting in concert, however, they could not have accomplished their mission. We feel, therefore, that

this was essential to the success of their endeavor. In the Military Code, banding together and the swearing of oaths are strictly forbidden. We would submit, however, that had insurgency been the original intention of these vassals of Takumi, they might well have displayed some defiance in the previous year when Takumi was punished and his castle and domains were declared forfeit. Yet on that occasion, they offered not the least opposition. On the present occasion, however, they could not have accomplished their mission had they not acted in concert; they had no choice but to band together in numbers. This can hardly be deemed the act of a band of insurgents.

Similar cases may well arise in the future, but they will differ one from another, depending upon the intentions of the individuals involved, and should be judged individually according to the merits and demerits of each case.

The foregoing is the unanimous opinion of this tribunal. The vassals of Takumi should, for the time being, be left in custody, and their case should be adjudicated at some later date.

TWELFTH MONTH, 23RD DAY

Commissioners of Temples and Shrines

      Nagai Iga-no-Kami Hisatomi

      Abe Hida-no-Kami Masataka

      Honda Danjō Shōhitsu Tadaharu

Inspectors General

      Sengoku Hōki-no-Kami Hisanao

      Andō Chikugo-no-Kami Shigeharu

      Kondō Bitchū-no-Kami Mochitaka

      Orii Awa-no-Kami Masatoki

City Magistrates

      Matsumae Izu-no-Kami Yoshihiro

      Yasuda Echizen-no-Kami Munesato

      Niwa Tōtōmi-no-Kami Nagamori

Superintendents of Finance

      Ogiwara Ōmi-no-Kami Shigehide

Kugai Inaba-no-Kami Masakata
Togawa Bizen-no-Kami Yasuhiro
Nakayama Izumo-no-Kami Tokiharu

At this point, nine days after the attack, what little that we know of official opinion suggests that those in positions of the greatest influence and power were leaning toward lenience. There were a great many people whom this decision would have pleased. But it would not have pleased everyone. The Uesugi, in particular, must have been outraged to hear the Advisory Opinion of the Tribunal, which recommended not only lenity for the ronin, but the utmost severity for themselves. Had not they been forced to stay their hand when they were about to counterattack? How could they be punished for obeying a command of the Council of Elders? A near-contemporary report of their reaction says, "Uesugi Danjō should by rights have launched a counterattack and stopped them dead, but to have done so would have created dreadful disorder in the city of Edo; and so he restrained himself and waited for the Shogunate to punish them. Yet what if perchance the Shogun should pardon them: How, then, could Danjō face his fellow daimyo?"

And so, according to this report, Uesugi Danjō made known his opposition to this opinion via two routes: "He time and again appealed through Yanagisawa Mino-no-Kami for the ronin to be dealt with severely," and he persuaded the Shogun's daughter to dispatch a messenger to the Shogun's mother, urging "that the vassals of Takumi-no-Kami be sentenced forthwith." The first of these forms of protest produced only "continued delay." But the second may have been more effective, for Uesugi Danjō stood at the head of a line of marriages that led directly to the Shogun.

Uesugi Danjō was not born an Uesugi; he was the natural son of Kira Kōzuke-no-Suke, adopted by the Uesugi when the sudden death of their previous lord had left them without an heir. And as the lord of an old and once-powerful warrior clan, Danjō was able to marry a sister of Tokugawa Tsunanori, head of the Kii branch of the House of Tokugawa; Tsunanori was, in turn, married to Tsuru Hime, the daughter of the Shogun. This meant that Danjō's sister-in-law was able to entreat not only her father, the Shogun himself, but also the Shogun's mother, whom he so doted upon that he had arranged for her to be promoted to First Rank in the Imperial Court.

"For if Uesugi Danjō should be shamed," Tsuru Hime wrote, "then my husband the Middle Counselor is bound to be regarded in a similar light. And so, lest anything disadvantageous to the realm transpire, onerous though I am sure you will find it, I should be most grateful if Your Ladyship of the First Rank could bring this to the attention of His Highness." Immediately after the messenger arrived, Her Ladyship of the First Rank appealed directly to her son, the Shogun. Thus it was that, just when the representations of certain others had made it seem more appropriate to delay, this word from Her Ladyship of the First Rank made it more difficult to delay.

The line of kinship was direct and strong, and could not be ignored. To what extent it influenced the final decision, we shall never know.

Such virtue may appear easy,
but in fact is difficult.

As the Twelfth Month wore on and the year drew to a close, everyone—
and especially, the Shogun—was spending more and more of their time
fulfilling year-end obligations and preparing for the festivities of the
New Year that would follow immediately thereafter. The ronin could
see that, given the season of the year, it was most unlikely that their
fate would be decided anytime soon. They had expected to know—
perhaps even to die—by the evening of the day they surrendered
themselves; now it appeared that a month could pass before anyone
would have time to give their case the attention it required. Near the
end of the month, Kuranosuke seemed to think that their longevity
called for an apology.

"For those of you on watch," he said to Den'emon, "indeed, for
everyone involved in looking after us, it must be a terrible strain that
this has gone on for so long. I do hope the matter will be resolved soon."

"Not at all," Den'emon replied. "When the watch changes and I return
home, the long walk actually helps me to sleep more soundly. And when
I wake up the next morning, I want to get back here as quickly as I can
to see all of you again. Even when I'm sleeping, embarrassed though I
am to admit it, I dream about you. I know, too, from all that I can see,
that even the menials who serve you your meals morning and evening
feel not the least bit put upon. They just want to do the very best they
can for you. So in the name of all the gods in Japan, really, you mustn't
feel the least bit apologetic. That, truly, is how all of us—even the very
least of us—feel."

+ + +

On the 28th, word filtered in from the outside world of another suicide, this one with a slightly disturbing aspect to it. Okabayashi Mokunosuke had been a Samurai Commander in Akō, enfeoffed at 1,000 koku per year. Only Kuranosuke was better recompensed; the other three Elders all received less than Mokunosuke. This is our first encounter with the man, however, as he never involved himself in any way, either positively or negatively, with Kuranosuke's plans to defend the castle or to commit mass suicide in protest. Even before the castle was surrendered, Mokunosuke sold off his weapons and the next day left Akō. Thereafter, he moved to Edo, where he was taken in and supported by his elder brother, Matsudaira Magozaemon, a bannerman and Commander of a Ten-Man Guard Unit. Mokunosuke had been adopted by his great-uncle, the previous Okabayashi Mokunosuke, who had no heir. Now he was returning to his natal family. But why he would commit suicide is something of a mystery. He himself left no clues, so we have only the report submitted by his brother Magozaemon to go on:

> Mokunosuke, while in the care of his brother Magozaemon, in the Eleventh Month of this year traveled to the capital region on personal business. He returned two days ago. Yesterday morning, he committed suicide. Upon investigation, I found no note of explanation. It may have been because his great-uncle, who adopted him, had been a vassal of Takumi Dono, and while Mokunosuke was away in the capital region, Kōzuke-no-Suke Dono had been killed. Mokunosuke may have committed suicide because he felt shamed in this connection.

The authorities to whom Magozaemon submitted this report did not question it; they ruled the cause of his suicide to be derangement and declared the case closed. Unofficial opinion, however, suggests that there may have been more to the matter than mere derangement. When Tōjō Shusetsu asked the ronin in custody at the Mizuno house about it, Kanzaki Yogorō told him, "The man was a congenital coward. His brothers probably forced him to do it." Other reports agree with Yogorō, and one goes so far as to say that he committed seppuku at the temple Seishōji in Atagoshita and that his younger brother Saemon, a ronin, served as his Second. Yet why should his brothers feel that Mokunosuke must die? Did they feel *that* greatly shamed to be related to a weakling? We shall never know. But given his previous behavior, it does seem unlikely that Mokunosuke would have had the courage to do the deed on his own initiative. When Horiuchi Den'emon mentioned having heard the story, even Yoshida Chūzaemon said, "Yes, that could very well be what happened."

◆ ◆ ◆

Ban Kōkei tells of yet another victim of the righteousness inspired in some people by the vengeance of the Akō ronin:

> One of the daughters of Ōno Kurōbei, the Elder of the Akō house who fled in the night, had been married to a samurai named Kajiura Heishichi, who lived in the adjacent domain of Okayama in the eastern part of the province of Bizen. They had three children and were a very close couple. But shortly after Ōno's flight, Kajiura, for no apparent reason, seems to have had a retirement cottage built on some unused land at the rear of their home. His wife expressed concern about the expense of this project. As in many domains that were financially straitened, the Kajiura were not receiving their full stipendiary allotment, which in any case was not great. Besides which, Heishichi was nowhere near old enough to be thinking of retirement. It seemed a needless expense, she told her husband. But he dismissed the matter, saying only that he had "something in mind."
>
> For more than a year, the little cottage stood empty, neither of them even mentioning its existence to the other. But then one day, an itinerant peddler passed their door, selling broadsheets listing the names of the Akō ronin who had taken the head of Kira Kōzuke-no-Suke. Kajiura bought a copy and read it through with great care. The name of Ōno Kurōbei was nowhere to be found on it, nor was

there even a name that resembled it. So his father-in-law's flight had not been a clever ruse, under cover of which he might plot revenge! Kurōbei's daughter was sick with shame, and she shut herself up in her room and would not get out of bed. After a time, however, her husband sent a servant to tell her that he had something he wished to say to her. She thought this strangely ceremonious, and when she went to him and found him sitting bolt upright in his most formal clothing, her suspicions were only heightened.

"I am deeply grateful to you," he began, "for the devotion with which you have managed this household through all these years of privation. There is, however, this matter of your father. It was he who was chiefly responsible for the domestic management of the domain, and for this he was handsomely rewarded; yet in the moment of the domain's greatest distress, he fled. Nor is his name to be found among those who took revenge for this Catastrophe. Such disloyalty is beyond description. You yourself are blameless; but for me to continue to keep company with the daughter of such a man would be shamefully contrary to the Way of the Warrior. From this day forward, I must sever all ties between us. I realize, of course, that you now have no home to which you can return. This is why I have built the little cottage at the back. I shall spend the rest of my life there. Your task shall be the raising of our three children. This will be our last meeting, ever."

Thereupon, he retreated to the cottage. And apart from an old servant woman upon whom he depended for all his needs, he never went near another woman. His friends urged him at least to take a mistress, but he told them, "My former wife is blameless. I left her only because it was my duty to do so. It would be inexcusable were I to do anything that might make her feel jealous." And thus he remained to the end of his life, they say. There was one occasion when his wife happened to see him strolling in the garden, and although she made no attempt to speak to him, she did open the shoji a crack and try to catch his eye. But he immediately turned heel and went indoors. Thereafter, she too took care to avoid him.

"Such virtue may appear easy," Kōkei tells us, "but in fact is difficult." I must confess that to me it does not even *appear* easy. And if it were anyone less reliable than Kōkei reporting it, I would be inclined just to dismiss the tale. But given the indubitable instances we have seen of the power of "such virtue," I must instead echo Chūzaemon and conclude that it "could very well be what happened."

◆ ◆ ◆

Not all the news from the outside world was so somber. Nakase Sukegorō, as a Commander of the Bodyguard, was frequently called on to accompany Etchū-no-Kami on his travels here and there in Edo; most recently, that duty had taken him to the mansion of the Elder Akimoto Tajima-no-Kami. While Sukegorō waited, to his surprise, a samurai of that household approached him and asked if he knew Horiuchi Den'emon—which, of course, he did. The man then introduced himself as the father of the wife of Okuda Magodayū and asked Sukegorō to tell Den'emon that Magodayū's children were safe in his care. The news came as an unexpected delight to Magodayū and to the other ronin as well. But Sukegorō was concerned that Magodayū's father-in-law had asked after Den'emon by name—which he was at a loss to explain. He felt that he should caution Den'emon; so many of the ronin were related to one another that Den'emon should take care in his dealings with them. Den'emon agreed and thanked Sukegorō for his advice. But in his own mind, he had decided that he had nothing to worry about; he was fully prepared to accept any consequences that his relations with the ronin might have.

◆ ◆ ◆

As we saw somewhat earlier, Tominomori Suke'emon's wife was the daughter of Suga Jizaemon, a Company Commander in the service of Tamura Ukyō-no-Daibu in Atagoshita, the very house where Takumi-no-Kami was taken to commit seppuku. We have seen, too, that Suke'emon and his wife had an infant son, Chōtarō, born the previous year at the farmstead of Karube Gohei in the village of Hirama. How the news reached Den'emon he does not say, but he now assured Suke'emon that his wife and son were safe in the care of her father. Which, in turn, inspired him to arrange a "meeting" with the little boy.

There was a tea master in the Tamura house named Kishi Sōboku, whom Den'emon had once met in the quarters of Emura Sessai, a physician in the Hosokawa house. Through this connection, he arranged to meet Chōtarō in Sōboku's quarters, in preparation for which he had a doll made to take to the boy. Den'emon's only comment was that the child greatly resembled Suke'emon. Suke'emon himself was, of course, delighted to hear of all this.

Later Den'emon also arranged to meet Suke'emon's mother at the home of Takeya Sōjirō, who once had had a connection with the Asano house and now came regularly to the Hosokawa mansion.

"I'm very grateful that you should look me up and very pleased to meet you," she said. "It must be the intercession of our clan deity that has brought us together. It was that same deity, though, who sent Suke'emon out on that night attack, so that I shall never see him again. Yet even to a woman like myself, when I heard that Takumi-no-Kami Dono had been made to commit seppuku and Kōzuke-no-Suke Dono had gone free, I could not but think that this was unjust. Suke'emon was born a man; he only did what was right for a man to do, I thought. To hear that he is well and is being looked after so thoughtfully—well I could hope for nothing better."

"I was at a loss for an answer," Den'emon says, "and tears came to my eyes. For a woman to say that this was unjust, and on our first meeting! A most exceptional woman, I must say, but only what one would expect of the mother of Suke'emon. Her father, they say, was Yamamoto Chōzaemon, a warrior who had been enfeoffed at 1,000 koku. Suke'emon's father, too, was a man of illustrious lineage and a relative of the rich Edo merchant Suminoe Sen'emon. This is what I hear from Fukuda Ryūkei.

"Yes, a samurai must raise his children with the greatest care, even if they are girls. I must tell my daughters all about this."

*I still hear nothing
from Edo.*

As the year came to an end, the roles of those on the fringes of the action likewise came to an end. Like the ronin, they would continue to wait; but unlike the ronin, the word everyone awaited would have no material effect upon their lives. Important though they had been when they were needed, the parts they had played were now played out, and they began to disperse and go their separate ways. Some hadn't far to go. Ōishi Mujin and his son Mitsuhira lived but a short distance from the Kira mansion in Honjo. Satō Jōemon would return to his room in the barracks of his patron, Suwa Iki-no-Kami. Hakura Itsuki would carry on as before in the lodgings provided him by the timber merchant Nakajima Gorōsaku—and never in his life mention his part in the success of the attack. Many of these people we'll not hear from again. But a few will remain visible, and occasionally active, personae in the drama that ensues.

◆ ◆ ◆

Terasaka Kichiemon, a foot soldier under the command of Yoshida Chūzaemon, had been a member of the pact from the very start. As we have seen, though, for reasons that no one ever states, he was dismissed from the group just outside the middle gate to Sengakuji and sent back to Chūzaemon's family in Harima. He did not set out immediately, as he had been told to do. He waited somewhere outside Sengakuji until the ronin emerged and made their way to the mansion of Sengoku Hōki-no-Kami; there, again, he waited, and then followed the

Hosokawa procession back to the lower mansion in Takanawa. Early in the morning of the 16th, he took to the Eastern Sea Road, and at quite a brisk pace, it would seem. Horibe Bungorō wrote to Jinzaburō: "Terai Genkei says that Terasaka Kichiemon Sama returned to Kyoto on the 25th of the Twelfth Month, and that he called upon Genkei Dono. I would very much like to know what passed between them and what they talked about."

We would all like to know what they talked about; but what we can know, at least, is that Kichiemon traveled from Edo to Kyoto in only ten days—two days less than the twelve that it normally took a strong man walking from dawn to dusk. Kichiemon may also have carried the three documents that Kuranosuke wished to leave with Genkei: the manifesto, a list of participants and their assignments, and another list ranking the value of their contributions. But neither Kuranosuke nor Genkei nor Kichiemon made any mention of such a mission; the question of how these documents got to Genkei must remain in the realm of speculation.

Yoshida Chūzaemon's wife, O-Rin, was more forthcoming. She said in a letter to a friend written at about the same time:

> As you say, all the talk that one hears is extremely favorable, and what a delight that is. And if their judgment should be likewise? Both Chūzaemon and Sawaemon, father and son, were resigned from the very start to whatever might become of them. But if by some chance I should hear that they have been judged favorably, I shall let you know straightaway. In Edo and everywhere else, all the talk is in their favor. Let their judgment be likewise, I pray, entreating the help of all the gods and Buddhas. For there is naught else I can do. . . .
>
> Toward the end of the year, Kichiemon returned here. He had wanted above all to stay with Chūzaemon. Both father and son consoled him, but insisted that he return. I am both impressed and delighted by his devotion.

Thereafter, Kichiemon and his wife lived a secluded life in Kameyama, in the service of Chūzaemon's wife and her daughter's family, the Itō. Not until three years later did he leave there, and then only because Honda Nakatsukasa, the lord of Himeji, was transferred to a new fief in Echigo Murakami, and the Itō family was forced to move with him. But that is a story that must wait until later.

✦ ✦ ✦

Chikamatsu Kanroku's man Jinzaburō—I am at a bit of a loss what to call him, because he was one of those men known as "vassal-farmers." Like other farmers, they tilled the soil, but they were not mere peasants. Many of them were descended from warriors who, when the wars ended, had "returned to the land"; and yet they remained the loyal vassals of their former commanders, who usually were the owners of that land. Although Kanroku was in service in Akō, he still owned the land in his home village of Hiruta that was tilled by Jinzaburō and his fellow "vassals"—which probably explains why Jinzaburō was so determined to follow Kanroku to Edo. As Kanroku told it:

> Jinzaburō's parents were people of some consequence and for generations had been the Headmen of Hiruta. I told him that until everyone had agreed about what we would do, he should prepare himself, but stay at home. He replied that he could see that we were on the verge of decision; but if he could be of no use to me, he was prepared to commit seppuku. So I brought him to Edo with me. His parents told him, "Serve him to your utmost; be prepared to abandon yourself body and soul." And that is exactly what he has done. At the time of the night attack, I brought him with me. But Kuranosuke had always said that no one who had not served Takumi-no-Kami was to join us, so he came only as far as the gate. And when we came out again, he had stuffed his clothes with mandarin oranges and rice cakes. "You must be thirsty," he said, and passed them out to everyone. When Hōki-no-Kami Sama summoned us, I expect that he followed us there and was hanging about somewhere near the guardhouse, which quite fills me

~ 665 ~

with pity. Everyone was saying that I should have given him my
surname and made him a samurai.

Jinzaburō had come to Edo with Chūzaemon and Kanroku in the
Second Month; he had been there for ten months by then. Now all the
people he had spent those months with were in custody. It was time to
return home to Hiruta.

♦ ♦ ♦

On the furthest fringe of the action was a woman we have heard not
a word from since news of the Catastrophe first reached Akō in the
previous year, Ōishi Kuranosuke's wife, O-Riku. In the summer of the
present year, prior to the birth of her now infant son, Daizaburō, she
returned from Yamashina to her ancestral home in the town of Toyooka
in the province of Tajima. And toward the end of the year, she wrote to
the Superior of the temple Jingūji in Akō. Hers is the last dated letter of
this year written by anyone we know:

> *I take the liberty to address you by way of this letter. The season is*
> *cold, but I hope nonetheless to hear that you remain well. Some while*
> *ago, I sent a man to Tōgorō. At the time, I was hoping that he might*
> *take the trouble to write, but alas I go on longing as much as ever*
> *to know what might be happening. I understand that you continue*
> *to pray that all will go well in Edo, which gives me both strength*
> *and hope. For I am certain that it was thanks to your prayers that*
> *Kuranosuke and the others succeeded in having their way with their*
> *enemy. One could hardly wish for any greater delight than that has*
> *given me.*
>
> *P.S. I expect that you, too, are so good as to be delighted by this.*
> *May what now follows be just as fortunate!—that is my constant*
> *prayer; for their fortunes in war have been strong, and they have*
> *made a name for themselves that will last through the ages. You*
> *may rest assured that everyone is well here. You will be pleased to*

hear, too, that Soren has taken vows and entered orders with no difficulty. I am extremely grateful that you have not forgotten us and remain so constant a correspondent. Although I hesitate to ask, please be so kind as to let Tōgorō and his family know that we send our best regards.

My, but it was a shock to hear about Magozaemon; I was terribly disappointed in him. But at least this makes us realize that anything can happen; it all depends upon circumstances.

TWELFTH MONTH, 27TH DAY   *Soren's mother*
To: Jingūji Sama
via his entourage

Thus stood matters at the end of the year Genroku 16 (1702). And thus they seem to have remained for O-Riku. Twenty days later, she wrote again to Jingūji: "I still hear nothing from Edo. What will happen there is my constant worry. That they succeeded in accomplishing their mission of course delights me. But now, I fear, all is up to the Will of Heaven."

The Vendetta of the 47 Ronin from Akō

PART III

Year of the Ram

Genroku 16 (1703)

CHAPTER

81

What do you think
will become of them?

The New Year had come, and the city was resplendent with sprays of pine and bamboo at every gate and door. And with the slowing of the hectic round of visits and observances, there came a welcome succession of mild, almost balmy days. It was spring in more than name only. The streets filled with people, and the people, as ever, were full of talk. This year, however, there seemed to be only one thing to talk about. Once the appropriate greetings had been exchanged, you were sure to be asked, "What do you think will become of them?" That *they* were paragons of military virtue had already been decided. That some of the greatest lords in the land had praised them extravagantly was known in every alleyway of the wards. But now what? Everyone thought that they knew that, too. But there was little agreement among them on this point.

"Whatever happens, at least their lives will be spared. Of that you can be sure."

"I wouldn't be so sure of that. Most of them will just be banished to an island for a while, but they may make one or two of the leaders commit seppuku."

"But if they execute even one of them for killing his lord's enemy, who's going to risk his life the next time this happens to some lord? It'd be the end of loyalty, throughout the whole land!"

"Yet if this group is allowed to live, there'll be some great houses humiliated. Don't you reckon that they'll be forced to sentence every one of them to death?"

"For quite apart from what we may *think* of these gentlemen, they can't let them get away with breaking the law."

Once this line of speculation had come full circle, and yielded its undesirable conclusion, they would leave off the larger questions of principle and move on to a more satisfying sort of gossip.

"I heard that Lord Hosokawa has gone to see every member of the Council of Elders, and he's asked to keep those seventeen men in his custody, permanently if necessary. And not just asked; he pleaded!"

"That's right! And he's had thirty-four swords made for them—seventeen long and seventeen short—magnificent blades, and fittings to match. Obviously, *he* thinks that they're going to be pardoned. And he's going to take every one of them into his service."

"It's the same with Lord Mizuno. He already had another lord in his custody when this happened, but then he heard that some of the Elders thought this must be too great a burden for him, that they thought they should move his nine ronin to some other house. Well, when he heard that, Lord Mizuno got in his palanquin and went as fast as he could to see the Elders, in person. 'It's no burden at all for me to look after those men,' he told them. 'I consider it an honor to have them in my house, and I'll be much obliged if you'll leave them right where they are.'"

No one had heard news of any similar sentiments on the part of Lord Hisamatsu and Lord Mōri, but all agreed that they, too, must be of like mind. And with four great lords on their side—including Hosokawa Etchū-no-Kami—how could anyone sentence them to death? No, there was no question of it; every one of them would live, not a one of them would die.

On any given day in the New Year's season of that Year of the Ram, no matter where you might be in the city, you were bound to hear some version of this conversation. But within the walls of the castle, where the decision would actually be made, the issues did not seem as simple as they did to those relishing the warmth of an early spring in the sunny streets of the wards.

◆ ◆ ◆

Rumor certainly was right about Hosokawa Etchū-no-Kami. The Hosokawa house records are unambiguous:

Tsunatoshi's delight in having these men in his custody was beyond measure, and he appealed to the Council of Elders, twice or thrice, asking that their lives be spared and they be left in his custody on a long-term basis. . . . In addition to which, kimono and formal linens bearing the family crest, as well as swords, both long and short, had been prepared for presentation to them on the occasion of their pardon.

When these appeals were made is not specified. I would guess, though, that it was after the Advisory Opinion of the Full Tribunal had been submitted, recommending that the ronin be left in custody. Rumor also had it that the other three daimyo followed suit, as they did in so many things, once they had heard what the Hosokawa were doing. But as far as I know, there is no documentary evidence of this.

We have seen, though, that there were equally impassioned appeals for the death of the ronin from equally influential quarters. And thus those empowered to decide the fate of the ronin would find themselves under strong pressure from diametrically opposed directions.

For the next few days, however, the duties and festivities of the New Year would ensure that no one, from the Shogun on down, would have time to spare for serious deliberation of any sort. There would now be a hiatus during which those most anxious to know what was in the offing would simply have to wait.

◆ ◆ ◆

But this is not to say that there was nothing festive about this New Year for the ronin. The Hosokawa, as we have come to expect, were the most generous and genuinely benevolent of the four daimyo houses. Etchū-no-Kami himself had commanded that they be fêted even more lavishly than his most honored guests. Thus on New Year's Day, all seventeen of the ronin in his custody were presented with complete new sets of clothing—formal linens, kimono, obi, even new loincloths. They would at least be festively dressed for the New Year. Etchū-no-Kami was unable to greet them in person; a man of his consequence was more than fully occupied with duties at the castle and at his own upper mansion. But Kuranosuke immediately asked where the upper mansion was located, whereupon the ronin bowed in unison, heads to the floor, in His Lordship's direction to express their gratitude. Thereafter, they did likewise in the direction of young Lord Naiki's apartments, and then in the direction of their own lord, buried at Sengakuji, and of his widow in Imai-chō.

The ronin were also informed that they would soon be moving, from the Arch-Windowed Rooms to the Actors' Room. The order clearly had come from His Lordship himself, for it was a distinguished delegation— two Elders, the Chief Adjutant, the Commander of the Bodyguard, and the Edo Liaison Officer—that came to explain the situation to the ronin: "Recent events being as sudden as they were, we simply installed you in these rooms with no forethought. But it is quite dark here and there is no garden, so we've been commanded to move you to rooms with a garden. Tomorrow, we will begin sprucing up those quarters, and carpenters will be coming. This might have made you wonder what was going on, so we've come to let you know in advance."

Their new rooms were bright and airy, the garden broad and filled with luxuriant trees surrounding a lovely pond. Here they could enjoy to the fullest all the subtle changes of spring that were just beginning to appear. Kuranosuke was deeply touched by His Lordship's thoughtfulness, and Yoshida Chūzaemon, from the main room, and Tominomori Suke'emon, from the anteroom, came forward to offer their thanks: "We could hardly be blessed with greater good fortune than you bestow upon us with your kind command. We are utterly at a loss for words with which to express the gratitude that we feel. We are much obliged to you, too, for the thoughtful care of the many samurai whom you have assigned to look after us, and particularly for the kind ministrations of Horiuchi Den'emon Dono."

"They are such well-spoken men," Den'emon thought. "I can see why it was *they* who were chosen to report to Sengoku Hōki-no-Kami."

♦ ♦ ♦

By contrast—although again as might be expected—the records of the Mizuno house suggest what now seems a strange mixture of magnanimity and wariness. They contain but six cryptic notations relating to the New Year. On New Year's morning, the ronin were to be served *o-zōni*, the traditional soup with which the year begins. They might have their hair cut and arranged if they wish. This would be done for them by foot soldiers, who were warned not allow the ronin to touch the scissors. For the first three days of the year, they were to be served sumptuous seven-course meals on two trays. Henceforth, they would also be provided with reading material—war tales, of course—with which to amuse themselves. And that is all we know about New Year's at the House of Mizuno.

◆ ◆ ◆

At the Hisamatsu house, Haga Seidayū makes no mention of the first and most festive days of the New Year: "There is no need to record what was done for the detainees at this time." But on the 5th, he reports, Hisamatsu Oki-no-Kami, lord of the domain, paid his first visit to the ronin, who were now at his middle mansion in Mita. Early that morning, the ronin were presented with new suits of clothing for the occasion—quilted under-robes, black formal kimono, and *tabi*. They were then transported in heavily guarded palanquins to the main entryway of the mansion, where their guards removed and racked their swords before escorting them to the anteroom of the reception chamber. His Lordship, too, removed his short sword and passed it to a member of his Bodyguard as he entered at the upper level of the chamber. No one in the room was armed when Oki-no-Kami proceeded to the middle level and addressed the ronin:

> *I should by rights have come to greet you last year, as soon as you were entrusted to our care; but I have not been well and have been unable even to pay my respects at the castle. I am pleased, though, to be able to offer you my felicitations today. I am deeply impressed by the devotion of each and every one of you on this recent occasion. After the long months of toil and privation you have endured, I trust that you will now be able to relax in comfort and good health. The law being what it is, you will, unfortunately, be subject to certain restrictions; and we shall be unable to offer you a proper banquet.*

But I have given instructions that for the duration of your stay with
us, you are to want for nothing; so if there is anything you require,
you mustn't hesitate to tell my men. I trust, too, that I shall soon
have the opportunity to talk with you again.

After expressing their gratitude to the Elder, Hattori Genzaemon,
the ronin were seen back to the entryway by two Inspectors, where they
again boarded palanquins and were returned to their quarters.

✦ ✦ ✦

In the records of the Mōri house, it is as though the Year of the Ram
had never come. They jump from the last day of the Twelfth Month—
when, for some reason, they reported to the Council of Elders that
Takebayashi Tadashichi's injuries were "half healed"—to the 22nd Day
of the First Month, without so much as a mention of New Year's Day
or even the season. The Mōri themselves would, of course, have celebrated, but if anything at all was done for the ronin, it was not deemed
worth mentioning.

✦ ✦ ✦

There was, however, one house where the New Year was not celebrated
at all. The records of the Uesugi read: "Genroku 16 [1703], Year of the
Ram. On New Year's Day, His Lordship rose to greet the first sunrise of
spring at his mansion in Sakurada; but owing to the incident in Honjo
in the Twelfth Month of the previous year, he was now in mourning, and
thus none of the New Year's observances were celebrated."

CHAPTER
82

*As the days passed, they grew
as close to one another as brothers.*

In any other month, the Military Tribunal would have met on the 2nd, 12th, and 22nd Days. In this First Month of the New Year, however, it would have been impossible for members of that court to escape their duties at the castle on the 2nd, and unlikely that they would have enough free time by the 12th to meet and deliberate a matter as serious as this. If they met on the 22nd, no record of it remains. What, then, *was* going on in the meantime?

From the records of the Hosokawa and the Uesugi, we know of the representations, both for and against the ronin, made by those houses—but nothing of the reception or outcome of these representations. All we can say for certain, therefore, is that sometime in the course of the First Month, a decision was made. But a full month was to pass before any word definitive enough to be deemed a verdict would issue from the castle.

♦ ♦ ♦

And so, while the ronin waited, they talked. As the Hosokawa house records tell us:

> *Their five custodians were eager to ask the ronin all about the vendetta and what they themselves had done, but from the very start, they had been warned that they must not. The ronin, too, wanted to talk about it, but felt that their success was due not so*

much to what any one of them had done, but to their good fortune and the help of the heavens. Even so, when some of their custodians questioned them in secret, they told them all that had happened. . . . Thus, as the days passed, they grew as close to one another as brothers, or as parent and child.

Much of what we know of this relationship we owe to one man, Horiuchi Den'emon. Not only did the ronin find a superb interlocutor and a staunch friend in Den'emon, but he was the only one of the five who recorded his conversations with them. We have met Den'emon on previous occasions and listened in on some of his conversations with the ronin; by now, they had been together for more than twenty days, and the tone of their exchanges had become noticeably more relaxed and personal.

✦ ✦ ✦

Den'emon was chatting with Ushioda Matanojō, when Hara Sōemon joined them. They then fell to talking desultorily about poetry.

"Do you know about Onodera Jūnai's wife's poems?" Matanojō asked.

"No, not at all," Den'emon replied.

"Sōemon Dono," Matanojō said, "you know them all. Write one down and show it to Den'emon Dono."

Sōemon laughed. "If Jūnai hears about this, he'll be very angry with me." And still smiling, he wrote:

fude no ato miru ni namida no shigure kite
iikaesubeki koto no ha mo nashi
Just to see the traces of your brush calls forth such a cold rain of tears,
that not a word can I think of with which to answer you.

Sōemon obviously had a finely tuned ear for poetry. Yet only six of his own compositions survive, two of which must date from this New Year's season. As we have seen, Sōemon was most of the time an amiable and mild-mannered man; but when necessary, he could be sharp and very directly spoken—as when he frightened Ōno Kurōbei so badly that he absconded. The two qualities are not incompatible. A contemporary writer describes Sōemon as one of those rare men who is capable of "saying the things that are difficult to say." His two New Year's poems, both written at the Hosokawa mansion, are perfect examples:

Year's End
nagaraete hana o mirubeki mi naraneba
nao oshimaruru toshi no kure kana
To live on and see the cherries bloom again: that is not our lot;
wherefore we mourn only the more the passing of this old year.

The Coming of Spring
omoiki ya kesa tatsu haru ni nagaraete
hitsuji no ayumi nao matan to wa
Who would have thought it: that we should survive until this morning,
the advent of spring, like lambs, still waiting to be led to slaughter.

Sōemon was looking the future straight in the face, stating beautifully, but without evasion, exactly what he saw and still managing to remain the affable, warm, cheerful man he had always been.

✦ ✦ ✦

Chūzaemon had been chaffing Den'emon, asking him why he was spending all his time in the anteroom with the younger men.

"Not at all," Den'emon said. "It's just that I don't want to force myself upon you gentlemen. But is there something in particular . . . ?"

No, Chūzaemon told him. It was just that Kuranosuke could hear his voice and thought that it would be nice if he would come in and talk with them, too. But when Den'emon went into the main room, it turned out that there *was* something they wanted to ask him about. Chūzaemon, Sōemon, and Yahei all came and sat down with him.

"Den'emon Dono, everyone says that you're very fond of horses. So could you explain something to us? It's said that some horses are good for traveling long distances and others are not. Why is that so?"

"I am, indeed, fond of horses," Den'emon said, "and have been since I was a boy. But horses, by nature, simply do not have strong hooves. You should not ride them over long distances. They may hold their heads up handsomely and look trim and fit, but no matter how healthy a horse may be overall, if you ride it for long distances, its hooves will bleed, and then it will be of no use to you when you really need it—in battle."

"Well, I can see that you know even more about horses than we were led to believe," Chūzaemon said.

Den'emon went on to tell them about some of the skilled riders whom he had known or heard of—including one Nakayama Kurōzaemon, whose sense of balance was so perfect that he could eat a bowl of gruel on horseback without spilling a drop. But then he returned to the subject of horses and battle.

"As I've said, riding is the most important of all the martial arts. A horse is a living creature; it knows perfectly well what sort of man is riding it. Learning to wield a lance, you can do by yourself; if you know the general principles, that will suffice. But riding takes practice. Nowadays, when there are so few horses, it is difficult to get enough practice, but if you put your mind to it, it is not impossible."

◆ ◆ ◆

From the very start, and with the very best of intentions, Etchū-no-Kami had commanded that the ronin be served a classic banquet menu, every day. "Two Soups and Five Sides," such meals were called colloquially, but they were a bit grander than that makes them sound. These were meals that filled three trays. On the main tray, there was one of the soups, two of the side dishes, and a bowl of rice. On the second tray were another soup and two more side dishes. And on the third tray, a main course of something broiled—usually fish or fowl of some sort. All of which was often followed by tea and sweets of several sorts. It is hardly surprising that Den'emon should tell us that Kuranosuke and the others had spoken to him about this.

"We've often mentioned this," Kuranosuke said, "but as you know, we've been ronin for some time now and have grown accustomed to eating only lightly. So we're finding it uncomfortable to eat such extravagant meals day in and day out. We've actually grown quite fond of brown rice and sardines. Could you by any chance have the cooks make our meals a bit lighter?"

"I know just what you mean," Den'emon said. "As your companions, we, too, have been served some of the same meals and found that they leave us rather uncomfortable. You are quite right, and we should like to do as you wish. But if the number of dishes were to change, His Lordship would be certain to hear of it, which makes it all but impossible for us to reduce the number."

"Well in that case, couldn't you make the dishes smaller, or at least simpler?" some of the others said. "Small bowls of soup, little plates of sliced sea slug in vinegar, a few rice bran pickles, that sort of thing?"

They discussed various ideas, Den'emon says, but there was also the problem of the cooks. Their duty was to make every dish as delectable as possible; they would not take kindly to any requests for simplicity.

The banqueting continued.

◆ ◆ ◆

One could easily get the impression that Den'emon was kindliness and benevolence personified, and for the most part that was true. But he tells one story on himself in which he was deeply irritated by one of the ronin, Kataoka Gengoemon: "I have a vest made of a deep-blue raw silk, which in summertime I wear unlined and in winter with the addition of a lining, the material for which is a plain brown fabric taken from the lining of an old surcoat. One day when I was wearing this, Kataoka Gengoemon came up to me."

"What is the material your vest is made of?" he asked.

"I think it's raw silk or something of the sort. Something the younger men are partial to these days, I'm told."

"Well, it's exquisitely tasteful," Gengoemon said, "and it harmonizes beautifully with the lining." Then he stroked the material softly with his fingertips as he admired it, which, Den'emon confesses, "made me feel dreadfully uncomfortable. I pay no attention to fashions of any sort; they come and they go, from one day to the next. And it's not just clothing."

Den'emon was not a hurtful man, but this former Page Boy delicately stroking his shoulder must have aroused strong feelings in him, for he did not just let the matter drop: "My father remembered when Hosokawa Tadaoki was still alive. Sansai Sama they called him, Sansai being his retirement name. As you probably know, Sansai Sama was a ruthless man, capable of extraordinary cruelty on the battlefield. But even in old age, he retained some of that sharpness, and one thing that irked him was samurai who were slaves to fads and fashions. One of his kinsmen, Hosokawa Gyōbu, had just come back from Edo wearing a very short surcoat. 'What's that thing you've got on?' Sansai Sama asked him. 'It's what all the bannermen in Edo are wearing,' Gyōbu said. 'It's short so it won't catch on the croup of a horse.' Sansai threw him an old coat, and said, 'Here, cut this up and have yours made a proper length.'

"So I can see why Takeda Shingen's men used to laugh at anyone who followed fashion and call him a 'sissy samurai,'" Den'emon said. "That was wartime, of course, but even now I can't help feeling queasy when someone admires my vest."

◆ ◆ ◆

Old Horibe Yahei told Den'emon, "My son Yasubei has a cousin, a ronin named Satō Jōemon. He's been patronized by a bannerman, Suwa Iki-no-Kami, and when Suwa was appointed Shogunal Magistrate for Nagasaki, he took Jōemon with him. And while they were there, Jōemon singlehandedly apprehended three foot soldiers who were stealing cargo from the harbor. Kuranosuke would not allow Jōemon to participate in the attack. But because I am such an old man, he came and helped me to get there. He's very manly. Unfortunately, though, he's an ugly fellow. If any lord were willing to take him into his service, Jōemon would strive with all his might to serve the man well. But I worry about him; he's an unfortunate fellow."

"No," Den'emon said, "you can rest easy on that score. Anyone as genuine as he is doesn't have to be handsome. He's certain to have his share of a warrior's good fortune. In fact, I would like to get to know him someday."

◆ ◆ ◆

While the young men were talking, Okuda Magodayū turned and said, "Den'emon Dono, I don't know *how* to commit seppuku. What's the proper way to do it?"

"To tell you the truth," Den'emon said, "I have never once seen it done. I've heard that they bring you a tray with a short sword on it and that you draw the tray toward you.... But do you do that *before* you slip your vest off your shoulder?" He put his hand up to the shoulder of his own vest while pondering this—whereupon Suke'emon, Jūrōzaemon, and some of the other men spoke up.

"Oh, come now! This is a waste of time! Any way you do it is just fine. Just stick out your head and let them cut it off." With that the discussion ended.

◆ ◆ ◆

By the 18th Day of the First Month, Hosokawa Etchū-no-Kami was at last able to make time to travel to his lower mansion in Takanawa and offer New Year's greetings to the ronin. With typical generosity, he also ordered that they be served an auspicious feast, the main course of which would be roast crane:

> I had hoped to offer you my New Year's felicitations somewhat sooner, but there are so many things one must do at the beginning of the year that until now I haven't been free to do as I would wish. I am pleased, though, that all of you have begun the year in good health and without mishap—and I am particularly delighted, as I expect that you will all be pardoned in the very near future. I've wanted to offer you some token of my felicitations, but could think of nothing special; so I hope you will enjoy this dinner of roast crane at your ease. I would be pleased to join you myself, but as you might find that a bit too formal for comfort, I've asked my Chief Elder, Nagaoka Kenmotsu, to join you in my stead.

After Kuranosuke thanked him profusely and all seventeen ronin bowed with heads to the floor, His Lordship added, "I hope in the near future to come back with my son Naiki and talk with you again, but tonight you must relax, enjoy yourselves, and banish all your cares." With which he left and returned to his upper mansion.

Nagaoka Kenmotsu then joined the group, and he turned out to be extremely congenial company. The ronin ate heartily, they say, and after their meal, drank just as heartily. And then, as they were about to break up and return to their rooms, Lord Naiki came to call upon them. New Year's felicitations and expressions of gratitude were again exchanged, and the young lord, too, before he left, promised that "we shall meet again soon."

CHAPTER
83

*The Shogun still felt it a pity
to punish these men.*

The records of all four daimyo houses note that on the 22nd Day of the First Month, they received a brief message from the Duty Elder Inaba Tango-no-Kami, summoning their Liaison Officers to his residence, "on official business." The most detailed of these entries, that in the Mōri house records, reads:

> *Upon arrival, the Elder's Adjutant, Okada Han'emon, informed us that we must have the detainees in our custody compose and submit genealogical records. These are to include their grandparents, even though they be dead, and all other relatives including cousins. If either their grandparents or their parents be dead, they are to give the year, month, and day of their death. These are to be written by the individuals themselves and signed with their monograms.*

At first, there seems to have been a bit of bureaucratic confusion. Some of the documents were sent back because they had not been signed properly, and then all of them were returned with the demand that the names and ages of their children be added. But by the 27th of the month, all documents were at last in order and in the hands of the Elders. It now remained only to await the outcome of this command. Everyone knew only too well what to expect; concerning which the Hosokawa house records are quite specific:

As a rule, the demand for genealogical records from those in detention means that they will soon be sentenced to death. Everyone was deeply distressed by this, especially those who had been close to the ronin since this past year—*they* were in a state of shock. The detainees themselves, however, had expected from the very start to die, and thus seemed not the least perturbed. Their only regret, they said, was that they would never be able to repay their great debt to us.

In short, a decision had been made; the Shogun must have decided—or been persuaded to decide—upon the death penalty. But why should this require such a complex bureaucratic exercise as the creation and collection of forty-six genealogical documents? I would guess that it was the system of guilt by association, or by relation, that made this necessary. The list of those to be punished would be based upon where the lines of guilt were drawn. In extreme cases, not only male children but wives and daughters and even more distant kin might be punished; in lesser cases, only male children of a certain age. With all the information it demanded, the Shogunate would need nothing further with which to draw up the list, once its limits had been decided.

✦ ✦ ✦

A decision had been made, but no one outside the castle had any idea *how* it had been made. And no one who was then inside the castle left any record of what he knew. As always, those who wished to know were forced to speculate on the basis of whatever clues they could glean outside the ramparts. The house records of the Shogun's Chief Adjutant, Yanagisawa (now Matsudaira) Mino-no-Kami Yoshiyasu, provide one such clue:

> *Having examined a series of possible precedents, the Elders arrived at a unanimous decision: "Although the aforementioned men were intent upon taking revenge upon an enemy, they got themselves up to look like commoners and day laborers, and late at night broke into the residence of another by stealth. This is not in keeping with the*

Way of the Warrior. They have behaved precisely like thieves in the night and should be punished as such. These forty-six men should be beheaded."

Eikeiji Sama [Yanagisawa Yoshiyasu], who was then serving as Adjutant to His Highness, found this most deplorable, but having at hand no appropriate precedent with which to argue against the Elders, he left matters as they stood. Yet even after departing the castle, he could not reconcile himself to the thought of His Highness sanctioning such a decision. Whereupon he summoned two of the Confucian scholars in his service, Shimura Sanzaemon and Ogyū Sōemon.

"Leaving aside for the moment our own land, have you ever, perchance, come across any precedent for such a case in other lands?"

Sanzaemon replied, "As old a scholar as I am, I can recall nothing of the sort in all recorded history. I would venture, therefore, that there is no relevant precedent."

He then asked the much younger Sōemon what he thought.

"Well," Sōemon replied, "it would appear that the participants in this deliberation are bogged down in minutiae and overlooking the essentials. The sages teach us, however, that essentials are far the more important, while the minutiae of a matter should be ignored. In this day and age, those on high hold the Way of Loyalty and Filiality to be of first importance in the governance of the land. Given which, it would be deplorable to execute, as though they were thieves, those whose very aim was to be loyal. If we set a precedent of punishing those determined to be Loyal and Filial as though they were thieves, what, then, are we to do with those whose intentions are dishonorable and disloyal? In the first place, therefore, we should leave events in other lands out of consideration, and adjudicate the matter in accord with the present-day political realities of our own land. If we permit these men to commit seppuku, then their own aims will have been achieved and it will set a good example for the public."

Eikeiji Sama was so exceptionally pleased with this opinion that the

following morning he set out for the castle an hour early to report
it to His Highness, who likewise was so impressed that he over-
turned instantly the decision of the Elders and commanded that
Kuranosuke and the others be permitted to commit seppuku and
their sons be banished to a distant island.

There is little doubt that Yanagisawa would have discussed the matter of the ronin with Ogyū Sōemon—the man we now know better as Ogyū Sorai. Whether this is a faithful representation of such a conversation is hard to say. But Yamazaki Yoshishige tells a story that suggests it might be:

Over the years, there have been several hypotheses as to how it was
decided that the ronin should commit seppuku. It will not do to
accept just any notion, but it is often said that it was the result of
Butsu Sorai's opinion. Yet in all the writings about the ronin, I have
never found any evidence of this. When the present Ogyū Sōemon
(in the service of the lord of Kōriyama) called upon me, however,
knowing my admiration of those Righteous Samurai, he brought with
him a valued volume handed down in his domain recording the deeds
of Eikeiji Sama, in which the aforementioned matter is made clear.

Who this contemporary of Yamazaki—also named Ogyū Sōemon—may have been I have yet to ascertain, but the text he showed Yamazaki is the very same as that I've just quoted, suggesting that at least the descendants of Sorai thought it authentic.

The details of Sorai's thoughts are spelt out more coherently, however, in a document now known as his "Legal Opinion," which he may well have composed to give Yanagisawa a written record of his reasoning:

Devotion to Duty is the Way by which we purify our own persons,
whereas the Law is a code of conduct to which all in the realm are
subject.

The forty-six gentlemen who lately took revenge upon their foe in the
name of their liege lord did so because they felt shamed as samurai.

荻生徂徠肖像

figure 28
Ogyū Sōemon (Sorai). (*Sentetsu zōden*, 1844)

In that they did so by Way of purifying their own persons, they may be said to have done their Duty; yet it was only within the confines of their own ranks that they were thus Duty-bound. In the final analysis, their motives were personal.

The facts of the matter are thus: in the first instance, Lord Naganori acted in disregard of his presence within the palace and was duly punished for this offense. Yet his vassals thereupon deemed Lord Kira his enemy and, with no official permit, plotted an attack upon him. Under the Law, this cannot be condoned.

These forty-six gentlemen should thus be adjudged guilty and sentenced to commit seppuku with all the honors due a samurai. If this be done, then neither shall the claims of the Uesugi house go for naught, nor shall the fidelity of these gentlemen be impugned. Such, I submit, would seem the most equitable disposition of this case. But should public interest be sacrificed to personal preference, thenceforth would the laws of the land be bereft of their force.

OGYŪ SŌEMON

The Yanagisawa house records tell us only that the Shogun was "impressed" when his Adjutant told him of Sorai's solution to the problem and that he overturned the decision to behead the ronin. But another version of the same colloquy—less reliable, but by no means a total fabrication—goes a bit further in describing its outcome: "But the Shogun still felt it a pity to punish these men who had proved themselves so loyal. He declared that he needed to ponder the matter further and did not issue the command that same day. And on the 1st Day of the Second Month, he discussed the matter with Prince-Abbot Kōben of the Rinnōji in Nikkō [and Kan'eiji in Ueno]."

This discussion with the Prince-Abbot actually took place. The 1st of the Second Month was the day traditionally set aside for the Prince-Abbot's New Year's visit, and it is duly reported in the *Veritable Records of the Tokugawa*: "On the 1st Day of the Second Month, the Nikkō Prince-Abbot, Kōben Hosshinnō, and other Tendai dignitaries came to offer their customary felicitations. When the formalities were finished, the Shogun entertained the Prince-Abbot in his private apartments. There were also performances of *Sarugaku* to which the Prince-Abbot's entire entourage were admitted."

Whether the Shogun knew it or not, I have no idea, but the Prince-Abbot had been one of the first of the eminences of that day to evince publicly his admiration for the ronin, which he did in the form of a Chinese poem, written in Nikkō on the 5th Day of the First Month:

> All the world rejoices in their act of fidelity;
> I plant a peony, noblest of flowers.
> Alike, we salute this age of peace;
> Each in our own way, we honor the coming New Year.

But Kōben was related to some of the most powerful ladies in the Women's Palace, and they, as we have seen, together with the Shogun's daughter Tsuru Hime, had urged strict punishment of the ronin. The Prince-Abbot's aunt Umenokōji had come to Edo in the service of the Shogun's wife, Nobuko; and he was also related to Tsuru Hime's mother, Kita no Maru Dono. It would have been difficult to predict what Kōben's answer might be when asked what he thought the fate of the ronin should be—whether he would be more moved by personal admiration or familial loyalty. What he said, however, betrays no trace of either; it is an intelligently argued opinion based upon widely accepted principles:

> *These men have endured extreme hardship for months and years on end; they have fervently persisted in their purpose; and now, finally, they have attained their goal: revenge upon the enemy of their lord. They have nothing further to wish for in this world. They have already surrendered themselves to the judgment of the authorities, and even if they should now be pardoned, they could hardly go to some other house and serve a second lord. Rather than consigning such uncommonly loyal vassals to starvation deep in some forest or desolate valley, the best way to ensure that their resolve not go for naught is for the Shogunate to grant them a death in keeping with*

*the Way of the Warrior. The proper exercise of the penal code is in
every way the most irreproachable course of action and of the greatest benefit to the public welfare of the realm.*

This, then, *may* approximate the way the decision for seppuku was
reached. A ruling was made by the Council of Elders, but the Shogun's
Chief Adjutant persuaded him to modify that decision before sanctioning it—the honor of seppuku would replace the humiliation of
beheading. The Shogun's sanction, however, turned out to be only tentative. He seems to have hoped that the Prince-Abbot, at the last moment,
might urge him to pardon the ronin as an act of mercy. Yet in the end,
it was the argument of the Prince-Abbot that convinced the Shogun to
stick to his decision for seppuku. Even this scenario involves a fair bit of
speculation. We know for certain, though, that the next day, preliminary
plans and preparations would be made. Two days later, the enactment of
those plans would begin. Three days later, it would all be over.

CHAPTER
84

*I just couldn't
imagine it.*

On the 3rd Day of the Second Month of Genroku 16, the Inspectorate delivered to the Heralds on duty in the castle, Hisanaga Naiki and Sakakibara Hachibei, the following note from Katō Etchū-no-Kami, Duty Officer of the Junior Council of Elders:

> To: Hisanaga Naiki
> Saitō Jizaemon
> Komakine Chōzaburō
> Akai Hei'emon
>
> *Tomorrow, the 4th, prior to the beginning of the Fourth Hour [10:00 A.M.], you are present yourselves at the castle.*
>
> SECOND MONTH, 3RD DAY

Hisanaga Naiki immediately dispatched a circular letter informing the other three men.

♦ ♦ ♦

Saitō Jizaemon seems not to have known why he was being summoned to the castle, but he decided that it would suffice if he were to wear an older suit of formal linens that day. He left his home in Komagome at the Fifth Hour (8:00 A.M.), allowing a full double-hour before his presence was required in the castle. Upon arrival, the four Heralds were joined by four Inspectors: Araki Jūzaemon, Sugita Gozaemon, Suzuki Jirōzaemon, and Kuru Jūzaemon. And although their presence was not explained, two of Kira's kinsmen had also been summoned, the bannermen Arakawa Tanba-no-Kami and Inoko Sadayū.

The four Inspectors, four Heralds, and two guests first were shown to the antechamber of the Blackwood Rooms; then, midway through the Fourth Hour (11:00 A.M.), another Inspector, Nagata Kizaemon, led them along the veranda to the Kerria Room. There they were shown into the presence of the full Council of Elders; the Duty Inspector General, Sengoku Hōki-no-Kami; and the City Magistrate, Niwa Tōtōmi-no-Kami. There was no discussion. Akimoto Tajima-no-Kami, Duty Officer of the Council of Elders, simply presented them with their orders: a team of one Inspector and one Herald would be sent as Shogunal Emissaries to each of the four daimyo houses to oversee the seppuku of the ronin in their custody.

To the Hosokawa	Araki Jūzaemon and Hisanaga Naiki
To the Hisamatsu	Sugita Gozaemon and Komakine Chōzaburō
To the Mōri	Suzuki Jirōzaemon and Saitō Jizaemon
To the Mizuno	Kuru Jūzaemon and Akai Hei'emon

Each of the four teams was also given a copy of the sentence that they were to read aloud to the ronin:

> *Asano Takumi, having been appointed official host to the Imperial Envoys, yet heedless of the solemnity of the occasion and his presence in the palace, was duly punished for his outrageous behavior. Kira Kōzuke, however, was deemed blameless. Whereupon forty-six of Takumi's vassals, claiming to wreak revenge upon their lord's enemy, joined in unlawful league, broke into the Kōzuke residence armed with assault weapons, and killed him. Such defiance of constituted authority is an egregious offense. You are therefore commanded to commit seppuku.*

> YEAR OF THE RAM [1703], SECOND MONTH, 4TH DAY

Each team was then handed a list of the Inspectors, Deputy Inspectors, and Sub-Inspectors who would accompany them, and assured that each of the daimyo houses would be sent a directive from the Council of Elders in advance of their arrival. The delivery of this document would be seen to straightaway by the Inspector Nagata Kizaemon. The directive read:

> *In connection with the sentencing of the vassals of Asano Takumi now in your custody, very shortly the Inspector ——— and the Herald ——— will call upon you. Your Lordship need not be present; this matter may be left to your vassals. Herewith the foregoing.*
>
> *Inaba Tango-no-Kami*
> *Akimoto Tajima-no-Kami*
> *Ogasawara Sado-no-Kami*
> *Tsuchiya Sagami-no-Kami*
> *Abe Bungo-no-Kami*

Finally, after fortifying themselves with a meal in the castle kitchens, they all set out midway through the Ninth Hour (1:00 p.m.). The four teams—by now grown to sizable entourages—probably remained together as far as the Sakurada Gate, and there spread out on their separate routes to Takanawa, Azabu, Mita East, and Mita West.

✦ ✦ ✦

Nothing further is said of Kira's kinsmen Arakawa Tanba-no-Kami and Inoko Sadayū. One presumes that they had been invited merely to witness the Shogunate's execution of "justice," word of which they could then carry to Kira's son in the House of Uesugi. We know, though, that this was not the last of their duties that day. Once dismissed at the castle, they did indeed go directly to the Uesugi Middle Mansion in Shirogane, for they had been commanded to escort their kinsman Kira Sahei, who was now living there, to the Military Tribunal. Once again, they were ushered into the presence of Sengoku Hōki-no-Kami, Niwa Tōtōmi-no-Kami, and Nagata Kizaemon, as well as a panel of six other Inspectors and seven Sub-Inspectors. Sengoku Hōki-no-Kami read the sentence:

KIRA SAHEI

Last year, when the vassals of Asano Takumi killed your father Kōzuke-no-Suke, your conduct on that occasion was indefensible. Your fief is thus declared forfeit, and you are hereby remanded to the custody of Suwa Aki-no-Kami.

With these few simple words, the House of Kira was abolished, and its young lord condemned to indefinite confinement. No further particulars or explanations were offered. The decision had been made before the court convened. Yet knowing that Sahei, only a boy of seventeen at the time, had been severely wounded on the night of the 14th Day of the Twelfth Month, and at one point had been left for dead, it is hard not to conclude that he was being punished as a surrogate for his adoptive father, whom the Shogun had failed to punish when he should have.

Sahei would not be allowed to return home that day. A detail of Suwa Aki-no-Kami's men were waiting at the Military Tribunal. Once the court was dismissed, they took Sahei into custody and escorted him directly to the Suwa mansion in Honjo. A few days later, on the 11th, he would be taken to Takashima Castle, six days up the Middle Mountain Road on the shores of Lake Suwa, high in the province of Shinano. There he would live, strictly constrained, for the duration of his detention, accompanied by only Sōda Magobei, the Elder of the Kira house who had fled through a hole in the wall on the night of the attack, and Yamayoshi Shinpachi, his one surviving childhood guardian. The Shogunate had at last fulfilled the Principle of Equal Punishment—but to the pain of an undeserving victim.

◆ ◆ ◆

There is one last event of the day that we wish we knew a great deal more about. Whether by accident or by design (one suspects the latter), the day of the punishment of the ronin and the punishment of Kira Sahei was also the last and most important day of the series of seven obsequies for Kira Kōzuke-no-Suke—his forty-ninth day. The requisite funds for these rites had been sent to the temple Banshōin two days earlier. All was in readiness. But who could attend? His widow and perhaps his daughters? An assortment of former vassals? Whoever else might be there, neither Kira's natural son nor his adoptive son was now free to mourn his father properly on this paramount day of the mourning process.

◆ ◆ ◆

Some people seem to have been warned in advance of what was to happen on the 4th, but apparently not everyone involved was told the news. This caused some confusion.

Late at night on the 3rd, when Horiuchi Den'emon and Yoshihiro Kazaemon were on duty in the Hosokawa Lower Mansion, Nagase Sukenoshin, an Adjutant to Etchū-no-Kami, came to their duty room.

"A letter has just come from the upper mansion," he said. "Tomorrow morning, we are to put out flower arrangements in each of the rooms of the ronin. The tea masters will come in the morning with their flowers. So I'll ask you two to meet them and show them where the flowers should go."

"That's a very thoughtful thing to do," Den'emon said. "I'm sure that they'll appreciate it." He seems to have been totally unaware that these flowers had deep symbolic significance. But just then, the ronin in the anteroom sent a serving monk to say, "None of us are asleep yet, and we just heard your voice, Den'emon. Do come in here, please."

"They seem to be on very friendly terms with you," Sukenoshin said, suspicious as always of anyone becoming *too* friendly with the detainees. Kazaemon came to Den'emon's rescue.

"Ichidayū and I are regularly on duty here, too," he said. "The three of us take it in turns. They called for Den'emon only because they heard his voice."

"Then you'd better hurry and see what they want," the Adjutant replied.

Normally, everyone would be in bed by this time. But Tominomori Suke'emon, Ōishi Sezaemon, and all the younger men were still up, talking of this and that.

"This matter will be resolved soon," they said, "so as our parting gift, we'd like put on a little show for you." They positioned some folding screens so the guard detail could not see them and performed a few Kabuki dances from the Sakai-chō theaters.

"Pardon us, please," they said to Okuda Magodayū and Ushioda Matanojō, who were lying down off to the side.

Magodayū and Matanojō laughed. "Even if this thing is resolved," Magodayū said, "with you making such a racket, they'll put the handcuffs on Kuranosuke tomorrow morning."

Den'emon was concerned, though, because the Adjutant Sukenoshin could see what was going on.

"It's very late now, and I think that you're disturbing Magodayū; so let's let it go at that."

"Please, just a little longer," they pleaded. But Den'emon left the room. He was later to regret his haste.

◆ ◆ ◆

The next morning, the 4th, when the tea masters had finished arranging the flowers, Kuranosuke said, "Den'emon Dono, won't *you* put the flowers in our room?"

"Why, of course," Den'emon said. He took the flowers and put them in place himself. All seventeen of the ronin came in and admired them. Then, after breakfast, word arrived that His Lordship Etchū-no-Kami would be coming to the lower mansion today. Everyone in the duty room began changing into more formal wear, but Den'emon was about to go off watch and return home. It was just then that Isogai Jūrōzaemon came to him.

"So the watch changes today?" Jūrōzaemon said. "I wonder what will transpire between now and when you return. I expect that the matter will be decided by then. We're all at a loss for words to express how grateful we are for all that you've done for us while we've been here— and especially you, Den'emon Dono. Every one of us here. . . ." He turned his head sharply to the side and hid his face. Then he continued: "Presumptuous though it is of me to say this, every one of us here feels so comfortable with you that we were hoping that the matter would be decided while you were on duty."

"If there are any orders forthcoming from the castle," Den'emon said, "we're sure to hear of it in advance; so even if I happen not to be on watch, I'll still be able to come back and be with you."

"Well, if that's how you see it, then by all the gods we'll take your word for it." Den'emon stopped briefly in the duty room, chatting with his colleagues, and then left the lower mansion, still strangely unaware of what was soon to happen.

◆ ◆ ◆

It was only the accident of a chance meeting that finally opened Den'emon's eyes. He was riding home when at Sukiyabashi, midway through the Ninth Hour (1:00 P.M.), he encountered his colleague Hirano Tan'emon riding in the opposite direction, obviously in a hurry and dressed more formally than usual. Den'emon stopped and asked him what was up.

"Emissaries from the castle—they'll be arriving at the lower mansion soon," Tan'emon told him. Finally, the truth struck home; Den'emon now realized what it all added up to. He turned his horse around and began riding back to Takanawa with Tan'emon.

But *how* had Den'emon failed to see the meaning of all the signs? The flowers; the Kabuki dances; the arrival of His Lordship; the disappointment of the ronin when he left for home at the end of his watch. Den'emon himself attempted to explain.

"I swear," he said, "I just couldn't imagine it. Everyone spoke so very favorably of them, saying that they were certain to be pardoned. And we ourselves were saying that they probably would come back to Kumamoto with us. It simply never occurred to us that they could be sentenced to commit seppuku."

*You may tell these men discreetly that this
redounds to the honor of them all.*

In a sense, it was the same at all four of the destinations visited by the emissaries. The advance couriers delivered precisely the same directive of notification, the only difference being the names of the emissaries being dispatched to each house. The teams of emissaries read out precisely the same sentence, the only difference being the names of the ronin that followed. But daimyo houses and their Corps of Vassals could be as individual as the individuals who composed them. The variety they displayed in their reception of the news and their reactions to it reveal in fascinating ways just how individual they could be.

♦ ♦ ♦

The Liaison Officers of all daimyo houses were in constant touch not only with one another, but also with contacts they had developed within the Shogunate. It must have been one such contact who, on the evening of the 3rd, got word to the Hosokawa house that the ronin in its custody would be sentenced on the morrow. Whether he was able to advise the Hosokawa what that sentence would be, we do not know. They seem to have assumed the worst: that it would be a sentence of death. Which is why Hosokawa Etchū-no-Kami commanded that flower arrangements be placed in the rooms of the ronin—a gentler forewarning, he hoped, than any words could be. It was no surprise, therefore, when two members of the Vanguard arrived at the Hosokawa Upper Mansion the next morning, the 4th. The message they bore read:

*In connection with the sentencing of the vassals of Asano Takumi now
in your custody, very shortly the Inspector Araki Jūzaemon and the
Herald Hisanaga Naiki will call upon you. Your Lordship need not be
present; this matter may be left to your vassals. Herewith the foregoing.*

> *Inaba Tango-no-Kami*
> *Akimoto Tajima-no-Kami*
> *Ogasawara Sado-no-Kami*
> *Tsuchiya Sagami-no-Kami*
> *Abe Bungo-no-Kami*

To: Hosokawa Etchū-no-Kami Dono

There could be no doubt now. However appropriate the message of
the flower arrangements may have been on the previous evening, only
words would now suffice. Before all else, Etchū-no-Kami paused to
write a quick note to Kuranosuke and dispatch it to Takanawa, with
orders that it be carried there as rapidly as possible:

*I had hoped to be able to send you news of a favorable verdict, that
you had been pardoned. I deeply regret, however, that we have just
received word from the Council of Elders that you shall instead be
sentenced. You must now write your parting words to your wives,
children, and kinfolk. We assure you, too, that we shall send your
bodies wherever you may wish. The emissaries should arrive this
afternoon. In the meantime, you may calmly prepare yourselves.*

An appropriate letter of acknowledgment was then composed and
sent to the Council of Elders, following which Etchū-no-Kami himself
acknowledged the notice with a brief visit to the mansion of the Duty
Elder of the month. And since the Elders had noted that he himself need
not be present, he assured them that he would not direct the process
personally but would convey any commands he might make through an
intermediary. That done, he left immediately for his lower mansion in
Takanawa. The same message was conveyed to the other Elders and to
the Shogun's Adjutants by his representative, Iida Saibei.

✦ ✦ ✦

It would have been no accident that Araki Jūzaemon was the Inspector appointed to head the Shogunate's mission to the Hosokawa house. Araki had also served as head of the mission sent to Akō to supervise the confiscation of the castle and lands of Asano Takumi-no-Kami. He had spent almost a month in the castle town, in the course of which he had worked closely with (and sometimes against) Kuranosuke; and it was he with whom Kuranosuke had made the pact that he persisted in keeping despite the urgings—and near mutiny—of the more hotheaded ronin. It would be too much to describe the two men as friends, but they certainly had developed great respect for each other. Araki Jūzaemon was the ideal leader of the detail sent to supervise the seppuku of the highest-ranking ronin, including, of course, the former Chief Elder Ōishi Kuranosuke.

✦ ✦ ✦

Horiuchi Den'emon had managed to ride fast enough to arrive ahead of Araki and his entourage. He left his horse in the care of the guards at the Meguro Gate, sent a servant to borrow a set of formal linens from his kinsman Kizaemon, and then, having changed, made his way to the quarters of the ronin:

> When I peeped into the anteroom, they were all eating. Owing to the circumstances, their meal had been served a bit early. Since I had left to return home that morning when the watch changed, I kept out of sight lest they think it ominous that I should be back. But the looks on their faces and their manner left little doubt that they all knew what was happening. As they ate, they exchanged glances and looked as though they wanted to finish as quickly as they could. A little later, Yagi Ichidayū came and said, "Emissaries will be coming, so you'll have to change into formal linens." He then gave everyone a complete new outfit: black silk kimono, pale-blue linen vest and trousers, obi, and *tabi*. At this point, I entered the room and helped Isogai

Jūrōzaemon, Tominomori Suke'emon, and some of the others tie the waistbands of their trousers.

Presently, Araki Jūzaemon, Hisanaga Naiki, and their attendants arrived. After appropriate greetings had been exchanged, they were shown into the room where the ronin were gathered, followed by a number of Etchū-no-Kami's ranking vassals who looked on from the aisle side of the room. Jūzaemon then read the sentence, the text of which they had been given in the castle:

> Asano Takumi, having been appointed official host to the Imperial Envoys, yet heedless of the solemnity of the occasion and his presence in the palace, was duly punished for his outrageous behavior. Kira Kōzuke, however, was deemed blameless. Whereupon forty-six of Takumi's vassals, claiming to wreak revenge upon their lord's enemy, joined in unlawful league, broke into the Kōzuke residence armed with assault weapons, and killed him. Such defiance of constituted authority is an egregious offense. You are therefore commanded to commit seppuku.
>
> YEAR OF THE RAM [1703], SECOND MONTH, 4TH DAY

Following which he read aloud the names of each of the seventeen ronin. In assent, Kuranosuke, speaking so softly that Den'emon could hardly hear him, replied, "Although we might have been sentenced to almost any punishment imaginable for our offense, we are extremely grateful to be commanded to commit seppuku." Yoshida Chūzaemon, too, said something of the same sort, Den'emon tells us, while all the others bowed with their heads to the floor.

Araki then spoke in confidential tones to Kuranosuke. "Kira Sahei, too, has been remanded to the custody of Suwa Aki-no-Kami. I am not officially authorized to tell you this," he explained, "but I expect that it will be cause for satisfaction to all of you." Then after a pause: "You may now, at your leisure, begin to prepare yourselves." The officials then left the room.

When the ronin were again alone, Kuranosuke, tears in his eyes, said, "This is such good news, such good news. Gather around everyone; I'll tell you what he told me." I have often wondered if this was Jūzaemon's way of telling Kuranosuke that he, too, had done his best to honor the "pact" that they had made almost two years earlier during the final inspection of the castle in Akō.

In the course of "preparing themselves," another source tells us, Kuranosuke turned to one of the Elders of the Hosokawa house and said, "In the sentence just read to us, they say we are guilty of joining in 'unlawful league.' Now if we had recruited even one outsider, then we might well be deemed an unlawful league. But those of us who joined forces are all vassals of Takumi-no-Kami, each one of us intending only to kill the enemy of our own late lord. That, I should think, can hardly be called unlawful," he said, smiling wryly. "Still, I am grateful that we are commanded to commit seppuku, as befits a samurai."

◆ ◆ ◆

The finale to the sentencing process was strangely celebratory. Horiuchi Den'emon's account of it seems perversely terse, but he does at least tell us that once the ronin were "prepared" (if ever one is "prepared" to die), saké was produced, cups were passed around, and "everyone" gathered and drank and talked. Just who "everyone" was, Den'emon does not tell us, although I imagine the group to include Hosokawa vassals as well as ronin. For another old Hosokawa vassal fills out the story in a beautiful way.

As they were about to break up, the little boy who always brought them their tea—a fledgling Tea Monk, his head already shaved—came in as usual. Kuranosuke lifted his cup from the tray, let it warm his palms for a moment, and then raised his eyes and smiled.

"We're going away today, you know?"

The boy nodded.

"I want you to be very good after we're gone. You see, we're going to become ghosts." Kuranosuke's voice had grown very soft. The boy seemed puzzled, unsure whether this was a joke or a confidence. Years later, he would realize it had been both.

"So if you're a good boy, and don't make too much noise, we'll all look after you." Then his face beamed with a broad grin.

"But if not—we'll come and give you an awful fright!"

♦ ♦ ♦

The Hisamatsu, too, had their contacts within the Shogunate. But the first notice they received of an impending judgment, their records tell us, came directly from Inaba Tango-no-Kami, Duty Officer of the month for the Council of Elders, who sometime on the 3rd advised them, "The ten men in your custody will soon be sentenced to commit seppuku, for which you should make the necessary preparations."

♦ ♦ ♦

The question of what was to be the fate of the ronin, and what they should be doing to prepare for that fate, had been a matter of concern almost from the time the Hisamatsu had taken the ronin into custody. But if anyone in the Hisamatsu house, like Den'emon in the Hosokawa house, felt that the ronin might eventually be pardoned, their thoughts were never recorded. There is brief mention of the possibility that they might be banished to a distant island. Most in the house, however, seemed to assume that they would be sentenced to commit seppuku. The Hisamatsu thus had made confidential contact with the Hosokawa, probably through their Liaison Officers, from whom they learnt that the man who would serve as Second for Ōishi Kuranosuke would be of higher rank than the rest. Accordingly, it was decided that the Second for Kuranosuke's son Ōishi Chikara would be Haga Seidayū, and that the other Seconds would be selected on the basis of ability, not rank. Seidayū was also commanded to draw up a general plan of procedure, a draft of which he had already submitted.

♦ ♦ ♦

Later the same day, the 3rd, the Inspectorate sent a Sub-Inspector with whom the Hisamatsu were in regular contact, Ikeda Jinbei. Jinbei's mission was not simply to inform; he had come, he said, to teach them "the proper procedure for seppuku as decreed from the time of our founding

Shogun, Gongen Sama [Tokugawa Ieyasu]." Following which he gave a demonstration of how to conduct the inspection of a head after it had been severed. Thereafter, food and drink was served, and it promised to be a convivial afternoon.

"Who is to serve as Second for Ōishi Chikara?" the Sub-Inspector asked. "I'd like to discuss this with him, as those who come after him will follow his example."

Seidayū replied, "I have been told confidentially that I shall be the Second for Ōishi. But we are well aware that the inspection of heads is a matter of great importance in the Way of the Warrior. Oki-no-Kami is the lord of a line quite as venerable as that of Gongen Sama; and many of his vassals are descended from warriors who served the house in those days. I doubt that any of them will have the least difficulty conducting the inspection of a head. We do appreciate your thoughtfulness, though, for which we thank you from the bottom of our hearts. And when Oki-no-Kami's Adjutants report this to him, I am sure that he, too, will be pleased to hear of it."

Jinbei clearly understood what Seidayū was telling him and dropped the subject immediately. Then, once he had finished his saké, he left.

The Adjutants later told Seidayū that His Lordship was most amused when they told him the story. "That's Seidayū!" he laughed. "He *would* say something like that."

◆ ◆ ◆

That evening, the meal served the ronin was even more splendid than usual, and the ranking Inspector of the Hisamatsu house joined them.

"We received confidential notification earlier today from the Council of Elders that Inspectors will be coming tomorrow to announce their decision," he told them. "I am certain that they shall have been deeply impressed by your deeds, and will come bearing tidings that will please you. We are all waiting in anticipation of a favorable judgment."

The ronin must have known that the man was lying to them, for they all sat with their hands properly folded and their faces devoid of expression as Horibe Yasubei replied: "We are very grateful for this notification. We have for long caused you great hardship as our custodians, and we are at a loss for words to express our gratitude to all of you who have been so kind to us. From the sounds of activity that we could hear outside our quarters this evening, we were expecting that the matter would be resolved either tonight or tomorrow." The others, we are told, were completely calm and comported themselves with great dignity.

◆ ◆ ◆

Early the next morning, on the 4th, the Liaison Officer in the Hisamatsu Upper Mansion received a note from one of his contacts in the Inspectorate, the Sub-Inspector Orihara Kohei: "Four Inspectors, twenty Deputy Inspectors, and twenty Sub-Inspectors have been notified that they should come to the castle on official business. I think this may mean that the matter of the men in your custody has been decided. For your information, I send you this confidential advisory."

His Lordship now commanded that preparations already in train, whether for banishment or for seppuku, be brought to a final state of readiness. In the case of banishment, those who would hand over the ronin to the Shogunate were to be notified. In the case of seppuku, not as many men would be required. But in addition to the Seconds, those who guard the site, and those who present the trays bearing the short swords, they would also need musketeers, foot soldiers, and men from the Department of Works to hang the curtains and attend to the bodies; then, too, there would be those in the funeral cortege. Haga Seidayū was directed to oversee these preparations, he being the man who had supervised all such arrangements since taking the ronin into custody last year. He would be assisted by the Hisamatsu Inspectors Watanabe Jinnojō and Miura Jirōemon.

In the meantime, at the middle mansion in Mita, the ronin were roused early. Once they had finished breakfast, they were allowed to bathe and have their hair done, and then were given complete new outfits, into which they changed as though they were just passing the time of another normal day—chatting, laughing, sipping tea, smoking.

At the Hisamatsu Upper Mansion, toward the end of the Hour of the Serpent (ca. 10:30–11:00 A.M.), the Sub-Inspector Suzuki Fumihira brought a letter signed by the full Council of Elders—the same letter that was sent to all the daimyo—saying that they would soon send Inspectors in connection with the sentencing of the ten ronin in their custody and that His Lordship need not be present. Appropriate acknowledgment was sent, but His Lordship announced nonetheless that he would go to the middle mansion and meet the Inspectors. Haga Seidayū, too, was ordered to drop what he was doing, go to the middle mansion, and instruct the other Seconds how to perform their duties in a way that would bring credit to the House of Hisamatsu. All the supervisors of the several details were likewise commanded to gather their people and proceed to Mita as inconspicuously as possible. This included even a detail from the kitchens, charged with preparing box lunches for both their own people and the functionaries from the castle.

◆ ◆ ◆

Midway through the Hour of the Ram (2:00 P.M.), the emissaries and their entourage arrived in Mita: the Inspector Sugita Gozaemon, the Herald Komakine Chōzaburō, five Deputy Inspectors, six Sub-Inspectors, and six Deputy Heralds. Once seated in the main reception chamber, they told their hosts that they need not rush, but they might now prepare to proceed, and then give notice when preparations were complete.

These preparations were completed with dispatch, but then a strange rumor arose in the Hisamatsu mansion that deterred them from notifying the emissaries. The retired Confucian scholar Hirata Kiken had for some reason gone to the mansion of the Duty Elder, Inaba Tango-no-Kami, and there were those who were saying that he was certain to return bearing news of a pardon. No one knew the source of the rumor; but if it should turn out to be true, it would be a great mistake to proceed. When Kiken returned with no knowledge of any such news, however, the emissaries were finally notified that preparations were complete.

The ronin were carried from their quarters to the vestibule in palanquins, and then escorted to the anteroom of the reception chambers. The emissaries invited them to cross the threshold into the main reception chamber, and they all slid forward into the room on their knees. Komakine Chōzaburō announced that they would now be sentenced, and Sugita Gozaemon read out the sentence "in resonant voice"—

precisely the same sentence as was read at the other three houses.

In assent, Yasubei responded, "Having attained all that a samurai could wish for, we are most grateful to be sentenced to commit seppuku."

"You may now, at your leisure, begin to prepare yourselves," Gozaemon said. The ronin were then escorted to the Vanguard duty room, where they would await their call to the courtyard. As far as we know, there was no brief moment of saké and good cheer at the Hisamatsu Middle Mansion.

◆ ◆ ◆

If anyone in the house of Mōri Kai-no-Kami was in touch with anyone in the castle, no mention of it is made in any of the house records. The first notification seems to have come on the 4th, the very day of the seppuku. A bit before midday, two members of the Vanguard arrived at the Mōri Upper Mansion bearing advance notice from the Council of Elders that emissaries would soon arrive at the lower mansion in connection with the sentencing of the ten men in the custody of the house. Was this yet another manifestation of the long-standing animosity between the Tokugawa and the Mōri, a failure to communicate for reasons of spite? Or just patchy record keeping? In any event, preliminary preparations had already been made, just in case the ronin should eventually be sentenced to seppuku. The site chosen was an open space before the viewing chamber at the mounted archery range. The tatami mats in this room had been resurfaced; the sliding doors would be removed for the occasion, the seats of the emissaries would be enclosed by folding screens, and the site of the seppuku itself would be hidden from view on three sides by curtains.

Yet the Mōri seem not to have known, prior to the arrival of the emissaries, whether the ronin would be sentenced to seppuku or to banishment. The Elders Tashiro Kaname and Tokita Gondayū immediately sent word of the notification to the main house of which they were a cadet branch, the Mōri of the domain of Hagi. Whatever the sentence, they said, they would require assistance from the lord of Hagi—for security either at the gates of the mansion in the case of seppuku or in the procession to the quayside in the case of banishment.

✦ ✦ ✦

At the beginning of the Eighth Hour (2:00 P.M.), those in the advance detail arrived from the castle and were shown to their places in the appropriate rooms: five Deputy Inspectors, seven Sub-Inspectors, and five Deputy Heralds. Shortly thereafter, the emissaries themselves arrived: the Inspector Suzuki Jirōzaemon and the Herald Saitō Jizaemon. Both Elders of the house, Kaname and Gondayū, went to the entryway to greet them and show them to the main reception chamber. On their way there, as they passed along the aisle, they caught sight of His Lordship Mōri Kai-no-Kami, whereupon the emissaries seemed almost to admonish Gondayū.

"The directive you were sent stated that Kai-no-Kami need not be present."

"Quite so," Gondayū replied. "I mentioned that to him, but His Lordship said that he intends only to greet you and then retire."

And just as Gondayū said, when the emissaries were seated in the main reception chamber, His Lordship and his heir the young lord entered and greeted them.

"As it said in the directive," Jirōzaemon repeated, "there is no need for you to be present. You are welcome to withdraw." Whereupon, after a strained exchange of pleasantries, His Lordship went within. Then, however, the emissaries were greeted again, this time by Mōri Daizen-no-Daibu, lord of the main house in Hagi, and his son. All that is recorded of this meeting is that Their Lordships immediately retreated.

✦ ✦ ✦

Once the emissaries were settled in their positions, they summoned the Mōri Elders, Kaname and Gondayū.

"We have come to sentence the ten men in your custody, so when you are prepared to proceed, please let us know. You might also tell your Seconds that we would wish them to perform their task calmly, without mishap." They asked, too, that the Elders prepare a list of all the Seconds, showing their ages and to whom they would be assigned.

A Deputy Inspector then asked Naitō Kakuzaemon, "Are your

preparations well in hand?"

"Well, we did not know beforehand what the sentence would be," Kakuzaemon said, "so I can't yet say that everything is in order. We have prepared the site, however. Would you be so good as to take a quick look at it?" Kōbe Jūdayū went with Kakuzaemon, but when he was shown the site at the mounted archery range, Jūdayū said, "It looks a bit cramped here. We had better ask the emissaries about this." Cramped in what way, we are not told. But for the seppuku of even one man, a space of 3-*ken* (18 feet, 5.5 meters) square is required, and it must be separated from the seats of the witnesses by at least the same distance. The emissaries decreed immediately that this site was inadequate; it must be moved to the courtyard of the main reception rooms.

◆ ◆ ◆

The change of site would take time. But in the interim, the emissaries were offered a full meal—which they declined, saying that it would interfere with their work. They were served tea and sweets instead.

This was also when the ronin were first notified—officially, at least—that they were to be sentenced. They may well have suspected that such was the case, but the Mōri have told us nothing of what the ronin thought or said before they were sentenced. They tell us only that the ronin had not bathed recently, and so were allowed to bathe before changing into completely new outfits—silk kimono, formal linen vest and trousers, loincloth, obi, and *tabi*.

The Elders were then recalled to the presence of the emissaries, who told them, "We are now ready to sentence the detainees, so when their preparations are complete, please have them come before us."

"All is in readiness," the Elders replied.

"That was fast," said the emissaries.

The ronin were then called from their quarters, one by one. Each boarded a palanquin guarded by two samurai, two members of the Mid-Corps of Pages, and two foot soldiers bearing hardwood staves. At the vestibule of the mansion, each alighted and was escorted from there to the Envoys' Room by two unarmed samurai. Here, for the first time since they had been taken into custody, all ten men were again together.

From there, they were summoned into the main reception chamber, where the emissaries sat, their swords at their sides. After Kōbe Jūdayū called out the names of all ten men, Saitō Jizaemon announced that they would now be sentenced, and Suzuki Jirōzaemon read out the sentence.

In assent, Okajima Yasoemon, younger brother of Hara Sōemon, replied that they were most grateful to be sentenced in keeping with warrior law, while all bowed with their heads to the floor. They were then taken to the Upper Chamber of the great entry hall, just within the vestibule, where they would await their call to the courtyard.

◆ ◆ ◆

The records of the Mizuno house have the least to tell us of its custody of the Akō ronin, and what they do tell us dwells overwhelmingly on details of the strict security that was maintained throughout. And yet, as we shall see, it was at the Mizuno house that one of the most touching—and significant—moments in the sentencing of the ronin was to take place.

◆ ◆ ◆

If there was any contact between the Mizuno and the castle on the 3rd, the day prior to the seppuku, it is not mentioned. Their records of the 4th tell much the same story as those of the other houses, although in less detail. Toward the end of the Hour of the Serpent (ca. 11:30 A.M.), a Sub-Inspector arrived bearing the same advance directive from the Council of Elders that had been sent to the other three houses. And early in the Hour of the Ram (ca. 1:00–1:30 P.M.), as promised in that directive, the Inspector Kuru Jūzaemon and the Herald Akai Hei'emon arrived, attended by five Deputy Inspectors, six Sub-Inspectors, and six Sub-Heralds. At the main gate of the Mizuno Middle Mansion, they were welcomed by an impressive force. Outside the barrier, before the gate, waited a Company Commander and two samurai in full formal linens as well as twenty foot soldiers bearing hardwood staves. As the emissaries entered, the samurai knelt, the foot soldiers bowed with their heads to the ground, and six more foot soldiers emerged within the barrier. Within the gate, a Liaison Officer stood on either side, and two Elders of the house stepped down to the gravel at the entrance to the vestibule—all in full formal linens. Of course, the double-layered fencing of heavy bamboo, built to prevent any escape, had been dismantled. As the emissaries mounted the steps, His Lordship Mizuno Kenmotsu came out to the edge of the vestibule to greet them. And as they moved on into the tatami-matted great hall, they were met by a Company Commander, a detail from the Horse Guards, and another from the Mid-Corps of Pages, who escorted them into the antechamber of the Envoys' Rooms. Here His Lordship excused himself and went within, and the emissaries were served tea and given a smoking tray. They were also handed a list that they had requested, giving the names and ages of the nine ronin.

What took place between this splendid welcome and the reading of the sentence to the ronin, the Mizuno records do not even mention. The next thing we know, the emissaries are seated before the alcove in the Upper Chamber of the Envoys' Rooms and the ronin are lined up facing them, freshly bathed and clad in their new finery. The sentence was read, and one of the ronin—not named—responded, "Although we might have been punished in any imaginable way, we are most grateful to be sentenced to commit seppuku." They filed out, and the emissaries summoned the Elders of the house.

"Now that the sentence has been read," said the emissaries, "you may prepare to proceed. There is no need to rush; you may take your time." And before the Elders left, a Deputy Inspector added: "Normally, Inspectors are not sent to supervise the seppuku of rear vassals, but on this occasion a special exception is being made. You may tell these men discreetly that this redounds to the honor of them all."

*The Second is no executioner;
he is the dying man's friend.*

Seppuku was a ritual. It hadn't always been. In the earliest known instances, men took their own lives on the battlefield to avoid capture by the enemy and possibly torture—or simply as a display of stubborn samurai pride. But by the Genroku era, seppuku had come to be regarded as the most honorable way for a warrior to die—whether of his own volition or as a punishment—and a multitude of conventions had been developed to guide participants at every step in the process.

The Akō ronin were being punished for what the Shogunate had decided to consider a crime. But so few people, other than those in positions of authority, considered them criminals that they were "awarded" a death of the most honorable sort—indeed, in some ways more honorable than those of their rank and the house they had served would normally have been entitled to. It will be well, therefore, to review some of the conventions that they will be subject to before entering upon a description of their individual deaths.

✦ ✦ ✦

This most honorable of deaths could not be accomplished alone. As is obvious from any pictorial depiction of such an occasion, it involved a great many people other than the man about to die. A man could, of course, cut open his abdomen in isolation, and then raise the sword to his neck and sever the carotid artery to hasten the moment of death. He might then be admired for his bravery and moral fiber, but solitary seppuku conferred upon him none of the ceremonial honor of the more elaborate rite.

The most important of the many executors of this rite were the Inspectors (*kenshi*) and the Seconds (*kaishaku*), both of whom we have already encountered. The Inspectors were in overall command of the detail appointed by the authorities to oversee the seppuku. Their first duty, therefore, was to read the sentence to the condemned. Ideally, this should be done in a firm and fluent voice, with particular attention to clarity in the final phrases, a voice that inspired not weakness but strength and courage.

The Inspectors must then inspect and approve the site and its appurtenances, for as we have seen in the case of Takumi-no-Kami, even the choice of an indoor or an outdoor site was determined by the rank of the condemned. Then, too, it had to be spacious enough to accommodate not only the participants, but also those who would witness the rite and those whose only task would be to secure the site.

Once the sentence was read and the site deemed to be in good order, the Inspectors asked all the participants and witnesses to take their places, and indicated that the first of the principals could be called. In the present instance, the ronin were summoned individually by senior members of the houses in which they were being held.

The names of the ronin were called in the order of their rank, this having been determined by each man's place in the list of signatures at the end of the manifesto submitted to the Shogunate. As each man was called, he was met by two Escorts. In a sense, the Escorts might be considered guards, but only in an emergency would they function as such. Like all participants in the rite, they wore full formal linens, although with their trousers bloused up above their knees. And they were unarmed, except, perhaps, for a small dagger concealed in the folds of their robes. When their man emerged, they guided him gently along the matted path to his seat on the dais, and then dropped back and waited, crouching quietly at the rear of the site throughout the rite. Thereafter, they retreated to the room where the principals were waiting and waited for the next man to be called. Only in the unlikely event of a man whose courage failed him, or a badly aimed stroke by a Second, would the Escorts ever be called upon to use physical force to achieve the ultimate aim of the mission.

✦ ✦ ✦

The first problem to confront the potential Second was how to respond to the command that he serve in this capacity. He should not accept with such enthusiasm that it appeared as though he were hoping to be asked. Yet neither should he act as though he were discommoded by the command. Initially, he should decline, for it was a thankless task. To do the job well in no way redounded to a Second's credit, yet to fail could only shame him. He had to decline gracefully, however, for no samurai dared admit to being so inept that he could not even sever a man's head. Perhaps the best way to go about it, for a younger man, was to protest that he lacked the experience of an older man; or, for an older man, to lament that he lacked the strength of a younger man. Neither tactic was likely to succeed, but at least he would have declined diplomatically.

In the case of the Akō ronin, their Seconds were at least spared the necessity of introducing themselves to their principals and discussing the procedure with them: all of that had been predetermined by the circumstances of their punishment. It had been decided that the ronin would commit seppuku in name only. The nuances of this procedure differed, depending upon the school of swordsmanship in which the Second was trained, but here in a general way is how it was done:

As the principal takes his seat, he greets the emissaries silently with his eyes and a slight nod. The Second, approaching the dais from the rear, kneels to his left and slightly behind him. His face is impassive, his palms resting lightly upon his thighs, his back straight. The principal loosens and removes his vest from his shoulders; slips his arms from his sleeves, first right and then left; and bares his abdomen. While he does this, an assistant approaches and presents him with a platform tray, upon which lies the blade of a short sword wrapped in thick edict paper, from which protrudes 1 or 2 inches of the sharp tip of the blade. The Second gently and slowly rises on his knees and, planting his right foot before him for firm balance, slowly reaches for the hilt of his sword. As he draws, gently and silently so as not to distract his victim, his left hand remains gripping the sheath, and then slides off to rest on his sash. When at last the tip of the blade clears the sheath, his right hand gracefully raises the sword, his body lifts, and his right foot slides to the rear. Now the sword is poised, almost horizontally, behind his head, still held with only one hand. Then, as the principal leans forward, either to draw the tray toward him or to grasp the blade, the Second's sword descends. His right foot again thrusts forward as the full force of his body is directed into the blow, and his left hand rises to meet and grasp the hilt, adding further power to the blade in its final arc as it strikes the back of the victim's neck. If he has gauged the force of the blow with unusual precision, the blade will stop just short of severing the head totally, leaving a narrow lap of skin that will prevent it rolling out of reach. The Second then retracts the blade, keeping it close to his body so as not to draw attention to the blood upon it; drops to one knee and wipes the blade clean with a quire of paper drawn from within his robe; reverses the grip of his right hand from overhand to underhand; and grasps the sheath with his left hand and quietly sheaths the weapon. Such is the nature of the Second's assistance, sparing his principal not only the agony of a prolonged death, but also the pain of thrusting a blade into his own body and pulling it the width of his abdomen. The Second is no executioner; he is the dying man's friend.

This is not to say, however, that there could be no conversation between principal and Second. One aspect of the honor of seppuku was that one's life would be terminated not by an outcast in a prison yard, but by a fellow samurai, ideally of rank comparable to one's own. As we shall see, some of the ronin did greet their Seconds and, in some cases, discreetly ask their rank. Some of the Seconds were indeed chosen for their rank, but even those chosen for their ability, whatever their rank, might answer simply, "I am of proper rank; you may set your mind at ease."

One last task of the Second was to present the head that he had just severed to the emissaries for inspection. The original purpose of this exercise was to ensure that no substitution had been made, that the person beheaded was indeed the intended victim. In the case of the Akō ronin, this was totally superfluous. But because it was so integral an element of seppuku procedure, some of the Seconds nonetheless presented the heads that they had severed for inspection. For this, there were several variant procedures.

If the principal was a man of exalted rank, the Second might have an assistant who would do this duty in his stead. For the Akō ronin, there were no assistants. Yet even when performed by the Second himself, there were various methods. Depending upon the monstrosity of the crime for which the principal was being punished, his head might be held upon the haft of the Second's sword or even upon the sharp edge of the blade. The most honorable way, however, was for the Second to spread another quire of paper on the palm of his left hand, grasp the topknot in the hair of the severed head with his right hand, place it upon the paper in his left hand, and hold it out to the Inspectors. This, I assume, would have been the way the heads of the Akō ronin were presented. Once the Inspectors signaled their satisfaction, the Second restored the head to its body and retired. The rest of the process was of no concern to the Inspectors, and they were freed from viewing it.

◆ ◆ ◆

Once the Second and the Escorts had withdrawn, a folding screen of six pure-white panels was drawn across the front of the dais, and behind it a team of foot soldiers, wearing bloused trousers but no linen vests, came out and wrapped the body and head in the spread that covered the dais. The body was then lifted onto a wooden storm door and carried by two soldiers out beyond the curtains surrounding the site. There it would be marked with an identification tag and placed in one of the burial urns or casks that had been ordered well in advance of the event—just in case.

At the same time, in preparation for the next principal, other members of this detail would be doing their best to camouflage all evidence of the bloody nature of what had just taken place. When a head is suddenly severed, great spurts of blood gush forth from the carotid artery, pumped by the still-beating heart. Depending upon the angle of the torso at that moment, these spouts can travel a considerable distance.

The foot soldiers and menials therefore kept a good supply of sand on hand to spread wherever the blood might fly beyond the limits of the dais. The dais itself, of course, was almost totally renewed, for which a fresh supply of tatami mats, quilts, spreads, and felts was stacked out of sight. Whatever had been soiled could quickly be replaced.

When all had been restored to its original state, the six-fold screen was again shifted to the side of the site, and control of the process returned to the Inspectors, whose first move was to signal the members of the daimyo house that the next man on the list may be summoned to the dais.

*You're absolutely right. There's no need to say
that these men "performed magnificently."*

Migita Saisuke was a middling member of the Hosokawa Corps of
Vassals. But as a scribe in the Directorate of the Domain, he must in
some way have been involved in the layout and installation of the site of
the seppuku and thus, in the suite of the Superintendent of Works, he
was one of those who witnessed the entire procedure. He was also one
of the many who could see that this was an event certain to "go down in
history." Saisuke decided that he could contribute to that process:

> *Saisuke silently scrutinized the entire scene, distinguishing beyond
> doubt the position and rank of everyone from the highest Shogunal
> Emissaries to the lowliest foot soldiers, ascertaining in minute detail
> the numbers of samurai on security duty, committing to memory
> everything he laid eyes upon; and when it was all over, sighing with
> sorrow and driven by a determination born of sadness, he rendered
> in this sketch precisely what he had seen. He then secreted it away
> with his family records, where it has been passed down by his descen-
> dants these hundred and some long years.*

Precisely what Saisuke "rendered in this sketch" remains a mystery—at least as far as the minutiae are concerned. His original sketch
no longer survives, but there are countless copies—or, rather, versions—ranging from simple bird's-eye views to full-color perspectival
paintings more than 1 yard wide. They are all equally useful, for they
are in complete agreement as regards the most important elements of

the scene—the layout of the site, the floor plan of the mansion, the participants, the seating arrangements. And they are all in agreement with the diagram preserved in the Hosokawa house records. The painters of the later copies omitted to depict the Nō stage and the pond at the rear of the site. But neither of these details is crucial to the action and probably they were thought to detract from the composition of the scene. In short, Migita Saisuke has bequeathed to us one of the most telling of all the documents depicting this episode, one that not only enables us to visualize the scene with astonishing accuracy and detail, but greatly enhances our understanding of the written records as well—not only those of the House of Hosokawa, but of all four daimyo.

♦ ♦ ♦

But first, before beginning to work our way through those records, a word of forewarning: the records of the four daimyo houses supply a wealth of detail about the rite of seppuku as they conducted it. But for reasons of reputation, perhaps, and possibly taste, neither the performance of the Seconds nor the end result of their work is mentioned in any of these records. The stroke of a sword might be so perfectly executed as to excite admiration; or too weak to cut more than halfway through the victim's neck; or miss the mark so totally as to strike his head or shoulder, forcing the Escorts to rush forward and support the man until the Second recovers himself. Nothing of this sort is ever mentioned in the records of the daimyo houses. All we are told is that so-and-so "committed seppuku" or such-and-such a Second "did his duty." These written records, then, take us no further than Saisuke's sketch—the sword poised, but yet to cut; the head soon to roll, but still intact; the dais and its surrounds still pristine. What happened next is left almost entirely to the imagination, and there has been no shortage of that. Tales abound of faulty aim, bungled attempts, perseverance despite painful mutilation, and the like. Yet none of these stories are confirmed by anyone who was present. Such mishaps must have occurred, for it is hard to imagine that all forty-six decapitations could have been performed with perfect precision. The total silence of the witnesses, however, leaves us with nothing but hearsay and fabrication.

And it means that we, too, must leave the blood, the gore, and perhaps a bit of inadvertent butchery to the imagination of the reader.

◆ ◆ ◆

The layout of the site described in the Hosokawa house records is exactly the same as that shown in Migita Saisuke's sketch. The ronin, at the far right, awaited their call in the Actors' Room—probably a corner of one of the rooms in which they had been quartered. The men who would serve as their Seconds waited in the adjacent aisle. From the gateway to these rooms, a pathway of rush matting had been laid out, allowing them to walk barefoot across the graveled courtyard, around the Nō stage, and to the white-curtained enclosure, within which was placed the dais upon which they would be seated. The dais itself was made up of three tatami mats laid out in parallel upon a base of rush matting. These mats were covered with a single sheet of white fabric, described alternatively as a spread (*furoshiki*) or a quilt (*awase futon*). On the far side of the enclosure, at the left of the sketch, was an exit through overlapping lengths of brush fencing, beyond which, out of sight of everyone in the courtyard, were stacks of fresh tatami, rush mats, and white spreads, as well as brooms and boxes of sand. Here, too, waited the foot soldiers who would need all these supplies to refurbish the site after each seppuku.

Directly opposite the dais, seated before a folding screen in the main reception room, were the two emissaries sent by the Council of Elders to supervise the rite, while at a slightly lower level, the veranda to this room had been spread with red felt as a seat for the Deputy Inspectors. Lower still, on a row of tatami mats at the base of the veranda, sat the Sub-Inspectors. On either side of these representatives of officialdom sat the several members of the House of Hosokawa who would witness the rite. On the same level as the emissaries but to their rear were the Chief Adjutant and three Elders of the house. Three lesser Adjutants sat on tatami mats to the left of the Sub-Inspectors, while to their right sat two Commanders of the Bodyguard, two Liaison Officers, and the suite of the Superintendent of Works—one of whom, of course, was Migita Saisuke. And at the very rear of the reception room, out of everyone's sight, but with a view of the courtyard, sat His Lordship Hosokawa Etchū-no-Kami, who, mindful of the Elders' stipulation that he "need not be present," had entered unobtrusively from the small reception room.

Once everyone was seated and all was in readiness, two members of the Great Guard, Yoshihiro Kazaemon and Yagi Ichidayū, were to call out the ronin one by one, each to be followed by his Second. Etchū-no-Kami had been careful to observe the etiquette of honor in his appointment of the Seconds. Kuranosuke, the Elder of his house, would be attended by a Company Commander, and the remaining ronin by members of His Lordship's Bodyguard. There was no favoritism in the selection process; the first sixteen men in the order of their precedence in the Bodyguard were assigned this duty.

Kazaemon and Ichidayū were stationed on either side of the gateway to the courtyard. One of them now called out, "Kuranosuke Dono. Come forward, please." As Kuranosuke stood, Ushioda Matanojō rose to his knees and shouted after him: "Kuranosuke Dono! We'll all be coming along right behind you!"

Kuranosuke looked back, smiled and nodded, and then continued on his way. Just beyond the gate, he was met by his two Escorts, both members of the Bodyguard, behind whom followed his Second, Yasuba Ippei. And here is where we come up against the unfortunate reticence of the compilers of the Hosokawa house records. The fullest version of their account reads as follows:

> When his Second had taken his place on the left, a Deputy Herald in full formal linens brought a platform tray upon which a lay a short sword, and placed it before him. Kuranosuke then took up the sword and committed seppuku. Once the Second had done his duty, a white folding screen was placed so as to prevent the emissaries from seeing the body. The body was then wrapped in the spread upon which it lay and removed. The three tatami mats were replaced, as they were in every instance. The process began at about the Seventh Hour and was completed midway through that hour [ca. 4:00–5:00 P.M.].

That is all. The official narrative is filled out a bit by Horiuchi Den'emon, who apparently was in or near the room where the ronin were waiting:

> *As one after another came forward, Kazaemon and Ichidayū would proclaim, "Kuranosuke Dono performed magnificently"; "Chūzaemon Dono performed magnificently." Which they repeated every time. Finally I told them, "There's no need to say they 'performed magnificently'; just call their names." The Seconds, too, were there, awaiting their turns. One of them, Ujiie Heikichi, heard me and, with a smile, said, "You're absolutely right. There's no need to say that these men 'performed magnificently.'"*

In contrast to the extreme reticence of the official Hosokawa house record, however, the compiler of one of those texts speaks out briefly in his own voice and with breathtaking frankness:

> *I hear that when the ronin committed seppuku, the menials charged with cleaning the tatami mats upon which blood had been spilled gathered together, tears in their eyes, and then sucked up and swallowed the blood. I mention this not just to praise the deeds of servants; such were the extremes of emotion to which everyone of whatever rank was moved by the virtue of these men. Useless though it may be, I record this to show how utterly downcast we all felt at that time and that place.*

For the wealth of detail that we do have, we can only be grateful. And yet . . . If only a few of the others who were there could have told us with equal candor what they had seen, thought, and felt that day, what richness and depth it would add to what we already know.

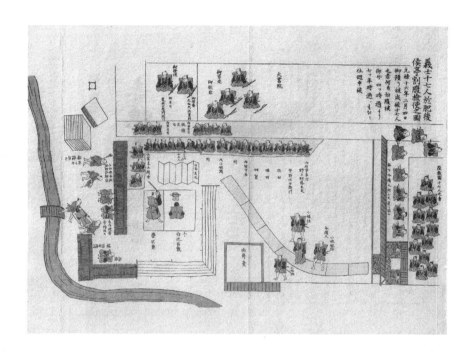

figure 29

A sketch of the site of the seppuku at the Hosokawa Lower Mansion. An
inscription on the sketch from which this was copied reads: "The original version
of this sketch was drawn by Migita Saisuke. In the Genroku era, Saisuke served
as Processional Guide for Lord Tsunatoshi and is said to have been on duty at the
time of the seppuku of the Righteous Samurai. His sketch was in the possession
of old Migita Shizan. On the 15th Day of the First Month of Kyōwa 2 [1802],
however, that sketch was lost to fire when old Migita's home burnt along with
countless other houses. This copy survived in the possession of Migita Shichirō."
(1703.2.4, copied late eighteenth century)

CHAPTER
88

~⚔~

Quite a sight that was, they say.

When last we left the ten ronin in the Hisamatsu Middle Mansion, they had just been sentenced in the main reception chamber and then escorted to the Vanguard duty room, where they awaited their call to the courtyard. They were now dressed in full formal linens and white, unlined kimono.

◆ ◆ ◆

The site of the seppuku in the Hisamatsu mansion was similar to but not quite the same as that at the Hosokawa house. Here, too, the site was laid out in the courtyard of the main reception room. These ronin being of lesser rank, the dais was made of only two tatami mats, placed in parallel on a base of rush matting. Covering the tatami was a large pale-blue quilt, 8 feet square and padded with cotton to deter the leakage of blood. A path of rush matting was laid out across the gravel leading to the dais, and the entire site was surrounded by pale-pink curtains.

The seating arrangements, too, were much the same as at the Hosokawa house: the emissaries at the front of the reception room, directly facing the dais, and the senior officers of the Hisamatsu house on the same level but to the left and rear of them. On the veranda and in the courtyard immediately below it sat the Deputy Inspectors and Sub-Inspectors, while in the courtyard, looking on from either side, were some of the lesser officers of the Hisamatsu Corps of Vassals: Company Commanders, Liaison Officers, Inspectors, and such. His Lordship, too, was present; but like Hosokawa Etchū-no-Kami, he though it politically wise to take the Council of Elders at their word and stay out of sight.

The ronin and their Escorts would enter the site from the left, and their Seconds from the right.

✦ ✦ ✦

Outside the Vanguard duty room, two Samurai Commanders were stationed, awaiting word that the rite could begin. At the command of the emissaries, Miura Jirōzaemon called out, "Ōishi Chikara Dono! Come forward, please." When Chikara stood, Horibe Yasubei, sitting immediately adjacent to him, looked up and said, "Chikara Dono, I'll be coming along right behind you." Their eyes met, and each smiled brightly at the other. Chikara then continued on his way, bowing to the two Company Commanders at the exit as he left.

From the opposite side of the courtyard, his Second, Haga Seidayū, emerged from within the curtain, walked slowly to the dais, and knelt at the rear to the left of the seat. His trousers were bloused above the knee, and he drew his right arm out from the shoulder of his vest and flipped the strap over his back.

As Chikara took his seat, he greeted the emissaries briefly, withdrew his arms from his vest and the sleeves of his kimono, and bared his abdomen. He then turned, nodded, and smiled at Seidayū. "Your rank?" he asked. Seidayū lied and told him what he wanted to hear. "You may set your mind at rest," he said. "I rank high enough to have my own lance bearer." In the meantime, a Deputy Herald had brought a platform tray that he placed before the dais. On it lay a short sword, wrapped in white paper and tied with twisted paper cord, the tip of the blade protruding about 5 inches. As Chikara reached forward to grasp the sword, Seidayū rose and severed his head. He then dropped to one knee, and, with his right hand, grasped the young man's head by his topknot and held it out to the emissaries for their inspection. A white folding screen was quickly placed before the dais to hide the workaday tasks that would follow.

No sooner had the screen been set in place than four liveried menials came out from behind the curtains and pulled the four corners of the quilt together, wrapping within it the body, the head, and the tray.

Seidayū then retreated, and the menials followed, carrying their load out through the exit between the curtains. A sharpened stake bearing Chikara's name had been prepared and was erected beside the bundle. The dais could now be replaced and the site refurbished.

Behind the curtains stood stacks of twenty tatami mats, thirty rush mats, and a pile of ten cotton-filled quilts, as well as several buckets of water and sand. The tatami were quickly replaced and covered with a new quilt. The problem of wayward blood was not so quickly dealt with. Some patches could be washed away; others might be obscured by sprinkling a layer of sand over them. But Seidayū tells us nothing of how that task was accomplished. His description of the event ends here.

◆ ◆ ◆

But I know a man named Ikeda Hajime, who remembers a story that his grandmother told when he was a child. Ikeda's mother died when she was only thirty-three, and his father, who worked for a bank, was very busy; so the children were raised by their grandmother. This is one of the stories she told them:

> I was married from the Arakawa house into the Ikeda house. The Arakawa were of much higher rank than the Ikeda, and if things had been as they were in the Edo period, such a marriage would never have been permitted. But Grandpa persisted, and so we were married.
>
> The Arakawa were Deputy Inspectors and for generations had been Masters of Swordsmanship in the Matsuyama domain. One of my ancestors was named Arakawa Jūdayū, and when the Akō ronin were in their custody, he served as Second for both Horibe Yasubei and Fuwa Kazuemon. They say that he was a very skilled swordsman.
>
> On the day of the seppuku, Ōishi Chikara, the eldest son of the leader, was the first to go. He was still very young and a fine figure of a man. When he was beheaded, a great gush of blood spurted out.

There was a plum tree in bloom in the corner of the garden, and blood flew all the way over there. Quite a sight that was, they say. Attending to his body took a long time.

Next was Horibe Yasubei, hero of the battle at Takadanobaba. He turned to the rear and said to Jūdayū, "Your rank?" "You've no worries," Jūdayū replied. But Yasubei continued to stare straight at him, and so Jūdayū lied. "I am in the Horse Guards," he said, "200 koku." If he had told his true rank, it would have shamed the house; thereafter, His Lordship praised him, saying, "Your impromptu response was superb." And he was rewarded. Each of the Seconds had mortuary tablets made for the ronin they had beheaded. In the Arakawa house, we had those tablets for a long time.

I was told these stories over and over again as a child, and I always wondered if they were true. So at a meeting of the Haiku Society, I asked the Governor about it, and he said, "It's true all right. It's clearly recorded, right there in our house records." The Governor of Ehime in those days was Hisamatsu Sadatake, heir to the last lord of the domain; but in Matsuyama, at meetings of the Haiku Society, we mingled with no concern for differences in rank.

The house records mention none of the others who followed, except to say that after Ōshima Hanbei had "assisted" Nakamura Kansuke, the emissaries announced that it would no longer be necessary to present the heads of the ronin for inspection.

◆ ◆ ◆

They also mention the last of the ronin, Ōtaka Gengo. Gengo must have noticed the same plum tree of which Ikeda's grandmother speaks, for before he was called, he asked his guards if he could borrow a writing brush. Not a proper brush with an inkstone, just one of those little brushes that travelers carry for jotting down notes, one that fits into a little wooden case with a bit of ink stored in it. As it happened, one of the guards had one, and Gengo used it to write his very last haiku on a sheet of paper from a quire that he carried:

ume de nomu / chaya mo arubeshi / shide no yama
Surely there's a teahouse where we'll drink beneath the plums,
on the mountain road to death.

The reason that both Seidayū and Jūdayū had to lie about their status was that the Hisamatsu chose their Seconds by entirely different criteria from those used by the Hosokawa. Hosokawa Etchū-no-Kami was genuinely respectful of the honor that accrued to a principal in having a Second whose rank was roughly equivalent to his own. As we have seen, he assigned a Company Commander to "assist" Kuranosuke and the first sixteen members of his Bodyguard to the others. Even old Horiuchi Den'emon was told that he might be asked to serve as a Second, simply because he had become such a close friend of the ronin while they were in custody. Their skill as swordsmen was not considered, only their rank or relationship. And each Second was to "assist" only one of the ronin.

The Hisamatsu did the exact opposite. In the first place, only five Seconds were appointed, each of whom had to "assist" two ronin. And these five were selected only for their repute as swordsmen. As we have seen, Haga Seidayū was excessively proud of his warrior-like qualities. And Arakawa Jūdayū was the Master of Swordsmanship in the Hisamatsu house, teacher to everyone in the Corps of Vassals and even to the lord of the domain, if he desired it. What the qualifications of the other three Seconds were, we are not told. We do know, though, that all of them were of very low rank, three of them Deputy Inspectors and two of them dismounted samurai in the Vanguard, all of them on stipends of less than 20 koku. The ronin in the custody of the Hisamatsu were not the highest-ranking members of their league, but more than half of them had been enfeoffed at 100 to 200 koku. Seidayū and Jūdayū were simply being considerate of the feelings of their principals when they lied about their rank.

◆ ◆ ◆

Seidayū was fully conscious of these differences. He even goes so far as to recount a story he had heard about a bungled beheading at the Hosokawa house:

I've heard that the Second for Hara Sōemon, in the custody of Hosokawa Etchū-no-Kami Sama, aimed too low and hit him square on the shoulder. This knocked him flat on his face. But he rose up again and braced himself, placing his hands together on the mat before him. "You haven't cut it off yet," he said. "Now calm down." And he let the man try again. Whether this is true or false, I don't know. But it is rumored that one of the Seconds in the service of Etchū Sama has been placed in Domiciliary Confinement for having failed to perform his duty properly.

Needless to say, no mention of such a bungled attempt is to be found in any of the Hosokawa house records. They tell us only that "they all met their end in the most admirable manner." But Seidayu's rumor is at least one that originated with and traveled among samurai directly involved in this massive exercise in seppuku. It may even be true.

*I am sorry that I must soil
your hands today.*

From the very start, matters had not gone smoothly at the Mōri house. The Elders claimed not to have known before the arrival of the emissaries whether the ronin would be sentenced to banishment or seppuku. And when His Lordship Mōri Kai-no-Kami greeted the emissaries, they responded with a curt reminder that his presence was not required. A bit later, when the Deputy Inspectors were shown the seppuku site that the Mōri had prepared, they decreed that it was too cramped and must be moved to the courtyard of the reception rooms.

Now, however, all seemed to be in readiness. The ten ronin and their Escorts were seated in the great entry hall, awaiting their call; the white curtains and screens had been moved; the dais was in place, while in the reception rooms and the courtyard all were seated, in much the same arrangement as at the Hosokawa and Hisamatsu houses. In the rearmost chamber of the reception rooms, Mōri Kai-no-Kami and his son watched, well out of sight of the censorious emissaries.

But then someone noticed—and brought it to the attention of the emissaries—that no blades had been prepared. The Mōri had assumed that since the ronin were to be beheaded before they could reach a sword, fans would suffice. And so they had wrapped ten fans in white paper to take the place of the swords. The emissaries advised them immediately that this would not be acceptable, that it did not show proper respect for the honor of the ronin, and that they must replace the fans with ten real swords. Somehow, they managed to do so. At last, Harada Shōgen, at the entrance to the courtyard, could call out, "Okajima Yasoemon!

Come forward, please." And Fukuhara Heima, at the rear exit of the site, could summon Sakaki Shōemon, the first of the five Seconds.

✦ ✦ ✦

The rite was not uneventful, and the Mōri seem to have been willing to mention some of its high points. They noted, first of all, the politeness of the ronin. Most of them, they said, in one way or another, greeted their Seconds in a friendly manner, either asking their names or assuring them that they might be at their ease. The seppuku of old Muramatsu Kihei, however, aroused particular admiration.

"May I ask your name?" he said to his Second.

"I am Tagami Gozaemon," the man replied.

"I am sorry that I must soil your hands today. But I am an old man and shall probably be quite clumsy. I must ask your forbearance for this."

The emissaries must have been touched by this, for despite all that they had thus far found fault with, one of them now exclaimed, "Splendid! Just splendid!"

✦ ✦ ✦

Of quite a different sort was the seppuku of Hazama Shinroku. What little we know about Shinroku suggests that he was an impetuous young man. His elder brother Jūjirō—something of a hero for having been the first to wound Kira with his lance—was to have inherited the position of his father, Hazama Kihei, in the Horse Guards. And Shinroku had been adopted as the heir of his father's cousin Satomura Tsūemon, also a member of the Akō Corps of Vassals. But Shinroku seems not to have got on well with the Satomura family, and he absconded to Edo. There he was taken in by his elder sister Suma, who was married to Chūdō Matasuke, a samurai in the service of Akimoto Tajima-no-Kami, whom we know well by now as a member of the Council of Elders. Strictly speaking, then, Shinroku was a runaway and thus a ronin at the time of the Catastrophe, but that technicality seems to have been ignored when he moved in with his father and brother and began to function as a member of the pact. His behavior at the time of his seppuku is of a piece with that of his earlier years.

~ 733 ~

The normal procedure would have been for Shinroku to take his seat on the dais, greet his Second, reach out and draw the platform tray and the sword toward him, slip his vest and robe from his shoulders and bare his abdomen, and, finally, reach forward and grasp the sword—at which point, his Second would sever his head. Shinroku did none of this. Instead, the moment the tray was placed before him, he snatched up the blade and drove it straight into his abdomen. His Second, Era Seikichi, was caught off guard, but recovered himself quickly enough to decapitate Shinroku without further disruption.

The process then continued as normal. But the emissaries were perplexed. It *looked* to them as though Shinroku had stabbed himself. But had he? They asked to examine the body—in order to do which the Sub-Inspectors had to remove it from its funerary cask. Upon inspection, though, they found that Shinroku not only had stabbed himself, but had managed to cut 6 or 7 inches across his abdomen. Hazama Shinroku was thus the only one of the forty-six ronin actually to commit seppuku.

♦ ♦ ♦

Less spectacularly, but still quite revealing, the Mōri noted that when the heads were held up for inspection, some of them had not been completely severed and had to be cut loose by the Seconds, probably with their short swords. All was not absolute perfection.

♦ ♦ ♦

It was well after the Seventh Hour (ca. 4:30 P.M.) by the time the rite was completed and the Shogunal officials were preparing to leave and return to the castle. But the Inspector Suzuki Jirōzaemon made a point of summoning the two Elders of the house, Tashiro Kaname and Tokita Gondayū, to thank them for their efforts: "These men have been in your custody for a very long time, throughout which you have shown uncommon care and consideration. And your execution of the sentence today—in particular, the skill with which your Seconds performed their duty—has been superb. All of which we shall duly report to the Council of Elders. We trust that you yourselves will pass this on to Kai-no-Kami."

Kaname and Gondayū then asked the emissaries what they should now do with the bodies of the ronin and their possessions, and were told that they might do as they please. Apparently, neither the emissaries nor the house Elders were yet aware of the consensus that every body and every thing should be sent to Sengakuji.

＋ ＋ ＋

Or perhaps I should say almost every man. For while Naitō Kakuzaemon and Kaneko Rokurōemon were supervising the dismantling of the site and the preparations for transfer of the bodies, they were told that two vassals of Akimoto Tajima-no-Kami had come, bearing a letter requesting that the body of Hazama Shinroku be handed over to another of Tajima-no-Kami's vassals, Chūdō Matasuke. The request could only have originated with Shinroku's sister Suma, who was married to Matasuke and, through her husband, had been able to borrow a bit of the power of the Council of Elders. It was a request that it would have been unwise to deny, and so the next morning, another vassal of Tajima-no-Kami arrived to collect the cask containing the body of Shinroku, along with his swords, lance, and coat of mail, as well as the clothes he had worn on the night of the attack. It is said that a similar request was sent to the Mizuno house, but that it arrived too late. The body of Suma's other brother, Hazama Jūjirō, had already been sent to Sengakuji.

＋ ＋ ＋

The Mōri house records, although fragmentary, are refreshingly open by comparison with those of the other houses. There is one matter, though—a lacuna, it seems to me—that I can't help wondering about. No one mentions, or even appears to have noticed, how ironic a twist of fate it was that Takebayashi Tadashichi should die at the hands of the Mōri. These people were descendants of Mōri Terumoto, the great warlord who had spared the life of Tadashichi's Chinese grandfather, Meng Erh-k'uan, after the horrific battle of Namwŏn in 1597, and then brought him safely to Japan. And strange it was, too, that Tadashichi's death should be witnessed by Asonuma Shinbei, descendant of the Mōri commander who had first captured Erh-k'uan, and then cared for him over the next few years in Hiroshima. Tadashichi himself never forgot his Chinese ancestors. Had the Mōri forgotten their own connection with his grandfather?

◆ ◆ ◆

The house records of the Mizuno contain the most cryptic description of the seppuku of any of those of the four daimyo houses. We are fortunate to be able to consult the sketch of the scene at the Hosokawa house and the written descriptions of those at the Hisamatsu and Mōri houses; with that wealth of foreknowledge, we can see from what the Mizuno tell us that they conducted the rite in almost precisely the same manner. The only differences at all worth remarking are that the principals were allowed to wear sandals when crossing the courtyard to the dais and that the dais itself was covered with not only a white quilt. but also a bolt of red felt.

We are fortunate, too, that a physician in the service of the Mizuno, Tōjō Shusetsu, almost immediately after the seppuku, compiled an account of the entire incident: *Sekijō shiwa*. Some of his account was, necessarily, based upon hearsay, but his knowledge of events at the Mizuno house was firsthand. He, too, has little to say about the rite itself—although he does note that not all the heads were completely severed and had to be "cut loose from below when presented to the emissaries for inspection." He does, however, illuminate the periphery in interesting ways.

◆ ◆ ◆

We have seen, for example, that the nine ronin in custody at the Mizuno house were the lowest ranking of those who participated in the attack. Yet some of them seem to have been inordinately concerned about their position within their own ranks. Kanzaki Yogorō was listed to be the last to commit seppuku—but he seems to have thought that he should be the second from the last.

"Why do I come after Mimura Jirōzaemon?" he asked. "I rank higher than him."

"When you were taken into custody, Sengoku Hōki-no-Kami Sama gave us a list," Yamakawa Kurōemon told him. "That's the order everyone is in, and there's nothing we can do now to change it."

"Well, all right, then, if that's the way it is," Yogorō grudgingly agreed.

◆ ◆ ◆

Yokogawa Kanpei was third from the last to die, but his death poem makes one wonder if he, too, might not have aspired to a higher place in the hierarchy:

> *mate shibashi shide ni chisoku wa arinutomo*
> *ware sakigakete michishirube sen*
> Wait! Just a moment! Some of us may go sooner and some later,
> but I'll take the lead and show you all the right way to go.

Other sources tell us that His Lordship Mizuno Kenmotsu won the admiration of his men in the way he selected those who were to serve as Seconds. *Hiyōroku*, a document produced within the Mizuno house, describes his arrival at the Mita mansion on the morning of the day of the seppuku:

> *At that time, he still had not appointed those who were to serve as Seconds that day. Two men of the Horse Guards, Shibata Sadaemon and Matsuzaki Gorōbei, had been told in advance that they would serve as his personal attendants, but everyone was wondering just what his intentions were now. Whereupon, as he mounted the steps to the entry hall, he turned and personally commanded that all eight of the men who had accompanied his palanquin, as well as one of his Samurai Commanders, were to serve as Seconds for the ronin in their custody. All of them expressed their acquiescence, and there on the gravel surrounds of the path drew their swords part way to show His Lordship. All were in possession of superb blades, and most of them highly skilled in the martial arts.*

Another source tells a similar story that is more revealing of His Lordship's reasoning. One of his Elders asked him to name the men who were to serve as Seconds:

> "No," His Lordship replied, "if I do that, then those who are selected will feel honored and those who have not been selected will lose face. After all, no one is accustomed to serving as a Second, much less has anyone become highly skilled at it. If you sever the head, the job is done. And even if you fail, it is nothing to be ashamed of. Just tell those who happen to be on duty today that they are to do it."
>
> The Elder did as he was told, and the samurai who were on duty that day were grateful. They executed their assignment calmly and with no fear of failure. As a result, all of them performed well.

Finally, Tōjō Shusetsu tells a story of a group of samurai, some old and some young, discussing the seppuku:

> One man said: "Kuranosuke and his men are a rare breed. I can think of no one, even in the distant past, who is their equal as Righteous Samurai. But to condemn them to death is just too pitiless and cruel. If they had placed them in the custody of daimyo, or banished them to an island, it would have done no damage whatever to the Shogunate's prestige or impaired its power to govern."
>
> Whereupon a wrinkled, old samurai spoke up: "It is indeed a pity, and I, too, wish their lives could have been spared. But sentencing them to seppuku may in the end have been for the best. A man may, throughout his lifetime, comport himself in ways that are both praiseworthy and righteous. But not everyone possesses the perfection of a sage; some are bound to go wrong. In the past, there have been those who, although renowned for their prowess on the battlefield, have foolishly gone down in defeat. Even if the ronin had been spared, how much longer would they have to live? As the old saying goes, 'To die here and now is no loss.' There could

be nothing finer for them than to commit seppuku and die a noble death in high repute."

Everyone agreed that the old man had a point.

CHAPTER
90

Just as the ronin desired.

News travels strange routes. At the temple Sengakuji, the monks' first inkling of what was to happen that day came just as they were beginning their midday meal. Suddenly, their local greengrocer burst into the refectory. "At the Hosokawa mansion, just up the hill—the ronin are about to commit seppuku!" he shouted. "Everyone was so shocked," Sekishi tells us, "that they lost their grip and dropped their chopsticks." What happened next, no one says. Not until much later in the day did news of all that had been going on that afternoon begin to make the rounds.

◆ ◆ ◆

The four daimyo houses had been in frequent touch with one another throughout their custody of the ronin, in the course of which the lesser three looked to the leadership of the greatest and most powerful of their number: Hosokawa Etchū-no-Kami. This we know from occasional mentions of their meetings in the records of all four daimyo. The decision to bury the ronin at the temple Sengakuji is but one more example of an agreement among the four that somehow coalesced in a manner that no one discussed.

Some of the house records note that inquiries about what should be done with the bodies of the ronin had at first been directed to the Council of Elders, to Sengoku Hōki-no-Kami, and even to the Inspectors sent as emissaries. Everyone replied, simply and unhelpfully, "Do as you please." But by the time something actually had to be done, all were agreed that their destination should be Sengakuji. That, too, may have been at the suggestion of the Hosokawa, for Horiuchi Den'emon has told us that the ronin, soon after their arrival, had asked to be buried together in a single hole by the grave of their lord.

And so, "just as the ronin desired," the Hosokawa sent their Chief Deputy Herald, Hirano Tan'emon, to Sengakuji to request the burial of the ronin (although not in a single hole, of course). Temple officials told him that they would reply as soon as the Commissioner of Temples and Shrines responded to their application for permission. A bit later, the Hosokawa sent Itō Kihei, a member of the Bodyguard, to ask that the funeral not be an elaborate formal ceremony, but something of a simpler sort, to which the temple agreed. The temple officials did ask, though, that the bodies not be sent before the middle of the Sixth Hour (ca. 7:00 P.M.), as they were not expecting to hear from the Commissioner of Temples and Shrines before then.

When the Mizuno sent a similar request, they were advised that the Hosokawa had already been in touch with the temple, and plans were in place to bury the ronin there, but that they should wait to see whether the Commissioner of Temples and Shrines would impose any restrictions.

Once permission had been granted, however, the temple was faced with a formidable logistical problem. According to the novice Hakumyō, "There was no place to bury them. But then the Bursar had a sudden inspiration. 'We'll clear away the bamboo thicket just next to the Asano graves'—which we then made haste to do. That done, however, Asano Dono's grave turned out to be at a lower level than the thicket. But there was no open land other than the thicket; so that was that, their graves would just have to be a little higher."

The Hisamatsu mention sending their Superintendent of Works as well as carpenters, to which Haga Seidayū adds that he also sent "men to help prepare the site." This suggests that the temple had had to ask the daimyo to send day laborers to clear the bamboo thicket, for this was no simple matter of cutting down trees. The root system of even the slenderest bamboo is an invasive maze of tough intertwining shoots. The entire network would have to be exposed and uprooted in order to restore the plot to its original state as workable soil. The Bursar's inspiration may have saved the day, but it could not have been accomplished as easily as Hakumyō makes it sound.

♦ ♦ ♦

The sun had gone below the hills at the rear of the temple well before the time bell began tolling the Sixth Hour (6:00 P.M.). By then, the monks were raising rows of white lanterns on either side of the stepped slope leading up to the middle gate. And in the broad quadrangle between the central hall and the foundation stones of the once-grand main gate, logs were laid out on the bare earth, upon which the palanquins carrying the bodies of the forty-six ronin could be lined up. It was not until the Hour of the Dog (ca. 7:00 P.M.), however, that messenger monks were dispatched to tell the daimyo that they might now send the dead. It would be nighttime when the funeral processions began arriving, but the way would be well lit and the temple well prepared.

♦ ♦ ♦

The funeral processions, although not as grand as those sent to take custody of the ronin, were similarly composed. The Hisamatsu had sent three hundred men to fetch the ronin, but dispatched only two hundred to bury them. In their solemnity, though, these processions were nonetheless impressive. There were, of course, individual palanquins for each of the dead, each carrying a funerary cask containing the body and head of a ronin, the short sword he had not been allowed to use, and the tray upon which the sword had been presented—all still wrapped and tied in the spread upon which he died. At least two of the houses, and perhaps others as well, had had new palanquins constructed for the occasion. To each was affixed a name tag.

The ronin were well attended, too, although on this journey there was no suggestion that their attendants were doubling as guards. A typical arrangement consisted of four foot soldiers and one or two samurai accompanying each palanquin, preceded by a large lantern atop a tall shaft and one or two hand-held lanterns. In the vanguard were three or four higher-ranking samurai on horseback, and a similar rear guard—which also included a column of foot soldiers, but no musketeers.

♦ ♦ ♦

The first to arrive were the seventeen men who had been in the custody of Hosokawa Etchū-no-Kami, his mansion being the closest to the temple. Then one after another came the processions of Mizuno Kenmotsu, Hisamatsu Oki-no-Kami, and Mōri Kai-no-Kami. The bodies in their casks remained just as they had been after their seppuku, still dressed in their formal linens and kimono; and so they would remain when buried. As they arrived, Ryōden, a temple Elder, examined them, one by one, presumably to verify each man's identity.

The process, Hakumyō tells us, began early in the Hour of the Boar (ca. 9:00 P.M.) and ended late in the Hour of the Ox (ca. 3:00 A.M.). What a full formal funeral—such as the Hosokawa requested *not* be performed—would have consisted of, I have no idea. The funeral that *was* performed consisted of three rites, all conducted by the Abbot himself: the Final Guidance, the granting of posthumous names, and the ceremony called Taking Up the Torch.

♦ ♦ ♦

Final Guidance (*indō*) refers to the last words of the Abbot to the departed, intended to guide them on their way to enlightenment in the next incarnation. Sengakuji being a Zen temple, the Abbot chose to recite a koan, one of those perversely illogical dialogues used by Zen masters to jolt disciples out of their mundane thoughts and shock them into enlightenment. Considering the nature of those he was addressing, the Abbot chose the "Sword Blade Koan" from the *Records of Rinzai* as his words of Final Guidance:

> The Master ascended the hall. A monk asked, "What is meant by this matter of the sword blade?"
>
> The Master said, "Fearful! Fearful!"
>
> The monk was about to speak, whereupon the Master struck him.

As it happened, this text was particularly appropriate, not only because the ronin had lived by the sword and died by the sword, but also because it provided two highly appropriate characters—sword (*ken* 剣) and blade (*nin* 刃) that could be used in every one of their posthumous names.

A Buddhist posthumous name (*hōmyō*) corresponds to the name that a monk is given when he takes vows while still living. When he first enters orders, a monk is given a two-character Taboo Name (*imina*), so called because originally, in China, this name was not to be spoken. Then, when a monk is deemed sufficiently advanced in his training to transmit the Buddha's teachings to others, he is given a two-character Way Name (*dōgō*), which is placed before his Taboo Name. In granting a posthumous name, however, both Taboo Name and Way Name are given simultaneously, and to them is attached a designation of ecclesiastical rank. Thus the formula followed by the Sengakuji Abbot in creating posthumous names for the ronin was "Blade-X, X-Sword, Lay Believer." Horibe Yasubei is NIN-Un Ki-KEN Shinji (BLADE-Cloud Gleam-SWORD Lay Believer), and Fuwa Kazuemon is NIN-Kan So-KEN Shinji (BLADE-Observe Founder-SWORD Lay Believer). And all the others are named similarly, except for Ōishi Kuranosuke, who, as their leader, was granted a slightly more elaborate name: Chūsei-in NIN-Kū Jō-KEN Koji (Loyal Leader BLADE-Void Pure-SWORD Lay Devotee).

The Abbot recited his Final Guidance text separately for each of the four groups of ronin as they arrived and were lined up in the quadrangle before the central hall. "Immediately thereafter," Haga Seidayū tells us, "they were taken to the graveyard and buried."

It must have been early in the process that the monk Taiun—an old disciple of the previous Abbot—had drawn up the plan of the graveyard, but no one mentions when the graves were actually dug and by whom. Seidayū's account is corroborated by another source that says, "After the Final Guidance, the ronin in their casks were buried," so the excavation must have been completed—or at least well under way—by the time the bodies were moved to the graveyard.

◆ ◆ ◆

The last of the three rites, Taking Up the Torch (*hinko no butsuji*), could have been performed only at the graveyard, but all we are told is that

（東京芝高輪泉岳寺）　四十七義士ノ墓全景

figure 30
The graveyard of the ronin at Sengakuji as Ōhashi Yoshizō would have seen it,
shown here in an early-twentieth-century postcard. (Private collection)

it took place. As its name suggests, it originates in an early form of the cremation ritual in which the officiating monk actually took up a torch and lit the pyre himself. In later years, this practice seems to have been simplified, using only a symbolic torch. And in the case of burials, the officiant would not even wield a symbolic torch, but instead a mattock. How this rite was performed at Sengakuji we have no idea. But this may well have been the occasion of the great gathering described by Sekishi, at which every monk in the temple was present, including all the novices, 161 of them, and probably many more men, high and low, from the four daimyo houses. How we wish that we knew what they saw.

◆ ◆ ◆

When it was all over, the carpenters from the four daimyo houses set to work. They built a sturdy 3-foot bamboo fence around each of the graves, leaving an opening at the front through which offerings could be made. When they finished, the lanterns before each grave were left burning through the rest of the night.

Come morning, Hakumyō tells us, laborers were sent from the kitchens to remove all the bamboo that had been cut down and dug out in the night. The rest of their day was spent "hauling away earth and stones, leveling the site, cleaning the graves, decorating them with flowers and offerings of incense." If you visit the graveyard today, you will see that the ronin now rest, respectfully, at a slightly lower level than their lord.

CHAPTER
91

————

Those seventeen brave men will serve us well
as guardian deities of this estate.

For the living, the seppuku of the ronin could not yet be shunted into the past. This seems to have been just as true for the townsfolk of Edo as for the samurai who were directly involved.

♦ ♦ ♦

Rumor had spread through the wards that day even faster than through the intelligence networks of the military houses. The deliverymen and shopkeepers would have been the first to notice when they found the gates of four great houses closed to them, and at an hour when normally there would be steady traffic into and out of the kitchens and store-houses of those mansions. Then later in the day came the four official delegations, spreading out from the castle. And, finally, the funeral processions to Sengakuji. By nightfall, the town had made up its mind what it thought and would make known its judgment in a most unusual and unexpected way.

Early the next morning, a Constable from the office of the City Magistrate encountered evidence of a crime that he had never before had to deal with. On his rounds through the Nihonbashi district, he was just crossing the great bridge that gives the neighborhood its name. This being the bridge that marks the starting point of all the highways that lead out of Edo, it was also one of the principal sites for the posting of government notices on signboards. Of course, a Constable who crosses the bridge nearly every morning seldom even notices these fixtures. But on the morning of the 5th, as he began the descent from the arch of the bridge, he noticed a long black smudge on the right-hand side of the foremost signboard. In Genroku, you see, the first article of the General Admonitions posted on all official notice boards read: "The Military and Civil arts, as well as Loyalty and Filiality, are to be encouraged. Proper decorum is to be observed." This entire article had been obliterated. For reasons that we can perhaps imagine, the vandal seems to have been particularly concerned that no trace of the word "loyalty" remain. A generation earlier, this injunction would have applied only to the military estate, but the present Shogun was proclaiming it applicable to all, townsmen included. So the townsmen were letting him know what they thought of his own treatment of the loyal.

The Constable returned immediately to Hatchobori to report this offense to his superior, who deemed it serious enough to bring to the attention of the Magistrate himself. Defacing an official decree is no mere misdemeanor. The Magistrate, in turn, assigned the case to the Special Investigator for Arson and Robbery, who immediately rounded up several suspects and sources, some of whom were questioned with considerable severity. Yet these efforts failed to turn up a single witness or the slightest clue to the crime. No one would admit even to having seen it. At the end of the day, they were left with no choice but to release everyone they had arrested and order the Department of Works to inscribe and install a new plaque.

I cannot imagine why the Magistrate thought *that* would resolve the matter. Surely either he or the Special Investigator should have kept the bridge under surveillance throughout the night. But apparently, neither of them did. And the next morning, the new notice board had been not simply defaced, but ripped from the earth and flung into the river. What was more, all the signboards bearing the same injunction in Shinagawa, Senju, Yotsuya—every entrance to the city—had been smeared with ink or pelted with mud. By now, even some of the officers in the Magistracy were whispering that this might be the result of official misjudgment. It would be damaging to governmental authority if the notice boards were not replaced at all. But perhaps some other worthy sentiment— for the time being, at least—could be substituted for the exhortation to loyalty. And this, they say, was when the first article of the General

Admonitions was changed to read: "Parents and children, brothers and sisters, husbands and wives, all kinsmen shall endeavor to live in harmony with one another; and even the lowliest of their servants shall be treated with kindness. Those in the service of a lord or master shall perform their appointed duties with all diligence."

◆ ◆ ◆

In the daimyo houses, there were far more mundane, but nonetheless demanding, tasks that remained. The Shogunate's highest-ranking officials—the Council of Elders, the Junior Council, the Adjutants, the Duty Inspector General—all had to be informed that the sentence rendered the previous day had been duly executed. The lord of each domain would himself report to the Duty Elder, and his senior officers would be delegated to inform the other Elders and ranking officials. Those officials, of course, knew full well that the sentence had been executed, but formal notification by gentlemen of consequence was considered of great importance.

And then there was the matter of gifts and financial considerations. Everyone from the Council of Elders, who first issued the sentence, down to the foot soldiers and liveried menials who attended to the bodies, was rewarded by all four daimyo houses, each in proportion to his rank and the rated wealth of the domain in question. The more exalted recipients were sent bolts of expensive fabrics in varying numbers, while those lower in rank than the Shogunal Emissaries were presented with descending amounts of cash.

Of course, Sengakuji, too, would be paid munificently, for both the ministrations on the day of the burial and the observances that would follow at the appointed intervals. On the day of the burial, the Hosokawa sent thirty gold pieces to the temple as a burial fee; the Hisamatsu, fifty pieces of silver; the Mōri, ten of silver; and the Mizuno, twenty of silver. The next day, the Hosokawa and the Hisamatsu each sent fifty more gold pieces, and the Mōri and the Mizuno sent twenty each.

The records of the Hisamatsu house note, too, that all five men who had served as Seconds were given three gold pieces to cover the cost of having the blades of their swords repaired. Perhaps the same was done in the other houses as well.

The most mundane task of all, however, was that, early that morning, the Hosokawa arranged to have seventeen very large stones hauled to Sengakuji, to be placed atop the grave mounds of the ronin who had been in their custody. The other three daimyo houses must have done the same, for such was the finishing touch to all forty-six graves— as a deterrent to grave robbery by unscrupulous souvenir seekers or impious profiteers.

♦ ♦ ♦

Another question that all four houses asked of those in authority was what to do with all the possessions of the ronin. At first, the answer to that, too, was that they could do as they pleased. But, again, a consensus somehow—somewhere—coalesced, and by the time of the burial, all four houses were agreed that everything, particularly the weapons, should be sent to Sengakuji.

The Hisamatsu were the most thoroughgoing in their execution of this agreement. They sent not only bows, arrows, swords, great swords, coats of mail, helmets, and the outfits worn on the night of the attack, but also all the clothing given to the ronin while in custody, and even their nightwear, bedding, buckets, and basins. All of which they packed into ten new baskets and portable chests for delivery to the temple.

The account that gives us the best sense, though, of what it felt like to those who had known the ronin, and now had to sort through the possessions of their dead friends, is that of Horiuchi Den'emon:

> That night, the house Elders told us, "There probably is written matter in the clothing and paper folds of these men. Check everything carefully, and if you find anything suspicious, let us see it." Hayashi Hyōsuke had gone to Sengakuji, so Murai Genbei, Yoshihiro Kazaemon, Yagi Ichidayū, and I lit candles, inspected everything, and put it in portable chests to be sent to Sengakuji. I myself inspected the effects of Kuranosuke Dono, Jūrōzaemon Dono, Jūnai Dono, and Gengoemon Dono.

We were told to inspect everything very carefully, but when I saw the tags with their names on them, it just made me weep; I couldn't even look at them. Some of us didn't inspect anything at all carefully. Many of their paper folds had handwritten talismans in them. When we showed them to Chūzaemon and Tōbei, they said, "Just put them back where they were." They were all resigned to dying, but nothing they had written was at all slapdash. For me to disturb any of it would be unforgivable, so I left most of their things just as they were.

When the job was done, we were served a meal, but I had no appetite. I mixed a bit of hot water with the rice, and then after the Ninth Hour [midnight] returned home. I felt totally drained of energy, but didn't sleep a wink that night.

◆ ◆ ◆

There were also those in the Hosokawa house who felt that the violent death of seventeen men in one of the main courtyards of the mansion had so polluted the place that it would have to be purified—a ritual that could be performed only by Buddhist monks. Again, Horiuchi Den'emon tells the story:

Thereafter, someone in the Directorate of the Domain sent word, informally, to the temple Shinzōin that they would soon be needed to purify the site of the seppuku. But that was not to be. When word of this reached His Lordship, he said, "That will not be necessary. Just leave things as they are. Those seventeen brave men will serve us well as guardian deities of this estate." Tears came to my eyes when I thought how gratified they would be to hear that, resting there beneath the grass.

I understand that the other three daimyo houses had their seppuku sites purified. I've also heard that Sengoku Hōki-no-Kami Sama resurfaced the tatami mats and re-papered the lower half of the sliding panels in the room where he received the ronin—most likely, I thought, because he felt that his position as Inspector General demanded special measures.

I hear, too, that when close friends visit, His Lordship now tells them that "this site of their seppuku is a place of historic significance."

At the Shinzōin, they thought it very strange that His Lordship should refuse to have so defiled a site purified. But the story has spread far and wide throughout the city, and everyone praises him for it—so the townsfolk tell me.

*We are as a single body with
four mouths to feed.*

The guilty were dead and buried, but those whose only crime was to be related to the guilty had yet to be dealt with. As we have seen, Onodera Jūnai repeatedly warned his wife, O-Tan, that she might be punished, and Ōishi Kuranosuke went so far as to write a formal letter of divorce so that O-Riku could not be forced to share his guilt. And his second son, Kichinoshin, took vows and entered holy orders to escape that fate. The documents no longer survive, but it is said that others, too, broke off relations with their families when the attack was finally decided upon. Those whose menfolk had not broken with them were now about to learn what their fate would be.

There was good reason that the first sets of genealogical records submitted by the ronin were sent back, stipulating that the names and ages of their children be added. Someone in the castle had realized, just in time, that most likely it would be the children who were punished after the ronin were dead. Using these records, a list was compiled of nineteen sons of the ronin; together with the decree specifying their punishment, the list was forwarded to the City Magistrate, Yasuda Echizen-no-Kami. The decree read:

> *Your fathers, on the pretext of avenging themselves upon their lord's enemy, and in an unlawful league of forty-six men, broke into the residence of Kira Kōzuke-no-Suke bearing assault weapons, and killed Kōzuke. For this egregious defiance of constituted authority,*

they were sentenced to commit seppuku. In consequence thereof,
their sons are now to be banished to a distant island.

YEAR OF THE RAM, SECOND MONTH, 4TH DAY

There must also have been an attachment sent with the decree, for the sentence was not to be applied unconditionally. The sentence makes it clear that no women and no male kin other than sons were to be punished. And only those sons aged fifteen or over were to be banished forthwith. Those under that age would be placed in the custody of their immediate families until they reached fifteen, at which age they, too, would be banished. Those sons who had entered holy orders would be spared banishment regardless of their age.

On the 5th Day, the Magistrate summoned all those on the list then resident in Edo to appear before him on the following morning, the 6th. He also ordered that the lords of the domains in which the others lived be instructed to execute the sentence in his stead.

Of the nineteen on the list, only four were of an age to be banished straightaway: Nakamura Chūzaburō (fifteen), Masé Sadahachi (twenty), Muramatsu Masaemon (twenty-three), and Yoshida Dennai (twenty-five). Muramatsu Masaemon was the only one of the four present, however, since Yoshida Dennai and Masé Sadahachi were living in Kameyama and Nakamura Chūzaburō in Shirakawa.

No official record survives of this day in court. But this is the version of it told in that same year by Sugimoto Yoshichika, a samurai in the service of the Kaga domain:

Item. *Muramatsu Masaemon was summoned to the court of the*
City Magistrate and there questioned.

"Didn't your father and your brother tell you about this plot?"

"I am in the service of Ogasawara Nagato-no-Kami,
Commander of the Bodyguard. Normally, they would have
told me their plans. But Nagato-no-Kami being an official
of the Shogunate, and I having been in his service for some
time, they seem purposely to have avoided telling me. Until

> *the attack actually took place, I knew nothing at all."*
>
> *The officials at the court of the Magistrate then informed him of his sentence, whereupon Masaemon said, "Since my father and my brother were sentenced to commit seppuku, I expected that I, too, should be found guilty of the same crime and sentenced likewise. But now, above all else, I must be grateful to you for sentencing me to banishment."*
>
> *"'Above all else . . .' That was a nice turn of phrase," they said in praise of him at the court of the Magistrate.*

Whatever else Masaemon may have had in mind, he left to the conjecture of the court. But that "nice turn of phrase" certainly made it clear that he had not said all that he may have wished to say.

✦ ✦ ✦

Carrying on from here, Sugimoto recounted another episode from that day in court, this one involving one of the younger sons who would not be sent away just yet. Yada Gorōemon's son, Sakujūrō, was only in his ninth year. His mother had died some time ago, and he had been raised by his father, who had not remarried. Since the previous year, however, he had been cared for by an uncle of his late mother, the bannerman Okabe Suruga-no-Kami:

> *He was a clever lad, and both the lord and his lady quite doted upon him. Then, on the 6th Day of the Second Month, word came from City Magistrate that the sons of the ronin were to be sentenced to banishment, and Sakujūrō was to present himself at court. Prior to this time, Okabe had given strict orders to his vassals that they were not to mention the death of the boy's father, Gorōemon. But now that he had been summoned, they feared that he might even take his own life. When Okabe's wife was fixing the boy's hair and helping him change his kimono, Sakujūrō asked, "Where are you taking me?"*
>
> *"The officials at the office of the City Magistrate want to see what*

~ 755 ~

sort of boy you are," Okabe said, "so you're not to be naughty, the way you are here sometimes; you must be very polite."

"I'll not misbehave," Sakujūrō said. "I know that my father was sentenced to commit seppuku. If that is what is to become of me now, I'd like you to have one of your men serve as my Second. Who is it that will cut off my head? There is something I'd like to say to him. Could you please tell me his name?"

Okabe and his wife were choked with tears and could say nothing in reply. Later, they were to regret that they had sent such lowly servants to attend the boy. Their women, too, wept until their voices gave out.

They put the boy in their lord's palanquin, and Okabe himself saw him off as far as the gate. When he arrived at the entrance hall of Yasuda Echizen-no-Kami, a Deputy told him, "Young you may be, but it is the law that you leave your swords here."

Sakujūrō appeared to think for a moment, and then asked, "Would there be any objection to my leaving them with a retainer?"

"You may do as you please," he was told. Whereupon he called his sandal bearer, handed his swords to him, and mounted the steps.

Sakujūrō was told that, as he was underage and had no mother, he would be placed in the custody of Okabe Suruga-no-Kami until he reached the age of fifteen. It is said, though, that he was displeased and wished that he had been sentenced to commit seppuku, the same as his father.

It was not until the Fourth Month, however, that Matsudaira Yamato-no-Kami was able to send Nakamura Chūzaburō under escort from Shirakawa to Edo, and Honda Nakatsukasa was able to send Yoshida Dennai and Masé Sadahachi from Himeji. And it was not until the 27th of that month that all four of the banished were brought to the wharves at Tsukudajima. There they were handed over to the Izu Deputy Ogasawara Hikodayū and put aboard a ship that, on the morning of the 28th, set sail for Ōshima. At least they were being sent to the largest and closest of the seven Izu islands. Ogawa Tsunemitsu continues the story:

> *Both Matsudaira Yamato-no-Kami and Honda Nakatsukasa-no-Daifu provided the men for whom they were responsible with nineteen pieces of gold and nineteen bales of rice each. It was the law that exiles were permitted to take only twenty pieces of gold and twenty bales of rice with them; and since these men were also to be provided with clothing and bedding and numerous other implements, these would be counted as their twentieth in cash and rice. In addition to which several members of both houses, whether out of a sense of duty or pity, had presented them with parting gifts. But Muramatsu Masaemon's guardian, Nagato-no-Kami, was of far lesser rank than these daimyo and did not possess the wealth that they did. He was able to give Masaemon only four pieces of gold and two bales of rice, which, even with the addition of parting gifts, did not come close to the maximum he was permitted. . . .*

> *As they began to row out of the harbor, Sadahachi, Dennai, and Chūzaburo turned to Masaemon and said, "We understand that you are short of money and rice, whereas we have been well provided for. But our fathers and brothers died together, and we are being banished to the same island, where we shall rot in the same soil together. Our money, needless to say, but even our clothing and equipment are not our personal possessions. We are as a single body with four mouths to feed. If we are to die of starvation or freeze to death, we shall all die together; or if one of us lives, we shall all live together."*

> *"I am much heartened by your words," Masaemon replied. "But since we all have to share this same miserable lot in life, I long for nothing more than the coming of death, whether by starvation or freezing." Even the sailors and oarsmen who heard him were moved to tears.*

> *It was the vile habit of the crews on these ships to plunder and divide up among themselves most of what their passengers' families had given them, leaving only a minute portion for the exiles to live on. But they touched nothing at all belonging to these four men. And the*

islanders on Ōshima, having heard that the sons of the Righteous
Samurai were coming to live among them, took pity on them and,
entirely of their own accord, joined forces to build a fine dwelling for
them. No sooner had their ship touched shore than everyone came
to welcome them, as heartily as if they were long-lost grandchildren;
and then they prepared a great feast for them.

Such is what we were told by one of the men who was on the ship,
after he returned.

We shall hear more of these four sons in due course.

◆ ◆ ◆

As we have seen, when Kira Sahei was disenfeoffed and remanded to
the custody of Suwa Aki-no-Kami, he was not even allowed to return
home; he was escorted directly from the Military Tribunal to the Suwa
mansion by a waiting detail of samurai sent by Aki-no-Kami.

In the seven days that followed, both he and his hosts prepared
themselves for their journey to Takashima Castle on the shore of
Lake Suwa, seat of the House of Suwa in the mountainous province
of Shinano. Sahei was not permitted a large suite, such as befitted the
head of the House of Kira and a son of Uesugi Danjō. His only companions would be one of the Elders of his house, Sōda Magobei, who
had proved his worth by fleeing through a hole in the wall on the night
of the attack, and Yamayoshi Shinpachi, a man of real worth who had
fought ferociously at Sahei's side and whose wounds even now were far
from fully healed. Nor could either of these men join him until proof of
their temple registration was forwarded from their ancestral homes in
Mikawa and Yonezawa.

Neither was Sahei allowed to take with him a great many of the necessities of daily life. His mother somehow managed to obtain permission
to send two portable chests filled with the bedding that he would need
to weather the highland winters—but little else.

In contrast, the Suwa house seems, above all, to have been intent
upon security. To escort these three men safely to their home domain,

the Suwa assembled an entourage of more than 130 men: samurai of all ranks, foot soldiers, menials, cooks—and, fortunately, two physicians to look after their two severely wounded guests. Sahei had hoped that his attendant surgeon, Kurisaki Dōyū, would be allowed to accompany him, but the Shogunate had told the Suwa that their own medical men would suffice.

On the morning of the 11th Day of the Second Month, this procession set forth, first heading for the river and crossing at the Ryōgoku Bridge; then following the long curve of the Outer Moat, past the Confucian Academy at Shōheizaka, through Ushigome and Ichigaya, and all the way around to the Yotsuya Gate; and finally leaving the city though Naitō Shinjuku via the Kōshū Highroad. They would travel the full length of this highway, more than 53 leagues (174 miles, 208 kilometers), to the point where it joined the Middle Mountain Road, a journey of six days and five nights though forty-four post stations.

The first stretch was relatively level, but as the Kantō Plain rises to hills and then mountains, travel slowed and the post stations crowded closer to one another. Just past Komakino, the procession entered one of the steepest of the cuts between these peaks. Here, with good reason, the Shogunate had placed one of the barriers that guarded the principal gateways to the Shogun's capital, the Kobotoke Checkpoint. The procession of a daimyo house, I presume, passed these barriers without having to seek special permission to travel to and from their lord's domain. But the three men being escorted to Suwa were required to stop at Kobotoke and present a pass identifying themselves and certifying the legitimacy of their journey. The checkpoint pass of Kira Sahei still survives:

> *Kira Sahei, having been remanded to my custody, is being dispatched to Shinshū Takashima, accompanied by two of his vassals. These three men shall be permitted to pass the checkpoint without hindrance. For future reference, herewith the foregoing.*
>
> GENROKU 16, SECOND MONTH, 11TH DAY   *Suwa Aki-no-Kami*
>   [sealed]
>
> To: The Inspectors at Kobotoke Checkpoint Barrier

The Suwa house had long experience in the entertainment of eminent prisoners of the Shogun. Seventy-seven years earlier, in Kan'ei 3 (1626), the Suwa had been entrusted with the care of Matsudaira Tadateru, the somewhat deranged sixth son of the founding Shogun, Tokugawa Ieyasu. Whatever his failings, however, Tadateru was a healthy man who lived to the age of ninety-three, more than fifty years of which he spent in Suwa. Owing to Tadateru's illustrious lineage, the Suwa (whom he far outranked) felt it necessary to provide him with special quarters, which they did by building an entirely new addition to their castle, the Southern Perimeter. This structure was, in essence, a purpose-built prison—comfortably appointed, no doubt, but accessible only by way of a narrow, heavily guarded bridge connected to the main body of the castle; surrounded by impassable, mosquito-infested marshland; and fitted with nine guard posts perched upon its walls to keep watch on an enclosure of only 43,000 square feet (4,000 square meters). I doubt that the thought of escape ever crossed Tadateru's mind.

Now the Southern Perimeter was to have a new occupant, Kira Sahei. Twenty-one years had passed since the death of Tadateru, and his prison was badly in need of repair and refurbishment. And so Shiga Rihei, an unfortunate samurai whose residence happened to lie within the castle walls, was forced to move elsewhere for two months, so that Sahei could be housed securely until the Southern Perimeter had been made ready for him. Sahei, alas, was not destined to find the Southern Perimeter as salubrious a home as Matsudaira Tadateru had.

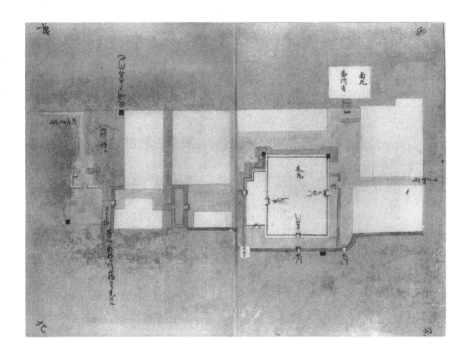

figure 31
Yamagata Daini's drawing of the floor plan of Takashima Castle.
The Southern Perimeter is the small square at the upper right.
(National Diet Library of Japan, Tokyo)

CHAPTER
93

When I heard that they really had sold them,
I was shocked.

At exactly the same time that the sons of the ronin were being sentenced to banishment at the office of the City Magistrate, a short distance away Hosokawa Etchū-no-Kami was addressing his men in the Hosokawa Upper Mansion on Daimyo Lane. Again, Horiuchi Den'emon describes the scene:

> On the 6th Day of the Second Month, all samurai were summoned to the upper mansion, where His Lordship addressed us personally.
>
> "All of you have worked long and tirelessly while these men were in our custody. And that goes for those of you here at the upper mansion as well; you've stood a great many additional watches and thus deserve just as much credit as everyone else.
>
> "Now, concerning those seventeen gallant men, there were considerable differences of opinion, even among those in authority, which is why it took them fifty days to decide their fate. I may have my doubts about their reasoning, but I expect that they found sentencing them to seppuku one of their most difficult decisions since the time of Gongen Sama. So when others ask what you think, there is no need for you to evade the question. For whatever the merits or demerits of the case, I've no doubt that all of them were gallant men. I trust that you will keep this in mind whenever you are discussing the matter."
>
> Everyone was very pleased that he referred to the ronin as "gallant"

*three times [actually, only twice]. It brings tears to my eyes to think
how grateful they must be, resting there in the shade of the grass.*

His Lordship seems also to have had advice intended for Den'emon
himself—although he would not have mentioned it in the presence of
any of the other samurai. Instead, he summoned his physician, Emura
Sessai, and asked him to carry the message confidentially to Den'emon,
who writes:

> *On the 9th Day of the Second Month, Emura Sessai called upon
> me at home. I was paying my respects to the mortuary tablet of one
> of my kinsmen when he arrived, and he told me that he had been a
> good friend of the man and remembered him well. He said, too, that
> he had been with His Lordship this morning and had heard that
> tomorrow we would observe a day of abstinence from meat and fish
> in honor of the first of the seven obsequies for the ronin, which I was
> pleased to hear. Then Sessai came to the point.*
>
> *"His Lordship said, 'I expect that the three old men [Hyōsuke,
> Genbei, and Den'emon] will be talking of nothing else, and prob-
> ably are feeling very downcast. How are they?' I told him, 'They
> are together day and night and talk of nothing else.' To which he
> replied, 'Den'emon, in particular, made many friends among them.
> I expect that he may be planning to visit the temple tomorrow. But
> if he were to do so just now, the monks might assume that he is
> there as my representative. And if talk of that sort were to be noised
> about, it would not look good for us in the eyes of the Shogunate.
> You had better go to Den'emon, tell him this, and ask him to post-
> pone his visit.'"*
>
> *"If that is how he feels," I said, "I shall certainly obey. As you know,
> I've felt drained of energy, and haven't been up to a temple visit. But
> tomorrow is the 10th, the first of seven obsequies, so I did think I
> might go, even if I had to hire a town litter to get there. But knowing
> how His Lordship feels, this actually seems a stroke of good fortune."*

"His Lordship says that this is only for Den'emon's ears," Sessai said.
"I am not to say anything about it to Hyōsuke and Genbei."

His Lordship then sent word to the temple, telling the monks much the same thing. Although he himself would like to attend, he said, he thought it best that he refrain from doing so, at least on this occasion. He would not be sending his Elders either, but he did intend to send one of his personal attendants, as no one was likely to recognize this man as his representative.

♦ ♦ ♦

At the temple, the stonecutters had been chipping away since the morning of the 6th. The raw stone had been delivered smartly, as ordered, the day before. Now the wooden stakes could be replaced; there would be a proper gravestone standing at every mound. Hakumyō does not tell us how long the job took, only that the weather held and the work was completed "before long." What seems to have concerned Hakumyō more than details of this sort is what he imagined to be unjust criticism of the temple, on at least three counts.

For one thing, a rumor seems have been making the rounds of the city, that the Abbot of Eiheiji, the head temple of the Sōtō school of Zen, had castigated the Abbot of Sengakuji for his conduct of the burial of the ronin. The Eiheiji Abbot had indeed been in Edo at the time, Hakumyō says, and had visited the temple three times. But Eiheiji himself said that he had come to "pay his respects." He had been entertained lavishly and had conversed long and amiably with Shūzan Oshō, the Abbot of Sengakuji. To say that he had interrogated him concerning Ōishi and threatened to dismiss him is unthinkable. Besides which, Sengakuji was one of the three main Sōtō Zen temples in the Kantō region. Even if our Abbot had been in the wrong, we monks needn't have worried what Eiheiji might think of it.

Then, too, there was the matter of the fence. While the stonecutters were at work on the gravestones, a team of carpenters was constructing a sturdy bamboo fence around the entire graveyard. For this, the Abbot was being accused of making it difficult for people who wished to visit the graves of the ronin and pay their respects. But this fence, Hakumyō says, was absolutely essential. From the morning after the ronin were buried, the temple had been overrun with sightseers. Nor had the temple acted without permission. When told of the situation, the Commissioner of Temples and Shrines had freely given his consent to the construction of the fence.

Whatever the merit of his first two complaints, it is difficult to escape the feeling that Hakumyō, in his third complaint, was trying too hard to justify something that looks suspiciously like a case of that familiar monkish vice: greed. Here is what Ogawa Tsunemitsu, a contemporary observer, had to say: "The weapons they carried and the armor they wore should have been preserved far into the future as valued treasures of the temple, and as proof of the valor of the Righteous Samurai buried there. But, sad to say, every sword, long and short, as well as every lance and great sword, without a single exception, had been sold off even before the first of the seven obsequies."

Ogawa goes on in this vein at some length, noting that none of the swords even found their way into the hands of the wives, children, or kinsmen of the ronin—or even other samurai who admired the fidelity of the ronin. But here is what Hakumyō has to say in defense of the temple:

> The weapons sent to us by the four daimyo houses would have done the ronin no good in their subsequent incarnations if nothing were to be done with them. And so we sold them to people who expressed a desire to have them, with the intention of using the proceeds in ways that would benefit the ronin in lives to come. We improved the surrounds of their graves and subsidized their perpetual maintenance; we financed rites, the merit of which was dedicated to them; and with what was left over, we rebuilt the main gate. This, after all, is why we again have a main gate. Of course, it was our rule that if anyone came with proof that they should be given the weapons, we would do so. . . . But there were a great many people who came to the Bursar or the kitchens claiming that they were relatives of the ronin. At first, we complied without verification. Before long, though, hundreds of them were coming, and so we became more stringent,

which angered many of those who were refused.

Probably we shall never know how all of this worked out in practice. Hakumyō accused Ogawa of being a writer who took whatever he heard at face value, without checking whether it was true or false. And Satō Jōemon tells us that he was able to retrieve Yasubei's great sword by taking the sheath to the temple and proving that it matched the weapon. But Horiuchi Den'emon says, "When I heard that they really had sold them, I was shocked." Of one thing we can be certain, though: any artifact that we now see in a museum or an exhibition that is labeled as belonging to one of the ronin is likely to be a fraud.

◆ ◆ ◆

I want to mention here a story told by Katashima Shin'enshi that I could never quite believe was true. But just a short while ago, I read an article in the newspaper that made me think that—like much else in *Sekijō gishinden*—this tale may actually contain more than just a grain of truth. It concerns Kai Shuso, Master of the hermitage Shūsuian at the temple Zuikōin in the north of Kyoto:

> *The Master of the Shūsuian had not seen Kuranosuke since he left Kyoto in the Tenth Month of the previous year. But they had corresponded in the interim, and when he heard that Kuranosuke and the others had accomplished their goal, and were now remanded to the custody of four daimyo houses, he heaved a sigh of deep emotion and murmured, "So they've actually done it, exactly as they said they would. And now they calmly await death. I've never heard the likes of it, past or present." He then decided that he must hasten to Edo in the hope of meeting with Kuranosuke one last time while he was still alive, and after their death bring back the bones of the ronin to be interred at Zuikoin, as they had so often requested. . . .*
>
> *When he arrived in Edo, having made the journey as rapidly as he could, he attempted in various ways to arrange a meeting with Kuranosuke. The law was strict and did not normally permit*

such visits. But it has always been applied more leniently to clerics, besides which the Master was a man of no common lineage.... Fortunately, through the good offices of someone sympathetic to him, on the evening of the 3rd Day of the Second Month, Kai Shuso was permitted to meet Kuranosuke.

Shin'enshi goes on at some length describing the emotions of the two men, and the scene ends with Kuranosuke asking that the locks of hair he has gathered—as well as the locks that had been gathered at the other three daimyo houses—be buried at Zuikōin.

It is easy to see, even from this short excerpt, why this tale was hard to believe. Shin'enshi's florid style does sometimes strain credulity. Yet as I said, there was a report in the news recently that has made me reconsider. On 14 December 1909, the anniversary of the attack on the Kira mansion, a group of students from the Kyoto Normal School went to Zuikōin to dedicate a pair of cherry trees to the memory of the Akō ronin. But when their teacher, Narita Kijūrō, began to dig a hole in which to plant the first tree, his shovel struck something hard. Further, more careful, investigation unearthed a cracked ceramic urn that was filled with hair. It was, of course, assumed that these were locks of hair collected from the forty-six ronin before their death. Once the trees were planted, and duly dedicated, Professor Narita obtained a new urn, transferred the contents of the old one to it, and reburied it.

Did Kai Shuso indeed go to Edo and collect these locks himself? And if not, who did? No record of such a visit is to be found in any other source. Even so, Shin'enshi's story no longer seems as implausible or impossible as it once did. And if Kai Shuso did actually go to Edo, it would have been at just this point in the narrative—the 16th or 17th of the Second Month—that he returned to Kyoto and buried the urn at the Zuikōin. Which is why I wanted to mention it here.

*In time of war, our men have more urgent concerns
than to fly to the aid of some helpless woman.*

Amid the almost ceaseless chorus of praise, it can be refreshing to hear
the occasional voice of a skeptic. Not the quibblers who thought that
there had been no quarrel, that Kira had not been the enemy of Takumi-
no-Kami, that only the ronin had been in the wrong; but, rather, those
who agreed that justice had been done, but thought that it might better
have been done a bit differently. The wife of Shimazu Awaji-no-Kami
was one such voice.

Lady Shimazu was born the daughter of a member of the Shimazu
main house, Shimazu Zusho Hisahiro. She was raised by the head of
that house, Shimazu Satsuma-no-Kami Tsunataka, and later became
the second wife of Shimazu Awaji-no-Kami Korehisa, head of a cadet
branch of the Shimazu and lord of the Sadohara domain. She bore him
his heir and two daughters.

In short, Lady Shimazu was a Shimazu not merely by marriage. She
was descended in the main line of that clan of fierce warriors, who for
more than six hundred years had ruled their domain at the southern tip
of Kyushu almost as an independent kingdom. And being a full-blooded
Shimazu, she considered herself as much a warrior as any of her menfolk.
Every morning, in the garden of her Edo mansion, she would muster her
Ladies-in-Waiting and maidservants, and lead them through a vigorous
round of halberd thrusts and parries, slashes and swipes.

"Feminine fragility and ineptitude are no excuse," she would tell
them. "Yes, there is peace in the land—for the time being, at least. But
the Shimazu, surely, have not fought their last battles. So you had better

get serious about learning to fight, for in time of war, our men have more urgent concerns than to fly to the aid of some helpless woman."

And for the wives of her vassals down in Kyushu, whom she could not lead personally, she wrote tracts and treatises to be printed and distributed in every corner of the domain: *A Woman's Guide to Battle Tactics and the Waging of War* (*Onna ikusadate buji narai shū*) and *Women Warriors in Full Battle Array* (*Onna musha momochidori*).

But the news that she had been hearing of the Akō ronin and their vendetta she found upsetting. Many, she feared, would fail to see what an alarming precedent this incident was setting. She summoned her Chief Elder, Ijūin Kumanosuke, and a record of her (one-sided) conversation with him survives:

> *"Kumanosuke Dono!" she said. "Your forebears have been vassals of the Shimazu for generation upon generation. Their feats of arms are famed throughout the land and are recorded in full detail, even in the official records of the Shogunate. They redound to the credit of you and all your kinsmen. Which is why I want to talk to you about something that is troubling me.*
>
> *"As you know, I am a staunch advocate of the martial arts. I devote the greatest part of my energies to developing my skill in weapons, and I try my best to encourage the women in my service to do the same, even those who have no natural talent for it. You may think this excessive in a woman, but let me tell you how I see it. This land is well governed, the world is at peace, and our suits of armor are stowed in their cases; we live in a rare age indeed. There are even men nowadays who spend their every moment practicing the more polite accomplishments. To be sure, there are those few who still endeavor to develop their skill in weapons, but even they may be led astray by their idle companions and succumb to the temptations of song and strings.*
>
> *"Now you may imagine that, for a woman, skill in the martial arts is quite unnecessary, for who nowadays would be so foolish as to challenge the authority of the Shogun? Yet when someone becomes*

the thrall of an uncontrollable grudge, dreadful things can happen.
In the not so distant past, there have been Inaba, Horiyama, Asano,
Oda. They all held personal grudges, were unable to restrain them-
selves, and lashed out with the sword—whereupon the noble houses
of which they were the lords were abolished, one and all.

"When Asano was forced to kill himself and Kira was left in peace,
Ōishi Kuranosuke, with forty-some other loyal vassals, attacked and
killed Kira. In a situation of that sort, could anyone born to a mili-
tary house, even a woman, just let the matter pass? But Lady Asano!
She left it entirely to her vassals to kill her enemy, and, worse still,
left them to commit seppuku while she lives out the rest of her life
in comfort. Can anyone say that that is as it should be? Yes, she is
a woman; but she ought nonetheless to have joined in the attack,
killed her husband's enemy, and offered up the head so as to assuage
the bitter resentment that he carried to the netherworld. Yet just to
ignore such an outrage, as though it had nothing to do with her—
that I find unforgivable! Over the years, there have been countless
occasions when husband and wife have died in battle together. If she
had joined the ronin in that spirit, who could possibly criticize her?"

Ijūin Kumanosuke's response is not recorded.

✦ ✦ ✦

Even the ronin themselves, for whom praise was all but universal,
were not regarded by everyone as paragons of perfection. A man of
honor should, after all, be quick to anger; yet nearly two years were to
pass before the ronin avenged their lord. This was a sore point with
Yamamoto Jōchō, author of *Hagakure* (1716), an influential treatise on
warrior morality, in which he says:

> *A certain man was shamed because, in a quarrel, he had failed to*
> *retaliate. To retaliate, you must simply rush straight in and fight*
> *until you are killed. Do this, and you will never be shamed. But if*

you feel that you must win the fight, then you will miss your chance. And if you worry that your opponents are too numerous, then time will pass and eventually you probably will decide to give it up. Even if your opponents number in the thousands, just make up your mind that you're going mow down every one of them, and go to it; then you'll have done your duty. You may even succeed.

When Asano Dono's ronin, after their night attack, failed to commit seppuku at Sengakuji, that was a mistake. Moreover, they waited far too long between the time their lord was killed and the time they attacked his enemy. If in the interim, Kira Dono had died of illness, that would have left them totally luckless. People from the capital are very clever and thus skilled at things that will win them praise, but they are incapable of acting impulsively, as in the Nagasaki brawl.

The night attack of the Soga brothers, likewise, was far too long and drawn out. When he spied the crest on those curtains, Jūrō Sukenari missed his chance. That was bad luck. But what Gorō said was splendid.

I wouldn't normally criticize like this; I mention these things only by way of elucidating the Way of the Warrior. For if you have not done your thinking beforehand, then, when the moment comes, you will have no time to think things through, and most likely you will end up being shamed. We listen to what people have to say, and we read books, in order to help us prepare in advance for such moments. The warrior, more than anyone, must remain constantly alert, for he knows not what might happen from one moment to the next. He must be thinking day and night what he would do, step by step, in any given situation. That could decide the outcome of a battle.

But escaping shame is quite another matter; for that, you need only die. Even when it seems that you cannot succeed, retaliate! Good sense has nothing to do with it. A man obsessed never thinks about the outcome of a battle. He attacks fanatically, as a madman determined to die. Do that, and you will awaken from your dreams.

Kuranosuke would never have agreed with Jōchō. And even Yasubei was eventually persuaded that it would avail him nothing to "die a dog's death." The Way of the Warrior was by no means the same for all warriors.

CHAPTER
95

At Ausaka no Seki
wakaretemo mata ausaka to tanomaneba
tague ya semashi shide no yamagoe
As we part with no hope we shall ever meet again at Ausaka,
Might I liken this to crossing the mountain pass to death?

ONODERA JŪNAI

On the night before his seppuku, Onodera Jūnai wrote a long letter to his wife, O-Tan, that he knew would be his last. He "managed to have [it] transmitted secretly," he says, which probably means that Horiuchi Den'emon posted it to Terai Genkei in Kyoto, so that Genkei could take it to O-Tan. Traveling at the usual speed of letters from Edo to Kyoto, she should have received it sometime around the 10th of the Second Month. These, then, are Jūnai's last words to the woman he wished never to be parted from, even in death—and perhaps her first confirmation of his impending death:

I leave with you this last missive, which I have managed to have transmitted secretly through Terai Genkei. No words can express our joy at having achieved the goal of taking the head of our late lord's enemy. I expect that you will have heard of it where you are by the 20th or 21st, and that you rejoice with us in the same spirit. Since then, I imagine, you'll have heard one thing and another, bit by bit, about all of us. I hear, too, that Gentatsu was to return early in the First Month, so I expect that you'll have been pleased to hear up-to-date, reliable news from him.

Item. On the night of the 15th in the last month of last year, we were taken into custody by Hosokawa Sama. We expected that our punishment would be meted out to us that very night; yet to our amazement, here we are: the old year has ended, the New Year's season has passed, and now, going into the Second Month, we are still drinking the saké of this mortal world—which, I need hardly say, feels very strange. We are not likely to enjoy such leisure much longer. Everyone is expecting that our fate will be decided today, and we are now just waiting to see what the verdict will be. Really, though, the success and perfection of our accomplishment is the greatest good fortune that a warrior could ever hope for. It all went so well that I can't help thinking Hachiman must have been on our side. I'm told that all the world praises us as models of fidelity, rare in this land of Japan. There could hardly be a better memento to take with us to the Netherworld.

Item. That night, even before any of us had removed our coats of mail, Etchū-no-Kami Sama honored us with a visit. He sat down close by us and told us that he was deeply impressed by the loyalty of our deed, particularly the composure with which we had accomplished it. I was gratified and delighted by these words, such a credit to a warrior's good name, coming from a great lord of his stature. And then there are the two men charged with our care, as well as several others, all of good lineage, who look after us in alternate watches night and day; and all the fine food, clothing, and whatnot that His Lordship has commanded we be provided with—everything anyone could ever need (except weapons, of course). Such rare kindness—indeed, extravagance—has made our sojourn here seem more like living in Paradise than in this mundane world. Those lords in whose custody Kōemon [Mōri], Gengo [Hisamatsu], and Kin'emon [Hisamatsu] have been remanded have all sought the advice of Etchū-no-Kami Sama, so I expect that they, too, have been well looked after.

Item. As I've warned you already, once we have been sentenced and put to death, you yourself may not escape punishment. I am *confident, though, that, given your resolve, you'll not break down and lose control of yourself. But if you do escape punishment and are living on the outskirts of the capital, then summon my sister Teiryū to come stay with you, and spend your few remaining years together comforting each other in your woes. That is all I would ask of you. You're already aware that you'll have no one to turn to for support, so you've no need to brood over that. Regrets, no matter how great, can do you no good. You must simply dismiss them from your mind and resign yourself to finding what pleasure you can in living a quiet, secluded life.*

Item. Kōemon, of course, fought very bravely, as did Kin'emon and Gengo. You may well have heard in a general way what went on, but I doubt that you'll have heard news of each individual's accomplishments. Quite apart from news of everyone else, I'm sure that you'll be wanting to hear about our immediate family, so I'll do my best to describe what we did. At sundown on the 14th, Kura Dono and I left our lodgings and went by town litter to Horibe Yahei's place. Until about midnight, we ate and drank and talked, and then we went on to Horibe Yasubei's place in Hayashi-chō, where we assembled our force. After the Seventh Hour [4:00 A.M.] we set out to attack the enemy. The distance was about 12 or 13 chō [0.9 mile (1.4 kilometers)]. The snow that had fallen the day before was frozen over with a coat of dawn frost, which gave us a firm footing. Lest we attract undue attention, we took neither lanterns nor torches; but the early morning moon was so brilliant that there was no chance of losing our way. We advanced to the corner of the enemy's property, where we divided into two groups, east and west, twenty-three men each, and attacked over the rooftops. It was decided that father and son should not attack together, so I attacked from the west and Kōemon went to the east. Gengo, Kōemon, and two or three others were first over the walls. As they leapt down from the rooftops, they declaimed their names in a great voice and made for the entrance hall. There they kicked down the doors and forced their way in. One of the three men on guard duty in the great hall, who rose up and fought back, Kōemon wounded high on the thigh and then cut him down. Immediately, they advanced within. A row of bows was arrayed in the alcove, I'm told, and Kōemon fought his way in and slashed every one of the bowstrings, before moving on. We were told that quite a few of the enemy were expert archers, and we should be prepared to be shot at, both indoors and out. We had all been warned confidentially to take care lest the enemy appear out of nowhere and shoot from behind. Cutting all those bowstrings was thus a wise precaution; but despite the simplicity of it, everyone was impressed. I trust that you, too, will delight in the timely wisdom of this deed. Kin'emon, master of the cruciform lance that he is, said, "This is the weapon for me; I'll fight out in the open where I can take on a great lot of them." So he did not join those who fought their way into the mansion, but secured the sector where there was a small gate called the New Gate. I'm told that he did just as he intended and felled every man who challenged him there. Gengo carried a long weapon called the great sword, and he wore a crimson under-robe and a black outer-robe with broad sleeves. He cut a particularly impressive figure, and he, too, took his toll of the enemy. Well, I'm sure that you can imagine how pleased I was with each and every one of our young men; they fought so well and so successfully. And I'm sure that you share my delight. There was no sense of rivalry between young and old. The task of the old men was to direct the young men and to keep a careful watch; for when you burst in upon the enemy and none of you may come out alive, everyone shares a single aim. Before we set out, we all swore an oath to one another that there would be no ranking of greater or lesser exploits. On the west, Chūzaemon and I served as aides to Ōishi Chikara. At this gate, Mimura Jirōzaemon battered down the wicket with two or three blows of a mallet; then the whole force surged in and fought their way straight into the foyer of Kōzuke-no-Suke Dono's retirement quarters. It seemed to me that even Tenma Hajun could not have withstood such a powerful force. After we had broken in, I was standing in front of the barrack block to the right of the gate when two men emerged. I killed the first with a single thrust of the lance, and Kihei felled the second. Kihei stayed to guard the gate, *and I moved on toward a rear entrance on the north and called out to the men on the other side of the rear wall who were guarding the mansion of Tsuchiya Chikara. While keeping watch there, two more of the enemy came at me, and I felled them both. Kataoka Gengoemon saw me kill one of them and shouted out, "Jūnai Dono, you did it!" The other one Ōishi Sezaemon saw. That one I could hear invoking the name of the Buddha as he fell. The sins of my old age, I suppose I must call them. All committed with the lance; I never laid a hand on the hilt of my sword.*

Item. To have died for killing the enemy of our lord will redound to the good name of our ancestors, which was one of my aims in doing this. So please place this letter before the memorial tablet of my father.

Item. The days are long, and we have nothing to do. We sleep when we please and rise when we please. We delight in drinking saké whenever we please, whether at bedtime or by day. The seventeen of us spend night and day discussing all that has happened, and those charged with our care join us in a friendly way, so we are never lonely. Today is the fiftieth day we've spent like this. Whenever I read out the poems that you've sent me, everyone is so deeply touched that their sleeves are drenched with tears. I've dashed off a great lot of them myself. I do hope that somehow I'll be able to write to you one more time. Please put your mind at rest, and let this poem help you to accept our fate.

> *mayowaji na ko to tomo ni yuku nochi no yo wa*
> *kokoro no yami mo haru no yo no tsuki*
> I'll stray not; for in that world to come, whither I go with my son
> this darkness of heart shall clear in the light of the spring moon.

And lest you think that, on the brink of death, I have forgotten my old home, here is another poem that came to me recently:

Seeing spring vegetables arrayed upon my dinner tray

musashino no yukima mo mietsu furusato no
imo ga kakine no kusa mo moyuran
Even here in Musashino, green gaps in the snow appear; at home,
by the fence wherein my love lives, herbs must now be sprouting.

The house of Etchū-no-Kami Sama is very large and comprises
great numbers of people, some of whom are devotees of poetry; so
there are those who are constantly asking me to tell them all about
Keian. I find it a bit embarrassing, not to say bizarre, to be spoken
of as though I were a known name in the Way of Poetry. But do pass
this story on to Keian.

Item. So far, none of the wives and children of our men have
been interrogated. Okuda Magodayū's father-in-law is a vassal
of Akimoto Tajima-no-Kami Sama, a member of the Council of
Elders. Magodayū's wife and children have been taken in by him,
apparently by command of Tajima-no-Kami Sama. The uncle of
Tominomori Suke'emon's wife is a vassal of Tamura Ukyō Sama.
And Honda Nakatsukasa has commanded Yoshida Chūzaemon's
son-in-law Itō Jūrōdayū to take in his wife and children. Everyone
seems quite grateful that these daimyo have been so kind as to use
their great might for the benefit of these wives and children. But
there is no one to take you in. What a terrible pity! I've informed
Ekōin Dono of your plight and asked his help; but no matter how
much one writes, one can never tell the whole of it. We shall just
have to leave it at that. Word that both father and son have cut open
their bellies will spread before long. There is little else you can do but
let this awaken you to the transience of life in this world of human-
ity. Respectfully,

YEAR OF THE RAM [1703], SECOND MONTH, 3RD DAY   *Jūnai*
To: O-Tan Dono

Unfortunately—indeed, tragically—none of O-Tan's letters to Jūnai
survive. We know that they corresponded while Jūnai was in custody
at the Hosokawa mansion, and she may well have written more often
than he had been able to do. But Jūnai was soon to die; he was able to

share her poems, and probably some of her news, with his comrades. But there was no way that he could have preserved her letters.

Jūnai was still unsure whether O-Tan would be punished for guilt by relationship, but he at least suggests a way that she might endure her loneliness if she does escape. O-Tan was about as alone in the world as anyone but an orphan could be. She had broken with her brother Tōbei when he defected from the pact. And now she was about to lose not only her husband and her adoptive son, but also her nephew Ōtaka Gengo, her cousin Masé Kyūdayū and his son, her nephew Okano Kin'emon, and, more distantly, Nakamura Kansuke, Hara Sōemon, and Okajima Yasoemon. If, as Jūnai suggests, his sister Teiryū were to move to Kyoto from Akō to live with O-Tan, the two women could at least console each other in their shared bereavement. O-Tan did entreat Teiryū, but Teiryū would not have it. Neither O-Tan's plea nor Teiryū's rejection survive, but Teiryū did discuss the matter—somewhat defensively, it seems to me—in her letters to the wife of Sakurai Kakuemon, a samurai in the service of Honda Noto-no-Kami, lord of Yamato Kōriyama, as well as to Kuranosuke's widow, O-Riku, in Toyooka. To Sakurai's wife, she wrote:

This is my sixty-fifth year. I haven't much longer to live; but having survived both of my brothers' children, I am all alone in the world. Jūnai is my brother; Kin'emon, my nephew. Masé Kyūdayū is my cousin, and his son went with him. Nakamura Kansuke, too, is a relative, and Hara Sōemon and Okajima Yasoemon are close kin of my late husband, Gengo's father. Altogether, nine of them went. I am all alone here in Akō and am staying, for the time being, with the family of the nursemaid who raised Gengo. Kin'emon's mother is living with her younger sister. Jūnai's widow remains where she was in Kyoto. She has written from Kyoto several times saying, "Come up here, come up here"; she has no one she can depend upon, living alone in Kyoto. But Gengo was of low rank, in addition to which he served every year in Edo; and now my medicine has run out. As a result, I no longer have the resources to live comfortably. Whatever would become of me, I cannot but wonder, if I were to go running hither and yon off in the East? So I've decided not to go up to Kyoto. I've lived here for more than fifty years now and have close relations with my temples. Kagakuji is the family temple of Takumi Sama. The Prelate there is very solicitous and kind to me. My own temple is Enrinji, and that Prelate, too, looks after me very well. For the time being, I'll just carry on here. So far, it has been my good fortune to live a long life, but I'm rather pessimistic what the future may hold.

To O-Riku she wrote, more concisely:

Jūnai's widow is living in Kyoto. "I beg you, please, come up and live with me," she writes. But everything is so unsettled nowadays, what if I were just to pull up and move to Kyoto? I couldn't have anything like the close relationship I have here with Enrinji Sama and Kagakuji Sama, so I am not at all inclined to move. I am sixty-five this year; I haven't much longer to live. Rather than run hither and yon, it seems to me better to place my trust in my two temples here.

The last of the seven obsequies for the ronin, their forty-ninth day, fell on the 22nd of the Third Month, by which time O-Tan must have been certain that Jūnai's sister would not come to live with her. O-Tan then entered the temple Ryōgakuin—some say to become a nun, some say to die. It may have been both. The only substantial reference to O-Tan's death, however, is buried in Ban Kōkei's long chapter on her, dealing mainly with her poetry. He says simply:

After Jūnai had been sentenced to death by seppuku, unable perhaps to endure her yearning for him, she ceased to eat and, after several days, passed away. Her grave is at Ryōgakuin, a dependency of the temple Honkokuji in Kyoto. On her gravestone, the date of her death is given as Year of the Ram, Genroku 16, Sixth Month, 18th Day. The temple Death Register, above her posthumous name, records her parting poem:

tsuma ya ko no matsuran mono o isogamashi
nani ka kono yo ni omoiokubeki
My husband and my son now await me; I must hasten on my way;
for what more have I to detain me here in this world?

The Death Register also notes that she took her own life. So perhaps
she may actually have died by the sword?

I cannot agree with Kōkei that she might have taken her life with a sword—an act not without precedent among samurai women, but totally out of character, it seems to me, with this most refined and tasteful of women.

The temple Ryōgakuin no longer exists, but the graves of O-Tan and her younger sister O-Iyo, who died in the previous year, still remain in dreary isolation, within a locked enclosure. If you wish to pay your respects, however, the custodians of the key, in the adjacent house, are kindly people who will cheerfully open the gate.

figure 32
O-Tan writing to Onodera Jūnai.
(*Akō gishi den issekiwa*, 1854)

I just feel empty and listless,
still living but little else.

Whatever became of the defectors? The question is often asked, but very few of them can be traced. Kuranosuke's cousin Shindō Genshirō, we know, did very well for himself. Received as the returning lord of Nishinoyama, profiting not only from the yield of his lands, but also from the pilgrims to the Inarizuka on his property, he probably was better off in Yamashina than he ever had been in Akō. Kuranosuke's uncle, Oyama Gengozaemon, we know less about, but he was at least able to retire comfortably in Kyoto. Yet these two are exceptions. Most of the others vanished without a trace. Some probably changed their names, so they would not be recognized as survivors of the Akō Corps of Vassals. Others gave up their status as samurai, stowed or sold their swords, and melted into the towns and villages as commoners or farmers.

There are two, however, whom we know a bit better than the others and who somehow managed to leave their mark: Ōno Kurōbei, the domain Elder who absconded in the night in a women's palanquin, and Kuranosuke's personal retainer, Seno'o Magozaemon.

♦ ♦ ♦

Kurōbei comes to our attention just now by way of a cache of moldering documents recently uncovered at the temple Jūrin'in in Kobe. One of them is a letter from Kurōbei's younger brother Itō Goemon to a man named Hinatsu Chōbei in Kyoto. In it, Goemon thanks Chōbei for having arranged the burial of Kurōbei in the graveyard at Kurodani—which allows us to date his death to the 6th Day of the Fourth Month, barely two months after the seppuku of the ronin.

The interim between Kurōbei's flight and his death two years later must have been a hectic time—needlessly so, it seems to me. He and his son Gun'emon may well have been planning to abscond as soon as they received their severance allowances, even before they were threatened by Hara Sōemon and his brother Okajima Yasoemon, for their household goods were already packed for transport. But their sudden departure in the night—abandoning Gun'emon's infant daughter to her nursemaid because she was crying—forced them to leave behind anything that they could not carry.

Many lower-ranking samurai were, of course, free to leave Akō once they had vacated their homes and collected their severance allowances. But for an Elder of the house to abscond before he had done the duties of his high office was by no means acceptable, either to his fellow officers or to the Shogunate's Inspectors. Kurōbei himself seems to have known the gravity of his offense, which he attempted, feebly, to excuse with a letter to his late lord's Adjutant and the Inspector General. He had retreated to the harbor village at Misaki, he said, to recover from illness—when, in fact, he was there to board a ship. This fooled no one. Kuranosuke did his best to rescue the man from his own foolishness. He had Kataoka Gengoemon speak to Kurōbei's brother Itō Goemon, but Goemon claimed he had no idea that Kurōbei had fled—and then he himself disappeared.

At first, Kurōbei seems not to have gone far, but news of his malfeasance must have preceded him. At his first stop, he was refused permission to settle in the coastal village of Aboshi; when he landed a bit farther on at Shikama, the temple Hontokuji refused him admittance to Kameyama. Eventually, he ended up in Omuro, near the gate of the temple Ninnaji in Kyoto. Itō Jinsai's son Baiu tells us that he lived there under the name of Ban Kansei, and at first gave the impression of a well-to-do ronin. But inevitably, his resources dwindled. He being an illegal fugitive, his family's household goods had been impounded, under orders that they were not to be returned until officially authorized. Seventy bundles belonging to Kurōbei were in the warehouse of Ōtsuya Jūemon, and ninety belonging to his son Gun'emon were with

Zaimokuya Shōbei. Kurōbei now needed those goods to sell and support himself, in consequence of which he began to make a nuisance of himself.

At first, he solicited the intercession of the Kyoto Liaison Officer of Toda Uneme-no-Kami. And when the Inspectors, who had supervised the surrender of Akō Castle, returned to Edo, Kurōbei waylaid them at Kakogawa and presented them with a written petition. But when these schemes failed, Itō Baiu tells us, Kurōbei then took to dealing in charcoal. Yet despite the financial acumen for which he had been valued in Akō, Kurōbei seems not to have been a successful merchant. Fortunately, Kuranosuke came to his rescue. Writing to Ochiai Yozaemon, just before the attack on the Kira mansion, Kuranosuke said:

> Concerning the impounded goods belonging to Ōno Kurōbei: A new castellan has been appointed in Akō, and we can no longer leave this matter unattended to. Fortunately, I have had word from an assistant to the Resident Intendant, who tells me that Kurōbei is living in straitened circumstances and wishes to retrieve these goods. And so I have sent word that I agree to grant his request. I shall collect all the documents related to the matter and send them on to you.

Four months later, Ōno Kurōbei died.

✦ ✦ ✦

The last we saw of Seno'o Magozaemon, he was staying in the house in Hirama on the farmstead of Karube Gohei. Tominomori Suke'emon had lived there immediately after the Catastrophe, and then, more than a year later, it had been refurbished for Kuranosuke's use when he moved to Edo to lead the attack. Kuranosuke was soon persuaded that it was perfectly safe for him to move into the center of the city, and certainly more efficient. Magozaemon, however, was to remain in Hirama, posing as the main occupant of the house after his "guest" had departed. Which he did—for a time; but then, early in the Twelfth Month, he disappeared, accompanied by Yano Isuke, the foot soldier who was posing as his retainer. Magozaemon was but one of many defectors, but his departure was particularly hurtful to Kuranosuke. Magozaemon was no mere factotum. Kuranosuke often had entrusted him with tasks that required both competence and confidentiality, and Magozaemon had never disappointed him. But on the night before the attack, Kuranosuke wrote to the monk Keikō at Kagakuji: "In Yamashina, I insisted that Magozaemon remain behind; but that only made him angry, and so in the end he came with us. I was actually pleased, and even thought that this would redound to my credit after our death. And then this . . ."

And now? Magozaemon seems eventually to have returned to Akō and changed his name to Kyūshin, which sounds like the name of an old man in retirement. He would, of course, have been known there, but did he imagine that no one in Akō would know what he had done and why he had returned there? Even more surprising, though, he then wrote to Kuranosuke's widow, O-Riku, in Toyooka. Magozaemon's letter does not survive, but O-Riku's reply does:

> I was delighted to read your recent letter. As you say, Kuranosuke Dono and our son were sentenced to commit seppuku. This has left me drained of all strength. Still it was the most favorable of all possible sentences. Kuranosuke Dono himself was permitted to commit seppuku at Sengakuji, and all the others at the houses where they had been held in custody. And their custodians were commanded to give them a proper burial. At Sengakuji, they performed all the appropriate rites; and I understand that their gravestones are inscribed with their familiar names, their formal names, and their posthumous names. Mohei has written to Saroku, telling him all the details. From all that we hear, it seems at least that all has turned out as they wished it would: that much I accept. And yet, I am sure that you can imagine how I feel. I expect that you, too, would like to go to Edo, but, with the prohibitions that are now in place, you cannot. If later these are relaxed, you should then be able to visit their graves. At the moment, I just feel empty and listless, still living but little else. Eventually, the time may come when I'll be able to talk about the misery and the pain. Fortunately, as you say, all women and daughters have been exonerated. What will become of Soren and Daizaburō, I don't yet know; nothing out of the ordinary, I expect. I

understand that rites were performed at Kagakuji. That is wonder-
ful. And I gather that you and Saroku went to the temple together. It
is like a dream to me to know this.

While writing this letter, I have received more detailed news from
Edo. Kuranosuke Dono, too, they say, committed seppuku at the
mansion of Etchū Sama. His Lordship appointed a Company
Commander to serve as Second for Kuranosuke Dono, and the
seppuku was performed to perfection. The other details are rather
unpleasant, and I find it difficult to speak of them. I shall write
again later and tell you all the rest. Sincerely,

SECOND MONTH, 26TH DAY   *Soren's mother*
To: Kyūshin Dono,
with respect

I hardly know what to make of this letter. It is a remarkably frank
confession of the anguish that O-Riku felt, just days after learning of
Kuranosuke's death. Yet why would she reveal her feelings so openly to
someone whom she knew had betrayed her husband? O-Riku was not
ignorant of Magozaemon's defection. Two months earlier, in her letter
to the Superior of the temple Jingūji in Akō, she stated quite plainly that
she was "shocked" to hear what Magozaemon had done and was "terribly
disappointed in him." Not a trace of this resentment appears here. I find
this something of a mystery.

CHAPTER 97

Until then, just another temple: Sengakuji

HAIFŪ YANAGIDARU

I can see why the monks at Sengakuji were beginning to have mixed feelings about their temple having become the posthumous home of the forty-seven Akō ronin. It was the ronin who, quite literally, put Sengakuji on the map. One cannot help noticing that, before the vendetta, few writers could even guess the correct characters with which to write the name of the temple. But every map of Edo published after the vendetta is annotated to show that "here are the graves of the forty-seven." Their sudden fame must at first have pleased the monks, and, as we have seen, it certainly helped to enrich the temple. But before long, the throngs of visitors may have come to seem more a nuisance than a distinction. Sengakuji was a teaching temple; the monks had work of their own to do. Hence that note of irritation in Hakumyō's defense of the need for a fence around the graveyard that could be entered only through a locked gate. Tōjō Shusetsu gives us a feeling for what it was like before the fence was built:

> *Old and young, men and women—the visitors come to pay their respects were innumerable, some weeping, some marveling that so many men had given up their lives in this ultimate act of loyalty.*
>
> *One day, I saw a woman there, going from grave to grave—"Ōishi Kuranosuke Dono, Ōishi Chikara Dono, Hara Sōemon Dono, Okajima Yasoemon Dono, Fuwa Kazuemon Dono, Katsuda Shinzaemon Dono"—all forty-six of their names she recited, placing a sprig of star anise on each grave.*

Another time, I saw an old woman of sixty-plus who had come to the graves and was telling her beads there, apparently for the benefit of the forty-six. As I turned to leave, she tugged at my sleeve to get my attention. "I wish people who have young children would tell them about this," she said to me, and then walked away. What sort of person might she have been? I wondered.

✦ ✦ ✦

Nor were the common run of visitors the only disturbers of the peace at Sengakuji. My friend the scholar Mitamura Engyo has found a document describing a *Hokke Senbu no Kuyō*—a rite in which a passage from the Lotus Sutra was chanted a thousand times over—sponsored by Yozei'in, the widow of Takumi-no-Kami, at the first of the seven obsequies for the ronin. Samurai from her home domain of Miyoshi were sent to maintain order, but apparently the crowds spilled over into the adjacent neighborhoods—a degree of adulation that the Commissioner of Temples and Shrines deemed inappropriate for those who had been punished for committing a crime. One reason, perhaps, why the Commissioner so readily approved the construction of a fence.

✦ ✦ ✦

One of the more charming graveyard scenes, though, is described by the *haikai* master Takarai Kikaku. In those days, the Urabon Festival—or O-Bon, as most people call it—lasted from the 13th to the 16th Day of the Seventh Month. Nowadays, the emphasis is very much on the festivities—the dancing, the celebratory foods, even the genial welcoming of the returning shades. But it originated in rites and offerings of propitiation to be performed on the 15th of the Seventh Month, intended to alleviate the suffering of a late loved one. I suspect that a bit more of this earlier spirit was still alive in the Genroku era than now, and this year was the First O-Bon for the ronin. As Kikaku tells it, they seem not to have been given the attention they deserved.

Kikaku's mother and father were buried at the temple Jōgyōji, on the road to Meguro, just past the lower mansion of the Hosokawa house, where seventeen of the ronin had so recently been held in custody. On the first day of O-Bon, Kikaku dutifully visited his parents' graves there. And since he had known some of the ronin quite well through his disciples Sentoku and Teisa, he decided that he would make a stop at Sengakuji on his way back into the city:

> On the 13th of the Seventh Month, I went to visit the graves at the temple Jōgyōji, and on the way back I descended the slope at Izarako and looked in through the gate of Sengakuji. It occurred to me that I might encounter the shades of my now renowned friends, returned for their First O-Bon; and, indeed, it did somehow feel as though they were right there before my very eyes—Shiyō [Gengo], Shunpan [Suke'emon], Chikuhei [Yogorō], and all the others. I had hoped to take flowers and water to their graves, but the grave-yard was closed to visitors. The weeds were so rank that I could hardly even make out the rows of stones. So I had to settle for send-ing them the feelings that filled my heart—and a reminder, in jest, that they were not to worry too much about the painful horrors of the Shura Hell.

Kikaku speaks lightly, but the thought seems to have stayed with him, for he goes on to say:

> When I contemplate the vanity of the human condition, I conclude that we've nothing in these guts of ours but shit and greed. As those wandering women used to sing, "Earth, Water, Fire, Wind, and Air—Sinew, Veins, Flesh, Bones, Skin covered with hair. Of these are our bodies made. How can we ever hope to escape them?" Everyone, of course—nobles, aristocrats, samurai, common folk, farmers, craftsmen, merchants, not to mention the myriad spirits of the departed who inhabit the Three Realms—every one of us wants to conceal our shit and greed. So we don ceremonial court caps, gird ourselves with swords, array ourselves in formal attire, ride about on horses, while the varieties of ecclesiastical costume are

infinite. Yet our lives on this earth yield naught but the fame of a snail and the fortune of a fly.

> *tarachine ni / shakusen kou wa / nakarikeri*
> Parents never demand that their children pay them back.

One sees Kikaku's point. If loving parents never demand that their children repay the money they "lend" them, how is it that a daimyo expects all these good men to die for him?

◆ ◆ ◆

And, of course, there are more Sengakuji poems, probably scores of them. Some of the best, though, are those gently humorous haiku-like verses named after their inventor, Karai Senryū. My own favorite is:

> *sore made wa / tada no tera nari / sengakuji*
> Until then, just another temple: Sengakuji.

Others play upon the posthumous names of the ronin, all of which contain the characters for "sword" and "blade":

> *sekitō mo / mukoshi de wa inu / shijū shichi*
> Even the gravestones are none of them unarmed: all forty-seven.

> *go-shukun wa / hitori mutō no / on-sekihi*
> His Lordship is the only one whose gravestone wears no sword.

When you read this next poem, imagine yourself moving from grave to grave to grave, reading the names as you go:

> *Sengakuji / yoko ni aruite / kutabireru*
> At Sengakuji, you have to walk sideways; it wears you out.

And remember how the Sengakuji monks who returned Kira's head made the Elders of the house write out a receipt for it?

> *mezurashii / shōmon no aru / sengakuji*
> A most unusual certificate they have here at Sengakuji.

And to the chagrin of all the monks:

> *hondō wa / mairite no nai / sengakuji*
> To the main hall: that's not where the worshippers go, at Sengakuji.

◆ ◆ ◆

I doubt that anyone at Sengakuji would now regard the graveyard of the ronin as anything but an asset. The fence that surrounds it today is of solid granite palings, barely 3 feet high, each carved with the name of a generous donor; and there is no gate, locked or otherwise, at the entrance. The monks might wish to clear away the graves of those once-great daimyo houses that no longer pay rent on the land that they occupy. But the ronin still attract a steady stream of visitors, and that can only accrue to the temple's benefit. Without them, Sengakuji would again be "just another temple."

figure 33
Yosa Buson's whimsical portrait of Takarai Kikaku.
(*Zoku Haika kijin dan,* 1832)

CHAPTER
98

I know of no record that Horiuchi Den'emon
ever returned to Edo.

The home domain of the House of Hosokawa lay 280 leagues (700 miles, 1,120 kilometers) to the west of Edo, in the province of Higo on the far shore of the island of Kyushu. For an entourage of 1,000 men to travel this distance usually took about a month. The first half of the journey would be by land, via the Eastern Sea Road, but skirting Kyoto, moving instead through Fushimi and on to Osaka. There they would board the domain's great fleet of ships and boats, sail the length of the Inland Sea to Tsurusaki on the near shore of Kyushu, debark, and follow the road through the mountains to their castle in Kumamoto. This year, their departure was set for the 25th Day of the Ninth Month.

Preparations were underway at least a month in advance, but these were routine matters and not the sort of thing that anyone felt they need enter in the house records. Horiuchi Den'emon, however, in his personal journal, tells of his farewell visit to the graves of the ronin at Sengakuji:

> I called at Sengakuji, taking incense money, and sent word in to the Abbot: "I am Horiuchi Den'emon, a vassal of Hosokawa Etchū-no-Kami, and was assigned to the vassals of Asano Takumi-no-Kami while they were in our custody. During that time, I was on friendly terms with all seventeen of them. I am about to leave Edo, and being an old man, I am not certain whether I shall be coming back, so I should like to bid them farewell. Could you kindly send someone to guide me to their graves?"

The Abbot sent one of the monks back with his reply: "That is most commendable of you. I should myself conduct you thither, but I have been very ill of late, so I shall send someone to guide you." Two monks came, one of whom had the key to the gate and the other who brought the water bucket, incense burner, and other equipment.

One enters the graveyard from the left of the quadrangle in front of the main hall of the temple, and they stand on a rise, slightly lower than the grave of Lord Naganori. All forty-six are buried together in the same place, and the graves are surrounded by a fence, the entrance to which is locked.

As I was about to leave, a samurai in formal linens came and said to me, "If you don't mind, might I, too, pay my respects?"

"You've come at a perfect time," I replied. "Please do come in." And he did so.

Den'emon was in the vanguard of the homeward-bound procession, and at the inlet to Lake Hamanako, it was he who organized and supervised the crossing from Maisaka to the checkpoint at Arai. Den'emon would have had his hands full on this stretch of the journey. He had arranged in advance, however, to part company with the procession when it turned off the Eastern Sea Road at Oiwake, just short of Kyoto. Etchū-no-Kami himself had given Den'emon permission to proceed directly into Kyoto and lodge at the residence of the Kyoto Liaison Officer. He could then visit Terai Genkei, the former personal physician to Asano Takumi-no-Kami; tell him all the news from Edo; and transmit the messages that the ronin had entrusted to him before their death. To Den'emon's surprise, however, Genkei came to call upon him the very next morning.

"How did you know that I was here?" Den'emon asked.

"I know a merchant named Izutsuya Chōzaemon," Genkei said. "He does business with your domain's residence here, and they told him that you would be coming. So I asked Chōzaemon to let me know as soon you arrived; he came last night to tell me." Den'emon, of course, returned Genkei's visit that same day, at his home on the west side of Yanagi no

Banba, just above Oshinokōji.

"His son Gentatsu was there with him, so we had a long, leisurely chat. I couldn't think what to take as gifts," Den'emon says, "so I gave them both short swords."

Genkei first thanked Den'emon for having visited his friend and fellow physician Utsumi Dōoku in Edo, and then told him of all the letters that he had received from Kuranosuke before his death, as well as a joint letter from Kuranosuke, Sōemon, and Jūnai.

"They said that they were treated better than they could ever have imagined by Etchū-no-Kami Sama and would remember that as long as they lived. They were truly blessed by heaven, they said, and their fortunes as warriors could not have been better. They found it all but impossible to express their feelings on paper," Genkei told him.

"If you've no objection, might I ask you for copies of those letters?"

"Why, that's no problem at all," Genkei said, and his son Gentatsu began by copying the joint letter. While he worked, Den'emon must have been reading the letters from Kuranosuke; for when Gentatsu had finished, Den'emon told him that, actually, he already had copies of the other letters and thus needn't trouble him to him to copy them. But then Genkei showed him the letter from Kuranosuke, dated the 6th Day of the Eighth Month, refusing him permission to participate in the attack, as it was not strictly speaking a battlefield. This was a letter that Den'emon had not seen, and again he asked Gentatsu to make a copy of it for him.

Den'emon then returned the favor and showed Genkei and Gentatsu the scroll on which he had been keeping his personal journal; Genkei, in turn, asked if he might copy that. Gentatsu must have worn out his writing brush that night.

When Den'emon finally bade farewell to Genkei and his son, they made a list of the addresses of people in Fushimi, Hachiman, and Osaka that he wished to call upon. He describes his stop in Fushimi thus:

> In Fushimi, Ryōgae-chō, Kataoka Gengoemon's wife and son were living in rented lodgings. Her younger brother greeted me, and through him she said, "I'm very grateful that you've come to call

upon us. I've heard how you were on friendly terms with Gengoemon for some time. I've been very ill of late, so I can't greet you personally. And Shinroku has gone to his writing lesson, which is rather far from here. If you were able to wait, I would send for him. But I understand that you are just passing through; that is unfortunate." To which her brother added simply, *"It can't be helped."* I made the proper greetings and left. I don't remember the man's name.

In Fushimi, Den'emon boarded the boat on the Yodo River for Osaka, but went only as far as the first stop:

I left the Yodogawa boat at Hachimanzan and called at Ōnishibō, which is just behind the main shrine. There he has a lovely room furnished with a curtained chamber. It was in the afternoon, and the midday meal was served along with various other treats. Ōnishibō appeared to be about twenty or so. Kuranosuke said that the benefice is transmitted in his lineage. The present Ōnishibō is his cousin, but Kuranosuke told the Shogunate that the boy was his nephew, probably to protect him from punishment as his close kin.

On the 15th of the Tenth Month, Den'emon arrived in Osaka, where he found Hara Sōemon's youngest brother, Wada Kiroku, living in lodgings rented from Yorozuya Jirōbei at Tenma, 9-Chōme. Kiroku was a ronin and was looking after Sōemon's four daughters. The two men went to Den'emon's lodgings and had a long leisurely talk; Etchū-no-Kami's departure was scheduled for the next day, however, so there was no time for anything more. Den'emon gave Kiroku a bit of gold, wishing that he were higher in rank so he might give him more. But Den'emon had at least managed to make contact with everyone on his list.

On the 16th Day of the Tenth Month, the Hosokawa fleet sailed from Osaka and arrived in Tsurusaki on the 21st. The procession then made its way across the mountains of Kyushu and arrived in Kumamoto on the 24th Day of the Tenth Month—a journey of twenty-nine days.

◆ ◆ ◆

I know of no record that Horiuchi Den'emon ever returned to Edo. It is possible that he did not. In 1706, three years after the death of the ronin, he resigned his official duties and retired to his small fief in the village of Sugi, more than 7 leagues north of the castle in Kumamoto. In a letter to Terai Genkei, dated Hōei 6 (1709), Eighth Month, 24th Day, he wrote that he was sixty-five years old and no longer made the trip to Edo. Den'emon's stated reason for retiring was illness. But if he was actually ill, it cannot have been a terribly threatening ailment that he suffered, for he lived to the age of eighty-three, dying in 1727. It seems likely that the villagers of Sugi were as fond of their no-longer-absent landlord as were the ronin in Edo. Den'emon and his wife were buried side by side, with identical gravestones, at the village Zen temple, and their graves are as well tended today as they were two centuries ago.

✦ ✦ ✦

Such, then, is what little we know of what transpired in the year of the death of the ronin. In more ways than one, that year was the end of an era. Genroku 16 (1703) was the last year of Genroku. The horrific earthquake that jolted Edo on the 22nd Day of the Eleventh Month, and started the fire that razed a great part of Honjo, made it clear that a new start was needed. The name of the era was changed from Genroku to Hōei, which for those of us who are following the story of the vendetta of the ronin from Akō means that we now enter the After Years.

PART IV

The After Years

*Since this evening, Sahei Sama has been unable to pass
urine, and his breath is rasping and rapid.*

Winters in the mountains of Shinshū, on the shores of Lake Suwa, are
bitterly cold. So cold that ice on the lake becomes thick enough to bear a
steady stream of horses and men, turning off the Middle Mountain Road
and crossing the frozen surface as a shortcut to the Kōshū Highroad
where it runs through the castle town—a scene that Eisen has painted
so beautifully that you can almost feel the chill in your bones.

Kira Sahei certainly would have felt the chill, for Takashima Castle,
on the far side of the lake, was the very fortress in which he was confined—clad only in cotton. The Southern Perimeter could not be seen
from this direction; it had no turret, and it lay beyond the rear ramparts
of the complex. As strictly sequestered as he was there, Sahei may never
even have seen the lake the castle faces—in any season.

◆ ◆ ◆

How Kira Sahei would have fared had he not been remanded in custody
must remain an open question. He had survived the attack of the ronin,
but the wounds sustained in his encounter with Fuwa Kazuemon were
deep and not yet fully healed. He seems, too, to have been troubled by
a chronic intestinal ailment. Nor would those six days en route in a
frigid palanquin have done him much good. On the 16th Day of the
Second Month, however, after his arrival in Suwa, Sahei was examined
thoroughly by two of the physicians in the Suwa household, both of
whom pronounced him in good health—or at least as good as could
be expected under the circumstances. By now, the worst of winter was

past, and the mild days of late spring were on their way. But even the warmth to come would be a mixed blessing where Sahei, Sōda Magobei, and Yamayoshi Shinpachi were housed. The front of the castle faced Lake Suwa, but the Southern Perimeter, at the rear, was surrounded by marshland—an excellent defense against enemy attack, but infested with mosquitoes. As we shall see, this was no minor irritant. It may even have been deadly.

♦ ♦ ♦

The spirit in which Kira Sahei was held in custody might be described as courteous rigor. The Suwa were well aware that Sahei was descended from forebears in the great House of Uesugi, once one of the most powerful in the land and still not to be trifled with. The Suwa, by contrast, were a small house, enfeoffed at only 30,000 *koku*, which made them chary of any conduct that might make the Shogunate think them lax in the performance of their duty. Sahei would be accorded the full measure of respect due someone of his rank and family. Everyone mentioning, or even writing, his name was to call him Sahei *Sama*. But there would be no relaxation of the strictness and severity demanded of a daimyo charged with detaining a prisoner of the Shogun. The Suwa were in no position to bend the rules, as the Hosokawa had done with the ronin in their custody.

Even before Sahei, Magobei, and Shinpachi left Edo, a long list of rules had been drawn up for the samurai who would be assigned to guard them, and to which all concerned were required to swear total obedience. Here are just a few of them:

> Item. *No one is to mention or discuss with others any matters concerning Sahei Sama, Magobei, or Shinpachi.*
>
> Item. *Magobei and Shinpachi are not being held in custody, but they are in touch with Sahei Sama. Everyone is to take care what he says in their presence.*
>
> Item. *If ever Sahei Sama is required to leave the Southern Perimeter, he is to be transported in a palanquin.*

Item. *No one is to behave impolitely toward Magobei or Shinpachi. But if ever they ask about matters pertaining to this house, they are to be told nothing. Simply reply that you do not know.*

Item. *No one is to speak loudly in the presence of Sahei Sama or say anything impolite, even in the guardhouse.*

Item. *As decreed, he is to wear only clothing made of cotton.*

Item. *If Sahei Sama appears to feel ill, even if he himself does not mention it, Jizaemon is to be informed immediately. A physician is to examine him every two or three days.*

Item. *Before entering the presence of Sahei Sama, all swords, fans, paper folds, toothpicks, and such are to be deposited in the guardhouse.*

Item. *All correspondence coming from or sent to Sahei Sama and his vassals is to be carefully inspected.*

The records have almost nothing to say about the daily lives of those forced to live under this regimen. Kira Sahei would not have been allowed to leave the Southern Perimeter, except under conditions of extreme emergency, such as fire. Magobei and Shinpachi were not to be treated as prisoners, yet neither is there any mention of either of them venturing forth. And given the detail of the records, it seems unlikely that anyone's departure would go unremarked.

How, then, would they pass those long empty days, just the three of them, under constant surveillance, in the confines of that small perimeter? The question seems to have occurred even to some of their custodians. When the Southern Perimeter was being refurbished, someone asked if one of the rooms should be furnished for ceremonial tea. The answer was "No." Others noted that Sahei was fond of painting and asked if he should be given the paper he would need for that pastime. And what about reading material? No answers to either of these questions are recorded, nor is there any further mention of books, painting, poems, *go*, *shōgi*, or even interesting conversations. There was no one comparable to Horiuchi Den'emon in the House of Suwa; no one would even have been allowed to befriend them. The lacunae are vast. All we can do is report a bit of what little the official records do tell us.

✦ ✦ ✦

Immediately upon their arrival in the Second Month of Genroku 16, Sahei, Magobei, and Shinpachi were relieved of their swords. The weapons were inspected, and then stored in a container that would be kept in the guardhouse. Once a year thereafter, a man named Asakura Riemon would be summoned to polish the blades.

Through the rest of the first year, the chief concerns of the record keepers seem to have been the clothing and the health of their charges, and to a lesser extent the routine of their guards. In the course of that year, each man was given first a lined cotton kimono, and later single-layer garments. In the Fifth Month, Sahei suffered a recurrence of his chronic ailment—*senki* it was called, which seems to mean abdominal pain in the region of the large intestine. He was prescribed medicine and is said to have recovered. Later in the year, he caught a cold and recovered. Come summer, all three were given fans. In autumn, Magobei and Shinpachi received surcoats. In winter, all three were given two new kimono each.

✦ ✦ ✦

The second year of Sahei's captivity (1704) had a new era name, changed from Genroku to Hōei because of a severe earthquake late in the previous year. On the 6th Day of the First Month, Watanabe Jizaemon, one of the Wardens, asked his superiors if Sahei should be served a traditional New Year's dinner. "No," they told him. "Just give him seven-herb gruel on the morning of the 7th. That will suffice." Neither would it be necessary for the guards to change into formal wear when serving this festive fare.

In the summer of this first year of Hōei, the mosquitoes were mentioned for the first time. Shinpachi told the guards that Sahei's quarters were swarming with them, and he wondered if he might burn some of the Korean incense that Sahei's mother had sent with him to drive away the insects. The problem was duly discussed, and finally it was decided that the incense may be burnt, but not by Sahei himself. A serving monk must be sent with a bowl in which *he* would light the incense. And one wonders: Why was Magobei given a mosquito net when he demanded one, yet neither Sahei nor Shinpachi was provided with any protection?

For the first time, too, someone seems to have noticed that Sahei was feeling depressed. And so on the 13th of the Seventh Month, he was given a box of sweets in the hope that that would cheer him up. It cannot have helped very much, for on the 15th of the Ninth Month he was again depressed, and this time was consoled with a packet of grapes.

This was also the year in which Sahei's natural father and adoptive mother—Uesugi Danjō and Kira's wife—died, only two months apart, in the Sixth and Eighth Months. On both occasions, his guards were told that they should behave with due respect for his bereavement.

Throughout the year, of course, there were the usual replacements of garments and the occasional minor illnesses.

♦ ♦ ♦

In the third year of Sahei's captivity, Hōei 2 (1705), someone in Edo decided that he should be congratulated upon greeting the New Year in good health. The text of this directive was written out and sent to Suwa, where it was read to Sahei on the 5th by Shiga Rihei.

Shortly thereafter, on the 16th of the First Month, word came from Edo that if Sahei should again be taken ill, the Suwa would be required to report it directly to the Shogunate. His guardians in Suwa must immediately send an account of what and how much he had eaten, his symptoms, the doctor's diagnosis, and what medicines he had been given.

Two months later, in what was a particularly cold spring, Sahei was for the first time allowed to use a *kotatsu* to warm himself.

What instigated this new concern for the health and comfort of the prisoner was not explained. But it certainly was timely, for by the autumn, Sahei was beginning to show clear signs of failing health. It had begun with a recurrence of his chronic intestinal pain, which persisted into the Tenth Month. Then, on the 20th of that month, in the middle

figure 34
Keisai Eisen, *View of Lake Suwa from Shiojiri Pass*. Takashima Castle stands on the
far shore of Lake Suwa. (From *Kiso Kaidō rokujūkyū tsugi*, ca. 1835)

~ *806* ~

of the night, he came down with severe fits of shivering and chills, followed by a high fever that did not subside until nearly the Eighth Hour (2:00 A.M.). The next day or two seems to have brought some relief; but from the 23rd through the end of the month, the attacks came nightly, varying only slightly, but with the chills growing steadily more intense. In the Eleventh Month, this pattern became so repetitive that on the 6th the official record simply refers the reader to "the journal kept by Rihei and Naoemon" for details. But by the Twelfth Month, Sahei's condition was being described in more extreme terms: the chills and trembling had grown "far worse" and the fever was now causing "profuse perspiration." Sahei's year-end gift of a new kimono was this time wrapped in formal presentation paper, but it was unlikely that he was well enough to appreciate the gesture.

◆ ◆ ◆

By the beginning of Sahei's fourth year in Suwa, Hōei 3 (1706), a steady stream of express couriers had been carrying news of his condition to the main house. And then we read:

> 19th Day. Since this evening, Sahei Sama has been unable to pass urine, and his breath is rasping and rapid. The Elders and the Adjutants met at the Southern Perimeter to discuss the matter. In consequence, the physicians Ryōan and Yōzen prepared medicines for him. These matters were reported by express courier to both Edo and Osaka. . . .

> 20th Day. Sahei Sama failed to recover. This morning, early in the Hour of the Hare [ca. 5:00 A.M.], he died.

Died of what? I know nothing of the pathology of malaria; but given the environment in which he was forced to live, the apparent weakness of his constitution, and the symptoms that he suffered, I cannot but suspect that Kira Sahei was a victim of the mosquitoes that swarmed about the Southern Perimeter of Takashima Castle. But none of the records venture any explanation of his death. We know only his symptoms and his fate.

◆ ◆ ◆

Whatever the cause, there was nothing that could be done about it without orders from Edo. All the senior officers gathered, well before sunrise. Morozumi Jūrōemon and Sawa Mohei were commanded to carry the news to Edo as soon as they could ready themselves (this was news too momentous to be carried by courier; samurai were required); they were under way even before the Hour of the Hare was out. And although the lake was still frozen solid, and it was no warmer within the Southern Perimeter, Sahei's body was "packed in salt."

Jūrōemon and Mohei must have traveled by express conveyance; they arrived in Edo before midday on the 22nd, only two and a half days en route. By nightfall of that day, the death of Kira Sahei had been reported to the Shogunate.

The recipient of that report, though, seems not to have thought it as urgent a matter as the Suwa house did. Not until six days later, on the 27th, was Ishigaya Shichinosuke, a member of the Shogun's Bodyguard, commanded to proceed to Suwa and investigate; and two more days were to pass before he departed.

Shichinosuke traveled by way of the Middle Mountain Road and arrived in Lower Suwa on the 3rd Day of the Second Month. That night, he lodged in the official inn, and at midday on the 4th made his way to the Willow Gate of the castle, where he was served a light soup before proceeding to the Southern Perimeter. Nothing is said of his inspection of the body, except that after completing it, he was served a magnificent meal of "three soups and nine sides." Late in the afternoon of the same day, Kira Sahei was buried at the temple Hokkeji. Shichinosuke and his entourage, having been duly rewarded, returned to their inn in Lower Suwa and on the morning of the 5th set out for Edo.

◆ ◆ ◆

The return trip of Sōda Magobei and Yamayoshi Shinpachi would be far more comfortable than that of their arrival. A detailed itinerary was drafted, listing not only the stations where they would lodge along the way, but even those where they would pause for refreshments—advance arrangements having been made at every stage of the journey.

Nor were they to return empty-handed. Their swords were, of course, returned to them, and those of Sahei as well. Each man was also presented with a fine kimono, the material having been sent from Osaka to be tailored in Suwa, and to go with it, a full set of formal linens, a new obi, and three pairs of tabi each.

Finally, on the 15th Day of the Second Month, almost a month after the death of their lord, Magobei and Shinpachi were to depart Suwa. They were first served a sumptuous meal of "two soups and five sides," and then given a stack of lacquered boxes filled with treats they could snack on until their next stop—in the unlikely event that they were still hungry. Watanabe Jizaemon and Shiga Rihei, their former Wardens, came to the Southern Perimeter, locked the gate, and then saw them off as far as the sally port of the castle. From there, they would be accompanied all the way to Edo by Ariga Genbei, Morozumi Han'emon, and Kosaka Hei'emon, as well as a number of foot soldiers, lackeys, and bearers, all clad in matching surcoats. It was nowhere near as grand a procession as when they had come to Suwa, but still impressive in its neatness. And this time, they were treated as honored guests rather than as semi-prisoners.

Their journey and their arrival at the Uesugi Middle Mansion in Shirogane were nowhere described. Sometime thereafter, however, Sōda Magobei returned to his ancestral home in the village of Kira, the province of Mikawa; Yamayoshi Shinpachi, to his birthplace in Yonezawa. We know nothing more of Magobei, except that he lived to the age of eighty-four, but we have not seen the last of Shinpachi.

◆ ◆ ◆

Before their departure, Magobei and Shinpachi pooled their resources and sent three gold pieces to the temple Hokkeji, where Sahei was buried, asking that a stone be erected at his grave—something made of natural stone rather than the traditional cut granite. The temple chose well. The stone still stands—a handsome asymmetrical rock, inscribed only with his posthumous name and the date of his death: Hōei 3, First Month, 20th Day. Sahei had just begun his twenty-first year.

CHAPTER
100

This domain is at the very heart
of the Snow Country.

Many of the people we knew when they were gathered in Edo now scattered to other corners of the land, some to pursue new careers, some to die. Some disappeared almost immediately; some remained in sight for years to come.

♦ ♦ ♦

The year after the seppuku, Hōei 1 (1704), Honda Nakatsukasa died, at the age of only thirty-nine, and was succeeded as lord of Himeji by his six-year-old son, Tadataka. The Shogunate, understandably, considered Himeji too strategic a domain to be entrusted to a child, and the Honda were moved to the domain of Murakami in the northwestern province of Echigo. This meant that the family of Itō Jūrōdayū, the husband of Yoshida Chūzaemon's eldest daughter, was forced to move with them. And at that point, it was a very large family indeed. In addition to Jūrōdayū's own wife and children, his wife's mother, the widow of Chūzaemon; his wife's younger sister; and Terasaka Kichiemon and his wife were living with him. Kichiemon describes their new situation briefly:

> *My wife and I are both well. And [Yoshida] Dennai's mother, even*
> *after moving here, still receives a yearly allowance in cash from His*
> *Lordship, for which we are very grateful. Chūzaemon's youngest*
> *daughter, radiant with the glory of her father's honor, is certain to*
> *find an excellent husband among the samurai of this house. . . .*

This domain is at the very heart of the Snow Country. From the Ninth Month through the Second Month of the next year, it is very difficult to get about. They say that the snow has been as deep as 10 feet in the past, but in the last four or five years, it has been only 3 or 4 feet deep. Nonetheless, it does make life difficult. How we miss the region of the capital!

◆ ◆ ◆

Once Kuranosuke and others of the command group arrived in Edo, Ōishi Mitsuhira, the second son of Ōishi Mujin, became an active participant in the plot. He had never been a vassal of Takumi-no-Kami, and thus could not join in the actual attack; but as an Ōishi, there was no doubt that he could be trusted. And being a ronin, he had no conflicting allegiances to deter him from abetting his kinsmen and their comrades. But what was to become of Mitsuhira now that all of them were dead?

The genealogies say nothing of how he happened to embark upon his subsequent career. One suspects the influence of the Konoe again, but no mention was made of it when, in Hōei 2 (1705), Mitsuhira became a vassal of Matsudaira Sanuki-no-Kami Yoritoyo, lord of Takamatsu Castle and the entire province of Sanuki. Thereafter, his rise was steady, from rations for twenty men at the outset to 300 koku by the time of his retirement. Mitsuhira paid no penalty for his considerable contribution to the Akō vendetta.

◆ ◆ ◆

The reader may recall how concerned old Horibe Yahei had been for the future of Yasubei's cousin Satō Jōemon. He was living on the patronage of a bannerman, Suwa Aki-no-Kami, at the time, but had no prospects for a more permanent career.

"He's very manly," Yahei had told Horiuchi Den'emon. "Unfortunately, though, he's an ugly fellow." But Den'emon was right to reassure Yahei that all would turn out well for him. Sometime after the death of the fifth Shogun, Jōemon was recruited into the growing Corps of Vassals of Manabe Akifusa, Chief Adjutant and Elder to both the sixth Shogun, Ienobu, and the seventh, Ietsugu. Who sponsored him, and when, we have no idea; but in 1714, Jōemon's name appears in the Manabe roster of vassals as a samurai on a stipend of "rations for fifteen men per year." And a samurai he remained, even after the eighth Shogun, Yoshimune, dismissed Manabe from office in 1717 and packed him off to the snowbound domain of Murakami, the fief formerly held by the Honda. Jōemon seems to have prospered there; still later, after a further move, Jōemon was promoted from Vanguard Commander to City Magistrate and was awarded a stipendiary increase of thirty bales per year. As late as 1734, when Jōemon would have been about sixty-five, his name still appears in the records of the Manabe house.

Like his cousin Horibe Yasubei, though in a very different way, Jōemon succeeded in escaping his ambiguous origins and establishing himself as a fully fledged samurai.

◆ ◆ ◆

The monks at Sengakuji, too, were as constantly on the move as Jōemon. Hakumyō, whose memoir we have cited so often, was a nineteen-year-old novice at the time of the vendetta. After completing his training, he stayed at Sengakuji until Kyōhō 3 (1718), after which he moved to Eiheiji in Echizen for further training at the home temple of Sōtō Zen. Seventeen years later (ca. 1735), after making the rounds of various other Zen temples in other parts of the land, he returned to Tosa to become the Superior of the temple Tōfukuji in the town of Sukumo at the far western tip of Shikoku. And there he remained until his death.

Hakumyō also tells us a bit about what became of his two fellow monks who had returned the severed head of Kira Kōzuke-no-Suke to his family. Ichidon, who was from the province of Musashi, later became the Superior of Jushōji in the village of Yōda, in Musashi. And Sekishi, who was from Wakasa, at some point returned there.

◆ ◆ ◆

Horiuchi Den'emon told us some time ago how Chikamatsu Kanroku regretted that he had not given his surname to his manservant Jinzaburō and made him a samurai. But Den'emon seems not to have known that Kanroku at least had managed to reward Jinzaburō in another way.

No documents survive, but we know that after he returned to Ōmi, Jinzaburō entered the service of the Chikamatsu main house and that Kanroku had left all the land held in his own name—valued at more than 160 koku—to the sixteen vassal-farmers who had tilled it while he was away in Akō. Quite as touching as the gift itself, though, is the fellow feeling with which these men accepted their gift. Never, even in the present day, has the land been divided into individual plots. The descendants of that band of warriors who became the original vassal-farmers continue to hold the land in common, as equals, and continue to till it together. And every year, on the 4th Day of the Second Month, they still meet to commemorate and mourn the death of their bene-factor, Chikamatsu Kanroku.

✦ ✦ ✦

The entry for the 3rd Day of the Sixth Month of Shōtoku 4 (1714) in the *Miyoshi Cadet Branch Records of a Dutiful Progeny* reads:

> Yōzei'in Sama failed to recover from her illness, and toward the end of the Hour of the Dog (ca. 9:00 P.M.), she passed away. On the 6th Day, her coffin was taken to Sengakuji, where she was buried. On the following day, obsequies were held and the temple was given offerings of fifty pieces of silver, to which were added another fifty pieces of the same, together with a list thereof, a total of a hundred pieces.

No mention of her illness appears in earlier entries, and no description of it accompanies the notice of her death. She died in the Miyoshi Middle Mansion, which had been her first home when she came to Edo as child of seven. She was only in her forty-sixth year.

Shortly thereafter, her lifelong Chamberlain, Ochiai Yozaemon, returned to Miyoshi, his "home" in the hills of the province of Bingo that he had not seen in almost forty years, since he had accompanied his young charge to Edo in Enpō 4 (1676). He lived in Miyoshi until Kyōhō 8 (1723), nine years after the death of Yōzei'in and three years after the Miyoshi domain had been reunited with Hiroshima for lack of an heir.

✦ ✦ ✦

Some of the women, too, fared well.

How it all came about is no longer known, but Tadami Suke'emon, the brother of Horibe Yahei's widow, Waka, was a vassal of Honda Magotarō, Chief Elder of the Fukui Matsudaira house. Through him, it was arranged that Waka be taken into the service of the retired head of the house of Niwa Wakasa-no-Kami, now known as Ryōtai'in. In this capacity, she adopted the name Takashima. No date is given for Waka's entry into service, but it must have been in the year of the seppuku, for her New Year's letter to the wife of Yahei's old friend Ōishi Mujin was written after she had moved to her new home in Nihonmatsu Castle. Happily, her daughter, Hori, and her adopted son, Bungorō, were able to continue to live with her.

And, once again, the Regental House of Konoe showed that it had not forgotten its connection with the House of Ōishi—dating back more than a century to the marriage of Shimo, Konoe Sakihisa's "misplaced seed," and Ōishi Kyūemon. This time, the Chancellor Konoe Motohiro came to the aid of the aging mother of Ōishi Sezaemon and took her into his service as an Elder. In this capacity, she adopted the name Toyama no Tsubone and remained with the Konoe in Kyoto until her death on the 26th Day of the Eleventh Month of Kyōhō 6 (1721).

But what of those women whose fate we have good reason to worry about, but whom no one ever mentions again? What, for example, became of the mother of Yatō Emoshichi, turned back from the checkpoint at Arai because her son hadn't known she would need a woman's checkpoint pass? And what ever became of Hara Sōemon's four young daughters, living in Osaka with their uncle, who was himself an indigent ronin? And O-Karu, still in her teens, whom Kuranosuke had made pregnant before he left for Edo? Did she ever bear the child she carried? Did she survive the birth? Reports of her death a few years later survive, but can we believe them? We shall never know.

✦ ✦ ✦

There must be many more such people, both in the thick of things and on the periphery, whose later life—or demise—was never recorded. There is one very formidable figure, however, whose death was to prove a turning point in the lives of a great many people we know. That was the fifth Shogun, Tokugawa Tsunayoshi, who died on the morning of the 10th Day of the First Month of Hōei 6 (1709), one more victim of a severe epidemic of measles. The entry for that day in the *Veritable Records of the Tokugawa* reads:

> *He had been bathed in saké [upon his supposed recovery], and his kinsmen and vassals, both of daimyo rank and lower, had gathered. Then at the Hour of the Hare [5:00 A.M.], his illness suddenly took a turn for the worse. He died in the main hall of the Palace, having lived through sixty-four illustrious years. The Elders came out and informed those in attendance what had happened, and that His Highness had left word of his wish that the Major Counselor [Ienobu] now strive faithfully to fulfill his duty. With which all, high and low, in a state of shock and grief, departed. At the time, all anyone had heard was that the Shogun was ill; but as the news spread, the common folk were astounded, and myriad baseless rumors began making the rounds.*

CHAPTER
101

Takumi Dono wasted the lives of a lot of good men
with one useless stroke of his sword.

Despite the temple's early attempts to discourage sightseers, the graves of the ronin, far from fading into collective forgetfulness, became a perennial attraction for both tourists and residents of Edo. But I know of only one daimyo who dared to visit the graveyard while the fifth Shogun, Tsunayoshi, still ruled and the ronin were still officially deemed criminals. This was Maeda Uneme Toshimasa, younger brother of Maeda Toshinao, lord of the Daishōji cadet branch of the "Million Koku Maeda." When Toshinao succeeded to the headship, he granted Uneme Toshimasa a fief of 10,000 koku in his own right. The domain was appropriately named Daishōji Shinden, because it consisted mainly of rice lands newly developed by peasants of the parent fief.

The records are not full enough to date precisely Uneme's visit to Sengakuji, but it was probably in the year 1708 that he paced up and down those rows of gravestones and remarked, "Takumi Dono wasted the lives of a lot of good men with one useless stroke of his sword. If he simply *had* to do it, he should just have jabbed the blade 5 or 6 inches into the man's gut." Uneme's words conjure up the image of a brash and irreverent young man, which jibes perfectly with what we know of him from other sources. He was also said to be "as beautiful as a court lady, and powerfully strong"; and if his penchant for formal wear of sky blue and cherry-blossom pink is any indication, he was a bit of a dandy as well.

One wonders, though, whether his visit to Sengakuji might not have been an inspiration to him. In 1709, after the death of the Shogun,

~ 817 ~

Uneme was appointed to serve as official host to the emissary sent by the Empress from Kyoto to attend the final obsequies—a duty similar to that which had led to Takumi's downfall. His colleague in this duty was Oda Kenmotsu Hidechika, a distant descendant of the great warlord Oda Nobunaga. Kenmotsu was of no higher rank, but because he was the elder, Uneme was careful always to ask his opinion and defer to his judgment. Kenmotsu, however, repaid deference with rudeness, deliberately withholding instructions sent from the Council of Elders, and at one point telling Uneme that he was behaving "like a two-year-old." Such insults may well have called to his mind the case of Takumi-no-Kami. That evening, at any rate, Uneme went to see his mother and told her, "There are some things that a warrior simply cannot abide, so I'll warn you: don't be shocked if you hear that something unexpected has happened."

The next day, both men arrived well before dawn at the temple in Ueno, where their aristocratic charges were waiting. When Uneme entered the duty room, he found Kenmotsu dozing, so he prodded him awake. Then he drew his short sword and "jabbed it deep into Kenmotsu's gut, twisting the blade sharply in the gash. With a groan, Kenmotsu attempted to stand, but fell forward. Hardly any blood emerged from the wound, but a great deal gushed from his mouth." Moments later, he expired. Uneme wiped his blade clean on an under-robe, sheathed it, and turned to his Chief Elder, Kimura Kuzaemon.

"Well, shall I commit suicide now?" he asked.

"No," the Elder replied. "You've done exactly what you wished to do. We'll tell them you've suddenly been taken ill, and then get you out of here." With that, he bundled Uneme into his palanquin and sent him home. Lord Nakayama, Third Rank, one of the delegation of court nobles, witnessed the whole scene, peeping through a crack between the sliding panels.

The commotion that ensued need hardly be described. Inspectors were dispatched from the castle to interrogate Uneme. He told them only that he had killed Kenmotsu because "he annoyed me." They concluded that Uneme was deranged; but since his victim had died, there was no escaping punishment on that account. He was placed in the custody of another daimyo, at whose mansion he would be commanded to commit seppuku on the evening of the morrow.

Tatami mats were laid out in the garden, but when the Inspector General and his entourage arrived to oversee the proceedings, he said, "I understand that in the case of Asano Takumi, such an arrangement was regarded as beneath the dignity of a daimyo. This being the case, I must ask you to cover the entire veranda of your reception rooms with felt and on it lay out six tatami mats. Over this, in successive layers, you are to place a purple spread, a bolt of felt, and a sheet of white cotton. Until we have finished reading the sentence to Uneme Sama, this place should be concealed by folding screens covered in white."

So Uneme was to die with far more of the dignity due a daimyo than had Takumi-no-Kami. But when they read the sentence to him— that he would be allowed to take his own life rather than suffer the humiliation of execution—he uttered none of the refined expressions of gratitude with which Takumi and the ronin had responded. He said only, "Well, let's hurry up and be done with it."

Four guards led him to the appointed place on the veranda. A short sword with no guard, wrapped in white paper, was placed before him. He raised it and bowed slightly, and then positioned the point just below his ribs on the left side of his abdomen, thrust it in, and drew it 4 or 5 inches to the right—whereupon his Second, with one powerful blow, severed his head.

He had persisted in his insolence to the very end, but at least he had wasted no other life than his own.

CHAPTER
102

*In fear and trembling,
I tender this humble request.*

I expect that O-Riku spoke for most of the widows of the ronin when she said, "I just feel empty and listless, still living but little else." That emptiness would never be made whole again, but at some point, these women's lives would again resume at least the outward appearance of normality. For those wives who were also the mothers of young sons, it was fear rather than peace or resignation that would begin to fill the emptiness—fear of the loss they were to suffer when their sons reached the age of fifteen and were taken away to be banished. And for those whose sons were already far away on an island, fear that they might not survive the hardships of that life long enough for their mothers ever to see them again.

Still, banishment does lack the finality of death. One could at least hope for an amnesty. But amnesties were unpredictable and never indiscriminate. One could not *just* wait and hope. There was a system of sorts. If one hoped for a pardon on the occasion of obsequies held at one of the Shogun's temples, for the benefit of some departed eminence, then a close relation of the condemned must write to either Kan'eiji or Zōjōji, stating their case, so that the name of the condemned could be entered on the temple's Amnesty Roll. This roster would then be submitted to the Commissioner of Temples and Shrines the next time an amnesty was in the offing. The earliest surviving example of such an appeal is this brief missive from Yoshida Chūzaemon's wife, O-Rin, written about a year after the seppuku of the ronin:

Memorandum

Last year, the life of Yoshida Dennai was graciously spared, and he was instead banished to a distant island—for which I am deeply grateful. I am now living with Itō Jūrōdayū, a vassal of Honda Nakatsukasa Taifu Sama. Inasmuch as Dennai is my only surviving son, I would be most grateful if in your infinite mercy you should kindly allow him to return home. In fear and trembling, I tender this humble request. Herewith the foregoing,

SECOND MONTH

Yoshida Dennai's mother
His elder sister
His younger sister

In the meantime, it is said, Takumi-no-Kami's widow, Yōzei'in; Asano Aki-no-Kami, lord of the main house in Hiroshima; and even Honda Nakatsukasa in Himeji had been writing to request amnesty for the children of the ronin; but none of these letters survive. Besides which, my friend Mitamura Engyo tells me that Yōzei'in's entreaties may have taken an entirely different form.

In a very small temple, the Kayōin, close by the Great Gate of the Shogunal Temple Zōjōji, there lived a nun named Senkei. We know very little about this woman, except that her temple was a dependency of Zōjōji and that she was a close friend of Yōzei'in, whom she was frequently seen visiting at the middle mansion of the Miyoshi domain. Senkei obviously had a great deal more freedom of movement than her friend, and she had a direct connection with one of the Shogun's mortuary temples. According to Engyo, many of the good works attributed to Yōzei'in were in fact executed by Senkei at her behest. It is quite likely, therefore, that Yōzei'in's appeal for amnesty was carried personally by Senkei to the appropriate prelate in Zōjōji, where, given the rank of its author and the temple's relationship with Senkei, it would have been given high priority.

But amnesty requires an occasion; in this case, the occasion was the death of the Shogun's mother. The effect, however, did not follow immediately upon the cause. Keishōin died, aged seventy-nine, on the 22nd

Day of the Sixth Month of Hōei 2 (1705). It was not until the memorial services held more than a year later, on the 12th Day of the Eighth Month of Hōei 3 (1706), that an amnesty was proclaimed in her name. Those to be pardoned included seven in the custody of daimyo, ten banished to islands, twenty-five expelled from Edo, seven in prison, one in custody of a guardian, one fugitive—and of these, ten would be required to take vows upon release and become monks. Unfortunately, this last condition was applied to the three young men who would be returning from Ōshima.

The first boat from the island arrived in Edo on the 7th Day of the Ninth Month. Two days later, on the 9th, Yoshida Dennai (now twenty-eight) and Muramatsu Masaemon (now twenty-six) were released from the office of the Izu Deputy. On the 16th, they both took vows at the temple Tōunji, just across the Edo River in Mejiro. Thereafter, they would be known as Keigaku and Musen, respectively.

On that same day, news of the amnesty reached Dennai's mother, far to the northwest in the province of Echigo. Terasaka Kichiemon, who by sheer chance happened to be in Edo when the amnesty was proclaimed, wrote to her immediately. On the 16th, as soon as his letter arrived, she herself wrote to Dennai:

> I have just heard from Kichiemon, so I'll send off a quick note straightaway. I am so grateful that you have been released from island banishment. The request came from an unexpected source, although I understand it was requested that you be pardoned on condition of becoming a monk. That is a pity. But at least you are all safe and sound. I look forward with such delight to seeing you again soon. Despite all, do try to make the best of everything there, and take care to speak agreeably. You can leave the minor matters to Kichiemon. From what Sahyōe Dono tells us, I expect that he, too, will be of help to you in some ways. He is really very thoughtful, and we must somehow thank him properly. Likewise with Uzaemon. A letter came from Sahyōe Dono just the day before yesterday. I think he will be going to Edo shortly. At any rate, I am so looking forward to seeing you soon. Be sure to discuss all the

details with Kichiemon. . . . Respectfully,

NINTH MONTH, 16TH DAY *From Mother*

To: Yoshida Dennai Dono,
with respect

Kichiemon himself made matters a bit clearer in a letter to an old
friend back in Harima, whom he addressed simply as "Shichiemon
Sama, in the village of Kibita."

> *Last year, on the occasion of obsequies held by the Shogunate, Dennai
> was released from island banishment. The decree reached the island
> in the Eighth Month, and in the Ninth Month, his ship arrived in
> Edo. Toward the end of the Tenth Month, once we had concluded
> all our business in Edo, I accompanied him home to Murakami
> in Echigo. I just happened to be in Edo under orders, when, quite
> unexpectedly, he was advised that he might return home. I was
> utterly delighted by his good fortune. It was the entreaty of the
> widow of a certain daimyo in Edo that made this possible. But he
> was commanded to take vows, shave his head, and now goes by the
> ecclesiastical name of Keigaku. This is the one thing that his mother
> and everyone else in the family regret, but there is nothing that can
> be done about it.*

A few days after the arrival of Dennai and Masaemon, the third of the
sons, Nakamura Chūzaburō, returned to Edo. Upon his release, he went
to the temple Sōgenji in Asakusa, where his younger brother had earlier
entered orders and where he, too, took vows. The two brothers obviously had discussed the matter of their ecclesiastical names: the younger
had taken the name Shunshō (Spring Pine), and so the elder decided
that he would become Shūchiku (Autumn Bamboo). Chūzaburō did
not remain in Edo, however. He headed north to Shirakawa, where his
mother was living. Five years later, he died.

The fourth son, Masé Sadahachi, would never return. He had died a
year before the amnesty, at the age of twenty-three, and was buried on
the island of Ōshima.

✦ ✦ ✦

Welcome though it was, the amnesty of Hōei 3 (1706) was as nothing compared with the amnesty of Hōei 6 (1709), proclaimed after the death of the Shogun, Tokugawa Tsunayoshi. This was to be a Grand Amnesty, but a Grand Amnesty of a new and special sort. In the past, amnesties proclaimed by the Shogunate applied only in those in lands directly under its jurisdiction. No one in the domain of a daimyo or a bannerman could ever be the beneficiary of an amnesty proclaimed by the Shogunate. This was unfair, and it was perceived as unfair; but it was not until the new Shogun, Ienobu, had taken office and his new adviser, Arai Hakuseki, officially had his ear that anything was done to right the wrong. Now the wrong *was* set right.

Tokugawa Ienobu personally examined the charges against those on the lists submitted by the temples Kan'eiji and Zōjōji, and on the 30th Day of the Second Month, he pardoned 92 of them, after which he pardoned another 3,737 persons in the domains of daimyo and lesser lords—a total of 3,829 pardons. The notice of this amnesty in the *Veritable Records of the Tokugawa* goes on to state specifically: "The vassals of Asano Takumi-no-Kami, claiming to avenge their lord, killed Kira Kōzuke-no-Suke and thus were sentenced to death. Their young children, who were remanded to the custody of their kin, are hereby pardoned."

There could be no ambiguity. All twenty children, wherever in the land they might be living, no longer needed to fear that they would be banished to an island when they reached the age of fifteen. There were unstated beneficiaries as well. That the underage children had been pardoned unconditionally meant that those who had been pardoned conditionally were now free from the conditions imposed upon them. Yoshida Dennai and Muramatsu Masaemon could now recant their vows as monks and return to secular life as samurai. They were warriors once again and free to perpetuate the lineages of their parents, which otherwise would have died out.

Asano Daigaku, too, was "freed." He had more than once been assured that he was *not* under sentence of detention while in the care of the main house in Hiroshima. But when the Council of Elders commanded all the lords of the land to submit the names of those in their custody, the Hiroshima house reported that Asano Daigaku was being held "in custody." The Elders' response gave the lie to their previous claims, for again the *Veritable Records of the Tokugawa* states explicitly that "Asano Daigaku Nagahiro and 1,149 others" were among those "previously banished or expelled but now pardoned." Once pardoned, he seems also to have been recalled to Edo, for on the 29th Day of the Ninth Month of Hōei 6 (1709), he departed from Hiroshima and on the 25th of the Tenth Month arrived in Edo. At first, he was housed in the Asano mansion in Aoyama and given a stipend of 2,000 bales per year. A year or so later, however, he was granted an audience with the Shogun, awarded a residence of his own in Aoyama, reinstated as a bannerman, and enfeoffed with lands in the nearby province of Awa valued at 500 koku. Throughout the remainder of his career, Asano Daigaku remained a member of the Reserve Force and was never assigned any official duties within the Shogunate. Thus was the Akō branch of the House of Asano at long last resuscitated—although no longer as the lords of Akō and at barely one-hundredth part of its previous wealth.

CHAPTER
103

*The boy . . . hardly listens to anything
his mother tells him.*

On the 2nd Day of the Third Month of Hōei 8 (1711), Kuranosuke's widow, O-Riku, now Kōrin'in, wrote a long letter full of family news to a woman in Okayama named Murao. Whether Murao was a relative or not we do not know, but she was clearly a woman to whom O-Riku felt she could speak frankly. Fascinating though her letter is, the only parts that need concern us are those in which O-Riku spoke of herself, Kuranosuke, and her children:

> *What Kuranosuke has accomplished is known even out here. He has made quite a name for himself throughout the land, which affords us a certain satisfaction. And yet, how I long for the good old days. I never cease wishing we could again be as we were back in Akō. . . .*
>
> *O-Ruri is thirteen this year, but so grown up that she looks fourteen or fifteen. She has become quite skilled at the koto; she can even read my letters to me, which she seems to enjoy. . . . Daizaburō, too, is in good health. He is big for his age and a very spirited boy. I spend all my days doing whatever I can for those two children. But they have no father, and their manners are not what they should be for children their age. The boy, in particular, hardly listens to anything his mother tells him. I would like people to speak well of them, but it keeps me going morning to night, just trying to look after them. You can imagine how I feel.*

Precisely two years and two days had passed since the amnesty proclaimed after the death of the fifth Shogun had freed Ōishi Daizaburō from the threat of banishment. The boy was now in his tenth year. O-Riku may well have begun to think about his future, but if so, she does not mention it in her letter. Others, however, had begun to discuss what might be done for the boy. The first were Terai Genkei, former personal physician to Takumi-no-Kami, and Ishizuka Gengobei, O-Riku's father and Chief Elder of the Toyooka domain. It was a disaster that brought these two men together.

In the year prior to the amnesty (1708), a dreadful fire had swept across the northern reaches of Kyoto, razing, among much else, the palaces of both the Emperor and the Retired Emperor. And, as chance would have it, Kyōgoku Kai-no-Kami, lord of Toyooka, had been assigned the task (and expense) of rebuilding the palace of the Retired Emperor. Kai-no-Kami, in turn, dispatched his Chief Elder, Ishizuka Gengobei, to Kyoto to supervise the works. Thus Gengobei was in Kyoto when the amnesty was proclaimed, and Genkei—who otherwise could not have known the man—was able to contact Gengobei easily and discuss the future of his grandson Daizaburō.

Genkei seems to have hoped that Gengobei could persuade Kai-no-Kami to take Daizaburō into his service. Gengobei allowed as how Kai-no-Kami would be loath to let the son of Kuranosuke go elsewhere, but Toyooka was a small domain and was now faced with the massive expense of rebuilding an Imperial Palace. This would not be a good time to suggest another major expenditure.

Genkei lived just to the south of the Imperial Palaces, and his home, too, had been burnt to the ground. After the fire, he had moved across the river, to the vicinity of the great temple Chion'in, which, again by pure chance, put him in touch with another possible benefactor. Just across the street from Genkei's new home was the residence of the Kyoto Liaison Officer of the Hosokawa house. It was there, in the course of his daily comings and goings, that Genkei happened to meet Yokota Zendayū, an old friend of Horiuchi Den'emon. Genkei thus was able to importune Zendayū to forward a personal letter to Den'emon along with the domain mail. He told Den'emon of his fruitless discussion with

Ishizuka Gengobei, and then offered another suggestion:

> *Ishizuka Gengobei has been here since the summer of last year as superintendent of a government construction project and will remain in Kyoto for the present. I encounter him frequently and gather that although Kai-no-Kami seems reluctant to let Daizaburō go elsewhere, his being a small house, we doubt that anything can be done for him. What I should like, therefore, is for your Great Lord to take him into his service. I know that in years past, you were a close friend of Kuranosuke. If someone like your good self were to take an interest in the matter, and put a word in His Lordship's ear, I would hope that when the boy grows up he might be received as a vassal by your Great Lord.*

Genkei could not have known, of course, that his request would catch Den'emon at a most inopportune moment. Den'emon replied:

> *As you say, if one were to put a word in the ear of Etchū-no-Kami, he would without a doubt give the command instantly—for Daizaburō Dono. But His Lordship is now in Edo, having been commanded to help rebuild the Shogun's temple in Ueno. And although he would certainly agree were he to hear of this, his Adjutants here are hard pressed with official business. They have no time to discuss such matters or even pass on the message to Etchū-no-Kami.*

Nor was Den'emon himself able to pass on the message. He was now sixty-five, retired, and no longer living in the castle town. Even so, he promised Genkei, he would tell his son Shōsuke, as well as his kinsmen and certain others he knew well, so that they could mention Genkei's proposal at a more propitious moment. As far as we know, however, nothing further concerning Daizaburō was heard from anyone in Kumamoto.

◆ ◆ ◆

The first line of the entry for Daizaburō in the Ōishi genealogies reads:

"Yoshiyasu's [Daizaburō] invitation to Hiroshima was arranged by Yoshimaro." Which is to say that, in the end, Daizaburō joined neither the Kyōgoku nor the Hosokawa Corps of Vassals, but instead was taken in by Asano Aki-no-Kami, lord of Hiroshima. And this move was planned and executed by Ōishi Gōemon Yoshimaro, the elder son of Ōishi Mujin. The anonymous genealogist goes on to explain:

Gōemon, too, could see that the Kyōgoku house might feel that it had a proprietary claim on Daizaburō; yet for a small domain with heavy obligations, it might prove financially burdensome to take on a new vassal whose illustrious lineage would require generous compensation. Diplomacy would be called for if this plan were to succeed.

Gōemon first discussed the matter with O-Riku's younger brother, Ishizuka Genpachi, who was then stationed in Edo. Genpachi seems to have agreed that it should be possible to assuage the pride of his domain if a concrete offer were forthcoming from the Asano. The next step, then, was for the two of them to take the proposal to the bannerman Asano Sahyōe Nagatake—an Ōishi by birth, but an Asano by adoption, as well as a cousin of the late Asano Takumi-no-Kami. Sahyōe, too, thought it a good plan and agreed to sound out the Edo Elder of the Hiroshima house, Kakizaki Tonomo. Nothing is recorded of the meeting of these two men, but the outcome must have been favorable, for negotiations thereafter became open and formal.

Kurima Chūbei, a Liaison Officer of the Hiroshima house, called upon his counterpart in the Kyōgoku house, stating only that the Asano Edo Elders had recommended to the main house that they move Daizaburō from Toyooka to Hiroshima. The Kyōgoku Elders flatly refused to countenance such a plan. Daizaburo must remain in Toyooka; the Kyōgoku could not be seen to bend under pressure from the more powerful domain. Negotiations thus had to be carried to a higher level.

Shimojō Chūbei, a bannerman known to both parties, was then called upon to carry a formal plea from Asano Aki-no-Kami, lord of Hiroshima, to Kyōgoku Kai-no-Kami, lord of Toyooka, requesting that Aki-no-Kami be allowed to reclaim Daizaburō, inasmuch as the boy was descended in a line of hereditary vassals of the Asano. Nothing was said about making a vassal of the boy, thus (nominally, at least) leaving open the possibility that the Kyōgoku might later invite him to join their Corps of Vassals. This time, the Kyōgoku acquiesced, whereupon the lords of the two houses exchanged visits and thanked each other in person. Plans could now be made for the journey from Toyooka to Hiroshima.

◆ ◆ ◆

The journey was planned so as to involve as many kinsmen of the Akō people as possible. Takebayashi Kansuke, an elder brother of Takebayashi Tadashichi, was sent from Hiroshima to Toyooka to accompany the boy. To accompany O-Riku and O-Ruri, the Kyōgoku house would send Tamura Sebei, a cousin of O-Riku; to welcome them when they reached Himeji, Hiroshima would send her uncle, Sassa Uzaemon.

Their departure was delayed, however, by the illness and death of O-Riku's father, Ishizuka Gengobei, who died on the 29th Day of the Seventh Month, aged seventy-three. Almost two months were to pass before the party could leave Toyooka.

Finally, early on the morning of the 23rd of the Ninth Month, the procession moved out from Toyooka and over the mountain road to Himeji. "There were more than a hundred people," O-Riku later wrote, "but there were no delays." By the evening of the 25th, they were in Himeji. There, they were met by O-Riku's aging uncle Sassa Uzaemon. And a short distance beyond Himeji, in Katashima, they were joined by Kuranosuke's old retainer Kasemura Kōshichi and his son Kōhachi. It would have been at least ten years since O-Riku had seen Kōshichi, but she did not neglect to call him back from Akō now that the House of Ōishi was to be reconstituted.

Toward the end of their ninth day of travel, the 1st Day of the Tenth Month, they arrived in Hiroshima. First, they were shown to the home that had been prepared for them in the Second Perimeter of the castle. Then, once they were settled, on the 6th Day, Daizaburō was summoned to the castle and officially inducted into the Asano Corps of Vassals at an enfeoffment of 1,500 koku, the same stipend that his father had received as Chief Elder of the Akō Cadet House. At the same time, Oyama Magoroku, a kinsman of Kuranosuke's uncle

Gengozaemon, was assigned to serve as Daizaburō's guardian until he should reach his majority. Three days later, on the 9th, the new vassal was granted his first audience with the lord of the domain, Asano Aki-no-Kami Yoshinaga.

After all the effort that so many friends and admirers of his father had expended on his behalf, this should have been the auspicious beginning of an illustrious career for Ōishi Daizaburō and a worthy sequel to the life of Ōishi Kuranosuke. Alas, it turned out to be nothing of the sort.

◆ ◆ ◆

This is not the place to begin a biography of Daizaburō. The Ōishi genealogies sum up the rest of his life in two brief paragraphs: one listing his marriages, and the other describing the illnesses of his later life. I shall follow their example.

In the second year of the Kyōhō era (1717), at the age of sixteen, Daizaburō celebrated his majority and changed his name to Tonoe. Four years later (Kyōhō 6 [1721]), at the behest of His Lordship, he married the daughter of Asano Tatewaki, one of the Elders of the domain. The next year, he divorced her. Then, in Kyōhō 15 (1730), he married a daughter of Okada Suke'emon, whom he divorced in Kyōhō 19 (1734). Eleven years later, in Enkyō 2 (1745), he married a daughter of Asano Hachirōzaemon, and two years later divorced her. None of these marriages produced any offspring.

The later life of Daizaburō/Tonoe is well encapsulated in an experience that a friend of Kanzawa Tokō told him about and that Tokō recorded in *Okinagusa*:

> *A friend of mine had gone to the Gion Shrine, and on the way back stopped at the teahouse Izutsuya. When he parted the curtain in the doorway, it looked as though everyone who worked there was hiding behind the screen in the anteroom, peering into the reception room.*
>
> *"What goes on?" he asked.*
>
> *"Yura-san's son has just arrived," they told him. "Have a look!"*

My friend peeped in, and there sat an old man, well over seventy, his nose eaten away by syphilis. To see this—and then recall the great name of his father, Yoshitaka! Hardly to be mentioned in the same day! This old man was the third son of Ōishi Kuranosuke Yoshitaka; his childhood name was Daizaburō. Later, he took the name Tonoe. After the official amnesty, he was taken into the service of the main house in Hiroshima, with the rank of Samurai Commander and an enfeoffment of 1,500 koku. Unlike his father, he accomplished nothing whatever throughout his life, and did nothing at all well. Recently, upon his retirement, he was demoted, and his stipend was cut by 300 koku. His adopted son succeeded him at 1,200 koku, with the rank of Company Commander. The man I heard this from was the Liaison Officer from Hiroshima.

The old man in the teahouse could not have been "well over seventy." Although he had first asked permission to retire while still in his thirties, permission was not granted until the 18th Day of the Third Month of Meiwa 5 (1768), when he was sixty-seven. The scene described by Tokō would have to have taken place sometime between then and the 14th Day of the Second Month of Meiwa 7 (1770), when Daizaburō/Tonoe died, aged sixty-nine. His decrepitude was more the result of dissipation than antiquity.

CHAPTER 104

I visited the actual sites of the action,
and I sought out the true details of the matter.

Several times in telling this tale, I have quoted a favorite old book of
mine, by Katashima Shin'enshi, *An Account of the Loyal Vassals from
Akō* (*Sekijō gishinden*). How this book came to be published is something of a story in its own right. The same prohibitions that applied to
the Kabuki and puppet theaters were applied just as strictly to books
on that still-sensitive subject, with the result that none of the earliest
accounts of the vendetta were ever printed. The only way you could
obtain a copy of one was to borrow it from a friend and copy it yourself.
Even then, one had to be careful. Another century would pass before
anyone could walk into a shop and purchase a printed book about the
Akō vendetta. But Katashima Shin'enshi had an idea how he might get
around this prohibition. He knew that he could not evade the law, but
he might avoid the worst of the damage it could do.

Shin'enshi was a ronin living in Osaka. We know nothing of his earlier life; but at the time of the Akō vendetta, he was making a modest
living as a writer of books on military matters. *Three Generations of
the Takeda Clan: A Military History* (*Takeda sandai gunki*) and *Japanese
Principles of Battle Planning* (*Bubi wakun*) probably are his best known
works. But like so many others, samurai and commoners alike, his imagination was arrested by the extraordinary daring and success of the Akō
vendetta, more so than by any of his earlier subjects. Shin'enshi was
more than just fascinated; he was determined to write an exhaustive
account of the operation—*and* publish it.

When he began work on this project, he does not say. It must not have been too long after the event, for the task as he describes it could not have been completed quickly. He first consulted all the works then circulating in manuscript that he could lay hands on. He lists twenty-two titles (some no longer extant)—all of which he had to have copied himself. And then, "For information these works failed to supply, I hastened to Akō; I spent time in Edo; and while in Kyoto, I went also to Yamashina, Murasakino, and the great complex of temples at Shijō. In all these places, I visited the actual sites of the action, and I sought out the true details of the matter, never once resorting to speculation or unfounded rumor."

Shin'enshi does not do himself justice with this brief description of his efforts. His travels would have taken him not only to the major cities he mentions, but to several of their surrounding villages as well. His text itself is testimony to the fact that he also found and made copies of several letters and other documents, all of them demonstrably authentic. We know, too, from materials in his book, that he must have made the acquaintance of Terai Genkei in Kyoto and Ochiai Yozaemon in Edo, as well as of relatives and friends of the ronin who were still alive and possessed firsthand knowledge of the people and events he was writing about. The synthesis of all this research, study, and detective work was a monumental narrative in fourteen volumes plus a preface, written in the florid phrases of a professional storyteller (Shin'enshi's enthusiasm seems to have affected his writing style as well).

Yet even when the manuscript was completed, the greatest problem still remained: How to publish it? More than fifteen years had passed since the vendetta, but the Shogunate was certain to ban any publication concerning the Akō ronin. The vendetta was, after all, a "crime," and it was illegal to publicize crime. Nevertheless, *Sekijō gishinden* was published, through a stroke of bold investment and fearless marketing on the part of Shin'enshi and his publisher.

Normally, considerable caution would be called for in the publication of a work of this size, especially if it was not subsidized by a patron. The printing and binding of books involved an enormous amount of skilled, and thus expensive, hand labor. The wood blocks for printing must be hand carved; every page, hand rubbed and folded; every cover, hand cut and pasted; every volume, hand sewn. If the publisher overestimated his market and produced too many copies, he could incur heavy losses. It was wisest, therefore, to begin with a relatively small printing, and if demand persisted, follow with a second and possibly a third printing.

Shin'enshi's publisher obviously knew that he had a best seller on his hands—a fifteen-volume best seller. And so he decided to invest heavily, sell fast, and run with the profits. First of all, he had a single printing, comprising a "vast number" of complete sets, made up in advance. Then, the books were transported quietly to dealers in "several major cities"—unfortunately, not named. And finally, with all the retail outlets fully stocked, the book was announced and displayed simultaneously in every city on the 4th Day of the Second Month of 1719—the seventeenth anniversary of the death of the ronin.

As predicted, *Sekijō gishinden* was an overnight success. Likewise, as predicted, the Shogunate was not amused. The book was banned, and the printing blocks were burnt. But it was too late. By the time the ban was issued, the entire printing had been sold. Shin'enshi and his publisher (who discreetly neglects to identify himself, or even his location) seem to have been chastised and possibly sentenced to a brief period of Domiciliary Confinement. This must have seemed a minor inconvenience, for by all reports, the book was an enormous financial success.

And a well-deserved success, I think; through their industry and daring, Shin'enshi and his publisher have bequeathed us the only published narrative of the Akō vendetta by someone who lived at the time of the events. The flamboyant style of the work has led some to question the veracity of Shin'enshi's account, yet virtually everything that can be checked against other sources is, in fact, highly accurate. There was so much fact still to be found at this time that there was hardly any need to falsify. We must be grateful to Katashima Shin'enshi for preserving so much of it for us.

*He had a terrible temper,
you know.*

As the years passed, the Inspectorate relaxed and eventually ceased bothering to ban Kabuki and puppet plays depicting the Akō vendetta. The names and the times and the places still had to be changed, of course. But it doesn't require the intellect of a sage to realize that someone called Yuranosuke is really Kuranosuke or that the court of the Kamakura Shogun is really the castle of the Tokugawa Shogun in Edo. So if you had chanced to attend the Kanya-za in Kobikichō when Yamamoto Kyōshirō was playing the role of "Yuranosuke," you would have found the theater packed and the audience enrapt.

And after the play, you might have overheard an interesting conversation between two of the spectators, a samurai and a doctor. The samurai, who recorded the story, unfortunately neglects to tell us his name. The doctor was Matsui Gyūan, who practiced mainly in the commoners' wards, but occasionally was summoned to the Sakurada mansion of the Hiroshima Asano house, for which he received a modest retainer from them. As they were leaving the theater, the samurai said to Gyūan: "The Hiroshima people must be very pleased; their forty-seven kinsmen have made quite a hit at the Kanya-za."

"Pleased? Far from it!" the doctor said. "You'll never hear so much as a murmur of those forty-seven in the Hiroshima house."

"Really? How so?"

"Well, don't forget: in the end, there were *only* 47. The other 250 ran away. There are too many people in Hiroshima—some of them in high places—whose kinsmen were *not* among the heroes. It makes life simpler not to mention it any more. Everyone gets along much better that way."

♦ ♦ ♦

Tominomori Chōtarō was barely a year old when Horiuchi Den'emon first "met" him; in his second year, the boy and his mother were moved to Minakuchi in the province of Ōmi, where later he would be taken into the service of the lord of that domain, Katō Sado-no-Kami. Den'emon would never see Chōtarō again, nor would he have known that eventually he would rise to become the Edo Liaison Officer of the Minakuchi domain. But attached to one of the many copies of Den'emon's memoir, we find a fascinating bit of memorabilia written by someone who did know the former Chōtarō, fifty years later, after he had inherited his father's name. Who the author of this snippet is, we do not know; but the story it tells is a delight, for it takes us back to the morning after the vendetta, when the ronin were passing through Hatchōbori on their way from Honjo to Sengakuji. Quite by chance, Tominomori Suke'emon encountered Ōshimaya Hachirōbei, a shopkeeper who used to supply the Asano Upper Mansion in Teppōzu, and asked him to take his helmet to his wife and mother in Kōjimachi, as a souvenir. The anonymous memoirist recalls:

> In the Hōreki era [1751–1763], when Tominomori Suke'emon II was Liaison Officer for Katō Sado-no-Kami, I got to know him quite well. At one of our meetings, when not many people were present, I told Suke'emon the story of his father's encounter with Ōshimaya Hachirōbei on the morning after the attack.
>
> Suke'emon struck his palm and said, "Well, that's a remarkable tale you tell. After my father's death, my mother and I were taken in by Sado-no-Kami and sent to live in his domain in Minakuchi. From the time I was two years old, I was granted a stipend of 100 koku, for which I am deeply indebted to Sado-no-Kami. When I was seven, I lost my mother; but she had always said, 'When you grow up, if ever you go to Edo, there is a townsman in Hatchōbori who was very kind to us; you must by all means look him up and thank

him.' At the time, she must have told me his name and where he lived, but I didn't remember. Hatchōbori, I remembered, of course; but when I did get to Edo, I walked all through that neighborhood, by various routes, but I hadn't a clue where to look or what to look for. And now you tell me! Please—introduce me to Hachirōbei!"

Suke'emon was utterly delighted; but unfortunately, I had to tell him that Hachirōbei had died in his eighties in the autumn of the previous year. He was terribly upset to hear this, and even the others in the room were weeping.

Some of the others said to him, "You probably remember very little of what your mother told you when you were a child, but you must have heard some interesting things from friends of hers."

"Yes, I did," Suke'emon replied. "In fact, a few of those who knew my mother are still alive. One thing I remember hearing from them was that Mother had no idea there was to be an attack that night until just the day before. She knew almost nothing of all that was going on. Ōishi Kuranosuke used to call occasionally at our lodgings in Kōjimachi. But our rooms were very small, and there were often many others there, so I never even saw Kuranosuke Dono. He would inquire politely whether Mother's husband was at home, her friends said, but she never knew what it was they talked about."

◆ ◆ ◆

People never stopped wondering *why* he had done it. To the ronin themselves, it hadn't seemed to matter much. Their lord had tried to kill Kira and failed. He must have had a good reason, but to them the reason was almost immaterial. Their duty was simply to finish the job. But everyone else went on wondering, as we still do. And so, when the bannerman Asano Daigaku was assigned duty in the Shogun's Bodyguard, his new colleagues were quick to ask: *Why* had Takumi-no-Kami tried to kill Kira? One of them, Ise no Sadatake, recorded Daigaku's answer:

Asano Takumi-no-Kami's younger brother, Asano Daigaku, lived into the Enkyō and Kan'en [1744–1750] eras. I once served with *him in the Bodyguard, at which time I heard him say: "He had a terrible temper, you know. His vassals urged him to send bribes to Kira, but Takumi-no-Kami would have none of it. A warrior, he said, does not fulfill his duty by buying the favor of others, whether with flattery or bribery." I have seen a brief mention of this in Ōishi's diary, written in his own hand.*

Sadatake was seriously mistaken, of course, in thinking that the Asano Daigaku he knew was the younger brother of Asano Takumi-no-Kami. Daigaku Nagahiro died in 1734, aged sixty-five, when Sadatake was only seventeen. And as we have seen, when Daigaku was recalled to Edo in 1709, restored to his status as a bannerman, and enfeoffed at 500 koku, he was never assigned official duties of any sort, but spent the remainder of his career as a member of the Reserve Force. Sadatake's colleague in the Shogun's Bodyguard must have been Daigaku Nagazumi, the son of Daigaku Nagahiro. Still, it is not without interest that this was the explanation that lived on in the lore of the Asano house.

*I'm afraid that's precisely
what happened.*

Far off in the North Country, 15 leagues (27.5 miles, 60 kilometers) upstream from the mouth of the Mogami River, lies the castle town of Shinjō, seat of the House of Tozawa, enfeoffed at 65,000 koku throughout the entire Edo period. The Shinjō Valley is narrow and deep, and all through the autumn, it fills with mist every morning. Then, as winter approaches and the days grow chill, winds blow in from the sea and up the river that at last clear away the mist, but are so strong that farmers have to erect straw barriers to protect their fields from being ravaged. Worst of all, though, are the snowstorms that begin in early winter and continue, regularly and relentlessly, for the next four months and more. The snow is deep, and life is bleak for much of the year in the domain of Shinjō.

There, in the windswept village of Furukuchi, an outpost of the domain on the south bank of the Mogami River, a monk named Kangetsu had just been appointed the new Superior of the rural temple Zennenji. Taguchi Gozaemon, a samurai from the castle town on his inspection round of the villages and their crops, stopped at the temple to make the acquaintance of the new cleric, and found him to be an interesting talker. One of the monk's stories, Gozaemon saw fit to record in his journal.

One night while a novice in Yonezawa, Kangetsu said, he was soaking in the tub of the neighborhood bathhouse, when he was joined by another bather. The man was large and powerfully built, probably in his mid-fifties, with a heavy growth of beard. And his body bore two ghastly, long scars. One stretched diagonally down the side of his face from above the eye to below the ear; the other ran the full width of his abdomen. Yet despite his formidable, even threatening, appearance, the man greeted his fellow bather affably. He was Yamayoshi Shinpachi, he told the novice, a vassal of the Uesugi house. In fact, Kangetsu later learnt, Shinpachi was Superintendent of Finance, a position of considerable responsibility in this fief of 150,000 koku, with its long history of financial distress. At first, their conversation was amiable and aimless, but Kangetsu eventually worked up the courage to broach the question he was aching to ask: "This is terribly abrupt of me, but may I ask how you happened to get those scars?"

"Oh, they're nothing to speak of," Shimpachi said. "I was once assigned duty in the Corps of Pages attached to Lord Kira Kōzuke-no-Suke. These are wounds from the night Takumi-no-Kami's men attacked us."

Kangetsu was so astonished that he could think of nothing more intelligent to say than, "My, is that so?" And then, "What was it like?"

"Well," Shinpachi began, "at first everyone was shouting, 'Fire, fire!' which created confusion enough. But when we realized that it was actually a vendetta, there was such chaos that we hardly knew who were the enemy and who were our friends. I was flailing about with my sword like someone trying to fight his way out of a cloud in the dead of night. This scar on my stomach looks dreadful, but it was only the sidelong thrust of a lance. It slit the skin, but it didn't go deep. The one over my ear, though—blood just poured out of it. It got in my eyes; it flowed all over my skin; it made my clothes so sticky that I could hardly move. So I pushed the flesh back together and bound up my head as tightly as I could. Then I took Lord Sahei on my shoulder—because he'd been wounded, too—and we fled to a house in the neighborhood. But first, I had one of my fellow Pages put on Lord Sahei's robe; I told him to announce himself as Sahei, and then fight to the death. And he did it. He went out there and died fighting, which is why many of Takumi's men thought they had killed Lord Sahei."

Kangetsu had one last question: "They say that Lord Kōzuke-no-Suke was killed in the charcoal shed. But is that really true?"

"I'm afraid that's precisely what happened," Shinpachi said, as a wry smile flickered across his face.

EPILOGUE

Tokyo, 1916

This is not the end of this story of a story. I somehow doubt that there ever will be an end to it. For my own part, though, this much must suffice. Fascinating though the aftermath may be, my first interest still lies in the facts of the matter. I leave the rest to others.

ŌHASHI YOSHIZŌ

THE VENDETTA OF THE 47 RONIN FROM AKŌ

GLOSSARY

Actors' Rooms . . . . Yakusha no Ma 役者の間

Allied Daimyo . . . . Tozama Daimyo 外様大名

Anteroom, Antechamber. . . . . Tsugi no Ma 次の間

Arch-Windowed Rooms . . . . Kushigata no Ma 櫛形の間

Armed Monks . . . . Bōkan 坊官

Bodyguard. . . . . Koshōgumi 小姓組

Bursar (of a Zen temple). . . . . Fūsu 副寺, 副司

Certificate of Appointment. . . . . Kokuinjō 黒印状

Checkpoint Passes for Women. . . . . Sekisho Onna Shōmon 関所女証文

Chief Adjutant . . . . Soba Yōnin 側用人

Chief of Clandestine Operations . . . . Shinobigashira 忍び頭

Circle of Talkers. . . . . Otogishū 御伽衆, Hanshishū 話衆

City Magistrate . . . . Machi Bugyō 町奉行

City Magistrate of Nagasaki . . . . Nagasaki Bugyō 長崎奉行

Clan Deity . . . . Ujigami 氏神

Commander of Mounted Samurai . . . . Bangashira 番頭, Kumigashira 組頭

Commander of Page Boys . . . . Kogoshōgashira 児小姓頭

Company Commander (of foot soldiers) . . . . Monogashira 物頭

Confidential Secretary. . . . . Naishō Yōnin 内証用人

Constable . . . . Dōshin 同心

Corner Guardhouse. Tsujiban 辻番

Corps of Pages . . . . Koshōgumi 小姓組

Corps of Vassals. . . . . Kashindan 家臣団, Kachū 家中

Council of Elders . . . . Rōjū 老中

Crampons . . . . Kasugai 鎹

Currency Exchange . . . . Satsuza 札座

Deputy (Commander). . . . . Yoriki 与力

Deputy Inspectors . . . . Kachi Metsuke 徒目付, Yokome 横目

Directive . . . . Hōsho 奉書

Distant Holdings . . . . Tobichi 飛地

District Deputy . . . . Gundai 郡代

Domiciliary Confinement . . . . Heimon 閉門

Eastern Sea Road . . . . Tōkaidō 東海道

Escort (to Seppukunin) . . . . Kaizoe(nin) 介添(人)

Express Conveyance . . . . Hayakago 早駕籠

Fealty, Fidelity, Loyalty . . . . Chū 忠, Chūgi 忠義

Filial Piety/Devotion, Filiality . . . . Kō 孝

Financial Officer . . . . Kanjō-kata 勘定方

Forestry Officer . . . . Yama Bugyō 山奉行

Fortunes of War . . . . Bu'un 武運

Full Formal Linens . . . . Asa Kamishimo 麻裃、上下

Genealogical Record . . . . Shinruigaki(sho) 親類書

Grand Amnesty . . . . Taisha 大赦

Great Sword . . . . Ōdachi 大太刀, Nodachi 野太刀

Guardian Deity . . . . Mamorigami 守神

Herald . . . . Tsukaiban 使番

Horse Guards . . . . Umamawari 馬廻

Imperial Envoys . . . . Chokushi 勅使, Inshi 院使

Inspector-General . . . . Ō-Metsuke 大目付

Inspectors . . . . Metsuke 目付, Yokome 横目

Izu Deputy . . . . Izu Daikan 伊豆代官

Junior Council (of Elders) . . . . Wakadoshiyori 若年寄 (Waka-Rōjū)

Kōshū High Road . . . . Kōshū Kaidō 甲州街道

Lackey . . . . Chūgen 中間

Law of the Land . . . . Tenka no Taihō 天下の大法

Letter Box . . . . Fubako 文箱

Life Guards . . . . Shoinban 書院番

Litigant's Inn . . . . Kuji Yado 公事宿

Liveried Menials . . . . Komono 小者

Local Lords . . . . Kokujin (Ryōshu) 国人(領主)

Maritime Officer . . . . Fune Bugyō 船奉行

Masters of Court Protocol . . . . Kōke 高家

Masters of Military Protocol . . . . Sōshaban 奏者番

Merrymakers . . . . Torioi 鳥追

Mid-Corps of Pages . . . . Chū-goshō 中小姓

Middle Mountain Road . . . . Nakasendō 中山道

Military Governor . . . . Shugo 守護

Military Household Service . . . . Buke Hōkō 武家奉公

Military Liaison Lodge . . . . Tensō Yashiki 伝奏屋敷

Military Tribunal. . . . . Hyōjōsho 評定所

Mino High Road . . . . Mino Kaidō 美濃街道

Mutual Aid Society . . . . Tanomoshikō 頼母子講

Neighborhood Watchman's Post . . . . Jinshinban(sho) 自身番(所)

Officer in Charge of Maps and Plans . . . . Ezu Bugyō 絵図奉行

Officer in Charge of Shogunal Benefactions . . . Shinmotsugakari 進物係

Page Boys . . . . Kogoshō 児小姓

Parting/Death Poem . . . . Jisei 辞世

Personal Attendants . . . . Konando 小納戸

Platform Tray. . . . . Sanbō 三方

Poem Strip . . . . Tanzaku 短冊

Premier Inn . . . . Honjin 本陣

Private Entrance. . . . . Nai- (Uchi-) Genkan 内玄関

Provisioner, Prefect of Provisions . . . . Daidokoro Bugyō 台所奉行

Rear Vassal. . . . . Matamono 又者, Baishin 陪臣

Reception Chamber (Main Chamber) . . . . Shoin 書院 (Dai Shoin 大)

Rental Permit. . . . . Yado Shōmon 宿証文

Reserve Force . . . . Yoriai 寄合, Kobushingumi 小普請組

Resident Deputies . . . . Daikan 代官

Resident Intendant . . . . Jitō 地頭

Restraint (judicial). . . . . Enryo 遠慮

Right of Audience . . . . O-Memie 御目見

Rural Overseer . . . . Ōjōya 大庄屋

Samurai Commander. Bangashira 番頭, Kumigashira 組頭

Sectarian Registry Records . . . . Shūmon Aratame-chō 宗門改帳

Serving Boy. . . . . Bōzu 坊主

Shogunal Deputy for Kyoto . . . . Kyoto Shoshidai 京都所司代

Southern Mountain Road . . . . Sanyōdō 山陽道

Sub-Inspectors . . . . Kobito Metsuke 小人目付

Special Investigator for Arson and Robbery . . . Hizuke Tōzoku Aratamekata 日付盗賊改方

Superintendent of Construction. . . . . Sakuji Bugyō 作事奉行

Superintendent of Finance . . . . Kanjō-gashira 勘定頭

Superintendent of Works . . . . Fushin Bugyō 普請奉行

NOTES

Abbreviations used in the notes and bibliography refer to the following sources.

AGJ   *Akō gishi jiten.* Edited by *Akō gishi jiten* Kankōkai. Kōbe: *Akō gishi jiten* Kankōkai, 1972.

AGS   *Akō gishi shiryō.* Edited by Chūō Gishikai and Watanabe Yosuke. 3 vols. Tokyo: Yūzankaku, 1931.

AGSS   *Akō gijin sansho.* Edited by Nabeta Shōzan. 3 vols. Tokyo: Kokusho Kankōkai, 1911–1912. Reprint, Tokyo: Nippon Sheru Shuppan, 1975. The pagination of vols. 1 and 2 of the reprint edition differs from that of the original edition because the publisher of the reprint foolishly excised several pages that it considered superfluous. The page numbers given in the notes, however, are those in this imperfect edition, because for many years the original edition was not available to the author.

AJUM   *Ōishi Jinja zō Akō-jō uketori monjo.* Edited by Iio Kuwashi. Tokyo: Shin Jinbutsu Ōraisha, 1993.

AS   *Akō shishi.* Edited by *Akō shishi* Hensan Senmon I'in. 7 vols. Akō: Akō-shi, 1981–1986.

CG   *Chūshingura.* Edited by Akō-shi Sōmubu *Shishi* Hensanshitsu. 7 vols. Akō: Akō-shi, 1987–2014.

KCS   *Kansei chōshū shokafu.* Edited by Takayanagi Kōju et al. 26 vols. Tokyo: *Zoku Gunsho ruijū* Kanseikai, 1962–1964.

KD   *Kokushi daijiten.* Edited by *Kokushi daijiten* Henshū I'inkai. 17 vols. Tokyo: Yoshikawa Kōbunkan, 1979–1997.

MEZ   *Mitamura Engyo zenshū.* Edited by Mori Senzō, Noma Kōshin, and Asakura Haruhiko. 28 vols. Tokyo: Chūō Kōronsha, 1975–1983.

MS   *Minō shishi.* Edited by *Minō shishi* Henshū I'inkai. 14 vols. Minō: Minō Shiyakusho, 1964–2005.

MSAGS *Mikan shinshū Akō gishi shiryō.* Edited by Sasaki Moritarō. Tokyo: Shin Jinbutsu Ōraisha, 1984.

NKBT *Nihon koten bungaku taikei.* 100 vols. Tokyo: Iwanami Shoten, 1957–1967.

NKBZ *Nihon koten bungaku zenshū.* 51 vols. Tokyo: Shōgakukan, 1971–1976.

NRCT *Nihon rekishi chimei taikei.* 51 vols. Tokyo: Heibonsha, 1981–2003.

NST *Nihon shisō taikei.* 67 vols. Tokyo: Iwanami Shoten, 1970–1981.

NZT *Nihon zuihitsu taisei.* Edited by Kurita Sōji. 72 vols., ser. 1–3, and supplements. Tokyo: Yoshikawa Kōbunkan, 1973–1979.

OGM *Ōishi-ke gishi monjo.* Edited by Iio Kuwashi and Sasaki Moritarō. Tokyo: Shin Jinbutsu Ōraisha, 1982.

OGS *Ōishi-ke gaiseki shiyōden.* Edited by Iio Kuwashi and Sasaki Moritarō. Tokyo: Shin Jinbutsu Ōraisha, 1979.

OKS *Ōishi-ke keizu seisan.* Edited by Iio Kuwashi and Sasaki Moritarō. Tokyo: Shin Jinbutsu Ōraisha, 1980.

SGD *Sekijō gishinden* (1719). By Katashima Shin'enshi (Ōno Takenori). 15 vols. Woodblock ed. publisher and place of publication unknown.

SN *Sekijō nenkan* (1851). Edited by Hiratsuka Hyōsai (1792–1875). 10 vols. Manuscript in the collection of Kokuritsu Kokkai Toshokan.

TJ *Tokugawa jikki.* Edited by Narushima Motonao (1778–1862). 7 vols. Tokyo: Keizai Zasshisha, 1902–1904.

YT *Yōkyoku taikan.* Edited by Sanari Kentarō. 7 vols. Tokyo: Meiji Shoin, 1953–1954.

Prologue

p.3 The prologue is based principally upon Akiyama, "*Gijin sansho no henja*"; Mori, "Nabeta Shōzan shokan shō"; Ōhashi Yoshizō, "*Akō gijin sansho yuraigaki*"; *Ōhashi Totsuan Sensei zenshū*; and Terada, *Ōhashi Totsuan Sensei den*.

p.4 **Black Ships:** The narrator voices a common perception of the arrival of Commodore Matthew Perry's squadron. For some of the more intelligent reactions, see Watanabe, "Opening of Japan as a Philosophical Question."

p.6 **As Nyoraishi says:** *Kashōki*, in *Tokugawa bungei ruijū*, 2:115.

p.10 **Shigeno Yasutsugu:** Shigeno (1827–1910) was the founder of the Institute for Historical Research at the University of Tokyo. On the influence of Ludwig Rieß (1861–1928), see Mehl, *History and the State in Nineteenth-Century Japan*, 97–102; 2nd ed., 113–19.

Benkei: Mythical vassal and devoted companion of Minamoto no Yoshitsune.

p.12 **Ōhashi Yoshizō:** Strangely little is recorded of the life of Ōhashi Yoshizō. The lives of his mother, father, grandfather, and uncles are richly documented and summarized in several works of reference; yet not even the birth and death dates of Yoshizō are to be found in any of them. Despite having lived well into the twentieth century, and having published at least eight books, his name appears in the *National Diet Library Directory of Authors Under Copyright* only because his *Guide to Graves of Old* was reprinted in 1992. Having searched, fruitlessly, every printed source I could lay hands on, I tried entering his name (as well as pen names) in several Internet search engines, most of which likewise yielded nothing. One of them, however, turned up a hand-bound pamphlet in the University of Tokyo Library made up of offprints from the *Journal of the Antiquarian Society* (*Shūkokaihō*), one of which was the article "Color Prints and Comic Theater" by Bishō Shōshi (The Smiling Scribbler)—one of Yoshizō's favorite noms de plume. This slender clue proved unexpectedly productive; the knowledge that Yoshizō had been a member of the Antiquarian Society led to the further discovery, through the catalogue of the Waseda University Library, of a privately printed directory of that society (*Senri sōshiki*), published in commemoration of its two hundredth meeting. In this directory, Yoshizō himself states that he was born in Edo in 1859 (Ansei 6.11.3), that his principal research interests are Chinese and Japanese history, that his antiquarian activities include visiting old graves and collecting woodblock prints, and that in 1935 he was living in the northwestern suburbs of Kyoto (Tōji'in Nishi-machi). His stated occupation, as a "member of the editorial staff of the Imperial Household Ministry," turns out to be a modest reference to his years of work compiling an encyclopedia of "loyalists" (*shishi*) who died for the cause of the Meiji Revolution (*Shūho Junnanroku-kō*, 3 vols. [1909; rpt., 1934]). Further examination of the journals of the Antiquarian Society reveals that he was a member of that group almost from its inception in January 1896 until it was forced to disband in July 1944, owing to "the depredations of the American demons and the English devils." Throughout those years, he was a regular contributor to the society's journal. He is not listed among the founders of the society, but his first article appears in the first issue of the journal to contain essays, as opposed to merely listing the artifacts exhibited at its meetings; and his last essay, "Speaking of Sushi," was published in 1943, his eighty-sixth year. He also contributed to nearly every issue of the journal *Bibliophilia* (*Hon dōraku*) from 1932 until its demise in 1940. A brief sketch of his life, together with a photograph, "The Last Son of Ōhashi Totsuan, Who Died for His Country," appeared in the 28 September 1915 issue of *Asahi shinbun*. But I have yet to find any record of Yoshizō's death. Nor have I any notion why so prolific and active a figure should so totally escape the attention of chroniclers of Japan's history and culture.

PART I. Year of the Serpent: Genroku 14 (1701)

CHAPTER 1

p.15 Several of the larger temples: Named in *Tokugawa jikki*, *Bukō nenpyō*, and *Ryūkō Sōjō nikki*. Ryūkō claims that his prayers and incantations must have been responsible for the cloud cover, thus sparing people the inauspicious sight of an eclipse.

p.16 The severed head of a woman: *Bukō nenpyō*, 1:101.

p.17 A precise account of the fifth Shogun's movements: In 1986, Futaki wrote, "In recent years there has been a steady growth in the study of the *Baku-han* system and the structure of power within the Edo Bakufu . . . , but the ceremonials that marked the progress of the year remain an unexplored field of study. Most descriptions are nothing more than summaries of the studies of Mitamura Engyo and materials in *Tokugawa reiten roku*" (*Kinsei kokka no shihai kōzō*, 390). This account suffers from the same limitations. It is based principally upon the very sketchy records of later years: *Ryūei hikan*; *Tokugawa reiten roku*; Ono, *Tokugawa seido shiryō*; and Ichioka, *Tokugawa seisei roku*.

Long before first light: This account of these processions to the dismounting ground is based closely upon, and in some passages translated from, Hori, *Geba no otonai*. See also the procession depicted in Hiroshige's *Kinokunizaka Akasaka Tameike enkei*, in *Meisho Edo hyakkei*.

p.18 **The exquisitely fashioned sprays of pine and bamboo:** The origin of these *kadomatsu*, still the traditional New Year's decoration in the Kantō region, is described in *Tokugawa seisei roku*:

In Genki 3 [1572], when Ieyasu was young and still went by the name Matsudaira, he fought in a battle against Takeda Shingen, at Mikatagahara, on the last day of the year. Most of the force was defeated by Shingen, but Ieyasu, through a clever stratagem, managed to elude the enemy. That evening, the Takeda sent him an ominously threatening New Year's poem:

まつかれてたけたくひなきあしたかな

It was of course intended that the poem be read:

松枯れて竹たぐひなき明日哉

matsu karete / take tagui naki / ashita kana

Come New Year's morn, the Pine [Matsudaira] shall wither and die, and the Bamboo [Takeda] shall flourish unrivaled.

But Sakai Tadatsugu 酒井忠次 (1527–1596), who happened to be with Ieyasu when the poem was delivered, saw that by changing the voicing and the spacing of a few syllables, the poem could be given an entirely different meaning:

松枯れで竹田首なき明日哉

matsu karede / takeda kubi naki / ashita kana

Come New Year's morn, the Pine shall wither not, but the Bamboo shall have no heads.

Thus, with appropriately altered diacritics, it was sent back to Shingen. And thus, we are told, began the Kantō tradition of decorating one's gate on New Year's Day with arrangements of luxuriant pine boughs and stalks of bamboo from which the leaves have been lopped and the tops sliced off.

p.22 **His first destination is the Women's Palace:** Based upon Inagaki, *Kōshō Edo buke shidan*, 26–28. Inagaki does not cite his source, and I have yet to track it down.

p.25 **Hare broth:** The story of this dish and its importance in the history of the Tokugawa house is told in several sources. The following version is based principally upon that in KCS 4:129.

In the year 1438, one of Ieyasu's distant ancestors, Tokugawa Sakyō-no-Suke Arichika, found himself on the losing side of an intra-familial quarrel (*Eikyō no ran*) between the Kyoto Shogun Ashikaga Yoshinori (1394–1441) and his kinsman the Kamakura Commander (Kamakura *Kubō*) Ashikaga Mochiuji (1398–1439), a dispute that eventually ended in full-scale warfare. Arichika himself never came near the battlefield; his unit's assignment was to defend the Kamakura Palace (Kamakura *Gosho*). But when Mochiuji was defeated and his son Yoshihisa, their immediate superior, absconded (to Ōgigaya) and left his men to fend for themselves, they were surrounded by forces loyal to the Shogun. Arichika's comrades—the Edo, the Miura, the Kasai—were all taken alive; but Arichika, his son Chikauji, and his grandson Yasuchika somehow managed to break out and escape. They fled first to their native village of Tokugawa in the Nitta district of the province of Kōzuke. There they lay low and listened for further news from Kamakura. But when they heard that orders had come from Kyoto to search every corner of Nitta, they knew that there was nowhere they could hide in their present condition. So they fled to the temple Seijōkōji in Fujisawa, where they shaved their heads, took vows, and adopted the monkish names Chōami, Tokuami, and Sukeami. Even then, it was too dangerous to remain in the Kantō, and so they decided to head west to Mikawa, taking a long back route through the mountains. By now winter had set in, and travel through the snow was painful and slow. But along the way, to their delight, in the tiny village of Hayashi in the province of Shinano, they happened upon another escaped comrade, Hayashi Tōsuke Mitsumasa, who like themselves had fled to his old homestead. Although Tōsuke had barely enough to feed himself, he insisted that his old friends lodge with him. And on the last day of the year 1439, in the midst of a blinding snowstorm, Tōsuke set out into the forest armed with bow and arrow, and miraculously managed to shoot a hare. Now he could at least serve his guests a festive bowl of hare broth to see in the New Year. The Tokugawa were delighted, not only with the unexpectedly hearty fare, but even more with Tōsuke's generosity and hospitality. When they moved on to Mikawa, they urged Tōsuke to join them, for he was certain to be discovered if he remained in Hayashi. We know now, of course, that the Tokugawa prospered in Mikawa. Yet they never forgot the kindness of Hayashi Tōsuke. As long as he and his progeny lived, they were always the first to be served New Year's saké, even before members of their immediate family. And on New Year's Day of every year thereafter, even after the Tokugawa had come to rule the entire land from their castle in Edo, the first thing served to those vassals and allies who came to offer their felicitations was a sip of hare broth such as Tōsuke had served them a few centuries earlier—a salutary reminder of the grave peril in which their rise to preeminence had begun.

CHAPTER 2

p.35 **Appointed official host to the two envoys from the Emperor:** Three sources describe this process: *Kōseki kenmonki* 1, AGSS 3:172; *Asano Naganori den*,

AGS 2:375; and *Ekisui renbei roku*, 26–27. The first of these is thought to have been compiled by Ochiai Yozaemon, Chamberlain to Naganori's widow, Yōzei'in; the second is the portion of the Asano house records that pertains to Naganori and is based to a certain extent upon Ochiai's account; and the third was compiled by an anonymous bannerman of the Shogunal house. The three sources in no way contradict one another, and each supplies bits of information not found in the others.

p.36 **The first to come to his aid:** *Asano Naganori den*, AGS 2:375.

Katō Tōtomi-no-Kami: This story first appears in *Akō shōshūki*, AGSS 2:423–24, and is repeated, much embroidered, in several later works. Kira's behavior on this mission is indisputably attested by Kato's co-host Tozawa Kazusa-no-Suke, whereas Katō's conversation with Takumi-no-Kami is not independently corroborated. On the basis of Tozawa's account, however, as corroborated by Ogasawara Nagato-no-Kami in conversation with Asano Aki-no-Kami, Fukumoto Nichinan is inclined to accept the report of Katō's visit as authentic. For details, see Fukumoto, *Shinsōroku*, 36–39.

p.37 **A stubborn streak of his own:** Muro Kyūsō calls him "obstinate, intractable," in *Akō gijin roku*, NST 27:274.

An Elder of the great Satake house: Okamoto Matatarō Mototomo (1661–1712). The passage quoted from *Okamoto Mototomo nikki* is excerpted in the Akita-ken Kōmonjo Kan newsletter *Komonjo kurabu*, December 2007, 2. For more detail, see Satō Hiroshi, "Akita-han *Okamoto Mototomo nikki* ni miru Akō jiken."

The more meager the gifts: *Akō shōshūki*, AGSS 2:423–24.

p.38 **Only such gifts as customary formalities required:** *Kōseki kenmonki* 1, AGSS 3:172–73. According to a contrary report, Takumi-no-Kami's Liaison Officers tell him, "Kira is the most distinguished of the Masters of Court Protocol, and as such it is his duty to instruct you in these matters. Yet to date, you have received no help whatever from him. Given which, it should hardly be necessary to send gifts. Surely it should suffice to send gifts, commensurate with the assistance you've been given, after your duties have been fulfilled" (*Asano Naganori den*, AGS 2:375–76).

The anonymous satirist: *Genroku sekenbanashi fūbun shū*, 197.

p.38 **The records of another daimyo house:** The records of the Tamura house, a cadet branch of the Daté in the northern domain of Ichinoseki, would seem to be the only surviving records of a daimyo's service as official host to the Imperial Envoys. Unfortunately, these records have never been published, but the contents of a draft journal compiled in 1849–1850 by Numata Nobumichi, an Elder of the Tamura house, are summarized, together with a detailed chronology, in Koiwa, "Numata-ke hon *Chokushi gochisō nikki* to sono shūhen." The fair copy of Numata's journal has not survived. Another document in the Tamura archives, *Chokushi hokkin chō*, describes aspects of the previous daimyo's service in the same capacity in 1829. Portions of this text, including several valuable diagrams, are excerpted in Saitō, *Akō gishi jissan*, 10–67 passim.

The system of notification billets used by the Tamura house is described in an article based upon *Chokushi gochisō nikki*: Iwashita, "Edo no chūshin shudan." The author's modestly phrased suggestion that his may be the first published study of this system of communication seems justified.

p.41 **A certain discord had arisen:** *Shōshūki*, AGSS 2:423; *Kōseki kenmonki* 1, AGSS 3:172. Kira's abusive treatment of Takumi-no-Kami is attested in *Horibe Yahei Akizane shiki*, AGS 1:231, and discussed in Tanaka Mitsurō, "Warukuchi wa satsugai dōzen," *Rongaibi* 26.

p.42 **Another very early start:** *Asano Naganori den*, AGSS 2:377–78. Takumi-no-Kami's indisposition is mentioned in the same source. The weather is described in *Ryūkō Sōjō nikki*, 2:94.

Face-to-face audience (taigan): *Ryūei hikan*, 1:104–5. This text describes practices current in the Kyōhō era (1716–1735).

CHAPTER 3

p.44 **Now you'll remember, won't you:** This chapter is based almost entirely upon the accounts of two participants in the action: *Kajikawa-shi hikki*, AGSS 2:273–79; and *Okado Denpachirō oboegaki*, NST 27:164–78. Other sources are noted in passing.

One of the larger allotments in the Wardens' Quarter: A detail of a Genroku-era map showing the location of Kajikawa's home is reproduced in Mayama, *Genroku Chūshingura*, 27.

p.46 **The only person who actually saw what happened:** Kajikawa is often described as the only eyewitness to the attack, but this cannot literally be true, as it took place immediately in front of Takumi-no-Kami's junior colleague Daté Sakyō-no-Daibu. Yet no record survives of Daté ever mentioning the matter, nor of his being questioned about it by either the Inspectorate or the Council of Elders. His silence seems a bit less mysterious, however, in light of the fact that the main house of the Daté in Sendai and the main house of the Asano in Hiroshima had not been on speaking terms (*futsū*) since 1596, when Daté no Masamune accused Asano Nagamasa of issuing orders in the name of Hideyoshi that he himself had originated. It thus may still have been Daté Sakyō's familial duty to feign ignorance of anything concerning a member of the Asano clan. For details, see Matsukata, "'Futsū' to 'tsūro,'" and "Asano-ke to Daté-ke no waboku no kokoromi to sono shippai." A draft of Masamune's letter to Nagamasa severing relations with him is transcribed in *Dai Nihon komonjo*, no. 3, vol. 2, *Daté-ke monjo*, 177–83. See also Kuroda, "Masamune no rihan," in *Asano Nagamasa to sono jidai*, 349–61.

p.47 **A full program of four dramas:** Listed, together with the names of the principal performers, in *Genroku nenkan*, AGS 1:12.

p.49 **Upper Chamber:** *Chūsei kōkanroku* assumes that the court nobles were in the immediate vicinity of the fracas: "For these ranking court nobles, who spend their days in the luxury of their palaces, concerned with naught but composing poems and making music; who have never heard of, much less seen, anyone attack another with a sword, it is hardly a wonder that they blanched with fright when separated only by a papered panel [*fusuma*] from such violence as this" (AGSS 3:422). The senior envoy, Yanagiwara Sukekado, is a bit more specific; he tells us that the attack took place in "the corridor adjacent" to the room in which the three envoys were waiting for the ceremonies to begin and that "the tumult was indescribable" (*Kantō gekō dōchū nikki*, unpublished but excerpted in AGS 1:39; also in a much fuller version excerpted in Hirai, "Chōtei kara mita," 18). *Mitsutsuna Kyō ki bekki* (1755) likewise speaks of "the retiring room facing upon the Great [Pine] Gallery" (Hirai, "Nentō chokushi no Kantō gekō," 130). The location of that room is positively identified in an official communication from the Shogunate to the court, which states that the envoys were "resting in the Upper Chamber" when Takumi-no-Kami attacked Kira (*Koga Michitomo Kō ki*, unpublished but excerpted in Hirai, "Chōtei kara mita," 20). Two chambers faced directly upon the Pine Gallery, the Upper and the Lower. The Upper, which was the closer of the two to the Whitewood Rooms, where the ceremony was to take place, was normally assigned to the Three Cadet Houses of the Tokugawa (*Gosanke*).

p.50 **One of the most powerful and formidable of the Shogun's bannermen:** "Yosōbei is a big man and very strong. He is highly skilled in the martial arts; indeed he ranks first among all bannermen" (*Ekisui renbei roku*, 49).

His own hands would be weapon enough: I am indebted to Jeroen Veldhuizen for his demonstration and explanation of the traditionally prescribed maneuvers (*kata*) for disarming an opponent who is wielding a sword.

p.52 **The quarrel is between *these* two gentlemen:** *Genroku sekenbanashi fūbunshū*, 198.

p.53 **Matsudaira Izumi-no-Kami Norimura:** This anecdote is told in variant versions in several different sources. This version is based principally upon the earliest of these reports, in *Akō shōshūki*, AGSS 2:428.

CHAPTER 4

p.56 **Kurisaki Dōyū:** Opinion seems divided whether Kurisaki's style should be pronounced "Dōyū" or "Dōu." The genesis of the latter pronunciation is described by Sugita Genpaku in *Rangaku koto hajime:* "The name 'Dō-u' is said to come from the Dutch word for 'dew' [*dauw*; J. *tsuyu*]. Thereafter, they say, it was written with the characters 道有" (NKBT 95:475). Matsumura Akira dismisses this notion as one of "several errors" in Genpaku's sketch of the history of Dutch medicine in Japan (NKBT 95:520). And since the only orthographic evidence that I know of for either reading—the handwritten romanizations of his name in the *Deshima Dagregisters*—is highly ambiguous, this book hews to the traditional "Dōyū."

p.57 **The old fort at Komorida:** *Kiyomasa ki*, 326–28.

The nursemaid of Kurisaki Utanosuke: Several variant but, in the main, consistent accounts survive of the flight abroad and subsequent career of Kurisaki Dōki. This version is based upon sources quoted in Koga, *Seiyō ijutsu denrai shi*, 23–42; and Takeuchi, "Nanban geka Kurisaki-ke," 23–40.

Someone who knew their secret betrayed them: Yamamoto quotes Hosokawa Tadatoshi's (1586–1641) description of Nagasaki as a place where "nothing you might wish to keep secret can ever be kept secret," in *Kyūtei seiji*, 230–31.

p.58 **The Jesuits and Nagasaki:** Concerning which, see Elison, *Deus Destroyed*, esp. chaps. 4 and 5.

Campo Japón: The vicissitudes of the Japanese settlement in Manila, the activities of its inhabitants, and their relations with the Spanish authorities are described in Iwao, *Nan'yō Nihonmachi*; Nelson, "Southeast Asian Politics and Society"; Paske-Smith, "Japanese Trade and Residence in the Philippines"; and Schurtz, *Manila Galleon*.

Japan's Wild West: Koga, *Seiyō ijutsu denrai shi*, 28.

p.59 **His progeny:** Dōki's third son apparently was a headstrong wastrel.

CHAPTER 5

p.61 **The Shogun was in his bath:** TJ 6:730; *Chūshin kiku junjū roku*, 2:6r–6v (unnumbered pages).

p.65 **There's been no *death* pollution:** Yanagiwara, *Kantō gekō*, AGS 1:39; Yanigiwara, *Zoku shi gushō*, 326; Konoe Motohiro, *Motohiro Kō ki*, AGS 1:34.

For a discussion of these sources and their relationship to one another, see Hirai, "Chōtei kara mita," 18, 28n.7.

The Imperial Response (chokutō): The description of this ceremony is based upon *Tokugawa Bakufu O-Nikki*, excerpt in CG 3:41–43.

p.66 Rumors of a swordfight began to spread: *Okado Denpachirō oboegaki*, NST 27:165.

p.69 Seki Kyūwa: There were more than three hundred *cha bōzu* in Edo Castle, but Kyūwa is one of the few whose lives we know anything about. He was descended in a family of minor warriors, based in the village of Seki in the province of Musashi, who had once been in the service of Tokugawa Ieyasu. Although Kyūwa was the second son, because of his tenuous connection with Ieyasu, a place was found for him in the castle. Kyūwa's eldest son succeeded to his father's post in the castle, and his second son became a *haikai* master, Saryūan Ri'ichi (1714–1783), who compiled the first commentary on Bashō's *Oku no hosomichi*. See *Nihon koten bungaku daijiten*, 6:205, s.v. "Ri'ichi."

Yosōbei questioned: *Kajikawa-shi hikki*, AGSS 2:276–77.

Asano and Kira interrogated: *Okado Denpachirō oboegaki*, NST 27:165–66.

We shall dispense with all deferential forms of address: Although the Inspectors rank much lower than either Takumi-no-Kami, a daimyo, or Kōzuke-no-Suke, a high-ranking bannerman, they speak on behalf of the Shogun and thus address these men as though they were their inferiors.

p.71 Shunted progressively up the chain of command: *Okado Denpachirō oboegaki*, NST 27:166.

p.72 The Shogun himself decided the fate of the two parties: *Akō shōshūki*, AGSS 2:426. Sugimoto Yoshichika not only is the author of this work, but also supplied Muro Kyūsō, who was then resident in Kanazawa, with much of the information the latter used in composing *Akō gijin roku*.

CHAPTER 6

p.74 The commotion outside the entry hall of the palace: *Asano Naganori den*, AGS 2:380.

They ... return to the Asano Upper Mansion: *Kōseki kenmonki 1*, AGSS 3:174–75; *Asano Naganori den*, AGS 2:380.

p.75 I wonder if I should refrain from participating: *Toda-ke goyō-tome*, in Usui,

Ōgaki-han to Chūshingura, 72. Toda's titular epithet is often glossed "Uneme-no-Shō," partly because the *kami* (Director) of this title is written with the character 正, the more familiar reading of which is *shō*; and partly because the Office of Palace Women (*Uneme no Tsukasa*) has been so long defunct that many have forgotten that this character, when used to denote the office's Director, should be read *kami*, which meticulous historians still consider the correct reading in this context.

Uneme-no-Kami sent to the Military Liaison Lodge: *Toda-ke goyō-tome*, 72.

p.75 **Kira Kōzuke-no-Suke Dono rebuked him on several occasions:** *Horibe Yahei Akizane shiki*, AGS 1:231. For an excellent discussion of how Kira's sharp rebukes at the Military Liaison Lodge probably provoked Takumi-no-Kami to watch for an opportunity to strike back, see Tanaka Mitsurō, "Warukuchi wa satsugai dōzen," *Rongaibi* 26. As Tanaka puts it, "The attack was decided upon but not planned in advance."

p.75 **His report is confirmed by . . . Kurisaki Dōyū:** *Kurisaki Dōyū kiroku*, CG 3:9a.

The official history: TJ 6:433.

p.77 **Withdraw in the most peaceable manner possible:** *Asano Naganori den*, AGS 2:381; *Kōseki kenmonki 1*, AGSS 3:177.

p.79 **Aki-no-Kami was already on stage:** *Asano Tsunanaga den*, AGS 2:524. The Nō text translated is that in NKBZ 33:280–90. The poem from *The Tale of Genji* quoted therein is in the "Sakaki" chapter in NKBZ 13:79.

p.81 **Principle of Equal Punishment:** This "principle" is discussed in many works on the history of Sengoku- and Edo-period Japan. Among the more useful in this context are Ishii, *Nihonjin no kokka seikatsu*, 73–108; Shimizu, *Kenka ryōseibai no tanjō*; Tanaka, "Kenka ryōseibai-hō no Genroku," *Rongaibi* 32; and Taniguchi, *Kinsei shakai to hō kihan*, 29–68.

p.82 **These two gentlemen were then dispatched to the Asano Upper Mansion:** *Akō-jō hikiwatashi oboegaki*, CG 3:57–58; *Kōseki kenmonki 1*, AGSS 3:177.

CHAPTER 7

p.84 **Express conveyance (*hayakago*):** In his series of prints *Tōkaidō gojūsan tsugi*, Hiroshige shows a *hayakago* employing only five bearers passing through the fifty-second post station, Kusatsu.

155 leagues: "League" is used throughout this book to translate the Japanese measure of distance *ri*. Both measures vary slightly, depending upon the time and place of their use, but as both most frequently denote a distance of about 2.5 miles (4 kilometers), they are here treated as near equivalents. The distance of 155 *ri* from Edo to Akō is considered mistaken by some scholars, who note that the distance by modern railway is the equivalent of 170 *ri*. But as this distance is calculated on the basis of the present rail route via Kyoto and Osaka, whereas the route traveled in the Genroku era bypassed both cities by a wide margin, the traditional distance of 155 *ri* is actually the more accurate. For routing details and precise distances, see Kishii, ed., *Shinshū Gokaidō saiken*, passim.

p.85 **Generous annual gratuities . . . to certain merchants in the transport business:** *Horiuchi Den'emon oboegaki*, AGSS 1:294. In Hara Sōemon's words: "Although such practices were prohibited by the authorities, Takumi-no-Kami had for years sent generous financial contributions to the merchants of Denma-chō, which is what enabled us to make these journeys without delay."

p.86 **The first two bearers of bad tidings:** Reports of the departure times of the men who carried the news to Akō vary considerably. Those given here are as stated in *Asano Naganori den*, AGS 2:381; and *Sōgenji kiroku*, 3. The Okayama operative is more precise but less authoritative; he has heard that Sōemon left "in the Fourth Hour" (ca. 9:00–11:00 P.M.; CG 3:88). Further details are as related by Akō samurai in the custody of Hisamatsu Oki-no-Kami and recorded in *Kikigaki*, 5.

Sōemon was loath to leave: This conversation is reported in *Sōgenji kiroku*, 2–3.

CHAPTER 8

p.88 **Their acquiescence to these orders was not immediately forthcoming:** These passages are based entirely upon *Okado Denpachirō oboegaki*, NST 27:164–78.

p.89 **Dōyū reached immediately for a sachet of medicine:** This description is based closely upon the physician's own account, *Kurisaki Dōyū kiroku*. The manuscript of this text is held in the library of the University of Tokyo. Although it has never been published in its entirety, the portion describing his treatment of Kira's wounds and all that followed is transcribed in CG 3:9–14.

p.95 **The Inspector General then took out the decree and read it:** *Asano Naganori den*, AGS 2:379.

Kira Kōzuke-no-Suke: The version of Kira's pardon quoted here appears in *Tokugawa Bakufu O-Nikki*, CG 3:42.

CHAPTER 9

p.100 He would remain in the duty room: This is Tamura's own description of his thoughts on the matter as he related them to a group of his senior vassals. They were recorded by Kitazato Mokunosuke. See CG 3:19–20.

p.101 By the midpoint of the Eighth Hour: *Ichinoseki-han kachū Nagaoka Shichirōbei kiroku*, CG 3:15.

p.103 It was to go down in history: Such was the verdict of Kudō Jūichibei Yukihiro, author of *Jijin roku*, in which he describes the Tamura preparations and procession in some detail, in *Bushidō zensho*, 10:324–28. The Tamura house records, upon which much of the following is based, are conveniently collected in CG 3:14–26.

When the Tamura force reached the castle: *Ichinoseki-han kachū Nagaoka Shichirōbei kiroku*, CG 3:15.

p.105 He is not likely to recover: *Ichinoseki-han kachū Kitazato Mokunosuke tebikae*, CG 3:22.

Takumi struck up a conversation with Magofusa: *Kōseki kenmonki* 1, AGSS 3:174; *Asano Naganori den*, AGS 2:380. The compiler of the latter comments that Takumi-no-Kami's remarks suggest that he believed he had killed Kira.

p.106 I should have told you about this problem beforehand: *Ichinoseki-han kachū Nagaoka Shichirōbei kiroku*, CG 3:19.

p.107 A letter of inquiry: *Ichinoseki-han kachū Nagaoka Shichirōbei kiroku*, CG 3:17.

p.108 We wish you to return to your duties immediately: *Okado Denpachirō oboegaki*, NST 27:168–69.

The famous glutton: *Genroku sekenbanashi fūbun shū*, 51–53.

p.109 A great surprise to Tamura: *Goyō tomegakinuke*, CG 3:25.

Denpachirō was the first to question this expedient: *Okado Denpachirō oboegaki*, NST 27:169–72.

p.111 The Tamura . . . had assumed that Takumi must commit seppuku indoors: *Ichinoseki-han kachū Kitazato Mokusuke tebikae*, CG 3:24.

The Shogunal decree: The version quoted here is from *Tokugawa Bakufu O-Nikki*, CG 3:42. Other versions in other sources differ slightly in wording, but are consistent in content.

p.112 The Tamura house records: *Goyō tomegakinuke*, CG 3:25.

The Asano house records: *Kōseki kenmonki* 1, AGSS 3:175; *Asano Naganori den*, AGS 2:382.

Suga Jizaemon: Jizaemon also witnessed and reported Takumi-no-Kami's conversation with Magofusa. Some writers prefer to read his surname as "Kan." I follow Mitamura Engyo in preferring "Suga," but we have no way of knowing which reading Jizaemon himself preferred.

p.114 Takumi-no-Kami's famous death poem: *Okado Denpachirō oboegaki*, NST 27:173–74.

p.115 His men lifted him into his burial urn: *Goyō tomegakinuke*, CG 3:25–26; *Kōseki kenmon ki* 1, AGSS 3:176–77; *Chūsei kōkanroku* 1, AGSS 3:425; *Asakichi ichiran ki*, AGSS 1:379; *Horibe hikki*, NST 27:180; *Ikeda-ke bunko*, CG 3:87–88.

CHAPTER 10

p.117 A life of ease (*shiri de tsukamu isshō no anraku*): Tanno, *Edo aheahe sōshi*, 9. For a brief but meticulous description of relationships of this sort among warriors, see Watanabe, "Sexuality and the Social Order," 307–9. See also Ujiie, *Bushidō to eros*, and "Nanshoku no henyō," in *Edo no sei fūzoku*, 127–52.

It should be noted, too, that being set apart as former lovers of their lord, seems to have engendered solidarity rather than jealousy among these men.

p.118 Utterly incomprehensible: *Horibe hikki*, NST 27:180.

p.119 A small flotilla of boats slipped up to the quayside steps: Horibe Yasubei to Kikkawa Mohei, Genroku 14.6.28, AGS 3:83–89; and CG 3:278–81.

It is tempting to see this raid at the Watergate as a late survival of the openly condoned looting by the rabble (*zōnin*) of the mansions of dispossessed daimyo in Muromachi-period Kyoto. For concrete examples of this practice, see Shimizu Katsuyuki, "Botsuraku daimyō no matsuro," in *Kenka ryōseibai no tanjō*, 87–92, and "Seiken kōsōgeki no naka no toshi minshū," in *Muromachi shakai no sōjō to chitsujo*, esp. 51–55. See also Hayami Shungyōsai's imaginatively detailed print of the Teppōzu Watergate in *Ehon Chūshingura*, ser. 2, 2:23v–24r.

p.121 A separate establishment of her own: An excellent reproduction of a recently discovered plan of the Asano Upper Mansion is included as a supplement to the exhibition catalogue *Chūshingura to hatamoto Asano-ke*. See also the diagrammatic exposition of this plan and the accompanying analysis by Shibuya Yōko,

"Akō Asano-ke 'Teppōzu kami yashiki zu' ni tsuite," 76, 77–79.

Kyūsō's account: Muro Kyūsō, *Akō gijin roku*, NST 27:292–93. Kyūsō's source is the Hiroshima samurai who were present at the time. The same is true of his subsequent description of Lady Asano cutting her hair.

p.122 *Records of a Dutiful Progeny*: Miyoshi bunke Seibiroku.

Her name was O-Ishi: SN 4:12v–13v (unnumbered pages).

p.123 Inaba-no-Kami died unexpectedly: MS 1:480.

Yonemura Gon'emon: Itō Bai'u, *Kenmon dansō*, 122–23.

p.125 Hyōe Hitachi: This particular appellation is not to be found in any of the Tokugawa genealogies, but it probably refers either to Tokugawa Ieyasu's tenth son, Yorinobu (1602–1671), or his eleventh and last son, Yorifusa (1603–1661). The former held the title of Hitachi-no-Suke, but he never set foot in the province of Hitachi and is more closely associated with the province of Kii. The latter was the first of the Tokugawa to rule the domain of Mito in Hitachi, which he did for more than fifty years, and his youthful title of Saemon-no-Kami identifies him (nominally) as an officer of the Hyōe-fu. He thus seems the more likely to have been styled Hyōe Hitachi. I am indebted to Professor Kasaya Kazuhiko for these observations.

p.126 Two official inquiries: *Asano Tsunanaga den*, AGS 2:525.

A very small detail of only fifteen men: *Kōseki kenmonki* 1, AGSS 3:178.

CHAPTER 11

p.128 Kagano Densuke: CG 3:81–82.

p.129 Kira's wounds: *Kurisaki kiroku*, CG 3:14.

p.130 He returned to Teppōzu: *Asano Tsunanaga den*, AGS 2:525–26.

They were now under sentence of Restraint (*enryo*): *Ekisui renbei roku*, 38–39.

Official enforcers of the confiscation: *Ekisui renbei roku*, 50–51; TJ 6:433. A vast cache of documents related to this project survives, many of which are conveniently collected in AJUM.

The size of the force that would be required: AJUM, 7. The Wakizaka, although required to send only 3,500 men, in fact sent a force of 4,545. The assignment was considered an event of such significance in the history of the house that artists were commissioned to produce a pictorial scroll of the procession, including even the ships that transported their cannon to Akō. Fortunately, this scroll was acquired in 1970 by the Ōishi Jinja in Akō when it was on the verge of being sold to the Museum of Fine Arts, Boston. Portions of it are reproduced in various exhibition catalogues, but no complete reproduction has been published.

p.131 **Sentenced Asano Daigaku to Domiciliary Confinement (*heimon*):** *Asano Naganori den*, AGS 2:386; TJ 6:433.

p.132 **After twelve years of marriage was still childless:** Takumi-no-Kami's near fatal attack of smallpox may have left him infertile. See Janetta, *Epidemics and Mortality in Early Modern Japan*, 189.

p.133 **Kira Kōzuke-no-Suke had *not* died:** *Horibe hikki*, NST 27:186–87.

CHAPTER 12

p.134 **The traveler:** *Tamenaka Ason shū*, 134.

Kajikawa Yosōbei . . . was again interrogated: *Kajikawa hikki*, AGSS 2:276–78.

p.136 **Virtually the entire population of the Asano Upper Mansion in Teppōzu had departed:** *Asano Tsunanaga den*, AGS 2:526–27.

Tominomori Suke'emon and Karube Gohei: The relationship between Gohei and Suke'emon is described in similar terms in several secondary works, but there seems to survive no single contemporary source upon which the story is based. The basic elements of the narrative are indisputable, but their textual basis can only be described as a patchwork. The best summary I have found is Murakami, "Akō rōshi to Kawasaki," and the details are interestingly analyzed in Tominomori Eiji, *Uron nari Suke'emon*. Yamazaki Yoshishige includes a sketch of Gohei's farmstead in *Akō gishi zuihitsu*, NZT, ser. 2, 24:110. Gohei's water route from Hirama to Teppōzu can clearly be traced on the painstakingly reconstructed bird's-eye view of Edo and environs included as a fold-out supplement to Tachikawa, *Ō-Edo chōkanzu*.

p.138 **The Rokugō River:** Now known as the Tamagawa.

CHAPTER 13

p.139 **Which turn Tōzaemon and Sanpei took:** Kishii, ed., *Shinshū Gokaidō saiken*, esp. 153–54 (Miya), 248–51 (Mino/Nagoya Kaidō).

p.140 One wise scholar: Fujita Tōko, "Bushi dochaku no gi."

Toda Izu-no-Kami: Izu-no-Kami (1646–1701) was a Unit Commander in the Shogun's Corps of Pages (Koshō Bangashira).

Make one last round of inspection: This episode is related by Yagi Akihiro (CG 1:51–52), who fails to cite his source. The resumption of the mansion is recorded in [Ōgaki-han Toda-shi] Banshū Akō ikkan oboegaki, CG 3:49, but nothing is said in this source of Izu-no-Kami's inspection prior to the transfer. For the time being, we shall just have to trust Professor Yagi.

p.141 Iyo-no-Kami thought it best to communicate his intentions: CG 3:82.

p.142 She took the name Yōzei'in: Asano Tsunanaga den, AGS 2:527. Most writers gloss Lady Asano's new name as Yōzei'in, but a few still hold out for Yōzen'in. It is likely that both are correct. For example, in Miwa Haruo's Naniwa-bushi performance of "Nanbuzaka no wakare," her name is glossed in the text as "Yōzen'in," but Miwa clearly chants "Yozei'in." The verbal version is simply what grammarians would call an i-onbin variant of the written version.

CHAPTER 14

p.143 Having urgent business: Hayami Tōzaemon and Kayano Sanpei to Ōtsukaya Koemon, Genroku 14.3.17, AGS 3:66. A local historian who saw the original letter says that it is in Tōzaemon's hand and that the unsteady characters betray the strain of days of hard travel without sleep. See Tada, "Kayano Sanpei no jijin," 14.

Written well before dawn: As time was reckoned in the Genroku era, the new day did not start at midnight, but at daybreak; thus the letter is dated "night of Third Month 17th Day."

p.144 Fushimi Road: Kishii, ed., Shinshū Gokaidō saiken, 166–67. It was also known as the Fushimi-Osaka Michi.

Jūnai's terse reply to Ōtsukaya: AGS 3:67.

p.145 Chinamen's Steps (Tōjin gangi 唐人雁木): The steps are so-called because this was where embassies from Korea disembarked en route to Kyoto. It was also the landing used by both the Yodo riverboat to Osaka and the ferry that traversed the mouth of the Katsura River. The steps are shown clearly in Tōkaidō bunken nobe ezu, 23:fold 17, and are described in the companion Kaisetsu-hen, 31–32.

Westlands Highroad: Kishii, ed., Shinshū Gokaidō saiken, 173–77. It was also known as the Saikoku Kaidō, Saikoku Hondō, and Yamazaki Kaidō.

For Sanpei, this was home: This description of the Kayano Valley is based principally upon the beautifully drawn and colored pictorial road map in *Yamazaki-dō bunken nobe ezu*, but also upon the experience of walking those portions of the old road that still exist.

p.146 The House of Kayano in the Kayano Valley: This summary of the history of the Kayano is based principally upon Inoue, *Ōsaka-fu zenshi*, 3:1160–78; Itō Tōgai, *Kayano Sanpei den*, AGSS 1:106–9; Mochizuki, "Kayano Sanpei no matsuei ni tsuite"; MS 1:96, 258–60, 286–87; MS 2:1–6, 271–99, 400–403; NRCT 28:183–305; Tada, "Kayano Sanpei no jijin"; SGD 4:21v–25v; and *Setsuyō gundan*.

That cluster of 11 villages in the valley: Ge'in, Hakunoshima, Ishimaru, Higashi Bōgashima, Nishi Bōgashima, Nyoidani, Imamiya, Nishijuku, Shiba, Higashi Ina, and Nishi Ina. Most of these names survive in some form on modern maps of the region.

p.148 Its old homestead in Shiba in the Kayano Valley: Fortunately, the Kayano homestead stands at the center of a stretch of the old Saikoku Kaidō that remains exactly where it was in the Genroku era. The *nagaya-mon* in which Sanpei lived (and died), and that forms the front wall of the property, also survives. For many years, the present-day Kayano family was unable to maintain this structure properly, for despite its recognition as an Ōsaka-fu Important Cultural Property, there were no funds forthcoming for its repair. Now, however, it has been transformed into a handsome and well-cared-for museum, the Kensen-tei, Kensen being Sanpei's style as a *haikai* poet.

CHAPTER 15

p.150 At the edge of the hamlet of Kuga: The Meiji-period map (1888) attached as a supplement to *Hyōgo-ken no chimei* 2, NRCT 29, shows the route to Akō as described here, branching off at Kuga, passing through the villages of Naba and Sakata, then rising to Takatori Pass. On current governmental maps, the winding course of the old upward slope is drawn more precisely—showing all its cliffs and switchbacks—but the hamlet of Kuga has disappeared, swallowed up, apparently, within the present town of Aioi.

The signpost that marks the turn-off to Akō and the inscription on it are clearly shown on a pictorial map entitled Kōteiki (1764), a detail of which is reproduced in Aioi shishi 2:669.

p.151 Bitter the nettle: *Akō gunshi*, 1.

Akō under the Ikeda: AS 2:35–71.

p.153 You are hereby directed to exchange domains: TJ 3:404; AS 2:132–64; *Asano-shi to Makabe*; "Asano-shi no furusato"; *Asano Akō bunke seibiroku*, quoted in AS 5:6–7 (manuscript in the possession of the Asano family).

p.154 The downward slope: The description of this segment of the route is based upon a map drawn by vassals of Wakizaka Awaji-no-Kami in preparation for their march from Tatsuno to Akō. The original is in the collection of the Okayama University Library, and a superb full-size color reproduction is included as a supplement to the exhibition catalogue *Akō-jō uketori to Tatsuno*.

p.156 The Hour of the Tiger: The ronin in the custody of the House of Hisamatsu say that Tōzaemon and Sanpei arrived at "*ushi no gekoku*" (ca. 3:00 A.M.; *Kikigaki*, 5); *Akō-jō hikiwatashi ikken* says "*tora no gokoku*" (ca. 4:00–5:00 A.M.; AGSS 2:492), whereas Okajima Yasoemon says they arrived at "*u no koku*" (ca. 5:00 A.M.; *Akō-jō hikiwatashi oboegaki*, CG 3:57). This narrative opts for the median, *tora no koku*, but probably no one knew precisely what time it was.

CHAPTER 16

p.157 The Ōishi and the Shindō: This chapter is based almost entirely upon the many genealogies collected in OGS and OKS. No attempt has been made to give page references for every detail, as this would produce an unmanageable number of notes, but significant supplementary materials are cited.

One reason that pre-Edo-period genealogical data is so hard to come by is that the Rokkaku branch of the Sasaki Genji, the regional overlords in southern Ōmi, demanded of all of their dependants that they surrender their genealogies to them. All these documents must have gone up in flames when Nobunaga razed the Rokkaku castle at Kannonjiyama. Members of the Tsugaru branch of the Ōishi house have striven to make good this loss, but with only partial success. The fruits of their efforts are collected in the two volumes cited in the preceding paragraph.

p.161 Konoe Sakihisa: Taniguchi Kengo, *Rurō no sengoku kizoku Konoe Sakihisa*.

p.162 Ōishi Yoshikatsu was taken into the service of Asano Uneme-no-Kami Nagashige; Hiratsuka Hyōsai (1792–1875) reckons that Yoshikatsu's uncle Hyōzaemon mediated his employment by Nagashige (SN), whereas Ōishi Kuranosuke says it was Akiyama Sensai who "spoke to Uneme Sama" on Yoshikatsu's behalf (Kuranosuke to Ōishi Mujin, Genroku 7.4.7, AGS 3:25). Perhaps both are correct?

p.163 What sort of a man was he: Many of the better-known comments on Kuranosuke's character are collected in Utsumi, *Shinsetsu Akō gishi roku*, 89–92. "Always had a friendly greeting and kind word" and "all the respect due a warrior": quoted in Kanzawa Tokō, *Okinagusa*, NZT, ser. 3, 1:154–55. Inoue Dan'emon: AGS 2:457–58. Onodera Jūnai to Onodera Jūbei, Genroku 14.4.7, in *Akō gishi no tegami*, 49–51.

What did he look like: Kuroda Hideo, "Ōishi Kuranosuke, Chikara zō no 'hakken,'" and "Ōishi Kuranosuke no shōzō." An excellent photograph of the images discussed in Kuroda's articles appears in *Toki o koete kataru mono*, 125.

CHAPTER 17

p.165 All that those on the scene tell us: *Akō-jō hikiwatashi ikken*, AGSS 2:492–93.

I take the liberty to inform you: Asano Daigaku to Ōishi Kuranosuke and Ōno Kurōbei, Genroku 14.3.14, in *Okajima oboegaki*, AGS 1:52–53.

p.166 Paper currency: For a detailed description of the use of paper money in transactions with Osaka salt merchants, see KD 11:773c.

Acting Elder: This title approximates but does not translate literally *nenban karō*. *Nenban* 年番 originally indicated that the holder of an office so designated served in that capacity only in alternate years. Later, it came to be applied to officials, like Ōno Kurōbei, who served continuously but whose appointment was neither for the duration of his lifetime nor hereditary. See Katayama Hakusen, quoted in Hiroyama, *Banshū Akō no shiro to machi*, 36.

p.167 Yosōbei expressed his gratitude for this reward: *Kajikawa-shi hikki*, AGSS 2:276, 278–79.

p.168 The unkind satirist: Quoted in Mayama, *Chūshingura chishi*, 520.

Shōda Shimōsa-no-Kami was dismissed from office: *Okado Denpachirō oboegaki*, NST 27:176–77; TJ 6:448. The suggestion that Okado's report may not be entirely incorrect is found in Yagi, CG 1:42–43.

p.169 Pandemonium at the Akō Currency Exchange: *Akō-jō hikiwatashi ikken*, AGSS 2:492–93; *Kōseki kenmonki* 1, AGSS 3:182b.

p.171 The entire Corps of Vassals was called to the castle: *Kōseki kenmonki* 1, AGSS 3:182.

Two letters were read aloud to them: The letters were from Tsuchiya Sagami-no-Kami to Toda Uneme-no-Kami and Asano Mino-no-Kami, and from Tamura Ukyō-no-Daibu to Asano Daigaku. See *Akō-jō hikiwatashi ikken*, AGS 1:53–54.

CHAPTER 18

p.173 Delayed their departure: *Matsuyama Kō Akō ki kikigaki*, CG 3:576–77.

Kira was *not* dead: *Horibe hikki*, NST 27:180–81.

p.174 Surrender his lord's castle: For a discussion of this dilemma, see Kasaya, *Kinsei buke shakai no seiji kōzō*, esp. 315–28; concerning this instance in particular, 317–20.

When two men quarrel: This principle is articulated in many sources. The version quoted here is from *Imagawa kana mokuroku* (1526), NST 21:195. See also Shimizu Katsuyuki, *Kenka ryōseibai no tanjō*.

p.175 The reports of one group of agents: "Okayama-han shinobi no hōkoku," CG 3:81–112.

p.176 Agents in disguise from both Himeji and Tatsuno: CG 3:95.

Two of the Iga men: CG 3:97.

Ikeda Iyo-no-Kami and Yanagisawa Dewa-no-Kami: CG 3:82.

p.177 Surrounded by contingents of armed men: *Kōseki kenmoki* 2, AGSS 3:226; *Chūsei kōkanroku* 2, AGSS 3:445–46; SGD 3:1r–5r.

Prepared to attack and annihilate them: *Chūsei kōkanroku* 2, AGSS 3:445–46.

CHAPTER 19

p.178 Certain to be opposed: See Mayama Seika's interestingly imagined discussion of the exchange rate between Ōishi Kuranosuke and Ōno Kurōbei, in *Genroku Chūshingura*, 99–108.

Okajima Yasoemon: *Akō-jō hikiwatashi oboegaki*, CG 3:56–66; AGS 1:51–68.

The process was far from orderly: *Itō Jūrōdayū Haruyuki kikigaki oboe*, 122–23.

p.179 Close attention to the sources: Enumerated and discussed in Tanaka Mitsurō, "Akō-jō nai'dai hyōjō' wa nakatta," *Rongaibi* 10.

The din of the greedy: *Itō Jūrōdayū Haruyuki kikigaki oboe*, 123.

A gentleman came to call: *Denpachirō oboegaki*, NST 27:177.

p.180 Kira's wife . . . had urged her husband to commit suicide: *Akō shōshūki*, AGSS

2:461. Another story reported in the same source says that one of the Uesugi Elders visited Kira, reiterated his wife's recommendation, and offered to serve as Second at his seppuku. When Kira declined to accept his offer, the Elder stayed on for two more days, waiting for him to change his mind, but finally left, warning Kira that his refusal could cause the downfall of the Uesugi house.

Memorial rites: *Horibe hikki*, NST 27:180.

CHAPTER 20

p.183 Asano Daigaku had been sentenced to Domiciliary Confinement: *Akō-jō hikiwatashi oboegaki*, CG 3:58; Okayama *shinobi* reports, CG 3:89.

The undercover agents from Okayama: Okayama *shinobi* reports, CG 3:89.

p.184 Those who sided with Kuranosuke: *Kikigaki*, 6.

p.185 Defending the castle against siege: The description of the attainder of Fukushima Masanori is based upon that in Kasaya, *Kinsei buke shakai no seiji kōzō*, 317–22. The principle involved was clearly articulated by Katashima Shin'enshi in 1719: "There is military precedent that when the defense of a castle is entrusted to a vassal, he may not surrender that castle without written orders from his lord. This is an ancient rule that still holds true today" (SGD 2:11v–12r).

p.186 Ōnishibō Kaku'un: For details of his career, see OKS, 117–18.

By the time this reaches you: Ōishi Kuranosuke to Ōnishibō Kaku'un, Genroku 14.3.21, AGSS 2:318. A diagram showing the location of this temple appears in Utsumi, *Shintei Toyooka to Ōishi Kuranosuke Fujin*, 112.

CHAPTER 21

p.188 Rumor ran rife in Edo: CG 3:83.

The movements of Horibe Yasubei: This description of Yasubei's plan is based upon *Horibe hikki*, NST 27:186–87; and *Kōseki kenmonki* 1, AGSS 3:181–82. The reason given for his failure follows Taniguchi Shinko, *Akō rōshi to Kira-tei uchiiri*, 61–62.

p.189 Chūemon finally came to the point of his visit: This episode is based entirely upon Yasubei's own account of it in his letter to Kikkawa Mohei, a close friend of Yasubei's late father, Genroku 14.6.28, AGS 3:86–87. This text is also reproduced in CG 3:280–81, but this version omits the extremely important postscript.

p.190 Akabori Tōemon: Tōemon is described in the no-longer-active Shibata Kenkyūjo website as an Adjutant (*yōyaku*) and Junior Elder (*chūrō*) of the Shibata domain in the Genroku era.

p.191 Horibe Yasubei was not born a Horibe: The best biography of Yasubei remains Fukumoto Nichinan, *Horibe Yasubei*, whereas the most up-to-date research on his early years is found in Tomizawa, "Horibe Yasubei no funkei no tomo."

Mizoguchi Shirōbei: His wife Ito, fifth daughter of Mizoguchi Hidekatsu, had died 1636.10.12. She could not have raised Yasubei after her husband's death, as claimed in some sources.

p.193 A shrine dedicated to ... Sugawara no Michizane: A two-page print of the shrine and the commoners' quarter at its base appears in volume 4 of *Edo meisho zue*. According to the description in this work, Yoritomo himself was the first to notice the resemblance of the stone to Michizane's ox.

Horiuchi Gendazaemon: Horiuchi's familiar name (*tsūshō*) appears in two forms: Genzaemon and Gendazaemon. I have preferred the latter not because of any evidence that it is the correct version, but partly because it is used in *Kangakusha denki shūsei*, and partly to distinguish him from others who go by the more usual Genzaemon. Very rarely, his surname is rendered as "Horinouchi."

Oda Nobunaga had kept a bodyguard: Ise no Sadatake, *Ansai zuihitsu*, 271.

This method of sword fighting was Yasubei's true métier: A copy of a portrait of Yasubei made for the archives of the Historiographical Institute of the University of Tokyo shows him seated, with his great sword lying immediately before him. The blade and the haft are of equal length. A full-page color reproduction of this portrait appears in *Egakareta Akō gishi*, 8. The techniques prescribed by one school of the use of this weapon are described in Shimazu, *Satsuma no hiken*.

p.194 A small tenement of his own: Ushigome Take-chō was later absorbed into Nando-machi, the name that neighborhood still bears. Yasubei's memory is preserved there by a small bar named Yasu-san.

p.196 Versions gleaned directly from the testimony of Yasubei and ... Satō Jōemon: Ogawa Tsunemitsu's description of the fight (*Chūsei kōkanroku wakusetsu* 2, AGSS 3:537–40), purports to be based upon the words of Nakayama Yasubei, Satō Jōemon, and members of the Horibe family. This claim is generally accepted as authentic, although there is no indication what form these "words" took. Saitō

Shigeru (*Akō gishi jissan*, 687–88) transcribes excerpts from *Nigatsu jūichinichi Takadanobaba deai kenka no koto*, purportedly a report submitted by Yasubei to the Matsudaira house on behalf of his deceased "uncle" Sugano Rokurōzaemon. According to Saitō, this document was discovered by Sasaki Moritarō (1906– 1983) in the Hosokawa Kōshaku-ke Bunko, but he gives no source, published or otherwise, for the excerpts that he prints. Nor does an Internet search of the holdings of the Eisei Bunko, the present-day successor of the Hosokawa Kōshaku-ke Bunko, yield any such title. These problems notwithstanding, the two sources are largely in agreement and thus seem the closest we shall ever come to a "true" description of a fight that took place more than three hundred years ago. This narrative is a composite of both sources.

Takadanobaba Mounted Archery Range: The range was a long, narrow stretch of land, about 1,230 feet (375 meters) in length from east to west and 260 feet (80 meters) wide from north to south. This area was further divided into four tracks that ran the full length of the plot and were separated from one another by earthen embankments intended to stop the flight of stray arrows. A two-page print in volume 4 of *Edo meisho zue* shows some, but not all, of these embankments planted with trees. This arrangement permitted those practicing mounted archery to use two of the tracks as a circular route, shooting on one leg and returning on the other. The track in between these two could then be safely used to practice unmounted target archery. Edo-period maps show the road by which Yasubei and Rokurōzaemon approached as entering the range slightly below the mid-point of its long southern boundary.

p.198 Kaiga Yazaemon tells the story of Yasusbei's adoption by Horibe Yahei: Yazaemon told this story while he, Yasubei, and eight other men were in custody at the mansion of Hisamatsu Oki-no-Kami. It was recorded by Haga Seidayū, a vassal of the Hisamatsu house, in *Haga Tomoshige oboegaki*, AGS 1:322–24.

The same story was told at the same time by the "young men" in custody at the Takanawa mansion of Hosokawa Etchū-no-Kami, where it was recorded by Horiuchi Den'emon, but Den'emon's version, although it agrees in large part with Haga's version, is more melodramatic and appears to draw upon an unidentified outside source. See *Horiuchi Den'emon oboegaki*, AGSS 1:311–13. The detention in custody of the Akō ronin is the subject of later chapters.

He was living as a ronin in the vicinity of Kobinata: Yazaemon (or, perhaps, Haga Seidayū) is mistaken here. Yasubei lived not in Kobinata but in Ushigome Take-chō, later renamed Nando-machi, the name it still bears.

p.200 His enfeoffment is 200 koku: Again mistaken. Horibe Yahei was enfeoffed at 300 *koku*, but when he retired, Yasubei succeeded him at 200 koku.

p.201 We know now: A hitherto obscure source recently has been introduced by

Tanaka Mitsurō in *Nagatsuta zasshi*, 2, 10, 14, 16, and 20 August 2018. In these articles, Tanaka summarizes a document entitled *Nakayama Yasubei—Horibe Yahei fushi keiyaku no tenmatsu*, which the editor thereof, Mibu Seigorō (Sekiun), has traced from a copy of Yasubei's own report of his adoption. Mibu published a limited edition of his tracing in Shibata in 1934, but even then it seems to have escaped the attention of those writing on the subject. Fortunately, however, a copy was acquired by the National Diet Library in Tokyo and can be consulted in the digital archives there. This document describes in considerable detail the negotiation of Yasubei's adoption, which involved, among others, Nakane Chōdayū, a close friend of Yasubei's "uncle" who had been killed at Takadanobaba, and Horiuchi Gendazaemon, Yasubei's teacher of swordsmanship.

His own son, Yaichibei, had been murdered: The story of Yaichibei's murder is best summarized in Fukumoto Nichinan, "Yaichibei no henshi," in *Horibe Yasubei*, 31–34. Nichinan bases his account principally upon a letter written by Yahei, which is reproduced in SN 1:24r–27v (unnumbered pages), and says that he also consulted *Chūsei kōkanroku*; *Mado no susabi*; *Nirō ryakuden*; Miyake Kanran, *Resshi hōshūroku*; and *Akō shijūshichi-shi den*.

CHAPTER 22

p.202 Tonomura Genzaemon set sail for Hiroshima: Some sources say that he sailed on the morning of the 20th. Both versions are probably close to correct. If he sailed just before dawn, it would still be considered the night of the 19th; if after dawn, the morning of 20th. Everyone agrees that he arrived on the 22nd. This account follows *Kōseki kenmonki* 1, AGSS 3:184; *Asano Naganori den*, AGS 2:290–91; *Asano Tsunanaga den*, AGS 2:527–28; and *Miyoshi bunke Seibiroku*, 589–92.

Genzaemon ranked as a Commander of Mounted Samurai (*bangashira*); he was enfeoffed at 400 koku, plus a 100-*koku* duty allowance (*yakuryō*).

Oki Gondayū Tadasuke: Oki Gondayū is described as an "Acting Elder" because he is listed as "*Karō-nami*" in "*Geihan shūyō*" *jinmei sakuin*, 35.

p.203 Lined up like teeth on a comb: SGD 3:1r.

p.204 Tokunaga Mataemon arrived in Akō from Miyoshi: *Kōseki kenmonki* 1, AGSS 3:185.

p.205 Itō Gōemon: *Asano Tsunanaga den*, AGS 2:531.

Tosa-no-Kami needed no convincing: *Kōseki kenmonki* 1, AGSS 3:189; *Akō-jō hikiwatashi oboegaki*, AGS 1:57–58. A longer letter to the same effect from the

Miyoshi Elders to Ōishi Kuranosuke and Ōno Kurōbei follows.

p.206 Toda Gengobei and Uemura Shichirōemon: *Kōseki kenmonki* 1, AGSS 3:187–88. Their entire mission is described in detail, with quotation of all relevant documents, in Shimizu Shun'ichi, *Chūshingura Ōgaki monogatari,* 56–63.

p.207 Finally confirmed beyond a doubt that Kira was still alive: No source reveals precisely when and from whom Kuranosuke learnt for certain that Kira was still alive. But his letter dated the 29th, quoted toward the end of this chapter, clearly presupposes Kira's continued existence, thus providing a terminus ad quem of Kuranosuke's uncertainty. That this date coincides with the arrival from Edo of Toda and Uemura is, to say the least, suggestive. In this surmise, I follow Tanaka Mitsurō, "Akō-jō no seihen," *Rongaibi* 9.

On the 28th: Muro Kyūsō, *Akō gijin roku,* NST 27:278–80; *Horibe hikki,* NST 27:181. A less dramatic, but in substance consistent, summary of the conflict is in *Kōseki kenmonki* 1, AGSS 3:183. Hara Sōemon describes the threat in his own words, which are reported in *Horiuchi Den'emon oboegaki,* AGSS 1:286–87. Fukumoto provides an interesting re-creation of the meeting, based upon Kyūsō's account, in *Shinsōroku,* 136–44.

p.208 Sōemon . . . was normally very placid: *Chūsei kōkanroku* 2, AGSS 3:432.

p.209 Kuranosuke's letter: This letter appears in slightly variant versions in several sources. This translation is based upon the version in *Kōseki kenmonki* 1, AGSS 3:190–91.

CHAPTER 23

p.211 Five men from Kameyama: This episode is mentioned in several sources, two of which are participant accounts: *Sekijō meiden,* AGSS 1:145; and *Horibe hikki,* NST 27:185. Its veracity is thus beyond doubt. The most detailed report of the event is found in *Sōgenji kiroku,* 3–6. This document appears to have been compiled by someone related to the leader of the group, Okano Jidayū (later Sakura Shinsuke), and thus may not be entirely objective; but the bare bones of the account are consistent with other versions, and the narrative is a great deal more circumstantial. This description is based upon all three of the foregoing texts, with occasional reference to Muro Kyūsō's account in *Akō gijin roku,* NST 27:323. I have also benefited from Tanaka Mitsurō's discussion of the episode in "Kaketsuketa Okano Jidayū: *Sōgenji kiroku* o chūshin ni," *Rongaibi* 54.

Both Okano Jidayū and Ōoka Seikurō are listed in a roster of Akō samurai dated Genroku 7 (1694), when Takumi-no-Kami was commanded to oversee and enforce the confiscation of Matsuyama Castle in the province of Bitchū;

their dismissal from the Akō Corps of Vassals must postdate this roster, but no record of the circumstances survives.

The secret agents from Okayama . . . reported a plot to defend Akō castle: Several mentions of such a possibility were made in these reports (CG 3:81–112), but they usually conclude that it was not likely to happen.

p.212 Hontokuji: *Hyōgo-ken no chimei* 2, NRCT 29:521.

p.213 Our foot soldiers are in a rebellious mood: For their plan to murder the Hagiwara brothers, see chapter 27.

p.214 His subsequent behavior: Okano Jidayū returned to Akō on the 6th Day of the Fourth Month and proposed detailed plans for a rebellion "as great as that in Shimabara." Again, his assistance is politely rejected. See *Sōgenji kiroku*, 5–6.

p.215 Muramatsu Kihei and his son Sandayū: *Kōseki kenmonki* 1, AGSS 3:181.

The home of one Kamishima Yasuke: Clearly marked on *Akō jōnai samurai yashiki kensū no zu*, supplement to AJUM.

p.216 Okano Jidayū happened upon Kihei and Sandayū: *Sōgenji kiroku*, 7.

The town was overrun with merchants: *Sōgenji kiroku*, 4.

Weaponry inherited from . . . the Ikeda: Listed in *Shiro-tsuki bugu chō*, AJUM, 200.

The castle's kitchen utensils had gone five days earlier: AS 2:269.

All of which went to a single buyer: Okayama *shinobi* reports, CG 3:106–7.

The Akō musketeers were allowed to keep their weapons: Okayama *shinobi* reports, CG 3:107.

Seventeen of the domain's ships were sold: Okayama *shinobi* reports, CG 3:95.

p.217 Store of lumber: Okayama *shinobi* reports, CG 3:100.

A severance allowance: *Kōseki kenmonki* 1, AGSS 3:194; Okayama *shinobi* reports, CG 3:100; *Akō-jō hikiwatashi ikken*, AGSS 2:499, 565–70. The foregoing contemporary sources give a detailed accounting of payments made, but say nothing about the disagreement between Kuranosuke and Kurōbei. As Fukumoto points out (*Shinsōroku*, 172), the first work to mention this is SGD 2:12v–14r. The date of composition (1719) raises questions of accuracy, but the statistical data in contemporary sources in no way vary from those on which Shin'enshi's later narrative is based. The suggestion that Kurobei's disagreement with Kuranosuke over severance allowances was what provoked Hara Sōemon to threaten him comes from Utsumi Sadajirō, author of the article on Kurōbei in *AGJ*, 355. See also Yamamoto, *"Chūshingura" no kessansho*, 63–67, in which he points out that in addition to their severance allowances, every man was paid his entire stipend for the year Genroku 14.

CHAPTER 24

p.218 The Kyoto residence of the Akō Liaison Officer: The house is clearly marked on *Genroku kyū-nen Kyōto dai ezu*.

p.219 Shogunal Magistrate: The staff of the Fushimi Bugyō was made up of ten Deputies (*yoriki*), fifty Constables (*dōshin*), and a variety of subordinate functionaries.

p.220 The "Murasaki Shikibu of our time": "Your poems have all the vitality of those by Murasaki Shikibu. Indeed it seems to me that you might even be Shikibu herself, returned to live in our midst" (Konze Keian to O-Tan Sama, undated, AGS 3:423).

They took their name from a village, Onodera: Onodera and Onodera, *Chūsei no Onodera-shi*.

p.222 I have no idea whether this will ever reach you: O-Tan to O-Riku, Genroku 14.3.24, AGS 3:69–70.

We've . . . dismissed some of the servants: Jūnai's staff at the Kyoto residence consisted of five foot soldiers (*ashigaru*) and five liveried menials (*komono*) sent from Akō (*Akō shōshūki*, AGSS 2:457); but like most samurai of his rank, he and O-Tan also would have had a few personal servants, some of whom were longtime retainers of the family. The dismissed servants probably had been hired locally. All these people vanish into the dim periphery as the focus of action shifts to Akō.

p.223 Jūnai . . . decided that his duty was to return to Akō: SGD 1:21r–v. The remainder of the episode is related by Jūnai himself in the letters that follow.

His manservant, Kyūemon: We know of this man only because Ōtaka Gengo once gave him a pipe case, which he inscribed with one of his own *hokku*, and this case later came into the possession of the writer and artist Santō Kyōden (1761–1816), thus perpetuating the memory of Kyūemon. See *Kinsei kiseki kō*, NZT, ser. 2, 3:771–72.

With this letter: Onodera Jūnai to Onodera Jūbei, Genroku 14.4.7, in *Akō gishi no tegami*, 49–51; AGSS 2:207–9; CG 3:269–70.

p.224 "I am of low rank," I told him: Jūnai is excessively modest in describing his rank. He was enfeoffed at 150 *koku* and received a 70-*koku* duty allowance, which would have placed him in the middle ranks of the Akō Corps of Vassals. He was, however, lower in rank than those of the command group, made up of Elders, Adjutants, Commanders of Mounted Samurai, and Company Commanders of Foot Soldiers.

p.225 Including a white robe: In which to die.

Your letters of the 6th and the 7th: Onodera Jūnai to O-Tan, Genroku 14.4.10, in *Akō gishi no tegami*, 51–53; AGSS 2:209–11; CG 3:270–72.

p.226 Mother hasn't much longer to live: Jūnai's mother died in the autumn of the following year, on Genroku 15.9.9, aged ninety-three.

O-Iyo is betrothed: Jūnai and O-Tan were childless, so they adopted O-Tan's younger sister O-Iyo as their daughter and Jūnai's nephew Kōemon as their son. Eventually, Kōemon was to marry O-Iyo, inherit Jūnai's position, and perpetuate the Onodera line. The reason Kōemon was not "likely to volunteer to have her" now was not the fault of O-Iyo but the loss of his own future prospects. O-Iyo, whose illness is nowhere specified but perhaps was tuberculosis, died about a year later, on Genroku 15.4.21.

p.227 Keian Dono: Konze Keian (1648–1729) was both physician and teacher of poetry composition to Jūnai and O-Tan. See Kansaku, "Genroku kamigata jige no kajin."

Chōbei has come . . . to fetch his daughter: Chōbei probably is a Kyoto townsman whose daughter was one of the young women doing "military household service" (*buke hōkō*) in Akō castle, with the aim of learning the more refined speech and manners of the military estate. It is likely that Jūnai arranged this opportunity for her. Her father, Chōbei, may have been a merchant with whom Jūnai had dealings, for he trusts the man to carry a substantial sum of money for him.

There must have been a number of young women from Kyoto in service at Akō Castle. The Okayama *shinobi*, in their report for the 23rd Day of the Third Month, mention that "the girls from the capital region in service at the castle will be sent home by ship" (CG 3:87).

p.228 Hanzaburō and Roku: Probably hereditary family servants.

Should serve as Liaison Officer in Akō: *Kōseki kenmonki* 2, AGSS 3:203.

CHAPTER 25

p.229 **The Council of Elders was quick to act:** *Kōseki kenmonki* 1, AGSS 3:186–87.

A suite of thirty-three attendants: Usui, *Ōgaki-han to Chūshingura*, 18.

More than a hundred men: Okayama *shinobi* report, dated 4.10, CG 3:103–4.

p.230 **Dan'emon's report of his colloquy with Kuranosuke:** *Asano Tsunanaga den*, AGS 2:574–76. "I appreciate the purport of His Lordship's command" translates *Tōzen no on-uke mōshiage sōrō*; and "I cannot guarantee our compliance" translates *Shika to on-uke e-mōshiagezu sōrō*.

p.231 **Four samurai from Tatsuno:** Okayama *shinobi* report, dated 4.11, CG 105.

p.232 **Instructed *not* to inform either of the Edo Elders:** *Akō gijin roku*, NST 27:280ff; *Horibe hikki*, NST 27:182ff.

There is no need for you to appeal to the Inspectors: *Horibe hikki*, NST 27:184.

Letter and a memorandum: *[Ōgaki-han Toda-shi] Banshū Akō ikkan oboegaki*, CG 3:48; *Kōseki kenmonki* 1, AGSS 3:198–201; *Kikigaki*, 8.

p.234 **Kuranosuke . . . summoned the fifty-four men:** *Kikigaki*, 8.

CHAPTER 26

p.235 **Nozaki Rokudayū sent the following report:** Okayama *shinobi* report, dated 4.12, CG 105–6.

Go'ō Hōin: KD 5:568–69, s.v. "Go'ō Hōin," plus thirty-six unnumbered pages of photographs between 572 and 573. See also Nakausa, "Hosokawa-ke kishōmon no sekai."

p.236 **Should a man take his own life:** *Jinkaishū* (1536), NST 21:215. For discussion of this principle, see Shimizu Katsuyuki, "Chūsei shakai no fukushū shudan to shite no jigai," in *Muromachi shakai no sōjō to chitsujo*, 29–49, and "Fukushū to shite no seppuku," in *Kenka ryōseibai no tanjō*, 43–50.

What his emissaries failed to do: Tanaka Mitsurō wisely suggests that Kuranosuke's ability to entertain simultaneously multiple solutions to a problem is probably what enabled him to adapt so readily to this setback. See "Akō-jō no seihen," *Rongaibi* 9.

p.238 Ōno Kurōbei . . . fled in the night: This episode is related in many different sources. There is no doubting its veracity, but I have avoided the more embroidered versions. This account is based principally upon *Kōseki kenmonki 2*, AGSS 3:203, 227–31.

CHAPTER 27

p.241 The Hagiwara brothers . . . sell their cannon: *Kōseki kenmonki 2*, AGSS 3:203–4.

p.242 Taguchi Sōen: *Kōseki kenmonki 2*, AGSS 3:204.

Peasants and village Headmen: *Kōseki kenmonki 2*, AGSS 3:204–5, supplemented by *Nabaya Kuzaemon oboegaki*, quoted in *Hyōgo-ken no chimei 2*, NRCT 29:734. The nuances of this relationship between peasants, Headmen, samurai, and domain officials are sensitively depicted in some of the historical fictions of Fujisawa Shūhei (1927–1997)—in particular, his long novel *Semishigure*.

CHAPTER 28

p.246 They went directly to the home of Ōishi Kuranosuke: Yasubei himself describes this meeting with Yasubei, Gunbei, and Magodayū, as well as those with Okuno Shōgen and the four Company Commanders, in *Horibe hikki*, NST 27:187–89. All dialogue is taken from this text.

At this time, and over the next several months, Okuda still went by the name of Hyōzaemon. Sometime in the Third Month of Genroku 15, however, he adopted the name of his father, Magodayū. Since this is the name by which he is most commonly known, in this book, for the sake of clarity, he is called Magodayū throughout.

p.248 All samurai housing had to be vacated: For a discussion of this process, as well as transcriptions of the few surviving inventories of movable fittings that each householder was required to submit, see *Akō rōnin aki-yashiki aratame-chō*.

His old manservant, Hachisuke: According to *Sekisui kyōdan* (AGSS 3:54), an often fanciful work, Hachisuke had been in the employ of the Ōishi since he was a child, when he was taken in by Kuranosuke's grandfather. Now an old man, though still in good health, he did not feel strong enough to accompany Kuranosuke on his subsequent moves.

The walk was refreshing: Kuranosuke to his father-in-law, Ishizuka Gengobei, Genroku 14.5.10, AGS 3:76–78.

CHAPTER 29

p.251 Final inspection of the castle and its grounds: There are several versions of this episode. The most complete, and probably the most reliable, is that in *Kōseki kenmonki* 2, AGSS 3:212–13. Others include *Horibe hikki*, NST 27:185a–b; Terasaka Kichiemon, *Terasaka shiki*, AGS 1:247; *Chūsei kōkanroku* 2, AGSS 3:442; and *Sekijō meiden*, AGSS 1:148–49. This narrative is based principally upon the first of these texts, but incorporates details from some of the others.

A suite of senior officers: Okuno Shōgen, Samurai Commander and Acting Elder; Tanaka Seibei, Adjutant; and Mase Kyūdayū, Inspector General.

p.252 Our Corps of Vassals is most reluctant to disperse: All versions agree that Kuranosuke hinted at the possibility of dire deeds following the surrender of the castle if they were offered no satisfaction of their grievance, but only *Sekijō meiden* (AGSS 1:148–49) states explicitly that they were prepared to die "with this castle as their pillow."

p.253 Laws of the Land: *Akō-jō meshiage no setsu no Bakufu jōjō*, CG 3:129–30.

p.255 Hara Sōemon remonstrates with the senior officers of the Wakizaka force: *Asahara Shigehide oboegaki*, AGS 1:289–90; *Itō Jūrōdayū Haruyuki kikigaki oboe*, 128.

They again summoned Kuranosuke to their lodgings: *Kōseki kenmonki* 2, AGSS 3:213.

p.256 It was a masterful stroke of negotiation: This interpretation follows that of Tanaka Mitsurō, "Akō-jō no seihen," *Rongaibi* 9, and "Iwayuru Asano-ke saikō undō no seikaku ni tsuite," *Rongaibi* 14.

A foot soldier from . . . Iehara: *Asahara Shigehide oboegaki*, AGS 1:289–90.

p.257 Kuranosuke looked out silently: SGD 3:5v–6v.

CHAPTER 30

p.259 The Wakizaka forces: The positions of the Wakizaka and Kinoshita forces are shown clearly on a map, drawn by Wakizaka samurai, that survives in the library of the University of Okayama. An excellent full-size reproduction is included as a supplement to the exhibition catalogue *Akō-jō uketori to Tatsuno*.

Certificate of Appointment: The great care exercised in handling this certificate, which bore the black-ink seal of the Shogun (*Kokuinjō*), can be followed in *Akō-jō on-uketori kakitome*, AGS 1:91, 115, 121–22, 134, 156, 159, 163, 198; and AJUM 20, 282, 284–85.

The surrender itself could not have been simpler: The most detailed documentary records of this process are *Akō-jō on-uketori kakitome*, AGS 1:69–218; *Akō-jō uketori zaiban goyō oboe*; *Akō-jō hikiwatashi ikken*, AGSS 2:492–578; and the many documents collected in AJUM. This narrative of the surrender is based principally upon the portion of *Akō-jō on-uketori kakitome* (AGS 1:191–204) that describes events on the 18th and 19th Days of the Fourth Month; *Kōseki kenmonki* 2, AGSS 3:217–21; *Chūsei kōkanroku* 2, AGSS 3:442–45; and various of the documents in AJUM.

The ronin in the custody of the Hisamatsu house at the end of the following year note that some of the men sent by Toda Uneme-no-Kami were present at the surrender and attempted to command the Akō samurai on duty within the castle, but that no one paid any attention to them and obeyed only those orders issued by Kuranosuke. See *Kikigaki*, 9.

p.261 **The dragon . . . that lies submerged:** *Chūsei kōkanroku* 2, AGSS 3:443.

There should be a banquet: The full menu is given in *Banshū Akō-jō on-uketori oboegaki*, AJUM 39–40; their abstention from celebratory saké is mentioned in *Akō-jō on-uketori kakitome*, AGS 1:199, and AS 5:161; and the "three lacquered trays" appear in AS 2:279. For a fuller description of such a meal, see chapter 82 and its notes.

The two daimyo composed their joint report: This letter, in the collection of the Tatsuno Shiritsu Rekishi Bunka Shiryōkan, is reproduced in the exhibition catalogue *Akō-jō uketori to Tatsuno*, photographically on 36 and in transcription on 76.

p.262 **Inoue Dan'emon . . . took the trouble to report . . . to the cadet house in Miyoshi:** *Kōseki kenmonki* 2, AGSS 3:220–21. Dan'emon's mention of the "illness" of Ōno Kurōbei is interpolated from his report to the Hiroshima main house, which, though less dramatic, in other respects is almost identical. See CG 3:130–31.

p.263 **He sought out Shindō Genshirō:** SGD 3:7v–8r. Katashima Shin'enshi reproduced the entire list on 8r–9r.

p.264 **He is a most extraordinary man:** *Kōseki kenmonki* 2, AGSS 3:221.

Many samurai were then free to leave Akō, but not all of them: *Akō-jō hikiwatashi ikken*, AGSS 2:508–10.

p.265 **After the surrender, new people garrisoned the castle:** *Akō-jō hikiwatashi*

Notes

ikken, AGSS 2:528–29.

Documents ... to be submitted ... to the Inspectors: *Akō-jō hikiwatashi ikken,* AGSS 2:535–37. The documents submitted to the Inspectors and the Resident Deputies are conveniently listed by Yagi, CG 1:81, and Taniguchi Shinko, *Akō rōshi no jitsuzō,* 48, 51.

A great-grandson of Mimura Bizen: Note attached to a letter, probably written in the Fifth Month of Genroku 14, from Mimura Jirōzaemon to Nonomura Heitazaemon, CG 3:273–74.

CHAPTER 31

p.267 **The paperwork would drag on:** The two principal sources pertaining to these activities are *Kōseki kenmonki* 2, AGSS 3:219–27; and *Akō-jō hikiwatashi ikken,* AGSS 2:525ff. Neither of these is a narrative description of the work that went on; both are collections of fragments and copies of documents arranged mainly by date. For a discussion of the relation between these two sources, see Tanaka Mitsurō, "*Akō-jō hikiwatashi ikken* to 'Chōmen kakitsuke no mokuroku,'" *Rongaibi* 52.

Checkpoint passes: Four of these passes are reproduced in *Akō-jō hikiwatashi ikken,* AGSS 2:534–35.

Rental permits: Kaiga Yazaemon's permit is reproduced in Saitō, *Akō gishi jissan,* 201. The original is one of the documents constituting the *Saitō monjo,* which were passed down in the family into which Yazaemon's daughter married, and now are held in the temple Honmyōji, at Higashiyama-Niōmon in Kyoto.

p.268 **A floor plan of the mansion:** *Akō-jō uketori zaiban goyō oboe,* 55; *Akō-jō hikiwatashi ikken,* AGS 1:174, 177. A copy of the plan submitted to the Inspectors, made by an artist in the employ of the Wakizaka, is reproduced in *Akō-jō uketori to Tatsuno,* 31.

Sectarian Registry Records: *Akō jō hikiwatashi ikken,* AGSS 2:534. Those records served both as a census of the local population and as proof that none of these registered were adherents of the proscribed sect, Christianity.

I have perused the letter: Ōishi Kuranosuke to Ishizuka Gengobei, Genroku 14.5.10, AGS 3:76–78. This letter has been edited to remove references to the departure of Kuranosuke's eldest son, Matsunojō (later Chikara), for a visit to Toyooka. It contains the only extant reference to this visit and nothing further is known of its purpose, dates, or duration.

Kumode Mohei, who is mentioned twice in this letter, was a retainer of Gengobei who carried Gengobei's letters to Kuranosuke over the mountain road from Toyooka to Himeji and then on to Akō. When Kuranosuke wrote to Gengobei, his letters were carried over the same route by Kuranosuke's retainer Senoo Magozaemon.

p.269 Pay us for this work in rice rations: Details in *Akō-jō hikiwatashi ikken*, AGSS 2:549–50. A year's rations for one man (*ichinin-buchi*) was calculated on the basis of 5 *gō* of rice per day, which amounted to 1.8 *koku* per year.

p.270 With this missive: Kuranosuke to Sugiura Tōbei and Maeda Ichiemon, Genroku 14.5.11, in *Akō-jō hikiwatashi ikken*, AGSS 2:537–38. Kuranosuke probably sent similar reports to Aki-no-Kami and Toda Uneme-no-Kami, but they no longer survive.

Both Asano Mino-no-Kami and Asano Sahyōe were bannerman of the Shogun, descended from the sons of Ōishi Tanomonosuke (1619–1683) and a daughter of Asano Naganao (1610–1672). Both of Tanomonosuke's sons were adopted by Naganao and granted demesnes of 3,000 koku at Wakasano and Iehara (pronounced "Eibara" by the locals), respectively. Mino-no-Kami was then lord of Wakasano and Sahyōe, lord of Iehara. Maeda and Sugiura were senior retainers of the two bannermen—perhaps Adjutants or Elders?

p.271 Until the 18th of the Fifth Month: Mimura Jirōzaemon to Nonomura Heitazaemon, undated, CG 3:273–74.

CHAPTER 32

p.273 The Reinstatement Movement: The argument of this discussion follows that of Tanaka Mitsurō, "Iwayuru Asano-ke saikō undō no seikaku ni tsuite," *Rongaibi* 14.

p.247 I take the liberty to address this brief missive to you: Ōishi Kuranosuke to Fumon'in, Genroku 14.5.12, in *Kōseki kenmonki* 2, AGSS 3:232–33.

p.275 The lords of both Hiroshima and Miyoshi would soon arrive in Osaka: They traveled via Osaka because they intended to complete their journey by ship.

Kuranosuke quickly drafted a letter to the lord of Hiroshima: Kuranosuke to Asano Aki-no-Kami, undated, in *Okajima oboegaki*, AGS 1:67–68.

p.277 Sōemon . . . spoke with Ōkubo Gendayū: *Kōseki kenmonki* 2, AGSS 3:229–30.

Kuranosuke's carbuncle: Described in his and Hara Sōemon's letter to Yasubei, Magodayū, and Gunbei, Genroku 14.6.12, in *Horibe hikki*, NST 27:197.

CHAPTER 33

p.278 Unpaid debts: *Akō-jō hikiwatashi ikken*, AGSS 2:540. These funds and Kuranosuke's disbursement of them are the subject of an extremely interesting book: Yamamoto, *"Chūshingura" no kessansho*.

p.279 Fujie Yūyō Heisuke Tadayasu: Fujie's (1685–1751) *Tōkyakumon* is quoted in Utsumi, *Shintei Toyooka to Ōishi Kuranosuke Fujin*, 21–22; and Fukumoto, *Shinsōroku*, 241. Fukumoto also notes that the original text was written in *kanbun*. But neither author says where or by whom it was held. The text seems to be untraceable; it is not listed in *Kokusho sōmokuroku* or in the online catalogues of any major library. Fujie's best known extant works are two regional gazetteers: *Akō gunshi* (1747) and *Tatsuno-shi*.

p.281 Katashima Shin'enshi waxes sentimental: SGD 4:3r.

p.282 Kuranosuke's reply: Ōishi Kuranosuke to Yūkai, Genroku 14.7.22, in *Akō gishi no tegami*, 76–79.

The two clerics "responded favorably": *Kōseki kenmonki* 4, AGSS 3:257–58.

Yūkai might attempt to contact Yanagisawa: Kuranosuke to Yūkai, Genroku 14.7.22, in *Akō gishi no tegami*, 76–79.

p.283 The conditions demanded by Kuranosuke: Kuranosuke to Yūkai, Genroku 14.7.22, in *Akō gishi no tegami*, 76–79 (edited slightly to minimize repetition).

CHAPTER 34

p.284 Genshirō . . . had moved to the village of Nishinoyama in Yamashina: SGD 4:1r–3v.

p.285 Inarizuka: Another version of this story reads:

The Inarizuka is adjacent to Kazan Jinja in Ōaza Nishinoyama. According to the Shrine History of Kazan Jinja, long ago there was a renowned swordsmith from Sanjō, Rokurō Munechika, who, wishing to penetrate the deepest mysteries of his art, came to pray at Kazan Jinja. On one such occasion, three Celestial Cherubs (dōji) appeared to him, scooped up some clay from Kazan, fashioned a hearth from it, and presented it to Munechika. Choked with tears of gratitude, Munechika purified himself and, using this hearth, forged a perfect treasure of a sword. As he had accomplished this through the aid of the Myōjin, and as the three Cherubs must have been foxes serving as the deity's emmisaries, he named the sword Kogitsune Maru, and the place where he tempered the blade was called

Inarizuka. (Kyōto-fu Yamashina-chō shi, 331)

The site of Munechika's forge is still marked by a commemorative plaque on Sanjō-dōri, a short distance west of the Miyako Hotel.

In the Nō play *Kokaji*, a single Cherub appears to Munechika, and after revealing himself as a fox and helping Munechika forge Kogitsune Maru, he "ascended to the clouds and returned to Inari no Miné" (NKBT 41:365–69).

p.287 Declaration of Guarantee: AGS 3:95–96. All the documents relating to Kuranosuke's move to Nishinoyama, including not only Genshirō's letter but also Kuranosuke's genealogical record (*shinruigaki*) and the submissions of the village Elders to the office of the Shogunate's regional administrator (*o-bugyōsho*), are collected in SN 4:1r–5v (unnumbered pages). One presumes that Hiratsuka Hyōsai, the editor of this work, had access to these archives because he himself was an official in the office of the Kyoto City Magistrate.

p.288 One letter that was waiting: Araki Jūzaemon to Ōishi Kuranosuke, in *Kōseki kenmonki* 4, AGSS 3:257. In SGD 4:2r–2v, Katashima Shin'enshi says that the letter was initially sent to Asano Mino-no-Kami, another of Kuranosuke's distant kinsmen, and that Araki called upon each of the Elders individually, because in joint session they would just agree with one another and thus their individual opinions would never be known. Kuranosuke, too, notes that "Araki Jūzaemon Dono has conveyed my request to the Council of Elders and the Junior Council of Elders, and their response was favorable" (Kuranosuke to Gunbei, Yasubei, and Magodayū, Genroku 14.7.13, in *Horibe hikki*, NST 27:199–201).

He answered a letter from his father-in-law: Kuranosuke to Ishizuka Gengobei, Genroku 14.7.13. This fascinating letter is transcribed in two sources: Saitō, *Akō gishi jissan*, 821–22; and *Akō "gishi" no tegami*, 86–88. The latter transcription is fuller and more accurate, but Saito's punctuation and interlinear notes offer useful suggestions as to what the illegible passages might be meant to say. Neither version is complete, nor do the two transcriptions always agree. As Kuranosuke himself notes in his final paragraph, he wrote when he was suffering "dizzy spells and felt unsteady on [his] feet," and thus feared that "at times this may seem incomprehensible." He was right. Lengthy illegible passages are indicated by ellipses.

Your letter of the 7th: Gengobei's letter to Kuranosuke has not survived.

p.289 The perfect place for a ronin to live: Perhaps because ronin were less subject to scrutiny and suspicion than in Kyoto? As he wrote to his adopted son, "I am unfamiliar with the capital region. I am not even sure but what it might be an unsuitable place for a ronin to reside" (Kuranosuke to Ōnishibō Kaku'un, Genroku 14.3.21, AGSS 2:318).

CHAPTER 35

p.292 Kuranosuke came personally . . . to see them off: *Horibe hikki,* NST 27:1989.

Everything went just as we three had hoped it would: Horibe Yasubei to Horibe Yahei, Genroku 14.4.19, AGS 3:73–74.

On their return: Yasubei to Kikkawa Mohei, Genroku 14.6.28, AGS 3:83–90. The three men set out from Akō on the 22nd Day of the Fourth Month and arrived in Edo on the 16th of the Fifth Month.

p.293 Yasubei did sometimes seem to hear only what he wished to hear: I am indebted to Tanaka Mitsurō for this insight into Yasubei's character. It makes many of the things he says and does seem more understandable. See Tanaka, "Iwayuru Asano-ke saikō undō no seikaku ni tsuite," *Rongaibi* 14, and "Horibe Yasubei no jinbutsuzō," *Rongaibi* 18.

Have you any thoughts where you will lodge: Yasubei to Ōishi Kuranosuke, Genroku 14.5.19, in *Horibe hikki,* NST 27:190–91. Although intended principally for Kuranosuke, this letter is also addressed to six other members of the command group: Okuno Shōgen, Yoshida Chūzaemon, Kawamura Denbei, Shindō Genshirō, Hara Sōemon, and Oyama Gengozaemon.

p.294 We hear all manner of interesting news: Yasubei to Oyama Gengozaemon, Genroku 14.6.18, in *Horibe hikki,* NST 27:192–94. This letter has been heavily edited to avoid repeating what Yasubei has said (often verbatim) in other letters.

Kobiki-chō: This neighborhood, near the present-day Kabuki-za, was the location of the residence of Asano Daigaku, and thus is frequently used as a code name for him.

p.295 This was their first meeting since returning from Akō: This conversation is reconstructed from three firsthand accounts of it, all by Yasubei: *Horibe hikki,* NST 27:186–87, 194–95; Yasubei to Gengozaemon, Genroku 14.6.18, NST 27:192–94; and Yasubei to Ōishi Kuranosuke, Genroku 14.8.8, NST 27:204–5.

p.297 Of the three of us, . . . I am the youngest: Yasubei was thirty-two at the time, Magodayū was fifty-five, and Gunbei's age is unknown.

p.298 Kuranosuke sent a brief note: Kuranosuke to Yasubei, Genroku 14.7.3, in *Horibe hikki,* NST 27:198–99.

I have read Yasubei Dono's letter to Gengoemon: Kuranosuke to Gunbei, Yasubei, and Magodayū, Genroku 14.7.13, in *Horibe hikki,* NST 27:199–201.

p.300 Yasubei was careful to preserve copies: Although most of the letters from Edo were signed by the "Edo Three," as they came to be called, it was Yasubei who wrote out, copied, and probably composed them.

CHAPTER 36

p.301 Zuikōin: This brief historical sketch is based upon Kanzawa Tokō, "Murasakino Zuikōin no koto," *Okinagusa*, NZT, ser. 3, 24:19–21. The temple, hermitage, and shrine are depicted in Hayami Shungyōsai, *Ehon Chūshingura*, ser. 1, 6:5v–6r; and a distant view is shown in Yamazaki Yoshishige, *Akō gishi zuihitsu*, NZT, ser. 2, 24:120.

Hideyoshi's brother-in-law Asano Nagamasa: Asano Nagakatsu had two daughters, one of whom, O-Ne (Nene), was married to Toyotomi Hideyoshi, and the other to Yasui Nagamasa, who was adopted as heir to the Asano house.

p.302 A second cousin of the late Haruyori: A genealogy of the Yamazaki house showing the descent of O-Ishi is found in SN 4:12r–13r (unnumbered pages). On 13v is a convenient list of the superiors of Zuikōin and their death dates.

p.303 Kai Shuso: This monk's proper ecclesiastical name is Ōshū Sōkai, but in his capacity as incumbent of the new Zen hermitage, this is abbreviated to Kai Shuso, or Master Kai.

Timberland for the temple: That is, a small mountain. See *Kingin ukeharai chō*, AGSS 3:134.

The path was overgrown with weeds: Katashima Shin'enshi's description of Zuikōin is in SGD 4:4v–5r.

p.305 He wrote again on the 22nd: Kuranosuke to Gunbei, Yasubei, and Magodayū, Genroku 14.7.22, in *Horibe hikki*, NST 27:201–2.

His reply is signed only by Yasubei himself: Yasubei to Kuranosuke, Genroku 14.8.8, in *Horibe hikki*, NST 27:202–6.

p.307 Commanding Kira to surrender his mansion: Yasubei, Gunbei, and Magodayū to Kuranosuke, Genroku 14.8.19, in *Horibe hikki*, NST 27:206–8; *Kōseki kenmonki* 4, AGSS 3:258.

Hachisuka Hida-no-Kami: His complaint is reported in Yasubei, Gunbei, and Magodayū to Kuranosuke, Genroku 14.8.19, in *Horibe hikki*, NST 27:206–8; *Kōseki kenmonki* 4, AGSS 3:258.

p.308 Circle of Talkers (*Otogi-shū, Hanashi-shū*): Kuwata, *Daimyō to otogishū*.

Hayato-no-Kami's ... blind masseur: Yasubei, Gunbei, and Magodayū to

Kuranosuke, Genroku 14.8.19, in *Horibe hikki*, NST 27:206–8.

p.309 **We understand fully your desire to await the decision:** Yasubei, Gunbei, and Magodayū to Kuranosuke, Genroku 14.8.19, in *Horibe hikki*, NST 27:206–8.

p.310 **This letter seems to have gone astray:** *Horibe hikki*, NST 27:209.

Both parties reacted to their uncertainty in the same way: *Horibe hikki*, NST 27:208.

Argue their case and urge him to make up his mind: *Horibe hikki*, NST 27:208.

p.311 **Sōemon and Genshirō dispatched a joint letter:** The letter has not survived, but it is described in *Horibe hikki*, NST 27:208.

I understand fully the devotion that you feel: Kuranosuke to Yasubei, Gunbei, and Magodayū, Genroku 14.10.5, in *Horibe hikki*, NST 27:209–10. Throughout this letter, Kuranosuke refers to Asano Daigaku by the code name "Bun Kō"; in like manner, Kira Kōzuke-no-Suke is called "Bokuichi-no-Suke." To avoid confusion, I have substituted their real names. Occasionally, I also have made slightly more explicit those matters that, for reasons of secrecy, Kuranosuke only hints at.

p.312 **Katashima Shin'enshi has described Kuranosuke:** SGD 2:1v.

Kuranosuke was on the road to Edo: *Horibe hikki*, in NST 27:211. The dates are specified in SGD 4:10r–v.

CHAPTER 37

p.313 **When Kuranosuke asked Hara Sōemon to go to Edo:** Sōemon's travel expenses are itemized in *Kingin ukeharai chō*, AGSS 3:135.

As Yasubei tells it: *Horibe hikki*, NST 27:208.

p.314 **Ōtaka Gengo had not been keen to travel in the company of Genshirō:** Ōtaka Gengo to Okajima Yasoemon, Genroku 14.9.14, AGS 3:106–7. Unfortunately, Gengo did not explain why he disliked Genshirō. Gengo's travel expenses are itemized in *Kingin ukeharai chō*, AGSS 3:135. No mention is made of any disbursement to Shindō; perhaps, being a man of means, he paid his own way.

A pledge to be signed by all: *Horibe hikki*, NST 27:210–11.

p.315 **They declined:** Yamamoto (*Akō jiken to shijū-roku shi*, 64) suggests that one reason the men from Kyoto declined to affix their monograms is that, because their travel expenses were financed from domainal funds disbursed by Kuranosuke, they were reluctant to sign the pledge without his approval.

p.316 Maebara Isuke: *Kōseki kenmonki* 4, AGSS 3:259. Isuke's family members, living and dead, are listed in his genealogical record (*shinruigaki*), transcribed in AGJ, 302.

Mid-Corps of Pages: In the Akō Corps of Vassals, the only samurai who ranked lower than the Mid-Corps of Pages were the Yokome or Kachi Metsuke. See Tanaka Mitsurō, "Asakusa Dōmei no shinsō: Kakyū bushi no iegara ishiki," *Rongaibi* 27.

The used-clothing market: In the Genroku era, Tomizawa-chō was the center of this thriving business. Maebara Isuke's "shop" probably consisted of little more than a mat spread out at the roadside upon which he displayed his wares whenever the weather permitted. See "Furugiya," in either *Edo-gaku jiten*, 243–45, or *Edo Tōkyō-gaku jiten*, 481–82.

CHAPTER 38

p.317 They lodged ... with Maekawa Chūdayū: *Kōseki kenmonki* 4, AGSS 3:259.

A meeting to be held on the 10th: *Horibe hikki*, NST 27:211–13. As Fukumoto points out (*Shinsōroku*, 276), Yasubei's description of this meeting is the only contemporary account of it, one result of which is that most early writers did not even know, and thus did not report, that Kuranosuke was in Edo in the Eleventh Month. Both Ochiai Yozaemon (*Kōseki kenmonki* 4, AGSS 3:258–59) and Ogawa Tsunemitsu (*Chūsei kōkanroku* 3, AGSS 3:448) describe Kuranosuke's visit to Edo, but neither mentions this meeting.

p.318 As Katashima Shin'enshi imagines it: SGD 4:13r.

p.319 Kuranosuke called upon ... Araki Jūzaemon and Sakakibara Uneme: *Horibe hikki*, NST 27:213.

Ogawa Tsunemitsu mentions Kuranosuke's visits to the Inspectors: *Chūsei kōkanroku* 3, AGSS 3:448.

The widow herself sewed a nightcap ... for him: *Horiuchi Den'emon oboegaki*, AGSS 1:304; SGD 4:14v.

p.320 Kazuemon's return to the fold: The best discussions of Fuwa Kazuemon's admittance into the group are Tanaka Mitsurō, "Fuwa Kazuemon wa kata-kimochi?" *Rongaibi* 31, and "Edo ni okeru 'dōshi' no shūdan no keisei: Fuwa Kazuemon wa itsu kamei shita ka?" *Rongaibi* 61.

He took Kazuemon with him: *Akō shōshūki*, AGSS 2:466.

p.321 Let's see you cut down one of these swallows: *Sekisui kyōdan*, AGSS 2:61–62.

p.322 *Tsujikiri* and *suemonokiri*: *Asano gishi no setsu*, transcribed in Kanzawa Tokō, *Okinagusa*, NZT, ser.3, 1:153–54.

p.323 Maebara Isuke . . . submitted a pledge: *Kōseki kenmonki* 4, AGSS 3:259.

Buy a house in Mita: *Kingin ukeharai chō*, AGSS 3:135.

CHAPTER 39

p.324 A place in the unit of Horse Guards: *Asano-ke bugenchō* (ca. 1699–1700), transcribed in *Akō gishi no tegami*, 388–408.

Heizaemon stabbed O-Hatsu and then himself: *Kōseki kenmonki* 4, AGSS 3:260; Sassa Kozaemon to Hayami Tōzaemon, Genroku 14.11.6, AGS 3:116–17; Sawaki Hikoemon and Sawaki Magoshichi to Hayami Tōzaemon, Genroku 14.11.9, AGS 3:121–22. My conjectures concerning the couple's "escape" and the location of their suicide are based entirely upon similar scenes in Chikamatsu Monzaemon's love suicide dramas: *Sonezaki shinjū* (1703) and *Shinjū Ten no Amijima* (1721).

p.325 The petition of Kira Kōzuke-no-Suke: *Horibe hikki*, NST 27:213.

His son Kira Sahei: Kira's son's familiar name (*tsūshō*) is often read "Sahyōe," but there are indications in contemporary sources that it was then pronounced "Sahei." Both Kuranosuke and Yasubei write the name 佐兵 (*Horibe hikki*, NST 27:202, 204), and in documents collected by a Liaison Officer of the Kuwana domain, it is written 佐平 (*Kuwana-han shoden oboegaki*, AGSS 2:360). I have preferred this pronunciation not only on the basis of this empirical evidence, but also because it helps to distinguish him from others of the same name who *do* pronounce it "Sahyōe."

p.326 His wife moved to . . . Shirogane: Mitamura, *Akō gishi ibun*, MEZ 16:389.

His first letter is addressed to Terai Genkei: Ōishi Kuranosuke to Terai Genkei, Genroku 14.12.25, AGSS 2:321–22.

p.327 To the Edo Three: Kuranosuke to Yasubei, Gunbei, and Magodayū, Genroku 14.12.25, in *Horibe hikki*, NST 27:220–21.

p.328 To Yahei: Kuranosuke to Horibe Yahei, Genroku 14.12.25, in *Horibe hikki*, NST 27:221–22.

CHAPTER 40

p.331 Monogram not affixed: Yasubei, Gunbei, and Magodayū to Kuranosuke, Genroku 14.12.27, in *Horibe hikki*, NST 27:217–19.

Yasubei has recorded what he knew of the story: *Horibe hikki*, NST 27:219–20; Yasubei and Magodayū to Ōtaka Gengo, Genroku 15.1.30, NST 27:236.

Gunbei had held a tenuous position: *Sekijō shiwa*, AGSS 1:240–41.

p.332 Uchida Saburōemon: Saburōemon's career is described in KCS 16:76–77.

p.334 The postscript of a letter: Yasubei and Magodayū to Gengo, Genroku 15.1.30, in *Horibe hikki*, NST 27:234–36.

p.335 Gengo, Sōemon, and the others seemed less shocked than sympathetic: Sōemon, Gengo, Matanojō, and Kansuke to Yasubei and Magodayū, Genroku 15.2.21, in *Horibe hikki*, NST 27:249–52.

The separate sheet: This separate document (*besshi*) has not survived. But in a narrative section of his record (*Horibe hikki*, NST 27:219–20), Yasubei describes the circumstances of Gunbei's defection in considerable detail, and it is clear that Sōemon and the others are familiar with these details. Perhaps Yasubei enclosed a copy of this description with his letter to Gengo in which he says that he will "write down all the details of the Takada incident" (Yasubei and Magodayū to Gengo, Genroku 15.1.30, NST 27:236).

p.336 Just before Saburōemon died: KCS 16:77.

He . . . never kept either promise: Such is the story that Ogawa Tsunemitsu reports in *Chūsei kōkanroku wakumon* 2, AGSS 3:542–43.

PART II. Year of the Horse: Genroku 15 (1702)

CHAPTER 41

p.341 The pledges of fifty-four men: *Kikigaki*, 6.

A single document, attached to a Goō Hōin: KD 5:568–69, s.v. "Goō Hōin," plus thirty-six unnumbered pages of photographs between 572 and 573. See also Nakausa, "Hosokawa-ke kishōmon no sekai."

A number of young people: Ushioda Matanojō and Nakamura Kansuke to Yasubei, Gunbei, and Magodayū, Genroku 14.12.10, in *Horibe hikki*, NST

27:213–14.

Ochiai Yozaemon reports: *Kōseki kenmonki* 4, AGSS 3:255.

p.342 The restoration of Asano Mino-no-Kami: Asano Mino-no-Kami, having been under sentence of Restraint (*enryo*) since the Third Month, was restored to the right of audience (*o-memie*) with the Shogun on the 28th Day of the Twelfth Month. By this time, he was more properly known as Asano Iki-no-Kami, having changed his *kanmei* on the 28th of the Eleventh Month out of respect for Yanagisawa Dewa-no-Kami Yasuaki (*Ekisui renbei roku*, 38), who had been granted the new name of Matsudaira Mino-no-Kami Yoshiyasu two days earlier, on the 26th (TJ 6:454–55).

The 130 signatories to the pact: Fukumoto names 130 signatories in *Shinsōroku*, 293–96. His list probably is a composite, for he cites no single source, as normally he does.

If there are matters: Ōishi Kuranosuke to Enrinji Yūkai, Genroku 15.1.11, AGS 3:134.

Ryūkō's "favorable response": *Kōseki kenmonki* 4, AGSS 3:258.

Sixty-five gold pieces: *Kingin ukeharai chō*, AGSS 3:134. These expenditures are analyzed in Yamamoto, "*Chūshingura*" *no kessansho*, 100–103.

p.343 Celebrate his majority: Ōishi Chikara to Jingūji, Genroku 14.12.27, AGS 3:129.

I am very grateful: Ōishi Kuranosuke to Ishizuka Gengobei, Genroku 15.1.27. This letter is mentioned in several secondary works, but I have yet to find a transcription of the text. This translation is based upon an excerpt in Saitō, *Akō gishi jissan*, 260–61.

p.344 Your letter of the 25th: Yasubei and Magodayū to Kuranosuke, Genroku 15.1.26, in *Horibe hikki*, NST 27:222–25. This letter has been edited extensively to increase clarity and reduce repetition.

p.346 Yasubei's father, Yahei, also wrote: Horibe Yahei to Kuranosuke, Genroku 15.1.26, in *Horibe hikki*, NST 27:228–29.

In my first letter: This letter has not survived.

p.347 Some only pretending: As suggested by Utsumi, *Shinsetsu Akō gishi roku*, 312.

CHAPTER 42

p.349 Kayano Valley: For the history of the Kayano house and the Kayano Valley, see chapter 14.

p.350 Thirty to forty days in a place called Kawabe in Mino: Kayano Sanpei to Kanzaki Yogorō, Genroku 14.9.1, AGS 3:99–101.

Katsuno'odera: This rendition of the name of the temple follows Katayama Hakusen, *Shiyō*, 19. It is now known more commonly as Katsuōji.

p.351 The poems they exchanged: Ōtaka Gengo, *Futatsu no take* (1702), AGS 3:436.

His impressions of the temple: Gengo, *Futatsu no take*, AGS 3:436.

Katsuno'ō yama: In reciting this poem, Gengo probably reverted to an earlier pronunciation, compressing the final *-no'o* to *-nō*—read as a single syllable—to satisfy the demands of prosody.

p.352 Ogawa Tsunemitsu says that "someone told him": *Chūsei kōkanroku* 1, AGSS 3:530.

As Katashima Shin'enshi imagines it: SGD 4:21v–25v.

p.353 Having spoken last year: Kayano Sanpei to Ōishi Kuranosuke, Genroku 15.1.13, CG 3:291; *Akō gishi no tegami*, 118. Katashima Shin'enshi quotes a covering note from Sanpei's father to Kuranosuke in which he says that he had no knowledge whatsoever of his son's intentions. See SGD 6:1r.

Last year: Sanpei to Kayano Shichirōzaemon, Genroku 15.1.14, CG 3:291–92; *Akō gishi no tegami*, 117.

p.355 Sanpei unsheathed his short sword: Precisely how Sanpei took his own life is nowhere even mentioned. Even in his letters to Kuranosuke and his father, he uses the word *jisatsu* (suicide), rather than "seppuku." Given the symbolic importance of seppuku in warrior culture, however, I have taken the liberty of assuming that seppuku was his chosen method. It is possible, too, that after the symbolic act of seppuku, he used his sword to sever a carotid artery, thus speeding his death in the absence of a Second. Yet to assume this much without evidence seems an imaginative leap too far. This description is based in part upon details in Saitō, *Akō gishi jissan*, 270. Saitō, unfortunately, does not cite his sources.

CHAPTER 43

p.356 The Yamashina meetings: *Yamashina kaigi* is usually construed as singular, referring to the meeting held in Yamashina on the 15th Day of the Second Month. It is here translated in the plural in order to emphasize the participants' perception of it as the culmination of a series of meetings.

We can ... reconstruct some of the schemes: Both Katashima Shin'enshi in 1719 and Fukumoto Nichinan in 1914 used the correspondence of Hara Sōemon and Ōtaka Gengo to construct their narratives of the Yamashina meetings, but both writers summarized this correspondence in the form of imagined dialogue. The content of these dialogues is not inaccurate, but in the present telling, I have preferred direct quotation from the letters.

On the 11th: Ōtaka Gengo to Yasubei, Magodayū, and Gunbei, Genroku 15.1.17, in *Horibe hikki*, NST 27:231–34.

p.358 Since coming here: Sōemon to Yasubei, Magodayū, and Gunbei, Genroku 15.1.15, in *Horibe hikki*, NST 27:229–30.

These people here say: Ōishi Kuranosuke to Yasubei, Magodayū, and Gunbei, Genroku 15.1.25, in *Horibe hikki*, NST 27:237–38.

p.359 "Strange to say," he wrote: Sōemon to Yasubei, Magodayū, and Gunbei, Genroku 15.1.24, in *Horibe hikki*, NST 27:238–41.

Sōemon wrote a nine-page letter to Kuranosuke: Gengo to Yasubei, Magodayū, and Gunbei, Genroku 15.3, in *Horibe hikki*, NST 27:241–44.

p.360 Over a span of three calendar years: Kuranosuke says simply that Domiciliary Confinement generally lasts for three years. However, he does not mean three full years, but rather *ashikake sannen*. Thus when one counts Genroku 14, the year of Takumi-no-Kami's death, as the first year, and Genroku 15 as the second year, then the third anniversary of his death is Genroku 16.3.14. This is the date that Kuranosuke wishes to make their final deadline.

p.361 Yoshida Chūzaemon: *Terasaka hikki*, AGSS 2:230–32.

p.362 On the 13th: Sōemon, Gengo, Ushioda Matanojō, and Nakamura Kansuke to Yasubei and Magodayū, Genroku 15.2.21, in *Horibe hikki*, NST 27:249–52.

p.363 As you so rightly say: Kuranosuke to Yasubei, Magodayū, and Horibe Yahei, Genroku 15.2.16, in *Horibe hikki*, NST 27:247–49.

To break our commitment would not be right: In the aforementioned letter, Kuranosuke frequently uses the phrase "break our commitment" (*koto o yaburu*), and in the context of his discussion of whether they should "abandon" Asano

Daigaku and attack before his case is decided, it sometimes sounds as though he means a commitment to Daigaku. Elsewhere, however, Sōemon makes it clear that the commitment in question is to the Bakufu, implied in Kuranosuke's appeal to the official Inspectors prior to the surrender of Akō Castle (*o-metsuke-chū e mōshitasserare, sono dan kōgi e oshi'idashitaru gi ni sōraeba*). See Sōemon to Yasubei and Magodayū, Genroku 15.4.2, in *Horibe hikki*, NST 27:256–58.

In their reply: Yasubei and Magodayū to Sōemon, Gengo, Matanojō, and Kansuke, Genroku 15.3.9, in *Horibe hikki*, NST 27:252–53.

In his personal record: *Horibe hikki*, NST 27:244–45.

CHAPTER 44

p.365 He would let certain people know: I am indebted to Tanaka Mitsurō, "Ōishi Kuranosuke no saigo tsūchō," *Rongaibi* 20, for the suggestion that Kuranosuke's activities described in this chapter constitute an "ultimatum" of sorts—a veiled warning that if the Council of Elders could not be persuaded to apply the Principle of Equal Punishment to Kira, thus restoring the honor of Asano Daigaku, then others might have to take the matter into their own hands.

p.366 He set out on the Fushimi Road: Ōishi Kuranosuke to Inoue Dan'emon, Genroku 15.3.27, MSAGS, 323–25. Ishibe is the fifty-first of the fifty-three post stations of the Eastern Sea Road (Tōkaidō).

Kuranosuke did leave behind a memorandum: "Kōjō no oboe," MSAGS, 317–18.

p.368 Kuranosuke wrote to Danemon: Genroku 15.3.27, MSAGS, 323–25. In the copy of this letter that survives, the addressee is given as "Nanigashi Sama" (A Certain Gentleman). This is probably because it was copied by a Hiroshima vassal who thought it best to conceal Inoue's identity. See Tanaka Mitsurō, "Ōishi Kuranosuke no saigo tsūchō," *Rongaibi* 20.

Kuranosuke's excursion to Ōgaki: *Kingin ukeharai chō*, AGSS 3:136.

p.369 Kuranosuke painted a chilling scene: A photograph of the scroll upon which the painting is mounted appears as a frontispiece to Usui Senkichi, *Ōgaki-han to Chūshingura*. Every effort has been made to trace the copyright holder of this image. For what little is known of previous owners, see also 57–59.

If Daigaku Dono is released on unfavorable terms: Kuranosuke to Kano Jibuemon, Genroku 15.4.25, MSAGS, 316–17.

p.371 **Yūkai arrived in Edo:** *Kingin ukeharai chō,* AGSS 3:136; *Terasaka hikki,* AGSS 2:233; *Horibe hikki,* NST 27:263.

p.372 **We have no choice now:** Kuranosuke to Terai Genkei, Genroku 14.12.25, AGSS 2:321–22. See also chapter 39.

CHAPTER 45

p.373 **Takebayashi: his forebears:** An undated and anonymous Edo-period *senryū,* probably playing upon the fact that Wu (J. Take)-lin 武林 (Warrior/Bamboo Grove) had once been called Hu-lin 虎林 (Tiger Grove). Reprinted in Rinoie, "Takebayashi Tadashichi," 256.

Descended of Chinese stock: This brief account of Tadashichi's ancestry is but a sketch of a very complex subject. It is by no means based upon exhaustive research into the many aspects of history that bear upon the matter, nor does it attempt to resolve any of the seeming contradictions that abound in the sources that survive. Anyone wishing to explore the matter further will find references to the sources I have consulted in Kan, "Mō Jikan to sono kōei," and "Mō Jikan to sono kōei: Hoi"; Kibe, "Hagi-han ni okeru Chōsenjin horyo"; Koyanagi, "Kira o utta Chūgokujin sansei"; Marumo, "Chōsenjin yokuryū"; *Nihon senshi;* Rinoie, *Sagashiateta nisennen mae no rūtsu,* chaps. 1–3, passim, and "Takebayashi Tadashichi"; and Tsuruzono et al., *Torai Chōsenjin.*

p.374 **The night described in *The Tales of Ise:*** *Ise monogatari* 6, NKBZ 8:138.

Will this rain: *Chōsen nichinichi ki o yomu,* 17, 18. See also Elison, "Priest Keinen and His Account of the Campaign in Korea."

p.376 **A more precise report:** *Mōri Hidemoto no ki.*

As the Mōri household records suggest: *Hagi-han batsuetsuroku* 4:141.

p.378 **Depicting the Beauties of Mount Misen:** *Geishū Itsukushima zue* 1:372–87.

CHAPTER 46

p.380 **The two men set out, bound for Akō:** Yasubei and Magodayû to Ōtaka Gengo, Genroku 15.1.30, in *Horibe hikki,* NST 27:234–35. Their departure date is mentioned in SGD 6:8r.

Ogawa Tsunemitsu describes him succinctly: *Chūsei kōkanroku* 1, AGSS 3:530–31.

p.381 Tadashichi and Kazuemon in Yamashina and Osaka: Ushioda Matanojō and Gengo to Yasubei and Magodayū, Genroku 15.5.17, in *Horibe hikki*, NST 27:267–69.

p.382 Kuranosuke . . . wrote to Okuno Shōgen: This letter has not survived, but is summarized briefly in *Sōgenji kiroku*, 10.

They stayed in Kameyama: *Sōgenji kiroku*, 9–10.

p.383 I've said nothing whatever about this: Hara Soemon to Yasubei and Magodayū, Genroku 15.4.2, in *Horibe hikki*, NST 27:256–58. Portions of this letter have been rearranged for greater clarity, but their meaning has in no way been altered.

p.384 We have both read with great care: Yasubei and Magodayū to Sōemon, Genroku 15.5.3, in *Horibe hikki*, NST 27:258–60.

p.385 I am sure that the delays have been wearisome: Ōishi Kuranosuke to Yasubei, Magodayū, Horibe Yahei, and Okuda Sadaemon, Genroku 15.5.21, in *Horibe hikki*, NST 27:265–66.

We can well imagine: Yasubei, Magodayū, Yahei, and Sadaemon to Kuranosuke, Genroku 15.6.15, in *Horibe hikki*, NST 27:266. This is the last of the letters collected in *Horibe hikki*.

p.386 Swore mutual solidarity . . . at a teahouse in Asakusa: *Horibe hikki*, NST 7:260.

Yasubei left Edo: Yasubei to Mizoguchi Sukeya et al., Genroku 15.11.20, AGS 3:187–89.
  In the absence of any explanation from Yasubei himself, speculation abounds as to what Yasubei intended to do in Kyoto. The most commonly propounded notion is that he was mustering a force to attack without Kuranosuke's knowledge. But as Tanaka Mitsurō points out, in the same letter, Yasubei states plainly that he has "discussed matters with Kuranosuke and others" ("Kamigata ni okeru Horibe Yasubei no katsudō," *Rongaibi* 24), and when news of Daigaku's "pardon" came, they then decided to attack. In a reading that avoids this potential for contradiction, Watanabe Yosuke suggests that Yasubei intended to "assemble the members of the radical faction and then seek Kuranosuke's understanding" of their plan (*Seishi Akō gishi*, 114).

CHAPTER 47

p.388 The Little Swordsmith's Shrine (Mi-tsurugi Sha): This small shrine commemorates the legend of Munechika, the "Little Swordsmith from Sanjō," whom the foxes of Fushimi Inari helped to forge a miraculous sword for presentation to the Emperor. In recognition of their assistance, Munechika named the blade Little Fox (Kogitsune Maru). Readers will recall that the same story is told of the foxes at the Inarizuka in Yamashina, which was owned by Shindō Genshirō. See chapter 34.

p.389 **Shumoku-machi:** The pleasure quarter in Fushimi was so named because the layout of its two streets resembled the T-shaped hammer (*shumoku*) used to sound the small chime (*dora*) used in Buddhist rituals.

Less virtuous ... but more typical of his time: In discussing the sources cited in this chapter, I have been guided by the acute analysis of Tanaka Mitsurō, "Ōishi hōtō no kyojitsu," *Rongaibi* 23.

O-Riku ... was to return to her home in Toyooka: Ōishi Kuranosuke to Ishizuka Gengobei, Genroku 15.1.27, translation based on Saitō, *Akō gishi jissan*, 260–61, and excerpted in chapter 41.

p.391 **When I first came to live in Fushimi:** Tachibana Nankei, *Hokusō sadan*, 18–19. Nankei is mistaken when he says that Kuranosuke's nom de plume was Uki. His nom de plume was Kashō (可笑); Uki was the name by which he went in the pleasure quarter, what we might call an *asobina* (遊び名).

The letters that Nankei mentions: Those that survive are collected in AGSS 1:430–35.

p.393 **Bugyō Dono:** Perhaps the Master of the Sasaya?

p.394 **Ōtaka Gengo has left us a series of five verses:** In the printed text, these are described as "linked verse" (*renga*); but in fact, they are not linked by prosody, as are true *renga*. The prosody of all five is the same: 5/7/5 syllables—they are what are now called haiku.

Satogeshiki: These songs have survived because they were collected by the retired daimyo of Hirado, Matsura Seizan (1760–1841), and recorded in his massive compendium, *Kasshi yawa*. Since then, they have been reprinted in countless sources. In the puppet drama *Irohagura mitsugumi sakazuki* (1773), Chikamatsu Hanji (1725–1783) depicts a special performance of "Satogeshiki." See *Chūshingura jōruri shū*, 468–69.

p.396 **Shindō Genshirō and his uncle Oyama Gengozaemon:** *Kōseki kenmonki* 4, AGSS 3:263.

O-Karu: Kuranosuke acknowledges O-Karu's pregnancy in a letter to Ōnishibō Kaku'un, Genroku 15.11.25, AGS 3:194–96, and mentions that he has written to Terai Genkei, asking that he, too, look to the well-being of O-Karu and his child by her (if it lives) after his death.

CHAPTER 48

p.398 Asano Daigaku is to be released from Domiciliary Confinement: This description of Daigaku's "pardon" and his journey from Edo to Hiroshima is based principally upon the records of the Hiroshima main house, *Asano Tsunanaga den (Kenmyō Kō seibiroku)*, AGS 2:535–39, with additional details from *Kōseki kenmonki* 4, AGSS 3:260–61. The various officials mentioned in this description are listed in *"Geihan shūyō" jinmei sakuin*.

A sketch map dating from the Shōtoku era (1711–1716) showing the location of the Hiroshima home of Asano Daigaku is reproduced in *Akō jiken to Hiroshima*, 25.

p.400 The fief that Daigaku no longer possessed: The compiler of the Asano house records reckons that Daigaku's enfeoffment as a bannerman must have been confiscated, but notes that he can find no documentary evidence of such a decree. "This requires further investigation," he concludes, in *Asano Tsunanaga den*, AGS 2:536–37. Elsewhere Daigaku is described as *"heimon seshi yoriai Daigaku Nagahiro"* (TJ 6:478), suggesting that he remained a member of the Reserve Force (*Yoriai*) when he was sentenced to Domiciliary Confinement.

Their present plan was to leave Edo: Terasaka Kichiemon, *Terasaka shiki*, AGS 1:251.

Chūzaemon wrote a quick letter: Yoshida Chūzaemon to Kaiga Yazaemon and Ōishi Kuranosuke, Genroku 15.7.18, in *Matsuyama-kō Akō ki kikigaki*, CG 3:580.

He summoned Yokogawa Kanpei: *Kingin ukeharai chō*, AGSS 3:136. It probably would have been Ōtsuka Koemon in Fushimi who made the arrangements for this journey, both financial and logistical.

p.402 And with Hachirōemon went Oki Gondayū: *Kōseki kenmonki* 4, AGSS 3:262–63.

CHAPTER 49

p.404 Ogata Kōrin stage-manages the entrance of [Nakamura Kuranosuke's] wife: Kanzawa Tokō, *Okinagusa*, NZT, ser. 3, 19:187–88.

p.405 The only surviving report: SGD 7:8r–11r.

The weather: *Edo-Meiji Kyōto no tenki hyō*, 96.

p.409 Minamoto no Yorimitsu's exhortation: *Rashōmon*, YT 5:3348–49.

The "Men's Dance": *Kosode Soga*, NKBZ 34:299–300.

p.410 The day's festivities: *Kingin ukeharai chō*, AGSS 3:137.

Ochiai Yozaemon . . . has left us a detailed description: *Kōseki kenmonki 4*, AGSS 3:261–64.

p.412 The 7th Day of Intercalary Eighth Month: The meeting held on that day is mentioned in Kasuya Kanzaemon and Okamoto Jirōzaemon to Ōishi Kuranosuke, Genroku 15.I-8.7, AGS 2:484. The only discussion of this meeting in any secondary source is Tanaka Mitsurō, "Genroku 15-nen 8-gatsu 7-nichi no kaigō," *Rongaibi* 37.

p.413 Memorandum of Verbal Declaration: Shindō Genshiro to Kuranosuke, Genroku 15.I-8.8, AGS 2:483.

Verbal Declaration: Oyama Gengozaemon to Kuranosuke, Genroku 15. I-8.10, AGS 2:484.

p.414 Genshirō was "most grateful": Genshiro to Kuranosuke, AGS 2:487–88.

Gengozaemon replied in a similar vein: Gengozaemon to Kuranosuke, AGS 2:487–88.

CHAPTER 50

p.415 He gave them eight gold pieces: *Kingin ukeharai chō*, AGSS 3:136; Yamamoto, "*Chūshingura*" *no kessansho*, 153–55.

They encountered the entourage of Asano Daigaku: SGD 7:10v.

They rented two pleasure craft: *Terasaka jiki*, CG 3:227.

p.416 Two poems by Kanzaki Yogorō: *Gijin isō*, AGSS 1:188.

A letter from old Horibe Yahei: Horibe Yahei to Ōishi Kuranosuke, Genroku 15.8.17, in *Horibe Yahei Akizane shiki*, AGS 1:226–27.

Broken promises: Kanzaki Yogorō, who must have been particularly outraged by these defections, compiled a collection of them that he called "Letters of broken promises to go east" (*Tōkō ihen no shojō*). Ochiai Yozaemon included this collection in *Kōseki kenmonki 5*, AGSS 3:291–304.

p.417 Four former Akō samurai: *Sōgenji kiroku*, 10.

Sakayori Sakuemon wrote: *Kōseki kenmonki 5*, AGSS 3:292.

p.418 Nagasawa Rokurōemon wrote: *Kōseki kenmonki* 5, AGSS 3:293.

p.419 Yazaemon himself described what they did: *Kikigaki*, 11–12.

Kuranosuke's written instructions to Yazaemon and Gengo: OGM, 41–49.

p.420 Go'ō Hōin: KD 5:568–69, s.v. "Go'ō Hōin," plus thirty-six unnumbered pages of photographs between 572 and 573. For photographs of some similar pledges, see also Nakausa, "Hosokawa-ke kishōmon no sekai."

p.423 The undercover agents from Okayama: CG 3:105.

Sixty-some according to one count: *Kōseki kenmonki* 1, AGSS 3:183. This was not unusual. A pledge dated 1646.10.28 displayed in the exhibition "Hosokawa-ke kishōmon no sekai" at the Eisei Bunko Museum bears sixty-eight signatures.

He set fire to the paper he had just been handed: *Sōgenji kiroku*, 10.

CHAPTER 51

p.425 Not all of them were cowards: *Kōseki kenmonki* 4, AGSS 3:264.

A vagrant samurai: Miyakawa Masayasu, *Miyakawanoya manpitsu*, vol. 5, NZT, ser. 1, 8:755–57.

p.427 Jūheiji had been parceling out this gold: SGD 7:5v.

p.428 I have read your letter to Gengo: Takebayashi Tadashichi to Watanabe Han'emon, Genroku 15.I-8.11, AGS 3:151–53.

p.429 I take the liberty to address you: Ōishi Kuranosuke to Terai Genkei, Genroku 15.8.6, in *Asano Naganori den furoku*, AGS 2:474–75.

CHAPTER 52

p.431 Katashima Shin'enshi seems to have been the only contemporary even to mention the move: SGD 7:11r–v. Kuranosuke did not tell everyone that he was bound for Bizen. His address on the list kept by the Fushimi brothel Sasaya is given as "Yamashina Nishinoyama; in the capital, Shijō no Dōjō, Bairin no tokoro" (AGSS 1:434).

p.432 His maternal kinsman Ikeda Genba: Like Kuranosuke, Ikeda Genba Yoshikatsu (1675–1704) was a grandson of Ikeda Dewa Yoshinari

(1606–1676), Chief Elder of the great Okayama domain. See OGS, 119–21.

The Yawata monk Shōsan: Kuranosuke intended to bequeath his property in Yamashina to his adopted son, Ōnishibō Kaku'un. Kaku'un, however, was only sixteen at the time, and thus the bequest was made in the name of his guardian, Ōnishibō Shōsan. See AGJ, 354.

Hirano Hanbei ... absconded with thirty gold pieces: Yokogawa Kanpei to Miharaya Chōzaemon and Miharaya Shichizaemon, Genroku 15.12, in *Akō gishi no tegami*, 247–52. Hirano's letter of defection is dated Genroku 15.I-8.24, AGS 2:488–89. In *Genroku nenchū Mizuno-ke komonjo komonjo*, Kanzaki Yogorō is quoted as saying that Kuranosuke "raised 130 or 140 *ryō* from the sale of his personal possessions, which he used to help support other members of the league" (AGSS 2:279–80). An illustration in *Sekijō gishin e-den* shows a group of merchants who call upon Kuranosuke at Bairin'an to inspect bundles of goods (mainly kimono) that he wishes to sell.

Sahyōe and Shichirōbei have been extremely gracious: Ōishi Kuranosuke to Mio Keigo, Genroku 15.12.13, AGS 3:244–46; OGS, 119–20. For Chikugo-no-Kami's refusal, see OGS, 41.

p.433 Kuranosuke would give each of them three gold pieces: *Kingin ukeharai chō*, AGSS 3:137–38; Yamamoto, "*Chūshingura*" *no kessansho*, 162–65.

Shōgen ... seems to have had second thoughts: This episode and its attendant circumstances are described in detail in *Sōgenji kiroku*, 11–12, and the reactions of Kuranosuke and other ronin in *Kikigaki*, 12. These and other sources are meticulously analyzed in Tanaka Mitsurō, "Toketa tesshin: Okuno Shōgen—datsumei no fushigi," *Rongaibi* 38, and "Zoku Toketa tesshin: *Sōgenji kiroku* ni miru tangan zokkō ron," *Rongaibi* 49.

p.435 His will of iron simply melted: *Sekijō meiden*, AGSS 1:149.

CHAPTER 53

p.436 They must now set out on a journey: Fukumoto (*Shinsōroku*, 382–84) has compiled a list of ronin in Kyoto, Osaka, and the western provinces; the groups in which they traveled; and the dates of their departure for Edo, which he says is based upon the most reliable sources.

Yatō Emoshichi: The story of Emoshichi's disappointment is told (tearfully) by Isogai Jūrōzaemon and is recorded in *Horiuchi Den'emon oboegaki*, AGSS 1:292–93.

p.437 He wrote to a friend in Akō: Yatō Chōsuke to Uemura Yozaemon, Genroku

14.10, CG 3:316.

In the postscript to another letter: Chōsuke to Hashimura Ikujūrō, Genroku 14.12.12, in Saitō, *Akō gishi jissan*, 272.

p.438 You can imagine how I would feel: Teiryū to the wife of Sakurai Kakuemon, Genroku 16.8.17, MSAGS, 362–65. Sakurai was a samurai (200 koku) in the service of Honda Noto-no-Kami, lord of Yamato Kōriyama; his wife was a cousin of Gengo's mother, Teiryū. See MSAGS, 343.

My decision to go down to Edo: Ōtaka Gengo to his mother, Teiryū, Genroku 15.9.5, in *Akō gishi no tegami*, 194–98.

p.442 Chikara . . . as a hostage: *Kikigaki*, 13.

p.443 Jūnai visited the Horikawa Academy: Itō Bai'u, *Kenmon dansō*, 252–53.

Jūnai's travel poems: *Gijin isō*, AGSS 1:185–90. Slightly variant versions appear in several other sources.

p.445 Write in his own hand a letter: CG 3:309; Takagi, *Zōho Mikudarihan*, 303–5.

p.446 The verse—written in Chinese: *Gishi monjō*, AGSS 1:430; Tachibana Nankei, *Hokusō sadan*, 19.

p.448 Later in the day it would rain: Only rain is mentioned for Genroku 15.10.7 in *Edo-Meiji Kyōto no tenki hyō*; details are from *Myōhō-in hinami no ki*.

CHAPTER 54

p.452 Arriving in Edo: *Gijin isō*, AGSS 1:186.

p.453 A small clump of moss: This talisman is mentioned in *Isogai Monroku oboegaki* (1786) as surviving in a collection of memorabilia held in the Hosokawa house. See "'Chūshingura to Hosokawa-ke' tenji risuto," supplement to *Eisei Bunko* 85 (winter 2013). The Soga brothers are thought to have avenged their father by killing Kudō Suketsune in 1193.

Kuranoske and Chūzaemon meet in Kamakura: Terasaka Kichiemon, *Terasaka shiki*, CG 3:228.

The Rokugō River: Now known as the Tamagawa.

Kuranosuke wrote to Suke'emon: Genroku 15.8.27, CG 3:300.

p.454 Every day, two or three men would come out from Edo: *Kikigaki*, 13.

A set of general orders: *Kōseki kenmonki* 4, AGSS 3:266–67.

p.455 We have more than fifty: Utsumi Sadajirō (*Shinsetsu*, 358) reckons there were fifty-five Akō ronin in Edo when Kuranosuke arrived. Further defections would eventually reduce that number to forty-seven.

p.456 Your own base in the region: *Horibe Yahei Akizane shiki*, AGS 1:222–23.

He moved to . . . the Oyamaya: *Kikigaki*, 13.

p.457 He describes his feelings: Onodera Jūnai to O-Tan, Genroku 15.11.3, excerpted in CG 318–23, and AGSS 2:212–19. There are significant variants in some passages of these two texts.

Kōemon: Kōemon is their adopted son, Gengo is Jūnai's nephew, and Kyūdayū and Kansuke are his cousins.

p.458 Haikata Kihei and Tōbei: O-Tan's younger and older brothers, respectively. Tōbei was a member of the Akō Corps of Vassals who originally signed a pledge and then defected. Thereafter, both Junai and O-Tan severed relations with him. Kihei seems to have been in the service of a bannerman in Edo.

p.461 Tōsuke and Keian: Tōsuke probably was a hereditary family servant. Konze Keian was a physician who also taught poetry composition to O-Tan and Jūnai.

Chikara Dono's lodgings: Ōishi Chikara was lodging at the Oyamaya in Nihonbashi Koku-chō. Kuranosuke would soon move there from the village of Hirama.

CHAPTER 55

p.462 A list of the places where the ronin lodged: Saitō has compiled an exhaustive list of this sort, complete with maps, in *Akō gishi jissan*, 298–306.

The ronin themselves tell us: The person who describes their meeting place and reports Kuranosuke's speech is not identified, but probably was Kaiga Yazaemon. See *Kikigaki*, 13.

In Hayashi-chō at the Second Bridge: The description of this location is not entirely accurate. Both places were closer to the Third Bridge, and only one was in Hayashi-chō; the other was in the next block, Tokuemon-chō.

p.463 Kanzaki Yogorō and Maebara Isuke: *Sekijō shiwa*, AGSS 1:229.

Mōri Koheita: *Terasaka hikki*, AGSS 2:236.

p.464 A map was made of the entire neighborhood: *Terasaka hikki*, AGSS 2:236. A surviving copy of one such map is reproduced in Saitō, *Akō gishi jissan*, 315.

A system of surveillance: *Terasaka hikki*, AGSS 2:235–36.

The turning of a waterwheel: *Chūsei kōkanroku* 3, AGSS 3:449.

Yoshida Chūzaemon laid down some . . . rules: Memorandum addressed to Horibe Yasubei and others, CG 3:301–2.

The "old men" . . . met: *Chūsei kōkanroku* 3, AGSS 3:453.

p.465 Memorandum of Instructions: *Kōseki kenmonki* 4, AGSS 3:266–69. Terasaka Kichiemon adds, "The foregoing statement was formulated by Yoshida Chūzaemon, written down, and then shown to Kuranosuke, who pronounced it excellent and in no way deficient. It was thereupon adopted as it stood" (*Terasaka shiki*, AGS 1:266).

p.467 We have managed to obtain a plan: Horibe Yasubei to Ōtaka Gengo, Genroku 15.1.30, in *Horibe hikki*, NST 27:235.

Terasaka Kichiemon . . . wrote: Terasaka Kichiemon, *Terasaka shiki*, in AGSS 2:236.

We managed to obtain two plans: *Kikigaki*, 13. Again, the speaker probably was Kaiga Yazaemon.

I have finally obtained: Ushioda Matanojō to Ōishi Mujin, Genroku 15?.10?.11, CG 3:312. The dating of this letter is uncertain because on Genroku 15.10.11, Matanojō was en route from Kyoto to Edo in the company of Kuranosuke and could not have written it on that day. But he *was* in Edo on Genroku 14.10.11, in which case this would be the earliest surviving mention of a plan. Or it could be that the month as stated is mistaken, and the letter should have been dated [15.]11.11.

Ōishi Mujin . . . had a brother-in-law: Genealogical record (*shinruigaki*) of Ōishi Sezaemon, holograph in Saitō, *Akō gishi jissan*, 676.

p.469 A copy of which survives: Photographic reproductions of this copy abound. See, for example, the frontispiece to Saitō, *Akō gishi jissan*.

This was what the ronin studied: *Kikigaki*, 13.

CHAPTER 56

p.470 Shimo and Konoe Sakihisa: See chapter 16.

Ōishi Gozaemon (Mujin Yoshifusa): *Ōishi Yoshifusa den*, OKS, 138–53, and especially the "Memorandum" (*oboe*), 143–44. Tanaka Mitsurō summarizes and analyzes the events described in this genealogy in "Ōishi Mujin no shintai," *Rongaibi* 28.

p.471 Yamada Sōhen: Yamada Sōyū, "Yamada Sōhen," and *Yamada Sōhen den*.

p.472 Hakura Itsuki: Hayashi, "Kage no kōensha Hakura Itsuki," in *Ōishi Kuranosuke hiwa*, 167–78. This chapter describes Itsuki's part in determining when Kira would be at home and quotes all relevant passages in *Myōhōin hinami no ki* pertaining to Itsuki.

Itsuki's surname is often read "Hagura." He would later become much better known by the name Kada no Azumamaro (1669–1736). As far as we know, he never mentioned his participation in the Akō vendetta as long as he lived.

Myōhōin: One of three Imperial Temples (*monzeki*) of the Tendai sect, the others being Shōren'in and Sanzen'in.

Ōinomikado Tsunemitsu: Tsunemitsu was related to Kira by marriage. His son Tsuneoto was married to Kira's youngest daughter, who had been adopted by the Uesugi so she could marry him as the daughter of a daimyo.

p.473 They are not exceptionally close friends: *Horibe Yahei Akizane oboegaki*, AGS 1:235–38. In this text, Yahei refers to Kira throughout by his code name, Boku-ichi. In reporting Yahei's speech, I have retained this appellation, but in dialogue have taken the liberty of substituting "Kira Dono," since neither Itsuki nor Gorōsaku would have known Kira's code name. Yahei also refers to Mitsuhira as "Ōishi-shi," which many later writers have mistakenly taken to mean Kuranosuke—a linguistic and historical impossibility.

p.474 Armed with two swords: Instead of only a short sword, which was the norm in social situations.

Light refreshments (*kōdan*): Perhaps a bowl of soba.

CHAPTER 57

p.476 Uesugi Danjō Daihitsu ... had been ill: This paragraph is based upon *Kōseki kenmonki* 4, AGSS 3:265.

p.477 Gengo was outfitted as a well-to-do merchant: The story of Gengo's study with Yamada Sōhen is based principally upon *Kōseki kenmonki* 4, AGSS 3:269, with additional details from *Chūsei kōkanroku* 3, AGSS 3:457–58; and *Sekijō shiwa*, AGSS 1:230. The *Kōseki* text says only that Gengo was introduced by an "intermediary" (*tsute*); in suggesting that the intermediary was Nakajima

Gorōsaku, I follow the lead of Tanaka Mitsurō, "Hakura rūto no jōhō kakunin," *Rongaibi* 48.

Postponed until the 5th of the Twelfth Month: The *Kōseki* text gives the new date as the 6th, but the ronin themselves say, "Gengo reported that Kōzuke-no-Suke Dono would have guests for tea on the 5th" (*Kikigaki*, 14). That date is corroborated in *Rakushidō nenroku*, 4:51–57, which describes the Shogun's visit to the residence of Yanagisawa Mino-no-Kami Yoshiyasu on the 5th, in deference to which the plan to attack on that day was canceled.

p.478 **The only item . . . that survives:** Kuranosuke's account book is in the possession of Hakone Jinja, Kanagawa-ken, Hakone-chō.

A list of the other documents: "Chōmen kakitsuke no mokuroku," in *Akō gishi no tegami*, 226–29. See also Tanaka Mitsurō, "Akō-jō hikiwatashi ikken to 'Chōmen kakitsuke no mokuroku,'" *Rongaibi* 52; and Satō Makoto, "*Kingin ukeharai chō saikō.*"

A large dossier labeled *The Surrender of Akō Castle: Akō-jō hikiwatashi ikken*, AGSS 2:492–578.

p.479 **With this brief missive:** Ōishi Kuranosuke to Ochiai Yozaemon, Genroku 15.11.29, AGS 3:197–99.

I have purposely refrained from asking after him: Lest in doing so, he implicate Asano Daigaku in the plot to kill Kira.

To further our cause (*ichigi no yōji*): This phrase, which is used repeatedly in Kuranosuke's letter to Yozaemon, is often taken as a reference to the vendetta. However, both Satō Makoto ("*Kingin ukeharai chō saikō,*" 30) and Yamamoto ("*Chūshingura*" no kessansho, 188) point out that it is used here in a much broader sense, referring to the entire range of Kuranosuke's endeavors: protesting the unfairness of Takumi-no-Kami's punishment, his efforts at reinstatement, and finally the attack on the Kira mansion.

5 kanme [= 90 ryō]: The exchange rate was calculated by Yamamoto in "*Chūshingura*" no kessansho, 195. Yamamoto notes that this sum neither is recorded as income at the beginning of Kuranosuke's personal account book nor appears in any of the documents he later turned over to Ochiai Yozaemon. Yamamoto suggests that this money probably was spent, when other funds had been exhausted, to buy such things as chain mail, metal helmet crowns, and specialized weapons—and that Kuranosuke refrained from linking such purchases to Yōzei'in's name lest such a document fall into the wrong hands and incriminate her. This does not explain, however, Kuranosuke's mention of such documentation in his letter.

p.480 **The mountain that was donated to Zuikōin:** The malfeasance of which Kuranosuke speaks probably refers to an attempt by the Superior to sell the mountain. This is why Kuranosuke entrusted the deed to this property to Yozaemon, and why he suggests that the Kyoto Liaison Officer of Yōzei'in's brother, Asano Tosa-no-Kami, from time to time remind the Superior of Zuikōin that he remains under scrutiny lest he attempt any further financial mischief.

p.481 **How goes it with the Yamashina property:** Kuranosuke to Shōsan, Genroku 15.11.25, excerpted in AGS 3:194–96.

p.482 **Gathered at a large teahouse:** Terasaka Kichiemon, *Terasaka shiki*, AGS 1:255; Toda Mosui, *Murasaki no hitomoto*, 241.

p.483 **The new oath:** The text of the oath is in Terasaka Kichiemon, *Terasaka shiki*, AGS 1:263–64.

CHAPTER 58

p.486 **The Shogun visits his Chief Adjutant:** *Rakushidō nenroku* 4:51–57; TJ 6:491.

I write to tell you: Kayano Wasuke to his kinsmen, Genroku 15.12.5, AGS 3:208–9.

p.487 **Kaiga Yazaemon says:** *Kikigaki*, 14. Some writers interpret this to mean that the gathering itself had been canceled, but Yazaemon clearly states that it was Kuranosuke who canceled the attack. And Kuranosuke himself wrote, on Genroku 15.12.14, to Terai Genkei: "There was a gathering the other day, but since there was to be a Shogunal progress that same day, we refrained from taking any action" (CG 3:399–400).

From south-by-east: *Chūsei kōkanroku* 3, AGSS 23:449. Mototoki was Sōemon's proper name (*imina*).

p.488 **Will you be coming here:** Ōishi Kuranosuke to Ōishi Mitsuhira, Genroku 15.12.7, CG 3:362–63.

Katashima Shin'enshi relates a version of the episode: SGD 9:5v–6r.

Now that the 5th has been postponed: Horibe Yahei to Ōishi Mitsuhira, Genroku 15.12.11, AGS 3:242.

p.489 **Masé Kyūdayū visits Kuranosuke and Itsuki:** CG 3:385–86; OGM, 258–60.

Yesterday when I called upon Kuranosuke: Yahei to Mitsuhira, Genroku 15.12.13, CG 3:384. In this letter, Yahei refers to Kuranosuke by the second of his noms de guerre, Kakei Gorōbei. For clarity, I have substituted his real name.

As for the matter in question: Hakura Itsuki to Mitsuhira, Genroku 15.12.13, CG 3:385–86. In assuming that Mitsuhira took this letter with him when he went to Kuranosuke's lodgings, I follow the construction of events in Tanaka Mitsurō, "Hakura rūto no jōhō kakunin," *Rongaibi* 48.

p.490 I write in haste: Tominomori Suke'emon to Ōishi Mujin. Genroku 15.12.13, CG 3:384–85.

Kaiga Yazaemon tells us: *Kikigaki*, 14.

He was to take them to Ochiai Yozaemon: *Kōseki kenmonki* 6, AGSS 3:325. Ochiai mistakenly calls him Jinshichi, rather than Jinzaburō.

p.491 Kira definitely had returned to Honjo: *Terasaka hikki*, AGSS 2:243.

Fortune had been working with them: *Kikigaki*, 14.

CHAPTER 59

p.492 By daybreak, it was snowing: Muraji Yajūrō, *Kaisekiki* 2, in AGSS 2:402.

Writing to wives: Some of the letters quoted here were written not on the eve of the actual attack, but in anticipation of the canceled attack on the 5th, and some even earlier. Several such letters survive, many of which make the same arguments. In this selection, I have attempted to represent the full range of the sentiments expressed.

Mori Mimasaka-no-Kami: Kanzaki Yogorō's genealogical record (*shinruigaki*), transcribed in AGJ, 240.

p.293 Sekijō meiden: AGSS 1:132–55.

The time of our attack draws near: Kanzaki Yogorō to Kanzaki Tōgorō, undated and unsourced, quoted in AGJ, 239.

I'm very sorry to hear: Yogorō to O-Katsu, Genroku 15.10.16, AGS 3:175–77.

p.494 When I was very young: Chikamatsu Kanroku to O-Uba and Sakubei, Genroku 15.11.21, CG 3:336–37; genealogical record, transcribed in AGJ, 256.

They were anything but well off: Kimura Okaemon to Kinashi Sōbei, Genroku 15.I-8.17, CG 3:304–5.

As I have told you in confidence: Kimura Okaemon to O-Tomé, undated, CG

3:386–87; genealogical record, transcribed in AGJ, 242.

p.495 The time has now come: Okano Kin'emon to his mother, Genroku 15.12.4, in CG 3:352–53

p.496 I do wish: Hazama Jūjirō to Watanabe Han'emon, Genroku 15.11.5, CG 3:323–25.

My poor woman there in Akō: The woman in question is described as *shō* 妾, a word usually translated as "mistress," but that in samurai families may have referred to a woman who was a wife in every respect except officially, either because she was not of samurai birth herself or because her family did not rank high enough for her relationship to the man she lived with to be sanctioned as a marriage by domain officialdom. Jūjirō, although of samurai birth, had not yet been admitted to the Akō Corps of Vassals and thus could not yet marry anyone, unless he were adopted into another family for that purpose.

I am delighted to say: Ōishi Kuranosuke to Terai Genkei, Genroku 15.12.14, in *Akō gishi no tegami*, 262–64. Katayama Hakusen, the editor of this volume of letters, suggests that the documents Kuranosuke enclosed with this missive were intended for use in the compilation of an account of the vendetta, a project Genkei and Kuranosuke had discussed, and that these materials were later used by Genkei's friend Miyake Kanran (1674–1718) in composing *Resshi hōshūroku*, AGSS 1:520–31.

The order of the sentences in the second paragraph of this letter has been altered for greater clarity.

p.497 The manifesto we intend to leave behind: *Kōseki kenmonki* 4, AGSS 3:280–81.

A list of assignments for the attack: *Kōseki kenmonki* 5, AGSS 3:302–4.

Their fidelity and their contribution to the cause: *Kōseki kenmonki* 5, AGSS 3:313–14.

The text written by Kanzaki Yogorō and Maebara Isuke: *Sekijō meiden*, AGSS 1:132–55.

Tominomori Suke'emon and Kuwaoka Teisa: The story of their meeting on the Ryōgoku Bridge is told in the biography of Teisa in Takeuchi Gengen'ichi, *Haika kijin dan*, 159–64, and is repeated by Aoyama Enkō in *Setsuya seiwa*, 25–27. Teisa is described in the opening lines of his biography as a man of integrity and honesty who had a great many close friends, some of them Akō ronin.

CHAPTER 60

p.499 Having given my retainers: Ōishi Kuranosuke to O-Tan, Genroku 15.12.10, in *Akō gishi no tegami*, 245–46; AGS 2:222–23.

p.500 Men of Jūnai's family: O-Tan lost seven of her male relatives as a result of the vendetta: Jūnai, her husband; Kōemon, her adopted son; Ōtaka Gengo, son of Jūnai's elder sister and biological brother of Kōemon; Okano Kin'emon, son of Jūnai's deceased younger brother; Masé Kyūdayū, Jūnai's cousin; Masé Magokurō, Kyūdayū's son; and Nakamura Kansuke, Kyūdayū's nephew. See their genealogies in Saitō, *Akō gishi jissan* 599, 600, 715, 725.

My own family: Utsumi lists seventeen Ōishi kinsmen in the Akō Corps of Vassals, all but one of whom (Kondō Genpachi) joined the original league. Only Kuranosuke, Chikara, and Sezaemon did not later defect. See *Shinsetsu Akō gishi roku*, 99–100.

My retainer Magozaemon absconded: Seno'o Magozaemon was the most senior of Kuranosuke's personal retainers and frequently was entrusted with highly responsible tasks. When Kuranosuke moved from Hirama into Edo, Magozaemon and a foot soldier, Yano Isuke, remained behind at Karube Gohei's farmstead, posing as the principal occupant of the house and his servant. On the 3rd Day of the Eleventh Month, they absconded together.

The merrymakers: In Edo, brightly costumed singers, wearing broad sedge hats and playing the shamisen, went from door to door begging at year's end. They were called *torioi* (literally, "bird chasers") after the raucous "music" made by peasants to chase away marauding birds at harvest time.

Oniō and Dōzaburō: The comparison is even more appropriate than is immediately apparent. Oniō and Dōzaburō were the faithful retainers of the Soga brothers; and when the brothers at last discovered the location of their enemy Kudō Suketsune, they sent Oniō and Dōzaburō back to their home village bearing letters to their kinfolk—just as Kuranosuke does here.

p.501 I take this opportunity: Onodera Jūnai to O-Tan, Genroku 15.12.12, in *Akō gishi no tegami*, 254–56; AGSS 2:219–21. Jūnai's letters as recorded in these two sources are virtually identical, but the slight variations in wording and formatting are sometimes interesting.

p.502 Should it be your lot to escape punishment: Jūnai did not divorce his wife, as Kuranosuke did, and thus is concerned lest the women related to him be punished along with the men.

I've purposely refrained from telling Jūbei: Junai's cousin Onodera Jūbei was a Deputy (*yoriki*) on the staff of the Kyoto City Magistrate. Thus Jūnai was careful to avoid any contact with Jūbei that might incriminate or cast suspicion upon him. Ōkura Kensai (1786–1843) notes that many of Jūnai's letters to O-Tan survive because after her death, they passed into the possession of "Jūnai's cousin Onodera Jūbei, who lives in Kitano" (AGSS 2:229).

p.503 Teiryū Sama and O-Chiyo: Teiryū was Jūnai's widowed elder sister and the mother of Ōtaka Gengo and Onodera Kōemon. O-Chiyo was Okano Kin'emon's younger sister and Jūnai's niece.

Saihōji Ryōkenbō and Ekōin Sama: Unidentified.

Poem strips: This is an inadequate translation of *tanzaku*, long thin strips of high-quality, often decorated, card made especially for the inscription of Japanese poems. The standard dimensions of present-day *tanzaku* are 14 by 2.5 inches.

p.504 This next short note: Jūnai to O-Tan, Genroku 15.12.13, in *Akō gishi no tegami*, 257; AGSS 2:221.

My letter of the 11th: This letter has not survived.

Mino-ya Tahei: Mino-ya was a merchant whom Jūnai and O-Tan obviously knew well and trusted, and who did business in both Kyoto and Edo. Perhaps, like Chōbei in chapter 24, he was someone with whom Jūnai had dealt as the Liaison Officer in Kyoto. Nothing is known of the nature of Mino-ya's business.

You've entrusted two gold pieces: Jūnai to O-Tan, Genroku 15.12.14, in *Akō gishi no tegami*, 258; AGSS 2:221–22.

CHAPTER 61

p.506 Satō Jōemon: See chapter 21. This chapter is based principally upon Jōemon's memoir of the attack, *Satō Jōemon oboegaki*.

City Magistrate of Nagasaki (*Nagasaki bugyō*): A complete list of appointees to this office is given in KD 10:579–82. In this list, Suwa's name is given as Hyōbu Yorikage 兵部頼蔭, most likely the name by which he was known before his promotion to Iki-no-Kami. Of incidental interest in this context is that Suwa was succeeded by Ōshima Ise-no-Kami, lord and benefactor of the Kayano family, concerning whom see chapters 14 and 42.

p.509 We hope tonight: Sugino Jūheiji to Chōjūrō, Genroku 15.12.14, quoted in Saitō, *Akō gishi jissan*, 757.

Gengo watched the house: *Kikigaki*, 14.

p.510 Kuranosuke and Jūnai . . . left Oyamaya for the last time: Onodera Jūnai to O-Tan, Genroku 16.2.3, AGSS 2:224–29.

p.511 The climactic scene of . . . *Tsuna*: *Tsuna* is an alternative title of the Nō play *Rashōmon*, the hero of which is the warrior Watanabe Tsuna. See YT 5:3355–56.

CHAPTER 62

p.514 The younger men . . . had turned up far too early: *Kikigaki*, 14.

The older men . . . had stopped . . . for a bowl of soba: Terasaka Kichiemon, *Terasaka shiki*, AGS 1:269.

Ōishi Mujin: Mujin's "armor" is described in OKS, 148–49; his request to join in the attack, in *Horiuchi Den'emon oboegaki*, AGSS 1:318.

Satō Jōemon: All descriptions of Jōemon's activities at Yasubei's lodgings are based upon his memoir of the attack, *Satō Jōemon oboegaki*.

p.515 A letter box: A sketch of the box appears in Yamazaki Yoshishige, *Akō gishi zuihitsu*, NZT, ser. 2, 24:30.

Declaration of the Vassals of Asano Takumi: The text translated here is that in *Akō gishi no tegami*, 264–67. This account of its history follows that of Yagi (CG 1:174–80), in which he analyzes minutely, and quite persuasively, the process by which Yahei's draft was transformed into the manifesto left behind at the Kira mansion. The traditional account is in *Nirō ryakuden* (1772), AGSS 2:293–96. The text from which "lord or father" is quoted is *Chu-hsi wen-chi*.

p.518 They could contrive to look something like a fire brigade: *Asano katakiuchi ki*, AGSS 2:127; *Akō shōshūki*, AGSS 2:439.

p.519 The Honjo time bell: Hashimoto, *Nihon no jikoku seido*, 233–37. A good general description of the system and its facilities is Urai, *Edo no jikoku to toki no kane*.

p.521 The guardhouse at the corner: *Sekijō shiwa*, AGSS 1:231.

CHAPTER 63

p.522 Jōemon did not return in time: Again, all description of Jōemon's activities is based upon his memoir of the attack, *Satō Jōemon oboegaki*.

Seishōji: One of the many temples in the huge Zōjōji complex in Shiba, facing Atagoshita Yabu no Kōji and the Sakuragawa, which flows alongside it.

p.523 Ōtaka Gengo and Hazama Jūjirō ... commandeered the two ladders: *Kōseki kenmonki* 4, AGSS 3:272.

Lists of the equipment: For example, *Chūsei kōkanroku* 4, AGSS 3:460.

As lightly as spiders: *Kanadehon Chūshingura*, in *Chūshingura jōruri shū*, 150.

p.524 Everyone went over the top: *Sekijō shiwa*, AGSS 1:231.

Guards emerged at once and were quickly overpowered: *Kikigaki*, 16; *Teibi zakki*, CG 3:435.

Kuranosuke would stay at the gate: *Kikigaki*, 15.

Okano Kin'emon ... assigned duty there: Onodera Jūnai to O-Tan, Genroku 16.2.3, in *Akō gishi no tegami*, 303–8.

p.525 Hayami Tōzaemon was a highly skilled archer: *Chūsei kōkanroku* 4, AGSS 3:461.

The planking of this gate: *Chūsei kōkanroku* 4, AGSS 3:461.

Sugino Jūheiji and Mimura Jirōzaemon ... began splintering those thin planks: *Kikigaki*, 16; *Chūsei kōkanroku* 4, AGSS 3:461; *Sekijō shiwa*, AGSS 1:231.

p.527 Ōtaka Gengo ... reached up from below to catch him: *Kōseki kenmonki* 4, AGSS 3:272; *Sekijō shiwa*, AGSS 1:231, says it was Yokogawa Kanpei. Jōemon was outside the wall and thus could not know who helped him down.

CHAPTER 64

p.529 After the ronin broke in at the two entrances: The sources for just about every aspect of this battle are multiple. To document every movement described here would be next to impossible. In composing this description, however, I have preferred above all the firsthand reports of the ronin and their victims, and then the accounts of people who were in a position to talk with the ronin following the attack. I have also consulted the writings of those less directly involved, but have used them only when they seem consistent with the experience of those who were there. The postattack letters of the ronin are conveniently collected in CG 3:399–426. All other firsthand sources are listed in the bibliography under the heading "Participant Accounts." Only notable exceptions to the foregoing will be listed separately.

p.535 A report in the hand of Takenaka Suke'emon: *Genroku jikki,* excerpt quoted in *Chūō Gishikai kaihō,* July 1994, 6–7.

CHAPTER 65

p.539 The search that ensued: See the first note to chapter 64.

p.541 Yamayoshi Shinpachi: Nakamura, *Yonezawa-damashii,* 159ff; Taguchi Gozaemon, *Dewa no Kuni Mogami-gun Shinjō korō oboegaki,* 115–16.

p.543 Fuwa Kazuemon entered the room: Fuwa Kazuemon to Sakura Shinsuke, undated, CG 3:423–26. Other descriptions of this encounter with Sahei and Shinpachi identify Takebayashi Tadashichi as the protagonist, but there seems no reason to doubt Kazuemon's firsthand description in writing to his father.

p.544 He heard a voice that he recognized: Muro Kyūsō, *Sundai itsuwa,* AGSS 2:290–91.

CHAPTER 66

p.545 Tōfu-ya ... presented himself at ... the Uesugi Upper Mansion: *Ōkuma Yaichiemon kikigaki,* AGSS 3:127; *Nomoto Chūzaemon kenmonsho,* AGS 1:380.

Hosoi Kōtaku ... climbed to the rooftop of his house: *Nirō ryakuden,* AGSS 2:296.

p.547 Spring cleaning (*susutori, susuharai,* or *susuhaki*): Literally "soot removal," but more generally the word refers to house cleaning in preparation for New Year's Day, which in the lunar calendar was also the first day of spring. Depending on the locality, the date varied, but in Edo, the 13th or 14th of the Twelfth Month was traditional. A page from an almanac dated Genroku 15 (1702), reproduced by Yamazaki in *Akō gishi zuihitsu,* describes the day of the attack (14th Day, Twelfth Month) as "*yometori, genpuku, susuharai yoshi*" (a good day for marriage, coming of age, and spring cleaning). See Yamazaki Yoshishige, *Akō gishi zuihitsu,* NZT, ser. 2, 24:31.

CHAPTER 67

p.550 We have just beheaded your lord, Kōzuke-no-Suke Dono: This episode is recounted in various of the sources referred to in the first note to chapter 64, most of which agree fundamentally and differ only in nuances. Some of the details of this account, however, are drawn from single sources, which are cited in the following notes.

Hearing what seemed to be the sound of voices: *Horiuchi Den'emon oboegaki*, AGSS 1:315.

p.551 A storeroom that opened in two directions: Yoshida Chūzaemon describes it thus in *Horiuchi Den'emon oboegaki*, AGSS 1:315.

The other entrance . . . was only 3 feet high: *Kikigaki*, 17.

Kazuemon brought his lantern closer: Fuwa Kazuemon to his father, Sakura Shinsuke, Genroku 16.12.24, CG 3:423–26.

p.552 He administered the ceremonial coup de grâce: *Horiuchi Den'emon oboegaki*, AGSS 1:289.

Whale Wave: *Satō Jōemon oboegaki*, 81.

The young men strode about: *Onodera Jūnai shinjōsho*, CG 3:431.

p.553 Ekōin: Also known as Muenji (Temple of the Unknown Dead) because it was built in the aftermath of the Great Meireki Fire of 1657 as a resting place for the more than 100,000 dead, most so badly burnt they could not be identified. The rear wall of the temple stood opposite the west walls of the Kira and Tsuchiya properties, but the only entrance was around the block, facing toward the Ryōgoku Bridge. The temple's refusal to admit the ronin is described briefly in *Kōseki kenmonki* 5, AGSS 3:306.

p.555 "Jūjirō Dono!" Tadashichi shouted at him angrily: *Satō Jōemon oboegaki*, 83; *Chūsei kōkanroku* 2, AGSS 3:531. This account combines elements from both sources, both of which originated with Jōemon, who witnessed the event.

Sakaya Jūbei: This story is repeated in several contemporary sources. The version related here is based upon that in *Asakichi ichiran ki*, AGSS 1:404–5; *Ekisui renbei roku*, 108–9; and *Sekijō shiwa*, AGSS 1:245–46.

p.558 A battle formation suitable for city streets: Based upon a diagram in AGS 1:391–93.

CHAPTER 68

p.560 The confusion in the Uesugi household: *Ōkuma Yaichiemon kikigaki*, CG 3:439–43; *Nomoto Chūzaemon kenmosho*, CG 3:443–48; AGS 1:380–90; *Yonezawa Shioi-ke oboegaki*, AGS 1:369–79.

p.562 **Sent Hatakeyama Shimōsa-no-Kami to Sakurada:** *Uesugi nenpu*, AGS 2:366–67; *Uesugi hennen monjo*, CG 3:448–49.

p.563 **How keen the House of Uesugi was:** *Sekijō shiwa*, AGSS 1:256–57.

When the detail from Sakurada finally arrived: *Nomoto Chūzaemon kenmosho*, CG 3:443–48; AGS 1:380–90.

p.565 **Several name tags, one of which read: "Ōishi Kuranosuke":** *Yonezawa Shioi-ke oboegaki*, AGS 1:378.

p.566 **Medical attention came in the form of Kurisaki Dōyū:** *Kurisaki Dōyū kiroku*, transcribed in Saitō, *Akō gishi jissan*, 443–44.

CHAPTER 69

p.569 *Atake Maru:* KD 1:225–26.

Do his best to tighten the formation: *Itō Jūrōdayū Haruyuki kikigaki oboe*, 147.

Bits and pieces of conversation: *Asano rōnin katakiuchi kikigaki*, CG 3:467.

p.570 **Hishiya Sanjūrō . . . offered some of them tea:** *Kōseki kenmonki* 4, AGSS 3:279.

p.571 **He pulled off his fire helmet:** *Horiuchi Den'emon oboegaki, furoku*, in AGSS 1:366–67. There is a drawing and description of the helmet in Yamazaki, *Akō gishi zuihitsu*, NZT, ser. 2, 24:52–54; and a photograph of it in Tominomori Eiji, *Uron nari Suke'emon*, 19. Yamazaki notes that even in his day, it was something of a rarity, because most of the gear belonging to the other ronin had been passed on to Sengakuji, where it was sold off "to cover the cost of their funeral."

p.572 **Those at the head of the procession halted:** CG 3:467.

Sakurai Sōemon . . . described it: AGSS 2:322–24.

p.574 **Three hundred men on fire watch at Zōjōji:** *Kōko sōshi*, excerpted in KB 1:99–101.

Their parley with the vassals of Matsudaira Mutsu-no-Kami: *Akō shōshūki*, AGSS 2:442.

p.575 **Haga Seidayū:** *Haga Seidayū oboegaki*, AGSS 3:103–4.

p.577 **They were greeted by . . . Takada Gunbei:** *Horiuchi Den'emon oboegaki*, AGSS 1:316–17.

CHAPTER 70

p.580 We are Yoshida Chūzaemon and Tominomori Suke'emon: The only firsthand reports of this interview are a short paragraph in Suke'emon's general description of the vendetta, CG 3:426–30; and two or three sentences in Chūzaemon's letter to his son-in-law, Itō Jūrōdayū, Genroku 16.2.2, CG 3:413–14. This narrative is based upon these souces and is filled out with details from *Kōseki kenmonki* 4, AGSS 3:279–82, 306–7; and *Chūsei kokan roku* 4, AGSS 3:475–76.

p.583 Hisamatsu Oki-no-Kami: Oki-no-Kami was one of the many daimyo and bannermen who were granted the "privilege" of using the surname Matsudaira. In this narrative, he is referred to only by his original surname, Hisamatsu. Many daimyo preferred to retain their original surnames and referred to themselves as Matsudaira only in situations where it was politically prudent to do so. The Shogunate, of course, addressed them only as Matsudaira.

p.585 Teisa spotted . . . a saké dealer: This episode continues from that begun in chapter 59, with Kuwaoka Teisa's encountering Tominomori Suke'emon on the Ryōgoku Bridge, and was originally told in the biography of Teisa in Takeuchi Gengen'ichi, *Haika kijin dan*, 159–64.

p.589 Thought it prudent to alter their present plan: Yura Futan, "Asano-ke gishi no setsu," in Kanzawa Tokō, *Okinagusa*, NZT, ser. 3, 19:148–49; *Kōseki kenmonki* 4, AGSS 3:287. The letter to Hisamatsu Oki-no-Kami has been edited slightly for greater clarity.

CHAPTER 71

p.591 Just past the Eighth Hour: *Nomoto Chūzaemon shomen*, Genroku 15.12.17, AGS 1:384.

Inspectors Abe Shikibu and Sugita Gozaemon . . . arrived at the Kira mansion: *Kōseki kenmonki* 6, AGSS 3:323.

The chaos that they encountered: See chapter 68.

A veritable battlefield: *Yonezawa Shioi-ke oboegaki*, AGS 1:376–77.

Their report: *Kira Honjo yashiki kenshi ikken*, CG 3:432–38.

p.592 Heima's embarrassingly lame excuse: *Chūsei kōkanroku* 4, AGSS 3:477. In another version, Kasuya Heima is asked about his own combat with the enemy, and his answer is the same. See Muraji Yajūrō, *Kaisekiki*, AGSS 2:410.

p.595 Saitō Kunai, Sōda Magobei, and Iwase Toneri: These are the men who absconded through a hole cut in the wall of the barracks. See chapter 64.

Under the circumstances: Arai Hakuseki's opinion is reported in Muro Kyūsō, *Sundai (Shundai) zatsuwa,* excerpted in AGSS 2:291–92.

CHAPTER 72

p.598 Sengakuji: This description of the temple is based upon the drawings and description of it in volume 1 of *Edo meisho zue.* The history of the temple, its place in the hierarchy of Zen temples, and its relationship to the House of Asano are described in an excellent article by Hirose Ryōkō, "Sengakuji to Asano-ke to Akō rōshi," in *Zusetsu Chūshingura,* 96–100.

The graveyard: Kawahara, *Tanbō,* 23–27.

p.599 They marched straight in: The twelve hours or so that the ronin spent at Sengakuji, as well as the aftermath of their stay, are recorded in detail in two extraordinary documents, both of them transcriptions of eyewitness accounts. The first of these, *Hakumyō waroku* (AGSS 3:118–26), is, as its title suggests, a record of conversations with a monk named Hakumyō, who in the spring of 1702, at the age of nineteen, had come to Sengakuji as a Sōtō Zen novice. The conversations in question were recorded more than fifty years later, after Hakumyō had become the abbot of a temple in the town of Sukumo in his home province of Tosa. But since everything he says is in agreement with other accounts, we must assume that his memory remained not only vivid but accurate. The second of these documents is of somewhat more unusual provenance. Its author, Sasakawa Tadaemon, was a samurai in the service of the Honda house in the Himeji domain, not far from Akō. He was also the husband of a younger sister of Fuwa Kazuemon, which doubtless accounts for his exceptional interest in the vendetta. He introduces his *Gishi jitsuroku* (CG 3:485–501) as follows:

> I first visited Sengakuji on the 29th Day of the Second Month of the Year of the Ram [1703]. At the temple, I happened to meet Kaishū, Prefect of the Kaishū Dormitory, and Zuisen of the same dormitory. Later, on the 4th of the Third Month, I invited these two monks, as well as Sekishi of the Shunryō Dormitory, to dine at an inn at Saiwaibashi, where I asked them to tell me what they knew.

By piecing together the observations of these four monks, we can reconstruct in considerable detail the scene at Sengakuji on that winter's morning, when the routine of the temple was disrupted by the arrival of a procession of blood-spattered ronin in possession of a severed head. Other sources are noted separately where used.

You're off to Harima: *Itō Jūrōdayū Haruyuki kikigaki oboe*, 146–47. For a penetrating, and highly persuasive, discussion of the reasons that Teresaka Kichiemon should be sent to Harima, see Tanaka Mitsurō, "Yoshida Chūzaemon no rōbai," *Rongaibi* 72, and "Mibun no kabe," *Rongaibi* 73. I quite agree with Tanaka that the controversy whether Kichiemon absconded or was sent away is a "fruitless dispute," and like him I have no intention of participating in it. Those wishing to review the details of this controversy should consult the meticulous description, analysis, and bibliography in Smith, "Trouble with Terasaka." See also Katayama, *Gishi: Terasaka Kichiemon*, which Tanaka considers the best work on the subject in Japanese.

p.604 Takada Gunbei wanted to present them with some saké: *Horiuchi Den'emon oboegaki*, AGSS 1:316–17.

p.608 Three Deputy Inspectors: *Chūsei kōkanroku* 5, AGSS 3:483.

CHAPTER 73

p.610 He would go to the temple and meet them: All episodes in which Satō Jōemon appears are drawn from his memoir, *Satō Jōemon oboegaki*.

p.612 Sub-Inspectors had walked the entire route: *Ekisui renbei roku*, 105–6.

p.614 The gate of the the Sengoku mansion: The episode of the ronin arriving at the mansion is a composite of descriptions in *Kōseki kenmonki* 6, AGSS 3:315–16; *Chūsei kōkanroku* 5, AGSS 3:484; *Haga Seidayū oboegaki*, AGSS 3:106–7; and *Ekisui renbei roku*, 105–6.

Our entire group has come: *Terasaka Kichiemon kakisute no utsushi*, in AGSS 2:381.

p.615 Seidayū . . . took advantage of the confusion: *Haga Seidayū oboegaki*, in AGSS 3:106–7. Seidayū speaks as though he were the only member of the Hisamatsu Corps of Vassals to infiltrate the Sengoku mansion; another document, however, describes how three other Hismatsu samurai were invited by "minor functionaries" of their acquaintance to witness the transfer of the first group of ronin to the Hosokawa house. See *Asano Takumi Dono kerai Matsudaira Oki-no-Kami e o-azuke ikken*, AGSS 2:91.

p.617 The interrogation began: There are multiple versions of this interrogation by Sengoku Hōki-no-Kami, most of which seem to be based upon a common but unidentified original source. The version followed here is that in *Kōseki kenmonki* 6, AGSS 3:316–20. That the ronin were interrogated is beyond doubt; it is possible, too, that the proceedings were transcribed. But there are obvious errors in some of the answers attributed to Kuranosuke and Chūzaemon, indicating that this text could not be a verbatim transcript. It is translated here simply to give the reader some idea of how contemporaries of the ronin imagined the event. The latter parts of these various versions differ considerably and thus have been omitted, rather than choosing one over another arbitrarily.

CHAPTER 74

p.623 Past the Fourth Hour: Details of the transfer are as described in *Hosokawa-ke o-azukari shimatsu ki*, AGS 2:11–13; and *Horiuchi Den'emon oboegaki*, AGSS 1:280–81.

Seidayū . . . thought them terribly overdressed: *Haga Seidayū oboegaki*, AGSS 3:107.

p.624 At the head of the procession: The composition of the Hosokawa formation is conveniently diagrammed in Saitō, *Akō gishi jissan*, 455.

p.625 The procession of the Hisamatsu: The composition of the Hisamatsu formation is described in *Asano Takumi Dono kerai Matsudaira Oki-no-Kami e o-azuke ikken*, AGSS 2:91; and *Haga Seidayū oboegaki*, AGSS 3:105–6.

p.626 Haga Seidayū was determined to practice what he had been preaching: *Haga Seidayū oboegaki*, AGSS 3:104. Other sources gloss his proper name as Tomohide, rather than Tomohisa.

For the benefit of his descendants: *Haga Seidayū oboegaki*, AGSS 3:107–8.

The procession entered the Hisamatsu Upper Mansion: *Haga Seidayū oboegaki*, AGSS 3:107–8.

p.627 The Mōri and the Mizuno houses: The house records and other sources pertaining to these two houses are listed under their names in the "Participant Accounts" section of the bibliography. A diagram of the Mōri formation is found in *Banshū Akō no jōshu Asano Takumi-no-Kami rōnin o-azukari ki*, 42–44; and that of the Mizuno formation, in *Mizuno-ke o-azukari kiroku*, AGS 2:110–11.

p.628 Each and every one of you has acted with consummate loyalty: *Kumamoto Hosokawa kafu*, AGS 2:53; *Horiuchi Den'emon oboegaki*, AGSS 1:281.

We did so only for the sake of appearances: The records of the Mōri house suggest that there may have been more to it than just appearances. A Deputy Inspector is said to have told the Mōri that the Shogunate, too, was concerned that the Uesugi might attack, and that they should maintain strict alert on their return journey. In response, the Mōri immediately sent for reinforcements. See

Akō rōnin o-azukari no ki, AGSS 2:17. But perhaps Hosokawa Etchū-no-Kami did not think the Uesugi as formidable a threat as some others did.

p.629 The Shinobazu Pond: This description of the pond in winter is based upon a woodblock print by Eisen (1790–1848), *Edo Hakkei: Shinobugaoka Bosetsu*.

Chōfukuji: Chōfukuji has long since been replaced by a different temple, Kannonji, which seems nonetheless to regard itself as the successor to the temple of Chikamatsu Kanroku's brother Bunryō.

CHAPTER 75

p.630 The severed head: This description of the return of Kira Kōzuke-no-Suke's head to Kira Sahei is based primarily upon the firsthand account of the Sengakuji monks who actually delivered it, as recorded in Sasakawa Tadaemon, *Gishi jitsuroku*, CG 3:485–501. Another account, in *Chūsei kōkanroku* 6, AGSS 3:490–92, agrees substantially with the record of Sasakawa's interview. The wording of the receipt differs slightly, depending upon the text in which it was transcribed.

p.633 Sōda Magobei: Readers may recall that Magobei was one of those who escaped by way of a hole battered through the outer wall of the barracks on the night of the 14th. Another escapee was Saitō Kunai, who is not introduced by name in this chapter, but is the other Elder who signed the receipt for Kira's head. Both men, using a razor, inflicted "wounds" on their own foreheads in the hope that they would be thought combatants; the investigating authorities were not deceived.

p.635 Body and head reunited: Some secondary works claim that Kurisaki Dōyū stitched Kira's severed head to his body before his burial, but I have yet to find any documentary evidence of this. On 24 January 2014, however, Sassa Shōju 佐々昌樹, the present Superior of Banshōin (twenty-fifth generation), told me that in Taishō 3 (1914), when the Banshōin and its graveyard were moved from Kagurazaka to their present location in Ochiai, his grandfather (twenty-third generation) actually inspected the remains of Kira and found that the head had indeed been sewn to the body.

p.636 Poems pasted to the doors of Kira's main gate: *Haifū yanagidaru; Akō seigi sankō*, 509. The latter text is not a reliable historical source, but as a contemporary document it likely reflects what people in Edo were thinking and saying at the time.

CHAPTER 76

p.638 The Hosokawa mansion: *Horiuchi Den'emon oboegaki*, AGSS 1:281–82.

p.639 Two large rooms: Isogai Jūrōzaemon was originally assigned to the main room, but for reasons unknown he arranged to change places with Hayami Tōzaemon and move to the anteroom. See *Horiuchi Den'emon oboegaki*, AGSS 1:283. The overall dimensions of these two rooms were 4 by 15 *ken* (ca. 24 by 90 feet).

The entries in *Den'emon oboegaki* are not arranged in strict chronological order. Thus it is impossible to tell when in the course of the custody of the ronin certain events that Den'emon describes occurred. I have attempted to report them in what seems to be chronological order, but cannot always be certain that I have guessed correctly.

p.640 The custody of the Hisamatsu: *Haga Seidayū oboegaki*, AGSS 3:108–10.

p.641 The custody of the Mōri: *Banshū Akō no jōshu Asano Takumi-no-Kami rōnin o-azukari ki*, 42–47.

p.642 At the Mōri house, the ronin were treated as prisoners: This is Fukumoto's summary of the attitude of their custodians, in *Shinsōroku*, 716.

The Mizuno house: *Mizuno-ke o-azukari kiroku*, AGS 2:111–16; *Hiyōroku*, 195–97.

p.643 A satirical poem that was making the rounds: *Sekijō shiwa*, AGSS 1:252. References to the Hosokawa and Mizuno are obvious: the *-kai* of *taikai* refers to Mōri Kai-no-Kami, and *oki* refers to Hisamatsu Oki-no-Kami.

CHAPTER 77

p.645 Sōemon offered to write a summary of the attack: This document survives and is transcribed in *Kōseki kenmonki 5*, AGSS 3:304–12; and *Akō gishi no tegami*, 285–92.

Den'emon says: Excerpts from *Den'emon oboegaki*, AGSS 1:283–90.

I was born into a family: A brief summary of Horiuchi Den'emon's career is included in *Sanbyaku han kashin jinmei jiten* 7:458–59.

p.647 I'm afraid that I'd have killed him: See chapter 22.

It broke 6 or 7 inches from the tip: See chapter 64.

p.648 We were about to cross the Shōgen Bridge: Actually, it was the Kanasugi

Bridge. The Shōgen Bridge spans the same canal, the Shinbori, on a street that runs parallel to the avenue that the ronin traveled.

Jūrōzaemon had got that menial to produce the candles: See chapter 64.

p.650 Oyamada Ikkan . . . had killed himself: This episode is reported in *Kōseki kenmonki* 6, AGSS 3:339; *Chūsei kōkanroku* 2, AGSS 3:541–42; Muraji Yajūrō, *Kaisekiki*, AGSS 2:417–18; *Akō shōshūki*, AGSS 2:469; and Miyake Kanran, *Resshi hōshūroku*, AGSS 1:530. This summary draws details from some of these, while winnowing out elements that seem implausible.

CHAPTER 78

p.651 Once word of the attack reached the castle: The Elders were notified not only by Sengoku Hōki-no-Kami, but also by Uesugi Danjō, Kira Sahei, the City Magistrate, and the Commissioner of Temples and Shrines.

Opinion was divided from the very start: TJ 6:499.

The Military Tribunal: For a concise description of the Hyōjōsho, see *Tokugawa Bakufu jiten*, 337–38.

Not a word was ever recorded: An anonymous work, *Mishima-shi zuihitsu*, purports to describe a meeting at which written opinions submitted by more than sixty senior officials of the Shogunate, as well as the Shogun himself, were discussed and evaluated. Despite the obvious inauthenticity of the work, Nabeta Shōzan includes it in his collection of documents because many of the arguments presented therein "make good sense" (AGSS 2:578–81). *Mishima-shi zuihitsu* will not be cited here, as most of the same arguments are also to be found in documents that are genuine.

Fukumoto provides a cogent review of this and other attempts to reconstruct the decision-making process in the absence of any documentary evidence in *Shinsōroku*, 738–41.

A memorial tendered by: The original text is *Fukushūron*, AGSS 1:17–18; the Japanese summary is in *Gobidan*, AGSS 1:88.

p.653 Advisory Opinion of the Full Tribunal: *Hyōjōsho ichiza zonjiyorisho*, AGSS 3:148–49. The authenticity of this document has been questioned, owing to the discrepancy between what it recommends and what was eventually decreed. In its favor, however, is the fact that it survives in *Mukōyama Seisai zakki*, a collection of documents copied directly from the Shogunate's archives. Mukōyama Seisai (1801–1856) served for many years as an *oku yūhitsu* in the Shogun's Private Secretariat, which allowed him open access to these archives. Over the years, he examined thoroughly the documents therein and copied a great many of those that he thought significant. One of them was this Advisory Opinion, the preservation of which by the Shogunate greatly strengthens the case for its authenticity. A photographic reproduction of Seisai's copy is published in *Mukōyama Seisai zakki*, 10:141–46.

p.655 The Uesugi . . . must have been outraged: *Genshōkanki*, 2:121.

CHAPTER 79

p.657 Year-end obligations: Taniguchi Shinko has compiled a useful summary of the Shogun's obligatory duties in the Twelfth Month of Genroku 15 and the First Month of Genroku 16, in *Akō rōshi to Kira-tei uchiiri*, 99–100.

Kuranosuke's apology: *Horiuchi Den'emon oboegaki*, AGSS 1:322.

The long walk: Den'emon lived in Daiku-machi, just across the Gofukubashi Bridge from the Hosokawa Upper Mansion, his normal duty station. He would have had to walk briskly for at least an hour, however, to reach his present duty station at the Lower Mansion in Takanawa.

p.658 Another suicide: The suicide of Okabayashi Mokunosuke is reported in *Kōseki kenmonki* 6, AGSS 3:339; *Chūsei kōkanroku* 2, AGSS 3:540–41; Muraji Yajūrō, *Kaisekiki*, AGSS 2:417; *Akō shōshūki*, AGSS 2:468–69; *Asano katakiuchi ki*, AGSS 2:147; *Sekijō shiwa*, AGSS 1:252; Maebara Isuke and Kanzaki Yogorō, *Sekijō meiden*, AGSS 1:136, 146; and *Horiuchi Den'emon oboegaki*, AGSS 1:323. This summary draws details from some of these, while winnowing out elements that seem implausible.

Mokunosuke sold off his weapons and the next day left Akō: Okayama *shinobi* reports, CG 3:99.

p.659 One of the daughters of Ōno Kurōbei: Ban Kōkei, *Kanden jihitsu*, NZT, ser. 1, 18:437–38. A near contemporary (ca. 1704) *kanbun* account of this episode appears in *Meiryō kōhan* 2, the text of which is transcribed and annotated in Wakabayashi, *Kinko shidan zenchūshaku*, 366–69. This telling is based principally upon Kōkei's text, with details from the *Meiryō kōhan* version.

p.661 Nakase Sukegorō: Sukegorō's unexpected encounter with Okuda Magodayū's father-in-law is reported in *Horiuchi Den'emon oboegaki*, AGSS 1:290–91. Sukegorō was a highly regarded vassal of the Hosokawa because thirty years earlier, at the age of only thirteen or fourteen, he succeeded in avenging the murder of his father. He was taken into service immediately thereafter. See *Horiuchi*

Den'emon oboegaki, AGSS 1:302.

Suga Jizaemon . . . in the service of Tamura Ukyō-no-Daibu: See chapter 9.

Chōtarō, born . . . in the village of Hirama: See chapter 12.

p.662 Den'emon meets Chōtarō and Suke'emon's mother: *Horiuchi Den'emon oboegaki,* AGSS 1:295–96.

CHAPTER 80

p.663 Terasaka Kichiemon . . . was dismissed from the group: See chapter 72 and its notes.

p.664 Terai Genkei says: Horibe Bungorō to Jinzaburō, Genroku 16.1.25. This letter is one document in a collection now known as "Jinzaburō monjo," and is transcribed in Nakajima, *Ōishi Kuranosuke,* 179–80. A more accurate transcription of this collection was posted on Satō Makoto's website, "Akō Gishi Shiryōkan," but he was forced to remove it when threatened with legal action by Nakajima—despite the fact that it was Satō who first transcribed the documents for inclusion in Nakajima's book.

The three documents: Described in a letter from Kuranosuke to Terai Genkei, Genroku 15.12.14, in *Akō gishi no tegami,* 262–64.

As you say: O-Rin to Seitei, Genroku 16.1.27, AGSS 1:375–76. In her letter, O-Rin used the code names for Kichiemon, Chūzaemon, and Sawaemon— Kizaemon, Tarōbei, and Saheita, respectively. To reduce confusion, I have substituted their real names.

p.665 Kichiemon and his wife lived a secluded life: *Itō Jūrōdayū Haruyuki kikigaki oboe,* 147.

Chikamatsu Kanroku's man Jinzaburō: *Horiuchi Den'emon oboegaki,* AGSS 1:291–92.

Vassal-farmers: KD 11:854, s.v. *Hikan-byakushō.*

p.666 I take the liberty to address you: O-Riku to Jingūji, Genroku 15.12.27, AGS 3:262–63, 278. Soren was the ecclesiastical name of Kuranosuke and O-Riku's second son, Kichinoshin (Kichichiyo), now in his twelfth year. He had taken vows and become a monk to avoid punishment through guilt-by-relation as a son of Kuranosuke. Tōgorō is unidentified.

PART III. Year of the Ram: Genroku 16 (1703)

CHAPTER 81

p.671 **The New Year had come:** *Asano katakiuchi ki,* AGSS 2:136–37.

Sprays of pine and bamboo: See the notes to chapter 1.

p.673 **Lord Hosokawa has gone to see every member of the Council of Elders:** *Kumamoto Hosokawa kafu,* AGS 2:54–55. The order of the first two sentences has been reversed.

Equally impassioned appeals: See chapter 77.

Commanded that they be fêted even more lavishly than his most honored guests: *Kumamoto Hosokawa kafu,* AGS 2:53.

Presented with complete new sets of clothing: *Kumamoto Hosokawa kafu,* AGS 2:54.

p.671 **They would soon be moving:** *Kumamoto Hosokawa kafu,* AGS 2:54–55; *Horiuchi Den'emon oboegaki,* AGSS 1:299–300.

The records of the Mizuno house: *Mizuno-ke o-azukari kiroku,* in AGS 2:112.

p.675 **At the Hisamatsu house:** *Haga Tomohisa kikigaki,* AGS 1:326–27; *Haga Seidayū oboegaki,* AGSS 3:113; *Hisamatsu-ke Akō o-azukarinin shimatsu ki,* in AGS 2:84–85; *Asano Takumi Dono kerai,* AGSS 2:109. The first three of these texts quote a version of Hisamatsu Oki-no-Kami's greeting to the ronin. In purport they are the same, but because they are quoted from memory, their wording differs. Thus the version "quoted" here is a composite of three variant texts.

No need to record what was done for the detainees: *Haga Seidayū oboegaki,* AGSS 3:113.

p.676 **In the records of the Mōri house:** *Banshū Akō no jōshu Asano Takumi-no-Kami rōnin o-azukari ki,* 49.

None of the New Year's observances were celebrated: *Uesugi nenpu,* AGS 2:367.

CHAPTER 82

p.677 Their five custodians were eager to ask the ronin: *Kumamoto Hosokawa kafu,* AGS 2:54.

They had been warned that they must not: *Horiuchi Den'emon oboegaki,* AGSS 1:282.

p.678 His conversations with them: See chapter 77.

Onodera Junai's wife's poems: *Horiuchi Den'emon oboegaki,* AGSS 1:304.

Only six of his own compositions survive: Mochizuki Hiroko, "Gishi no shiika," 91.

A contemporary writer: The anonymous author of *Asano katakiuchi ki,* dated Genroku 16.3, only a month after the death of the ronin. See AGSS 2:149.

p.679 Year's End: *Asano katakiuchi ki,* AGSS 2:136.

The Coming of Spring: *Chūsei kōkanroku* 6, AGSS 3:495. There is hidden depth in this poem in Hara Sōemon's reinterpretation of the zodiacal designation of the year *(hitsuji no toshi)* as Year of the Lamb rather than the Ram.

Everyone says that you're very fond of horses: This passage is a composite of two conversations on the same subject, in *Horiuchi Den'emon oboegaki,* AGSS 1:308–9, 335. Iron horseshoes did not come into common use in Japan until the late nineteenth century. Which is why Den'emon warns that riding for long distances is harmful to a horse's hooves; in his day, even the hooves of warhorses would not have been protected with metal.

p.680 Have the cooks make our meals a bit lighter: *Horiuchi Den'emon oboegaki,* AGSS 1:314. An excellent double-page photograph of a meal such as those the ronin were served appears in *Ryōri: Bessatsu Taiyō* 14 (1976): 22–23.

p.681 A vest made of a deep-blue raw silk: Kataoka Gengoemon's admiration of Den'emon's vest is recounted in *Horiuchi Den'emon oboegaki,* AGSS 1:360–61. Den'emon's description of Hosokawa Sansai is an excerpt from a much longer discourse.

p.682 Old Horibei Yahei told Den'emon: *Horiuchi Den'emon oboegaki,* AGSS 1:326.

p.683 I don't know *how* to commit seppuku: *Horiuchi Den'emon oboegaki,* AGSS 1:341.

I had hoped to offer you: *Seichū bukan,* 494–98. This work is not considered a reliable historical source, but it has been handed down in the line of the Horibe who were in the service of the Hosokawa at the time of the Akō Incident, and many passages in this chapter are in close agreement with the Hosokawa house records. I suspect, too, that the author of this report may have been a member of the Hosokawa Corps of Vassals, for he ends his description of the evening by saying: "Oki-no-Kami Dono, Kai-no-Kami Dono, and Kenmotsu Dono, too, offered New Year's greetings to the ronin in their custody, and banqueted them as well; but what they did was nothing to compare with this feast of roast crane at the House of Hosokawa." The chapter also includes a complete menu of the meal served the ronin.

Another description of the same occasion appears in *Akō shōshū ki*, AGSS 2:477–78. This version, however, places the date of the dinner much later, on the 2nd Day of the Second Month.

CHAPTER 83

p.685 **The records of all four daimyo houses:** *Banshū Akō no jōshū Asano Takumi-no-Kami rōnin o-azukari ki*, 49; *Kumamoto Hosokawa kafu*, AGS 2:55; *Matsudaira (Hisamatsu) Oki-no-Kami e o-azuke ikken*, AGSS 2:108-9; *Mizuno-ke o-azukari kiroku*, AGS 2:130.

Genealogical records: Copies of all these documents survive and are transcribed under the entries for each of the ronin in AGJ.

p.686 **The house records of the Shogun's Chief Adjutant:** *Yanagisawa-ke hizō jikki*, in *Kai sōsho*, 3:64–65.

p.687 **The much younger Sōemon:** Ogyū Sōemon was thirty-eight years old at the time.

p.688 **Yamazaki Yoshishige tells a story:** *Kairoku*, 322–23.

Butsu Sorai: Sorai traced his ancestry to the ancient Mononobe clan, and thus was sometimes known by the surname Butsu, the Sino-Japanese pronunciation of the "Mono" of Mononobe.

His "Legal Opinion": AGSS 3:150.

p.690 **Another version:** *Gobidan*, AGSS 1:88–89.

All the world rejoices: Prince-Abbot Kōben's poem is quoted in Mitamura Engyo, MEZ 16:162. Elsewhere (MEZ 8:325–26), Engyo cites the source of the poem as *Go-nenpu*; but there are many works bearing this title, and unfortunately Engyo does not specify which of them he refers to.

Some of the most powerful ladies in the Women's Palace: Engyo (MEZ

16:163–64) points out that Kōben Hosshinnō owed his special relationship with the Shogun to the fact that he had powerful relatives in the Women's Palace.

These men have endured extreme hardship: TJ 6:499–500.

CHAPTER 84

p.693 Saitō Jizaemon . . . summoned to the castle: *Seppuku o-shioki go-yō Chōfu-han tomegaki,* CG 3:655–59.

His home in Komagome: Mayama, *Chūshingura chishi,* 549.

Araki Jūzaemon: At some point shortly after the seppuku of the ronin, Araki changed his familiar name (*tsūshō*) from Jūzaemon to Jūemon, with the result that he appears under both names in the records of this event, depending upon which name the individual authors knew him by at the time they were writing. To reduce confusion, he is here referred to only as Jūzaemon. This may also help make it clear that he was the same Inspector who had been sent to Akō the previous year to supervise the surrender of the castle.

p.694 You are therefore commanded to commit seppuku: *Chōfu-han tomegaki,* CG 3:656–57.

A list of the Inspectors: *Kōseki kenmonki* 6, AGSS 3:327–28.

p.695 A directive from the Council of Elders: Quoted in *Kōseki kenmonki* 6, AGSS 3:327.

Kira Sahei [summoned] to the Military Tribunal: *Kōseki kenmonki* 6, AGSS 3:326.

p.696 Kira Sahei's sentence: *Akō shōshūki,* AGSS 2:487. This source notes that Sahei was then living in the Uesugi Middle Mansion, not in the Kira residence in Honjo.

The requisite funds for these rites: *Uesugi nenpu,* AGS 2:367.

p.699 Den'emon failed to see the meaning: *Horiuchi Den'emon oboegaki,* AGSS 1:332–35.

CHAPTER 85

p.700 The same directive of notification . . . the same sentence: The text of the directive is recorded in *Kōseki kenmonki* 6, AGSS 3:327; and the sentence, in

Seppuku o-shioki go-yō Chōfu-han tomegaki, CG 3:656–57.

The Hosokawa house: This section is based upon *Horiuchi Den'emon oboegaki*, AGSS 1:279–368, esp. 336–37; *Hosokawa-ke o-azukari shimatsu ki*, in AGS 2:3–51; *Kumamoto Hosokawa kafu*, AGS 2:52–57; and *O-azukenin kiroku*, in *Higo bunken sōsho*, 4:341–52.

p.701 I had hoped: Hosokawa Etchū-no-Kami to Ōishi Kuranosuke, undated, AGS 2:55.

An appropriate letter of acknowledgment: AGS 2:28–29.

p.703 Kuranosuke . . . replied: *Akō shōshūki*, AGSS 2:470.

p.704 Another old Hosokawa vassal: The story of this unidentified vassal is based upon *Mimibukuro* 1:145.

p.705 The Hisamatsu: This section is based upon *Asano Takumi Dono kerai: Matsudaira Oki-no-Kami Dono e o-azuke ikken*, AGSS 2:67–124; *Haga Seidayū oboegaki*, AGSS 3:101–18; *Haga Tomohisa kikigaki*, AGS 1:302–55; and *Kikigaki*.

p.708 In resonant voice: *Haga Seidayū oboegaki*, AGSS 3:116.

p.709 The house of Mōri Kai-no-Kami: This section is based upon *Akō rōnin o-azukari no ki*, AGSS 2:14–35; *Banshū Akō no jōshu Asano Takumi-no-Kami rōnin o-azukari ki*; *Chōfu o-azukari gishi ikken*, CG 3:570–75; and *Fuchū-kō tomegaki*, CG 3:558–69.

The long-standing animosity between the Tokugawa and the Mōri: Their enmity originated in Tokugawa Ieyasu's post-Sekigahara settlement in which the vast holdings of Mōri Terumoto (1553–1625) were reduced from seven to only two provinces, causing great financial and social upheaval in the domain. The Mōri considered this grossly unjust, because Terumoto, although he was the figurehead commander of the Toyotomi force, never made a move against Ieyasu. Throughout the entire battle of Sekigahara, he and the men under his command had remained in Osaka Castle. Legend has it that it became customary throughout the Edo period for the Elders of the Mōri house, at their annual New Year's festivities, to ask their lord, "Is this to be the year that we overthrow the Shogunate?" (*kotoshi wa tōbaku no ki ikani*), to which their lord would reply, "It is still too soon" (*jiki nao hayai*). This long-remembered animosity was, of course, a strong motivating force behind the participation of Chōshū in the Meiji Revolution.

p.711 A space of 3-*ken* square: Kudō, *Jijin roku*, in *Bushidō zensho*, 10:278.

p.712 The Mizuno house: This section is based upon *Hiyōroku, Kōtokuben*,

Hanpiroku; Mizuno-ke o-azukari kiroku, AGS 2:107–36; and *Sekijō shiwa*, AGSS 1: 253–65. The relationship between rank and punishment is discussed in Hiramatsu, *Kinsei keiji soshōhō no kenkyū*, 430–35.

CHAPTER 86

p.714 Seppuku was a ritual: Technical details of the procedure are taken from Kudō, *Jijin roku*.

p.715 The Inspectors and the Seconds: "Inspector" is an almost literal translation of *kenshi*, and the senior members of the four teams of emissaries were themselves members of the Shogunal Inspectorate (*metsuke*). Their colleagues the Heralds (*tsukaiban*), too, had long shared many of the duties of the *metsuke* and worked closely with them.

"Second," however, is less than ideal as a translation of *kaishaku*. The word *can* mean "a person who aids or supports another, an assistant," which closely approximates the literal meaning of *kaishaku*; but the long use of "second" in the context of European-style dueling may suggest to some readers that the two functions are analogous, which they are not. I use the word here only for lack of a more appropriate one.

The Inspectors were in overall command: Kudō, *Jijin roku*, in *Bushidō zensho*, 10:300.

p.716 The nuances of this procedure: This description is based upon a demonstration and explanation, by Professor Glenn Stockwell of Waseda University, of the proper procedure (*kata*) for *kaishaku* as prescribed in the traditions of the Musō Jikiden Ryū of *Iaidō*, of which Professor Stockwell is the current *iemoto*. Minor adjustments from Kudō, *Jijin roku*, in *Bushidō zensho*, 10:299, have been made to adapt this description to the case of the Akō ronin, for whom seppuku was not volitional but a punishment, and thus only nominal.

CHAPTER 87

p.720 Saisuke silently scrutinized the entire scene: Quoted from the description of a copy of Saisuke's sketch by Iioka Yoshiaki, dated Bunka 13 (1816).11.15, AGSS 1:4. The textual history of this sketch is discussed by Satō Makoto, "Hosokawa-tei gishi seppuku zu," *Akō gishi shiryōkan* 64; and Tanaka Mitsurō, "Hosokawa-tei gishi seppuku zu, 1 & 2," *Nagatsuta zasshi*, 2007. Unfortunately these essays are no longer posted on the Internet.

More recently, a hitherto unknown version of the sketch has come to light, the owner of which maintains that it was copied from Saisuke's original and that all other extant versions are based upon it. This may be so, but the evidence is not conclusive. See Ōno, "Ōishi Kuranosuke-ra seppuku no genzu shinshutsu," 99–103. A copy of this sketch is used to illustrate the text of this chapter.

A floor plan of this wing of the actual Hosokawa Lower Mansion is published by the Kumamoto Prefectural Library on the weblog "Shirogane-tei," *Shinshindō no tawagoto nichiroku*, 23 January 2013, http://blog.goo.ne.jp/ shinshindoh/e/e60042b3cea3614c73f7f6e65e290ff2.

p.721 **The diagram preserved in the Hosokawa house records:** *Hosokawa-ke o-azukari shimatsu ki*, AGS 2:34–35.

Such mishaps must have occurred: Several such failures are described in the chapters on "Escorts" and "Seconds" in Kudō, *Jijin roku*, in *Bushidō zensho*, 10: 293–94, 301–3.

Nothing but hearsay and fabrication: Fukumoto has compiled very thorough lists of these reports and their sources, in *Shinsōroku*, 791–93, 798–800, 806–7, 811.

p.722 **The site described in the Hosokawa house records:** Four texts describe the seppuku of the ronin: *Hosokawa kafu*, MSAGS, 75–88; *Hosokawa-ke o-azukari shimatsu ki*, AGS 2:3–51; *Kumamoto Hosokawa kafu*, AGS 2:52–57; and *O-azukarinin kiroku*, in *Higo bunken sōsho*, 4:431–52.

The dais itself: There is a hierarchy of honor in the number and arrangement of the tatami mats used as a dais. Three mats are, of course, more prestigious than two, but the configuration in which they are arranged is also significant. The four levels in this hierarchy are illustrated in Kudō, *Jijinroku*, in *Bushidō zensho*, 10:255–56.

p.723 **The fullest version:** *Hosokawa-ke o-azukari shimatsu ki*, AGS 2:33. The time span stated here seems unrealistic. To complete the process in one hour would require that each seppuku be executed in only three and a half minutes.

841 **The official narrative is filled out:** *Horiuchi Den'emon oboegaki*, AGSS 1:342. Den'emon saw none of the ronin commit seppuku, and thus has nothing to add to the record of those events.

Ujiie Heikichi: Heikichi was the Second assigned to "assist" Tominomori Suke'emon.

The compiler of one of those texts speaks out briefly in his own voice: *Hosokawa kafu*, MSAGS, 85. The phrase translated as "sucked up and swallowed the blood" is *chi o susurishi* (血を歃りし). This character was once used to denote the ancient practice of smearing the lips with or drinking the blood of a living sacrifice when making a promise or swearing an oath. In Edo-period texts, it was sometimes read as *chisusuru*, or simply *nomu*. See Ueda Mannen, ed., *Daijiten*, 5597; Ozaki Yūjirō et al. eds., *Kadokawa Daijigen*, 4634; and Morohashi Tetsuji, ed., *Dai kanwa jiten*, 16131 (6:635d–36a).

CHAPTER 88

p.726 **The site of the seppuku:** Haga Seidayū provides detailed and annotated floor plans of the sites of both sentencing and seppuku in *Haga Tomohisa kikigaki*, AGS 1:328–30, 340–42.

A large pale-blue quilt: *Haga Tomohisa kikigaki*, AGS 1:350.

The seating arrangements: *Matsuyama sōdan*, AGSS 3:153.

p.727 **Chikara Dono; I'll be coming along right behind you:** *Haga Seidayū oboegaki*, AGSS 3:116–17.

Seidayū's description of Ōishi Chikara's seppuku: *Matsuyama sōdan*, AGSS 3:153; *Haga Seidayū oboegaki*, AGSS 3:116–17.

p.728 **A sharpened stake:** *Matsuyama sōdan*, AGSS 3:153.

Arakawa Jūdayū: Jūdayū was a Deputy Inspector, a very low rank in the Hisamatsu house, for which he was paid 12 *koku* and rations for three per year. He was indeed the Second for both Horibe Yasubei and Fuwa Kazuemon.
Ikeda Hajime's reminiscence of his grandmother's story was removed from the Internet on 8 June 2014.

p.729 **No longer be necessary to present the heads of the ronin for inspection:** *Matsuyama sōdan*, AGSS 3:153. These inspections ceased with the second seppuku. *Haga Seidayū oboegaki*, AGSS 3:117.

p.730 **Surely there's a teahouse:** *Matsuyama sōdan*, AGSS 3:155.

Horiuchi Den'emon . . . might be asked to serve as a Second: *Horiuchi Den'emon oboegaki*, AGSS 1:337.

The Hisamatsu Seconds: *Matsuyama sōdan*, AGSS 3:152.

p.731 **A bungled beheading at the Hosokawa house:** *Haga Tomohisa kikigaki*, AGS 1:351–52.

They all met their end in the most admirable manner (*Izure mo shinmyō naru saigo no tei nari***):** *Kumamoto Hosokawa kafu*, AGS 2:57.

CHAPTER 89

p.732 **Matters had not gone smoothly:** See chapter 85.

All were seated: Annotated floor plans of the sites of both sentencing and seppuku are included in *Fuchū-kō tomegaki*, CG 3:566–69; and *Banshū Akō no jōshu Asano Takumi-no-Kami ronin o-azukari ki*, 53, 56.

Mōri Kai-no-Kami and his son watched: *Fuchū-kō tomegaki*, CG 3:565.

No blades had been prepared: *Fuchū-kō tomegaki*, CG 3:566; *Banshū Akō no jōshu Asano Takumi-no-Kami ronin o-azukari ki*, 54. The Hisamatsu had prepared both fans and swords, but seem to have learnt in good time that only swords would be acceptable; as reported in *Matsuyama sōdan*, AGSS 3:154.

Harada Shōgen and Fukuhara Heima: *Banshū Akō no jōshu Asano Takumi-no-Kami ronin o-azukari ki*, 52.

p.733 **The politeness of the ronin:** *Banshū Akō no jōshu Asano Takumi-no-Kami ronin o-azukari ki*, 55; *Fuchū-han o-azukari gishi ikken*, CG 3:573.

Muramatsu Kihei: *Banshū Akō no jōshu Asano Takumi-no-Kami ronin o-azukari ki*, 55; *Fuchū-han o-azukari gishi ikken*, CG 3:573.

Hazama Shinroku: Biographical data taken from genealogical records (*shin-ruigaki*) submitted by Hazama Kihei, Jūjirō, and Shinroku, AGJ, 271, 273, 275. Seppuku described in *Banshū Akō no jōshu Asano Takumi-no-Kami ronin o-azukari ki*, 55; and *Fuchū-han o-azukari gishi ikken*, CG 3:573–74.

p.734 **Some of them had not been completely severed:** *Banshū Akō no jōshu Asano Takumi-no-Kami ronin o-azukari ki*, 54; *Fuchū o-azukari gishi ikken*, CG 3:573.

The Shogunal officials . . . thank them for their efforts: *Banshū Akō no jōshu Asano Takumi-no-Kami ronin o-azukari ki*, 55; *Fuchū-han o-azukari gishi ikken*, CG 3:574.

p.735 **The body of Hazama Shinroku:** *Banshū Akō no jōshu Asano Takumi-no-Kami ronin o-azukari ki*, 57; *Fuchū-han o-azukari gishi ikken*, CG 3:573–74.

A similar request was sent to the Mizuno house: *Sekijō shiwa*, AGSS 1:254.

Takebayashi Tadashichi: See chapter 45.

p.736 **The house records of the Mizuno:** The seppuku is described only in *Mizuno-ke o-azukari kiroku*, AGS 2:119–23.

Not all the heads were completely severed: *Sekijō shiwa*, AGSS 1:254.

Kanzaki Yogorō was listed to be the last: *Sekijō shiwa*, AGSS 1:255. Yogoro was a Deputy Inspector (*kachi metsuke* [5 *koku*, 5 *ryō*, 3 *nin*]), a very low rank in the hierarchy of a daimyo house. But Mimura Jirōzaemon was only a Kitchen Officer (*daidokoro yakunin* [7 *koku*, 2 *nin*]).

p.737 Sengoku Hōki-no-Kami gave us a list: These lists were based upon the order of the signatures on the manifesto submitted to the Shogunate, with minor modifications to avoid placing members of the same family in the custody of the same daimyo.

Wait!: *Hiyōroku*, 199. Yokogawa Kanpei, too, was a Deputy Inspector (5 *ryō*, 3 *nin*). Some lists place him fourth, rather than third, from last.

Mizuno Kenmotsu won the admiration of his men: *Hiyōroku*, 202; *Isetsu machimachi*, NZT, ser. 1, 17:86.

p.738 A group of samurai . . . discussing the seppuku: *Sekijō shiwa*, AGSS 1:262.

CHAPTER 90

p.740 Their local greengrocer: Sasakawa Tadaemon, *Gishi jitsuroku*, CG 3:499.

p.741 Buried together in a single hole: *Horiuchi Den'emon oboegaki*, AGSS 1:285.

Just as the ronin desired: *Hosokawa kafu*, MSAGS, 87.

The Hosokawa sent . . . Hirano Tan'emon to Sengakuji: *Hosokawa-ke o-azu-kari shimatsu ki*, AGS 2:46–47.

The Mizuno sent a similar request: *Mizuno-ke o-azukari kiroku*, AGS 2:122.

There was no place to bury them: *Hakumyō waroku*, AGSS 3:122.

Haga Seidayū adds: *Haga Seidayū oboegaki*, AGSS 3:117.

p.742 The sun had gone below the hills: Sunset on 20 March 2016, the solar equivalent of lunar 4th Day Second Month, was at 5:53 P.M.

White lanterns on the slope; logs on the bare earth: Sasakawa Tadaemon, *Gishi jitsuroku*, CG 3:499.

Messenger monks were dispatched: *Mizuno-ke o-azukari kiroku*, AGS 2:123.

The funeral processions: See, for example, the diagram of a typical procession in *Mizuno-ke o-azukari kiroku*, AGS 2:123.

The Hisamatsu . . . dispatched only two hundred to bury them: *Haga Tomohisa kikigaki,* AGS 1:345–47.

All still wrapped and tied: The Hisamatsu state explicitly that the bundles were secured with rope, in *Hisamatsu-ke Akō o-azukarinin shimatsuki,* AGS 2:96

p.743 The bodies in their casks: Sasakawa Tadaemon, *Gishi jitsuroku,* CG 3:499.

Ryōden, a temple Elder: "Temple Elder" is a translation of convenience, for I have no idea what the nature of this monk's office was. His title was *chōrō,* which normally means the Superior of a Zen temple. But we know from numerous mentions in several different texts that Shūzan Chōon Oshō held that office. And Hakumyō mentions by name three more *chōrō.* Yet even a present-day Sengakuji monk from whom I sought enlightenment said that he could not imagine what the function of these "Elders" might have been, as no comparable office or title now exists.

The process . . . began early in the Hour of the Boar: *Hakumyō waroku,* in AGSS 3:122.

The funeral that *was* performed: *Hakumyō waroku,* AGSS 3:122; Sasakawa Tadaemon, *Gishi jitsuroku,* CG 3:499.

The "Sword Blade Koan" from the *Records of Rinzai:* Linji Yixuan, *Zen Teachings of Master Lin-chi,* 16. In his notes, Watson adds that the sword referred to here is "the sword of wisdom that cuts through and annihilates all discriminative thinking."

p.744 A Buddhist posthumous name: For further detail, see *Shinpan Bukkyōgaku jiten,* 406, s.v. *hōmyō.* The posthumous names of the ronin are listed in many works. One of the most convenient is the list in Fukumoto, *Shinsōroku,* 815–18.

Recited his Final Guidance text separately: Sasakawa Tadaemon, *Gishi jitsuroku,* CG 3:499; *Asano Takumi Dono kerai: Matsudaira Oki-no-Kami Dono e o-azuke ikken,* AGSS 2:122.

Immediately thereafter, . . . they were . . . buried: *Haga Tomohisa kikigaki,* in AGS 1:348.

The monk Taiun: *Hakumyō waroku,* AGSS 3:122. A photograph showing a wooden burial cask about to be placed in a hole about 3 feet square is published in *Shashin de miru Hyakunen mae no Nihon,* 64. Unfortunately, it is impossible to see how deep the hole is.

Seidayū's account is corroborated: *Matsuyama sōdan,* AGSS 3:154.

Taking Up the Torch: *Shinpan Bukkyōgaku jiten,* 302–3, s.v. *sō.*

p.746 The great gathering: Sasakawa Tadaemon, *Gishi jitsuroku*, CG 3:499.

Laborers were sent . . . to remove all the bamboo: *Hakumyō waroku*, AGSS 3:125.

The ronin now rest . . . at a slightly lower level: Horiuchi Den'emon notes that this had already been accomplished when he visited the graveyard, in *Horiuchi Den'emon oboegaki*, AGSS 1:348.

CHAPTER 91

p.748 A long black smudge: *Genshōkanki*, 2:121.

p.749 Gifts and financial considerations: *Hosokawa-ke o-azukari shimatsu ki*, AGS 2:448–49; *Banshū Akō no jōshu Asano Takumi-no-Kami rōnin o-azukari ki*, 58; *Matsuyama sōdan*, AGSS 1:154–55; *Haga Tomohisa kikigaki*, AGS 1:352–53.

Sengakuji would be paid munificently: *Hosokawa-ke o-azukari shimatsu ki*, AGS 2:47; *Mizuno-ke o-azukari kiroku*, AGS 2:123–24.

The cost of having the blades of their swords repaired: *Haga Tomohisa kikigaki*, AGS 1:348.

p.750 The Hisamatsu were the most thoroughgoing: *Haga Tomohisa kikigaki*, AGS 1:348.

Den'emon inspects the possessions of the ronin: *Horiuchi Den'emon oboegaki*, AGSS 1:343–44.

p.751 It would have to be purified: *Horiuchi Den'emon oboegaki*, AGSS 1:342. This translation incorporates minor elements from two variant versions of the same text. The incident is also mentioned more briefly in *Kumamoto Hosokawa kafu*, AGS 2:57.

The temple Shinzōin: Shinzōin is one of a cluster of small temples a short distance to the northeast of the Hosokawa Lower Mansion. The nature of its connection with the Hosokawa house is unknown.

CHAPTER 92

p.753 Only crime was to be related to the guilty: For a concise summary of the history of this concept, see KD 2:400, s.v. *enza*.

Genealogical records . . . were sent back: See chapter 83.

Your fathers: No primary source survives that contains this decree. However, all contemporary secondary sources agree precisely on the wording of it, which is as quoted here.

p.754 **The Magistrate summoned:** Owing to the lack of primary sources, the account that follows is based principally upon two early secondary reports: *Akō shōshūki*, AGSS 2:475–77; and *Chūsei kōkanroku* 7, AGSS 3:506–9.

Only four were of an age to be banished straightaway: Yagi has compiled a very useful chart of all the sons of the ronin, showing the age and ultimate fate of each, in CG 1:304–5.

Muramatsu Masaemon was summoned to the court: *Akō shōshūki*, AGSS 2:476.

Ogasawara Nagato-no-Kami: Nagato-no-Kami (1640–1720) was a bannerman enfeoffed at 3,000 koku. Masaemon's position in the service of Nagato-no-Kami, which made it possible for him to care for his mother, was what persuaded his father, Muramatsu Kihei, to allow his first son, Sandayū, to join him in the vendetta. Masaemon's banishment must have left their mother with no one to support her. See chapter 23.

p.755 **Above all else, I must be grateful to you (*Mazu wa katajikenaku zonji-tatematsuru*):** I am extremely grateful to Professor Umezawa Fumiko for helping me to understand why officials at the court of the City Magistrate found Masaemon's use of *Mazu wa* such a "nice turn of phrase."

Yada Sakujūrō: *Akō shōshūki*, AGSS 2:476–77.

p.757 **Ogawa Tsunemitsu continues the story:** *Chūsei kōkanroku* 7, AGSS 3:507–9.

p.758 **When Kira Sahei was disenfeoffed:** See chapter 84.

p.759 **An entourage of more than 130 men:** This description is based upon *Suwa-ke goyōjō tomechō*, AGS 2:161–244, passim.

The Kōshū Highroad: Kishii, ed., *Shinshū Gokaidō saiken*, 201–16.

The checkpoint pass of Kira Sahei: Transcribed in CG 3:663. Original in Hachiōji-shi Kyōdo Shiryōkan.

p.760 **The Southern Perimeter:** Imai, *Suwa Takashima-jō*, 138–39, 208. The Southern Perimeter is clearly shown in a plan of the castle drawn by Yamagata Daini and published in *Shuzu gōketsuki*, 544–45.

CHAPTER 93

p.762 All samurai were summoned to the upper mansion: *Horiuchi Den'emon oboegaki,* AGSS 1:344.

p.763 The first of the seven obsequies (*nanananuka*): *Horiuchi Den'emon oboegaki,* AGSS 1:344–45. These obsequies are seven services held at seven-day intervals following a person's death. The practice originates in an ancient belief that the subsequent incarnation of the deceased is decided in the court of King Enma in seven successive hearings, at the last of which a verdict is rendered. It was thus thought beneficial to create merit and dedicate it to the deceased on the days those hearings were being held.

The three old men: Hayashi Hyōsuke, Murai Genbei, and Horiuchi Den'emon were assigned to serve in rotation as intermediaries between the ronin and the Hosokawa house. See chapter 76.

p.764 The stonecutters: *Hakumyō waroku,* AGSS 3:126.

What seems to have concerned Hakumyō: *Hakumyō waroku,* AGSS 3:124–25. The first and third of his complaints are discussed in some detail in *Chūsei kōkanroku* 8, AGSS 3:586–87, a work with which Hakumyō strongly takes issue.

p.766 Satō Jōemon ... was able to retrieve Yasubei's great sword: *Satō Jōemon oboegaki,* 69.

I was shocked: *Horiuchi Den'emon oboegaki,* AGSS 1:318–19.

Any artifact ... labeled as belonging to one of the ronin: Mitamura Engyo, "Sengakuji no hōbutsukan," MEZ 16:268–84.

A story told by Katashima Shin'enshi: SGD 12:7r–9v. Shin'enshi mistakenly refers to Kai Shuso as the Superior of Zuikōin. In fact, he was Master of the hermitage Shūsuian, a dependency of Zuikōin located within the temple walls. I have corrected the text accordingly. See chapter 36.

p.767 Shin'enshi's florid style does sometimes strain credulity: Kanzawa Tokō makes this point in *Okinagusa,* NZT, ser. 3, 6:22, and in commentary on Tokō's own text of *Horiuchi Den'emon oboegaki,* in *Shintei zōho Shiseki shūran,* 312–13.

A group of students from the Kyoto Normal School: Saitō, *Akō gishi jissan,* 225.

CHAPTER 94

p.769 She summoned . . . Ijūin Kumanosuke: This episode is based upon, and in part translated from, *Semetewagusa*, 153–55. Kumanosuke was the *tsuke-karō* of the Sadohara cadet house, an Elder appointed not by the lord of that domain but by the main house of the Shimazu to keep a watchful eye on the cadet house.

p.770 *Hagakure*: NST 26:237. Yamamoto Shin'emon Tsunetomo (1659–1719) took vows and entered lay orders after the death of his lord, Nabeshima Mitsushige, in 1700. Thereafter, he went by the name Jōchō, which is simply the Sino-Japanese reading of his formal name, Tsunetomo.

p.771 When he spied the crest on those curtains: Jūrō could then have killed their enemy, Kudō Suketsune, but he refrained from doing so to allow his brother Gorō to join him in the attack. Gorō told his brother that he should have killed Suketsune when he had the chance; but that he nonetheless appreciated the chance to join him. See NST 26:595, supplementary note to 237.

I wouldn't normally criticize: Tanaka Mitsurō paraphrases this passage: "I know that to speak critically of these people from a position of safety may seem irresponsible; I do so only by way of considering how a warrior should live in an age of peace" (*Nagatsuta zasshi*, 15 November 2016). Tanaka also notes that Jōchō's critique of the conduct of the ronin is "a blend of admiration, envy, and jealousy."

CHAPTER 95

p.773 I leave with you this last missive: Onodera Jūnai to O-Tan, Genroku 16.2.3: AGSS 2:224–29; CG 3:419–23; *Akō gishi no tegami*, 303–8. Two paragraphs of this letter referring to unidentified acquaintances and relatives have been excised.

p.778 None of O-Tan's letters to Jūnai survive: The caption in the upper-right-hand corner of the picture reads: "In a volume entitled *Ruikinshū*, my friend Shimizu Sekijō has collected all surviving holograph letters written by the wife of Onodera Hidekazu and sent to her husband. One need only read these letters to know what sort of person she was." The author of this caption is quite mistaken. *Ruikinshū* contains no letters from O-Tan, only poems. Incidentally, Shimizu Sekijō was the grandfather of our narrator, Ōhashi Yoshizō.

p.779 This is my sixty-fifth year: Teiryū to the wife of Sakurai Kakuemon, MSAGS, 359–65. This text has been augmented slightly to identify some of the people mentioned in it.

p.780 Jūnai's widow is living in Kyoto: Teiryū to O-Riku, AGS 3:301–4.

O-Tan's death: Evidence relating to O-Tan's death is meager and contradictory. The most influential source is Ban Kōkei's brief comment, quoted from his chapter on her in *Kinsei kijin den*, 78–79, and even he suggests that the mention of her suicide (*jimetsu*) might mean that she used a sword. Other sources claim unequivocally that she either used a sword, died of an illness, or simply entered the temple to become a nun. Tanaka Mitsurō suggests an interesting, though entirely speculative, explanation of this inconsistency, in "Tan-jo no shi," *Rongaibi* 64. O-Tan may have entered the temple and become a nun, intending to spend her days at devotions on Jūnai's behalf. But being debilitated from the stress of the previous two years, she fell ill, took to her bed, lost interest in food, and ultimately died.

CHAPTER 96

p.783 Shindō Genshirō: See chapter 34.

Ōno Kurōbei . . . who absconded in the night: See chapter 26.

A letter from Itō Gōemon to Hinatsu Chōbei: This letter has never been published, but is described briefly in Hirao, *Horobiyuku mono no bi*, 243.

p.784 Kurōbei . . . attempted to excuse himself: *Akō-jō hikiwatashi ikken*, AGSS 2:544–46.

Refused permission to settle: Maebara Isuke and Kanzaki Yogorō, *Sekijō meiden*, AGSS 1:145–46; Hirao, *Horobiyuku mono no bi*, 242.

Gave the impression of a well-to-do ronin: Itō Bai'u, *Kenmon dansō*, 254–55.

His household goods had been impounded: Maebara Isuke and Kanzaki Yogorō, *Sekijō meiden*, AGSS 1:146.

p.785 Kurōbei then took to dealing in charcoal: Itō Bai'u, *Kenmon dansō*, 254.

Concerning the impounded goods: Ōishi Kuranosuke to Ochiai Yozaemon, Genroku 16.11.29, AGS 3:197–99.

p.786 In Yamashina: Kuranosuke to (Kagakuji) Keikō, Genroku 15.12.13, CG 3:381–84.

I was delighted: O-Riku (Soren's mother) to Kyūshin (Seno'o Magozaemon), Genroku 16.2.26, AGSS 2:329–30.

Mohei has written to Saroku: Probably Kumode Mohei and Muroi Saroku, trusted retainers of the Ishizuka and Ōishi families, respectively.

p.787 In her letter to the Superior: O-Riku to Jingūji, Genroku 15.12.27, AGS 3:262–63. See also chapter 80.

CHAPTER 97

p.788 Before the fence was built: *Sekijō shiwa*, AGSS 1:262.

p.789 My friend the scholar Mitamura Engyo: Engyo and our narrator, Ōhashi Yoshizō, were fellow members of the Antiquarian Society (Shūko Kai) and regular contributors to its journal. Unfortunately, Engyō does not cite the source of his description of the *Hokke Senbu* sponsored by Yōzei'in. See MEZ 16:268–71.

p.790 Kikaku dutifully visited his parents' graves: His mother died in 1687, and his father in 1693.

Make a stop at Sengakuji: "Matsu no chiri," in *Kikaku "Ruikōji,"* ed. Watanabe, 109–12. See also Fukumoto Ichirō, *Haiku Chūshingura*, 222–24.

As those wandering women [kairai] used to sing: Their song mentions only the Five Elements (*gorin*) and the Five Fleshly Components (*gotai*); I have spelt out the content of those terms in order to make their message a bit clearer.

p.791 Parents never demand: This interpretation of Kikaku's poem follows that in "Matsu no chiri," 111–12.

Sengakuji senryū: Abe, *Edo senryū de yomu Chūshingura*, 169–85; Kitajima, *Edo senryū de yomu Chūshingura monogatari*, 349–64.

CHAPTER 98

p.794 The domain's great fleet: A few excellent paintings of the domain's fleet, as well as of their lord's homeward procession, were displayed at the Haneda Kūkō Bijutsukan from 4 April through 5 July 2015. They must now be viewed at the Hosokawa family archive, Eisei Bunko, in Tokyo.

I called at Sengakuji: Horiuchi Den'emon oboegaki, AGSS 1:348–52.

p.798 He was sixty-five years old: Horiuchi Den'emon to Terai Genkei, Hōei 6 (1709).10.24, in *Horiuchi Den'emon oboegaki*, AGSS 1:355–56. The village of Sugi has long since been incorporated into the town of Yamaga. The temple where Den'emon and his wife are buried was a Sōtō Zen temple in the Genroku era, but later became affiliated with the Nichiren sect and was renamed Nichirinji.

PART IV. The After Years

CHAPTER 99

p.801 **Kira Sahei certainly would have felt the chill:** This chapter is based upon three records of the Suwa house: *Suwa-ke goyōjō tomechō, Suwa-ke goyōbeya nikki,* and *Kira Sahei azuke Suwa-ke shojichō,* all of which are conveniently collected in AGS 2:161–244, 245–72, 273–85, respectively.

p.802 **The front of the castle faced Lake Suwa:** In the Edo period, Takashima Castle appeared to be floating on Lake Suwa, as it does in Keisai Eisen's print. What with decades of landfill and dense construction, however, the castle is now far removed from the shoreline, and can hardly be seen from the water's edge.

The Southern Perimeter was surrounded by marshland: Yamagata Daini's drawing in *Shuzu gōketsuki* is not to scale. The Southern Perimeter was much smaller in comparison with the main body of the castle than he shows it to be.

p.807 **These matters were reported by express courier to both Edo and Osaka:** Many of the earlier couriers, too, were sent to Osaka. This suggests that someone in a position of considerable authority in the Suwa house was at that time away from Edo. But I have yet to ascertain who that person was or why he was in Osaka.

CHAPTER 100

p.811 **Kichiemon describes their new situation:** Terasaka Kichiemon to Shichiemon, Hōei 4 (1707).2.15, transcribed in Fukushima, "Tokutomi Sohō-shi no Terasaka tōbō setsu wa bōdan nari," 43–44.

p.812 **Ōishi Mitsuhira:** OKS, 192–95, 305.

Satō Jōemon: Tomizawa, "Horibe Yasubei no funkei no tomo." Jōemon actually changed his familiar name (*tsūshō*) at least twice after reaching his majority. Before leaving Shibata for Edo, he was known as Satō Shingoemon. Sometime before the attack on the Kira mansion, he changed his name to Jōemon, the name by which he was known to the Akō ronin. And sometime before his appearance in the records of the Manabe house, he changed it again to Kakubei. Tomizawa adduces documentary proof that all these names refer to the same person. Throughout this book, however, he is called Jōemon, the name by which

he was known to most of the others who figure in the narrative.
For Horibe Yahei's conversation with Horiuchi Den'emon, see chapter 82; on Jōemon's origins, see chapter 21.

p.813 The monks at Sengakuji: *Hakumyō waroku,* AGSS 3:123, 126.

Chikamatsu Kanroku regretted: *Horiuchi Den'emon oboegaki,* AGSS 1:291–92.

p.814 Kanroku had left all the land: AGJ, 393, s.v. Jinzaburō. On vassal-farmers, see KD 11:854, s.v. *Hikan-byakushō.*

The sixteen vassal-farmers: See chapter 80.

Yōzei'in Sama . . . passed away: *Miyoshi bunke Seibiroku,* 672–73.

p.815 Horibe Yahei's widow: [Horibe] Waka to Myōei [wife of Ōishi Mujin], Genroku 17 (1704).1.25, OGM, 254–57.

The aging mother of Ōishi Sezaemon: OKS, 155. On the Konoe–Ōishi connection, see also chapters 16 and 56.

p.816 Tokugawa Tsunayoshi . . . died: TJ 6:722.

A severe epidemic of measles: Ōgimachi Machiko, *Matsukage nikki,* 948–49.

CHAPTER 101

p.817 Maeda Uneme Toshimasa: This episode is based upon excerpts from various records of the Maeda house that have been arranged in chronological order in *Kaga-han shiryō,* 5:817–38. Another version of the story in this source claims that Uneme slit the throat of Oda Kenmotsu (1662–1709).

p.818 They concluded that Uneme was deranged: When a crime was committed by a lord deemed to be deranged (*ranshin*), the man himself might be punished, but his domain would not be abolished, thus making his vassals ronin. In this case, Uneme's newly created Daishōji Shinden fief was not confiscated but returned, its Corps of Vassals intact, to the Daishōji domain, of which it was originally a part. Takumi-no-Kami's vassals were doomed not only by the extreme anger of the Shogun but also by their own lord's insistence that he was "not at all deranged." See chapter 3.

CHAPTER 102

p.820 I just feel empty and listless: O-Riku to Senoʻo Magozaemon, Genroku 16.2.26, AGSS 2:329–30. See chapter 97.

Amnesties were unpredictable: KD 7:173–74, s.v. *sha*.

p.821 Memorandum: CG 3:665. This letter has no addressee, but it probably was sent either to Kanʻeiji or to Zōjōji. It was common practice to route such requests for amnesty through the Shogunal temples to the Commissioner of Temples and Shrines. See Taniguchi Shinko, *Akō rōshi to Kira-tei uchiiri*, 112.

A nun named Senkei: Mitamura Engyo, "Hōyō nado mo uchiwa ni," MNZ 16:270–71.

An amnesty was proclaimed in her name: TJ 6:627.

p.822 I have just heard from Kichiemon: Dennai's mother to Yoshida Dennai, Hōei 3 (1706).9.16: CG 3:665–66. Dennai's mother was then living in the castle town of Murakami in the province of Echigo, whither her son-in-law Itō Jūrōdayū had moved when, after the death of Honda Nakatsukasa, his young heir was commanded to leave Himeji and move to the lesser domain.

p.823 Last year: Terasaka Kichiemon to Shichiemon, Hōei 4 (1707).2.15. This letter survived in the family of Ogura Kametarō, a twentieth-century descendant of Shichiemon, and was published, both photographically and in transcription. The present whereabouts of the letter is unknown. See Fukushima Shirō, "Tokutomi Sohō-shi no Terasaka tōbō setsu wa bōdan nari," 43–44.

p.824 The amnesty . . . proclaimed after the death of Shogun Tokugawa Tsunayoshi: TJ 7:14; KD 7:173–74, s.v. *sha*.

Asano Daigaku Nagahiro . . . now pardoned: TJ 7:51, 122.

CHAPTER 103

p.826 What Kuranosuke has accomplished: Kōrinʼin to Murao Dono, Hōei 8 (1711).3.2, AGSS 2:324–27. See also Tanaka Mitsurō's discussion in *Nagatsuta zasshi*, 6 December 2005. The passage concerning Kuranosuke is taken from a postscript that precedes the main text of the letter in the original. Note, too, that Hōei 8 does not become Shōtoku 1 (1711) until the Fourth Month of that year.

p.827 Terai Genkei, Ishizuka Gengobei, and Horiuchi Denʻemon: This episode is based upon, and in part translated from, an exchange of letters between Terai

Genkei and Horiuchi Den'emon, Hōei 6 (1709).8.24 and Hōei 6.10.24, respectively, in *Horiuchi Den'emon oboegaki,* CG 3:552–55 and AGSS 1:354–56. These texts are taken from two different copies of *Den'emon oboekaki,* and in places differ considerably. I have therefore consulted both texts in tandem, and at times have been forced to prefer one version over the other.

p.829 Yoshiyasu's (Daizaburō's) invitation to Hiroshima: OKS, 92–94.

p.830 The journey from Toyooka to Hiroshima: Many of the details of Ōishi Daizaburō's journey are recorded in a collection of documents discovered by accident in the home of a deceased Hiroshima historian that was about to be demolished. These documents remain in the possession of the owner of the demolition firm and have never been published. The journey they describe, however, is conveniently summarized in Setodani, *Chūshingura o ikita onna,* 290–306.

There were more than a hundred people: O-Riku to Ōishi Shōji, Shōtoku 3 (1713).10.8, AGS 3:311–13.

p.831 The Ōishi genealogies sum up the rest of his life: OKS, 94. The dates of his marriages are listed in AGJ 349; and Setodani, *Chūshingura o ikita onna,* 334–35. These two sources do not always agree.

A friend of mine: Kanzawa Tokō, *Okinagusa,* NZT, ser. 3, 5:416, augmented by OKS.

The teahouse Izutsuya: This shop still exists, on Shijō just across from Gion. It now deals in herbal teas, and its proprietors claim descent from Hara Sōemon. A long description and explication of its connection with Kuranosuke is found in *Karaku meishō zue: Higashiyama no bu,* 1:30.

p.832 Later, he took the name Tonoe: This name, 外衛, is susceptible of many pronunciations, among them "Sotoe," "Gai'e," "Ge'ei," and "Ge'e." I follow Tokō because his is the only premodern phonetic rendition of the name I have found.

CHAPTER 104

p.833 *Sekijō gishinden:* This section is based principally upon the front matter to SGD: *Jijo, Hanrei,* and *Inshō mokuroku,* and Konta Yōzō, *Edo no kinsho,* 139–45.

Kanzawa Tokō (*Okinagusa,* NZT, ser. 3, 6:22) says that Terai Genkei vouchsafed a great deal of his knowledge of the vendetta to Katashima Shin'enshi, because he himself was reluctant to write about the lord he had served, lest it appear unseemly of him to do so. Tokō's view of *Gishinden* is that it is fundamentally sound and accurate, but that Shin'enshi's occasional lapses into a too-florid style, in the eyes of some readers, detracts from its air of authenticity.

CHAPTER 105

p.836 As the years passed: *Kanadehon Chūshingura*, still the quintessential dramatic treatment of the Akō vendetta, was first performed as a puppet play on 1748.8.14 at the Takemoto-za in Osaka. In 1749, it was performed as Kabuki at the Morita-za in Edo, and immediately thereafter at the Ichimura-za and the Nakamura (Kanya)-za, both also in Edo. The Kanya-za performance mentioned in this anecdote is not dated. Both puppet and Kabuki versions are still regularly performed and remain enormously popular.

Their forty-seven kinsmen have made quite a hit: *Horiuchi Den'emon oboegaki, furoku*, AGSS 1:368.

It makes life simpler not to mention it: In this connection, see Tanaka Mitsurō, "'Fugishi no matsuro' ni tsuite," *Rongaibi* 58. In this essay, he reminds us that the Hiroshima authorities had tried their best to prevent the attack. From their point of view, to be what is now called "disloyal" (*fugishi*) was to do exactly as the Hiroshima authorities wished everyone to do. Tanaka also suggests that "it was probably taboo in Hiroshima to praise the '*gishi*' and denigrate the '*fugishi*.'"

p.837 Tominomori Suke'emon II: *Horiuchi Den'emon oboegaki, furoku*, in AGSS 1:366–67. Tominomori Eiji speculates that the author of this attachment may have been a son of Den'emon who became a Liaison Officer of the Hosokawa house and knew Suke'emon II through that connection. See Tominomori, *Uron nari Suke'emon*, 94–95.

His father's encounter with Ōshimaya Hachirōbei: See chapter 69.

p.839 Ōishi's diary: No such document has survived.

Sadatake is seriously mistaken: Ise no Sadatake, *Ansai zuihitsu* 1:149. It is astonishing that Sadatake should make such an error. He must have been one of the most learned men of the Edo period, especially as regards military matters.

Daigaku Nagazumi: Asano Daigaku Nagazumi (1707–1754) was assigned to the Bodyguard (Koshōgumi) in 1745.9.13. See KCS 5:349.

CHAPTER 106

p.840 Kangetsu . . . was soaking in the tub: The encounter in the bathtub between Kangetsu and Shinpachi is reported in Taguchi Gozaemon, *Dewa no Kuni Mogami-gun Shinjō korō oboegaki*, 215–16.

A heavy growth of beard: Shinpachi was granted special permission to grow a beard in order to soften the appearance of the gash on his face.

BIBLIOGRAPHY

Participant Accounts

HOSOKAWA-KE

Higo bunken sōsho. Edited by Kojō Teikichi, Uno Tōfū, and Mutō Itsuo. 6 vols. Tokyo: Ryūbunkan, 1910.

Horiuchi Den'emon oboegaki (1703). In AGSS 1:279–368; *Higo bunken sōsho* 4:289–340; *Akō gishi shinsō: Horiuchi Den'emon shuki, Asano Takumi-no-Kami kerai o-azukari no setsu oboegaki.* Edited by Mizuno Sadakichi. Kawasaki: Nippon Gidōkai, 1936; *Shintei zōho Shiseki shūran, Zokuhen* 8. Edited by Kondō Heijō, 165–326. Kyoto: Rinsen Shoten, 1967.

Hosokawa kafu—Tsunatoshi-fu shō. In MSAGS, 75–88.

Hosokawa-ke o-azukari shimatsu ki (1703). In AGS 2:3–51.

Kumamoto Hosokawa kafu—Hosokawa Tsunatoshi-fu. In AGS 2:52–57.

O-azukenin kiroku. In *Higo bunken sōsho,* 4:341–52.

HISAMATSU-KE

Asano Takumi Dono kerai: Matsudaira Oki-no-Kami Dono e o-azuke ikken (1703). In AGSS 2:67–124.

Haga Seidayū oboegaki (1703). In AGSS 3:101–18.

Haga Tomohisa kikigaki (1703). In AGS 1:302–55.

Kikigaki (1703). Edited by Akō-shi Sōmubu *Shishi* Hensanshitsu. Akō: Akō-shi, 1993.

Matsuyama sōdan (1703). Excerpt in AGSS 3:151–58.

MŌRI-KE

Akō rōnin o-azukari no ki: Mōri-ke kiroku. In AGSS 2:14–35.

Asano Takumi kerai o-shioki ōsetsukerare-sōrō setsu goyō ai-tsutome-sōrō kakitome. In CG 3:655–59.

Banshū Akō no jōshu Asano Takumi-no-Kami rōnin o-azukari ki: Chōfu-han o-azukari kiroku. Edited by Yagi Akihiro. Akō: Akō Shiritsu Rekishi Hakubutsukan, 1999.

Chōfu o-azukari gishi ikken. In CG 3:570–75.

Fuchū-kō tomegaki. In CG 3:558–69.

MIZUNO-KE

Asano Sama go-kerai kyūnin o-azukari ikken (1702–1703). In CG 3:605–16.

Genroku nenchū Mizuno-ke Kenmotsu, Asano gishi o-azukari komonjo: Jūnigatsu jūshichi-nichi yoru Kanzaki Yogorō monogatari. In AGSS 2:279–84.

Hiyōroku, Kōtokuben, Hanpiroku. Edited (respectively) by Kitajima Masamoto, Murakami Tadashi, and Kanai Madoka. *Nihon shiryō sensho* 7. Tokyo: Kondō Shuppansha, 1971. Excerpt (1702–1703) in CG 3:616–20.

Mizuno-ke o-azukari kiroku. In AGS 2:107–36.

Sekijō shiwa (1703). Compiled by Tōjō Shusetsu, physician to the House of Mizuno. In AGSS 1:203–65.

TAMURA-KE

Asano Naganori azukari zashiki, seppuku no ba ezu (1701). In CG 3:19, 20–21.

Goyō tomegakinuke (1701.3.14). In CG 3:24–26.

Ichinoseki kachū Kitazato Mokunosuke tebikae (1701). In CG 3:19–24; AGS 1:42–48.

Ichinoseki-han kachū Nagaoka Shichirōbei kiroku (1701). In CG 3:14–19; AGSS 2:9–14; *Iwate shigaku kenkyū* 46 (1966).

ASANO-KE

Asano Naganori den. Excerpt in AGS 2:375–466.

Asano Naganori den furoku. Excerpt in AGS 2:467–523.

Asano Tsunanaga den. Excerpt in AGS 2:524–89. The original title of this work is *Kenmyō Kō Seibiroku*, but it is referred to in the notes by the revised (and clearer) title given to it by the editors of AGS.

Miyoshi bunke Seibiroku (covering 1614–1720). Edited by Hiroshima-ken, Futami-gun, Miyoshi-shi Shiryō Sōran Henshū I'inkai. Miyoshi: Hiroshima-ken, Futami-gun, Miyoshi-shi Shiryō Sōran Kankōkai, 1980.

UESUGI-KE

Hennen monjo, 44. Excerpts in CG 3:448–49, 476–85.

Nomoto Chūzaemon kenmonsho. In CG 3:443–48; AGS 1:380–90.

Ōkuma Yaichiemon kikigaki. In CG 3:439–43; AGSS 3:127–33.

Tsunanori Kō go-nenpu, 23. Excerpt in CG 3:449–50.

Uesugi nenpu. Excerpt in AGS 2:360–72.

Yonezawa Shioi-ke oboegaki. In AGS 1:369–79.

BAKUFU

Teibi zakki (1702). In CG 3:432–38. The postattack report of Abe Shikibu and Sugita Gozaemon, the Inspectors sent to investigate.

Individual Participant Accounts

Akō "gishi" no tegami. Edited by Akō Shiritsu Rekishi Hakubutsukan. Akō: Akō Shiritsu Rekishi Hakubutsukan, 2001.

Akō gishi no tegami. Edited by Katayama Hakusen. Akō: *Akō gishi no tegami* Kankōkai, 1970.

Akō rōnin aki-yashiki aratame-chō (1701). Edited by Yagi Akihiro. Akō: Akō Shiritsu Rekishi Hakubutsukan, 1993.

Akō-jō hikiwatashi ikken (1701). In AGSS 2:492–578.

Akō-jō uketori zaiban goyō oboe (1701). Edited by Yagi Akihiro. Tatsuno: Tatsuno Shiritsu Rekishi Bunka Shiryōkan, 1995.

Asahara Shigehide oboegaki (1701–1703). Edited by Asahara Hidemasa. In AGS 1:286–301.

Hakumyō waroku (1755). In AGSS 3:118–26.

Hara Sōemon. *Uchiiri jikkyō oboegaki.* In *Akō gishi no tegami,* ed. Katayama, 285–92.

Horibe Taketsune hikki (1702). In NST 27:180–270.

Horibe Yahei Akizane shiki (1702). In AGS 1:221–46; *Shintei Horibe Akizane oboegaki.* Edited by Satō Makoto. Tokyo: Rinjinkan, 2001.

Itō Jūrōdayū Haruyuki kikigaki oboe (1743). Transcribed in *Terasaka setsuen roku,* 120–48. As its title suggests, this text is an attempt to reconstruct from memory a collection of reminiscences related by Terasaka Kichiemon (1665–1747) and recorded over several years by Itō Jūrōdayū, the son-in-law of Kichiemon's commander and patron Yoshida Chūzaemon. The original manuscript was destroyed by fire in 1741, but as Kichiemon was still alive and well, Jūrōdayū was able to enlist his aid in reconstructing the text whenever his service in the House of Honda took him to Edo, where Kichiemon was then living.

Kajikawa-shi hikki (1701?). In AGSS 2:273–79.

Kurisaki Dōyū kiroku (1701–1702). Excerpt in CG 3:9–14.

Maebara Isuke and Kanzaki Yogorō. *Sekijō meiden* (1702). In AGSS 1:132–55.

Nakayama Yasubei—Horibe Yahei fushi keiyaku no tenmatsu. Edited by Mibu Seigorō (Sekiun). Shibata: Kyōdo Kenkyūsha, 1934.

Ochiai Yozaemon. *Kōseki kenmonki.* In AGSS 3:172–362.

[Ōgaki-han Toda-shi] Banshū Akō ikkan oboegaki. In CG 3:48–56.

Ōishi Kuranosuke. *Azukeokisōrō Kingin ukeharai chō* (1702). In AGSS 3:143–140.

Okado Denpachirō oboegaki (post-1701). In NST 27:163–78.

Okajima Tsuneshige oboegaki (1701). In AGS 1:51–68.

Onodera Jūnai. *Mōshiagesho.* In CG 3:430–32.

Sasakawa Tadaemon. *Gishi jitsuroku: Sengakuji sō kikigaki.* In CG 3:485–501.

Satō [Jōemon] Isshō oboegaki. Edited by Nakajima Yasuo. Tokyo: Chūō Gishikai, 2002. A revised and enlarged edition of this work, published under the new but rather misleading title *Akō gishi uchiiri jūgunki* (Tokyo: Chūō Gishikai, 2013), contains a very useful essay by Professor Tomizawa Nobuaki on the ancestry and career of Satō Jōemon.

Terasaka Kichiemon. *Terasaka Kichiemon kakisute.* In AGSS 2:377–82.

———. *Terasaka shiki.* In AGS 1:247–78.

Terasaka Nobuyuki hikki. In AGSS 2:230–58; AGS 1:279–85. The latter text transcribes only a list of the children of the ronin, which is not included in the former text.

Terasaka Nobuyuki jiki. In CG 3:224–41.

Toda-ke goyō-tome (1701). Manuscript in the collection of Tokyo Daigaku Shiryō Hensanjo. Excerpt in Usui Senkichi. *Ōgaki-han to Chūshingura: Akō kaijō made no yakuwari.* Ōgaki: Ōgaki-shi Bunka-zai Hogo Kyōkai, 2003.

Tominomori Suke'emon and Isogai Jūrōzaemon. *Tominomori Suke'emon hikki.* In CG 3:426–30. Written at the request of and submitted to Horiuchi Den'emon.

Yanagiwara Motomitsu. *Zoku shi gushō.* Shintei zōho Kokushi taikei 15. Tokyo: Yoshikawa Kōbunkan, 1966.

Contemporary Accounts, House Records, and Other Premodern Sources

Akō rōnin aki-yashiki aratame-chō (1701). Edited by Yagi Akihiro. Akō: Akō Shiritsu Rekishi Hakubutsukan, 1993.

Akō seigi sankō (1704). Edited by Nishi Yasuo. Okayama: Techōsha, 1991.

Asakichi ichiran ki (1703). In AGSS 1:377–413.

Asano katakiuchi ki (1703). In AGSS 2:125–66.

Chōsen nichinichi ki o yomu: Shinshū sō ga mita Hideyoshi no Chōsen shinryaku. Edited by Chōsen nichinichi ki Kenkyūkai. Kyoto: Hōzōkan, 2000.

Chūsei seiji shakai shisō. Edited by Ishii Susumu et al. NST 21.

Chūshingura no emakimono. Edited by Akō Shiritsu Rekishi Hakubutsukan. Akō: Akō Shiritsu Rekishi Hakubutsukan, 2002.

Dai Nihon komonjo: Iewake, no. 3. Vol. 2, *Date-ke monjo.* Edited by Tōkyō Teikoku Daigaku. Tokyo: Tokyō Teikoku Daigaku Bunka Daigaku Shiryō Hensangakari, 1908.

Dokai kōshū ki (1690). Edited by Kanai Madoka. Tokyo: Jinbutsu Ōraisha, 1967. In his introduction to this work, Kanai also transcribes the entries on Asano Takumi-no-Kami in *Kanchō gosei* (1701) and *Shoshō renzoku ki* (1699), both manuscripts in the collection of Tokyo Daigaku Shiryō Hensanjo.

Edo machikata kakiage: Bunsei no machi no yōsu (3), Azabu-hen. Edited by Hasegawa Masatsugu. Tokyo: Minato-ku Minato Toshokan, 1995.

Ekisui renbei roku (1703). Edited by Saitō Shigeru. Tokyo: Nippon Sakimori Kyōkai Hotta Bunko Hanpubu, 1974.

Geishū Itsukushima zue. Edited by Okada Kiyoshi. 2 vols. Kyoto: Rinsen Shoten, 1995.

Genroku sekenbanashi fūbun shū (1694–1703). Edited by Hasegawa Tsuyoshi. Iwanami bunko 270. Tokyo: Iwanami Shoten, 1994.

Genshōkanki (1722?). Edited by Yano Kimikazu and Nakayama Yūshō. *Kiyō: Kyōritsu Joshi Tanki Daigaku Bunka* 22 (1979): 123–64; 23 (1980): 74–124.

Gokaidō nobe ezu (1807). Edited by Kodama Kōta. 103 vols. Tokyo: Tokyo Bijutsu, 1976–2002.

Hagi-han batsuetsuroku. Edited by Yamaguchi Monjokan. 5 vols. Yamaguchi: Yamaguchi Monjokan, 1971.

Hayami Shungyōsai (1767–1823). *Ehon Chūshingura.* 20 vols., ser. 1 and 2. Kyoto: Yoshinoya Jinbei, 1800, 1808.

Higo Hosokawa-ke samurai-chō. Edited by Matsumoto Sumio. 4 vols. Kumamoto: Hosokawa Hanseishi Kenkyūkai, 1977–1979.

Ihon Asano fukushū ki (1702). In AGSS 2:259–73.

Ise no Sadatake (1717–1784). *Ansai zuihitsu. Shintei zōho Kojitsu sōsho* 8 and 9. Tokyo: Meiji Tosho Shuppan and Yoshikawa Kōbunkan, 1952, 1953.

Kaga-han shiryō. Edited by Heki Ken. 15 vols. Tokyo: Ishiguro Bunkichi, 1929–1943.

Karaku meishō zue, Higashiyama no bu. 5 vols. Osaka: Kawachiya Kihei, 1863.

Kira Sahei azuke Suwa-ke shojichō. In AGS 2:273–85.

Kiyomasa ki. Edited by Tsunoda Bun'ei and Gorai Shigeru. *Shintei zōho Shiseki shūran* 39. Kyoto: Rinsen Shoten, 1967.

Kuwana-han shoden oboegaki (1702). In AGSS 2:359–67.

Mimibukuro (?–1814). Edited by Suzuki Tōzō. Tōyō bunko 207 and 208. Tokyo: Heibonsha, 1972.

Mishima-shi zuihitsu. In AGSS 2:578–81

Miyakawa Masayasu. *Miyakawanoya manpitsu.* In NZT, ser. 1, 8.

Miyake Kanran (1674–1718). *Resshi hōshūroku.* In AGSS 1:520–31.

Mizuma Sentoku (1662–1726). *Sentoku zuihitsu* (1718). In *Haisho sōkan.* Vol. 4. Kyoto: Rinsen Shoten, 1988.

Mōri Hidemoto no ki. Edited by Kurokawa Mamichi. In *Kokushi sōsho.* Vol. 19. Tokyo: Kokushi Kenkyūkai, 1915.

Mukōyama Seisai zakki. Edited by Harigaya Takeshi and Ōguchi Yūjirō. 47 vols. Tokyo: Yumani Shobō, 2001–2004.

Muraji Yajūrō. *Kaisekiki* (1708). In AGSS 2:384–422.

Muro Kyūsō (1658–1734). *Akō gijin roku* (1703; rev. ed., 1709). In NST 27:274–370.

———. *Sundai (Shundai) zatsuwa.* Edited by Mori Senzō. Tokyo: Iwanami Shoten, 1936.

Ogawa Tsunemitsu. *Chūsei kōkanroku* (1708). In AGSS 3:410–553.

Ōgimachi Machiko. *Matsukage nikki.* In *Yanagisawa-ke no kotengaku (jō): "Matsukage nikki."* Edited, translated, and annotated by Miyakawa Yōko. Tokyo: Shintensha, 2007.

(Ogyū) Sorai Butsu Shigenori (1666–1728). *Ritsurei taishō teihon Minritsu kokujikai.* Edited by Uchida Tomo'o and Hihara Toshikuni. Tokyo: Sōbunsha, 1966.

Ōkura Kensai (1757–1844). *Myōkaigo hyō.* In AGSS 2:254–58.

Ōta Gyūichi (1527–1613). *Shinchō-kō ki* (ca. 1598?). Edited by Okuno Takahiro and Iwasawa Yoshihiko. Tokyo: Kadokawa Shoten, 1969.

Ryūei hikan. Edited by Shiseki Kenkyūkai. Vol. 1, *Naikaku Bunko shozō shiseki sōkan.* Tokyo: Kyūko Shoin, 1981.

Ryūkō Sōjō nikki. Edited by Nagashima Fukutarō and Hayashi Ryōshō. 3 vols. Tokyo: Zoku Gunsho ruijū Kanseikai, 1969.

Saitō Gesshin (1804–1878). *Zōtei Bukō nenpyō* (1849–1850). Edited by Kaneko Mitsuharu. 2 vols. Tokyo: Heibonsha, 1968.

——— et al. *Edo meisho zue.* 7 vols. Edo: Suharaya Ihachi, 1834–1836.

Saji Kazuma Tametsuna. *Myōkaigo.* In AGSS 2:166–98.

Semetewagusa. Edited by Hotta Shōzō and Kawakami Tasuke. Tokyo: Kokushi Kenkyūkai, 1917.

Sugimoto Yoshichika. *Akō shōshūki* (1703). In AGSS 2:423–91.

Suwa-ke goyōbeya nikki. In AGS 2:245–72.

Suwa-ke goyōjō tomechō. In AGS 2:161–244.

Tachibana Nankei (1754–1806). *Hokusō sadan.* Edited by Nagai Hidenori. Tokyo: Yūhōdō Bunko, 1910.

Taguchi Gozaemon. *Dewa no Kuni Mogami-gun Shinjō korō oboegaki* (1716–1735). Edited by Tokiwa Kintarō. Shinjō: Kyū Shinjō Hanshu Tozawa-ke, 1918. Reprint, Shinjō: Shinjō-shi Kyōiku I'inkai, 1972.

Takeuchi Gengen'ichi. *Haika kijin dan* (1816), *Zoku Haika kijindan* (1832). Edited by Kira Sueo. Tokyo: Iwanami Shoten, 1987.

Tamenaka Ason shū. In *Shikashū taisei.* Edited by Waka Bungaku Kenkyūkai. Vol. 2, *Chūko II.* Tokyo: Meiji Shoin, 1973–1976.

Tanki manroku: Kokuritsu Kokkai Toshokan zōhan. 2 vols. Tokyo: Yoshikawa Kōbunkan, 1993, 1994.

Toda Mosui (1629–1706). *Murasaki no hitomoto.* In *Toda Mosui zenshū.* Tokyo: Kokusho Kankōkai, 1969.

Tōkaidō bunken nobe ezu (1806). Edited by Kodama Kōta. 24 vols. Tokyo: Tōkyō Bijitsu, 1977–1985.

Tsunanori Kō, Uesugi-ke go-nenpu. Vol. 6. Yonezawa: Yonezawa Onkokai, 1978.

Yamagata Daini (1725–1767). *Shuzu gōketsuki* (ca. 1764). Edited by Yamori Kazuhiko. Tokyo: Meicho Shuppan, 1974.

Yamamoto Tsunetomo (1659-1719). *Hagakure* (1716). Edited by Sagara Tōru and Satō Masahide. NST 26.

Yamazaki-dōri bunken nobe ezu (1806). Edited by Kodama Kōta et al. 2 vols. Tokyo: Tōkyō Bijitsu, 1978.

Yanagisawa Yoshiyasu (1658-1714). *Rakushidō nenroku.* Edited by Miyakawa Yōko. *Shiryō sanshū* 174 and 176. Tokyo: Yagi Shoten, 2014, 2015.

Yanagisawa-ke hizō jikki. In *Kai sōsho.* Kōfu: *Kai sōsho* Kankōkai, 1934.

Later Accounts

Aoyama Enkō (Nobumitsu, 1807–1871). *Akō shijūshichi-shi den* (1851). In *Nihon kyōiku bunko, kōgihen jō*. Vol. 6. Tokyo: Dōbunkan, 1910.

———. *Gijin isō* (1866). In AGSS 1:184–202.

———. *Setsuya seiwa*. Edo: Yamashiroya Sahyōe, 1866.

Ban Kōkei (1733–1806). *Kinsei kijin den* (1790). Edited by Nakano Mitsutoshi. Tokyo: Chūō Kōron Shinsha, 2005.

———. *Kanden jihitsu*. In NZT, ser. 1, 18.

Chūshin kiku junjū roku. 24 vols. Manuscript in the collection of Kokuritsu Kokkai Toshokan.

Fujie Yūyō (1685–1751). *Banshū Akō gunshi* (1727). In AS 5:607–32.

Fujita Tōko (1806–1855). "Bushi dochaku no gi." In *Fujita Tōko zenshū*, edited by Takasu Yoshijirō, 6:258–97. Tokyo: Shōkasha, 1936.

Hiratsuka Hyōsai (1792–1875). *Sekijō nenkan* (1851). Manuscript in the collection of Kokuritsu Kokkai Toshokan.

Hori Hidenari. *Geba no otonai*. In NZT, ser. 2, 22.

Ichioka Masakazu. *Tokugawa seisei roku*. Tokyo: Heibonsha, 1989.

Itō Bai'u (1683–1745). *Kenmon dansō* (?–1738). Edited by Kamei Nobuaki. Tokyo: Iwanami Shoten, 1940.

Itō Tōgai (1670–1736). *Kayano Sanpei den*. In AGSS 1:106–9.

Kanzawa Tokō (Yohei Sadamoto, 1710–1795). *Sekijō gishi hen sankō* (1775–1793). 9 vols. Manuscript in the collection of Kyoto Furitsu Sōgo Shiryōkan.

Koiwa Hiroaki. "Numata-ke hon *Chokushi gochisō nikki* to sono shūhen." *Ichinoseki-shi Hakubutsukan kenkyū hōkoku*, no. 6 (2003): 57–69.

Kudō Jūichibei Yukihiro (1800–1868). *Jijin roku* (1840). In *Bushidō zensho*, 10:273–348. Tokyo: Jidaisha, 1943.

Mikuma Katen (1730–1794). *Zoku Kinsei kijin den* (1798). Edited by Nakano Mitsutoshi. Tokyo: Chūō Kōron Shinsha, 2006.

Ono Kiyoshi. *Tokugawa seido shiryō*. Tokyo: Ono Kiyoshi, 1927.

Seppuku kuketsu (1840). In *Bushidō zensho*, 10:249–72. Tokyo: Jidaisha, 1943.

Sōgenji kiroku. Manuscript in the collection of the temple Sōgenji, Hyōgo-ken, Sasayama-shi, Furuichi. The author and the date of composition are unknown. The only extant copy bears a colophon that reads: "Copied Hōreki 14 [1764] by Keirin, maternal great-grandson of Fuwa Kazuemon." The text is transcribed

Bibliography

as "Genroku katakiuchi no kiroku" (www.gem.hi-ho.ne.jp/sogenji/chuushin-gura/ako2.htm) and a photographic reproduction of the manuscript is available (www.gem.hi-ho.ne.jp/sogenji/chuushingura /genroku-no-kiroku.htm).

Tokugawa reiten roku. Edited by Tokugawa Reimeikai. Tokyo: Hara Shobō, 1982.

Wakabayashi Tsutomu. *Kinko shidan zenchūshaku.* Tokyo: Taishūkan Shoten, 2001.

Yamazaki Yoshishige (1796–1856). *Akō gishi zuihitsu* (1819). In NZT, ser. 2, 24:1–136.

———. *Kairoku* (1820–1837). Edited by Itō Chikara and Motoori Seizō. Tokyo: Kokusho Kankōkai, 1915.

Selected Secondary Sources

Abe Tatsuji. *Edo senryū de yomu Chūshingura.* Tokyo: Bungei Shunjū, 2002.

Aioi shishi. Edited by *Aioi shishi* Hensan Senmon I'inkai. 8 vols. Aioi: Aioi-shi Kyōiku I'inkai, 1984–1995.

Akashi Saburō. *Jiriki kyūsai no kenkyū.* Tokyo: Yūhikaku, 1961.

Akiyama Kakuya. "*Gijin sansho* no henja Nabeta Mitsuyoshi-Ō." *Kokugakuin zasshi* 22, no. 3 (1916): 54–62.

Akō gunshi. Edited by Shiritsu Akō-gun Kyōikukai. Akō: Shiritsu Akō-gun Kyōikukai, 1908.

Akō jiken to Hiroshima: Shirarezaru Chūshingura. Edited by Zaidan Hōjin Hiroshima-shi Bunka Zaidan Hiroshima-jō. Hiroshima: Hiroshima-shi Shimin-kyoku, 2006.

Akō no chimei. Edited by Akō-shi Sōmubu *Shishi* Hensanshitsu. Akō: Akō-shi, 1985.

Akō-jō uketori to Tatsuno. Edited by Tatsuno Shiritsu Rekishi Bunka Shiryōkan. Tatsuno: Tatsuno-shi Kyōiku I'inkai, 2000.

Aoki Akihiro and Kobayashi Kikuhiko. *Uesugi to Kira kara mita Akō jiken.* Yonezawa: Yonezawa Shinyō Kinko, 2018.

"Asano-shi no furusato." Special issue, *Jōyō geibun*, December 2002.

Asano-shi to Makabe. Edited by Makabe-chō Rekishi Minzoku Shiryōkan. Makabe: Makabe-chō Rekishi Minzoku Shiryōkan, 1999.

Bitō Masahide. *Genroku jidai.* Tokyo: Shōgakukan, 1975.

Chūshingura jōruri shū. Edited by Ozawa Yoshikuni. Tokyo: Teikoku Bunko, 1929.

Chūshingura to hatamoto Asano-ke. Tatsuno: Tatsuno Shiritsu Tatsuno Rekishi Bunka Shiryōkan, 2009.

Doi Sakuji. *Hiroshima-han.* Tokyo: Yoshikawa Kōbunkan, 2015.

Edo fukugenzu. Tokyo: Tōkyō-to, 1989.

Edo Tōkyō-gaku jiten. Edited by Ogi Shinzō et al. Tokyo: Sanseidō, 1987.

Edo-gaku jiten. Edited by Nishiyama Matsunosuke et al. Tokyo: Kōbundō, 1984.

Egakareta Akō gishi. Edited by Kiso Kokoro. Akō: Akō Shiritsu Rekishi Hakubutsukan, 2012.

Elison, George. *Deus Destroyed: The Image of Christianity in Early Modern Japan.* Cambridge, Mass.: Harvard University Press, 1988.

―――. "The Priest Keinen and His Account of the Campaign in Korea, 1597–1598: An Introduction." In *Nihon kyōiku shi ronsō,* edited by Motoyama Yukihiko Kyōju Taikan Kinen Ronbunshū Henshū I'inkai, 25–41. Kyoto: Shibunkaku, 1988.

Eshita Hirohiko. *Shichinin no Kichiemon.* Tokyo: Sōbunsha, 1999.

Fukumoto Ichirō. *Haiku Chūshingura.* Tokyo: Shinchōsha, 1991.

Fukumoto Nichinan (Makoto). *Genroku kaikyo shinsōroku.* Tokyo: Tōadō Shobō, 1914. As Henry Smith points out, this work "remains even today the single most exhaustive study of the Akō incident" ("Trouble with Terasaka," 31). It is also valuable for the author's scrupulous citation of his sources and his occasional discussions of their value.

―――. *Horibe Yasubei.* Tokyo: Chūō Gishi Kai, 1917.

Fukushima Shirō. *Seishi Chūshingura.* Tokyo: Chūō Kōron Sha, 1992.

―――. "Tokutomi Sohō-shi no Terasaka tōbō setsu wa bōdan nari." *Nippon oyobi Nipponjin,* no. 218 (1931): 1–26.

Furukawa Aitetsu. *Sendai-han no futsū to Chūshingura.* Sendai: Ōsaki Hachimangū, 2010.

Futaki Ken'ichi. *Kinsei kokka no shihai kōzō.* Tokyo: Yūzankaku, 1986.

"Geihan shūyō" jinmei sakuin. Edited by Takahashi Shin'ichi. Hiroshima, 1990.

Hashimoto Manpei. *Nihon no jikoku seido.* Tokyo: Haniwa Shobō, 1978.

Hayashi Naosuke. *Ōishi Kuranosuke hiwa.* Kōbe: Privately published, 1992.

Hirai Seiji. "Chōtei kara mita Akō jiken." *Rekishi hyōron,* September 2006, 16–28.

―――. "Edo jidai ni okeru nentō chokushi no kantō gekō." *Ōkurayama ronsō,* March 1988, 110–40.

Hiramatsu Yoshirō. *Kinsei keiji soshōhō no kenkyū.* Tokyo: Sōbunsha, 1960.

Hirao Kojō. *Horobiyuku mono no bi: Akō rōshi no shiseikan.* Tokyo: Sankōsha, 1984.

Hiroyama Gyōdō. *Akō engyō shi.* Akō: Akō Shiyakusho, 1968.

———. *Banshū Akō no shiro to machi.* Tokyo: Yūzankaku, 1982.

Iio Kuwashi. *Chūshingura: Jidai o ugokashita otokotachi.* Kōbe: Kōbe Shinbun, 2002. Iio was a prolific writer, and some of his work appears in more than one of the following volumes. Despite the repetitiveness, however, he had a broader knowledge of the sources than did most of his contemporaries and was little affected by the biases that detract from the work of others who consider themselves specialists in the subject.

———. *Chūshingura no shinsō.* Tokyo: Shin Jinbutsu Ōraisha, 1995.

———. *Genroku Chūshingura: Sono omote to ura.* Akō: Ōishi Jinja, 1975.

———. *Igai shi Chūshingura.* Tokyo: Shin Jinbutsu Ōraisha, 1982.

———. *Jitsuroku Chūshingura.* Kōbe: Kōbe Shinbun, 1998.

———. *Ōishi Kuranoske no sugao.* Tokyo: Shin Jinbutsu Ōraisha, 1999.

———. *Za Chūshingura.* Tokyo: Shin Jinbutsu Ōraisha, 1985.

Ikuta Kunio, Sasano Shirō, and Habuka Hisao. "Genroku 14-nen Akō-jō uketori ni kan suru ikkōsatsu: Jujōshi no soshiki to gyōretsu ni miru kinsei jōkamachi no toshi kōzō." *Nihon Kenchiku Gakkai keikakukei ronbun shū* (1999): 329–35.

Imai Hiroki. *Suwa Takashima-jō.* Suwa: Suwa-shi Kyōiku I'inkai, 1970.

Imao Tetsuya. *Kira no kubi.* Tokyo: Heibonsha, 1987.

Imari annai. Edited by Nishiyama Jitsuichi. Imari: Imari Shōkōkai, 1927.

Inagaki Shisei. *Kōshō Edo buke shidan.* Tokyo: Kawade Shobō Shinsha, 1993.

Inoue Masaru. *Ōsaka-fu zenshi.* Osaka: Seibundō, 1922.

Ishii Shirō. *Nihonjin no kokka seikatsu.* Tokyo: Tōkyō Daigaku Shuppankai, 1986.

Itō Takeo. *Akō gishi Terasaka setsuen roku.* Akō: Kōkoku Shifūkai, 1935.

Iwao Seiichi. *Nan'yō Nihonmachi no kenkyū.* Tokyo: Iwanami Shoten, 1966.

Iwashita Tetsunori. "Edo no chūshin shudan 'chūshin tefuda.'" In *Kenryokusha to Edo no kusuri: Ninjin, budōshu, o-soba no o-kusuri,* 95–114. Tokyo: Hokuju Shuppan, 1998.

Jannetta, Ann Bowman. *Epidemics and Mortality in Early Modern Japan.* Princeton: Princeton University Press, 1987.

Kangakusha denki shūsei. Edited by Takebayashi Kan'ichi. Tokyo: Meicho Kankōkai, 1969.

Kani Hiroaki. "Mō Jikan to sono kōei." *Shigaku* 74, no. 4 (2006): 97–107.

————. "Mō Jikan to sono kōei: Hoi." *Shigaku* 75, nos. 1–2 (2007): 143–51.

Kansaku Ken'ichi. "Genroku kamigata jige no kajin: Konze Keian no ba'ai." In *Edo bungaku no bōken*, edited by Ōwa Yasuhiro, 74–93. Tokyo: Kanrin Shobō, 2007.

Kasaya Kazuhiko. *Edo o-rusuiyaku: Kinsei no gaikōkan.* Tokyo: Yoshikawa Kōbunkan, 2000.

————. *Kinsei buke shakai no seiji kōzō.* Tokyo: Yoshikawa Kōbunkan, 1993.

Katayama Hakusen. *Gishi: Terasaka Kichiemon: Shijū-roku shi ka, shijū-shichi shi ka.* Akō: Kagakuji, 1962.

————. *Ōishi Kuranosuke to Ryōsetsu Oshō.* Akō: Kagakuji, 1962.

————. *Shiyō: Ōtaka Gengo.* Akō: Kagakuji, 1972.

Katō gunshi. Yashiro: Katō-gun Kyōikukai, 1923.

Kawahara Yoshitsugu. *Tanbō: Edo daimyō hatamoto no haka.* Tokyo: Mainichi Shinbunsha, 1993.

Kibe Kazuaki. "Hagi-han ni okeru Chōsenjin horyo to buke shakai." *Rekishi hyōron*, September 1999, 47–59.

Kikuchi Hideo. *Edo Tōkyō chimei jiten.* Tokyo: Sekkasha, 1965.

Kikumura Norihiko. *Akō rōshi uchiiri igo.* Tokyo: Jinbutsu Ōraisha, 1965.

Kishii Yoshie. *Sanyōdō.* Tokyo: Chūō Kōron Sha, 1975.

————, ed. *Shinshū Gokaidō saiken.* Tokyo: Seiabō, 1959.

Kitagawa Tadahiko. "Teraoka Hei'emon no seiritsu." *Geinōshi kenkyū* 90 (1985).

Kitajima Hirotoshi. *Edo senryū de yomu Chūshingura monogatari.* Tokyo: Gurafusha, 2002.

Koga Jūjirō. *Seiyō ijutsu denrai shi.* Tokyo: Nisshin Shoin, 1942.

Kokaji. In *Yōkyokushū.* Edited by Yokomichi Mario and Omote Akira. NKBT 41. Tokyo: Iwanami Shoten, 1963.

Komiya Kiyora. *Edo bakufu no nikki to girei shiryō.* Tokyo: Yoshikawa Kōbunkan, 2006.

Kondō Ken and Satō Makoto. *Higo-han sanbyaku-koku Mera-ke: Horibe Yahei no kaishakunin Mera Ichiemon to sono zokufu.* Fukuoka: Karansha, 2013.

Konta Yōzō. *Edo no kinsho.* Tokyo: Yoshikawa Kōbunkan, 1981.

Koyanagi Yūichirō. "Kira o utta Chūgokujin sansei." In *NHK rekishi dokyumento*, 5:18–55. Tokyo: Nippon Hōsō Shuppan Kyōkai, 1987.

Kuroda Hideo. "Ōishi Kuranosuke, Chikara zō no 'hakken.'" *Rekishi hyōron*,

September 2001.

——. "Ōishi Kuranosuke no shōzō: Tokubetsu ten 'Toki o Koete Kataru Mono' kara." *Hon no tabibito*, December 2001.

Kuroda Kazuko. *Asano Nagamasa to sono jidai*. Tokyo: Azekura Shobō, 2000.

Kuwata Tadachika. *Daimyō to otogishū*. Rev. ed. Tokyo: Yūseidō, 1969.

Kyōdo kankei shiryō mokuroku. Edited by Akō Shiritsu Toshokan. Akō: Akō Shiritsu Toshokan, 1990.

Kyōto-fu Yamashina-chō shi. Kyoto: Kyōto-fu Yamashina-chō Yakuba, 1930.

Langenfeldt, Gösta. *The Historic Origin of the Eight Hours Day: Studies in English Traditionalism*. Stockholm: Almqvist & Wiksell, 1954.

Linji Yixuan. *The Zen Teachings of Master Lin-chi: A Translation of the Lin-chi lu*. Translated by Burton Watson. Boston: Shambhala, 1993.

Marumo Takeshige. "Bunroku, Keichō no eki ni okeru Chōsenjin yokuryū ni kan suru shiryō." *Kokushigaku*, July 1953, 44–55.

Matsudaira Tarō. *Kōtei Edo jidai seido no kenkyū*. Tokyo: Kashiwa Shobō, 1971.

Matsukata Fuyuko. "Asano-ke to Daté-ke no waboku no kokoromi to sono shippai." *Nihon rekishi*, October 1997.

——. "'Futsū' to 'tsūro.'" *Nihon rekishi*, November 1994.

——. "Kinsei chū-kōki daimyo shakai no kōzō." In *Buke yashiki: Kūkan to shakai*, edited by Mizaki Katsumi and Yoshida Nobuyuki. Tokyo: Yamakawa Shuppansha, 1994.

Mayama Seika. *Chūshingura chishi (Edo no bu)*. In *Mayama Seika zenshū*. Vol. 5 (suppl.). Tokyo: Kōdansha, 1977.

——. *Genroku Chūshingura*. In *Mayama Seika zenshū*. Vol. 1. Tokyo: Kōdansha, 1975.

Mehl, Margaret. *History and the State in Nineteenth-Century Japan*. London: Macmillan, 1998.

——. *History and the State in Nineteenth-Century Japan: The World, the Nation and the Search for a Modern Past*. 2nd ed. Copenhagen: Sound Book Press, 2017.

Mimura Seizaburō (Chikusei). *Kinsei nōsho den*. Tokyo: Futami Shobō, 1944.

Mitamura Engyo. *Akō gishi ibun*. In MEZ 16.

——. *Genroku kaikyo betsuroku*. In MEZ 16.

——. *Yoko kara mita Akō gishi*. In MEZ 16.

Mochizuki Hiroko. "Gishi no shiika." *Kiyō: Kariya-jō*, no. 1 (2010): 61–103.

Mochizuki Kodō. "Kayano Sanpei no matsuei ni tsuite." *Ōsaka Shidankai-hō* 2, no. 2 (1931): 17–20.

Mori Senzō. "Nabeta Shōzan shokan shō." In *Mori Senzō chosaku shū, zokuhen*, 7: 401–8. Tokyo: Chūō Kōron Sha, 1993.

———. "Seppuku to kaishaku to." *Risō Nippon*, March 1943, 91–94. Reprinted as "Seppuku no sho *Jijinroku*." In *Mori Senzō zenshū*, 11:382–89. Tokyo: Chūō Kōron Sha, 1971.

Murakami Tadashi. "Akō rōshi to Kawasaki." *Rekishi kōron*, December 1980, 112–13.

Naishi Masahiko. *Sengoku no jinkei*. Tokyo: Kōdansha, 2016.

Nakajima Yasuo. *Chūshingura uchiiri o sasaeta hachinin no shōgen*. Tokyo: Seishun Shuppansha, 2002.

———. *Genroku shijūshichi shi no hikari to kage*. Tokyo: Seishun Shuppansha, 1999.

———. *Ōishi Kuranosuke: Saigo no misshi*. Tokyo: Sangokan, 2000.

———. *Ōishi Kuranosuke no shōgai*. Tokyo: Sangokan, 1998.

Nakamura Tadao. *Yonezawa-damashii: Yonezawa shidan*. Yonezawa: Nakamura Tadao, 1943.

Nakausa Yuri. "Hosokawa-ke kishōmon no sekai." *Eisei Bunko* 90 (2015): 7–9.

Nelson, Thomas. "Southeast Asian Politics and Society as Seen Through the Japanese Communities." In *Japan Memory Project Conference Proceedings, Academic Year 2001–2002*, 296–309. Tokyo: Historiographical Institute, University of Tokyo, 2003.

Nihon koten bungaku daijiten. Edited by Nihon koten bungaku daijiten Henshū I'inkai. 6 vols. Tokyo: Iwanami Shoten, 1983–1985.

Nihon senshi: Chōsen no eki. Edited by Sanbō Honbu. 3 vols. Tokyo: Hakubunsha, 1924.

Nishimura Yutaka. *Takadanobaba to Yasubei no omokage*. Tokyo: Seikeidō, 1933.

Noguchi Takehiko. *Chūshingura: Akō jiken: Shijitsu no nikusei*. Tokyo: Chikuma Shobō, 1994.

———. *Chūshingura made: "Kenka" kara mita Nihonjin*. Tokyo: Kōdansha, 2013.

———. *Hana no Chūshingura*. Tokyo: Kōdansha, 2015.

Ōhashi Totsuan Sensei zenshū. Edited by Terada Takeshi. 3 vols. Tokyo: Shibundō, 1938–1943.

Ōhashi Yoshizō (Bishō Shōshi). "Akō gijin sansho yuraigaki." In AGSS 2:582.

Ōmi Kurimoto [Kurita] gunshi. Kusatsu: Shiga-ken Kurita-gun Yakusho, 1940.

Ōno Mizuo. "Ōishi Kuranosuke-ra seppuku no genzu shinshutsu." *Nihon rekishi,* December 2008, 99–103.

Onodera Hikojirō and Onodera Hiroshi. *Chūsei no Onodera-shi: Sono denshō to rekishi.* Sendai: Sōei Shuppan, 1993.

Ōta Yoshihisa. *Akō gishi jikki.* Tokyo: Gakugei Shoin, 1934.

Ōtaka-ke kaden shū. Edited by Saitō Hanzō. Tokyo: Kōdansha Shuppan Sābisu Sentā, 1970.

Paske-Smith, M. T. "The Japanese Trade and Residence in the Philippines Before and During the Spanish Occupation." *Transactions of the Asiatic Society of Japan* 42 (1914): 685–710.

Rinoie Masafumi. *Sagashiateta nisennen mae no rūtsu.* Tokyo: Tokuma Shoten, 1980.

———. "Takebayashi Tadashichi wa Mōshi no matsuei." *Rekishi tokuhon,* December 1981, 252–57.

Saitō Shigeru. *Akō gishi jissan.* Tokyo: *Akō gishi jissan* Hanpukai, 1975.

Sanbyaku han kashin jinmei jiten. Edited by *Kashin jinmei jiten* Hensan I'inkai. 7 vols. Tokyo: Shin Jinbutsu Ōraisha, 1987–1989.

Sasaki Moritarō. *Genroku jiken shimatsu ki: Ōishi Kuranosuke no nazo.* Tokyo: Shin Jinbutsu Ōraisha, 1975.

Satō Hiroshi. "Akita-han *Okamoto Mototomo nikki* ni miru Akō jiken." *Kiyō: Kariya-jō,* no. 1 (2010): 155–59.

Satō Makoto. *Akō Gishi Shiryōkan* (www.age.ne.jp/x/satomako/TOP). For some time now, this site has been undergoing "gradual renewal," and thus many items previously available, though still listed in the contents, are no longer accessible. Even so, much valuable material has been restored, and one hopes that progress will continue.

———. "Haga Seidayū oboegaki o yomu." *Rinjin* 27 (2014): 108–19.

———. "Kingin ukeharai chō saikō." *Gunsho* 56 (2002): 21–33.

Schurtz, William Lytle. *The Manila Galleon.* New York: Dutton, 1959.

Setodani Akira. *Chūshingura o ikita onna: Kuranosuke no tsuma Riku to sono shūhen.* Toyooka: Hokuseisha, 2005.

———. "Riku to Tajima no kōkogaku" (www.eonet.ne.jp/~his-tajima/index.htm). The late author, an archaeologist and former director of the Toyooka Shiritsu Shutsudo Bunka-zai Kanri Sentā, maintained a strong side interest in the life of Ishizuka Riku, the wife of Ōishi Kuranosuke, who was a native of

Toyooka. Many of his writings, both published and unpublished, are collected on this site, which one hopes will be kept active long after the author's untimely demise.

Setsuyō gundan. Edited by Ashida Koreto. *Dai Nihon chishi taikei* 25. Tokyo: Yūzankaku, 1930.

Shashin de miru Hyakunen mae no Nihon. Edited by Watanabe Mariko. Vol. 1, *Kurashi*. Tokyo: Mārusha, 1996.

Shida Gishū. *Haiku to haijin to*. Tokyo: Shūbunkan, 1942.

Shigeno Yasutsugu. *Akō gishi jitsuwa* (1889). In *Meiji bungaku zenshū*, 78:3–61. Tokyo: Chikuma Shobō, 1976.

Shimazu Yoshihide. *Satsuma no hiken: Nodachi no Jigenryū*. Tokyo: Shinchōsha, 2005.

Shimizu Katsuyuki. *Kenka ryōseibai no tanjō*. Tokyo: Kōdansha, 2006.

———. *Muromachi shakai no sōjō to chitsujo*. Tokyo: Yoshikawa Kōbunkan, 2004.

Shimizu Shun'ichi. *Chūshingura Ōgaki monogatari*. Ōgaki: Ōgaki-shi Bunka-zai Hogo Kyōkai, 2001.

Shinpan Bukkyōgaku jiten. Edited by Taya Raishun et al. Kyoto: Hōzōkan, 1995.

Shiraishi Tsutomu and Taguchi Yasuko. *Edo-Meiji Kyōto no tenki hyō: Nijō-ke nainai gobansho hinami no ki*. Vol. 1. Tokyo: Keio Gijuku Daigaku Mita Meidia Sentā, 1998.

Smith, Henry D., II. "The Capacity of Chūshingura: Three Hundred Years of Chūshingura." *Monumenta Nipponica* 58, no. 1 (2003): 1–42.

———. "The Trouble with Terasaka: The Forty-Seventh Rōnin and the Chūshingura Imagination." *Nichibunken Japan Review* 16 (2004): 3–65.

Sugita Genpaku. *Rangaku koto hajime* (1815). NKBT 95.

Tachikawa Hakushō (Hiroaki). *Ō-Edo chōkanzu*. Tokyo: Asahi Shinbun Shuppan, 2013.

Tada Sahei. "Kayano Sanpei no jijin." *Kamigata* 12, December 1931.

Tahara Tsuguo. *Akō shijū-roku shi ron*. Tokyo: Yoshikawa Kōbunkan, 1978.

Takagi Tadashi. *Zōho Mikudarihan: Edo no rien to josei-tachi*. Tokyo: Heibonsha, 1999.

Takeuchi Shin'ichi. "Nanban geka Kurisaki-ke keifu to Echizen Kurisaki-ke ni tsuite." *Jakuetsu kyōdo kenkyū* 14, no. 2 (1969): 23–40.

Tanaka Mitsurō. *Rongaibi* (www.7b.biglobe.ne.jp/~longivy/). Although the author has ceased to add new material to this site, the seventy-nine essays collected under the rubric "Akō jiken kankei" remain some of the most thoughtful, penetrating, and unbiased writing on this subject. Tanaka continues, however, to comment, albeit infrequently, on his weblog *Nagatsuta zasshi* (http://longivy.at.webry.info/).

Tanaka Yoshinobu. *Genroku no kisai: Takarai Kikaku*. Tokyo: Shintensha, 2000.

Taniguchi Kengo. *Rurō no sengoku kizoku Konoe Sakihisa: Tenka ittō ni honrō sareta shōgai*. Tokyo: Chūō Kōron Sha, 1994.

Taniguchi Shinko. *Akō rōshi no jitsuzō*. Tokyo: Yoshikawa Kōbunkan, 2006.

———. *Akō rōshi to Kira-tei uchiiri*. Tokyo: Yoshikawa Kōbunkan, 2013.

———. *Bushidō kō: Kenka, katakiuchi, burei uchi*. Tokyo: Kadokawa Gakugei Shuppan, 2007.

———. *Kinsei shakai to hō kihan: Meiyō, mibun, jitsuryoku kōshi*. Tokyo: Yoshikawa Kōbunkan, 2005.

Tanno Shirō. *Edo aheahe sōshi*. Tokyo: Kawade Shobō Shinsha, 1985.

Terada Takeshi. *Ōhashi Totsuan Sensei den*. Tokyo: Shibundō, 1936.

Toki o koete kataru mono: Shiryō to bijutsu no meihō. Edited by Tokyo Kokuritsu Bijutsukan and Tokyo Daigaku Shiryō Hensanjo. Tokyo: Tokyo Daigaku Shiryō Hensanjo, 2001.

Tokugawa Bakufu jiten. Edited by Takeuchi Makoto. Tokyo: Tōkyōdō Shuppan, 2003.

Tokugawa bungei ruijū. 12 vols. Tokyo: Kokusho Kankōkai, 1914–1916.

Tominomori Eiji. *Uron nari Suke'emon: Aru Akō rōshi to sono matsuei*. Tokyo: Sōshisha, 2002.

Tomizawa Nobuaki. "Horibe Yasubei no funkei no tomo: Satō Jōemon no shutsuji ni tsuite." In *Akō gishi uchiiri jūgunki: Satō Jōemon oboegaki*, edited by Chūō Gishi Kai, 106–43. Tokyo: Chūō Gishikai, 2013.

Tsuruzono Yutaka et al. *Nihon kinsei shoki ni okeru torai Chōsenjin no kenkyū: Hagi-han o chūshin ni*. Kanazawa: Kanazawa Daigaku Kyōyōbu, 1991.

Ujiie Mikito. *Bushi manyuaru*. Tokyo: Medeia Fuakutorii, 2012.

———. *Bushidō to eros*. Tokyo: Kōdansha, 1995.

———. *Edo no sei fūzoku*. Tokyo: Kōdansha, 1998.

———. *Katakiuchi: Fukushū no sahō*. Tokyo: Chūō Koronsha, 2007.

Urai Sachiko. *Edo no jikoku to toki no kane*. Tokyo: Iwata Shoin, 2002.

Usui Senkichi. *Ōgaki-han to Chūshingura: Akō kaijō made no yakuwari*. Ōgaki: Ōgaki-shi Bunka-zai Hogo Kyōkai, 2003.

Utsumi Sadajirō. *Shinsetsu Akō gishi roku*. Tokyo: Hakubisha, 1933.

————. *Shintei Toyooka to Ōishi Kuranosuke Fujin.* Edited by Setodani Akira. Toyooka: *Toyooka to Ōishi Kuranosuke Fujin* Fukkoku Kankōkai, 2001.

Wakita Osamu. *Genroku no shakai.* Tokyo: Hanawa Shobō, 1980.

Watanabe Hiroshi. "Sexuality and the Social Order." In *A History of Japanese Political Thought, 1600–1901,* translated by David Noble, 293–313. Tokyo: LTCB International Library Trust/International House of Japan, 2012.

————. "The Opening of Japan as a Philosophical Question." In *A History of Japanese Political Thought, 1600–1901,* translated by David Noble, 333–51. Tokyo: LTCB International Library Trust/International House of Japan, 2012.

Watanabe Tamotsu. *Chūshingura: Mō hitotsu no rekishi kankaku.* Tokyo: Hakusuisha, 1981.

Watanabe Yosuke. *Seishi Akō gishi.* Edited by Izutsu Chōsaku. Tokyo: Kōwadō, 1931.

Watanabe Yuriko, ed. *Kikaku "Ruikōji."* Tokyo: Shinsuisha, 2012.

Wilkinson, Endymion. *Chinese History: A Manual.* Cambridge, Mass.: Harvard University Asia Center, 1998.

Yada Sōun. *Edo kara Tokyo e.* 9 vols. Tokyo: Chūō Kōron Sha, 1998–1999.

Yagi Akihiro. *Chūshingura.* Vol. 1 [*Shijitsu, honmon hen*]. Akō: Akō-shi Sōmubu Shishi Hensanshitsu, 1989.

Yamada Aiken. *Chūretsu Akō gishi no sōkyo.* Tokyo: Chūseidō, 1915.

Yamada Sōyū. "Yamada Sōhen." In *Chadō zenshū.* Vol. 11. Osaka: Sōgensha, 1937.

————. *Yamada Sōhen den.* Osaka: Chi'in Hakkōsho, 1928.

Yamamoto Hirofumi. *Akō jiken to shijū-roku shi.* Tokyo: Yoshikawa Kōbunkan, 2013.

————. *"Chūshingura" no kessansho.* Tokyo: Shinchōsha, 2012.

————. *Edo-jō no kyūtei seiji: Kumamoto-han Hosokawa Tadaoki-Tadatoshi fushi no ōfuku shojō.* Tokyo: Kōdansha, 1996.

————. *Kore ga hontō no "Chūshingura": Akō rōshi uchiiri jiken no shinsō.* Tokyo: Shōgakukan, 2012.

————. *Seppuku: Nihonjin no sekinin no torikata.* Tokyo: Kōbunsha, 2003.

————. "Toyotomi seiken no 'shinan' ni tsuite [: Asano Nagamasa to Daté Masamune]." In *Bakuhan-sei no seiritsu to kinsei no kokusei.* Tokyo: Azekura Shobō, 1990.

Zusetsu Chūshingura. Edited by Nishiyama Matsunosuke. Tokyo: Kawade Shobō Shinsha, 1998.